# Crime and Criminality

The que
ing in a
address.
to devel
and why
criminol
spective

- a co
  iour
- an a
  tion
- an e
  to 'J
- an e
  risk
  tech

Addressi
theoreti
dents tal
forensic

**Sandie**
until lat
forensic
cal psyc
criminological and investigative psychology. Sandie is currently a visiting lecturer in psychology at the University of South Wales and a freelance writer on
psychology.

# Crime and Criminality

A multidisciplinary approach

Sandie Taylor

Routledge
Taylor & Francis Group

LONDON AND NEW YORK

First published 2016
by Routledge
2 Park Square, Milton Park, Abingdon, Oxon, OX14 4RN

and by Routledge
711 Third Avenue, New York, NY 10017

*Routledge is an imprint of the Taylor & Francis Group, an informa business*

*British Library Cataloguing in Publication Data*
A catalogue record for this book is available from the British Library

*Library of Congress Cataloging-in-Publication Data*
Taylor, Sandie.
Crime and criminality: a multidisciplinary approach / Sandie Taylor. – First Edition.
pages cm
Includes bibliographical references.
ISBN 978-1-138-88861-6 (hardback) – ISBN 978-1-138-88862-3 (pbk.)
– ISBN 978-1-315-71329-8 (ebook) 1. Criminal psychology. 2. Criminal
behavior. 3. Criminology. I. Title.
HV6080.T38 2016
364–dc23
2015019536

ISBN: 978-1-138-88861-6 (hbk)
ISBN: 978-1-138-88862-3 (pbk)
ISBN: 978-1-315-71329-8 (ebk)

Typeset in Bembo by
Servis Filmsetting Ltd, Stockport, Cheshire

MIX
Paper from
responsible sources
FSC
www.fsc.org   FSC® C013056

Printed and bound in Great Britain by
TJ International Ltd, Padstow, Cornwall

In loving memory of my dad, Alexander Taylor

# Contents

# Plates

# Figures

# Tables

# Boxes

# Acknowledgements

I would like to acknowledge the following people for all their help with this project. I would like to thank Thomas Sutton for providing me with the opportunity of publishing and for being so positive about what I had written. Also Heidi Lee who has been an especially helpful editor who has offered her advice and useful comments. She also helped to move things along. Thanks also to Cambridge Cognition Ltd., David Canter, *The Oklahoman*, thelaw-pages.com and Taylor & Francis for their kind permission to reproduce previously published material in this book.

I would also like to acknowledge my father who read through the early chapters and provided encouragement, and whose artistic influence I hope rubbed off on me in my production of the figures. Also my mother who kept asking me where I was up to. Finally, I would like to thank Professor Lance Workman who made a number of useful suggestions and corrections with his editor's cap on. Lance's knowledge of the writing and publishing process helped in the progression of this book and he provided much support in this. He also provided a great deal of guidance in the development of the Acknowledgements section.

# Introduction

**Crime** and **criminality** have long captured the imagination of the media and of the public at large. Despite this attention, people often struggle to define what actually constitutes a criminal act. We have long been able to identify behaviours which we feel contravene morality, and certainly have no difficulty recognising when someone has behaved unfairly towards us. To report a crime to the police, however, requires more than identifying unfair treatment and someone who is behaving immorally (see Chapters 1 and 2). So what is it that guides our acknowledgement of a crime and belief that someone has acted criminally? These are important questions but the answers are not so readily forthcoming. In order to understand crime and criminality it is necessary to explore how our concept of crime developed through social, religious and legal change, and more importantly their interaction (see Part I, Chapters 1 and 2). To help understand crime and criminality, the adoption of a multi-disciplinary approach will be taken in this textbook. In addition to utilising a multidisciplinary approach, a recurrent theme of this textbook will be the relationship between **nature** (i.e. our biology) and **nurture** (i.e. our environment) in explaining criminality. In order to progress a **nature–nurture** under-standing of crime and criminality, a plethora of theories and research findings from a variety of academic disciplines will be presented (with Part II presenting **nature-** and **nurture-driven** explanations and a nature–nurture interaction).

## Why is a multidisciplinary approach informative?

Theories of crime and criminality have been forthcoming from many different academic disciplines, which is why a multidisciplinary approach would provide a profound understanding of the area. Each academic discipline has its own domain of understanding, which is influenced by research findings, and these findings, in turn, are partially determined by the research method of inquiry used. A good example of this can be demonstrated by the use of quantitative versus qualitative research methods of investigation. In the case of quantitative, an experimental design might be used as a means of studying the effects of age on memory tasks: hypothesising, for example, that younger adults can recall more information than those over 80. Experiments are highly controlled so that the observations/findings can be attributed to the variable being studied. In contrast, a typical qualitative method of research might involve an open unstructured interview, where the information is subjectively analysed (in cases of a clinical interview the clinician often uses clinical lore based on decades of research). Different academic disciplines can be separated according to the method of research adopted – a research paradigm indicative of the discipline. Despite this there is a degree of overlap of quantitative and qualitative methods used by all academic disciplines which will be considered in this textbook. The following academic disciplines, will at times, be referred to where relevant to the topic of discussion:

- Law
- Economics
- Political Science
- Religious Studies
- History
- Philosophy
- Social Anthropology
- Criminology
- Sociology
- Feminist Studies
- Psychology
- Psychiatry
- Neuroscience/Neurochemistry/Neurocognition/Neurobiology
- Biology/Physiology/Biochemistry
- Genetics
- Evolution.

For our purposes of clarification here in the introduction, however, the three major academic disciplines offering an explanation of criminality considered in this text will be defined: psychology, criminology and sociology. Social scientists in psychology, criminology and sociology have all developed their theories about why an individual commits crime and initiates a life-cycle of criminality – some theories more than others are based on evidential information but have all tried to account for why a minority of individuals take to leading a criminal lifestyle.

### Psychology

A succinct definition of psychology is that it involves the study of mind and behaviour. How this is undertaken depends on the subdisciplines within psychology. The main subdisciplines within psychology relevant to this textbook are:

- Developmental: study of individuals from birth to senescence.
- Biological: study of physiological processes.
- Cognitive: study of perception, memory, thought and language.
- Social: study of how individuals interact in different situations.
- Personality and Individual Differences: study of how we develop a personality including temperament and intelligence and why we differ.
- Clinical: study of mental and physical (and the interaction between the two) well-being of individuals also addressing questions of 'what', 'how' and 'why' mental disturbance occurs.
- Forensic: study of the interface between law and psychology involving the areas of police and prison.
- Investigative: study of the linkages between victim, perpetrator and the crime scene.

As can be seen the domains within psychology are vast and offer theories about criminals and criminality based on quantitative and qualitative research methods. Theories and models derived within psychology are both **nature-** and **nurture-**driven, with many suggesting the existence of a nature–nurture interaction.

## Criminology

Succinctly defined, criminology is the study of crime. Others have added that it is the scientific study of both criminals and their crimes. There is, however, an overlap between criminology and psychology with regard to intellectual content. Criminology is a social science studying aspects of behaviour that contravene the law – such behaviours are considered to be deviant. Criminologists, however, also study deviant behaviours which are not criminal in their own right, but when studied can help to provide further understanding of criminal behaviour. These behaviours might include prescription drug abuse, alcoholism, deviant sexual practises and gambling. The main subdisciplines within criminology relevant to this textbook are:

- *Criminal psychology*: the study of psychological phenomena in the area of crime.
- *Criminal psycho- and neuropathology*: the study of criminals with psycho-pathological problems such as psychopaths.
- *Criminal anthropology*: the study of bodily characteristics of criminals.
- *Criminal sociology*: the study of social phenomenon within the context of society and the physical environment.
- *Penology*: the study of **punishment** and its significance and weighting in society.
- *Critical criminology*: the study of how different classes interact and the oppression and manipulation of the lower classes; how capitalism controls perceptions of crime and what it is to be criminal; how conceptions of

crime have evolved but are still largely defined by the ruling classes and the application of Marxist ideology.

Criminologists prefer to regard themselves as scientists because they collect data about crime and test out their hypotheses. In this way there is overlap with quantitative and qualitative research methods and their theories can be considered to be both nature- and nurture-derived depending on the subdivision of interest.

## Sociology

Succinctly defined, sociology is the study of the impact of groups and societies on human social life. Sociology not only studies the impact of society on individuals but how society actually functions. Different types of relationship within the context of informal and formal socialising agents are considered as the infrastructure of society, and it is to these that society continues to thrive. Sociologists are interested in the attachments to groups and social institutions that individuals develop over time. Moreover, sociologists study how our behaviours follow the rules of these social institutions and what happens to those who fail to do so. Research methods used are primarily qualitative, although quantitative methods are used in the more scientifically oriented subdivisions. The main subdisciplines within sociology relevant to this textbook are:

- Historical: the study of social groups, social events and social facts.
- Sociology of knowledge: the study of social phenomena; how our knowledge is influenced by society.
- Criminology: the study of criminal behaviour in relation to individuals and groups; origins of crime and its causes; control of crime by different organisations.
- Sociology of religion: the study of how the structure of religion influences social behaviour and the role it plays in society.
- Sociology of economy: the study of how economic activities interface with socio-cultural variables.
- Political: the study of political ideology as part of the social system.
- Sociology of law: the study of law and the legal system as a way of social control; links with moral order to maintain society and its perpetuation through regulations and rules.
- Urban: the study of urban life and how it interfaces with urbanisation; dysfunction of which causes crime and corruption.
- Sociology theory and methods: the application of research methods to test sociologically driven theories.

You will notice there is an overlap between sociology and criminology. Criminologists are generally perceived as being sociologists who specialise in the area of crime and criminality because they adopt a sociological dogma. Nevertheless, there are criminologists who consider themselves as separate from sociology, on the grounds of theoretical and methodological differences. In the 'theory and methods' subdivision, both quantitative and qualitative research methods are adopted. Most sociological research, however, uses qualitative methods and, in particular, social constructionism (see Chapter 1). The theories derived from sociology tend to be nurture-driven.

The advantages of adopting a multidisciplinary approach to understanding crime and criminality are numerous. The major contribution, however, of using a multidisciplinary approach is the wide-ranging, multi-levelled, profound and in-depth analysis this enables. This further allows us to engage in the speculation of a nature, nurture or nature–nurture interactive explanation of criminality and the purpose crime serves.

## Nature–nurture spectrum

As mentioned previously, theories concerning human behaviour (and misbehaviour) will be considered as those supporting a nature (where the individual is predisposed in some biological/genetic capacity to behave criminally) or nurture (where they do so due to environmental influences) approach. Is it nature or nurture? This is a long and on-going debate which tends to be negotiated by suggesting that behaviour is the outcome of a nature–nurture interaction. The debate then becomes a matter of 'what is the nature of that interaction?'. This is a theme that weaves its way throughout the fabric of this textbook.

Occasionally a behaviour that appears to be developed from an environmental factor can be essentially nature driven. School boys, for example, physically fighting while school girls spreading nasty rumours can be explained using both evolutionary psychology and biology (nature approaches). Hence what initially appears as differences in strategy between the sexes due to **socialisation** processes is a difference driven by nature. Likewise inheritance of the 'warrior' gene (see Chapters 3 and 7) can influence future criminal behaviour (and in some individuals is implicated in murder) but this is not set in stone as it depends on what type of childhood the individual experienced. If it was an unhappy and abusive childhood, then this interacts with having the 'warrior' gene which can lead to criminality – nurture-driven. An attempt throughout this textbook is therefore made to ascertain which of the two assumptions (i.e. **nature drives nurture** or **nurture drives nature**) applies more readily towards understanding different aspects of criminality.

Research supporting nature and nurture approaches to understanding crime, criminality and different types of criminal is discussed in Parts II and III. Different types of criminal have different needs and motivations. In Part III (and Chapter 11 of Part IV) we will examine the research evidence available from various disciplines in order to expound the relationship between nature and nurture for different types of criminal. We will also consider the timelines of criminality by examining the behaviour of young children. We will use case studies (from different countries) throughout to help illustrate the type of crimes committed and their level of seriousness. Therefore a multi-cultural approach will be adopted to help understand the pervasiveness of *mala in se* crimes (see Chapter 1).

## Multi-cultural approach

A multi-cultural approach is used to explain the many types of crime committed (especially *mala in se* crimes) and the processes involved in committing crime and the induction to criminality. It is argued that these processes cross-over into many different cultures and across countries. A multidisciplinary approach of theories, models and research findings is considered to be applicable cross-culturally. Despite the multi-cultural aspect of this textbook it is, however, UK centred, meaning that many aspects of the law, legal system and legislations passed will be of British origin. Where deemed appropriate, references to other legal systems in other countries will be highlighted for comparison purposes. Much reference throughout this textbook, however, is made to the US as they too adopt the **adversarial system** (see Chapters 1, 2, 13 and 15). In explaining the origin of the adversarial system, and how this contrasts with the **inquisitorial system of law** (see Chapters 1, 2 and 13), reference is made to European countries. Hence despite a UK emphasis in terms of law, **jurisprudence** and penology, there is discussion of how other countries are similar and different. In discussing these similarities and differences we will consider the criminal investigation process which is defined by the Criminal Investigations and Procedures Act of 1996 as 'An inquiry to ascertain if an offence has been committed, to identify who is responsible, and to gather admissible evidence to be placed before a judicial authority'.

## Understanding the criminal investigation process

As pointed out by Monckton-Smith, Adams, Hart and Webb (2013), three aims underlie the definition of criminal investigation, 'to ascertain if an offence has been committed . . . to identify who committed the crime . . . to gather admissible evidence' (p. 2). Gathering admissible evidence is an important feature of police work but they rely on other professionals to provide evidence and this often includes professionals from the social sciences. Providing evidence of the status of an offender's state of mind before, during and after the crime event usually involves the assessment from a forensic psychologist. Forensic psychologists work within the confines of statutes and laws as well as their professional body, which in the UK is the British Psychological Society. Such assessments are strongly connected to the **concept of dangerousness**, and so their assessments are designed to detect the offender's capability of understanding the seriousness of their criminal behaviour and to identify factors which put them at risk of repeating their crimes. These assessments provide the courts with information about the offender's mental state, and offer invaluable information concerning the best option for the judge (if the case progresses this far). Other valuable investigative techniques include **offender profiling** and, more specifically, geographical profiling. These methods help police to focus on specific information and can potentially be useful in tracking down serial killers. In Part IV we explore the assessment and treatment of **dangerous offenders** including serial killers, which also provides an understanding of what makes these offenders behave in the way they do and what motivations initiate and perpetuate their need for committing serious and dangerous crimes. These discussions also provide a nature–nurture angle by speculating about the possible causes of their criminal behaviour.

The investigative process is important as it helps us understand how the facts of a criminal case evolve. The different types of evidence considered by the police and criminal justice system per se very much involves the social sciences. Social sciences, such as psychology, have contributed towards ways of improving methods of attaining information from both witnesses and suspects. In Part V we will explore the importance of eyewitness testimony which has become a contentious topic – especially when it is submitted as uncorroborated evidence. Uncorroborated confessions can also be troublesome when presented in the courtroom. Suspects may confess to crimes for many different reasons (which is interesting in its own right and can provide us with insightful speculation about the individual) but this does not necessarily mean that police have apprehended the true culprit. Those who are psychologically vulnerable may confess to a crime they did not commit, and yet believe that they are responsible – why this occurs is interesting but it is essential that this is identified so that a miscarriage of justice can be avoided. One way to help reduce such travesties of justice is to adopt the cognitive interview (in the case of witnesses – see Chapter 14) and the ethical interrogation method (in the case of suspects – see Chapter 15). Both these methods of obtaining information will be considered within the context of police investigation.

In Part VI, one chapter is devoted towards understanding the remit of the law – what it is designed to achieve. Interestingly all laws across different countries make use of five legal concepts (**retribution, punishment, deterrence,** protection of the public and **rehabilitation** – see Chapter 16) or the 'Big 5'. These concepts are used in social policy making, and interact in such a way that a careful balance is maintained. In order to understand why certain criminal behaviours are more likely to be perceived as having an environmental or an innate cause, the extent of interaction between the Big 5 can be informative. For example, if there are forms of rehabilitation which work for an offender then there is the underlying assumption that change is possible – usually in the guise of changing an environmental factor or teaching techniques to control certain elements of an offender's temperament such as anger. The temperament does not change but how the offender deals with feelings of anger can help to control it. Thus rehabilitation can provide a link with how we interpret the nature–nurture debate. Hence the type of balance between the Big 5 legal concepts a society adopts provides an indication of how certain crimes and criminal behaviour are perceived and whether the underlying causes can be traced back to an environmental or innate explanation – or, as will become clearer towards the end of this text, a complicated interaction between the two.

How and why laws are first developed and what their function was (and still is today) can be considered under the banner of 'law drives criminality'. Three different speculations of this relationship will be explored further in Chapter 17:

• criminality occurs out of the way we define crime;
• laws arise out of morality;
• socialisation drives law abiding behaviour but can also cause criminality.

These three hypotheses bring a sense of understanding to the development of laws and how they are maintained within society from one generation to the next. The following is a breakdown of the parts and the chapters therein.

## Breakdown of parts and chapters

### Part I What is crime?

In Part I there are two chapters devoted to developing an understanding of what is meant by criminal behaviour and how we define and categorise crime.

### Chapter I Defining and examining crime from different perspectives

Crime is defined using legal terms, social constructionism and psychological concepts. Our understanding of crime and criminal behaviour is traced, historically, back to when some semblance of law was being established. This establishment of law will also be considered within the context of religion. The role of religion in the perception of crimes considered as immoral and against the human moral code will be considered historically and within a cross-cultural framework. Religion and its direct and indirect influence over law, within a contemporary context, is reviewed using a consensus approach to what is morally acceptable behaviour. This is also linked with cross-cultural traditions considered in some cases to derive from religious practise. A cross-cultural review of serious crime and sentencing tariffs is used to highlight the similarities in the approach to punishment and attitudes towards those who commit crimes against the human moral code.

*Chapter 2 Concepts in crime definition influencing crime classification*

Concepts of seriousness and harm will be addressed with reference to how people make judgements about different crimes. Seriousness and the issue of harm are fundamental concepts used in the grading of crime, but like the definition of crime itself, these terms are difficult to pin-down. There is a long history of debate concerning the concept of harm and how it should be used in the classification of crime. Some harmful behaviour is considered responsible for changing society's perception of morality, thereby causing a decline of moral standards. By this measure, such behaviours might be considered as harmful to society. This debate will be reviewed in detail and how it has created a problem for legislating against legal immoral behaviours that are potentially harmful to society. Concepts of seriousness and harm are at the heart of crime classification and contribute to definitions that are legally and socially formulated. A consensus view of what constitutes criminal behaviour exists within society, and it is this that determines whether we decide to report such behaviours to the police. Some behaviours, considered as immoral or sinful that cause harm to the individual, remain unreported to the police because those responsible for such behaviours are unlikely to incriminate themselves. These behaviours or 'crimes' have been labelled as victimless crimes because the victim of these acts remains anonymous. How crimes are classified will be reviewed and compared with the legal definitions of *mala in se* (behaviours considered to be against the human moral code) and ***mala prohibita*** (behaviours that are prohibited by statutory law) crime.

## Part II Nature–nurture explanations of criminal behaviour

The **nature–nurture controversy** in relation to understanding human behaviour per se is not a new debate; nor is its application to the criminal mind. Whilst the **nurture** element of the debate is concerned with environmental factors of development that impact on future behaviour, such as upbringing and peer interactions, the nature approach examines the impact of biological factors, such as the influence of our **genes** and prenatal development, on behaviour. What is interesting about all of these approaches is that it is difficult to find one that can explain all. Even more interesting is the observation that many explanations can be linked: in other words they are not mutually exclusive. Some of the environmentally driven explanations, for example, have an underlying biological element. Part II will explore biological and evolutionary factors (Chapter 3); learning, social and developmental approaches (Chapter 4) and decision-making processes by criminals (Chapter 5).

### Chapter 3 Biological constraints and evolutionary factors

The consideration of a biological perspective on why particular individuals commit *mala in se* crimes (behaviours considered to be against the human moral code), has led to a variety of explanations: genetic mutation or conditions arising from prenatal aberration; brain damage, impairment or unusual 'wiring'; neurochemical and/or biochemical problems and evolutionary angles.

### Chapter 4 Social, learning and developmental approaches to understanding criminality

Environmentally based perspectives have also led to a variety of explanations: family background and upbringing; socialisation; attachment; different or faulty cognition; peer group influence; subcultural mores; deprivation and poverty; marginalisation and substance abuse (certainly the reasons for initiation of usage). The notion of risk, protection, vulnerability and resilience factors are important and help to provide explanations of why some individuals succumb to criminal lifestyles and others do not.

### Chapter 5 Decision-making processes by criminals

The type of cognitive processing involved in decision making is extended to criminals. The way we normally make decisions is explored in relation to models of decision-making used by economists and by psychologists. The problems associated with the complex models relying on the use of probability theory will be compared with simple 'rule of thumb' approaches such as **heuristics**. These approaches will be considered in the use of criminal decision-making – whether a crime needs to take place and the odds of gaining more and also escaping the crime scene by selecting suitable locations to burgle. Whether criminals have brains that are 'wired' differently from the rest of us will be explored using memory models from psychology and brain scans from neuroscience. The existence of a criminal personality type is considered with reference to typical thinking patterns and social attributions made by criminals.

### Part III Different types of crime and criminal with a focus on nature, nurture and nature–nurture

Part III is concerned with nature–nurture research and declaring the boundaries of the debate. We will be concerned with providing the evidence for the **nature–nurture controversy** through consideration of different types of criminality and criminal. The types of crime and criminal addressed in this part (also overlapping with dangerous offenders and serial killers in Part

IV), have received much attention through both biologically and socially oriented research. For this reason they are considered to be relevant to the nature–nurture debate.

### Chapter 6 White-collar criminals and their crimes

What **white-collar crime** is and the nature of decision making undertaken by white-collar criminals will be considered by drawing upon notions of a **criminal personality** and biological differences. Differences in the structure and function of the brains of white-collar criminals when making decisions in their workplace, for example, will be considered. The type of working environment in which they flourish is discussed in relation to their approach to leadership qualities and decision making in high risk situations such as successful companies and businesses.

### Chapter 7 Psychopaths and their crimes

What psychopathy is will be explained and differentiated from antisocial personality disorder. The developmental pathway of **criminal psychopaths** will be traced by beginning with children who exhibit antisocial behaviour from a very young age and who continue to battle to control their aggressive, antisocial and criminal behaviour throughout their lifespan. Evidence to demonstrate both nature and nurture elements influencing their behaviour will be considered, including brain imaging and neurochemical studies providing clear evidence of structural, functional and organic abnormality at variance from the 'norm'. Treatment packages and their clinical effectiveness in terms of reduced **recidivism** and decreased risk of dangerousness will be reviewed.

### Chapter 8 Sex offenders and their crimes

The generic category of the sex offender will be examined. This includes a host of different type of sex offender as stipulated in the Diagnostic Statistical Manual of Mental Disorder (DSM-5) (American Psychiatric Association 2013) including rapists, paedophiles and paraphiliacs. Sex offending will be considered in terms of the purpose it serves for those who offend in this way. The motivation for committing sexual offences underlies the purpose it serves, and it is this motivation that enables psychologists, criminologists and feminists to categorise sex offenders into different groups and apply different perspectives of explanation. Different treatments will be reviewed and evaluated for effectiveness in terms of recidivism and risk reduction. Discussions of morality, moral development, empathy and **Theory of Mind** are linked here in the same way as in Chapter 7.

### Chapter 9 Female offenders and their crimes

The gender divide for criminality and committing certain types of crime will be addressed and why the age of crime preponderance is similar across the sexes. Different perspectives will be discussed: sociological, feminist, psychological, biological and evolutionary. Examples of different types of crime committed by males and females across the lifespan will be reviewed using genuine criminal cases. Why more violent crimes are committed by men will be compared with speculations of what has 'gone wrong' with women who also engage in violence. The notion of females being more empathic than their male counterparts is discussed in terms of developing a more defined pro-social personality profile.

### Chapter 10 Delinquents and their crimes

**Delinquency** fuels the nature–nurture debate further by asking the question of whether delinquency is merely a label for naughty behaviour which the family, peers and society per se regard as less serious criminal behaviour warranting non–custodial sentences (often restricted to cautioning or at its most extreme a 'criminal behaviour order' and a 'crime prevention injunction'). Social issues, deviance and subcultural elements and familial interactions provide robust support for a nurture stance while research findings on individual differences, personality and temperament offer evidence for a gene–environmental interaction. Different treatments and social interventions to promote pro-social behaviour is reviewed in relation to morality, moral development, empathy and Theory of Mind.

### Part IV Prediction of criminal behaviour

In Part III different types of criminal were considered and explanations from research findings in psychology, sociology, criminology, feminist studies, biology and neuroscience were sought in order to establish possible reasons why offenders commit the crimes that they do. Examining the research in this way helps to build a picture of different types of criminal that might prove useful in predicting who is most likely to reoffend and continue to be a danger to society. In Part IV, predictability of dangerous offenders and their level of risk for repeating the same crime will be considered in relation to the different methods of assessment. These different methods will be evaluated for their effectiveness and successful outcomes. Clinicians, practitioners and forensic psychologists assess the mental health of criminals using their professional skills and different inventories to test for personality and intelligence, especially if it is suspected that there might be a mental health issue. In cases of crimes involving extreme violence, deviancy or murder, questions regarding the offender's level of dangerousness and risk of recidivism are asked.

## Chapter 11 Dangerousness, risk assessment and the mentally and personality-disordered offender

The **concept of dangerousness** and risk assessment in relation to those with a personality disorder, in particular the psychopath, and individuals who are considered to have a mental disorder is examined. The ethical debate of what you do with someone who has a mental disorder – prison (as punishment) or secure hospital (as rehabilitation and incapacitation for **public safety**) will be addressed using perspectives from law, criminology, sociology and psychology. Furthermore, the issue of whether an offender with a personality disorder should be perceived as ill and therefore unable to take responsibility for their actions will be examined. Often when dangerousness is discussed, the question of whether someone is 'bad, mad or sad' provokes differences of opinion.

## Chapter 12 Offender profiling: serial killers

The question of whether serial killers can be categorised and profiled using crime scene evidence is discussed in relation to reliability and validity of the profiles constructed by profilers. The different profiles of mass murder killers, spree killers and serial killers will be considered through the eyes of the FBI and the British approach to offence profiling. Profiling will be evaluated in terms of its credibility as a reliable tool for predicting who the killer might be and where he or she resides. What drives or motivates a serial killer and how this is implied through physical evidence and the victim's body, will also be reviewed. **Offender profiling** will be evaluated in terms of its value as a useful system for classifying serial killers. Furthermore, key similarities and differences in *modus operandi* (i.e. the method of killing used) adopted by serial killers will be discussed with reference to offender profiling approaches.

## Part V Reliability of investigative processes

In Part IV, issues concerning the predictability of criminal behaviour were considered in relation to dangerousness and offender profiling. Methods of assessing dangerous offenders and detecting serial killers were evaluated for their effectiveness and accuracy as measured by detection rates. In Part V, the theme of investigative strategies used by police to apprehend offenders will continue. The investigative strategies adopted by police involve finding evidence that can be used in court to prove beyond reasonable doubt that the suspect detained and arrested is the perpetrator. There are different sources from which evidential information is derived which will be the topic of discussion in the following chapters.

## Chapter 13 Eyewitness testimony and extra-legal defendant characteristics

Research findings from the social sciences concerning eyewitness testimony will be considered. In particular the salience of eyewitness testimony in court will be traced historically to the law and linked to the way our legal system operates. Research investigating the fallibility of eyewitness memory in relation to what is known about how human memory functions will be addressed as 'estimator' variables. System variables involving the way in which investigators attain eyewitness accounts, such as constructing facial composites, selecting suspects from mug shots and identifying suspects in a line-up, will be evaluated for their reliability and impact on the malleability of memory traces. Post-event information and the misleading effects it might have on memories for events, will be considered by referring to research on biased perception, stereotypes and irrelevant or non-evidential information about a defendant such as physical appearance (i.e. **extra-legal defendant characteristics**).

## Chapter 14 Cognitive interview

The adoption of the cognitive interview, which was designed using psychological principles of how human memory operates, is discussed. Based on interrogative and interview procedures, the objective of the cognitive interview is to recover information about an event from suspects and witnesses respectively. Police interviewers should follow the set stages of the cognitive interview procedure so as to obtain uncontaminated information about a criminal event. Its application is especially useful in attaining information from children and those who are vulnerable to accepting information from police investigators.

## Chapter 15 Confessions

The theme of attaining evidence that can be used in court is continued by concentrating on confessions. Confessions will be considered for their reliability by introducing forensic techniques of ascertaining the authenticity of confessions made by suspects. Different police interrogation styles, such as the standard police interview and the Reid model, will be examined in relation to the ethical style of interrogation called the PEACE model. The PEACE model will be defined and examined and its effectiveness considered. Police attitudes towards the importance of attaining a confession is explored in relation to their ability to detect when a suspect is lying. The underlying intentions for confessing to crime will be highlighted by considering personality (e.g. an antisocial personality), vulnerability (e.g. those considered mentally impaired) and self-sacrifice (e.g. protecting someone else or conscience offloading). Methods for assessing susceptible suspects and measures taken to protect them from confessing to crimes they did not commit will be viewed in relation to aspects of police law.

## Part VI Discussion about the function of law, its impact on antisocial behaviour and its origins

The question of how criminality can be defined is examined by considering how laws developed and what their purpose was. While previous chapters presented the case and evidence for causes of crime and criminality and the different strategies used to apprehend criminals, in this part the evidence is considered within the confines of the workings of law and the major legal concepts used. How these came about and why will be explored by focusing on our ancestral past.

### Chapter 16 'Big 5' legal concepts

What the law is for (and the consequences of contravening it) will be discussed in consideration of the 'Big 5' legal concepts: retribution, punishment, deterrence (individual and general), protection of the public and rehabilitation. The balance between factors of the Big 5 will be discussed in terms of their underlying implications for society's perceptions of crime and criminality. There is a constant balance between these five concepts in the political arena. One example where this is plain to see is in law and policy making. Depending on the political **zeitgeist** and public opinion, the hardliners will want policies favouring a tough approach to policing and punishment of criminals thus supporting a retributive stance. This would be the opposite point of view for the more soft-line politicians emphasising community-based punishments and the rehabilitation of criminals. These points of view have a complex impact on whether a person sees the criminal as arising mainly out of nurture or nature circumstances. People favouring the rehabilitative approach, for example, will view treatment and social intervention schemes as effective because the underlying causes of criminal behaviour are essentially socially/nurture driven. In the case of a nature driven explanation of criminality, opinions are more likely to err on the side of the criminal being innately wicked or evil, and there is nothing that will remedy this unfortunate disposition. In this case rehabilitation is regarded as ineffective, and the best line of action would then be to protect the public by imprisoning such individuals for a very long time.

### Chapter 17 Law drives criminality

As the law defines what it is to be deviant and a law-breaker, it could be argued that the law drives criminality, thereby supporting a nurture account. In this chapter three speculations about how the law developed are explored: first, criminality occurs because of the way we define crime; second, law arises out of morality, and third, socialisation drives law abiding behaviour but can also cause criminality. For the first; notions of cooperation and reciprocal altruism that played a major role for hominids in our ancestral past is derived from an evolutionary psychology approach. For the second, reference is made again to cooperation and reciprocal altruism and how these interacted to develop morality: this approach perceives morality as an innate development. For the third, socialisation of appropriate behaviour led to the instilment of **moral reasoning**. Criminal parents espousing deviant attitudes are likely to socialise their children in a way that perpetuates these deviant values. These children are therefore more likely to contravene the law because of their experience of inappropriate and deviant socialisation.

## Concluding comments

This concluding commentary draws conclusions from all chapters about the causes of different types of crime, why people commit crime and what initiates criminality.

As previously outlined there will be different theoretical approaches considered throughout this textbook – some described as falling into the nature or the nurture camp but many more supporting an interaction between the two. These theoretical approaches will derive from a number of different academic disciplines. The question therefore that we should be asking is to what extent does nature drive nurture or nurture drive nature when it comes to criminality? This is by no means an easy question to answer. A good starting point must surely be with an understanding of how crime and criminality are defined in law. And this is where we will begin our exploration into the world of crime and criminality.

# Part I

# What is crime?

# What is crime?

# Chapter 1

# Defining and examining crime from different perspectives

How we define **crime** and **criminality** is of interest to both professionals and the layperson. Many disciplines, such as law, criminology, sociology and psychology, have provided definitions of what we mean by crime and criminality. In this chapter we will explore these different approaches and their understanding of crime and criminality. The introduction points us to how we are readily influenced by the media in our construction of what constitutes a crime and criminal behaviour, but it is the legal approach for a definition and understanding of crime and criminal behaviour that we will address first. Two important aspects of crime definition using a legal stance is the distinction between Latin terms *actus reus* (wrongful act comprising the physical component of a crime) and *mens rea* (a guilty state of mind necessary for proving guilt). In this chapter we will explore the use of *actus reus* and *mens rea* in the determination of an individual's guilt. Circumstances where criminal responsibility can be mitigated against, such as age of criminal responsibility, impact of mental impairment and learning disability, ignorance or mistake of fact or law and acting in self-defence, will be explained. We will also explore within the legal approach, separate issues contextualising how law and punishment evolved. British laws can be traced back to King Henry VII in the late 1400s where a distinction between *mala in se* (morally wrong behaviour) and *mala prohibita* (legislative laws) was made. It is *mala in se* crimes, such as murder, where the role of religion had taken a strong lead in the determination of an individual's punishment, and still continues to have a presence today in the form of Canon Law and Islamic Sharia. Religion plays an important role in formulating a consensus understanding of how we should behave and live our lives – in effect influencing our understanding of morality. This has had both a direct and indirect influence on English law and the laws of other countries. Using a cross-cultural perspective of laws and religious influence, we will explore the similarities and differences in **jurisprudence** (the study and theory of law) towards various types of crime. In particular, we will focus on serious crimes against the human moral code such as murder, rape, assault and genocide.

Since sociological and criminological perspectives of crime and criminality have made an impact on our understanding of how particular behaviours are perceived as criminal, in this chapter we will consider the four main approaches – consensus; conflict and critical criminology; social interactionism, including **labelling; and discourse analysis**. These perspectives originate out of a social constructionist ideology which are used as a methodological foundation for understanding crime and criminality. Although these approaches are considered primarily as arising from a sociological (and criminological) perspective, there is an extensive overlap with psychology (i.e. labelling and discourse analysis).

Psychology is our final discipline considered in this chapter. The three main areas of psychology addressing crime and criminality are psycho-legal, criminological and forensic psychology. Despite their common interest in criminal behaviour there are subtle differences in the areas of focus which will be addressed in this chapter. The definitions and understanding of crime and criminal behaviour used in psychology is generic across these three areas. Different aspects of the definition, however, might be considered differently depending on whether a psycho-legal, criminological or forensic psychological approach is taken.

## Introduction

Psychologists, sociologists and criminologists have provided subtly different definitions of crime and criminal behaviour, but arguably none of these quite captures the 'essence' of what constitutes a crime and criminal behaviour. The difficulty of defining crime becomes obvious when asked the question of what is meant by the term crime. Children, for example, develop social construc-tions of robbers but, according to Dorling, Gordon, Hillyard, Pantazis *et al.* (2008), crimes and criminals are mere fictions that are constructed in order to exist. They argued that 'crime has no ontological reality; it is a "myth" of everyday life' (p.7). Dorling *et al.* (2008) are using the term ontological in this context to mean that crime does not exist in a literal sense but rather as a figurative concept. This might be one reason why it is difficult to describe the defining elements of criminal conduct but easier to provide examples of different types of crime. When asked to provide examples of different crimes, there appears to be a consensus of the types of crime that are remembered and these tend to be serious and punishable crimes like murder or burglary for instance.

What makes serious and punishable crimes most memorable has been attrib-uted to how information about serious crime is disseminated by the mass media (Chermak 1995). Chermak showed that the media focus on reporting serious crime, such as murder, which then becomes over-represented at the expense of property related crimes – the public then perceive serious crime as more preva-lent in society than other crimes. As this public perception is not supported by the data presented in the crime statistics and the Crime Survey for England and Wales (CSEW, formally known as the British Crime Survey (BCS) prior to 2012), a consensus conception of what constitutes crime is created by the media. The BCS figures of 2009/10 formulated using interview data from respondents in 45,000 households, were analysed for serious (i.e. crimes against the person and robbery) and less serious (i.e. theft, burglary and vandalism) crime prevalence rates. Flatley, Kershaw, Smith, Chaplin and Moon (2010) found a 22 per cent prevalence rate for serious crimes versus a 66 per cent prevalence rate for crimes considered to be less serious. What these figures tell us is the nature of crimes that people are more likely to experience rather than the serious crimes communicated by the media. Hence Chermak's findings suggest that we recall serious crimes when asked for a definition of crime because of a consensus understanding of crime provided by media coverage.

Identifying the factors that constitute a criminal act is not something we regularly think about – which might explain why we find it difficult to define what crime actually is. An example in Box 1.1 highlights the questions we should be asking when deciding whether a crime had taken place or not. Although this is a fictitious example it demonstrates the importance of an individual's perception of the situation and the factors considered in the determination of whether the incident is reported as a crime or not.

## Box 1.1

### An incident that could be a crime but at which point is it perceived as a crime?

If a man took £50 out of a friend's wallet, kept in a drawer and failed to inform the owner and pay the sum back, has a crime been committed?

If the friend did not intend to deprive the owner of the money, then does this behaviour constitute a crime?

Assuming that the owner fails to notice the money missing then does this imply that no crime had occurred?

Assuming that the owner notices the money is missing (and realises his friend had taken it) but fails to inform the police then is this a 'no crime' situation?

If the owner informs the police but the police are not convinced that the money was stolen, then does this imply a no crime situation?

If the police decide not to prosecute against the friend, because he is on medication that has effects on behaviour, then does this imply that no crime has taken place?

If the friend's case was discharged on the grounds of police pressure to confess to taking the £50 then does this mean that no crime had taken place?

| If the friend is prosecuted and convicted of stealing £50, now has a crime been committed?

The stages and scenarios in Box 1.1 illustrate how the process of defining crime is multifaceted: the individual who commits a crime (i.e. the actor), the crime committed (i.e. the act) and the context (i.e. the physical and social environment, circumstances and provocation) all influence whether or not a crime is considered to have taken place. According to Quinney (1970) this suggests that a 'crime' is a socially defined phenomenon that cannot be isolated from the social context in which it occurred. Even the terms used to describe individuals who commit crime (i.e. criminal, offender, perpetrator, felon, culprit or delinquent) are derived from a social process known as **labelling** (to describe or classify someone in a word or short phrase). Labelling influences how behaviour is perceived by the observer and whether it is considered to be a criminal act. Once the behaviour is labelled as a criminal act, it is then the observer's decision to inform the police.

Reporting to the police that a crime has occurred is the first stage towards acknowledging a criminal event and implying that we know when a crime has been committed. Knowing when a criminal act has occurred, however, can be a **tautological** problem as demonstrated in Figure 1.1.

Hence defining crime is difficult, but Andrews and Bonta (1998) have nevertheless introduced a succinct working definition as '[a]ntisocial acts that place the actor at risk of becoming the focus of the attention of the criminal and juvenile professionals'. Of course some might consider this definition to be tautological. Andrews and Bonta (1998) elaborated further by offering four definitions of crime and criminal behaviour using legal, moral, social and psychological perspectives. In the case of a legal perspective, criminal behaviour is prohibited by the law of the land and is punishable using the legal processes

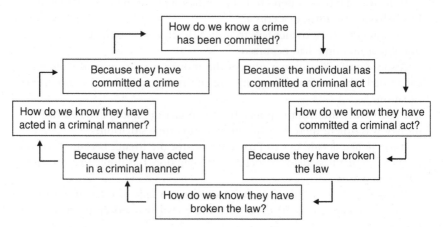

*Figure 1.1* Tautological argument of knowing when a criminal act was committed

of that law. Adler, Mueller and Laufer (2004) defined crime as 'the violation of some law that causes harm to others'. Crowther (2007) defined crime as consisting of acts that contravene the law and are therefore punishable by the criminal justice system. Crowther (2007), however, also recognised that a legal definition can be limited given that laws are not consistently standardised across different countries. This makes direct comparisons of what constitutes criminal behaviour across different countries less reliable. In the case of a moral perspective, criminal behaviour that violates norms stipulated in religious and moral doctrine is considered to be punishable by a supreme spiritual being such as God. A social perspective views criminal behaviours as a violation of socially defined behaviours. These socially defined behaviours are based on our customs and traditions, which is why it is considered fitting that individuals who contravene these should be punished by the community. A psychological approach considers the actions of an individual as criminal if the rewards received from their criminal actions are at the expense of causing harm or loss to others (Andrews and Bonta 1998).

Because these four definitions consider different perspectives, Andrews and Bonta in 2006 conceded that there is no single satisfactory definition that captures the essence of a crime. It is difficult to endorse one type of definition to suit all, given that each country has its own cultural context that impact on morals, values and beliefs about crime and criminal behaviour. A socially constructed understanding of crime might be more appropriate than a legal definition, but it is nevertheless important to understand the legal stance on criminality given that the law is there to apprehend and punish offenders. There are three approaches to understanding crime and criminal behaviour that will be considered in the next section: the legal approach, the sociological and criminological approach (i.e. social constructionism) and the psychological approach (psycho-legal; criminological (or criminal) and forensic psychology).

## Definitions of crime and criminal behaviour

### The legal approach

Legal processes prescribed in Acts of Law (legislations that have been passed by Parliament and considered as part of law) are used by the criminal justice system to apprehend, prosecute and sentence individuals who have contravened the law. In the UK police are involved in the investigation of crimes with the objective of solving the case by apprehending and arresting the perpetrator. Once there is enough evidence on which to arrest the individual suspected of committing the crime (i.e. the suspect), a court case is prepared, and the suspect now known as the defendant, attends the courtroom and awaits his or her verdict. If found guilty then the judge decides the type of punishment – hence the defendant is sentenced. If the defendant is sentenced to imprisonment then

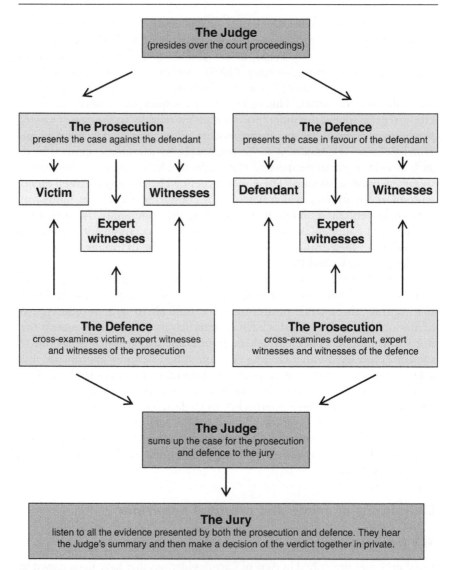

*Figure 1.2* Outline of a typical courtroom procedure
Taylor 2015. Reproduced with kind permission from Taylor and Francis.

he or she becomes a prisoner. In the UK the courtroom procedure is highly stylised as shown in Figure 1.2.

Legal processes, however, differ cross-culturally (Andrews and Bonta 2006) and do so as a consequence of variations in cultural infrastructure (Crowther 2007). Despite these variations, McGuire (2004) has argued that there is international congruency in the definition of serious crime and in the treatment by the criminal justice system of individuals who commit serious crimes such as murder and sex offences. Cross-cultural differences of legal implementation and practice, however, are a recognised problem that the International Criminal Court (ICC) has tried to overcome. The ICC Statute was adopted in Rome in 1998 as a declaration with intent to subject different state sovereignty to an international criminal jurisdiction.

According to Cassese (1999), the ICC Statute or Roman Statute, as it is also known, can be considered in two ways: first, as an international treaty law, and second, in terms of its contribution towards **substantive** (statutory or written law) and **procedural** (rules governing how all aspects of a court case are conducted) international criminal law. As an international treaty, the Roman Statute discusses the political and diplomatic variations across different countries and is upfront in highlighting the problems it faces at solving anomalies in the major issues of law. It is in substantive international law that the Roman Statute has made advances (Cassese 1999). One of the main differences between national law and international law relates to the principle of specificity. This principle requires that criminal rules have clarity and transparency which means that core elements of a crime must be detailed and defined. This can be seen in the case of a murder charge, where details of what constitutes murder in the first degree are separate from manslaughter. Likewise the type of sentence and length of sentence are clarified and made transparent to the assailant. This is often the case in national laws where the accused is well-informed of why his or her behaviour is prohibited, but this is less defined in international laws.

What constitutes a crime is defined under *corpus delicti*, which literally means 'body of crime'. *Corpus delicti* can be broken down into two elements both of which must be present for an act to be legally considered as a crime: *actus reus* ('guilty act') and *mens rea* ('guilty mind' – see next section). These two elements must be proven in a court of law in order to satisfy *corpus delicti*. The Roman Statute has considered *actus reus* and *mens rea* as important elements in deciding whether an individual acted in a manner that contravenes the law. *Mens rea* in particular has been considered under the principle of specificity, where a shared international understanding has received tighter clarification.

### Actus reus and mens rea

Actus reus has been defined in the Webster's New World Law Dictionary as:

> voluntary and wrongful act or omission that constitutes the physical components of a crime. Because a person cannot be punished for bad thoughts . . . there can be no criminal liability without *actus reus*.
>
> (2010 p.13)

According to Giles (1990, p.1) *actus reus* also 'consists of whatever circumstances and consequences are recognised for liability for the offence in question – in other words all the elements of an offence other than the mental element'. This guilty act can be against another person or property or could involve failing to act when legally required to do so (i.e. a doctor not saving a person's life even though they had taken the Hippocratic oath to save lives regardless of circumstance). However, it is not enough to commit a guilty act for it to constitute criminal behaviour. The Latin maxim *'actus non facitreum nisi mens sit rea'* states this well – meaning an act does not make a person guilty unless the mind is guilty. There has to be *mens rea* which suggests criminal intent: a guilty mind. *Mens rea* has been defined in the Webster's New World Law Dictionary as:

> defendant's guilty state of mind, as an element in proving the crime with which he or she is charged.
>
> (2010 p.178)

The terms *actus reus* and *mens rea* were first introduced by Aristotle in 350 BC in Book One of *Rhetoric*. There have been many translations of his work over the years, but Wexler's (2010) summary of Aristotle's writings on the usage of *actus reus* and *mens rea* in relation to 'injustices', 'missings of the mark' and 'bad luck' is most informative. For instance, in the case of an 'injustice' where a bad act had been intentionally committed then both *actus reus* and *mens rea* are present but for acts that are considered as 'missings of the mark', only *actus reus* is present. For acts of 'bad luck', neither *actus reus* or *mens rea* are present. Acts categorised by Aristotle as 'injustices' involve a bad act committed intentionally with ill will to the victim. While acts of 'missings of the mark' are also bad acts that are intentionally committed, in such cases, however, there is no ill will to the victim. This is further elaborated through the use of the Greek words *mochthêrias* and *ponêrias*, which refer to 'wickedness' and 'badness' respectively. Wexler (2010) claimed it is *ponêrias* that is used for acts of 'injustice' whilst 'missings of the mark' could have been avoided. In other words, Aristotle reserved the word badness for acts committed intentionally and *mochthêrias* or wickedness for unavoidable events that occurred through bad luck.

An example of a guilty act with guilty intent is a man who, without provocation, stalks and attacks a stranger with a knife which causes grievous bodily harm. Provided there are no mental health issues, the man is guilty with intent to cause harm to an individual. The *actus reus* is the attack on the victim and the *mens rea* is the intent to cause harm and knowing that his actions will do this. According to Giles (1990), 'intention must first be distinguished from motive' (p.8) when considering the liability of an individual's actions. Giles (1990) illustrates this through the case of Steane who in 1947 was charged 'with intent to assist the enemy' (pp.8–9). Steane was an actor and lived in Germany before the outbreak of World War II. When war began, Joseph Goebbels had Steane arrested, assaulted and coerced him into broadcasting misleading information in English on Germany's behalf. At the end of the war Steane was charged by Mr Justice Henn-Collins with 'doing acts likely to assist the enemy with

*Plate 1.1* Justice
© ER_09. Image used under license from Shutterstock.com. Available at http://www.shutterstock.com/pic.mhtml?id=3381 1846&src=id

intent to assist the enemy'. In Steane's defence it was argued that, 'his intent was not to assist the enemy but to save his family'. This defence saved Steane from being convicted as a traitor and receiving a sentence of life in prison: his *mens rea* presented by the defence helped commute his sentence to three years in prison.

Although *mens rea* is a familiar element of national laws it remained unaddressed and undefined in international law until 1998 when the Roman Statute was founded (Cassese 1999). In a report outlining the modes of liability for genocide, war crimes and crimes against humanity, the International Criminal Law Services (ICLS) devised in-depth definitions of individual criminal responsibility for international use. The forms of criminal responsibility included the stages of:

1  planning;
2  instigating;
3  ordering;
4  committing (direct perpetration);
5  aiding and abetting in the planning, preparation or execution of a crime;
6  joint criminal enterprise (which is considered to be a form of commission);
7  superior/command responsibility;
8  co-perpetration (joint perpetration) (considered as commission);
9  indirect perpetration (considered as commission);
10 indirect co-perpetration (considered as commission) (ICLS 2011, p.4).

Box 1.2 examines details of how *actus reus* and *mens rea* are applied to each of the above stages by the ICLS.

## Box 1.2

### Describes how *actus reus* and *mens rea* are involved in stages 1 to 10 by ICLS

In the case of the planning stage of a crime, *actus reus* refers to an individual organising and implementing the crime whereas the *mens rea* asserts that the accused intended and willingly planned and was aware of the crime.

In the case of instigation of a crime, *actus reus* refers to the instigation of the crime by encouraging an individual to break the law whereas *mens rea* asserts that it was the accused's intention to enable the crime to occur while showing awareness of the likely consequences following the criminal act.

In the case of ordering of a crime, *actus reus* refers to an individual in authority who orders others to break the law whereas *mens rea* asserts that the accused would be knowledgeable of the consequences of the order given.

In the case of committing (direct perpetration) of a crime, *actus reus* refers to an individual actually committing the crime that contravenes the law whereas *mens rea* asserts that the accused intended for the crime to be committed.

In the case of aiding and abetting of a crime, *actus reus* refers to assisting and supporting the perpetrator to contravene the law whereas *mens rea* asserts that the individual was aware of the consequences the assistance provided would cause.

In the case of joint criminal enterprise (JCE), *actus reus* refers to more than one individual involved in the planning and enactment of the crime whereas *mens rea* asserts that any individual involved in planning and committing the crime is just as liable and intended for the common plan to be operationalised.

In the case of direct perpetration, *actus reus* refers to the perpetrator being liable for carrying out the criminal act whereas *mens rea* asserts that the crime was committed intentionally and knowingly.

In the case of indirect perpetration, *actus reus* refers to the accused as not actually carrying out the crime but inducing another individual to do so whereas *mens rea* asserts that the accused in this case was responsible for making another individual perform the criminal act.

In the case of indirect co-perpetration, *actus reus* refers to two or more individuals organising a crime, each with their own role to perform whereas *mens rea* asserts that each individual acted intentionally with full knowledge of how the plan was to be implemented and the importance of their role in the plan and the consequences concerning the success of the crime if they failed to play their part.

---

ICLS dissolved in 2013 and all publication copyrights have been transferred to the Institute for International Criminal Investigations (IICI) who in turn has made these publications public.

Defining *actus reus* and *mens rea* for international jurisdiction serves the dual purpose of standardising what is meant by these terms and how they are implemented in the course of collating evidence for both national and international criminal prosecution. In Article 30 of the Roman Statute, *mens rea* is defined as consisting of 'intent' and 'knowledge' of a criminal perpetration. Cassese (1999), however, suggested the inclusion of 'recklessness' as another element of **culpability**. Cassese (1999) provided the following example to highlight the need for recklessness: A person who shells a town without intending to kill any civilians but takes the risk and decision to proceed knowing that there is a high probability that civilians will be killed (who are subsequently killed after the act) is culpable for reckless behaviour (see Boxes 11.10 and 11.11).

The combination of *actus reus* and *mens rea* for the most part operate in tandem, but there are examples where multiple factors are considered which can lead to mitigation of responsibility. Examples where an individual is exempt from criminal responsibility include: age; mental impairment and learning difficulty; ignorance or mistake of fact; and self-defence – each of these will be considered in turn.

## AGE OF CRIMINAL RESPONSIBILITY

A minor (i.e. a child under the age of criminal responsibility) is considered incapable of understanding his or her actions and hence is exempt from criminal responsibility. There is much variation across countries in the age set for criminal responsibility. The lowest set age of 7 is found in Switzerland, Nigeria and South Africa, followed closely at 8 years in Sri Lanka. In England and Wales, Northern Ireland, Australia and New Zealand the minimum age of criminal responsibility is 10 years, whereas in Scotland the age of criminal responsibility has increased from 8 to 12 (since the amendment to the Criminal Justice and Licensing (Scotland) Act 2010). In The Netherlands, Canada, Greece and Turkey this is also set at 12. Other countries have a higher minimum age, such as in Sweden, where it is set at 15; in Spain and Poland it is 16; in France, Belgium and most American states it is 18 and finally in Japan it is set at 20.

In England and Wales, children 10–17 years can be taken to court for committing a crime, but they stand trial in youth courts, are sentenced differently from adults and spend their sentence in special secure centres rather than prison (see Box 4.3 for discussion of child-killers Thompson and Venables). It has been argued that the age of 10 set in England and Wales is low in comparison to many other countries, but the jurisdiction for juveniles operates differently to that for adults which means they are not subjected to the same treatment and punishment. Offenders aged 18 and over, however, are considered as adults and expected to stand trial in adult courts. Recently, there has been lobbying for the age of criminal responsibility in England and Wales to be raised to 12, however, the Ministry of Justice in 2010 rejected this on the grounds that children of ages 10 to 12 understand the difference between behaving badly and committing a serious wrongful act. Whether the age of criminal responsibility should be raised is an on-going debate but in March 2012 it was reported in the national press that MPs are lobbying for the age of criminal responsibility to be raised to 14 years of age to be on a par with the European average. In 2011 there were 40,000 offences committed by 10–14 year olds of which 5,600 experienced the juvenile criminal justice system (Doyle 2012).

Even though the age of exemption from criminal responsibility varies across many countries, it is important to consider what happens to those between the age of 10 and 18 as a way of understanding why these differences in age of responsibility exist. In England and Wales this age group is not under the jurisdiction of an adult court but of special courts serving juveniles. As can be seen in Box 1.3, despite the fact that the age of exemption from criminal responsibility being set at 18 in the state of California, the introduction of Proposition 21 means that in some cases a minor can be tried in an adult court. Young Japanese offenders below 20 are under the jurisdiction of the Family Court rather than the criminal court. Recent amendments to Japan's Juvenile Law in 2000, has promoted tougher measures to reduce juvenile **delinquency**. Japan has seen a transition towards **deterrence** using threats of strict punishment such that children below 14 can now be tried through the criminal justice system rather than the welfare route that was previously endorsed (Sasaki 2005). In

China, the juvenile system deals with children between 14 and 18 years, but they can still be sentenced to life imprisonment for serious crimes. The age of exemption from criminal responsibility has been raised to 18 in Peru, Brazil and Columbia, but children aged 12 to 18 years can be convicted of crimes under the jurisdiction of a juvenile justice system. Hence we can see that there is much variation in the age of exemption from criminal responsibility which reflects a limited international consensus of when an understanding of criminal behaviour is considered to develop.

## Box 1.3

### A case of Californian treatment of juveniles

In California, children under the age of 14 who commit an illegal act are considered incapable of committing this when there is little evidence to suggest they were aware of the wrongfulness of their behaviour (Californian Penal Code (PC) 26). In the state of California there is a category of offences known as status offences whereby those under 18 who commit certain types of crimes are tried as minors. Their juvenile laws have the role of *parens patriae* which when translated from Latin means 'the parenthood of the state'. In Californian law this implies that the state can help those unable to protect themselves (i.e. children) using rulings from legislated statutes. *Parens patriae* is a means of allowing a person under 18 years to be considered a minor and therefore under the jurisdiction of the juvenile court. However, since the introduction of Proposition 21 (a get-tough-on-crime initiative especially in the case of gang members and juvenile offenders), under 18 year olds can be tried in an adult court. This was demonstrated by 14 year old Tony Hicks who murdered Tariq Khamisa in 1995 and stood trial as an adult and received a 25 year prison sentence. A new label for these minors now tried in adult courts was introduced – 'youthful offenders'. A 14 year old or older will be tried in an adult court for: murder (Section 197 of the PC), sex offences such as rape (Section 261 of the PC), spousal rape (Section 262 of the PC), forcible sex offences (Section 264.1 of the PC) and forcible lewd and lascivious acts on a child under 14 (Section 288 of the PC), forcible sexual penetration (Section 289 of the PC), sodomy or oral copulation by force, violence, duress . . . (Section 286 or 288a of the PC). The consequences for a child of 14 or older who commits any of the above offences is to be tried in an adult court and sentenced in the same way as an adult offender. Under these circumstances there is no juvenile court or special juvenile detainment centre. There are, however, fitness hearings held for juvenile offenders prior to going to court as a way of ascertaining whether they should be charged as juveniles or adults.

In the UK the debate surrounding the set-point age of criminal responsibility has drawn upon recent research released by the Royal Society, suggesting that the neural circuits of the brain continue to develop throughout adolescence (Mackintosh 2011). Evidence from neuroscience studies supports the view that the brain of a 10–15 year old is immature for many important functions such as memory, suggestibility, decision making and impulsivity (Mackintosh 2011). It is possible that in the future, setting an appropriate age of criminal responsibility that is internationally recognised might no longer rest on national politics but on evidence from neuroscience. For further reading see *Cipriani (2009) Children's Rights and the Minimum Age of Criminal Responsibility: A Global Perspective and the Justice for Children Briefing No. 4, The Minimum Age of Criminal Responsibility.*

## MENTALLY IMPAIRED AND LEARNING DISABILITY

According to the Crown Prosecution Service (CPS), an individual who is a suspect or has committed a crime and is known to have a disability or disorder of the mind is referred to as a **mentally disordered offender**. The Mental Health Act (MHA) 2007 introduced amendments to the MHA 1983 that changed the definition of mental disorder to 'any disorder or disability of the mind' – hence providing a more generic guideline. Today, 'any disorder or disability of the mind', encompasses a number of established clinical mental health classifications such as personality and autistic spectrum disorders, learning disabilities and mental illnesses such as schizophrenia, depression and bipolar disorder. The definition used to describe a learning disability by the MHA 2007 is 'a state of arrested or incomplete development of the mind which includes significant impairment of intelligence and social functioning' (Section 2(3) of the Mental Health Act 2007).

In English law every individual is presumed to be sane and therefore accountable for his or her actions. Hence it is the responsibility of the defence to demonstrate insanity at the time of the offence, with the prosecution's role being to establish *mens rea* beyond reasonable doubt. There are specific requirements for *mens rea* which the prosecutor has to fulfil. In the case of an offender with a mental disorder the prosecutor must provide evidence of their ability to develop a *mens rea*. Normally the service of an independent medical assessor is used for this purpose and the report of the individual's mental health helps decide their fitness to plead. To establish grounds for absence of *mens rea*, an individual who is impaired of mind (usually associated with low intelligence) must show an inability to know right from wrong. An individual might also experience a psychotic episode during the committal of an offence (i.e. as in schizophrenia or bipolar depression) which compromised their ability to know right from wrong at that time (see Chapter 11).

## IGNORANCE OR MISTAKE OF FACT OR LAW

In English law there are two important elements regarding ignorance: mistake of fact and mistake of law. In the case of mistake of law there are three types of mistake (Singh 2011):

- mistake of law of the country;
- mistake of foreign law;
- mistake of private right of the parties.

In the case of 'mistake of law of the country', ignorance is rarely an accepted defence for violating the law. This is because all citizens (i.e. with the exception of minors and the mentally impaired) are presumed to be familiar with and know and understand the law. While citizens are expected to know their own law they are not expected to know the law in other countries and so if they contravene the law in another country then the offence can be treated as a mistake of fact (Singh 2011). In the case of a 'mistake of fact' ignorance can be used as a defence for committing a criminal act – in other words, there is proof of *actus reus* but not *mens rea* (i.e. the unlawful act occurred but there was no intention to act unlawfully). Ignorance or mistake of fact can be used as a defence provided that:

- the ignorance or mistake negates the purpose, knowledge, belief, recklessness or negligence required to establish a material element of the offence;
- the law provides that the state of mind established by such ignorance or mistake constitutes a defence (Randall 2007).

An example where criminal responsibility is not taken into account occurs when the perpetrator is unaware that they have broken the law on the grounds of mistake of fact. Hence an adult who unknowingly had sexual intercourse with an under-aged adolescent demonstrates the concept of mistake of fact. In this case the perpetrator did not consciously choose to break the law and should not be perceived as morally blameworthy. Furthermore, a mistake of fact can be unilateral when the 'mistake as to the identity of the person contracted with' is one-sided (Singh 2011). This example highlights a mistake of fact where the act was carried out as a consequence of unconscious ignorance. Simons (2011) provides an example of mistake of law using the British case of Regina v. Smith. The defendant lived in rented accommodation and had installed wall panels and floor boards to improve the property. When he vacated the property, he damaged the wall panels and floor boards and was later convicted of causing damage under the Criminal Damage Act. In this case the defendant believed that he was damaging his own property (i.e. the wall panels and floors) that he had installed. Under the property law once the wall panels and floors were installed they came under the ownership of the landlord.

The defendant therefore was causing damage to the property of another. The court concluded that despite the *actus reus* of damaging property belonging to another, there was little evidence to support an underlying *mens rea* for this as the defendant believed that the property he was damaging belonged to himself. This example illustrates the defence of ignorance of the law regarding property ownership since this was not made 'reasonably known to the defendant' before he committed the act.

### ACTING IN SELF-DEFENCE

Acting in self-defence against an attacker will also exempt an individual from prosecution because the attacker's actions caused and forced the individual to retaliate. If the retaliation consisted of **reasonable force**, then a person is not culpable. The case of Tony Martin highlights the challenges that courts face when considering what is not meant by 'reasonable force'. In 1999 Martin received a custodial sentence for murder after shooting two burglars at his home. He confessed to shooting in self-defence but had not intended to kill anyone – hence there was *actus reus* but no *mens rea*. His sentence was later commuted to manslaughter. This case highlights the problem of defining reasonable force in situations of self-defence, as there are no guidelines provided by the criminal justice system. A victim becomes culpable once the force used in defence of self and property exceeds what is considered to be reasonable force: the problem, however, concerns awareness of the boundaries between reasonable and unreasonable force.

As an exemption from criminal responsibility how the law defines reasonable force and its use in self-defence, is clearly a difficult one to resolve. The Criminal Justice and Immigration Act of 2008 says that homeowners who use 'reasonable force' to protect themselves against intruders should not be prosecuted, providing they use no more force than is absolutely necessary. Kenneth Clarke, the UK Justice Secretary, caused controversy when he made the comment in 2011 that householders can 'use whatever force necessary' to protect themselves and their homes. On the 29 June 2011, however, he was forced to retract this comment stating that he had meant 'reasonable and proportionate' use of force should be advocated. Kenneth Clarke's initial comment illustrates the difficulty that even Ministers have in describing what reasonable force entails. Note that whilst the term 'reasonable and proportionate force' is in line with the Criminal Justice and Immigration Act of 2008, it is, however, arguably no more helpful in clarifying what is considered to be reasonable force.

All the above four factors that can lead to exemption from criminal responsibility have problems of clarity and definition. The way in which they are assessed can be tricky even in cases which appear to be straightforward such as being the initial victim. Furthermore, having an internationally set age of criminal responsibility ignores individual differences in the development of children. If set too high there is cause to suspect that some young perpetrators might 'get off' lightly, whereas if set too low there could be genuine grounds for concern that some offenders are too young to understand the consequences of their actions. There are assessments for individuals with mental impairment and learning disability which have been rigorously subjected to reliable testing but even with this in place there are individuals who are misdiagnosed or who somehow fail to be assessed for mental issues. Following the right procedures and systems can help prevent offenders entitled to exemption from remaining undetected, but this can only be successful when the law brings clarity to what constitutes exemption from criminal responsibility.

While legal concepts of *actus reus* and *mens rea* are used to establish whether a crime had been committed intentionally, it is the distinction between *mala in se* and *mala prohibita* which helps to categorise the type of crime committed. *Mala in se* and *mala prohibita* are used to classify the level of seriousness of criminal acts. These terms have important historical implications for the basis of crime classification in English law and the laws of other countries throughout the world. Because it relates to generally perceived moral conduct, *mala in se* in particular has been influenced by religion and continues to be linked with religious teachings of human morality. Hence knowledge of *mala in se* is pivotal to understanding the historical foundations of our legal systems. In brief, crimes which contravene human moral codes are known as *mala in se*. Crimes which contravene statutes of law are known as *mala prohibita* (plural case for *prohibitum*). What is actually meant by *mala in se* and *mala prohibita* will be discussed next with reference to their historical use.

### Mala in se and mala prohibita

In the late 1400s during the reign of Henry VII, legal reference to the terms *mala in se* and *mala prohibita* was first introduced and later formalised in the legal publication of *The Commentaries* by Sir William Blackstone during the 1760s (Blackstone, 1765–1769). Blackstone described and explained the *mala in se* and *mala prohibita* distinction as:

> [D]ivine or natural duties [do not] receive any stronger sanction from being also declared to be duties by the law of the land. The case is the same . . . to crimes and misdemeanours . . . forbidden by the superior laws, . . . therefore . . . *mala in se*, . . . legislature in all these cases acts only . . . in subordination to the great lawgiver (p.54).

Put simply, this means that because *mala in se* crimes contravene human moral codes which are forbidden from a higher authority, such as God in the case of Christianity, statutory laws (or laws of the land) cannot add to the level of punishment reserved for *mala in se* crimes. Statutory laws are perceived as inferior to the laws of the Divine and its powers are therefore limited. A more

up-to-date definition of how *mala in se* and *mala prohibita* are related to crime
is provided in the MSN Encarta (2007) where:

> Crimes . . . classified as *mala in se*, which includes acts, such as murder, so
> offensive to morals . . .; and *mala prohibita*, which are violations of specific
> regulatory statutes, such as traffic violations, that ordinarily would not be
> punishable in the absence of statutory enactments prohibiting the commis-
> sion of such acts (p.4).

Downes and Rock (2003) claimed that all crimes can be divided into *mala in
se* and *mala prohibita* and according to Davis (2006), 'legal scholars have used
the terms *mala prohibita* and *mala in se* to draw the distinction between legally
proscribed and morally proscribed offences' (pp. 270–89). In other words,
*mala in se* is used to signify crimes that are wrong in their own right, whereas
*mala prohibita* refers to crimes that are wrong because they are prohibited by
the law (Mojo Law, 2008). Hence *mala prohibita* crimes are criminalised by
statute for the purpose of regulating the behaviours of the populace (Lehman
and Phelps 2005), whereas *mala in se* crimes include behaviours that cause
harm to a person and to the property of others (i.e. crimes such as murder,
rape, aggravated burglary, theft and arson). (Blackstone's conception of *mala
in se* (1765–1769) involved the laws of God and connected *mala in se* to
notions of evil and sin. Although Blackstone clearly considered the Ten
Commandments in his writings of the legal system and law per se, there was
one Commandment which he omitted to consider as *mala in se* – the seventh
Commandment regarding theft. As far as Blackstone was concerned, theft was
a matter for *mala prohibita*. However, his legacy of theft as an example of *mala
prohibita* has not been adhered to and many contemporary legal writers have
considered it as *mala in se* – as is reflected in the recording of theft in crime
statistics).

This distinction between crimes of *mala in se* and *mala prohibita* is further
reflected in the severity of punishment awarded – severe and less severe respectively. Even within crimes of *mala in se*, there are gradations of seriousness and
extremity, as is demonstrated in serial killings or murders involving unusual
**modus operandi** (i.e. 'method of operation' such as the use of torture to execute
their crime).

In the case of *mala prohibita*, Lehman and Phelps (2005) considered actions
such as violation of driving laws, trespassing, gambling, drug abuse and drug
trafficking as typical examples of prohibited crimes. Hagan (1998) argued that
laws governing less serious offences of *mala prohibita* are designed to maintain
the **status quo** within a given society and in so doing provide a more predictable and ordered place for its citizens to reside. A definition of *mala prohibita*
provided in Black's Law Dictionary (Black, Nolan, and Nolan-Haley 1990,
p.960) states that, 'an act which is not inherently immoral, but becomes so
because its commission is expressly forbidden by positive law'.

If *mala in se* and *mala prohibita* are meant to be mutually exclusive categories (which not everyone agrees is the case), then it should be easy to separate different types of crime according to seriousness: *mala prohibita* offences should include all that falls outside of what offences constitute *mala in se* (Davis 2006). Downes and Rock (2003) claimed that although these categories are mutually exclusive, there has to be flexibility to enable some criminal conduct to shift from one category into the other. A good example of this is the shift in attitude, condemnation and punishment towards drink driving. Drink driving is an act prohibited by law which carries negative consequences if caught (i.e. *mala prohibita*), however, it also receives moral condemnation if another individual is harmed due to the driver having blood levels of alcohol over the acceptable legal limit set (arguably *mala in se*). According to Moore (1996), dynamic changes in law can be initiated through social pressure and the lobbying of government for a change in the status of particular crimes so as to reflect public opinion and the prevailing social **zeitgeist** or 'spirit of the times' (see Sociology and criminology: Social constructionism later in this chapter).

Nevertheless, even with social pressure and lobbying government to change the status of particular crimes, there remains little change of attitude towards *mala in se* crimes. Why this is the case might be answered by addressing the influence of religion in dictating which crimes contravene the human moral code. Furthermore, religious influence (whatever the domination) spans many different countries – could this explain why there are more cross-cultural similarities in punishment for *mala in se* crimes than there are differences? As these are important concepts to the development of laws, discussion of their relevance to the history and evolution of English law and jurisprudence, and their association with religion will be considered next.

### History of English law and the role of religion

In Britain, prior to William the Conqueror in 1066, there was no separation between law courts and **ecclesiastical courts** (courts held as supreme governor of the Church used for religious matters). The bishops and priests sat and headed the courts and dispensed punishments such as excommunication for 'sacred offences' (Oakley 1923, cited in Jeffery 1957; Potter 2012). Bishops and priests investigated cases, acted as judge and jury and made all the decisions including the nature of punishment. This approach to legal procedure is known as the **inquisitorial system** which many countries continue to use. The inquisitorial system operates differently from current English law in the way evidence is collected and prepared for trial and the composition of the judiciary (i.e. trial by jury was not used in the early days of the inquisitorial system of law). The **adversarial system** used in English law uses a host of legal professionals to gather evidence (i.e. police) and present their case (i.e. on the one side lawyers for the prosecution and on the other for the defence) to a jury (i.e. consisting of 12 individuals who listen to the evidence for both sides of the case and collectively decide whether the defendant is guilty or not). In seventh century England, the Anglo-Saxon King Ethelbert introduced the Rochester Book which consisted of a list of fines and compensations for many types of losses (e.g. loss of an ear was awarded a sum of money that could be negotiated by the families concerned). This system according to Potter (2012), however, lacked any moral underpinnings simply because disputes were settled using ideals of commodity. This meant that perpetrators repaid their victims according to a sum considered suitable by the victim's family which encouraged an arbitrary monetary system rather than remorse based on the acknowledgement of wrongdoing. It did, however, introduce a form of regulation that helped reduce the number of pre-existing blood feuds. Box 1.4 provides a brief history of how laws were conceived from times of antiquity and the gradual increase in regulatory rulings and systems of compensation.

After Ethelbert's reign, a two-tiered system of law court was introduced in the 900s by King Ethelstan, known as the Hundreds and the Shire courts. The Hundreds courts were equivalent to local town courts, which dealt with less serious offences, unlike the Shire courts that had a Bishop or a representative of the King known as a Shire-reeve (from which the term 'sheriff' was eventually derived). If an offence was religious related, then a Bishop would preside over the court and decide the accused's guilt or innocence using evidence provided by 'witnesses' under oath. This was an effective and just system as far as the church was concerned, as lying under oath meant mortal sin and condemnation. King Ethelstan was head adjudicator of the law and by 925 had introduced a series of law codes. An example of this would be a thief who stole more than eight pence was punished physically (i.e. by mutilation such as the removal of hands and arms).

## Box 1.4

### A history of law timeline from antiquity

Twenty-first century BC in Sumer: Law Codes in 57 Articles under King Ur-Nammu compiled to help protect and preserve personal rights. Prescribed penalties for specific cases that provided a formalised system of punishments.

Twentieth century BC in Sumer: 50 Articles in the law code of the *Lipit-Istar* in Sumer compiled to help protect and preserve personal rights. Prescribed penalties for specific cases that provided a formalised system of punishments.

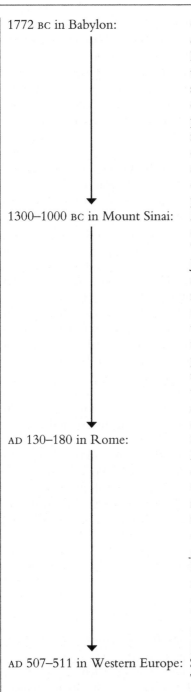

| | |
|---|---|
| 1772 BC in Babylon: | Code of Hammurabi provided codes of conduct that were religious in nature. Developed a standardised legal system to protect the vulnerable, establish a system of punishment equitable with the crime committed and to provide foster placements for juvenile delinquents from dysfunctional families. Used corporal punishment and confinement and trepanation (old surgical practice of cutting a hole in the skull) to cure those possessed by a demon. |
| 1300–1000 BC in Mount Sinai: | Mosaic Law based on the first five books of the Old Testament encapsulated in the Torah that contained 365 prohibitions. Judges officiated over the courts of justice and ruled that society must take some responsibility for crimes committed. Officials trained in cross-examination worked in Temples of Justice. Introduced the concept of righteousness and perpetrators who behaved inherently bad were punished by beheading; prostitutes were burned; kidnappers were stoned; assault warranted flogging and property crimes received a fine (O'Connor 2010). |
| AD 130–180 in Rome: | Systematised laws across the Roman Empire contained legal concepts and rules of law stipulated in the Commentaries of Gaius on the Twelve Tables which was regarded as a tort (i.e. a civil wrong arising from an act or failure to act). Concept of dominion had close links with *pater familias* (who is the male head of the household and has authority over its members) where property matters were dealt with by the *pater* (Daube 1969). The *pater* would receive compensation if there was a breach of law concerning his property. |
| AD 507–511 in Western Europe: | Salic Law is one example of the Teutonic Laws. It is a law of penal and procedural code and contains lists of fines (composition) for different offences. |

> It includes civil law enactments such as daughters forbidden from inheriting land. There were other Teutonic laws belonging to various Germanic tribes. These too had a system of monetary compensations that befitted the seriousness of the crime committed.

Bishops adjudicating Shire courts during the 900s, however, had their own system of trial and punishment such as the **Trial by Ordeal**. One example of the Trial by Ordeal involved the accused holding a hot iron rod, whose burns were then bandaged and checked a couple of days later for healing (therefore not guilty) or festering (therefore guilty). Another example involved immersing the accused into holy water. If they sank they were innocent but if they floated they were guilty.

William the Conqueror in 1066 kept the law as it was, but changed the method of ordeal to trial by combat. In 1154 Henry II introduced a common law and royal justices who were given authority to ensure the Shire courts were operating according to his common law (Potter 2012). Henry II also introduced 'juries of presentment' who were representatives from local communities, reporting while under oath, all crimes committed in their area to the Justice of the Shire (Potter 2012). As the clergy were in holy orders, they remained exempt from common law but under the jurisdiction of Canon Law (see Box 1.5). This meant that if they committed serious offences, the Cleric would be ordered by the Bishop to purge his sin. A commoner could also claim to be a Cleric, thereby 'removing his soul' from the secular authorities of the King, which remained until King John in 1215 gave the seal of approval to a legal document known as the Magna Carta. No longer could Clerics preside over trials of ordeal which was substantiated further by Pope Innocent III's ban on priests from blessing ordeals in 1215. Blessing ordeals was a holy ritual performed by priests who used prayer and holy water to save the accused's soul and was even applied to the weapon of ordeal such as the 'hot rod' (Pilarczyk 1996).

## Box 1.5

### Canon Law

Canon Law has its own legal system consisting of courts, lawyers and judges and a legal doctrine with codes of practice and uses panels of judges that direct an investigation using the inquisitorial approach (see Chapter 13). This is different from the adversarial approach used in Britain, which enlists a single judge to control the court and instruct a jury to consider the evidence presented by barristers. Although Canon Law existed before the thirteenth century, it was not until after the Magna Carta that it developed more fully by a monk called Gratian who edited *The Harmony of Discordant Canons* (Guyer 2012). In modern England and Wales, Christian Canon Law is similar to **civil law** (laws of the state or nation) and there are 1,752 religious codes or canons written before 1983 that are used by the Roman Catholic Church today as a legal guide governing behaviours for followers to uphold. This includes acceptable and forbidden behaviours which could potentially conflict with law and/or be a part of it. Canon law is regarded as a human law inspired by the word of God which has the legislative authority to regulate the internal structure and function of the Roman Catholic Church and the British Parliament for the Church of England. Hence the jurisdiction of Canon Law in modern England and Wales is limited to the clergy and matters of the Church. The canons continue to provide codifications of acceptable behaviour from which core principles in **civil law** derive (Arnold-Baker 2008; Fromont 2001).

With the introduction of the Magna Carta and Pope Innocent III's ban on priests blessing ordeals, English law diverged from the European inquisitorial approach (which used torture to obtain confessions) to the adversarial system of trial by jury (Potter 2012). In modern Britain, the use of trials by ordeal certainly no longer occurs, but this is not the case worldwide. The Integrated Regional Information Networks (IRIN) established by the United Nations to document events contravening humanitarian rights, reported in 2007 the use of red-hot metal placed on the limbs of four youths aged 16–26 accused of robbery in Liberia. This **Trial by Ordeal** was witnessed and condoned by people living in the village of Klay. The verdict of 'not guilty' was based on the expressions of pain portrayed by the four youths. The role of religion continues to influence law in specific countries including Canon Law used by the Roman Catholic Church and Islamic Sharia operating in Muslim countries (see Box 1.6).

## Box 1.6

### Islamic Sharia

Sharia is the sacred law of Islam, and Muslims believe Sharia is God's law (Otto 2008) and that it derives from two sacred books within Islamic Law. The first is the *Qur'an* which encapsulates the divine revelations and the second is the *Sunnah* which contains the life example set by the Prophet Muhammad. A doctrine in Islam known as *Ilmul Yaqin* has two components: what is good or *Husna* (must be done) and what is evil or *Qubh* (must not be done). The principles underlying *Husna* and *Qubh* known as *Shariats* are pervasive and influence every aspect of a Muslim's life, including sexuality. For example, in Iran homosexuality is prohibited in law and is considered an immoral behaviour that is against religious belief, which is why it receives the death penalty. To escape the death penalty in Iran, many homosexuals are resorting to extreme measures, such as sex change operations, which are legal courtesy of Ayatollah Khomeini, who in 1979 passed a religious edict allowing individuals to be diagnosed as transsexuals. It was suggested in the BBC broadcast 'Transsexual in Iran' that many gay individuals take advantage of this to be with their gay partner (Barford 2008). Islamic Sharia, scholars have argued, is akin to common law but also influences a few aspects of civil law (Badr 1978; El-Gamal 2006; Makdisi 1999). The extent to which Sharia dictates common law depends on the Islamic country considered. In secular Muslim countries (for example Turkey, Mali and Kazakhstan) religious interference in law is prohibited (Otto 2008). Muslim countries like Pakistan, Afghanistan, Egypt, Sudan, Malaysia and Morocco have legal systems that are influenced by Sharia but are still governed by the rules of state law. These countries have modernised their legal systems such that there are robust differences between the law and classical Sharia (Otto 2008). Finally there are countries endorsing classical Sharia such as Saudi Arabia and other states of the Gulf region. In these countries there are no constitutions, legislatures or common law, and those in power, have no authority to change this since classical Sharia is adopted as the ruling word of the land (Otto 2008). Sharia law also has influences in the secular states of the West. In a recent report, for example, it was estimated that 85 Sharia councils were operating in Britain in 2009 (Talwar 2012). Sharia councils have operated in Britain alongside civil and common law since 1982, and despite having no legal powers to implement penalties, their use has tripled in the last five years with 200–300 cases processed per month.

The historical connection between law and religion in Britain was apparent even before William the Conqueror. Although defendants are tried in a court of law, religion continues to influence our morality and the morality of society. It prescribes what is considered to be 'good' and 'bad' behaviour so much so that we are **socialised** by our parents to instil a code of conduct conforming with the mores and values of society (which are based on past teachings from the church). Whilst each country has its own laws, there is still an overarching commonality on what constitutes morality and moral behaviour. Furthermore, the usage of *mala in se* and *mala prohibita*, transcends culture. *Mala in se* and *mala prohibita* are utilised in modern day jurisprudence. The **philosophy of equity** (or just desserts) where the punishment fits the crime lends itself to jurisprudence (see Appendix for the England and Wales listings of different sentence tariffs for 2011 by thelawpages), and does so cross-culturally. Cross-culturally there is a general trend for *mala in se* crimes (crimes considered against the human moral code) to receive the highest sentence tariffs. Cross-cultural similarity in the jurisprudence of *mala in se* crimes provides further support of the division between *mala in se* and *mala prohibita*, therefore evidence for cross-cultural similarities in punishment for *mala in se* crimes will be considered in more detail next.

### Cross-cultural similarities in punishment for mala in se crimes

It is interesting to note that cross-culturally, *mala in se* crimes, such as homicide, have a sentence tariff of imprisonment (usually a life sentence). In the case of **dangerous offenders** (see Chapter 11), in England and Wales up until 3 December 2012, an indeterminate sentence of Imprisonment for Public Protection (IPP) was used which meant that the offender remained imprisoned indefinitely until the Home Secretary agreed that he or she was no longer dangerous and a threat to society (Dessecker 2004; and see pp. 46, 440–2, 628–9). As is the case with the majority of countries, England and Wales have life imprisonment as a mandatory sentence for crimes such as murder, rape, treason, genocide, crimes against humanity, drug trafficking and terrorism. These crimes are considered as *mala in se* as they are serious offences that cause harm to victims (this connection will be discussed further in Chapter 2). There are, however, some exceptions to the rule such as honour killings, considered a cultural practice (mistakenly viewed as religious practices by some) but is nevertheless illegal and a *mala in se* crime under English law (see Box 1.7).

Countries that do not endorse a mandatory life sentence nevertheless have prison sentences varying in length of incarceration depending on the seriousness of the offence. Hence although life imprisonment is not endorsed in countries such as Bolivia, Brazil, Colombia, Spain, Uruguay and Venezuela, a prison sentence could be a maximum of 30 years and in Bosnia and Herzegovina, Croatia and Serbia this could potentially be 40 years. Mexico, with 60 years, is the highest (Amnesty International 2010).

### Box 1.7

#### Cultural Practices against the Common Law of the adopted country

An important question to address is what happens when a culture-based practice against a woman is committed in a country such as Britain, where it is considered to be a *mala in se* crime: a *mala in se* crime that warrants a punishment within the high sentence tariff. This is a major problem in contemporary British society, where we are increasingly becoming multi-cultural which means we both assimilate and accommodate cultural traditions from different countries and yet reject others which contravene our law.

According to Sheybani (1987), perpetrators of family honour killings are perceived as heroes in their homeland. In cultures where honour killings are acceptable, women are perceived as pivotal to the successful reputation of the family. There are cases, however, where this concept is misused (even within that cultural framework) in favour of the husband achieving his aims, such as in the case of the stoning of Soraya M., accused of flirting so that he could marry a younger woman (Sahebjam 1990). Honour killings committed in a country where it is a *mala in se* criminal act causes conflict between cultural practice and the law of the land which is problematic. Immigrants bring with them their morally acceptable tradition of honour killing which is unacceptable to their adopted host country. Often when perpetrators are charged with murder they claim that they were adhering to their cultural heritage where honour killings are recognised as an acceptable solution to a family problem.

The Gaza Community Mental Health Programme (GCMHP) was founded in 1990 to help communities deal with mental health issues using principles of justice, humanity and implementation of human rights. In 2000, the GCMHP announced that in a culture of honour killings, a man who refrains from 'washing shame with blood' is 'a coward who is not worthy of living' (Feldner 2000). This bears testament to the integral connection between following tradition and being accepted socially. Furthermore, perpetrators of such acts sometimes use the argument of ignorance of the law as a form of defence (see the third factor of exemption from criminal responsibility).

All of these arguments are unsupported under English common law and perpetrators of honour killings are charged and sentenced with murder accordingly. In some Arab states, however, it is codified in penal law that honour murderers will receive a lenient sentence (Feldner 2000). In 2005 the Crown Prosecution Service stated that there were more than a dozen honour killings in the UK for 2004–5 (Gupta 2008). Based on figures from 39 regional police constabularies in the UK, there were 2283 cases of honour killings in 2010. For example, Iftikhar Ahmed and his wife Farzana Ahmed were convicted of committing an honour killing of their daughter Shafilea Ahmed in 2003. Strong evidence that they murdered their daughter convinced jurors of their guilt and they were given custodial sentences of at least 25 years each in August 2012. This sentence is consistent with jurisprudence under English common law.

Some countries have life sentences or long imprisonment and simultaneously practice capital punishment – in 58 nations that actively practice capital punishment, homicide could mean the death penalty (Amnesty International 2010). In the US 33 out of 50 states currently use the death penalty as a legal sentence (Death Penalty Information Centre 2012). A murderer could receive the electric chair as an optional method of execution in the following States of America: Texas, Alabama, Nebraska, Tennessee, Virginia, South Carolina, Florida and Kentucky but would be hanged in Iran, Iraq, Japan, Malaysia, Pakistan, Lebanon, Egypt, India and Singapore (Eriksrud and Trana 2010). The methods of state directed execution may vary cross-culturally but homicide, a *mala in se* classified crime, will usually receive the death penalty in these countries.

Legislation for sentence tariff varies cross-culturally, but what remains consistent is the high price for homicide. This, in part, originated from the traditional law practices in antiquity where *mala in se* crimes deserved appropriate justice in line with the **philosophy of equity**: a retributive equation of just deserts where the punishment suits the seriousness and gravity of the crime committed (Furnham 2003; Lerner 1980). This high price for homicide is seen as fair and appears to reflect the philosophy behind the thinking in jurisprudence and penology (i.e. the punishment of crime and prison management). In Canada, as with many countries, there is a distinction between first and second degree murder. For a first degree murder conviction and a second degree murder conviction (e.g. in cases where the offender was previously convicted of murder), offenders are ineligible for parole for 25 years. In comparison, for cases of second degree murder without mitigating circumstances, this is between 10–25 years. First degree murderers aged 16/17 are ineligible for parole until 10 years has been served, whereas with second degree murder this is seven years. Offenders convicted of first or second degree murder at the age of 14/15 years must serve 5–7 years before they are eligible for parole (Criminal Code of Canada: Sentencing – Imprisonment for Life 2012). In England and Wales murder and manslaughter are the equivalents to first and second degree murder respectively, whereas in Scotland this distinction is referred to as murder and culpable homicide. In Scotland, murder is intentional, whereas for culpable homicide the victim's death is accidental. Despite the semantic differences for these two types of homicide, the underlying principles of why they are classified in these ways are similar: they consider *actus reus, mens rea, mala in se* and *mala prohibita*. To recap, these terms refer to the actual crime committed, the intention behind the crime and a crime that contravenes the human moral code or is against the statutory law respectively.

In South Africa, a first-time offence of murder is subject to 15 years imprisonment but increments to 20 years if it is a second conviction of murder and to 25 years for a third conviction. In the case of rape this is ten years imprisonment at least for a first offence increasing to 15 years for a second and 20 years minimum for a third rape conviction. Crimes of smuggling firearms, explosives and ammunition, dealing in drugs, extortion, fraud, forgery and theft receive a similar sentence tariff to murder. Breaking and entering with intent to commit a crime warrants a five year prison sentence for a first offence which increases to seven years for a second conviction and to at least ten years for a third. Alternatively, Japan and Singapore, in common with 33 states of America, are the only other industrial democracies to maintain the death penalty (Marikkar

2009). In Japan the death penalty is reserved for *mala in se* crimes, such as murder and treason, and is executed by hanging. The Japanese Penal Code provides a list of 17 offences warranting the death penalty (e.g. murder, arson, robbery, kidnapping and hijacking) but there are no sentencing guidelines for judges to use. Hence the penalty for murder for instance could be death by hanging, life imprisonment or a prison sentence of three years or more. The sentence decision could rest on the presence of a multitude of mitigatory factors (Marikkar 2009).

Hence it can be seen that even cross-culturally the seriousness or the gravity of the offence and the harm endured by the victim are important considerations for penal decisions. These examples illustrate how concepts of seriousness and harm are considered in the sentencing of perpetrators of *mala in se crimes*, and more importantly, how similar these crimes are processed across cultures. Although in America, complicated Federal Sentencing Guidelines (based on the Sentencing Reform Act of 1984) are used where crimes are divided into four sentencing zones, a similar pattern of sentencing based on **crime seriousness** occurs in the same way as for many other countries. The four sentencing zones are called A, B, C and D where the sentence length increments as the seriousness of the crime committed increases. In zone A sentences range from 0–6 months; zone B sentences are more than zone A but no longer than 12 months; zone C sentences are above zone B but with a minimum penalty of 12 months; and zone D sentences are above zone C. Each zone has its own offence level which interacts with the offender's criminal history points. Offence level 43 in zone D warrants a life imprisonment whatever the offender's criminal history points are (U.S.S.G. 5A, 2009).

In England and Wales, a crime classified in America under zone D is now likely to receive a life sentence whereas before December 2012 this could also incur an IPP if the offender was considered dangerous and at high risk of repeating the same crime (known as **recidivism**). In Britain the incarceration of **dangerous offenders** is often considered as both a form of punishment and a preventive measure. By this is meant that dangerous offenders are incarcerated to prevent them from reoffending while serving their sentence thereby protecting the public. Similarly, in Germany there are penal sanctions for dangerous offenders with the objectives of deterrence and public protection. There is a difference, however, in countries such as Germany, Austria, Belgium and Switzerland in the philosophy behind these sanctions. These sanctions rely on a criminal court conviction but very often take into account the potential for there being future guilt from further criminal activities. Hence such sentences are designed to prevent any serious crimes from being committed in the future even if they have not been committed already (Bohlander 2008). This is different in Britain where the philosophy behind the sanction is to punish dangerous offenders for the crime(s) they have been found guilty of, and not the consideration of crimes they might commit in future. Once incarcerated, however, these offenders will need to demonstrate that they are safe to release back into the community on completion of their sentence.

What appears to be in common cross-culturally is that crimes are classed either as *mala in se* or *mala prohibita*. This is interesting because the difference between doing an act that is prohibited by law differs from an act that contravenes the human moral code. This raises the question of whether individuals who commit acts of *mala in se* are different morally, empathically and/or biologically from those who limit themselves to less serious misdemeanours (see Chapters 2, 3 and 4).

The legal approach to defining and understanding crime and criminal behaviour is an obvious starting point but it fails to address the processes involved in perceiving specific behaviours as criminal. Indeed while the legal approach provides a 'guideline' of what behaviours contravene the law, it is not always obvious to people where to draw the line between criminal or morally dubious behaviour. The processes involved in making that decision are socially defined and therefore require a socially oriented approach. This is provided by our next approach which derives from the disciplines of sociology and criminology. Many of the ideas expressed in the following sections are sociological but have found their way into the thinking of many criminologists and some psychologists.

### The sociological and criminological approach (social constructionism)

Both sociologists and criminologists use the method of social constructionism as a means to obtaining data that could help describe and explain criminal behaviour. A definition of the constructionist approach used is that of Rafter (1990) where, '[c]onstructionism is an approach that analyses the processes by which social information is produced, disseminated, verified and disconfirmed' (p.1). Thus constructionists are more concerned with processes that produce offenders than with the offenders themselves. Men and women, for example, are socialised differently, which has an impact on how they behave. There are expectations of how women and men should behave and such expectations extend to class and race. Gemignani and Peňa (2007/2008) defined social constructionism as 'constructs as coming from social interactions defined within local contexts of knowledge, power dynamics, cultural practices, and language' (p. 277).

Social constructionism became very popular in the US following the publication of Berger and Luckmann's book *The Social Construction of Reality* in 1966. This book offered a radical approach to understanding our knowledge of facts, rules, mores, definitions and interpretations of everyday reality. They argued that knowledge concerning everyday reality originates through social interactions. Common perceptions of reality are reinforced through people interacting and sharing their knowledge, and it is this transmission of information that becomes the accepted objective reality for future generations. Berger and Luckmann claimed that this objective reality is transmitted across generations, providing a consensual and unquestionable interpretation of the social world that becomes institutionalised and a part of human tradition.

In relation to the criminal justice system, Rafter (1990) stated that a social constructionist approach

> investigates how the facts of crime and crime control are produced. Asking how we arrive at knowledge within the field, it explores relationships among social structures, law, criminal acts, and perception (p.1).

The Dutch abolitionist (i.e. a supporter of abolishing slavery) lawyer and critical criminologist, Louk Hulsman (1986), used social constructionism as a means to understanding how the criminal justice system defines and disseminates a uniform definition of crime. He stated that:

> Categories of 'crime' are given by the criminal justice system rather than by victims of society . . . makes it necessary to abandon the notion of 'crime' as a tool in the conceptual framework of criminology. Crime has no ontological reality. Crime is not the object but the product of criminal policy (pp. 34–5).

Hulsman's perspective has been incorporated into the work of Dorling *et al.* (2008) who criticised criminology for perpetuating the myth of crime. Despite there being guidelines to determine whether or not a crime had been committed, such as *actus reus* and *mens rea*, Dorling *et al.* (2008) continued to argue that there is no ontological reality of crime and that the notion of a guilty mind applies primarily to the individual. It is this aspect of the law that causes problems in determining liability in cases beyond the individual – a good example being corporate manslaughter. Tombs (2008) considered the problematic tendency of the law to focus on individual rather than organisational *mens rea* which biases the true nature of criminal activity. An example of this is the *Herald of Free Enterprise* assistant bosun, Mark Stanley, convicted of manslaughter for the Zeebrugge ferry disaster of 1987 where he failed to close the bow doors before the moorings were dropped. There were numerous errors concerning a lack of communication in the workplace but when Townsend Thoresen was accused of corporate manslaughter the case collapsed after the jury were directed to acquit the company – thus failing to punish the executives in charge. Reiman (1998) expanded the debate using the argument of intentional murder versus indirect harms which has relevancy to this case. A murderer who intends to kill for instance has a guilty mind and represents the archetypal criminal. The executive of an organisation might not have the intention to kill and yet is aware that his or her actions could potentially kill people therefore causing indirect harm. Reiman (1998) asks the question of whether indirect harm should be treated any differently by the law than the harm inflicted directly: morally they are the same but indirect harm is considered to be more a regulatory than a criminal offence. Why the difference? In the Zeebrugge ferry disaster, the individuals brought to justice are those at the chalk-face (i.e. the assistant bosun) rather than executives of the company who represent the organisation. The executives have corporate responsibility and therefore are equally responsible for the deaths caused by the Zeebrugge ferry incident. For their role in perhaps knowingly endorsing faulty systems and procedures should they be held accountable for corporate manslaughter?

By adopting a social constructionist framework, Jaspers and Fraser (1984) argued that people use a common reality to understand crime and criminality – one which society has created for them. This means that people share a consensus reality explanation of which behaviours cause harm to others and which therefore constitute a criminal offence. Unfortunately this consensus reality explanation of how perpetrators should be treated by the legal system only extends to those who are culpable with an intention to harm. This might account for why there is a difference in the legal treatment of perpetrators who are indirectly culpable – they are not perceived as intending to cause harm to others. In the example of the executive of an organisation who is responsible for the deaths of many people resulting from his or her neglect to ensure safety measures, there is no *mens rea* and therefore no intention to harm others. The case therefore becomes one of failing to follow correct protocol that contravenes regulatory rules of law (*mala prohibita*) which consequently changes the nature of the offence.

Social constructs are used to inform and interpret the behaviours of individuals such that they can be ascribed a label (a description or classification). Christie (2004) highlighted two problems for criminology – disseminating the processes involved in labelling and how labelling is applied to specific behaviours such that they become criminalised. Once these processes are understood, Christie (2004) argued that the criminalisation of specific behaviours could be 'abandoned' and crime would therefore no longer exist. This radical and extreme social constructionist viewpoint would relinquish the need for labelling specific types of behaviour as criminal and the problem of separating behaviours labelled antisocial, deviant or morally offensive. For example, an antisocial act can be an illicit or a licit behaviour and simultaneously be morally offensive (see Box 1.8). Furthermore, a criminal behaviour might break the law without being considered as morally offensive. In the next section these different behaviours will be explored in the context of social constructionism.

### Is antisocial, deviant and morally offensive behaviour different from criminal behaviour?

Differentiating between criminal behaviour and what is simply considered antisocial, deviant or morally offensive behaviour is a difficult task. Are these differently categorised behaviours part of the same thing? Are they to be considered on a sliding scale where morally offensive behaviour is not as bad as criminal behaviour? Is all criminal behaviour morally offensive, deviant or antisocial? These questions are even harder to answer when different types of crime are thrown into the equation. Social constructionists view criminal behaviour as acts that contravene the law but only do so because of a social consensus. A consensus reality of what constitutes criminal behaviour that is shared from one generation to the next, determines the defining characteristics of the criminal label. This is also true for other labels such as antisocial, deviant or morally offensive behaviour. These labels, however, are not always mutually exclusive as can be seen in the selection of behaviours in Box 1.8. (It is important to note that there are likely to be cross-cultural variations concerning the behaviours listed in Box 1.8 and also differences of judgement across the British public barring criminal behaviours).

As demonstrated in Box 1.8, the different behaviours can be classified under multiple categories such as morally offensive, antisocial and deviant, and yet not be regarded as criminal behaviour. Deviant behaviour quite often can be seen as morally offensive behaviour depending on factors such as the age of the person witnessing the behaviours in question and who is performing these behaviours. If the son who sleeps in the same bed as his mother happens to be an adult in his 50s then this might be perceived as morally inappropriate. This behaviour becomes criminal behaviour if the son rapes his mother, but remains non-normative behaviour if both are consenting individuals and no harm is incurred to either party. There are many behaviours that can be perceived as deviant or non-normative and yet cause no harm. Under these circumstances such behaviours are benign, and whilst teetering on the border of what is considered to be appropriate and inappropriate behaviour they can be largely ignored. This takes on the sentiment of what goes on behind closed doors is private (see Chapter 2 for discussion on the harm debate).

## Box 1.8

**British-based examples of what could be considered as criminal, morally offensive, antisocial or deviant behaviours**

### Criminal Behaviour

An adult–child sexual relationship (also morally offensive and sexually deviant behaviour).

An individual who physically abuses a child (also morally offensive and deviant behaviour).

An individual who deals and sells cannabis on the streets (also antisocial and morally offensive behaviour).

An adult male who urinates in a public place (also antisocial and morally offensive behaviour).

An individual who downloads and distributes child pornography (also morally offensive and sexually deviant behaviour).

### Morally Offensive Behaviour

A promiscuous female adult.

An individual who shouts out profanities in church during a sermon (also antisocial behaviour).

An individual who sunbathes naked in their garden but can be seen by the neighbours.

An individual who gestures in a rude way (also antisocial behaviour).

Two adults kissing and touching each other inappropriately on a public bus.

### Antisocial Behaviour

An individual who shouts verbal abuse and belittles his/her partner in public (also morally offensive).

An individual who plays music very loud during the day.

A drunken individual who litters his neighbour's garden.

An individual who knocks on people's doors and runs away.

A group of young adolescents 'hanging-out' together late at night shouting and play fighting.

### Deviant Behaviour

An individual masturbates while watching the 'Telly-Tubbies' (also morally offensive behaviour).

An adult male who sleeps in the same bed as his mother (also morally offensive behaviour).

An individual who is aroused when watching animals mate (also morally offensive behaviour).

An individual who self-mutilates for sexual arousal (also morally offensive behaviour).

Individuals who find sleeping in a graveyard relaxing (also antisocial and morally offensive behaviour).

In another example an individual who has an active social nightlife might consider adolescents shouting and play fighting late at night as socially acceptable, simply because this behaviour is constructed and compared with the baseline level of their tolerated nightlife activity. In contrast a person who lives a quiet lifestyle and whose bedtime is early at night might consider such behaviour antisocial. Hence the perception of what constitutes antisocial, morally offensive or deviant behaviour is partially an individual's judgement made at their discretion. Given how easy it is to confuse the boundaries of these categories, it is not surprising that people have difficulties separating criminal from antisocial, deviant or morally offensive behaviours. Despite a consensual understanding within society of what should constitute criminal behaviour and hence a crime, the definition is not always clear. In addition to this there is another level of understanding and definition – that arising from an individual's social construction of the world based on their own experiences and type of **socialisation** encountered. If the law can provide the rules thereby arming society with guidelines of what constitutes criminal and non-criminal behaviour, then our social world and how we interact within it governs our perceptions of which behaviours can be construed as licit or illicit.

This is further compounded by differences in personal perception and statutory laws across other cultures. There are cross-cultural differences in attitude towards behaviours considered as morally offensive for instance. In some countries religion directly or indirectly dictates how individuals should behave. In Islamic countries where the legal system is influenced by Sharia, such as in Afghanistan, a single or married woman who is promiscuous could be punished by death in the name of an honour killing. The distinction between law and Islamic Sharia in Afghanistan, for example, can be less defined when considering what is acceptable behaviour and behaviour that is expected to be performed (i.e. known as *Husna* Shariat). Furthermore, there are cultural traditions, such as honour killings, which can be confused with Islamic Sharia. Honour killings are normally carried out by families who feel a female family member has caused shame to their family name, which can easily be considered the opposite of a *Husna* Shariat (see section on the role of religion in *mala in se* crimes). This is illustrated by the case of two women in Afghanistan who were murdered in 2011 because they committed adultery (Mail Online 2011). Even though the law was used to apprehend the perpetrators, this case highlights the pervasiveness of cultural and traditional ideals arising from social constructs of Sharia interpretation. The next section explores the processes involved in how we use social constructs to guide our interpretations of behaviours construed as criminal acts.

### When does behaviour become a crime statistic?

As Figure 1.3 suggests, reporting a crime relies on a social construction of what constitutes a crime. An individual has to perceive the behaviour as contravening the law – in other words that they have been 'crimed against'. This social construction continues when the crime is reported to the police, who recode the event as a crime and then decide the nature of investigation and pooling of their resources required.

An individual's initial interpretation of a situation is crucial in determining whether they have been a victim of a crime. From the viewpoint of social constructionism, there is no ontological reality of crime and yet society perpetuates the myth of crime (Dorling *et al.* 2008). As has been argued by Berger

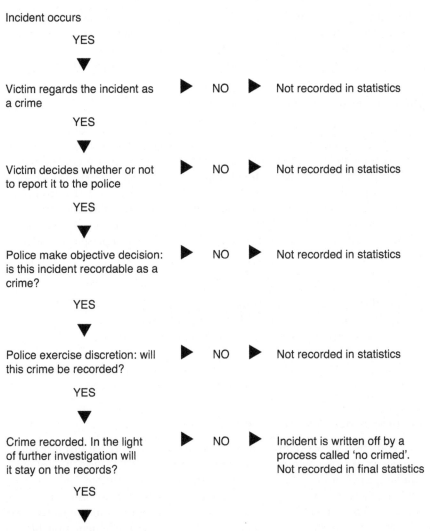

Incident occurs

YES

▼

Victim regards the incident as    ▶    NO    ▶    Not recorded in statistics
a crime

YES

▼

Victim decides whether or not    ▶    NO    ▶    Not recorded in statistics
to report it to the police

YES

▼

Police make objective decision:    ▶    NO    ▶    Not recorded in statistics
is this incident recordable as a
crime?

YES

▼

Police exercise discretion: will    ▶    NO    ▶    Not recorded in statistics
this crime be recorded?

YES

▼

Crime recorded. In the light    ▶    NO    ▶    Incident is written off by a
of further investigation will                        process called 'no crimed'.
it stay on the records?                              Not recorded in final statistics

YES

▼

HO collates details. Incident
appears as a crime in the final statistics

*Figure 1.3* The process of collating crime statistics from reporting to recording

and Luckmann (1966), people adopt existing social constructs of reality and this includes constructs of criminality. The criminalisation of specific types of behaviour is a social construct of what is inappropriate social conduct that has traditionally been considered as unacceptable behaviour. The social construct of criminality is pervasive and infiltrates all levels of society, although, social constructionists would argue that not everyone subscribes to the consensus understanding and perspective of crime that predominates in Britain. There are different perspectives arising from the discipline of sociology (used in criminology) which address how society can influence criminality and be responsible for creating the opportunities to commit crimes. In the next section these different perspectives for understanding crime will be considered.

## Different perspectives for understanding crime

While the law offers a definition of behaviours that constitute criminal acts that break the law, sociology and criminology, alternatively, focus on groups and organisations and how these influence each other and impact on the individual within society (i.e. a **macro-level explanation**). Defining crime is a social conception which is why many definitions of what crime is derive from sociology. Thus in this section much attention is paid to the different approaches within sociology to defining crime and explaining criminality. Definitions of crime and criminality vary depending on the sociological perspective adopted such as:

1    consensus view;
2    conflict and critical criminology;
3    symbolic interactionism and **Labelling Theory**;
4    discourse analysis (considered a contemporary approach).

The origins of these approaches will be discussed and their merits evaluated within the context of crime and criminality.

### CONSENSUS VIEW (TALCOTT PARSONS)

The consensus view originates from the functionalist approach first introduced by Talcott Parsons, which in its heyday during the 1950s was the dominant thinking in sociology. Parsons (1951) argued that institutions and structures within society function independently and co-dependently to ensure the system (or society) operates effectively to create a sense of equilibrium and **status quo**. Therefore any change that occurs (i.e. through the implementation of new institutions or subsystems) within society does so in an orderly, consensual and evolutionary manner. The example of the criminal justice system illustrates this well. Different branches of the criminal justice system have a role to perform, such as law enforcement and punishment, to those who fail to conform to society's code of conduct. Parsons described society's evolution as a continuous process of change to institutions, subsystems and legislation. Changes to legislation influence the status of statutory crimes (i.e. *mala prohibita*), as their classification depends on the current beliefs and opinions within society. Changes to statutory law permit criminalised behaviours to become decriminalised and vice versa. For example, the Wolfenden Committee Report of 1957 instigated a change to the Sexual Offences Act in 1967, whereby homosexual acts among consenting male adults over 21 years were decriminalised. In England and Wales, the Sexual Offences (Amendment) Act in 2000 reduced the age of consent for homosexual acts to 16. Child prostitution and sexual intercourse with a consenting individual under the age of 16, however, were criminalised in England and Wales as a consequence of the Contagious Diseases Act 1864.

Both examples illustrate the decriminalisation and criminalisation of crime status resulting from changes to *mala prohibita* laws. The consensus view maintains that the law is justified in identifying and controlling individuals who do not conform and abide by society's rules and mores. As rules change, however, legislations evolve in keeping with consensus ideology. For instance individuals can be found guilty and penalised for crimes contravening statutory laws, whether intentionally or unintentionally committed, which is considered equitable under consensus thinking. Hence legislation is in a constant battle to keep up with the changes to people's behaviour, which occurs when new technology is introduced (e.g. technological advances that create opportunities to commit different types of crime). With further opportunities for criminal activity, legislation is introduced to force individuals to conform to the new consensus stipulated in *mala prohibita* laws. An illustration of this is infringements of copyright laws, an area recently seeing new legislations (see Box 1.9).

## Box 1.9

### Effects of new technology on behaviour and the need for further legislation

With the introduction of video recording equipment and computers that could be used to download images, films and music from the internet, new legislation against piracy invoked changes to statutory laws. Piracy is theft and therefore illegal, which is why images, films and music are subject to copyrights that require the permission of the copyright owner for their use. Since the 1980s changes to copyright legislation were made to combat the increase of copied videos sold on the black market. Other measures introduced by the film industry relied on using technologies that blocked content from being copied successfully. With increasing use of the internet for downloading films and music onto DVDs and CDs, it has become increasingly difficult for copyright owners to protect their productions from piracy. Harris Interactive was commissioned to do market research on behalf of the British Phonographic Industry (BPI) in 2010, and found that piracy from the internet is increasing. A survey showed that 29% of 5,000 people sampled used rogue sites to download music (Robinson 2010). In the Harris Interactive Report in 2010, it was estimated that three in every four music tracks were downloaded from illegal rogue sites which outweighed the one billion legally downloaded numbers of individual tracks (Robinson 2010). In Britain, the Digital Economy Act 2010 was implemented to target illegal downloaders. One recent amendment due in 2013 (but now delayed until 2015) by the Culture Secretary, Jeremy Hunt, is the formality of sending warning letters advising illegal downloaders on how to avoid piracy (Crookes 2012). Internet Service Providers perceive this new legislation as an infringement of people's privacy as they will have to police their customers' patterns of internet use (Crookes 2012). Advances in technology have demanded new legislations in statutory law to combat the influx of high-tech crimes like infiltrating government computer files, cyber-laundering, spreading of viruses/worms/Trojans, scams, illegal trading, fraud, defamatory libel, cyber-staking and cyber-terrorism. An example of a Cyber Espionage Network operating in 2009 from China, demonstrated how it is possible to infiltrate official government computer systems. Private national documents belonging to government agencies, such as foreign ministries, were downloaded from 1295 computers in 103 countries (Glaister 2009). It is difficult to police these computer-based crimes, but the Home Office introduced a multi-agency unit in 2001 called the National Hi-Tech Crime Unit which consisted of representatives from the National Crime Squad, the Association of Chief of Police Officers and the National Criminal Intelligence Service. The role of the National Hi-Tech Crime Unit is to detect criminal activity on the internet.

There is, however, an alternative to strict copyright rulings on the use of copyrighted material known as open source and fair use, both of which have blurred the boundaries of free-use, limited use and granted use through the copyrighters. In the case of open source, the term generally refers to software programmes released for general use by the public free of charge. An open source code is available to enable users to access and improve the original programme. Open-source-based software are designed by programmers who have no self-financial interest or proprietary ownership in their product. Instead they use their programming skills to design and develop 'bug-free' software that the general public can use. These products are further subjected to 'bug' elimination by a peer review process where programmers consider the feedback from users of the product, modify the source code and redistribute it. It is this process which enables the product to continuously improve and therefore evolve into a more effective piece of software. Open source software programmes offer an alternative to commercially developed programmes which can be expensive to purchase and maintain licensing fees. Fair use can be perceived as a go-between open source and strict copyrights requiring permission from the copyright holder. Fair use is a doctrine which enables a person to have limited access to material that is copyrighted without having to seek permission of use by the holder(s). Fair use involves copying copyrighted material for the purpose of commentary, criticism or parody. Ascertaining what fair use is not always straightforward and sometimes involves a decision from the court. Two

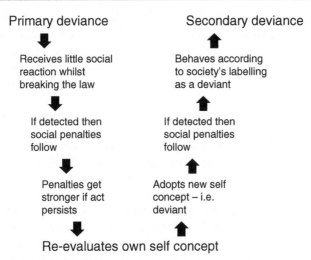

*Figure 1.4* Lemert's Labelling Theory
Lemert 1967

values of the deviant subculture become the dominant model of thought and behaviour for these individuals (see subcultures in Chapter 10). The individual becomes absorbed by the deviant subculture and justifies his or her membership through having a deviant lifestyle which further cements their membership. Both Becker (1963) and Lemert (1967) outlined the process of labelling via a series of stages which eventually lead to membership of a deviant subculture: entry to primary deviancy; establishing a self-fulfilling prophesy (where the individual believes the label, incorporates the label to form a new self-identity) and entering the world of secondary deviancy (which usually involves the adoption of behaviour and values befitting the new identity). Such membership to subcultures often results in the individual disembarking and disengaging from mainstream culture and going subterranean or underground. Figure 1.4 shows the relationship between primary and secondary deviance outlined in Lemert's (1967) Labelling Theory perspective.

Postmodern investigative methods of studying pervasive labelling and stereotyping of individuals, such as discourse analysis, is adopted in contemporary approaches that comprise the next section.

## DISCOURSE ANALYSIS (HAROLD GARFINKEL)

Although the term discourse analysis was first formally introduced by Zellig Harris in 1952 in relation to transformational grammar, in 1967 sociologist Harold Garfinkel extended its use to conversational analysis using the approach of ethnomethodology (a method of studying linguistic communication).

Garfinkel (2002) claimed that ethnomethodology is concerned with studying the way people behave as a means to establishing social order. In 1967, he suggested that the goal of ethnomethodology should be to document how people interpret and make sense of their social world. This approach has been used to investigate how people perceive criminality by deconstructing what they say.

Worrall (1990) used discourse analysis to deconstruct the perceptions held by medical and legal professionals towards women who commit offences. The perceptions held by magistrates and psychiatrists about women who offend, reflected the working domains of their professions as did their reasons for why women offend. Worrall found that magistrates, for example, perceived female offenders as lacking common sense while psychiatrists used the medical model to attribute female criminality to mental illness or mental states of helplessness. Welch, Fenwick and Roberts (1997) using discourse analysis, concluded that ideology has an impact on definition. Hence when the discourse of politicians and law enforcers were compared with intellectuals such as academics, the opinions expressed by politicians and law enforcers were taken more seriously and had a greater impact than those expressed by academics. Welch et al. (1997) attributed this to the credibility placed on the positions of power and prestige carried by the politicians and law enforcers which meant that their point of view became the dominant ideology. Furthermore, politicians and law enforcers often chose to ignore any possible connections between social conditions and crime, and would even distort the situation to suit their ideology. Hence through use of discourse analysis it was suggested that academics had little opportunity to introduce their findings of a link between social conditions and crime to such politicians and law enforcers (Welch et al. 1997). Discourse analysis was also used by Protess (1993) to highlight the role of the mass media in disseminating the ideology of those in power. Protess (1993) compared two Chicago newspapers: The Tribune and The Sun Times. Words like hate crime, racial disturbance, racial crime and inter-racial crime were searched using the Lexis-Nexis database, and the information in the hate crime articles was compared to the hate crime data. The majority of victims of hate crimes came from ethnic minority groups but the media portrayal of the number of Black offenders and White victims told a different story – a story which increased the number of Black offenders and the number of White victims (Protess 1993). Glassner (1999) argued that the American media caters for a mainstream American audience which led to biased reporting of crime in the newspapers. Glassner (1999) found that Black victims tended to under-report their experiences to the police which exaggerated the number of recorded White victims. The media then reports these statistics which perpetuates the fear of crime among White Americans.

Each perspective has its merits in explaining crime and criminal behaviour, and the processes involved in the development of criminality. As a reminder, Table 1.1 offers a summary of the key points for each perspective.

*Table 1.1* Summary of the four sociological (and criminological) perspectives

| Different sociological (and criminological) approaches | Description and example |
| --- | --- |
| Consensus | Institutions and structures within society function harmoniously to maintain status quo. Morals, values, beliefs and appropriate behaviours are defined by society and the majority of citizens agree to abide by these norms. Those who commit crimes are punished accordingly. A suicide bomber would be considered a terrorist and punished under the consensus approach. |
| Conflict and critical criminology | Capitalism creates a fragmented and dysfunctional society. The unequal distribution of wealth causes disharmony as different groups ('the haves and have nots') compete to achieve their conflicting goals. The powerful classes in society determine what normative and deviant behaviour is and how society and law treat individuals who are classed as deviant. A suicide bomber would be considered a freedom fighter and symbolise heroism or represent a martyr under the conflict approach. |
| Social interactionism and labelling | People interpret, add meaning and respond to the behaviour of others and adjust their own behaviour accordingly. Social processes, such as labelling, cause individuals to self-fulfil the prophesy of the label. Meanings attributed to behaviour generate responses to the behaviour and not the behaviour itself. A suicide bomber labelled as a terrorist will identify with the label and behave in a manner expected of a terrorist. |
| Discourse analysis (contemporary view example) | Used in the context of conversational analysis, people's behaviours are studied to ascertain how they create social order. What people say and do is deconstructed to analyse how they perceive their social world. Perception of criminality is no exception to this approach. Different professions have their own perceptions that reflect the attitudes of their working domain. The reality of how society and the different components comprising society perceive and attribute cause to a suicide bomber's actions would be deconstructed using discourse analysis. The explanations would vary depending on who is asked. A politician might perceive the act as defiance to a democratic regime whereas a psychiatrist might consider the person as mentally unstable. |

While sociology and criminology offer a **macro-level explanation** of crime and understanding criminal behaviour, psychology concentrates on the individual and how the individual interacts with other people within society per se (i.e. a **micro-level explanation**). Psychologists are primarily concerned with how and why individuals become criminal and with methods of assessing this and ways of increasing the reliability of investigative procedures within the definition of the law.

Our next section is concerned with the psychological perspective of defining crime and criminal behaviour. The three subsections of psychology specifically addressing criminal issues are psycho-legal, criminological and forensic psychology which will be discussed in turn.

### The psychological approach (psycho-legal, criminological and forensic)

As psychology is a discipline concerning itself with the study of individual development and behaviour, it comes as no surprise that some psychologists direct their attentions towards explaining why people commit crime. As a consequence there have been a number of definitions of crime, criminal behaviour and criminality in common use by psychologists. Crime has been defined succinctly by Blackburn (1993) as 'acts attracting legal punishment. [They] are offences against the community' (p. 5). Blackburn, however, also pointed out that crimes should involve a conscious element of breaking the rules. As we have seen earlier in the extended definition of crime offered by Andrews and Bonta (1998), there are a number of ways in which to consider crime worth reiterating here. They argue that crime consists of criminal behaviour that is prohibited by the law and therefore punishable; a violation of the moral or religious code punishable only by a supreme spiritual being; a violation of society's norms, values, attitudes and mores punishable by the community and finally a psychological stance where an individual's actions are considered to be criminal if they violate others by causing harm and loss in exchange for rewards. Hence criminal behaviour can be considered as, '[a]ntisocial acts that place the actor at risk of becoming the focus of the attention of the criminal and juvenile professionals' (Andrews and Bonta 1998).

In the case of criminality, definitions used generally focus on specific personality traits that might influence an individual to commit crime. Gottfredson and Hirschi (1990) claimed that criminality could be described as a strategic behaviour that shows itself as low self-control, egocentrism and a lack of empathy to the suffering of others. This description has parallels with Yochelson and Samenow's (1984) typical **criminal personality** – described as having a set way of thinking and decision making (see Chapter 5). Criminality is a main focus of attention for psychologists who try to explain how individuals become initiated into a life of crime and all that is associated with this such as a criminal lifestyle. They use different psychological theories to explain how individuals become criminal (see Figure 1.5).

Throughout this textbook, theories from these different areas within psychology are used to explain why certain individuals become criminals therefore brief descriptions of each will be provided here:

*   Evolutionary psychologists study the ways and means the mind of modern day man developed from our ancestral past. This involves the examination of environmental pressures (such as the availability of food resources) and how these influenced human nature.

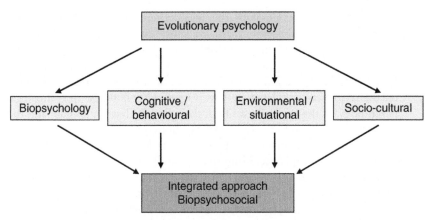

*Figure 1.5* The main theoretical approaches for understanding offending behaviour
Taylor 2015. Reproduced with kind permission from Taylor and Francis.

- Bio-psychologists study how our physiology and biochemistry, genetics and brain structure and function impact on our behaviour.
- Cognitive psychologists study the workings of the mind while behavioural psychologists consider how this influences our behaviour.
- Environmental psychologists study how environmental factors influence our behaviour. For example does increasing heat make us more inclined to be aggressive. Psychologists considering a situational approach concentrate on how personality interacts with the situations individuals encounter.
- Psychologists interested in the socio-cultural aspects of behaviour consider the impact that society, social norms, social groups, culture and our socialisation have on the development and shaping of our personality.
- Biopsychosocial psychologists promote an integrated approach to understanding behaviour. As the term implies this triangulates different theoretical explanations to account for criminality.

These approaches are very informative and influence theoretical understanding of why people commit crimes. Furthermore, psychologists specialising in the study of crime, criminal behaviour and criminality incorporate these different approaches within psychology to develop their fields. Within psychology the three main areas concerned with crime and criminality are: psycho-legal, criminological and forensic psychology. Although the focus on aspects of criminal behaviour and criminality may differ slightly across these three areas, there is considerable overlap of topical interest and in the professional practice itself. In brief, however, these areas can be described as follows:

- Psycho-legal psychology is concerned with the interface between the criminal justice legal system and human behaviour. This lends itself to psychologists interacting with the legal system and researching aspects of the criminal justice system that are more directly linked with human behaviour – offenders and non-offenders. According to Small (1993), psycho-legal psychologists are expert witnesses, evaluators or clinicians. Psycho-legal psychologists work within the definitions of crime and criminal behaviour as stipulated in law. Ogloff (2000) states, '[psycho-legal psychology] is the scientific study of the effects of law on people; and the effect people have on the law. Legal psychology also includes the application of the study and practice of psychology to legal institutions and people who come into contact with the law' (p. 467).

- Criminal psychology is concerned with the interactions between criminology, criminal justice and psychology, usually involving the study of the motivations, thoughts, intentions and actions of offenders. It looks at various causes and explanations of different criminal behaviours and research documenting the most effective punishments and treatments currently available.

- Forensic psychology is more closely focused on offender assessment and treatment within a forensic setting – hence dealing with legal aspects of behaviour and mental issues. The British Psychological Society (BPS) in 2013 expanded on this as, 'Forensic Psychology is devoted to psychological aspects of legal processes in courts. The term is also often used to refer to investigative and criminological psychology; applying psychological theory to criminal investigation, understanding psychological problems associated with criminal behaviour and the treatment of those who have committed offences'. Blackburn (1996) argues that forensic psychology is the 'direct provision of psychological information to the courts, that is, to psychology in the courts' (p. 7).

(It should be noted, however, that the terms psycho-legal, criminological and forensic psychology are often used interchangeably, and according to Otto and Fulero (2006) these labels can be used to refer to, 'the application of psychological research, theory, or practice to the legal system or legal issues' (cited in Greene and Drew 2008, p. 3)).

Given that psychology examines crime and criminality using a micro-level explanation, the theoretical focus and nature of practice is directed at the individual and the individual's interactions with others within the confines of society. This means that questions of how and why an individual becomes criminal are addressed through different theoretical approaches within psychology. These then determine the methods of assessing offenders used by forensic psychologists for instance. A psycho-legal psychologist might be asked to evaluate the likelihood of culpability of a suspect by applying psychological evidence to ascertain an offender's *mens rea* and state of mind. In some countries and States in the US where the death penalty exists, expert evidence from psycho-legal psychologists is important in the evaluation of culpability, *mens rea* and state of mind at the time of the offence and current fitness to stand trial (Cunningham 2006). As pointed out by Cunningham (2006) the 'probability of acts of criminal violence' is reframed by the state (and sometimes inexplicably by the defence), as a question of whether the defendant is 'dangerous', or will be a 'danger' in the future' (p. 211). Forensic psychologists can also perform this role which adds further credence to the point raised by Otto and Fulero (2006) of there being an interchangeable usage of terms within psychology when it becomes involved with legal issues. It has become increasingly common for those working in the field to be referred to as forensic psychologists and to represent forensic psychology. Whatever the reference, 'one common feature is the knowledge of the lawbreaker that it attracts legal punishment [. . .] rulebreaking is a meaningful [. . .] focus' (Blackburn 1993, p. 17).

## Summary

- There are problems with definitions of crime and criminality provided by psychology, sociology, criminology and law. Difficulties of providing a single interpretation and definition of crime and criminality occur when using examples of behaviours that could potentially be interpreted as criminal acts or behaviours that are morally offensive, deviant and/or antisocial but not necessarily criminal. Hence a legal position provides a good starting point for clarifying what criminality is. The legal perspective includes Latin terms such as *actus reus* and *mens rea* and *mala in se* and *mala prohibita*. *Actus reus* refers to the criminal act itself whereas *mens rea* refers to the intention to commit a crime. Both terms are less straightforward than they appear. *Mens rea* in particular can be ambiguous and difficult to ascertain as demonstrated under the rule concerning legal responsibility. A child under the age of 10 and a mentally impaired individual are considered as being incapable of understanding the wrongfulness of their actions and are therefore not considered responsible for their criminal behaviour.
- There are also ambiguities with the terms *mala in se* and *mala prohibita*. *Mala in se* refers to crimes regarded as heinous that not only break the law but contravene the human moral code. In contrast, *mala prohibita* is statutory law that is determined by government and Parliament (in Britain) but can be changed depending on the **zeitgeist**. Despite forming separate categories, *mala in se* and *mala prohibita* are not always considered to be mutually exclusive. Nevertheless, *mala in se* and *mala prohibita* categories of crime are reasonably reliable and provide a good benchmark for defining crime and guiding the criminal justice system. There is cross-cultural consistency in *mala in se* crimes reflected in the type of punishment crimes of this nature receive – ranging from capital punishment to long-term incarceration.
- The role of religion in law and its relevance to ascertaining *mala in se* crimes is seen throughout the history of law development and across many

cultures. Consistency of attitude and punishment towards perpetrators of crimes against the human moral code (or *mala in se* crimes) and the sentencing tariffs used is similar cross-culturally. Religion can have a direct or indirect effect on the law and nature of punishment depending on the country in question. In countries where there is a direct influence of religion on common law, jurisprudence for *mala in se* crimes can be more extreme than is the case for countries where common law presides over religion. Nevertheless, religion influences how we are expected to behave instilled through socialisation by our parents.

- Social constructionism considers crime as a society shared social construct. Crime and criminality are perceived as deviations from a consensus reality – where behaviours constituting criminal conduct are perceived as contravening an agreed set of social rules or law. Behaviours perceived as criminal acts can also be labelled as antisocial, deviant and morally offensive but antisocial, deviant and morally offensive behaviours can also be mutually exclusive from criminal behaviours. Social constructionists highlight the difficulty involved in separating such behaviours that can often overlap as a consequence of problems regarding a consensus reality. Social constructionists argue that the defining characteristics of crime and our perceptions of crime and criminality are disseminated down from those in government and the workings of the legal system. These perceptions influence our personal judgements of whether we report an event perceived as a crime to the police.
- Different sociological perspectives (also used by criminologists) influence our perceptions of crime and criminality and, depending on the view adopted, a suicide bomber, for example, might be perceived as a terrorist or freedom fighter. Sociological perspectives such as consensus, conflict and critical criminology, symbolic interactionism and labelling and discourse analysis have different frameworks for understanding crime and criminality. Whereas the consensus perspective provides an agreed reality that labels specific behaviours as criminal, a conflict and critical criminological perspective interprets these same behaviours as non-criminal – hence there are different social constructions of reality.
- Whether events are reported to the police as crimes depends on how they are perceived by the public. These events are perceived and interpreted using social constructions derived from a consensus reality. Police then decide whether to record the event as a crime. Further decisions are made concerning the deployment of their resources and the level of investigation priority the crime deserves – all decided under the guise of police ideology which reflects that of the government and *mala prohibita*.
- Psychological approaches overlap with sociological ones in that they also use labelling and discourse analysis (i.e. social constructionism) but also make use of a legal definition and framework for understanding crime and criminal behaviour. The psychological stance to understanding crime and

criminality is focused on the individual and how that individual interacts with others within a societal framework. By focusing on the individual, the approach to understanding crime and criminality depends largely on methods of assessment and treatment through all levels of the criminal justice system. Different terms such as psycho-legal, criminological and forensic psychology have been used interchangeably, which is understandable given the degree of overlapping content.

## Questions for discussion

1    In what way would you expect to find differences in the recording of crime under a consensus versus a conflict driven ideology?
2    If there was no written *mala prohibita* (acts that are considered as crimes because the law defines them as such), would we still be punishing individuals for breaking the human moral law?
3    Is it a coincidence that practically all countries reserve harsh punishments for *mala in se* (acts considered to be against the human moral code) crimes?

# Chapter 2

# Concepts in crime definition influencing crime classification

In Chapter 1, the problems associated with defining crime and criminality were discussed with reference to the law, sociological and criminological (i.e. social constructionism), and psychological theory. In this chapter, we consider the different ways that crime is recorded. Before it can be recorded as a crime, however, it has to be reported by an individual who perceives the actions of another individual or institution as criminal conduct and therefore a crime. In other words the individual has to consider that he or she is a victim and what has happened to them is a crime. Therefore we now have a victim and perpetrator. As we have seen in Chapter 1, defining a crime is difficult. We will pursue the difficulties involved in crime definition further in this chapter through the consideration of our perceptions of crime seriousness. Once we have decided that a crime has occurred and the police have recorded the incident as a crime, the police have to further decide how the crime will be investigated and the resources needed. How this decision is made is based on a re-coding of the **recorded crime** based on its level of seriousness and harm incurred to the victim. This re-coding also determines how the offence should be classified: serious or non-serious. This is reflected in how crime is measured and presented in the crime statistics. In this chapter we will discover the different crime measures used in the UK (in particular England and Wales) and the US. In both the UK and US, the methods are surprisingly similar: police based recorded figures and a victimisation survey. The method of crime data collation, and its significance in evaluating the prevalence of crime in England and Wales, provides criminologists with a table of serious and non-serious crimes dating back to when crime was first recorded. This provides criminologists with a history of crime trends that could be used to make future predictions about crime levels. While this information is readily available for public scrutiny (in the Home Office publication of crime statistics and in government websites online), the release of such information can cause unnecessary fear of crime and lead to **moral panics** that call for swift legislative change. This will be explored using the **Megan's Law** in the US as an example of how public reaction can lead to changes in the law. How the media reports crime and exacerbates fear which leads to moral panics will also be considered here. Strongly linked with crime prevalence is criminal careers which will also be examined. As the criminal career is defined by its onset, duration and termination, it will influence crime rates and the nature of crime statistics (i.e. rising or falling crime rates). Different stages of the criminal career will be outlined using primarily psychological research to explain it. Given that criminal careers will have an impact on crime levels, we will also explore short-term crime fluctuations with long-term crime patterns (which appear to currently suggest a reduction in crime) in the UK and US. Crime statistics are classified into crimes that are serious and non-serious using the concept of crime seriousness and harm. These terms were alluded to in Chapter 1, but will be elaborated further in this chapter. The importance of concepts, such as seriousness and harm, will be discussed in the context of crime reporting and recording. These perceptions are strongly influenced by judgements of behaviours considered as harmful – part of a debate that has existed since the late nineteenth century. Associated with this are crimes of *mala in se* and *mala prohibita*, because as we saw in Chapter 1, *mala in se* crimes are considered as crimes which contravene the human moral code – hence these are serious crimes with harmful consequences for the victim. We will focus on how crime seriousness is calculated and what makes an offence serious by alluding to *mala in se* and the **harm principle**. Different types of harm are considered and why this has a long history of debating the cut-off point across what should be considered as harmful or just immoral behaviour and therefore not criminal behaviour. This is further associated with the debate of what constitutes victimless crimes and whether these should be classified as criminal or immoral behaviours.

## Introduction

The classification of crime is influenced by the way society defines it (as discussed in Chapter 1) and our perceptions of **crime seriousness**. To illustrate this point further, consider the four crimes listed below. The probability of ordering these crimes, from least to most serious, in the same way, is highly likely given that we are **socialised** into accepting a shared consensus ideology of crime seriousness.

- Residential burglary – stealing £1,000 worth in goods.
- Aggravated residential burglary – stealing £1,000 worth in goods and physically assaulting the home owner.
- Fraud – laundering £1,000 from employees' pension funds.
- Murder – killing a stranger for £1,000 worth of jewellery.

Using a continuum of least to progressively more serious, it is clear that residential burglary and fraud are not as serious as aggravated burglary and murder.

As both aggravated burglary and murder involve physical contact and harm towards the victim (in the case of murder the loss of life is the most extreme form of harm possible), the weighting of seriousness is highest for these crimes. While residential burglary can cause psychological harm to the owner, as their privacy has been invaded, there is no physical harm involved and likewise for fraud, a crime committed at a distance from the victim and the victim's home. Furthermore, in the case of laundering £1000 from employees' pension funds, the loss of money is distributed and diluted such that individuals are less likely to be aware of the deficit. Given these criteria, a consensus order of least to most serious crime is likely to be fraud, burglary, aggravated burglary and murder.

According to the consensus approach, individuals are **socialised** to accept the morals and values of society, and in so doing become law abiding citizens. Parents are responsible for instilling these morals and values through the process of **socialisation**, which is cemented through other socialising agents such as educational establishments and the law (see Chapter 4). Furthermore, the consensus view provides a common perception of what is considered to be right or wrong and behaviours that contravene the law. Another example demonstrating the pervasiveness of a consensus approach towards crime and criminality, was the public condemnation towards illegal phone hacking committed in 2011 by numerous journalists and private investigators working for the *News of the World* 'red-top' tabloid. Journalists and private investigators were allegedly hacking into mobile phones to obtain private and personal information that could be published in *News of the World*. They targeted a variety of individuals including celebrities, victims and the families of victims from the London bombings of 7 July 2005, known as 7/7. *The Guardian* newspaper claimed that some journalists working for the *News of the World* had deleted voicemail messages from Milly Dowler's mobile phone, whose murder was currently being investigated by police – this accusation was later retracted by *The Guardian* in December 2011. Further accusations of phone hacking were made by at least 4,000 individuals, and the *News of the World* were allegedly making payments to police in exchange for sensitive investigative material. Although mobile phone hacking is in breach of privacy laws, it was the hacking of mobile phones belonging to deceased victims that was considered particularly unacceptable and led to public concern. Despite on-going enquiries, the *News of the World* tabloid was dissolved by Rupert Murdoch in 2011. *The Daily Telegraph* newspaper on Friday 8 July 2011 published the front-page headline, 'Goodbye, Cruel World' (Winnett 2011). The privacy laws were breached but the main public condemnation was directed towards the tactic of hacking into the phones belonging to victims of crime.

How crimes, such as phone hacking, are rated for seriousness depends on the extent of harm victims experience and their perception of the event as a serious transgression (similarly if an eyewitness also perceives the event as a serious transgression). Victim and witness perceptions of an event as a serious transgression will influence their decisions to report to the police. Under the adversarial system (see Chapters 1 and 13), crimes are reported to the police by the public (i.e. victims of crimes and eyewitnesses to crimes). Bottomly and Pease (1986) claimed that 77–96 per cent of **recorded crime** comes to light through reports from the public. In the US, eyewitnesses for example, are responsible for reporting 27 per cent of violent crimes according to the US Bureau of Justice Statistics (2003). Aggregate data of crimes reported to the police by victims, however, can be problematic (see Chapter 1) as:

- Figures can be biased given that not all victims report events to the police;
- Police recode reported events and might decide:
  1 not to record the event as a crime;
  2 not to investigate the incident further.

In Britain crime was first recorded in 1805, initially using court statistics, such as the number of convictions and number of prisoners, and in 1857 using police records of known criminals. Court and prison statistics provide further information as to the number and type of offences committed and offenders processed by the criminal justice system. Whereas court statistics give an indication of the numbers of offenders sentenced for different types of crime, prison statistics provide information about the extent of prisoners serving sentences and the composition of the prison population. Information from all police regions in England and Wales is disseminated in the annual Home Office (HO) publication, *Criminal Statistics for England and Wales*. This contains a mixture of indictable (or serious crime known as notifiable because it is processed by the Crown Court and jury) and non-indictable (or less serious crime that is usually processed by the magistrates court or a judge and is referred to as summary crime), solved and unsolved crime. Notifiable offences in the Criminal Statistics for England and Wales publication are divided into eight categories:

- violence against the person
- sex offences
- robbery
- burglary
- theft
- fraud/forgery
- criminal damage
- other.

The collation of crime-related information, such as the numbers of sex offences or burglary, can be measured in different ways. Counting the number of criminal events and the number of offenders are measures used by the HO in their publication of crime statistics. Two other measures of crime data are prevalence and incidence. Prevalence of crime for instance, informs researchers of the number of individuals committing crime at any point in time, as opposed to crime incidence, which provides a measure of the number of crimes committed by an individual. Whichever method is used to record crime (and this does vary across police forces), an unspecified figure of crime, known as the 'dark figure of crime', will continue to exist and to cause an underestimation of the true extent of crime – in part due to members of the public failing to report a crime (Bottomly and Pease 1986). According to Bottomly and Pease (1986) there are various reasons why people fail to report a crime:

- they might not know that a crime has occurred;
- they did not notice it;
- they were distracted;
- they did not perceive the crime to be serious enough to warrant police investigation;
- they were unaware that the behaviour constituted a criminal act (hence crime statistics are socially constructed).

Furthermore, police might disagree with a victim's perception of the event and conclude that a crime had not occurred or is trivial (Hough and Mayhew 1985). A trivial event might be perceived by the police as an ineffective use of their police resources, and given that they have a finite budget, decisions of resource allocation are based on a system of priority and urgency. The Metropolitan Police, for example, introduced a point system to indicate solvability of certain crimes but was later abandoned. Instead a counting method where the number of offences committed or the number of offences involving more than one victim was used. Since counting methods varied considerably across many police forces, there has been a call for their standardisation. The Smith Review (see next section) in 2006 emphasised that the differences in police practice has led to variations of reporting, recording and counting rules adopted by different police forces throughout England and Wales. Uniformity of police recording methods therefore has been placed at the top of the agenda for standardised police practice. Crime statistics obtained from police records and information from the British Crime Survey (BCS) provide the HO with a useful indicator of the frequency and nature of crime occurring in Britain today. In the police crime statistics serious and non-serious crimes are classified separately and there are further sub-categories of serious crime, which will be considered in the next section on crime classification.

## Classification of crime from statistics

In the UK the two main sources of statistical crime data are derived from police recorded crime figures and the British Crime Survey (renamed as Crime Survey for England and Wales (CSEW) in 2012). In the US a system known as Uniform Crime Reports is adopted which has a strong degree of overlap in the way crime is classified and recorded in the UK. There is also the National Crime Victimization Survey which is similar to the CSEW in England and Wales. All four methods of collating crime data will be described, and the advantages and disadvantages of police recorded crime figures and data from the CSEW in England and Wales compared.

### Police crime statistics

The Quarterly Update is a spin-off from the annual *Crime in England and Wales Bulletin* which publishes a public document on the government website of the most recent figures of recorded crime by the police (Table 2.1 shows crime figures for 2013 and 2014). This table typically shows the format of the different crime categories and their sub-categories of data derived from 43 territorial police forces of England and Wales (including the British Transport Police). Police recording of crime has been criticised for lacking consistency and standardisation, which has led to concerns over the reliability and validity of the crime statistics presented to the HO. The concerns of police recording of crime emanate from disparities in the way offences are considered by the different police forces (i.e. whether an offence is recorded depends on the counting rules adopted). The Home Office Counting Rules and the National Crime Recording Standard (NCRS) govern police recording practice, which have been revised in 2011 (HO 2011). In 1998, the Home Office Counting Rules for Recorded Crime allowed the inclusion of additional summary offences and specified that offences be counted towards a victim-based bias – in other words the number of victims is counted instead of the number of offences. The motive for including additional summary offences was to decrease the likelihood of any notifiable offence being downgraded to a summary offence and therefore go unrecorded. The consequence of introducing additional summary offences meant an increase in recorded crimes per se. The NCRS was introduced by the Association of Chief Police Officers (ACPO) in 2002 to work in collaboration with the HO. The agenda of the NCRS was to standardise the methods of recording crime across different police forces. A victim-oriented approach was taken, whereby police were required to record any allegation of crime reported by a victim provided there was no reliable evidence to suggest the contrary (Simmons, Legg and Hosking 2003).

The Audit Commission in 2007 published its assessment of police recording practice stating that, 'The police have continued to make significant improvements in crime recording performance and now have better quality crime data than ever before'.

It was reported by the HO in 2011 that in 2003/04 38 police forces were assessed as 'good' or 'excellent' for the quality of crime data obtained and the remaining five forces as 'fair'. In the 2005/06 and 2006/07 audits there were no police forces rated as having 'poor' crime data. Although the national audit programme was dissolved in 2007/08, the National Crime Recording Steering Group (NCRSG) headed by Professor Adrian Smith in 2006, was organised to achieve consistency in crime recording across all police forces. Police forces are monitored by a Force Crime Registrar (FCR) who ensures the counting rules are implemented and followed through a Data Quality Audit Manual (DQAM) which is also subject to review. Maintaining high quality recorded crime data has been helped through the introduction of a new data collection programme in 2011/12 – known as the Home Office Data Hub. This is designed to calibrate the Management Information Systems used by the different police forces which make it easier to collate data and offer alternative ways of analysing information.

Crimes considered and presented by the HO (Table 2.1) and the CSEW (Table 2.2), divide into personal and property based offences. Personal offences

*Table 2.1* Number of crimes recorded by the police in England and Wales between 2013 and 2014

| **Numbers and percentage changes** | **England and Wales, recorded crime** | | |
| --- | --- | --- | --- |
| *Offence group* | *Jan 2013 to Dec 2013* | *Jan 2014 to Dec 2014* | *% change between years* |
| Violence against the person offences | 614,410 | 740,802 | 21 |
| Violence against the person – with injury | 315,396 | 362,852 | 15 |
| Violence against the person – without injury | 298,462 | 377,435 | 26 |
| Sexual offences | 60,837 | 80,262 | 32 |
| Rape | 19,066 | 26,703 | 40 |
| Other sexual offences | 41,738 | 53,559 | 28 |
| Robbery offences | 59,426 | 51,585 | −13 |
| Robbery of business property | 5,783 | 5,778 | 0 |
| Robbery of personal property | 45,807 | 45,807 | −15 |
| Theft offences | 1,861,670 | 1,770,401 | −5 |
| Burglary offences | 447,235 | 419,350 | −6 |
| Domestic burglary | 217,486 | 200,785 | −8 |
| Non-domestic burglary | 229,749 | 218,565 | −5 |
| Vehicle offences | 378,130 | 353,308 | −7 |
| Theft from the person | 104,725 | 80,728 | −23 |
| Bicycle theft | 96,662 | 94,251 | −2 |
| Fraud offences | 207,168 | 224,947 | 9 |
| Criminal damage and arson | 510,708 | 499,885 | −2 |
| Drug offences | 201,172 | 178,719 | −11 |
| Miscellaneous crimes against society | 44,002 | 50,120 | 14 |
| **Total recorded crime all offences** | **3,711,511** | **3,769,175** | **2** |
| of which: Firearm offences | 4,927 | 4,860 | 4 |

Statistical Bulletin 2015

Table 2.2 Number of crimes and risk of being a victim in England and Wales between 2013 and 2014 based on CSEW interviews

| Offence group | Interviews from Jan 2013 to Dec 2013 | Interviews from Jan 2014 to Dec 2014 | % change between years |
|---|---|---|---|
| Criminal damage | 1,524,000 | 1,404,000 | −8 |
| Domestic burglary | 812,000 | 796,000 | −2 |
| Vehicle-related theft | 962,000 | 906,000 | 2 |
| Bicycle theft | 373,000 | 395,000 | 6 |
| Other household theft | 803,000 | 780,000 | −9 |
| Theft from the person | 560,000 | 476,800 | −15 |
| Other theft of personal property | 928,000 | 768,000 | −17 |
| All violence | 1,354,000 | 1,316,000 | −3 |
| with injury | 720,000 | 621,000 | −14 |
| without injury | 634,000 | 695,000 | 10 |
| **All CSEW crime** | **7,549,000** | **6,949,000** | |

| | Percentage risk of being a victim once or more and % point change | | |
|---|---|---|---|
| Criminal damage | 4.4 | 3.9 | −0.5 |
| Domestic burglary | 2.7 | 2.7 | 0.0 |
| Vehicle-related theft | 4.4 | 4.1 | −0.3 |
| Bicycle theft | 2.7 | 2.7 | 0.0 |
| Other household theft | 2.8 | 2.6 | −0.2 |
| Theft from the person | 1.1 | 1.0 | −0.2 |
| Other theft of personal property | 1.8 | 1.5 | −0.3 |
| All violence | 1.9 | 1.8 | −0.1 |
| with injury | 1.1 | 0.9 | −0.2 |
| without injury | 0.9 | 1.0 | −0.1 |

Source: Statistical Bulletin 2015

refer to crimes involving contact with people whether directly (physical contact like, for example, assault or mugging) or indirectly (no physical contact such as stalking). Property crimes usually involve damage, break-in or burglary to a building (residential or commercial). While burglary is an invasion of an individual's privacy and causes damage to a property, it does not involve hurting anyone (although it could be argued to cause psychological harm). If, however, the parameters are modified to include a scuffle between the homeowner and burglar and the homeowner is physically hurt then this becomes aggravated burglary. This offence now enters the realm of a personal crime, despite it originally being a property crime. An interesting question is whether this offence is a *mala in se* (i.e. act against the human moral code) or *mala prohibita* (i.e. act against statutory law) crime? Should the perpetrator be perceived as breaking the human moral code (given that a person was harmed) or perceived as performing a prohibited act (i.e. forced entry)? The main differences between personal and property crimes are the extent of contact with a person and the element of hurt (or harm) to the person whether this occurred directly or indirectly. Criminal acts therefore cannot always be conveniently classified into one or the other. It is useful to consider the differences between crimes of *mala in se* and *mala prohibita* and compare this with the way that recorded crime is presented in the annual HO publication, *Crime in England and Wales Bulletin*.

## Box 2.1

**Compares the two fundamental divisions of crime for concepts of crime seriousness and harm and recording of crime**

| *Mala in se* | *Mala prohibita* |
|---|---|
| Break the human moral code (e.g. murder) | Prohibited by the law (e.g. burglary) |
| Tend to be personal crimes (e.g. mugging) | Tend to be property and traffic crimes (e.g. vandalism and failing to stop at a red traffic light) |
| High level of seriousness (e.g. rape) | Not so high level of seriousness (e.g. shoplifting) |
| Seriousness based on harm (e.g. aggravated assault) | Seriousness based on carrying out a prohibited act (e.g. criminal damage) |
| Behaviour considered immoral (e.g. child pornography) | Behaviour considered immoral only insofar that it is prohibited (e.g. curb crawling) |
| Criminal behaviour that is immoral causes harm (e.g. paedophilia) | Some immoral behaviour could potentially cause harm (e.g. deviant sexual practices) |
| Such crimes receive high tariff punishment (e.g. life imprisonment for murder) | Such crimes tend to receive low tariff punishment (e.g. probation order for drink driving) |

When offences are listed under the two main categories of personal and property crimes, the reasoning for doing this becomes clearer as the concepts of *mala in se* and *mala prohibita* are used. The understanding that *mala in se* crimes are personal crimes that break the human moral code, implies a high level of seriousness (i.e. direct physical and psychological harm). For *mala prohibita*, the nature of crime committed is less serious (i.e. less direct and indirect harm (if any) to the individual). As discussed in Chapter 1, crimes of a personal nature are regarded as morally wrong and therefore can be considered as immoral behaviours. There are immoral behaviours that are not only deemed harmful to the individual and to others, but to the morality of society. In relation to the last point under *mala in se* in Box 2.1, it is a consistent finding within and across cultures that *mala in se* crimes are considered to be serious crimes warranting long-term custodial sentences. Unless there is an element of unsound mind the offender will be imprisoned. If the offender is deemed to be of unsound mind at the time of the crime, then they are likely to be incarcerated in a special secure unit or prison hospital until 'safe' to be transferred to prison. It is interesting that cross-culturally the pattern of sentencing for serious crime causing harm to the victim is strikingly similar. It could be argued therefore that almost the same classifications of *mala in se* crime are utilised (see Chapter 1 for discussion of cross-cultural similarities of sentencing criminals).

What does vary across countries are the types of offences considered to constitute *mala prohibita* crime. Although the laws in most European countries are similar, there are differences in the degree of latitude towards the regulation of immoral behaviour – in particular the boundaries of society's tolerance towards immoral conduct. Differences, for example, arise in the extent society tolerates prostitution, drug taking and gambling.

Countries such as The Netherlands have very permissive attitudes towards the sex industry and drug consumption. Both of these immoral behaviours test the boundaries of tolerance, and in The Netherlands the tolerance happens to be more liberal than most countries in Europe. The sex industry is overt and competitively sold in an open market. Drugs, in particular marijuana, can be purchased freely in cafes. Gunning (1993) who was the President of the Dutch National Committee on Drug Prevention reported that statistics for cannabis use during 1984–92 rose by 250 per cent. At the same time gun-shootings increased by 40 per cent, armed robbery by 69 per cent and car theft by 62 per cent. Although these trends appeared to co-vary, Gunning reminds us of the problems involved with inferring causation from correlation. In The Netherlands, individuals involved in the sex industry and drug use are not considered as victims or of warranting the attention of legal intervention in the name of preserving society's morality. If other countries are considered, it becomes clear that the law of the land (*mala prohibita*) determines what constitutes immoral behaviour and whether it is also an offence.

Dividing crimes into personal and property categories is rather rudimentary, given that the two types of offence are inconsistently mutually exclusive – especially when *mala in se*, *mala prohibita*, *mens rea* and concepts of seriousness and harm are included. Recorded crime figures published by the HO only include notifiable crimes, which is why the personal and property crimes recorded are of a serious nature. Clearly there is a consensus between the police and the HO concerning definitions of serious crime. Recorded crime figures can also be useful as a guide to long-term crime trends (i.e. informative for legal and social policy making). Figure 2.1, for instance, represents the data for victims of homicide in Scotland in 2000–2001 and 2009–2010. In

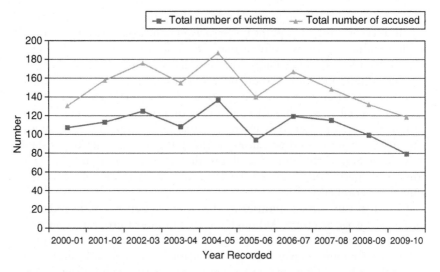

*Figure 2.1* Recorded numbers of accused and victims of homicide in Scotland from 2000–01 and 2009–10

The Scottish Government 2010

2009–2010 there were 79 victims of homicide – a drop of 20 from the preceding year and the lowest number of victims of homicide recorded in the last ten years in Scotland. Figure 2.1 also informs us that 118 were accused of homicide between 2009 and 2010.

### The Crime Survey for England and Wales

The CSEW is administered to a cross-selection of households in Britain where a responsible person in each household is expected to respond to questions about their experiences of crime in the past year. The CSEW is a type of victimisation survey providing criminologists with statistical information about crime, criminal and victim trends over the year and previous years (Table 2.2 shows the number of crimes and risk of being a victim derived from the CSEW). Despite the domination of non-serious crime, the CSEW is considered a more reliable measure of crime trends than are police records. There have been changes to the CSEW programme (known as the British Crime Survey prior to 2012) over the years that have resulted in the collation of new information:

- In 1982 when it was first introduced, one person of at least 16 years of age in 11,000 households in England and Wales was interviewed and asked questions about victimisation throughout the 1970s. Offences were divided into personal (robberies, assaults and sex crimes) and household (burglary, vandalism and car related) offences.

- In 1988 an ethnic minority (booster) sample of 1,349 Afro-Caribbean and Asian people was introduced. Victimisation in the workplace was also introduced.
- In 1992 a booster sample of children (12–15 years) was included.
- In 1994 computer-assisted personal interviewing helped improve confidentiality.
- Prior to 2001, the survey was conducted at two year intervals but is now a continuous survey.
- In 2010 the survey extended the sample to include children of 10–15 years of age (Fitzpatrick, Grant, Bolling, Owen and Millard 2010).
- In 2012 the BCS became known as the Crime Survey for England and Wales (CSEW).

### Summary of the advantages and disadvantages of police statistics and the CSEW

See Table 2.3 for a summary of UK police statistics and the CSEW.

In the US there are similar means of gathering crime data although the processes of data collection might be slightly different. In the next section we will explore the two major means of collecting crime data in the US: Uniform Crime Reports (UCR) by the Federal Bureau Investigation and National Crime Victimization Survey (NCVS) by the Bureau of Justice Statistics.

*Table 2.3* Summary of the advantages and disadvantages of police statistics and the CSEW's statistics

|  | Police Statistics | CSEW |
| --- | --- | --- |
| Advantages | Provide data at a local level<br><br>A good measure of serious crime | Provides a good measure of long term trends for common crimes<br>Provides a measure of crimes not reported to the police<br>Provides information on repeat victimisation<br>Can do risk analyses for different demographic groups |
| Disadvantages | Underestimates figures as much crime is not reported<br>Less serious crime is under-represented<br>Trends are influenced by legislation, reporting to the police, recording methods and counting rules and operational deployment | Excludes homicide, commercial crime, 'victimless' crimes (those who are unlikely to report themselves to the police) and crimes against the homeless or those in communal living<br>Difficult to identify trends or demographic variations for serious crimes |

## Federal Bureau Investigation (FBI) in the US

The Uniform Crime Reports (UCR) Program developed in 1929 by the International Association of Chiefs of Police has become a valuable source of information regarding criminal activity in the US. It has been used by the FBI in North America since 1930 as a provider of reliable crime statistics published in four annual publications: *Crime in the United States*; *National Incident-Based Reporting System*; *Law Enforcement Officers Killed and Assaulted*; *Hate Crime Statistics*. Data for these publications are received from more than 18,000 voluntarily participating agencies including county, state and federal law enforcement agencies. The crime data they acquire is submitted via a state UCR Program or the FBI UCR Program. This covers eight offences that are considered to be serious, frequently committed and reliably reported to the police. These crime data are submitted to the FBI via the law enforcement agencies which are further divided into Part I or index crimes and Part II or less serious crimes. Index crimes include the following serious offences:

- murder and non-negligent manslaughter
- forcible rape
- robbery
- aggravated assault
- burglary
- larceny–theft
- motor vehicle theft
- arson.

These index crimes can provide law enforcers with data covering numerous areas and with crime patterns and trends over time. In the US index crime information is available in the guise of colour coded online crime maps. More recently (in January 2011) this has been adopted in Britain as a means of accessing local-level information about burglary prone areas. In the case of Part II or less serious crimes arrest data is used.

### Bureau of Justice Statistics (BJS) in the US

Another crime measure adopted in the US is known as the National Crime Victimization Survey (NCVS). This has been run by the Bureau of Justice Statistics (BJS) since 1973. As the name suggests, the NCVS uses survey methods to ascertain information concerning crime incidents, victims and any obvious crime trends. The collated data provides information about the frequency of occurrence and the nature of crimes relating to sexual assault, rape, aggravated assault, personal robbery residential burglary, theft and motor vehicle theft for instance. Commercial crimes and homicide, however, are excluded. Household members in a nationally representative sample of households are interviewed by personnel from the US Census Bureau. It is estimated that 150,000 interviews of persons aged from 12 onwards take place annually, and that the selected households remain in the sample for three years while at the same time new households join the survey. Information about victimisation is collected regardless of having been reported to the police or not. From this information it is possible to ascertain reasons why 'victims' failed to report a crime to the police. In a similar vein to the CSEW, the NCVS provides information about the victims such as sex, age, marital status, ethnicity, educational background and income. Offender information provided considers sex, ethnicity and age, but also the relationship to the victim. The NCVS includes crime demographics such as the time and place of occurrence, type of weapons used and the consequences of the crime. Another parallel with the CSEW is the notion of supplements added periodically which means that new topics of inquiry are introduced such as school crime for instance. Despite running since 1973, it was not until 1995 that data from the NCVS was first published in a BJS bulletin. This includes an annual report called *Criminal Victimization in the United States,* which covers a wide range of areas captured in the NCVS (i.e. weapon crime, crimes against women and urban crime).

The NCVS was designed as a measure of crime in the US to complement the UCR Program. There are similarities and differences between the two measures. They are similar because they measure the same categories of serious crimes such as rape, aggravated assault, robbery, burglary, theft and motor vehicle theft. They differ, however, in a number of ways. The UCR and NCVS were developed to serve different purposes: in the case of the UCR Program the main purpose is to collate reliable criminal justice statistics useful to law enforcers while the NCVS serves to provide information about crime, the victims and offenders involved. While the NCVS provides information about both reported and non-reported crime, the UCR records information about homicide, commercial crimes, arson and crimes against children below the age of twelve. Furthermore, the UCR focuses on reported crimes but uses arrest data for crimes such as sexual assault and 'simple' assault.

The definition of burglary differs: for the UCR this is unlawful entry or attempted entry to commit further crime but for the NCVS this is defined as entry or attempted entry into a residential property without the right to be there. Property crimes (including theft, motor-vehicle theft and burglary) are calculated by the UCR on the basis of number of crimes per 100,000 persons unlike the NCVS which uses the criteria of number of crimes per 1,000 households. It is possible to ascertain crime trends using data from both the UCR and NCVS, however, due to differences of data collection and definition used there may be inconsistencies in crime patterns. This is only to be expected given that the UCR uses actual counts of crimes reported by the law enforcement agencies. It is possible to overcome crime trend disparity across the UCR and NCVS through checking for evidence that the crime discussed in the NCVS occurs in the UCR figures hence resulting in long-term trend consistency. Furthermore, when crimes defined in the same way by the UCR and NCVS are considered only, the long-term trends show increasing consistency.

Both the UCR and NCVS provide useful information albeit slightly different. The UCR in particular provides a reasonably accurate indication of the extent of crime and the nature of crime occurring across the US (including details of homicide). The NCVS offers information about the demographics of victimisation and non-reported crime. Hence it is possible to use both types of measure to increase awareness of crime trends and the type of crime occurring in the US.

Information from police statistics and the CSEW in England and Wales, and the UCR and NCVS in the US can be accessed by the public. For instance local-level data about burglary prone areas can be accessed through HO documents and government websites. While this is informative it can be a double-edged sword – information versus cause for public concern. Public concern can be expressed in the form of **moral panics** and fear of crime. This will be considered next as it is of particular relevance to the attitudes towards crime and criminality held by the public and the discrepancy often observed between these attitudes and the reality of crime prevalence.

## Moral panics and fear of crime

Public attitudes towards crime can be influential in determining the direction of political manifestos and in the determination of how criminal justice is administered in the short and long term. The relationship between public opinion and the election process of officials for positions within the criminal justice system is most obvious in the US. A good example is the public reaction towards paedophilia and the resulting series of modifications to legislation – **Megan's Law** and the legal requirement of paedophiles to declare their presence to their neighbourhood (Schwartz and Cellini (1997); see also Box 8.11). In some states of America, the method of informing the neighbourhood of a paedophile's presence is more extremely enforced than others – in Louisiana this could mean displaying a sign in the front of the house or distributing leaflets to neighbours (Solomon, Lee and Batchelder 2007).

Changes to legislation often arise from an extreme form of public opinion encapsulated in **moral panics**. The term was introduced by Stanley Cohen (1972) to describe a cultural clash between in-groups and out-groups, fuelled by media coverage, speculation and condemnation, which in turn is disseminated to the general public (see Chapter 10 for further discussion). The differences of attitude, ethos and behaviour across distinct groups of people, is often reported out of proportion with the true extent of cultural clashes that do occur. Bauman (2000) stated:

> Our time is auspicious for scapegoats – be they the politicians making a mess of their private lives, criminals creeping out of the mean streets and

rough districts, or 'foreigners in our midst' . . . 'investigative' tabloid journalists fishing for conspiracies . . . for plausible new causes of 'moral panics'
ferocious enough to release . . . fear and anger (pp. 38–9).

Bauman is intonating that we have become a society who fears crime, which
is in part due to the way it is reported by the media. This results in fear of
crime and a culture of moral panics that lead to demands for modification
to existing legislation (i.e. an increase of police power and police presence).
Cohen's original application of moral panics was used to describe youth crime
in Britain during the 1960s. The 'Mods' and 'Rockers', two distinct groups of
youths with their own in-group attitudes and subculture, reportedly clashed
and fought regularly in towns such as Brighton during the weekends and holi-
days. These clashes caused distress, fear and anger for local residents of these
towns which were further exacerbated by the media. In *Policing the Crisis*, Hall,
Critcher, Jefferson, Clarke and Roberts (1978) introduced a more profound
understanding of moral panics, which placed this concept at the heart of a
political phenomenon. Hall *et al.* (1978) used moral panics to describe street
crime such as muggings. Fuelled by media coverage, moral panics lead to a
demand for new legislation against crime and a call for increased policing.
Hall *et al.* further speculated that the mass media became an 'instrument of
state control', which documented street mugging in a manner representing 'an
index of the disintegration of social order' (Valier 2002, p.122). The media
therefore interpreted events contiguous with a consensus framework: one
which depicted a common moral condemnation towards crime (Hall *et al.*
1978; Valier 2000).

According to Valier (2002), the public understanding of crime is generated
through the media's depiction of it, which then arouses anxiety and fear. This
anxiety and fear causes a moral panic whereupon the dominant public opinion
(i.e. that which reflects a consensus view of society) demands that crime be
tackled strategically through new appropriate legislation – legislation increasing the power of police to subdue offenders from further criminality. Given
that the media tend to report high-profile violent crimes, the public are more
likely to remember these events which heighten their fear of crime (Innes
2004). These serious violent crimes occur less frequently than suggested by
the media (Williams 2004), however, their media coverage results in moral
panics. Moral panics can therefore accelerate the need for further regulation
of behaviour through new rules of law (Hall *et al.* 1978). An example of this is
demonstrated by the Conservative's successful election of Margaret Thatcher
as Prime Minister in 1979. Britain became increasingly rule bound as more
legislation was introduced to regulate society – as Hall (1980, p.3) stated, 'drifting into a law and order society'. Such views are typically founded in a critical
criminological ideology (see Chapter 1), but nevertheless provide an alternative point of view to understanding the impact of media and moral panics in
the evolution of law.

Public anxieties and fear towards crime have been investigated using numerous indices. One method is to compare England and Wales with other countries. This approach was taken by van Dijk, van Kesteren and Smit (2007). The questions they addressed included the level of 'safety experienced on the streets after dark', beliefs of 'the likelihood of house burglary in the coming year' and 'the extent of burglar alarm systems used by households'. They found that England and Wales generally exceeded the fears experienced for these questions by a large margin when compared with countries such as Australia, the US, Canada, Ireland and Scotland. This was supported by the BBC's (19 July 2007) report that despite statistics showing a decrease in crime, people in Britain have the highest levels of fear of crime in Europe. The Home Secretary, Jacqui Smith, claimed that the British public refuted the accuracy of statistical crime data to the extent where 65 per cent believed crime is still rising. The CSEW is another method of investigating fear of crime as it enables people to rate their levels of fear (Allen 2004). Povey, Ellis and Nichols (2003) found support from the CSEW suggesting a decrease in the extent of crime per se since the mid-1990s, and yet the public continue to disbelieve the figures.

Between 2010 and 2011 the CSEW revealed that in England and Wales 11 per cent of respondents showed high levels of worry about burglary and 13 per cent towards violent crime – these figures were not significantly different from the previous year. There remains, however, a small cohort of individuals who harbour a high level of fear and anxiety towards violent crime. Who these individuals are likely to be and where they most likely reside are important questions to address, as the answers will help uncover the relationship between perceptions of fear of crime and the likelihood of having been victimised or becoming a victim. There have been various surveys conducted over the years looking at fear of crime in England and Wales. In addition to studying different areas within England and Wales, researchers have provided a breakdown of those most likely to fear crime by sex, age, class and occupation. Past research has included international, national and regional crime surveys:

- International

    1   Junger-Tas, Terlouw and Klein (1994) conducted an international study of youth crime coordinated by the Dutch Ministry of Justice, which also comprised of five national studies based on England and Wales, Holland, Portugal, Spain and Sweden. England and Wales had the lowest violent crime rate among the 14–21 year olds but these findings did not support the tough approach to law and order at the time.

- National

    1   BCS 1982 found twice as many burglaries as that recorded by the police; five times more wounding; 12 times more theft; 13 times more

vandalism and five times more violence against the person; four times more criminal damage to property. People living in inner-city areas had an increased risk of victimisation; young men living in inner-city areas were most at risk; those living in flats were less safe than those living in houses; those in council accommodation were more at risk, and those who were at home less often were more at risk than individuals who remained at home.

2   BCS 1988 found 14 per cent of workers experienced verbal abuse, especially female workers; people working for welfare services, nurses and female office managers were susceptible to attack; teachers, social workers, nurses, pub managers and security men were more likely to experience threats. Ethnic groups reported higher rates of victimisation than Whites for threats, robbery and theft.

3   BCS 1992 found that repeat victimisation is a result of specific areas being easy targets; repeat victimisation for violent offences where 17 per cent experienced three or more incidents and in 43 per cent of these cases, victims were mugged by a stranger.

4   BCS 1994 found that police figures were four times lower than BCS estimates (3.1 million recorded crimes versus 11.6 million of which 41 per cent were reported to the police). The increase in BCS crimes across many types of offence suggests that the reporting rate of offences to police is falling or that the areas most prone to crime are uninsured and therefore less likely to gain by reporting to police.

5   BCS 2001 found that individuals living in inner-city and council estates who had experienced frequent victimisation and vandalism were more fearful of crime. Those in unskilled occupations who lived in less affluent areas and in council homes experienced higher levels of fear.

6   BCS 2003–5 found that Asian and Black respondents had higher levels of fear for burglary, car and violent crime (Allen 2006). Allen also found that women were more concerned about burglary than men (by 4 per cent). Individuals with good qualifications were less concerned about violent crime than those without qualifications (11 per cent and 20 per cent respectively).

7   BCS 2010–11 found that fear of crime for burglary was 10 per cent, for violent crime 13 per cent and car crime 10 per cent. Perceived likelihood of being a victim of burglary and violent crime was 13 per cent and for car crime this was 17 per cent. Vandalism of a vehicle or property was 6.1 per cent; vehicle crime was 5.4 per cent; violent crime such as wounding, assault with minor injury or no injury and robbery was 3.1 per cent; 2.6 per cent experienced burglary and 1.1 per cent theft. 2.5 per cent of women aged 16–59 and 0.5 per cent of men experienced a sexual assault. 60 per cent believed crime had

risen nationally whereas 28 per cent were convinced of local increases in crime rate.

8   CSEW 2011–12 found no statistically significant differences in crime figures and fear of crime to that of the 2010–11 BCS.

• Regional

1   Merseyside Crime Survey (Kinsey 1984) found a high risk of victimisation for the socially disadvantaged in the North; in the inner-city areas crime was the second largest social problem; fear of crime was highest among the economically vulnerable; working class women were compromised most because of their low standard of accommodation and 20 per cent did not venture out at night.

2   Islington Crime Survey 1986 (Jones, Maclean and Young) found that fear of crime was high for burglary, robbery, rape and vandalism. Women aged 16–24 were more likely to be raped than older women and women were more frequently victims of offences such as theft.

3   Manchester Survey of Female Victims 1986 found that of 226 sexual assaults, 47 per cent knew their attacker and of 152 rapes, 57 per cent knew their attacker.

4   The London Borough of Newham Crime Survey 1987 found that women were more likely to fear crime than men; 68 per cent of women worried about being sexually assaulted and remained indoors at night; 22 per cent of respondents had been a victim at least once.

5   City-centre Victim Surveys in Coventry (Ramsay 1989) found that victimisation decreases with age possibly due to changes in lifestyle – young people are more likely to go out and therefore are more at risk of coming into contact with criminal events (Gottfredson 1984). The victimisation figures were low (assault was 2 per cent; being mugged was 3 per cent and insulted by strangers was 12 per cent) but the fear of crime level was high (37 per cent were worried about being insulted by strangers; 50 per cent about being assaulted and 59 per cent of being mugged). Women were fearful of being sexually assaulted (60 per cent). Ramsay (1989) found that fear of crime increased as the seriousness of the offence increased. Hence the extent of fear is linked with the perceived seriousness of the offence (see section on concept of seriousness for further definitions).

6   A survey conducted in a village in Worcestershire (Yarwood and Gardner 2000) found that individuals living in rural areas were less fearful of crime. As many as 91 per cent claimed that they felt safe alone at home and 65 per cent had no concerns about walking alone at night.

7   Vanderveen (2006) cited a study of London taxi drivers (Mourato, Saynor and Hart 2004), where 33 per cent claimed that fear of crime affected their work.

These findings are revealing but must also be carefully considered. The problem of comparing different studies and different individuals is whether the same variables are being controlled, measured and analysed. As suggested by Jefferson and Holloway (2000), fear of crime has a different meaning for men and women. While women are more concerned about sexual attack, men are fearful of assault. Furthermore, young men, despite statistics suggesting they are most likely to be victims of violent crime, appear to be affected least by these probabilities. Different explanations for this have been put forward, but the assumption by Goodey (1997) that boys suffer emotional vulnerability which leads them to behave in a fearless and aggressive manner towards others, appears to explain why they ignore their risk of victimisation. In order to account for female fear, Ferraro (1995) introduced the notion of 'shadow of sexual assault'. Ferraro argued that while women fear the possibility of being sexually assaulted, they are actually more fearful of other crimes such as burglary with assault (i.e. aggravated burglary). As rape receives much attention by the media, it has a shadowing effect on how women perceive other crimes (Ferraro 1995).

There is also an age difference in the extent of fear of crime experienced by individuals: the elderly, for example, in past studies were found to be the most fearful of crime. O'Bryant, Donnermeyer and Stafford (1991) claimed that the elderly were more likely to use problems of frailty and vulnerability as explanations for this, when in fact physical assault or economic loss would be more incapacitating. Recent research findings, however, indicate that there has been a shift from the elderly being most fearful of being assaulted to them being less fearful than younger people (Moore and Shepherd 2007; Ferraro 1995). Goodey (2005) reported that the environment is partly responsible for this shift. It is not age that is necessarily the factor causing fear of crime but living alone and being susceptible to victimisation. Cohen and Felson (1979) introduced the **Routine Activities Theory** which made the point that staying indoors does not necessarily protect an individual from crime if the perpetrator perceives there being less risk of detection when the individual lives alone and is vulnerable.

Another factor considered in crime surveys is residential stability. The questions set specifically address the level of social cohesion and social community bonds inherent within neighbourhoods (Vanderveen 2006). According to Vanderveen, an area that has a high crime rate is less likely to have strong social bonds, hence making it a hostile environment to live in. The notion of 'Broken Windows', a theory introduced by Wilson and Kelling (1982), suggests that these environments are strongly linked with a culture of deviant behaviour. Broken Windows has become a metaphor describing a series of events likely to follow if a community is perceived by a potential criminal as a wasteland that no one cares about. Hence in the words of Wilson and Kelling (1982), 'if a window in a building is broken and is left unrepaired, all the rest of the windows will soon be broken' (p.2). It is assumed from this that potential criminals consider their environmental surroundings and accommodate their behaviour according to what they see. In a high rise block of flats for example where the communal areas are clean and tidy, tenants are less likely to throw litter because they could be held accountable for their actions. This seemingly ordered and cared about physical environment begets accountability unlike zones where there is disorder. It is argued that, in areas where there is disorder, crime is more likely.

Out of the Broken Windows theory a community policing strategy arose based on order maintenance. A former New York City mayor, Rudolph Giuliani, implemented a 'zero tolerance' policy based on the Broken Windows notion. In 1994 changes were seen in New York City such as cleaning graffiti off walls and in subway cars, picking up litter and checking and moving people on who committed antisocial acts. Basically the aim was to reduce behaviours that could be conceived of as 'quality of life crime' – hence by clearing up petty crime (i.e. public drunkenness, jaywalking, loitering and vagrancy) a better quality of life would be attained for many people. This also includes the reduction of what is known as victimless crime where some individuals indulge in illicit immoral and antisocial behaviour such as consuming and selling drugs on the streets or curb crawling for prostitutes.

Victimless crime is a topic we will return to later in this chapter (see Box 2.7). Through the enforcement of laws dealing with minor criminal acts, it is argued that more serious crime can be prevented. In fact this is what Giuliani found. During the 1990s violent crime in New York City fell by 51 per cent and homicide more impressively by 72 per cent. More recently in 2014, Giuliani's police commissioner, William Bratton has been asked to return to New York City to consider new policy based on the Broken Windows' philosophy (Kirchner 2014).' Successes have been found in other areas too. Doran and Lees (2005) applied the Broken Windows theory to communities where limited **crime prevention** initiatives provided opportunities for offenders to operate which led to increased public fear of crime. These communities have seen reduced crime and a less fearful public.

Ultimately, however, it is an individual's perceived risk of victimisation rather than the actual risk of victimisation which influences levels of fear of crime. The extent of correlation between perceived and actual risk has been debated. Vanderveen (2006), for example, claimed that perceived and actual risk does not correlate and refers to this as the fear–victimisation paradox. Others, such as Ferraro (1995), believed that perceived risk induces fear of crime while Chadee, Austen and Ditton (2007) differentiated between an individual's group and personal level of risk. This allows for individuals who are classified as part of a group which is statistically more likely to be victimised, to perceive their personal risk level either in accordance with or differently from their group risk. Of importance to the calculation of group risk level, is the level of crime committed in the neighbourhood where an individual resides. The level of crime committed is linked with how many offenders commit crime and the number of offences they committed. In the next section we consider factors that encourage individuals to lead criminal lives based on the idea of **criminal career pathways** (studies by psychologists), and notions of

**persistence** and **desistance** in crime (desistance in crime will also be discussed further in Chapter 5).

### Criminal careers

A criminal career can be divided into three parts – onset, duration and desistance (or an end) and defined as 'the longitudinal sequence of offences committed by an individual offender' (Farrington 1992, p.521). The notion of criminal careers has been useful in determining **risk factors** for who is likely to offend, for how long and how often. Farrington argued that most offences are committed by a 'certain proportion of the population' (p.521) – known as prevalence and is not to be confused with the number of offences offenders commit (i.e. the frequency). Offenders vary in the frequency and seriousness of offences they commit, which can be accounted for using a criminal career approach. Farrington and West (1990) reported that the frequency of offending peaks at 17 years, and that childhood predictors of prevalence included parents with a criminal record who had poor parenting skills and limited income; impulsivity; low intelligence; poor achievement at school and antisocial behaviour. Using a criminal career approach, Farrington (1986) claimed that this peak in the frequency of offences at 17 years was a reflection of variations in prevalence rather than the number of crimes individual offenders committed. This was based on evidence indicating consistency in the frequency of offences committed during an offender's criminal career. Furthermore, Farrington and Hawkins (1991) compared prevalence, onset of and desistance from offending using 67 correlates. They found that robust correlates of prevalence were inconsistent with correlates predicting onset and desistance – hence suggesting that the likely factors accounting for prevalence, onset and desistence were incompatible.

It is through longitudinal studies like Farrington and West (1990) and Kolvin, Miller, Fleeting and Kolvin (1988) that the following factors were found to be important in the assessment of criminal career longevity and variation:

- onset date of criminality;
- likely recurrence of further crime based on a history of offending;
- frequency of crimes committed;
- number of years intervening onset and desistence (total length of criminal career);
- time period between crimes committed (i.e. intermittency);
- different types of crime committed;
- specialisation in the types of crime committed or presence of crime-switching;
- type of sentence given for a current offence.

At close inspection of these factors and the data derived from Farrington and West's (1990) study, boys convicted at 10–11 years averaged a criminal career length of 11 years and five months, which depreciated to two years and nine months when first convicted at 17 years. These findings suggest that the earlier boys are convicted for offending, the more persistent offenders they become and the longer their criminal career. As many as 73.6 per cent of 17–24 year olds who had a prior conviction between the age of 10–16 were reconvicted. In comparison with 16 per cent who did not have a criminal record as a juvenile, the age onset of offending is clearly a statistically significant factor in explaining these figures (Farrington and West 1990).

The longevity of criminal careers taken at 32 years and from the age of desistence averaged five years and eight months, and occurred between 17 and 23 years of age with a record of four offences. Farrington and West's research also suggested that a small cohort is responsible for committing most of the recorded offences. This was substantiated in the figures for **recidivism**. Of those who committed a first offence, 68 per cent reoffended before the age of 32, and for those who committed a second offence as many as 71.2 per cent had reoffended again. This further increased to 80 per cent for a fourth offence. Past offending would appear to be a reliable predictor of future offending, but findings by Nagin and Farrington (1992) fail to provide evidence to support this. Using the notion of persistent heterogeneity which can be considered as a stable construct describing an inclination towards criminality – hence age, criminal parents and poor parenting skills, low intelligence, impulsivity and antisocial behaviour – was found to best account for criminality rather than a history of convictions per se. This favours Farrington's statement that, 'there tends to be persistence of an underlying "antisocial personality" from childhood to adulthood' (Farrington 1992, p.532).

Farrington, Coid, Harnett, Jolliffe et al. (2006) did a follow up of the Cambridge Study of Delinquent Development (see Chapters 3, 4 and 10) and reported an update of the findings from the 1973 results as a Home Office Research Study. The aims of this report were to document convictions up to the age of 50 and life success to the age of 48. They found that 41 per cent of the males in the study had been convicted for crimes spanning on average a nine year period. They further found that those who had been convicted at an early age tended to persist in crime and maintain a criminal career throughout their life. Those who offended by 10–16 years were responsible for three-quarters of all crime convictions (77 per cent). They found that persisters convicted before and after 21 years of age led successful lives in 42 per cent of cases by 32 years, and 65 per cent of cases at the age of 48. In the case of desisters convicted before the age of 21, this was 79 per cent at the age of 32 and 96 per cent by 48 years of age. In the case of offenders convicted after the age of 21, life success was 69 per cent at 32 and 84 per cent at 48. For non-convicted men this was 90 per cent and 95 per cent respectively. These statistics suggest that desisters lead successful lives at an earlier age than persisters. They also reported that measures of family criminality, poor parenting skills, poverty, risk-taking and low school achievement were important risk factors for criminality between the ages of eight and ten. Their findings alluded to there being criminogenic families where fathers, mothers, brothers and sisters were also convicted for crimes (see Chapter 3). The average age of conviction for fathers was 30 and mothers 35. This would appear contrary to the evidence that offending is a young person's game; however, these figures need to be put into context. These fathers and mothers would have been in their teens during World War II and their criminal records might have been destroyed with the 'weeding' (i.e. term used to describe the deletion of old criminal records) of files introduced in 1958. Previously it had been found by Farrington, Lambert and West (1998) that criminal careers had longevity – an average of 16 and 15 years for the fathers and mothers respectively.

Clingempeel and Henggeler (2003) were interested in why some delinquent adolescents continue to commit offences during adulthood. They considered **risk** and **protective factors** experienced by persisters and desisters and assessed the difference between the two groups. They conducted a longitudinal study consisting of 80 juvenile delinquents, and assessed the differences between those who persisted or desisted from a criminal career. Persisters consistently reported having poor relationships with their peers and psychiatric problems. Clingempeel and Henggeler (2003) applied six months of therapeutic intervention using Multisystemic Therapy for the treatment of substance abuse and dependency issues. This therapy involved an amalgamation of approaches but ultimately aimed to improve offenders' self-esteem by improving their problem solving, social and life skills. After treatment, desisters reported no criminal activity but claimed that they 'did not get involved in many fights'. Their comments suggested that they committed minor offences but resisted the temptation to commit serious crimes. Persisters alternatively reported more serious crimes committed, poor relationships with peers, less job satisfaction and more psychiatric problems. Clingempeel and Henggeler (2003) concluded that,

> With few exceptions, these differences remained statistically significant after [controlling] for treatment condition (p.319) . . . interventions designed to promote relationship building skills with pro-social peers may be important components of treatment programs focusing on aggressive juveniles (p.320).

Clingempeel and Henggeler (2003) controlled for variables such as gender, race, number of siblings and parental education, and despite this they attained significant differences between desisters and persisters regarding the protective factor of sustaining close emotional relationships. This offered resiliency against further serious criminality. It is interesting that desisters and persisters differed in this one major protective factor, as previous research alludes to gender being an important contributory protective factor against criminality. One reason why girls are portrayed as being more law abiding than boys links with their socialisation of sex-role acceptance (see Chapter 9). Furthermore, findings indicate a difference in prevalence across gender for developmental psycho-pathological conditions such as conduct disorder (CD); Attention Deficit Hyperactivity Disorder (ADHD) and other Oppositional Defiant Disorders (ODD) (see Chapter 7). Recently, however, prevalence differences for devel-opmental disorders across gender have been questioned using the **gender par-adox** first introduced by Taylor and Ounsted (1972), and references to an increasing ladette culture (see Box 2.2).

DeLisi and Vaughn (2007) also considered factors inducing delin-quent youths to persist in a life of crime. By focusing on levels of self-control exhibited in their cohort of 723 incarcerated delinquents, they found that:

- career criminals had lower levels of self-esteem than controls (non-career offenders);
- self-control played an important role in predicting a career criminal (i.e. low self-control increased the odds of being a career criminal);
- low self-control is a sensitive measure in the prediction of chronic criminality;
- low self-esteem was a stronger predictor of career criminality than other demographic factors such as gender, age, ethnicity, socio-economic status and any psychiatric problems (i.e. mental illness, trauma or ADHD).

These findings support previous research singling self-control as an important factor in crime persistence. Benda (2003) identified low self-control as a major predictor of recidivism (reoffending) among 601 adult male boot camp leavers whose onset of criminal behaviour started before or after 10 years of age. The impact of low self-control for criminality, regardless of whether the onset of criminal behaviour was before or after the age of 10, exceeded the contribution of risk factors such as poor family attachment, delinquent peers, gang membership, being abused and drug abuse. Similar findings reported by Evans, Brown and Killian (2002) demonstrated the importance of high self-control in the avoidance of impulsive decision making among juvenile delinquents. A robust link between low self-control and serious offending such as homicide (Piquero, MacDonald, Dobrin, Daigle and Cullen 2005) and chronic serious offending (Piquero, Moffitt and Wright 2007) was found.

Given that criminal careers can be short lived or last a life-time in the case of some offenders, it is no surprise therefore that this will have an impact on recorded crime. The persistence and desistance from crime featured in crimi-nal careers will no doubt influence short-term and long-term crime trends. This will be presented in short-term crime trends as fluctuation points where the crime rate will appear to have increased or decreased. Criminal careers, however, are not the only cause of crime fluctuations. In the next section crime fluctuations and crime reduction will be examined in relation to short-term and long-term crime trends.

---

## Box 2.2

### Gender paradox – ladette culture

Taylor and Ounsted (1972) first used the term 'gender paradox' to describe the greater prevalence of medical conditions for one of the genders – usually boys – but at the same time the gender with the least prevalence for the condition exhibiting the most serious symptoms. Eme (1992) speculated that this principle might generalise to disruptive behaviour. Loeber and Stouthamer-Loeber (1998) stated that, 'in disorders with an unequal sex ratio, those with the lower prevalence rate tended to be more seriously affected'. When considered more closely, this statement suggests that a quantity approach of presenting numbers of boys and girls afflicted with developmental disorders, leads to the deduction that more boys than girls exhibit behavioural and psychological problems (which includes criminal behaviour). If a quality approach is used, then it becomes apparent that girls exhibit problems to a more serious level than boys. For example, Szatmari, Boyle and Offord (1989) demonstrated that girls diagnosed with ADHD were 40 times more likely to develop CD than boys. Loeber and Keenan (1994) claimed that girls were more likely to have aggressive tendencies, ADHD, depression and substance abuse if diagnosed with CD than boys. Hence despite the frequency of disorders for boys being greater than for girls, the extent of distress experienced by girls might be higher. This gender paradox effect was further supported by a study based on a sample of 1423 (674 boys and 749 girls) aged 11–18 years who had co-occurring behaviours for depression and delinquency (Diamantopoulou, Verhulst and van der Ende 2011). Diamantopoulou *et al.* (2011) found that more girls than boys had co-occurring behaviours for depression and delinquency which continued into adolescence and adulthood. As symptoms of depression decreased and delinquency increased during adolescence, outcomes for females were poorer in adulthood than it was for males. Furthermore, the underlying prognosis differed across gender: for males it was childhood aggression whereas for females it was childhood depression and delinquency. An interesting study by Devaud, Jeannin, Narring, Ferron and Michaud (1998) reported that adolescent girls who were preoccupied with their weight and image also had **comorbidity** for increased violence. They believed that the underlying causes of their violent behaviour was overlooked and confounded by psychiatric diagnoses of aggression.

Reports of increasing violent offences committed by adolescent girls have been attributed to a 'ladette' culture (Ministry of Justice 2009). Ladette culture has been defined as 'girls or women who behave in "laddish" or "boyish" ways' (Jackson 2006, p.343). Jackson and Tinkler (2007) speculated that the ladette is 'taking space once regarded the principal or sole preserve of men' (p.254). Denscombe (2001) commented that the increase in risk-taking behaviour in females has led to a ladette culture where drinking and violence results in arrest. Slack (2009) reported that girls of 18 or under were responsible for 58,000 crimes in 2008, which translated to seven crimes committed per hour. Slack (2009) further reported that within the last four years violent offences by adolescent girls had risen by 50 per cent. In 2006, Chelsea O'Mahoney (who was 14 years old at the time of her offence) was found guilty of manslaughter and given eight years youth detention. She claimed that beating homeless and vulnerable people with her gang of female friends was a common occurrence and that these events were filmed so that they could re-experience what they had done. Slack (2009) reported many similar incidents of female violence.

Denscombe (2001) argued that increases of risk-taking behaviour in females, typical of the ladette culture, are a likely reaction against female sex roles and traditional female stereotypes. It is also plausible that the gender paradox argument is applicable here, as most females do not behave aggressively or violently towards other people. The typical portrayal of aggression in females is indirect or verbal aggression, such as backbiting and spreading nasty rumours, unlike males who use physical force (Bjorkqvist, Lagerspetz and Kaukiainen 1992; Pakaslahti and Keltikangas-Jarvinen 1998). If the gender paradox is correct, then one possibility is that females who are prone to violent tendencies will exhibit more extreme and serious forms of antisocial conduct – which appears to account for the extreme antisocial behaviour of O'Mahoney.

## Crime fluctuations and reduction

It is interesting that trends in crime rate in both England and Wales and North America suggest a reduction in the number of offences recorded by police, certainly since 2010. In fact a report by Rosenfield (2002) suggests that, in the US, crime rates, after peaking in the early 1990s, have been falling for almost a decade. The big question is whether these crime figures are a true reflection of the extent of crime occurring. In England and Wales the crime trend also suggests that crime is still falling. A report in June 2014 submitted to the House of Commons Justice Committee, examined police recorded crime figures and the estimated figures from the CSEW, finding that both methods of measuring the extent of crime committed, agreed with the drop in crime rate observed. The CSEW indicated a 10 per cent reduction of crimes against households between 2012 and 2013. This was also the lowest estimate since the survey

began in 1981. In the case of recorded crime, police figures co-occur by showing a 3 per cent reduction. This included crime reduction across most of the
categories used in recording crime. There were, however, some crimes where
there was an increase such as shoplifting (4 per cent rise) and theft from the
person (7 per cent rise). Sexual offences rose by 17 per cent, partly explained
by the recent spate of investigations of historical sexual abuse driven by
'Project Yewtree'. Another type of crime seeing a rise of 34 per cent in 2013
is fraud. This rise was attributed to the improved centralised recording system
police use and the effectiveness of Action Fraud set up to investigate national
fraud and internet crime in the UK. Hence the conclusion is that records show
a decline in crime rate for certain types of crime but an increase for others.

There are also reoffending figures published by the Ministry of Justice
which are useful in explaining crime trends. However, these figures suggest little change between 2008 and 2010 (reoffending rate at 35.9 per cent)
against the baseline level of 40.9 per cent in 2000. In 2012 the reoffending
rate was 35.4 per cent, a less than 1 per cent decrease from 2010. Similar
findings have been reported by Probation Trusts and local authorities. In
2010 the overall prison population was 85,400, which has remained relatively constant at 85,285 in 2014. So how can we account for a continued
reduction in crime rates in England and Wales given that reoffending rates
remain high and fewer Probation Trusts and local authorities are reporting
a decrease in reoffending coupled with a constant prison population figure?
The fall in crime is a complicated phenomenon to explain as there are many
factors other than crime rate, reconviction figures and prison population to
consider. Arguably, there are factors such as demographics, social policy and
societal structure as well as overarching cultural values and attitudes, which all
interplay in developing the criminal mind-set and in creating the opportunities to commit crime. Mills and Roberts (2012) considered the structures of
other countries and suggested that where there are lower rates of poverty and
inequality there tends to be fewer violent crimes and lower prison populations. Internationally, the crime trend appears to be the same – falling crime
rates. In 2012 the Ministry of Justice produced a document, 'Comparing
International Criminal Justice Systems', claiming that falling crime rates are
largely an international trend which suggests that reduction in crime rates is
likely to be independent of justice systems and policies endorsed in different
countries. Nevertheless crime can be sensitive to the national policies put
in place. Laycock (1991) for instance claims that without the legislation for
compulsory housing security systems installed in new builds, figures for burglary would rise again, just as this legislation has helped to reduce residential
burglary in the first place. This would suggest that crime trends are sensitive
to national and local policy.

According to Donohue (1998) there are many random factors influencing
the extent of crime, so much so that explaining the figures at any point in time
is difficult. He explains how random events tend to escalate the crime rate and

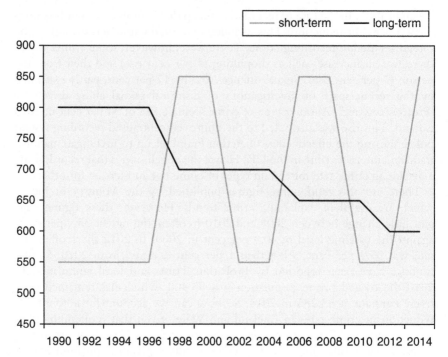

*Figure 2.2* Fictitious short-term fluctuations superimposed over long-term trends

innovate social policy to depress it. These will certainly have an effect on short-term fluctuations of crime. It is therefore important to focus on long-term trends in crime as the short-term fluctuations detract from the more stable and reliable crime patterns and what might be causing them. One way of viewing the interaction between short-term fluctuations and long-term trends is by using a graph format. Figure 2.2 is a fictitious demonstration of how short-term fluctuations can occur superimposed over long-term trends.

By looking at long-term crime patterns it should be easier to identify the stable variables underlying criminal activity. For example if the overall long-term crime rate remains constant over a period of many years, then it is a matter of what policy or system has also been in situ long term. Donohue (1998) created a number of possible models of long-term patterns for homicide in the US. Based on national crime homicide patterns (taken from UCR) from 1950 to 1997 he revealed that murder rose annually at a rate of 4.4 per cent between 1950 and 1977 but fell at a rate of 0.6 per cent between 1977 and 1997. At the same time he noted short-term homicide fluctuations around this trend. Hence two long-term homicide trends are identifiable: 1950–1977 and 1977–1997. According to Donohue this means that long-term explanations are required for these two long-term trends while variable explanations are needed for the short-term fluctuations which are likely to be caused by short-lived influences, such as a new drug gang moving into an area who then move away, or empty slum houses occupied by criminals which are then redeveloped for residential living. Donohue suggests that an increase of prison incarceration during the 1977 downward trend might account for the reduction in homicide but at the same time not explaining the significant drop in crime observed since 1993. This latter downward trend appears to be a short-term fluctuation because the long-term trend suggests a slow downward decline. Donohue suggests that one model of homicide prediction for the future is that it will be a very long time before homicide rates will be as low as the 1950s and early 1960s. It must be remembered, however, that Donohue's findings are based on figures up until 1997.

More recently, Rosenfield (2002) showed that homicide rates in the US were continuing to fall in 2000. Explanations vary from policing, prison expansion, firearms policy, the state of the economy and well-functioning social institutions which ultimately contribute towards the regulation of social behaviour – all of the above work in combination to reduce crime. The last point concerning functional social institutions relates to the notion of legitimacy. Here, people have confidence in social institutions which results in them being more inclined to follow the rules, and in doing so are less likely to behave criminally (based on the work of Gary LaFree 1998).

We have seen how crimes are recorded, how individuals might become involved in a life of crime through the notion of criminal careers and how crime statistics reflect both long- and short-term trends. Why crimes are categorised in the way they are (e.g. serious and non-serious crime) requires further exploration. What is it that makes a sexual offence a serious crime warranting a high sentence tariff? How do we determine what is a serious crime? What is it that makes us form a consensus of what is a serious crime? These questions are addressed in the following sections on crime seriousness and the harm debate – but first the concept of crime seriousness.

### Concept of crime seriousness

The concept of crime seriousness has received much attention from criminologists and sociologists. Crime seriousness is not so easily defined but Rossi, Waite, Bose and Berk (1974) have summarised succinctly what it entails in the following quote:

> The seriousness of criminal acts represents a conceptual dimension of criminality indispensable in every day discourse, in legal theory, and practice and in sociological work (p.224).

This statement emphasises the consistency in definition of crime seriousness across diverse professions such as law enforcers, magistrates and social workers. It implies a consensus or common understanding of crime seriousness instilled through the process of informal and formal socialisation (see Chapter 4). Crime seriousness therefore refers to the way people perceive different crimes: some crimes will be considered as more serious than others. It is not surprising therefore that crime seriousness is at the very core of **jurisprudence** and is used in conjunction with other factors (like mitigation and aggravation) for sentencing defendants who are found guilty of committing a crime. Crime seriousness is important in determining the type and length of sentence determined by the judiciary (Wilkins 1980). Wilkins, however, observed inconsistencies in its use and cites a case in 1983 where one of the defendants received a sentence of five years unlike his co-accused who received probation despite having a criminal record.

There appears to be an agreement both within and across cultures as to what constitutes serious crime, but the problem lies in how crime seriousness is measured reliably. To address this effectively, a historical review of Thurstone's work on the Laws of Comparative Judgement, in 1927 (Thurstone 1927a), the works of Coombs in 1967 and Krus, Sherman and Kennedy in 1977 is required. Louis Thurstone perfected a method whereby paired comparisons across 19 different criminal offences were made: each offence was paired with all other offences to produce a total of 171 pairs. At the University of Chicago, 266 students provided Thurstone with volumes of data which were converted to a linear scale, now known as the Thurstone Scale. This was a cumbersome feat of analysis considering that calculations were done by hand in 1927 (Thurstone 1927b). His findings showed that it was possible to devise a scale with psychometric properties designed to highlight the seriousness of different crimes using student judgements. Interestingly, crimes with the highest ratings of seriousness coincided with criminal acts considered to be *mala in se* crimes. Crimes against the person, like for example rape, homicide, kidnapping, arson, assault, battery and abortion (still a crime in 1927) were considered to be the more serious offences. Other crimes (at the time) like adultery and seduction also scored relatively high.

Coombs in 1967 replicated Thurstone's study by adopting the same methodology and list of crimes with students from the University of Michigan about 40 years later. The same crimes were considered to be serious and despite the actual scores being lower than those found in Thurstone's study; the scoring went in the same direction. Krus *et al.* (1977) carried out the same study on 209 students at the University of Southern California and compared their findings with Thurstone's and Coombs'. Although there were differences across the three selected decades, the same crimes that topped the seriousness list in 1926 and 1966 remained at the top in 1976.

The perceived seriousness of other acts, such as abortion and adultery, had decreased over time in line with the fact that for many countries these acts were no longer considered to be criminal. Krus *et al.* (1977) speculated that the well-publicised Lindbergh case of 1932 was a causal factor in heightening seriousness ratings for kidnapping, so much so that it rose to third place. The 20-month-old son of the famous aviator, Charles Lindbergh, was kidnapped on 1 March 1932. A series of ransom notes were received before his body was found partially buried. As this case was investigated well in to 1934 by the FBI, there was considerable media coverage and public outcry. An example of a serious crime that was down-rated in 1966 and 1976 was bootlegging. During the Prohibition years, when in North America alcohol production and consumption was illegal, bootleggers (those who made their own alcoholic beverages and sold their produce on the black market) who usually worked under the guise of the Mafia made millions of dollars while breaking the law. Hence bootlegging was considered a serious offence during this time as was reflected in Thurstone's ratings. What Krus *et al.* have captured in their comparative study is that perceptions of crime seriousness can change as a consequence of the **zeitgeist** (spirit of the times) but the nature of change is usually small and reserved for the less serious crimes. Serious crime considered as *mala in se* continue to be perceived as serious, and warrant appropriate punishment in accordance with a just deserts philosophy.

Sellin and Wolfgang (1964) considered the different crimes reported in the UCR such as murder, rape, robbery, aggravated assault, burglary and motor vehicle theft. The crimes reported were simply recorded as numbers with no indications of seriousness of injury or property loss; hence Sellin and Wolfgang devised a list of crimes varying in the kind of injury or harm experienced by the victim or damage incurred to property. A thousand students were asked to assign a number indicating the level of seriousness they believed each listed crime warranted. Sellin and Wolfgang's findings led to a scale of seriousness for 141 offences in 1964 which later increased to 204 in a follow-up study in 1985 by Wolfgang, Figlio, Tracy and Singer. Levi and Jones replicated their work in 1985 using a British-based sample. Levi and Jones (1985) argued that basing seriousness scores on a student population has problems of generalisability to the general public. Levi and Jones questioned whether Sellin and Wolfgang extrapolated their data beyond its predictive validity and explored this possibility by comparing the public with various branches of the justice system like the police. They found that the public and police shared similar rankings of seriousness but the public had a tendency to rate most crimes higher than the police.

O'Connell and Whelan (1996) followed in the footsteps of Levi and Jones but this time compared an Irish cohort with Levi and Jones' 'British-based' population sample. O'Connell and Whelan chose 1,000 names at random from the 1992 electoral register for the Dublin area. Ten cases of offences selected from the 14 used in Levi and Jones' seriousness survey were altered slightly to suit terms used in Irish culture like for instance social security was substituted with social welfare and police officer with Garda officer. Respondents rated each offence for crime seriousness using a scale of 1–11, where '1' represented not serious at all and '11' extremely serious. Findings were comparable with Levi and Jones' results despite population and time sampling differences. The first five top serious rankings of 'murder', 'corrupt policeman', 'mugging', 'assault of a policeman' and 'fraud on the public' were very similar. Slight differences occurred with ranked positions of offences considered as less serious. For example, burglary is rated eighth in the British-based sample but seventh in the Irish cohort.

There were, however, some differences which need to be explained. The question is whether these differences are due to confounding variables like when or where the surveys were conducted. It is plausible that the large standard deviations attached to crime seriousness ratings relate to offences that have seen some change in public attitude and to legislation. Ratings of offences involving the sale of marijuana, benefits fraud and underage sex have large standard deviations and had changed rank positions across the two surveys. Underage sex is taken more seriously in Ireland, which might reflect a cultural bias towards Catholic beliefs and practice. In this case the seriousness of underage sex might be considered as immoral behaviour rather than as being harmful to the individual. This dissonance between dimensions of immoral behaviour and the impact it has on the individual is more likely to cause change to perceptions of seriousness than in cases where the two are strongly correlated. In Britain, the laws against child abuse and underage sex have become more regulated and stringently enforced since the prevalence of child abuse was highlighted by the media and Esther Rantzen's introduction of ChildLine in 1986 – a telephone network devoted to helping children in crisis. At the Child Witness Conference in 1986, held at Cambridge University, psychological evidence was presented which portrayed children as reliable witnesses (Hedderman 1987). Representatives of the Crown Court and campaigners such as Esther Rantzen debated the need for an amendment in the corroboration rulings of cases involving children. This was presented to Parliament before the Criminal Justice Bill in 1986 in time for changes to the 1988 Criminal Justice Act (CJA). In section 34 of the CJA 1988, the statutory provision that prevented courts from accepting uncorroborated evidence of unsworn children was repealed. It further enabled evidence from one child to corroborate another's. These events not only reflect a change in public opinion but also induce changes to the perceptions of crime seriousness – in this case child abuse and children's rights (see Box 2.3).

## Box 2.3

### Changed perceptions of crime seriousness

Erikson (1966) discussed how social norms towards a crime can be altered through social manipulation. In Salem, Massachusetts during the 1860s, there was concern about witchcraft being practiced as a consequence of reduced church attendance. This led to a moral panic and the reporting of any person displaying eccentric behaviour or demonstrating healing powers for the sick using herbal remedies. Once reported they were subjected to an unfair trial that led to death by hanging or burning. This social engineering of perceived crime seriousness occurs in today's climate too. For instance, Caplow and Simon (1999) claimed that the level of dangerousness attributed towards drugs has heightened public awareness and caused undue moral panic to the extent where drug taking was perceived as a social threat. It is under these circumstances that the actual crime and legal, victim and general public perceptions can be inconsistent with the perceptions maintained by the perpetrators of these offences.

Kidnapping and child abuse are perceived as serious offences, but with events such as the Soham murders in 2003, moral panics have led to tighter child protection legislation. In England, Ian Huntley was convicted for murdering Jessica Chapman and Holly Wells in 2003. Ian Huntley was working as a school caretaker at the Soham Village College but unbeknownst to his employers, he had a criminal record of rape and child abuse. David Blunkett, the Home Secretary at this time, ordered an inquiry into the vetting system used for individuals working with children – this became known as the Bichard Inquiry. The Safeguarding Vulnerable Groups Act 2006 was introduced as a consequence of the Bichard Inquiry Report in 2004 (Bichard 2004). Furthermore, the Independent Safeguarding Authority (ISA) was introduced as a means to 'vetting and barring' people applying to work with children. Lists kept track of people who were convicted of specified criminal offences, such as sexual offences, violence and mistreatment of children. Once on this list, an individual would be barred from working with children for at least one year to a maximum of ten years. It was reported in the Bichard Inquiry Report that at the time of Huntley's conviction, there was 'widespread public disquiet when it became clear that he had been known to the authorities over a period of years' (p.1). From 1995–1999 Huntley had eight allegations of sexual offences against him which failed to materialise during his vetting check. The Bichard Report commented on a systemic and corporate failure of the management of police intelligence systems. The Humberside Police were ignorant of how to use their local intelligence system effectively and as a consequence they had problems of 'weeding', 'reviewing' and 'deletion' of files – many records were destroyed unwittingly. The Child Protection Database (CPD) was also unreliable because information was not recorded and records were not effectively reviewed for ten years. Problems concerning the Criminal Records Bureau (CRB) were also apparent. The Bichard Report recommended a register of those wanting to work with children and vulnerable adults. CRB checks would become more vigorous and used extensively – no longer for criminal records only but for the Department for Education and Skills and the Protection of Children Act List. A Code of Practice was introduced in the Police Reform Act 2002 to ensure standardised record keeping which involved the creation, review, retention and deletion of information and information sharing with other agencies, such as Social Services. All these changes to legislation were made as a consequence of public disquiet and moral panics urging that poor vetting could not be repeated in the future. Moral panics arise out of public perceptions of crime seriousness.

More recently, in 2012, allegations of child molestation and rape were made of the late Jimmy Savile. He allegedly molested at least 30 under-aged girls, and in some cases raped them, in his dressing room at the BBC centre. Rumours circulated at the BBC of Savile's behaviour over decades, but other presenters such as Janet Street-Porter claimed that the BBC was very male chauvinistic which created the opportunity for Savile to abuse underage girls. Janet Street-Porter appeared on Question Time and said, 'people in the BBC knew what was going on. I heard the rumours but I was working in an environment that was totally male . . . if I said to someone at the BBC higher up than me this was going on – they wouldn't have taken any notice of me whatsoever'. (*The Independent*, 9 October 2012). Investigations by the police and the BBC found evidence favouring Savile's victims (see Chapter 7). It is possible that tighter regulations in the Light Entertainment section of the BBC might result from these investigations. Given that there is public disquiet over the Savile case as witnessed by the removal of street names (i.e. Savile's Row), charities wanting to remove his name and David Cameron's suggestion of posthumously stripping Savile of his knighthood (although the Cabinet Office informed that when an individual dies, they cease to be a member of the order – hence there is no knighthood to revoke) (Hall 2012).

Caplow and Simon's (1999) example of incongruences in perpetrators' perceptions of their behaviour with that of the law and public opinion, led to the investigation of how perpetrators initially develop these views. If perpetrators refuse to believe that their behaviour contravenes the law and constitutes a serious criminal act, then they are more likely to continue offending. This approach is of particular use if we want to know the developmental criminal pathways that offenders pursue. For instance, it is useful to know the progressive pathway a delinquent is likely to consider from the way he or she perceives the seriousness of different crimes in the first place. Through the adoption of this approach researchers are provided with a methodological basis for testing the order of seriousness that perpetrators commit crimes. Ramchand, MacDonald, Haviland, Morral *et al.* (2009). considered the importance of probability as a measure of whether an individual is more likely to commit a less serious criminal act first before progressing to serious crime or vice visa. This is based on the Revealed Preference Theory used in economic purchasing habits of consumers, which Ramchand *et al.* (2009) adopted in their study of how perpetrators perceived crime seriousness.

The underlying assumption in their study is based on the adage that criminal behaviour will escalate in severity over time. This was assumed by numerous researchers in the field such as Farrington in 1986 and Le Blanc and Loeber in 1998 (see Criminal careers). Individuals start their criminal careers by doing a petty crime and progress to doing more serious crimes. Ramchand *et al.* (2009, p.14) make the following assumption:

> If within some population group, the seriousness of crime A is generally less than the seriousness of crime B, then the probability of an individual from that group committing crime A before he commits crime B is greater than the probability he commits crime B before he commits crime A.

Ramchand *et al.* (2009) investigated this assumption using the Bradley-Terry model (Bradley and Terry 1952) which can best be explained through the example of sport performance prediction (see Box 2.4).

---

## Box 2.4

### The Bradley-Terry model in sport performance prediction

The Bradley-Terry model considers each football team in the Premier League and provides an estimate to indicate that team's ability derived from the frequency with which it has won and lost games against competitors. Each team has such an estimate – the higher the estimate the better the team's performance. These estimates can be further used to gauge which team might win despite not having played against each other yet.

---

This principle and procedure has been applied to criminality. Through estimating which type of crime is more likely to be committed first and thereafter how further crimes escalate in seriousness, is useful for predicting the future course of an offender's criminal career. Crime seriousness scores of offences occurring over time within individuals can be calculated using the Bradley-Terry model. Through analyses of results obtained from 449 adolescents from the Adolescent Outcomes Project (Ramchand, Morral, and Becker 2009), similar rankings of crime seriousness were found. Crime seriousness rankings across the two groups of adolescents placed violent crimes against the person as more serious than property based or drug related crimes hence showing consistency in their perceptions of serious crime. Perpetrators rated drug offences as less serious crimes than the general public – the Bradley-Terry model showed that estimates for drug offences from both groups were placed as less serious than burglary. This reinforces the finding that the adolescents in this study engaged in crimes involving drugs before going onto more serious crimes such as burglary. The Bradley-Terry model has proven a useful method for understanding the development and progression of criminal careers.

## What makes an offence serious?

In Chapter 1, the distinction between *mala in se* and *mala prohibita* crimes was considered in the light of severity and the seriousness attributed to the criminal behaviour. A heavy weighting of seriousness was placed on *mala in se* crimes, so much so, that cross-culturally they were perceived as heinous acts that contravened the human moral code. *Mala prohibita* crimes on the other hand are acts that are prohibited by the law. Given this definition we can expect a crime perceived as serious to contravene the human moral code. Although this is a good starting point, it fails to provide an underlying basis that can be used for making decisions of seriousness. In order to answer the question of what makes an offence serious it is important to consider the nature of crimes categorised as *mala in se*. What is it about *mala in se* crimes that are essentially different from crimes that are merely prohibited by law? The underlying key factor appears to be the extent of contact and harm caused to the victim (Mill 1859).

The extent of contact with a potential victim, however, is not an all or nothing affair – in the case of burglary, no physical contact between the burglar and victim can still induce fear and anxiety. The consequences of burglary can have adverse psychological effects on victims such as being able to continue living alone or continuing to trust strangers. Psychological damage can therefore be intrinsically related to the extent of hurt or harm endured by the victim. Indeed, the **harm principle** is central to understanding how seriousness is attributed to different crimes. The harm principle has been debated since John Stuart Mill's essay 'On Liberty' in 1859 where he stated, 'That the only purpose for which power can be rightfully exercised over any member of a civilised community, against his will, is to prevent harm to others'.

The sentiment of this statement appears to be simple but even Mill made adjustments by adding and excluding clauses and offering mitigations to the rule. Mill referred to the prevention of harm to others, but was unclear about what was actually meant by the term harm. Harm to the individual can be construed in different ways such as physical, psychological, emotional and financial/economic. In Box 2.5, different ways of thinking about harm to the individual are discussed.

## Box 2.5

### Thoughts about different types of harm to the individual

Physical harm is the easiest type of harm to account for as its effects can be seen. If a careless driver causes a collision and the innocent driver of the other car suffers serious injury requiring medical care as a consequence, then it is clear that the negligent driver has caused physical harm to this person (regardless of intent). Reparation to the victim can then be calculated on the basis of medical costs and the lasting effects of the injuries (including loss of work and salary). Calculating reparation, however, can be problematic. For example, how can reparation be calculated effectively for someone who has lost both eyes as opposed to one eye? Double the reparation costs? Would this be equitable reparation given that the impact of losing both eyes is much greater than losing one eye (blindness is more serious than visual impairment and is an indication of more individual harm incurred). An additional problem in the calculation of reparation is the longevity of physical harm endured. Does short-lived harm mean the victim has endured less harm?

Despite the problems associated with identifying physical harm and its longevity, it often can be measured objectively, but what of the psychological– emotional costs? How can this be quantified objectively? Assuming it can via psychological assessment, what if this contradicts the victim's personal perception of psychological harm? Does this mean they are lying, misguided, malingering, deluded or suffering from hypochondria? Who are we as assessors of the psychological condition to say that we are any more correct in our assessment and therefore perception of the person's psychology than they are themselves? If there is congruency between the assessor's and victim's perception of psychological harm, then how is this translated in terms of reparation within the confines of an equity model? There is also the problem of cross-consistency from individual to individual in the interpretation of harm. This leads to different threshold levels for tolerance of what is harmful behaviour: when psychological and physical harm are considered, the assessment of what is harmful behaviour becomes a multi-layered one.

Hillyard and Tombs (2008) considered other forms of harm such as financial/economic harm involving loss of property or cash. Thus fraud, malpractice, price fixing and regressive governmental policies become harmful crimes. They further separated sexual harm from physical and psychological harm. The notion of cultural safety, originally introduced by Alvesalo in 1999 is concerned with the issues that could potentially be important to the general public. In particular, questions regarding how much knowledge the public should be privy to are debated. Therefore sensitive information is weighed against what individuals need to know and the potential harm caused to individuals by sharing or burying such information.

Harm to an individual that has been inflicted by another individual is just one type of harm. A broader remit of the definition of harm includes social, environmental, economic and cultural injustices and inequalities. Social and environmental harm have been suggested by Hillyard and Tombs (2007) as offering a broader picture of the causes of human suffering. This might include numerous harms incurred to individuals, their communities and society per se. Therefore such harms can be caused not just from the activities of other individuals, but from corporations, social institutions and the overarching polit-ical ideologies and regimes in power (see the Conflict approach in Chapter 1).

A new branch to the discipline of criminology launched officially in 2005 at the European Society of Criminology is, 'supranational criminology' and has become an important area of consideration since the concept of globalisation has taken off. Globalisation is the concept used to describe how the modern world has become closer as a consequence of advanced technological developments in communication systems. Hence the world has become analogous to a 'global village' (McLuhan 1962; 1964). With advanced communication comes an awareness of other people's suffering in different parts of the world. Trafficking of women for the sex trade and of human body parts (e.g. kidney organs) discussed later in this chapter, has developed as a new type of organised criminal activity. Other crimes such as the smuggling of drugs and weapons, the laundering of money and the contamination of our ecosystem (air, soil and water) have an impact on us all whether directly or indirectly. Supranational criminology examines crimes committed in the international arena which cause harm on a large scale and often grossly violate human rights. Annette Smeulers (2006), one of the founders of supranational criminology, summarises it as:

> an interdisciplinary research area with close links to criminology, sociology, psychology, history, philosophy, political science and law, amongst them. This extremely broad research program can be split into several core issues and central questions, which all signify a specific research area (p.3).

There are six main research areas which include the way in which international crimes can be defined and measured; the social costs involved; how the causes can be investigated; how they can be dealt with and what preventative strategies can be put in place.

Social harm, therefore, can be construed as harm incurred to individuals through the failings of social institutions and corporations to follow health and safety regulations, or as a result of negligence. Also we can include governmental prioritisation of societal issues as a key point influencing the health of the nation. For instance, figures of mortality in any one given year, and the different causes, can be considered important to how government and other political regimes deploy their money and resources to solving or improving the health of its citizens. This extends to the decisions made by the United Nations (UN) in its plight to prioritise harms caused by civil war, nuclear weaponry and terrorism. Roberts (2009) illustrated this very point by comparing the figures for deaths arising out of terrorism with deaths from infectious diseases. From 2002 to 2005, the combined number of deaths due to terrorism was 2,722. This compares to 1,940,000; 4,272,000 and 5,406,507 deaths from measles, malaria and diarrhoea, respectively. There is a vaccine available to cure measles, tablets to prevent malaria and provisions, such as bed nets, to prevent being bitten by mosquitoes whilst asleep at night. Diarrhoea is often a consequence of poor sanitary conditions which can be tackled through improvements made to living standards and to a higher quality of medical care. Very often countries with high levels of infectious diseases have problems of civil war, terrorism and cartel domination. This, however, is not always the case as it could be a consequence of environmental contamination due to pollutants emanating from corporations with inadequate systems for dealing with their waste products. Therefore social harm in this capacity derives from a failure of corporations to follow regulatory rulings – in other words statutory law. This means these social harms are a consequence of *mala prohibita* crimes. Civil war, however, is currently a major disruption in many countries. There have been serious injustices to people of specific ethnic origins and/or religious faiths. In its extreme form injustices have involved genocide, torture and slavery which have seriously contravened the human rights of these people. Such crimes cause severe social harm and contravene the human moral code – hence making these *mala in se* crimes (see Chapters 1 and 11).

The issue of harm, whether it is caused by individuals or by social institutions, is not always easily defined, but it is recognised that there are different types of harm. Harm has been at the heart of a long-term debate concerning the separation between harm to the individual and harm to society. More specifically, at which point does harm to an individual extrapolate to harming society per se? This will be our main focus in the next section, the harm debate.

### What is the harm debate?

The harm debate in part rests on the assumption that there are two levels of harm: harm to the individual and harm to society. As pointed out by S. Box (1983), however, not all serious harm to the individual or society constitutes a crime. For instance, **corporate crime** is often excluded from a 'just deserts' punishment agenda. Although increasingly perpetrators of corporate crime are forced to be accountable, their level of punishment is often disproportionately lenient when compared with the seriousness and social harm incurred to individuals and society. As we saw in Chapter 1, cases where there have been charges of manslaughter, such as the Zeebrugge ferry disaster of 1987 and in 1997 the Southall train crash, the individuals brought to justice were often employees (i.e. assistant boatswain and train driver respectively) instead of those in managerial positions who are equally culpable for contravening laws of regulation and health and safety (Tombs 1995).

Harcourt (1999) outlined three criteria as a guide to understanding how the legal enforcement of regulation rules on specific behaviour operates:

1   justifiable cause for reducing an individual's freedom if the consequences of their behaviour harms others (known as the **harm principle**);
2   justifiable cause for reducing an individual's activities if it prevents serious offences to others (known as the offence principle);
3   not justifiable to reduce harmless behaviour simply because it is perceived as immoral.

These criteria were central to the understanding of why behaviour needs to be regulated by laws. The harm principle introduced by John Stuart Mill was a reaction to legal moralism advocated by Lord James Stephen. The legal moralist stance supported legal intervention as a justifiable method of policing immoral behaviour, regardless of whether it was conducted privately and consensually. In 1963 Hart explored the original harm principle of Mill in his book *Law, Liberty and Morality* which addressed the question of whether there should be any legal enforcement on morality. This happened to coincide with the Wolfenden Report (1957) which was based on a committee formed to review homosexual acts and prostitution – whether they should be considered as criminal. Lord Devlin (1965) made it very clear that he considered acts of homosexuality and prostitution as immoral and these behaviours should therefore continue to be illegal. These acts according to Lord Devlin, contravene the law and anyone caught behaving in this way should be punished under the criminal law accordingly.

The debate between Hart and Devlin was a repeat of the very same discourse that took place between Mill and Lord Stephen in the nineteenth century. Lord Stephen in 1873 claimed, 'here are acts of wickedness so gross and outrageous that, self-protection apart, they must be prevented as far as possible at any cost to the offender, and punished, if they occur, with exemplary severity' (cited in Harcourt 1999, p.6). If such acts are so serious and cause harm, can they be regarded as *mala in se* crimes? Two important factors to consider when answering this question, is whether the behaviour is consensual and if it causes harm to the individuals concerned. If the behaviour is consensual and fails to cause any harm, then by all accounts it should not be a *mala in se* crime. Both Lords Stephen and Devlin took the view that any behaviour considered immoral (regardless of being consensual and causing no individual harm) is degrading society's level of moral standard – hence inducing social harm. If such behaviour is allowed to continue unpunished then standards of behavioural conduct will be undermined.

As regards to immoral behaviour of a sexual nature, Devlin considered fornication, adultery, homosexuality and bigamy as being dangerous to society and should therefore be prohibited. However, he considered fornication and adultery as very difficult, if not impossible, to police and eradicate, and it is for this reason that Devlin claimed fornication and adultery should remain devoid of legal intervention. Devlin further claimed that there should be regulations on brothels and the running of any form of commercialised sex. Lords Stephen and Devlin urged the legitimacy of criminal law to intervene in immoral but privately practiced behaviours as a means of preserving the morality of society. Mill, Hart and the Wolfenden Report believed that criminal justice should be reserved for the protection of the public from physical and psychological harm rather than to police the private affairs of individuals. Geis (1972) argued there are grounds for legal intervention when substantial harm has been caused to individuals or society or for the self-protection and protection of others. The problem with this approach is one of defining concepts like self-protection and the prevention of harm to others. To help clarify this Lord Devlin asked three important questions and answered using a legal moralist ideology (see Box 2.6).

## Box 2.6

### Lord Devlin's three questions with answers

Lord Devlin's Three Questions with Answers:

Q1.  Has society the right to pass judgement at all on matters of morals? Ought there to be public morality or are morals a matter of private judgement?

A1.  Society does have the right to pass judgement on morals. What makes a number of individuals into a society is precisely a shared morality – a common agreement about good and evil.

Q2.  If society has the right to pass judgement, has it the right to use the weapons of the law to enforce it?

A2.  Society does have the right to use the law to enforce morality in the same way as it uses it to safeguard anything else.

Q3.  If so, ought it to use that weapon in all cases or only in some?

A3.  Society reserves the right to use the law at its discretion depending on the case specifics.

According to Lord Devlin the law should not be used to punish behaviours lying within the boundaries of tolerance in order to preserve individual rights and freedom, and to maintain the integrity of society.

The question of why particular sexual behaviours were regarded as morally unacceptable will be discussed in the next section. What happens when immoral behaviour becomes hidden from mainstream cultural values and becomes subterranean immoral behaviour will be explored in relation to victimless crimes (also known as crimes of the market place and consensual crimes).

### Immoral behaviour in relation to victimless crimes

Subterranean immoral behaviour is difficult to quantify by virtue of it being hidden from the rest of society. Mill (see pp. 110–11) and Herbert Lionel Adolphus Hart, a legal philosopher and Professor of Jurisprudence, argued that immoral behaviour that is consensual, conducted privately and that is harmless to those participating in the behaviour should be allowed to continue without legal intervention or any sanction, while Lords Stephen and Devlin advocated that such behaviours affect the morality of society. Individuals indulging in

*Plate 2.1* Searching for equity

© Robyn Mackenzie. Image used under license from Shutterstock.com. Available at http://www.shutterstock.com/pic.mhtml?id=27084115&src=id

immoral behaviour according to Lords Stephen and Devlin fail to see themselves as victims; hence these crimes have become known as victimless crimes (see Box 2.7 for examples). In victimless crimes:

- there is no victim therefore no complaint;
- they are willing victims;
- they refuse to incriminate themselves;
- these behaviours occur in private

---

## Box 2.7

### Examples of commonly labelled victimless crimes

- Abortion (where foetus would be viable if born);
- Prostitution and/or soliciting for prostitution;
- Buying and using illicit drugs;
- Consumption of pornography (not involving children or coercion);
- Arranging unlicensed fights between animals or humans to gain monies;
- Public nudity and fornication (Williams 1997);
- Assisted suicide;
- Using buildings in urban areas to BASE jump;
- Wearing no helmet on a motorbike or bicycle;
- Wearing no seatbelt when driving a vehicle;
- Inability of those to give consent to participate in various activities (e.g. animals, children, mentally ill and those under the influence of alcohol) (Liberal Democratic Party webpage 2009);
- Being a member of the Russian mob, a Colombia drug cartel, or a biker gang (Naylor 2002).

---

The inability to give consent is an interesting point. As victimless crimes are considered to be consensual crimes (because all participants give their consent to be involved in unlawful activity), there must be situations where some of the participants have not given their informed consent. This begs the question of why these participants were unable to give their informed consent. As the point raised in Box 2.7 suggests there are participants who are unable to provide consent such as animals, children, mentally ill, the addicted and intoxicated. This is a contracted list as there are others who might be severely disabled, unconscious, forced into participation or have been misinformed about the issues involved. In the case of animals, obtaining consent is not possible. Animals can be used for sexual purposes as is in the case of zoophilia, better known as bestiality. Here the animal is used to fulfil the sexual desire of an individual and might involve penetration, which could be uncomfortable for the animal concerned (see Chapter 8). Animals, however, can be involved in victimless crimes. Unlicensed prize fights usually involving cockerels can be a bloodied event as these birds will often continue fighting to the death – likewise with dog fights. These criminal activities involve owners who wage their animals against other owners' animals in the hope of winning money derived from the bets made by an observing audience.

In the case of sexual assaults in the guise of rape fantasy, it is acceptable behaviour provided all participants give their informed consent. There are cases, however, where obtaining consent is difficult such as would be the case where the 'victim' is unconscious, drugged or intoxicated. Being misinformed of intent can have very serious consequences. Under these situations the participant has given informed consent to the activities described, but unknowingly has signed up to something very different. In organised crime set ups there are many examples where individuals have been promised one thing only to be presented with something else which they would not have provided any consent for had they known. For example, in Moldova, there is an organised criminal network where Moldavian women were recruited into the sex industry. This was achieved by misinforming them about work opportunities abroad. Another such scam involved the men who were promised jobs of painting and ironing trousers as illegal 'guest workers'. The reality was very different. Their passports were confiscated and they were each trapped into donating one of their kidneys. Human trafficking for organs such as kidneys is considered a victimless crime simply because some people benefit at the expense of others (Scheper-Hughes 2014).

Consenting individuals indulging in victimless crimes do not perceive themselves as being harmed, like for example gamblers who fail to see their addiction as causing their money problems, marital discord, homelessness, and so on. In the case of gambling, individual harm results from an inability to curb the addictive behaviour which has consequences for others. But does it also have harmful consequences for society in terms of moral standards? One argument is that victimless crimes such as drug abuse can lead to other more serious types of criminal behaviour, and the alternative is that victimless crimes should be conceived of as harmless behaviour which if decriminalised would decrease the escalation to serious criminality (see Box 2.8).

## Box 2.8

### What ways can victimless crimes impact on other types of crime?

A direct link between victimless crimes and other crime was forged by Rudy Giuliani, the former Mayor of New York. He attributed the reduction of homicide rate to the police policy of zero tolerance for minor offences. Bowling (1999) found that the rise and fall of homicide rates correlated with the rise and fall of crack cocaine use. The rise and fall of crack cocaine use, and the demand and sustainability of the drug-trade, was linked with the introduction of community-based initiatives such as providing education, advice on conflict resolution tactics, assertiveness training, leadership skills and effective welfare services. Bowling, furthermore, provided an example of a victimless crime such as consuming illicit drugs driving more serious crime like murder.

There are debates, however, concerning the validity of the concept of 'victimless crimes'. While some criminologists believe in the existence of victimless crimes and how they can lead to serious crimes such as mugging and murder, others have questioned the need to punish individuals who commit consensual acts causing little or no harm to others. This is a diluted form of the Mill-Stephen and Hart-Devlin harm debate where the issue is one of social harm affecting the morality of society. Naylor (2002) has made rather controversial comments about why victimless crimes should be decriminalised and perceived as market-based crimes. When interviewed for the McGill Reporter by Daniel McCabe in 2002, Naylor stated, 'I would take all the drug legislation away from the criminal code and move it to the regulatory side . . . strip it . . . to . . . a broad consensus that something is wrong'. Naylor further commented, 'If someone wants to smoke a joint, there is no clear social consensus on whether that's right or not'. He argued that those who want to take drugs will look for another means to obtaining their supplies if their usual drug dealer is apprehended. Naylor (2002), in his book *Wages of Crime: Black Markets, Illegal Finance and the Underworld Economy*, claimed that, 'Unless it can be established that a drug user . . . was forcibly held down and injected, not once, not twice, but often enough to create a heroin addiction, it must be assumed the user is just as much a consensual participant in the criminal marketplace as anyone on the supply side.' Naylor concludes that the extent of policing allocated towards victimless crimes (or market-based crimes) and the time spent on law enforcement should be focused on crimes involving real victims of crimes such as theft, assault, sexual offences and homicide.

These two points of view arise from discourse about harm and consensual behaviour. An individual's intention to act in a particular way that causes no harm to others can be perceived as contravening the law, if it is considered to degrade the morality of society (thereby taking Lords Stephen and Devlin's stance) or as consensual behaviour conducted privately as a form of right to express individuality and free will (therefore supporting Mill and Hart's sentiment).

Were Lords Stephen and Devlin right to consider legal moralism in relation to the very moral infrastructure of society? According to Devlin, legal moralism and a shared morality in society is what maintains social cohesion. When Giuliani was mayor in New York City (see Box 2.8) he was responsible for the police initiative of apprehending public drunks as it was believed that they were causing social harm to local communities. The reasoning behind this was that small-time disorder can be the cause of serious crime. Major Giuliani also instructed police to target people urinating, drinking and begging for money in public (Bratton 1996), all in the name of harm (harms related to alcohol, social harm to the community and the transition and escalation to serious crime). The social harm of alcohol and drug use is further explored in Box 2.9.

## Box 2.9

### The harm of alcohol and drug use

In Mill's time the issue of harm in relation to alcohol consumption was ambiguous: supporting the temperance movement by taxing on alcohol but simultaneously believing in an individual's right to consume alcohol in private. His ambiguous legacy lives on even today – where the harm debate offers no guidance on how to treat alcohol consumption and alcoholism. A similar debate rages over drug usage, although illicit drug use is a victimless crime (Schur 1976, 1980). Packer (1968) argued that scientific evidence suggests that marijuana causes less individual harm than alcohol or cigarettes; however, more recent research alludes to it having carcinogenic properties (Hashibe, Morgenstern, Cui, Tashkin et al. 2006; Tashkin 2005). Other social harms have been attributed to marijuana, such as progressing onto harder drugs like heroin, causing aggressive behaviour and other antisocial behaviour. However, Packer (1968) and Kaplan (1970) believed that there is little evidence of marijuana causing individual or social harm. In the current climate, the prevailing attitude suggests that usage of marijuana in the long term can cause psychosis (Moore, Zammit, Lingford-Hughes et al. 2007) and that harder drugs such as heroin can lead to acquisitive crime (i.e. stealing goods to trade for money to buy drugs) to support the addiction (Bennett, Holloway and Williams 2001; Lader, Singleton and Meltzer 2000).

Proponents against drug prohibition have come to accept that the law is very much in favour of banning illicit drug use, however, they also realise that preventing drug consumption is an impossible feat (during the Prohibition period in America people still managed to consume alcohol in secrecy and bootleggers had a market for their illegal distilleries and alcohol distribution). The new buzz-word has been harm reduction, and there is a passive acceptance that there will always be individuals using drugs and that there will be casualties as a consequence.

Nadelmann (1999) claimed that harm reduction is about introducing drug policies designed to reduce the harm element incurred by drug usage as far as possible. Harm reduction policies in Holland and Britain were adopted back in the 1970s and 1980s respectively. The idea was to make drug use as safe as possible for drug users and drug addicts. In Britain there was a public health approach where needle exchange programmes were in place to help prevent the spread of AIDS and hepatitis. Additionally, methadone was available to help heroin addicts reduce their dependency on heroin. Other programmes such as Outreach aim to reduce substance abuse through education, prevention, awareness, rehab and detox and to provide financial help. Not everyone is happy with the notion of harm reduction. In America, McCaffrey (1998, 1999) refers to the harm reduction movement as a group of individuals who are in support of the legalisation of drugs. It appears that the harm debate has modernised and is now more concerned with which harms should be prioritised.

Individuals indulging in immoral behaviour classified as victimless crimes such as prostitution, drug use, pornography and some forms of fornication (consider the impeachment of President Clinton on the grounds that his fornication caused political harm) all involve a degree of individual harm and social harm to the morality of society.

As pointed out by Harcourt (1999), the debate now focuses on different types of harm, extent of harm and the level of tolerance shown by society and the willingness of society to pay the costs of these harms both economically and socially. It appears that Lords Stephen and Devlin's ideology of legal moralism supersedes civil liberties to practice immoral behaviour regardless of whether it causes harm to the individual or society

## Summary

- The two main sources of crime data – police recorded crime and the CSEW – were considered using recent historical reference regarding their establishment and evolution. Both police and CSEW data offer information at a national level but there are also local surveys conducted which provide an indication of the extent of criminal activity in specified areas. The US approach of Uniform Crime Reports and the NCVS have a similar classificatory system of crime seriousness to Britain, which suggests that perceptions of how crime is ordered from least to most serious, tends to be universal. The differentiation between personal and property crime in the statistical data reflects a *mala in se* and *mala prohibita* divide.
- Information regarding fear of crime is also collected from CSEW, police data and other surveys conducted. Fear of crime data is very informative and provides an indicator of who within the population is most likely to experience fear. The information collected also releases a breakdown of factors such as age, whether an individual is living alone and the type of residential property. The type of person who fears crime and those statistically more at risk of becoming a victim is incongruent, as the data

shows that younger males have a higher probability of being assaulted than females or older age groups. Similar findings in the US are shown by the NCVS.

- Fear of crime can lead to moral panics. Moral panics normally derive from perceptions that there is an unprecedented increase in certain types of crime both locally and nationally, which increases people's vulnerability to victimisation. Moral panics send the message to police and crime enforcers that there is a need for new legislation to tackle crime, and modifications to old legislation – especially concerning the level of police power.

- The level of criminal activity can be measured in different ways – it can be counted in terms of number of criminal events or the number of offenders committing crime. Farrington uses the term prevalence to account for the certain proportion of the population who commit crime. Using the notion of criminal careers, Farrington (1986) explained previous findings of there being a peak of crime at 17 years of age. Criminal careers can be considered as having onset, persistence and desistence stages. Different factors are known to influence when an individual starts a criminal career and what prevents them from desisting from further criminal activity. One influential factor is the age at which an offender commits his or her first crime. Farrington and West (1990) found that 73.6 per cent of 17–24 year olds who started offending at 10–16 were reconvicted in comparison with 16 per cent without a criminal record as a juvenile. The age of onset was crucial in determining an offender's ability to desist from further crime. Other factors involved parental criminality and poor nurturance, impulsive and antisocial behaviour. **Risk** and **protective factors** such as low self-control (Benda 2003) and the ability to form good emotional relationships (Clingempeel and Henggeler 2003) respectively were also important in predicting recidivism and criminal career longevity.

- Comparisons of annual crime statistics provide information about crime trends. There can be short-term crime fluctuations over a period of time but also underlying long-term crime patterns. Short-term and long-term crime patterns suggest a reduction in crime in many different countries, including the UK and US. The long-term crime trend, however, is a slow reduction in crime. Short-term fluctuations suggest a rapid decline in crime. Long-term crime trends are more indicative of the true nature of the extent of crime, and should be understood within the context of a variety of factors such as policing, prison expansion, firearms policy (in the US), the economy and functional social institutions. When social institutions are functioning well, people, according to LaFree (1998), have confidence in them and as a consequence are less inclined to break the rules and commit crime – known as legitimacy.

- The gender paradox is used to describe why there is prevalence of medical and behavioural conditions in one gender (usually boys) and yet when the other gender experiences the condition, the symptoms exhibited are far more serious and extreme. For instance girls diagnosed with ADHD have a likelihood of developing CD up to 40 times more than boys – despite prevalence for ADHD and CD being higher in boys. The gender paradox can be used to explain ladette culture. Denscombe (2001) argued that risk-taking behaviour in females might be a reaction against traditional female stereotypes.

- The concepts of crime seriousness and how this is established and the harm issue were considered as a means of understanding the difference between *mala in se* and *mala prohibita* crimes. These concepts are used implicitly in our daily interpretation of crime. Nevertheless these concepts are difficult to define when considered at a profound level, as it becomes clear that what constitutes seriousness is based on harm but what constitutes harm is ambiguous. Despite deconstructing the term 'harm', it still remains a problem to what it actually is and at what level it is being considered: individual, others or society. Ultimately what is decreed as a serious crime causing harm to an individual (including social harm) or to others or to society influences how it is categorised in law: *mala in se* or *mala prohibita*. This categorisation can be seen reflected in the way that crime statistics are recorded by the police. It is this that influences our perceptions of crime dangerousness and seriousness. This reflects society's consensus of what it is to be criminal, deviant or immoral (or all) and what the unified response to such individuals is. Additionally, this influences whether the individual showing such behaviour should be punished and the nature of punishment severity. The answers complete a full-circle, which can be considered as a complicated tautology.

- The harm debate began with Mill and Lord Stephen in the late nineteenth century and continued between Hart and Lord Devlin in the 1960s. Lords Stephen and Devlin argued for legal intervention to behaviours that lowered the morality of society (i.e. immoral behaviours encapsulated in victimless crimes) whereas Mill and Hart claimed that consensual acts performed in privacy and causing no harm to others should be ignored by the justice system and reconsidered as non-criminal behaviour. This debate is still important today and impacts on social policy and legal legislation. The Liberal Democratic Party in 2009 had a list of what they considered to be victimless crimes on their website.

- Some criminologists believe that victimless crimes can lead to further crime which can escalate in terms of seriousness – this perspective was endorsed by Rudy Giuliani, the former mayor of New York who took a zero tolerance approach to minor offences such as drunken disorderly behaviour in public spaces in the 1990s. Decreasing homicide rates correlated with a fall in crack cocaine use. Naylor (2002) endorses the opposite to the tough approach on victimless crimes and claims that policing and law enforcement measures should be directed towards crimes that involve real victims – after all, drug users, gamblers and prostitutes perform these behaviours of their own volition. Others have the approach of harm reduction through the use of needle exchange and Outreach programmes designed to change individuals' behaviour and reduce health risks. McCaffrey (1998) considers harm reduction as a means towards the legalisation of drugs. The harm debate appears to be just as important for today's social policy and legislation as it was during Mill-Stephen and Hart-Devlin's day.

## Questions for discussion

1   Is there any way of considering crime seriousness other than the levels of harm incurred?
2   Can the classifications of different crimes based on concepts of seriousness and harm be considered a tautology? Discuss.
3   Are the classifications of offence type as recorded by the police and published by the HO flawed? Do they represent a consensus approach to understanding crime?

# Part II

# Nature–nurture explanations of criminal behaviour

# Chapter 3

# Biological constraints and evolutionary factors

In Part I, Chapters 1 and 2 addressed the issue of how we define crime and criminality, and the ways in which it can be measured and classified (based on concepts closely linked with crime definition). In Part II, the main emphasis for Chapters 3 and 4 is to provide explanations of the causes of criminality. These explanations can be divided into essentially **nature** (Chapter 3) and **nurture** (Chapter 4) but as we shall find explanations based on research findings tend to suggest a nature–nurture interaction. In other words we are looking at interactions between genes and the environment. Chapter 5 addresses the decision making processes commonly used by offenders, and how these differ from non-criminals. The basis of these decisions will be considered using research findings supporting a nature and/or nurture stance. As the emphasis in Chapter 3 is to present explanations airing towards the contribution of our genes to criminal behaviour, it is important to understand biological concepts and terms used in this area. We begin this chapter by considering the contribution of our genes and **chromosomes** in the understanding of criminality which enable certain individuals to embrace a criminal mind-set expressed through antisocial and violent behaviour. One way of studying the relationship between genes and criminality is to consider individuals of varying degrees of relatedness. By considering family members across generations, identical and non-identical twins and adoptees, it is possible to observe a relationship between closeness of genetic inheritance and criminal behaviour. The research findings suggest that the closer in similarity of genetic inheritance individuals are then the more likely they will behave similarly. Thus in the case of identical twins, who share 100 per cent of their genes, the trend is that they will behave more similarly than non-identical twins and other family members. An environmental contribution towards criminal behaviour can be derived from adoptees who are more likely to become criminals if the natural parent is a criminal but even more so if both biological and adoptive parents are criminal. We will also focus on research showing genetic and chromosomal differences between criminals and non-criminals. Different anomalies of gene coding and chromosome replication for example, and how these impact on violent and criminal behaviour are explained in relation to faulty genes (i.e. MAOA) and conditions that include extra or missing **sex chromosomes** (i.e. XXY, XYY and XO). The influence of other biological factors including bio-neurochemicals, such as hormones, have offered an understanding of the mechanisms enabling criminal behaviour to occur. In this chapter we will consider some of these hormones in particular testosterone and how this interacts with other hormones. We will see how it is difficult to disentangle the effects of these different hormones as they operate interdependently. Brain studies (i.e. using EEG, MRI and fMRI and PET scans) investigating structural and functional brain anomalies in criminal and violent individuals, provides further evidence of differences between individuals who live criminal lifestyles and those who do not. In particular we will focus on specific criminals with personality disorders such as antisocial personality disorder and its extreme form, known as psychopathy, to demonstrate how functionally and structurally different their brains are from non-criminals. Finally, an evolutionary approach to understanding the reasons why males tend to be more violent than females is used as an overarching explanation for criminal behaviour per se. This is explained using Charles Darwin's evolutionary account as well as more recent concepts of parental investment.

## Introduction

The belief that **genes** significantly influence our behaviour is referred to as biological determinism. Biological determinism is controversial and has long been the subject of debate. Recently, however, there has been a big step forward in our understanding of the relationship between genes and behaviour due to the findings of the Human Genome Project (which finished sequencing the entire human genome in 2003). In order to comprehend the significance of the Human Genome Project to our understanding of human behaviour, it is important to define the terms **DNA** and genes. Both terms are important for understanding the contribution biological psychology has made towards explaining criminality. DNA, abbreviated from deoxyribonucleic acid, is the substance of life itself and is a molecule that stores all genetic information in our cells transmitted during reproduction. A portion of the DNA known as a gene has its particular place on a **chromosome** and is considered to be one of many building blocks providing direction to development. Hence a chromosome is a threadlike structure in the **nucleus** of cells housing our genetic information – coded in the DNA.

Another important concept is that of **polymorphism** which refers to the multiple forms of a single gene that can exist in an individual. In other words there is one of two or more alternative forms of a gene (i.e. an **allele**) residing at the same **locus** (i.e. specific position) on a chromosome. Having more than one form of the gene (an allele) indicates the complexity of gene contribution towards the development of observable physical characteristics such as eye and hair colour. Genes code for our physical make-up (i.e. known as the **phenotype**) but the course of development this takes can be modified prenatally and by the environment. Given that phenotypic characteristics like hair and eye colour demand more than one gene then clearly there must be many more genes involved in the development of human behaviour. To search for one all-encapsulating gene to explain one type of behaviour is likely to be a fruitless and futile task which is why geneticists look for many genes **co-inherited** with a trait within families. There has been a host of findings in relation to the impact of polymorphic genes on mental illness and behavioural problems including criminality. Such findings often find their way (in a simplified form) into the mass media. An example of this was a news item that appeared in *The Scotsman* in 2004 by Reynolds titled, 'Spite? It's All Down to the Nasty Genes'. In this article antisocial behaviour was explained away by having bad genes that lead to a life of crime. This headline suggests that we can explain the emotion of spite purely by consideration of our genetic code – which arguably presents a simplified view of a complex internal state.

A good example of how difficult it really is to disentangle the effects of genes from the effects of the environment is the case reported in the Daily Mail in 2011. Marlene and Alan Wright described how their adoption of two half-brothers aged seven and five years born of the same heroin-addicted mother led to later problems of delinquency and brushes with the law. Before their adoption, both boys were neglected and subjected to physical and mental abuse. Despite the provision of a loving and caring upbringing by the Wrights, however, both boys developed into heroin addicts and committed violent crime. The Wright's account sparked the debate of whether, 'a child from the wrong side of the tracks can be transformed by the love of a devoted family – or will their genetic make-up, and horrific experiences in early years, blight their lives?' (Courtenay-Smith 2011, 32–33). At school they were described as hyperactive, disruptive in class with a reputation for fighting. As adolescents both boys abused drugs and eventually became heroin addicts. They stole and were violent towards their adoptive parents and in later years committed serious crime for which they received indeterminate sentences (i.e. no set length of imprisonment). One explanation for their behaviour offered by a psychiatrist described how being subjected to heroin during prenatal development made them susceptible to addiction. This is a plausible explanation as a foetus receives substances from the mother's blood which diffuse across the umbilical cord to the placenta. As heroin molecules are small enough to diffuse from the placenta into the circulatory system of the developing foetus, newborns are often born with a craving for heroin. In the case of the two boys, there is no information or knowledge of this having occurred but the symptoms of hyperactivity and asymptomatic drug addiction were strongly indicated. Asymptomatic refers to the delayed appearance of symptoms such as drug susceptibility, which normally appear at a later stage of development.

This is an interesting example of how the inter-uterine environment can influence the morphology (i.e. structuring of phenotypic characteristics such as skeletal development) and congenital (i.e. characteristics acquired prenatally not through inheritance) development of the foetus. This case illustrates that a child can be born with a propensity towards a particular form of behaviour. That behaviour, however, is not necessarily influenced by the genes since in this case the drug influenced the intra-uterine environment which can also be used as an explanation for the criminal behaviour.

The biological impact on an individual's behaviour is often investigated by considering such cases as the above – that is, through examining similarities in behaviour among family members and, in particular, twins and adoptees. There have been numerous studies investigating the similarity of behaviour across varying levels of genetic relatedness. The underlying reasoning for conducting research in this way is to determine the likelihood of related individuals having the same problems or conditions: a **comorbidity** likeness. For example if the mother has depression we might ask how likely is it that her son or daughter will also have depression? Or if one identical twin has schizophrenia, what are the chances that the other twin will exhibit similar symptoms. This idea has also extended to criminal behaviour, in particular to violent offending and antisocial behaviour. The assumption is that the closer one is genetically to another, the more alike behaviourally they will be. It is assumed that children are more similar to their biological parents with whom they share 50 per cent of their genes by common descent than they are to unrelated adoptive parents with whom they share no genes by common descent. Likewise identical twins who share 100 per cent of their genes will be more similar to each other than to their other siblings with whom they share 50 per cent of their genes. Of course geneticists know that some genes can appear to skip generations so much so that the grandson looks more like his grandmother than his parents. This is explained by the grandson having a number of genes in common with the grandmother that express themselves more obviously thereby creating the illusion of greater similarity.

It is clear from such research that genes play an important role in our behaviour; however, to understand the extent of their contribution it is important to go back to basics and compare the genetic and chromosomal differences across the sexes. Humans have 46 chromosomes (23 pairs) and one of these pairs is known as the **sex chromosomes.** In females there are two 'X' chromosomes but for males the pair consists of an 'X' and 'Y' chromosome. This difference determines our sex development and is responsible for prenatal developmental differences. Geneticists have found evidence, based on the differences of the sex chromosome complement across the sexes, of a male vulnerability towards particular syndromes and conditions. This is based on sex-linked inheritance, a process where genes carried on the X chromosome in males have no analogous genes on the Y chromosome to counteract any effects of faulty genes activated by the X chromosome (hence the X chromosome has an extra 'arm' in comparison with the Y chromosome). The implication of this is that an increased number of males will suffer the symptoms of genetic disorders caused by the missing 'q' arm of the 'Y' chromosome (i.e. bottom right arm). This means that if there are any faulty genes carried on the corresponding 'q' arm of the 'X' chromosome inherited from the mother, males are likely to inherit these because they are missing the protection of the matched 'q' arm that would be present on the other 'X' chromosome that females have. Hence males would show the gene's inherited traits while females act as carriers of the gene.

The influence of the 'Y' chromosome can also have an impact on the development of the male brain which might explain differences of cognition, personality and temperament, sexual and behavioural qualities expressed across the sexes. The difference, for example, between male and female performance scores on Baron-Cohen et al.'s 'Reading the Mind in the Eyes' Test (where emotional states have to be interpreted purely from seeing a series of pictures of people's eyes) is well established. Females are superior at interpreting emotion displayed in the eyes whereas males consistently score lower on this task and individuals with autism perform worse still (Baron-Cohen, Jolliffe, Mortimore and Robertson 1997). A connection has been made by Baron-Cohen regarding the masculinisation of the brain in normal males and how this is responsible for the difference between male and female brain function for specific tasks. Males have been shown to be superior at visual spatial skills for example. This is just one consequence of having a 'Y' chromosome that is responsible for the secretion of male androgens such as testosterone during embryonic development, resulting in the masculinisation of the brain. Consideration of the crime statistics brings the importance of this sex difference in development to light. It is clear that males commit more crime than females (see Chapters 1 and 9) and they commit the vast majority of homicides (Buss 2005). The extent to which this is a consequence of having a 'Y' chromosome, however, is still debated.

Given the contribution of genes and chromosomes to human behaviour, studying violent, antisocial and criminal behaviour among related individuals is an obvious empirical step to take. In the next section, individuals who are related to varying degrees will be explored. Researchers have explored family lineages, identical and fraternal twins and adoptees for criminality and have shown that individuals who are closer in their genetic composition tend to be more similar in their behaviour. This **genotype** contribution is also influenced by shared prenatal factors such as experiencing the same intra-uterine environment – as found in the prenatal development of twins.

## Impact of genetic relatedness and influence on comorbidity

It is important to establish to what extent both **nature** (i.e. the genes) and **nurture** (i.e. the environment) contribute towards an individual's development and whether it is possible to separate the two. Additionally, we might ask how the two interact – might nature drive nurture and vice versa. These are the questions of interest and not whether criminality is a consequence of nature or nurture. An insightful statement was made by Lange in 1931, 'the natural tendencies one is born with, the surrounding world he grows up in, these are essentials, these are destiny'. What Lange was saying here is that we are born with certain traits and these, in interaction with our environment, shape our behaviour and internal state. To this end Lange was not dismissing the importance of social factors but instead endorsing **biosocial interactionism**.

Biosocial interactionism views nature (your genes) and nurture (your environment/upbringing) as interdependent and can be used to account for temperament, social responsiveness to others and emotionality for example. These traits are apparent after birth and play a significant role in subsequent development but their effects depend on the opportunities and reactions of different social environments. A child may, for example, be **socialised** by its parents but the way parents socialise the child is shaped partly by the characteristics of the child as well as those of the parents. This means that parents react to the temperament that a child is born with and do not, contrary to popular belief, generally treat all of their children the same (Harris, 1995; 1998). Genes influence our behaviour in one of three ways and frequently do so by having profound effects on the immediate environment. Most behavioural geneticists consider that our genes can exert passive, active and evocative effects on our behaviour by affecting our social environment (Scarr 1996). In the next section, passive, active and evocative effects will be explored in relation to behaviours that can lead to criminality. As Scarr (1996) pointed out, the passive, active and evocative effects of our genes influence our immediate environment which underlies an important **gene–environment interaction**.

### Gene–environment interaction

#### Passive effects

In the case of passive effects, children's home environments are largely dictated by the parents and, since children share 50 per cent of their genes with each of their parents, it is likely that parents will create a home supportive of the child's combination of genes known as the **genotype**. A good example of this is a home environment where the children have musical parents who practise playing their instruments, write music and have musical manuscripts on their bookshelves. This enriched musical environment is likely to encourage the child to become musical themselves. This, in effect, serves to reinforce the child's genetic endowment of musical ability and demonstrates the important interaction between genes and the immediate environment (the former having a multiplier effect on the latter). Arguably this would equally apply to a home environment where children are surrounded by guns owned by their father, stolen goods, written plans of bank robberies and gangs of criminal friends visiting.

## Active effects

Genes can affect the environment in an active way which can be observed in children who seek environments that are compatible with their genetic make-up – considered a form of niche picking. This can be seen in children who become friends with like-minded individuals, nicely expressed by the adage, 'birds of a feather flock together'. Children will seek peers who are similar, and being drawn to others with similar criminal inclinations is no exception. A famous example of this type of friendship occurred between two boys, Jon Venables and Robert Thompson, known as truants and troublesome in class. Their delinquent behaviour led to the infamous torture and murder of a two year old called James Bulger in 1993 (see Chapter 1 for discussion on age of criminal responsibility and Box 4.3).

## Evocative effects

An evocative relationship is the gene–environment interaction which is studied the most by researchers in the field. This occurs when a trait in the child, such as a temperamental factor, causes other people to react in a particular way therefore reinforcing the expression of the trait. A simple example of this is when temperamentally 'easy going' babies who smile and respond in a friendly sociable manner elicit positive reactions from other people. This, in turn, reinforces the genetic predisposition to be an 'easy baby' and all the behaviours that this encapsulates.

In support of the concept of an evocative interaction, Lakatos, Toth, Nemoda, Ney et al. (2000) found that infant attachment to the mother at 12–13 months was influenced by the DRD4 gene which plays an important role in the production of dopamine (a chemical messenger that carries signals between nerve cells). Researchers looked at DRD4 in detail and in particular its common and less common structural format. The common form of the DRD4 gene is a 4-repeat allele and the atypical form a 7-repeat allele. The 7-repeat allele is more common in infants with a disorganised pattern of attachment, the equivalent to D-infants as classified in Ainsworth's Strange Situation Experiment (see Box 3.1; see also Chapter 4).

## Box 3.1

### Ainsworth's Strange Situation Experiment

During the Strange Situation Experiment an infant is observed interacting with their mother in a playroom which is recorded. A stranger then enters the room whilst mother leaves but later returns, after leaving the infant alone with the stranger. The infant's behaviour and interaction with the stranger and mother are compared. A **securely attached** infant will want to be with mother, is unhappy at her departure and wary of the stranger but is pleased and approaches her on her return. Some infants are insecurely attached to the mother and show different types of behaviour towards the mother in the Strange Situation Experiment. This is discussed in more detail in Chapter 4, but of relevance here is one type of insecure attachment – exhibited by infants known as D-infants. D-infants have difficulty settling into regular daily routines (such as eating and sleeping) and show wariness and anxiety towards strangers. Other types of insecurely attached infants treat strangers in the same way as the mother and are not too bothered by her absence. D-infants, however, tend to be more disruptive in their daily functioning than other types of insecurely attached infants. It is clear that the 7-repeat allele form of the DRD4 gene is likely to play a role in the development of difficult, and some forms of insecure, attachments.

Humans possess two alleles of each gene (one from each parent) and the chance of having at least one 7-repeat allele is 71 per cent for D-infants and 29 per cent for non-D-infants. Lakatos, Nemoda, Birkas, Ronai et al. (2003) found that the 7-repeat DRD4 allele influences wariness of strangers. This explained the typical behaviours of the disorganised baby (i.e. cries, unfriendly and is difficult to settle) and why these types of behaviour particularly attracted less friendly attention from others – which in effect is reinforcing the negative effects of the **genotype**. This is a good example of an evocative gene relationship with the environment as parents control how they interact with their infant and this then may or may not reinforce the infant's pattern of attachment.

As a robust gene–environment interaction is responsible for shaping our behaviour, investigating individual relatedness both genetically and for similarity of family context has provided insight in to the contribution of each factor. It is not surprising therefore that very often family, twin and adoptee studies consider specific types of temperament and personality as pre-requisite factors for criminality. These will be considered in turn, beginning with the family.

### Family studies

In relation to criminality, family studies tend to look at the distribution of anti-social behaviour in biological relatives of offenders and non-offenders. An early controversial study was conducted by Dugdale who published his findings in 1877 in an article titled, 'The Jukes: A study in Crime, Pauperism, Disease and Heredity'. The Juke family were known for their generations of deviants who plagued the New York state in the Ulster County. Dugdale was interested to find out if heredity or one's environment had causal and contributory effects for criminality, pauperism, disease and social malaise. Dugdale (1877) claimed that,

The nature of the investigation necessitated the study of families through successive generations, to master the full sequence of phenomena and include the entire facts embraced in the two main branches of inquiry into which the subject necessarily divides itself: The heredity that fixes the organic characteristics of the individual, and the environment which affects modifications in that heredity (p.12).

His method involved a survey asking questions on areas of heredity, income, intelligence, education and the nature of criminality across generations of the Juke family. Dugdale made connections between crime and pauperism and assumed a relationship between prostitution and illegitimacy speculating that any offspring would have been neglected, uneducated and unaware of their true parentage. An association was also made between what he called exhaustion and intemperance (self-indulgence) which affected the ability to make sensible decisions. Dugdale believed that disease and extinction would have repercussions for the future family lineage and demonstrated this by tracing Juke members born since the 1700s. The first Juke member had a combination of legitimate and illegitimate children – two boys and six girls. Two of his sons married his daughters incestuously and so Dugdale concentrated on these lineages. At the time of his study in total there were 709 family members of the Jukes studied, 540 of Juke blood and 169 through family reconstitution. There were 335 out of the 535 children born who were legitimate, 106 illegitimate and 84 unknowns. Dugdale's analysis of the data resulted in five findings:

1   Heredity played a major role in physical and mental capacity which created the future pathway.
2   Behavioural conduct relying on moral understanding was mainly shaped by the environment and not determined by physical and mental capacity.
3   The environmental context experienced was causal in developing habits which could potentially become hereditary such as pauperism.
4   Heredity tends to produce an environment aiding in the perpetuation of that heredity.
5   The environment is responsible in determining an individual's path in life which makes heredity an organised consequence of an unchanging consistent environment.

His conclusions alluded to genes having passive, active and evocative effects on behaviour. Dugdale was ahead of his time and his research addressed the role of a gene–environment interaction in criminal behaviour.

Over 100 years later, by concentrating on one family in the same way as Dugdale had, Brunner, Nelen, Breakefield, Ropers and van Oost (1993) found a wealth of information about a mutated gene responsible for criminality. In this Dutch family the presence of a mutated gene responsible for monoamine oxidase A (MAOA) production was found to be associated with aggressive criminal behaviour. The males in this family lineage had an MAOA deficiency which resulted in low concentrations of spinal serotonin (5-HIAA). Low concentrations of spinal serotonin are usually found in association with impulsive aggressiveness therefore providing a direct link between genetics and antisocial behaviour. MAOA deficiency in the Dutch family studied by Brunner *et al.* (1993) was used as an explanation for the family's history of violence and antisocial behaviour. We will return to MAOA later in this chapter but it is also discussed in Chapter 7 in reference to psychopaths.

Other researchers have also considered antisocial and criminal behaviour among family members by examining, for example, the extent of crime younger members of families commit and whether their parents and siblings offended in the past or are current offenders. Ferguson (1952) studied 1,349 boys in Glasgow who had left school at the age of 14, finding that, by the age of 18, 12 per cent of these boys had been convicted for theft and burglary. By linking the boys' criminal activities to other family members who had committed crimes, Ferguson was able to show a direct relationship between the number of criminal relatives and the percentage of boys who had committed crime. For example, 9 per cent committed crime if no other family member was convicted; increasing to 15 per cent if there was one member convicted; 30 per cent if two were convicted and 44 per cent if three or more were convicted. Furthermore, the probability of being convicted depended on who in the family had offended. If the father had offended then the likelihood of conviction was 24 per cent per cent, which increased to 33 per cent and 38 per cent for an older and younger brother respectively.

Other factors were considered but Ferguson was able to calculate a likelihood of criminal activity based on convicted family members only. Ferguson concluded that there appears to be a strong genetic link between the male members of the family and criminality. This does not, however, fully account for the father having the least impact on probability of conviction when compared with an older or younger brother. A possible explanation for this difference might relate to the impact of modelling and **socialisation** from one sibling to another. This idea has been put forward in the **Group Socialisation Theory** by Judith Harris in 1998 (see Chapter 4). She effectively claimed that siblings and peers can have more of an impact on children's behaviours than parents and pits the Group Socialisation Theory against the Nurture Assumption (i.e. that parents predominantly socialise their children). If this is the case then nurture (i.e. the social influence of brothers) might account for the increased influence of brothers on brothers than fathers on sons, which further suggest a gene–environment interaction. Similarly from a study of 120 Birmingham families, Wilson (1987) demonstrated that criminal activities run in families. Of these families, 47 per cent had at least one convicted parent and for 56 out of the 120 families who had one convicted parent, 180 sons (translating to 45 per cent) were convicted. In the case of the remaining 64 families without a parental conviction, 39 (translating to 19 per cent) of the 203 sons were convicted – suggesting a genetic link in behaviour between parents and sons.

The Cambridge Study conducted by West and Farrington (1973, 1977) is often cited as an informative longitudinal investigation into the behaviour of 411 boys in the South London area aged 8–46 years (see Chapters 2, 4 and 10). Having convicted fathers, mothers, brothers or sisters predicted convictions of the boys; however, using an odds ratio (OR) calculation they were able to determine the extent of the risk of offending. OR is a statistical measure used for calculating the likelihood (or the odds) of something occurring to two different groups – hence the *ratio* of the odds for the first group and the odds for the second group are considered. A host of OR calculations were made across the different familial relations such as older brother or older sister, mother or father. This analysis showed that boys who had criminal fathers were twice as likely to become delinquent as those boys with non-criminal fathers. They also found that a parent convicted before the son was 10 years old was a good predictor of future criminal and antisocial behaviour. This finding was supported by Cloninger, Christiansen, Reich and Gottesman (1978) for delinquent females who had more socially deviant relatives in the family tree. In America the equivalent findings came in the way of longitudinal research conducted by Robins, West and Herjanic (1975) and by McCord (1977), where both studies showed a pattern of delinquency in children who had criminal parents.

In a study funded by the US Office of Juvenile Justice and Delinquency Prevention, the US National Institute of Mental Health and the US National Institute on Drug Abuse, Farrington, Jolliffe, Loeber, Stouthamer-Loeber and Kalb (2001) investigated offending and antisocial behaviour in 1,517 boys in first, fourth and seventh grades. They were assessed every six months for three years using information provided from the boys themselves, their mothers and teachers. Predictive reports from parents, the prevalence of arrests and the inter-relationships of arrested relatives were considered using OR calculations. The main conclusions drawn were:

- a high proportion of arrested individuals came from within identified criminal families (117 families in total) – hence 597 of those arrested (43 per cent of arrests) were from these families;
- if one relative was arrested, the likelihood of another member of the same family tree experiencing a similar fate increased;
- arrested fathers tended to be with arrested mothers, arrested uncles with arrested aunts which continued as far back as grandfathers and grandmothers;
- all types of arrested relatives influenced whether the boys in the study became delinquents but it was the father's arrest that had the most impact on whether boys were delinquent.

Farrington *et al.* (2001) proposed a host of possible explanations for the findings, one including an intergenerational continuity explanation whereby multiple **risk factors** present themselves to these families time and time again like poverty, family discord and parental criminality – all factors indicative of antisocial behaviour. Parental criminality is a factor which plays a robust role in offspring criminality – but where does parental criminality arise from? Farrington *et al.* (2001) applied the concept of **assortative mating** to help explain a genetic connection between parental and offspring criminality. In this context assortative mating refers to female offenders having male offenders as sexual partners. Whatever the reason for assortative mating, however, this does beg the question of what are they passing on to their offspring? Farrington *et al.* (2001) further proposed an imitation effect of antisocial behaviour among family members – but here again we might ask what was responsible for causing this antisocial behaviour in the first place (i.e. nature or nurture)? Another proposal by Farrington *et al.* was that these parents used poor child rearing methods which led to inappropriate socialisation and immature moral development in their offspring. Lastly, Farrington *et al.* proposed a less likely explanation that criminal parentage and offspring delinquency relates to police and court procedures (simply because they are likely to have had a criminal record). They concluded that, although the findings are enlightening, a clear answer as to why offending occurs in families remains unsubstantiated. It would appear, however, that from some of the proposals suggested a gene–environment relationship exists. A more difficult question to address is the direction of influence – when it comes to criminality – does **nature drive nurture** or **nurture drive nature**? Familial studies clearly show a gene–environment relationship, but the data are difficult to disentangle – perhaps twin and adoptee studies might provide further insight.

### Twin studies

There are two types of twins: monozygotic (MZ) and dizygotic (DZ). MZ twins are often referred to as identical twins and share the same genetic blueprint (i.e. sharing 100 per cent of their genes) and inter-uterine environment. DZ twins known as fraternal twins alternatively, have a different genetic blueprint from one another. DZ twins are like their other siblings because they share 50 per cent of their genes but they experience the same inter-uterine environment.

The logic behind twin studies rests on the assumption that the more genes shared the increased likelihood of similarity across behavioural traits. Therefore, as MZ twins share 100 per cent of their genes, they should behave in an almost identical way. DZ twins, however, share fewer genes and should be less similar than MZ twins but more alike than single birth siblings due to a shared inter-uterine environment – any differences of behaviour within DZ twin pairings can therefore be attributed to environmental effects. It is possible to estimate the proportion of difference between MZ and DZ pairs known as the

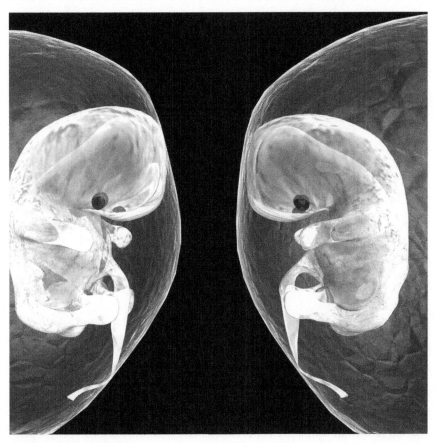

*Plate 3.1* Embryonic twins
© Christian Darkin. Image used under license from Shutterstock.com. Available at http://www. shutterstock.com/pic.mhtml?id=1105033&src=id

heritability of the trait. This has been studied in relation to behavioural traits of criminality, aggressiveness and assertiveness.

Christiansen (1977) studied a sample of 3,586 twin pairs (MZ and DZ) in Denmark and found that 52 per cent of MZ twins versus 22 per cent of DZ twins showed **pairwise concordance** for criminal behaviour. This means that if one MZ twin exhibits criminal tendencies then the probability of the other twin showing criminal traits increases. In the case of DZ twins this pairwise concordance was significantly reduced. This favours the view that MZ twins inherit biological characteristics that increase their risk for criminality. A study investigating heritability estimates for aggressiveness and assertiveness in MZ and DZ twins was conducted in 1986 by Rushton, Fulker, Neale, Nias and Eysenck. Aggressiveness was assessed using the Interpersonal Behaviour Survey on 90 MZ and 46 DZ male twins. Heritability estimates calculated for MZ and

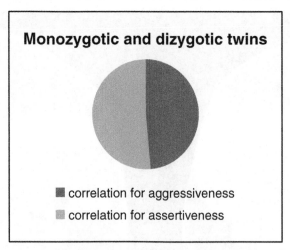

*Figure 3.1* Heritability estimates calculated for MZ and DZ twins combined
Adapted from Rushton *et al.* 1986

DZ twins combined were +0.34 and +0.36 for aggressiveness and assertiveness respectively. These figures represent correlations and suggest that when scores for MZ and DZ twins are combined together the genetic contribution towards aggressiveness and assertiveness is not that high (see Figure 3.1).

When correlations were calculated for aggressiveness, a score of +0.33 for MZ twins and +0.16 for DZ twins was found. In the case of assertiveness this was +0.44 for MZ twins and +0.26 for DZ twins. These correlations suggest that there is more similarity between MZ twins on dimensions of aggressiveness and assertiveness than is the case for DZ twins (see Figure 3.2).

In another study by Tellegen, Lykken, Bouchard, Wilcox *et al.* (1988) a heritability estimate of +0.44 was attained for aggression as assessed using the Multidimensional Personality Questionnaire on 331 male and female twins. Again, however, when within class correlations were considered a score of +0.43 was found for MZ twins and +0.14 for DZ twins. The results from both of these studies have heritability estimates going in the predicted direction. In other words, it appears that MZ twins are more behaviourally alike for aggressiveness and assertiveness than are DZ twins. This is what would be expected if the speculation that genes influence criminality is upheld.

Raine in 1993 found that a concordance rate for offending is higher amongst identical than fraternal twins and that adoptees showed a closer behavioural and criminal resemblance to biological than adoptive parents. According to Raine (1993), if the average concordance rates are considered across 13 twin studies conducted up to 1993 using a meta-analysis approach (a research method where findings from studies investigating the same variables in a similar way are combined to produce a very large sample), then for MZ twins this

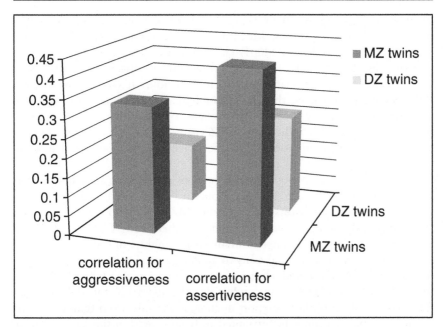

*Figure 3.2* Heritability estimates calculated for MZ and DZ twins separately
Adapted from Rushton *et al.* 1986

is 51.5 per cent and for DZ twins this is 20.6 per cent. Studies that have been conducted since 1993 confirmed higher concordance rates in MZ than DZ twins for aggressive and antisocial behaviour (Eley, Lichtenstein and Stevenson 1999).

It is assumed that for MZ, same-sex DZ and different-sex DZ twins the environment shared is equal, known as the 'equal environment assumption' (EEA). The EEA is, however, problematic. Clearly MZ twins will experience a more similar environment than same-sex or different-sex DZ twins (and likewise the same is true of same-sex DZ versus different-sex DZ twins) for various reasons – one possible cause relating to the similarity of physiognomy (i.e. outward physical appearance). Moreover, MZ twins elicit similar responses from others which reinforces similarities in their behavioural traits (Joseph 2006). Finally, as Carey (1992) had previously suggested, MZ twins are more likely to imitate each other than DZ twins and this, in turn, could lead to an overestimation of genetic influences.

This is not always the case as pointed out by Schachter and Stone (1985) who demonstrated that some twins try to 'de-identify' or be different from each other or even adopt opposing roles such as being dominant or submissive (Moilanen 1987). These effects are likely to reduce heritability estimates especially in MZ twins. Those supporting the method of twin studies and EEA further comment on how MZ twins create similar environments for themselves by virtue of their genetic identicalness on dimensions such as behaviour (Plomin, DeFries, McClearn and McGuffin 2008). Interestingly, Hay, McStephen and Levy (2001) claimed that, despite being treated more similarly by parents and peers, it is the genetic identicalness of MZ twins that is causal in the similarities of their behaviour. If MZ twins do share more similar experiences, then it is possible that genetic influences could be overestimated. Equally, however, the effects of assortative mating could be overestimating genetic influences in DZ twins: hence violations of EEA and assortative mating assumptions could be cancelling each other out to some extent.

An obvious question to ask is whether twins reared apart are different from each other? Grove, Eckert, Heston, Bouchard *et al.* (1990) considered concordance of antisocial factors for 32 pairs of MZ twins who were reared apart and adopted by strangers soon after birth. In their study Grove *et al.* (1990) considered the genetic influences involved in conduct disorder (a condition exhibiting similar behavioural traits to adult antisocial behaviours but occurring during childhood) and adult antisocial behaviours (see Chapter 7). They found a correlation of +0.41 in conduct disorder and +0.28 for adult antisocial behaviours. These findings support documented results from traditional twin studies and hence cannot be attributed to being reared in the same environment. We now turn to adoption studies which further examine the gene–environment relationship in criminality, but this time through consideration of the degree of similarity children have with their absent biological parents and adoptive parents.

### Adoption studies

Children adopted and nurtured by non-biological parents are known as adoptees. The logic underlying adoption studies is to enable the dissemination of nature–nurture factors such as parental genetics and socialisation influences. The assumption is that if adoptees resemble their biological parents more than their adoptive parents on a variety of behavioural factors then there is evidence for a genetic link. In relation to the investigation of criminality, the study design typically used is to compare the offspring of criminal and non-criminal natural parents with criminal and non-criminal adoptive parents. Findings from such research typically demonstrate a trend of varying biological contribution as shown by Hutchings and Mednick (1975). They compared 143 Danish adoptees of biologically criminal parents with 143 controls (i.e. non-criminal biological parents) and found:

- 36 per cent of sons became criminal if they had criminal biological and adoptive fathers;
- 21 per cent of sons became criminal if they had a criminal biological father;
- 12 per cent of sons became criminal if they had a criminal adoptive father;

- 11 per cent of sons became criminal if they had non-criminal biological and adoptive parents.

In 1984 Mednick, Gabrielle and Hutchings found figures suggesting a similar trend to Hutching and Mednick's study when they considered 14,427 adoptees (of which 981 males and 212 females had multiple convictions as compared with the remaining number who had no criminal record):

- 24.5 per cent of sons became criminal if they had criminal biological and adoptive parents;
- 20 per cent of sons became criminal if they had a criminal biological parent;
- 14.7 per cent of sons became criminal if they had a criminal adoptive parent;
- 13.5 per cent of sons became criminal if they had non-criminal biological and adoptive parents.

Subsequent analysis of these findings revealed that the relationship between criminal convictions of the biological parents and convictions in the adoptees was significant for property related but not violent offences. It was considered that perhaps a different type of genetic predisposition holds true for violent behaviour than other criminal acts. Mednick *et al.* (1984) concluded that:

- having a criminal biological parent predisposes sons to committing crimes;
- having adoptive parents who were also criminal had a cumulative effect;
- having adoptive parents who were criminal did not significantly influence their sons' behaviour from those with neither biological nor adoptive non-criminal parents.

Potential genetic influences on criminal behaviour might also occur indirectly via their effects on mental health. Heston (1966) compared a sample of 47 adoptees whose biological mother had schizophrenia with a control group. Heston found that five of the 47 adoptees became schizophrenic and 23.4 per cent had been incarcerated for violent offences. The suggestion here is that mental illness, in this case schizophrenia, and violent criminal behaviour can have a common genetic origin. Moffitt (1987) previously made a similar connection when parental mental illness was found to increase violent offending. Through analysing data from Mednick *et al.*'s 1984 Danish adoption study further, Moffit found no increase in violent offending among adoptees whose biological parents had criminal records. The outcome differed, however, when the biological father and mother were considered for criminality and any psychiatric condition − a threefold increase in violent offending was reported for the adopted offspring.

Results from these adoption studies are interesting and provide evidence that contributes further to the nature–nurture debate, but what are these studies actually telling us? These findings are consistent with both a genetic influence on criminal behaviour and a gene–environment interaction. The important comparison here is with the adopted offspring (who later became criminals) whose biological and adoptive parents were non-criminal (i.e. could be considered a control group). In both studies the difference in the rate of criminality between the control group and those who had a criminal adoptive parent was about 1 per cent. Hence only a minority of the adopted children whose adoptive parents were criminal became criminal. This suggests the influence of a criminal adoptive parent is no more significant than miscellaneous factors such as interacting with delinquent peers. The next important comparison is between the gene and gene–environment interaction. It is clear in both studies that the environment is having an additive contribution: as much as 15 per cent in Hutchings and Mednick's study and 5 per cent in Mednick et al.'s study. This implies that the environment (i.e. nurture) has an additive effect on the way we behave and might possibly be an example of nurture driving nature. Despite the small effect that nurture appears to be having, it is nevertheless a robust finding and cannot be ignored.

In Sweden, Bohman (1978) looked at criminality and alcoholism rates among 2,324 adoptees and had access to records belonging to the biological parents. The adopted children who had a criminal non-alcoholic biological father were no more likely to be criminal than those whose biological father was crime-free (12.5 per cent and 12 per cent respectively). Alcoholism and its heritability have been considered in numerous adoption studies where two types of alcoholism emerged: Type 1 and Type 2. Type 1 alcoholism was found to have a late onset, to be influenced by the environment provided by the adoptive parents and to be less likely to cause criminality (Cloninger, Bohman and Sigvardsson 1981). Alternatively, Type 2 alcoholism appears to be influenced by genes, and individuals with this type of alcoholism had an early onset and exhibited criminal tendencies. Adoptees with Type 2 alcoholism also showed a heredity influence passed on from the biological father to son, regardless of environmental factors (Sigvardsson, Bohman and Cloninger 1996). They further found that alcoholic biological parents were twice as likely to have violent offspring in comparison with non-alcoholic parents. Interestingly, this was not the case for property crimes which suggests this genetic influence is limited to violent offenders.

Findings from family, twin and adoptee studies are increasingly being supported and enhanced by recent developments in molecular genetics such as the MAOA mutated gene discussed earlier. Research into prenatal factors, however, also provides insight to how non-genetic factors might influence the development of criminality. For instance, how influenza experienced in the second trimester of prenatal development can increase the developing embryo's risk of violent offending later in life but not property related offending has been demonstrated by Mednick, Machon, Huttunen and Bonett (1988). This is based on research that looked at children born in Helsinki after the 1957 influenza epidemic. The criminal register was used to check for property and violent offending which helped forge a link between the mother having suffered influenza during the second trimester and her offspring later committing violent offences. Influenza is an example of a teratogen, which derives from the Greek word meaning the 'creation of a monster'. A teratogen is any non-genetic agent that can be passed on from the mother to the foetus and cause disturbance to the natural course of prenatal development. Influenza is just one example of a teratogen that is linked with future criminality but there have been others found to be equally influential. It has therefore been suggested that teratogens can impact on neurological and brain development thereby potentially altering the 'wiring' of the developing embryo's and foetus' brain functioning.

In the next section the theme of genetic transmission for criminality will be continued by considering research investigating the influence of genes and chromosomes on behaviour. It is important to understand the structure, function and formation of genes and chromosomes before evidence favouring a nature approach can be fully appreciated.

## The influence of genes and chromosomes for criminality

The influence of genes on human behaviour has long been debated between **nativists** (advocating a nature approach) and **environmentalists** (advocating a nurture approach). In recent years extreme determinism as was once advocated by nativists has been attenuated by the prevailing academic **zeitgeist** and, in psychological circles there is strong consensus of a gene–environment interaction. For many decades the burden of proof lay with the nativists having to provide evidence to substantiate their position to the environmentalists – a task which has become easier since new technological advances in genetics have been developed. Our understanding of the Human Genome, the mechanisms of DNA replication and the consequences of gene mutation for human development have become unrecognisable from previous 'biological' explanations of criminality. In current academia there is no place for serious discussion of Lombroso's (1911) characterisations of criminals as resembling ancestral (i.e. pre-human) forms of life, known as atavism, or Sheldon's (1942) relationship between bodily shapes (i.e. morphology) and temperament. In the case of Lombroso's theory of atavism, individuals who had distinctive and deviant features, such as many moles on the face, exceptionally hairy faces (especially females) or one joined eyebrow, were more likely to be criminals. He based his work on correlations between criminality and atavistic characteristics of poverty-stricken individuals. Unfortunately, correlations do not predict causality and in this case it could be more a matter of the poor stealing food to stave off starvation. Similarly, Sheldon's descriptions of three types of body shape and how one in particular, known as the mesomorph, normally associated with a criminal temperament could also be confounded by other variables. Sheldon described, for example, the mesomorph as being of medium structure and height and tending to be muscular which helped them excel in strength, mobility and speed. It might be that individuals of this physique find it easier to commit criminal acts that involve agility and strength, rather than having a criminal mind-set as a consequence of their body structure. With advances made in the way genes can be understood from molecular genetics, also known as **neurogenetics** (Raine, cited in Wilson and Petersilia 2002), the biological bases of criminality can be explored more scientifically. This provides evidence for a gene contribution to behaviour without excluding the importance of a gene–environment interaction. In the next section we consider the contribution of neurogenetics to understanding criminality.

### Molecular genetics (neurogenetics) associated with criminality

The Human Genome Project is important for understanding our human blueprint and its constituent parts (i.e. bases, genes, DNA and chromosomes). This has provided in-depth information regarding the cellular structure of the human body and how and where genes and chromosomes are located within the **nucleus** of every cell. Our genetic information (i.e. genes) is encoded on our DNA which is divided into two parts:

1   Chemical base-pairs called adenine, guanine, cytosine and thymine that make up our genetic code. The base-pairs have set bonding so that adenine bonds with thymine and cytosine bonds with guanine.
2   Sugar-phosphate bonds which make the attachment of the base-pairs possible.

The human karyotype (i.e. an individual's chromosomal profile) comprises 23 pairs of chromosomes which house our DNA. Chromosome pairs 1–22 are labelled autosomal because they represent the non-sex chromosomes and a pair of each chromosome (i.e. referred to as diploid) resides in almost all human cells – one from the mother and one from the father. The twenty-third pair consists of the **sex chromosomes** and, whilst they likewise occur in almost all of our body cells, in the case of sperm and egg cells (ova), which contain half of our chromosomes only, they occur singly. Such sperm and egg cells are therefore said to be haploid. This is to ensure that the correct number of 46 chromosomes arise when the ovum is fertilised by the sperm to create a **zygote** which then becomes the developing foetus. The mechanisms of gene transmission and replication are complicated but it is important to be familiar with these processes in order to understand the profound effects on our behaviour that gene and chromosome mutations can cause (see Box 3.2).

## Box 3.2

### Gene transmission and replication in relation to chromosomes

Genes per se occupy 2 per cent of the genome with the areas in between being non-coding regions providing structure for the chromosome. Genes are split into exons (expressed DNA sequences) and introns (intervening sequences). DNA contains the instructions for genes to be replicated via **messenger ribonucleic acid** (mRNA) which includes the exon and intron sequences. The mRNA separates from the DNA and a process of splicing begins where the introns are removed so that all the exons are joined together. The spliced mRNA then goes to a subcomponent in the cell (i.e. called an organelle) known as the ribosome where protein production begins in the form of codons (protein units of three RNA bases). Each codon is responsible for a specific amino acid and in humans there is a similarity of 99.9 per cent in the way these **nucleotide** bases combine which leaves very little variation (0.1 per cent). The 0.1 per cent of variation translates to 3 billion bases and is enough to enable genetic differences across individuals. Guo and Adkins (2008) found that three million variations of bases in the genome are possible – these bases are referred to as single nucleotide polymorphisms (SNPs) and it is these SNPs which influence gene expression and can be used as markers. A marker refers to a gene whose location and function is known. Sexual human reproduction enables variation in our genetic make-up and it is through the process of **meiosis** that this can occur. Meiosis is responsible for **gamete** (i.e. sperm and ovum cells) production and operates by two mechanisms: independent assortment and recombination. In the case of independent assortment, the 23 chromosomes from the mother and 23 from the father are divided so that one chromosome from each of the 23 pairs will form a gamete through the process of meiosis. A gamete can have any one combination of 23 chromosomes giving rise to a possible 8.4 million combinations. Recombination works differently. This is the exchange of segments along the chromosome between two **homologous chromosomes** as a part of gamete formation. Once this exchange has taken place then segments are recombined: segments are often thousands of base-pairs long. DNA sequences that are close together are considered to be spatially linked and because of this recombination process such linkage is called linkage disequilibrium.

There are different types of polymorphisms (i.e. occurring in many different forms) and one has already been considered – SNP. In addition to SNP there are variable numbers of tandem repeats (VNTR) referring to a repetitive sequence and short tandem repeats (STR). The difference between VNTR and STR is that for the former there could be repetitions of

10–200 bases whereas in the latter there are normally repetitions of only 2–5 bases. The most commonly researched polymorphisms in humans are SNPs. The example provided by Guo and Adkins (2008) is the following DNA sections pertaining to two separate people: CCAATTA and CCAACTA. Here there is one single nucleotide change – hence there are two alleles (T and C) for this SNP example. During meiosis genes in close proximity on a chromosome tend to remain together in comparison to genes that are distant from each. It is therefore assumed that when a trait (under investigation) is passed on with the gene which acts as a genetic marker, the gene responsible for the trait is proximate to the genetic marker. If the trait happens to be responsible for a specific condition and is present with the genetic marker, then we know that the locus point for a putative gene is proximate to our marker and if this occurs consistently it is possible to gauge the whereabouts of the disease causing gene. There is another important consideration for understanding the expression of a gene and that is the penetrance of a trait which can be anywhere from 1 to 100 per cent. An incomplete penetrance has repercussions for the extent to which the trait is expressed. This means that if there is 100 per cent penetrance then it is very likely that a trait will be fully expressed phenotypically. In the case of 10 per cent penetrance despite there being some presence of the gene for the trait, phenotypically it is absent. A good analogy here is two people exposed to the same cold virus but one shows the symptoms and the other does not. Whether the trait is expressed phenotypically is further complicated by the fact that there could be more than one locus point for the alleles responsible. This has been found to be the case for tuberous sclerosis (TSC1 at 9q34 on chromosome 9 and TSC2 at 16p13 on chromosome 16) and breast cancer (BRCA1 on chromosome 13 and BRCA2 on chromosome 17). A good analogy is to consider the way information is stored on a CD or computer hard drive. The information is fragmented and stored in a non-contiguous way, such that a small and specifically located scratch on a CD might affect all of the recorded songs instead of a few. These are the problems that geneticists face when trying to locate genes contributing to specific traits and it is obvious that the more complex the human trait is then the more difficult their task – behaviour versus, for example, hair colour.

Adopting the marker technique described in Box 3.2, Caspi, McClay, Moffitt, Mill et al. (2002) found a direct gene–environment relationship accounting for violent behaviour in male children from New Zealand. These children were maltreated and had low levels of monoamine oxidase A (MAOA) activity. A control group who had normal levels of MAOA and were not maltreated did not behave violently. The children who had been maltreated had the VNTR 3 or 5 repeat in MAOA. As MAOA codes for an enzyme that metabolises **neurotransmitters** (see Bio-neurochemistry, p. 149) such as dopamine, noradrenaline and cerebrospinal serotonin, low levels of MAOA will cause levels of cerebrospinal serotonin to increase. An increased level of cerebrospinal serotonin is linked with aggressive behaviour (see Bio-neurochemistry) as demonstrated in the Dutch family study (Brunner *et al.* 1993) discussed earlier. Guo, Ou, Roettger and Shih (2008) showed in their study that the VNTR 2 repeat in MAOA was associated with delinquent behaviour but only when participants failed at school therefore having to repeat the year (i.e. a gene–environment relationship). They used a delinquency scale focusing on violent delinquent behaviour which was compatible with the classification of violent offences among **recorded crime** statistics. In this study 2,524 siblings were taken from the National Longitudinal Study of Adolescent Health in grades 7 to 12 in 1994–95 (representing Wave I). In Wave II home interviews were made from 1995–96 whereas in Wave III interviews were held during 2001–02 and DNA measures had been taken. Guo *et al.* (2008) concluded that a 2 repeat in MAOA might be more predictive for violent delinquent behaviour than for non-violent delinquent behaviour. These findings implicated the 2-repeat in MAOA specifically in violent delinquent behaviour rather than delinquency per se. This suggests that the 2-repeat in MAOA figures more strongly in acts of violence than in delinquency in general.

In another study Guo, Roettger and Shih (2007) found evidence of DAT1 and DRD2 genes contributing to serious and violent delinquency in both adolescents and adults. In this study 2,500 adolescents and adults from the National Longitudinal Study of Adolescent Health participated and volunteered DNA samples. DAT, the dopamine transporter protein, controls the quantity and longevity of dopamine D2 receptor activation (hence DRD2). Dopamine levels have been implicated in aggressive behaviour. For instance drugs targeting the D2 receptors effectively reduce violent behaviour (Brizer 1988). The 10 repeat allele located on the DAT1 gene has been linked to ADHD, a condition where children have numerous symptoms:

- problems with attention
- hyperactivity
- impulsiveness (Barkley 1997).

It is the symptom of impulsivity which can lead to misbehaviour and delinquency. Guo *et al.* (2007) claimed that the 10-repeat allele on DAT1 could be used as a linked measure of serious and violent delinquency. In the case of the HPRT gene, a direct relationship between developmental delay, self-harming behaviour and aggressive tendencies towards others (Anderson and Ernst 1994) was discovered alongside a complete lack of the enzyme HPRT (resulting in abnormal uric acid metabolism that affects the central nervous system). This was caused by a mutation or deletion of the HPRT gene on the X chromosome (Stout and Caskey 1989) which means that this is an **X-linked disorder** known as Lesch-Nyhan. Here we can see a direct link between a gene and aggressive behaviour.

Thus far problems of gene codings and their mutations have been considered from research in the field of **neurogenetics** but anomalies of chromosome replication also occur and affect behaviour – specifically criminal behaviour.

### Chromosome anomalies associated with criminality

As stated earlier, we are born with the normal complement of 23 chromosome pairs (46 chromosomes) which contain our genes. One pair of chromosomes contains genetic information about our sex (chromosome pair 23) which in males is XY and females XX.

Occasionally, however, errors of meiosis cause additive or deleterious effects on the number of **sex chromosomes** present in gametes. For instance gametes can have XY or YY (in the case of males) and XX or O (a missing X chromosome in the case of females) chromosomes so that when fertilisation occurs, the sex chromosome complement could become XXX, XXY, XYY or XO or OX assuming the gamete from the other partner has the normal X or Y chromosome. It becomes more complicated than this if the partner also has faulty sex chromosome numbers in their gametes – here one could potentially have a **zygote** with XXXX, XXXY or XXYY!

The most commonly studied sex chromosomal anomalies are Klinefelter's syndrome (XXY), Double Y male (XYY), Triple X syndrome (XXX) and Turner's syndrome (XO). In the case of Klinefelter's syndrome the XX combination results from division failure during meiosis of the female's gamete formation. For XYY syndrome, the YY combination occurs during a division failure in meiosis of the male's gamete formation. Triple X syndrome also occurs due to an error of division during meiosis but the XX combination could potentially come from the mother or father which is also true of Turner's syndrome that has a missing X.

The X chromosome is larger than the Y chromosome and houses more genetic information. It is now known that in humans the X chromosome houses approximately 1,500 genes in comparison to the meagre 350 genes of the Y chromosome (Vallender and Lahn 2004). It is interesting to note that there are areas on the Y chromosome known as PAR1 and PAR2 (used for recombination during meiosis) and other non-recombining (NRY) areas. The non-recombining areas are interesting because they are expressed either throughout the body or in the testes and are passed down the paternal line to male offspring in an unchanged form. Since an area in this non-recombining zone known as the sex-determining region (Sry) encodes for maleness and affects dopamine production, any dysfunction of this might be a contributory factor for male prevalence of ADHD (Biederman 2005). Furthermore, since Sry is on the non-recombining area of the Y chromosome, this will be passed down from father to son, which accounts for why males are more vulnerable to ADHD and how it is kept in the male to male lineage. Götz, Johnstone and Ratcliffe (1999) suggested that the Y chromosome, especially in XYY syndrome, can be instrumental in raising the risk for antisocial behaviour as a consequence of over NRY gene expression.

Given that the X chromosome houses more genes than the Y chromosome, a reasonable assumption to make would be that Triple X syndrome is more detrimental and disadvantageous to these females than an extra Y chromosome is to males. Fortunately for Triple X sufferers, numerous studies have shown the extra X chromosome to be inactive (Hutt 1972). Zang (1984) showed, however, that intelligence decreases as the number of sex chromosomes increase and this is regardless of whether the chromosome is an X or a Y. In fact this is a robust observation found in Klinefelter's syndrome, Triple X and Double Y male syndrome. Hutt (1972) claimed the Y chromosome can never be masked by additional X chromosomes – this is due to the Sry on the NRY area of the Y chromosome which determines the male sex. This explains why a male with XXY or XXXY is still male. In Box 3.3 Klinefelter's syndrome, Double Y male and Turner's syndrome are discussed in relation to the likelihood of antisocial behaviour. Individuals with any one of these genetic conditions considered in Box 3.3 can be prone to antisocial behaviour and indulge in criminal activity but it does not necessarily follow that they will.

## Box 3.3

### Klinefelter's syndrome, Double Y male and Turner's syndrome

#### Klinefelter's syndrome (XXY)

Incidence of Klinefelter's syndrome is now estimated at 1.72 per 1,000 male births. Nielsen et al. (1969) found in their study that 13 of the 34 XXY males had expressed criminal traits or had been criminalised compared to the control of 16 XY males who showed no criminal traits. Götz, Johnstone and Ratcliffe (1999) recruited 13 males with XXY and 45 XY males from the Edinburgh Neonatal Survey for interview at the age of 20 years. They found that the XXY males portrayed increasing antisocial behaviour during adolescence and had a disorganised career record. In adulthood, however, only a small number fitted a diagnosis of antisocial behaviour disorder. The number of convictions across the two groups of men was consistent.

#### Double Y male (XYY)

The incidence of Double Y syndrome is estimated at 1 per 1,000 male births. With regard to social communication, interaction and adaptation,

Linden and Bender (2002) showed that children with XYY found it difficult to control their anger outbursts in the way of tantrums. Men with XYY are often studied in connection with risk of psychopathology. This line of assumption stems from research in a maximum security state hospital in Carstairs, Scotland for individuals with dangerous behaviour coupled with mental health issues. Jacobs, Brunton, Melville, Brittain and McClemont (1965) tested 197 of the hospital patients, finding eight of whom had the XYY karyotype. They calculated that this was thirty times higher than the expected prevalence within the general population. This was also confirmed to be the case in a study by Witkin, Mednick and Schulsinger (1976). Although this does support the contention that more men who are XYY have criminal convictions, no indicators as to why this is so were provided by these studies. Another common finding is that men with XYY have a lower IQ (intelligence quotient) and might be more easily persuaded into a life of deviancy or simply find it difficult to evade capture due to their lower IQ and general disorganisation that their condition brings. Soudek and Laroya (2008) measured the length of the Y chromosome in 84 male criminals and 38 male members of staff within a psychiatric hospital, concluding that the Y chromosome was significantly longer in the criminal sample of men. Gosavi, Gajbe, Meshram and Chimurkar (2009) examined blood lymphocyte cultures for genetic information and found an association with an individual with the XYY karyotype and them behaving criminally. Furthermore, Steen (1996) previously showed that men with the XYY karyotype were unable, 'to metabolize several different chemicals that transmit nerve impulses to the brain. . . . This impairment is due to a direct result of an X-linked mutation that disables an enzyme called MAOA' (p.234). This increases the amounts of serotonin, dopamine and noradrenalin in the brain, all of which have been associated with impulsivity behaviours. Impulsivity has been associated with the inability to control emotions and impulses effectively which, in turn, might influence antisocial and violent behaviour (Steen 1996).

### Turner's syndrome (XO or OX)

Incidence of Turner's syndrome is 1 in 2,000 females. Hutt (1972) cited a study conducted by Kaplan in 1967 that indicated a relationship between the absence of the X chromosome and juvenile delinquency. Interestingly, researchers have found a difference between Turners' girls who have inherited the X chromosome from the mother or from the father. It appears that when the X chromosome comes from the father then the girls tend to function more normally and have fewer socio-emotional problems than those whose X chromosome came from the mother. This has been explained by the fact that some genes are inactive and therefore do not express themselves. These genes are known as **imprinted** genes and for some imprinted genes to be 'switched on' they must come from the mother's X chromosome and for others they must come from the father's X chromosome. Hence some girls with Turner's syndrome can be problem-free, unlike others expressing socio-emotional problems that can lead to delinquency.

The inheritance of genes and chromosomes clearly influences behaviour but it is the instructions to produce bio-chemicals in the form of hormones, enzymes and neurotransmitters which directly influences our behaviour on a day-to-day basis. If there are problems with gene coding such that a mutation occurs or if there is a deletion on a chromosome normally housing genes important in the production of a specific enzyme (as is the case of Lesch-Nyhan), then there can be direct and serious implications to the normal functioning of an individual. This will be discussed as part of our coverage of bio-neurochemistry.

## Bio-neurochemistry

Bio-neurochemistry involves studying brain and neural chemistry and the impact that our own biology has on the workings of the brain. We might, for example, ask what effect testosterone has on the human brain. There have been numerous studies showing a relationship between our bio-neurochemistry and aggressive and antisocial behaviour. Of particular interest to psychologists as far as the relationship between our bio-neurochemistry and behaviour is concerned are hormones and neurotransmitters.

- Hormones are chemicals secreted by organs of the body known as endocrine glands. They have lasting effects on the central nervous system and other sites in the body.
- Neurons connect with other neurons, neighbouring cells or muscle tissue but there is a gap between them known as a synapse. Hence communication between cells has to traverse this synapse by a chemical transmitter. Neurotransmitters are therefore substances that act as vehicles of communication across synaptic gaps between one neuron and another (Toates 2011).

Hormones that have been considered important for their role in antisocial behaviour are those secreted by the gonads (androgens and oestrogens), the adrenals (adrenaline, noradrenaline and adrenocorticotropic hormone – often known as ACTH) and the pancreas (insulin). How these hormones affect our body and brain is complicated because different hormones have independent and interdependent actions with other hormones: it is this that confounds attributions of cause and effect to a specific hormone for aggressive or antisocial behaviour. Nevertheless researchers in this area have tried to ascertain the functions of specific hormones and their importance in behaviour. The first of these hormones considered is testosterone, a male androgen which has frequently been implicated in aggressive behaviour.

### Testosterone and aggression

Evolutionary psychologists have explained why males are considered to be more aggressive than females using concepts of sexual selection and male to male competition (see section on evolutionary factors). Research findings implicate the male androgen, testosterone, as being mainly responsible for sex differences in levels of aggressiveness. Olweus (1987), for example, found a positive correlation between circulating levels of testosterone and behavioural traits such as impatience and irritability. Boys with high levels were less tolerant of being frustrated and coped with this by behaving antisocially. More recent studies have found a relationship between high levels of testosterone in the brain and aggression and impulsivity in adult males (Coccaro, Beresford, Minar, Kaskow and Geracioti 2007). Testosterone was also found to have a direct link with provoked aggression and an indirect one with unprovoked aggression. In other words testosterone played a major role in situations causing an individual to feel aggrieved but less so when the provoking stimulus was more distant. Others have demonstrated a link between high levels of testosterone and aggressive prisoners which was higher still in violent rapists (Ehrenkranz, Bliss and Sheard 1974). Prothrow-Stith and Spivak (1999) found certain individuals diagnosed with violent personality disorders to have high testosterone but low serotonin levels.

Boyd (2000) considered an evolutionary perspective to explain the effects of testosterone on young men. Boyd conducted a study spanning the US, Canada and the UK looking at age factors on aggression. Violence was shown to increase at 15 years of age and to peak before 20 but then to decline after 30 years – hence violence was rarely observed in 40 year olds. This pattern was consistently found across different countries and time periods, although the frequency of homicide in the UK was one-tenth of that found in the US. Boyd further made the bold statement that higher levels of testosterone are a good indicator of homicide. He found, for example, that pre-pubescence males and females have similar rates of homicide, but by 13 years male homicide rates were twice that of females and the gap continued to widen, reaching a factor of four times by 16 years. Testosterone, Boyd argued, is a significant indicator in male sexuality which peaks during adolescence when sexual competition is highest among peers. In adolescence when testosterone is high, the potential for violence increased.

Raine et al. (1997) claimed that neurophysiological measures, such as high testosterone and low serotonin during childhood, can be used to predict later violence and criminality in adulthood. This claim has been researched further by Sanchez-Martin, Fano and Ahedo et al. (2000) in a study where male and female pre-schoolers were recorded in two situations: playing and socially interacting with each other. Sanchez-Martin *et al.* (2000) were particularly interested in aggressive behaviour in both types of situations and took samples of saliva to measure levels of testosterone. The levels of testosterone were higher in boys than girls and a positive correlation between higher levels of testosterone and aggressive behaviour under conditions of social interaction were found for boys. Dabbs and Morris (1990) revealed in their study of 4,462 males that high levels of testosterone correlated with delinquency and excessive aggressive behaviour. Again, childhood and adolescence factors, such as being in trouble with teachers at school, played an important role (Dabbs, Carr, Frady and Riad 1995).

Using saliva to measure testosterone levels was a method also adopted by Dabbs *et al.* (1995) on 692 male prisoners who were sentenced for having committed violent, sexual or property related crimes. Levels of testosterone were higher for prisoners who had committed violent or sexual crimes and in those prisoners who frequently violated prison rules using direct confrontation. Banks and Dabbs (1996) showed that adult delinquents when compared and matched for demographic and personality factors with college students had higher levels of testosterone. High testosterone levels were also found in 61 Type 2 alcoholic males, each showing antisocial behaviour (Stalenheim, Eriksson, von Knorring *et al.* 1998). The men in this study who were alcohol free, hospitalised or in prison had high levels of testosterone and scored positively for antisocial personality disorder (as indicated by Robert Hare's 'Psychopathy Checklist' – see Chapter 7).

According to Kalin (1999) higher levels of testosterone are associated with offensive or impulsive forms of aggression whereas defensive aggression experienced under situations of fear is controlled by high levels of the stress releasing hormone cortisol. Hence these two types of aggression have different underlying biological mechanisms. Other hormones found to be implicated in criminal behaviour include female hormones controlling the menstrual cycle and insulin discussed next.

## Other hormones and criminality

### Menstrual hormones

In females hormonal changes during the menstrual cycle can cause pre-menstrual tension (PMT) which, in severe cases, can lead to irritability. PMT, it is believed by some researchers, can make females vulnerable to deviancy. Dalton (1961), for example, showed an association between time in the menstrual cycle and likelihood of committing crime. It was found that of the 156 female prisoners interviewed in his study, 49 per cent committed their crime either eight days before menstruation or during it. It was also found that of the 63 per cent of women experiencing PMT whilst in prison, 54 per cent of them had violated prison rules. PMT and its effects on behaviour in women have been taken seriously in British courts and used in pleas of diminished responsibility.

## Insulin

Insulin is a hormone secreted by the pancreas involved in the regulation of glucose in the body. Increased insulin production, however, has been found to link with criminal behaviour. In cases of hypoglycaemia where the body and in particular the brain, is starved of glucose, secretion of insulin increases and symptoms of impaired brain functioning including decreased concentration and increased irritability coincide. Aggressive behaviour can be associated with glucose dysfunction and it has been shown that for some habitual violent offenders their recovery from hypoglycaemia is sluggish. Virkkunen (1988) found that some murderers had lower levels of cholesterol coinciding with higher levels of insulin and reduced serotonin. This highlights the interdependency of hormones and why it is difficult to attribute cause and effect to one hormone alone.

Hormones play an important role in behaviour but of equal influence are neurotransmitters such as noradrenaline, serotonin and dopamine.

## Noradrenaline, serotonin, dopamine and aggression

Testosterone can also inhibit the activity of MAO which, as previously discussed, metabolises the neurotransmitters noradrenaline, serotonin and dopamine. If MAO is inhibited then there is a build-up of noradrenaline which increases with aggression (Rubin 1987). Rubin (1987) found that having a history of violent behaviour correlated with high levels of noradrenaline in the brain and circulating in the body. Zuckerman (1984) found low levels of MAO to be associated with under socialisation, sensation seeking and impulsivity – all factors considered to influence an individual's temperament. Low MAO production is correlated with high levels of cerebrospinal serotonin which, in turn, has been associated with violent behaviour. Interestingly, some studies have shown that low levels of cerebrospinal serotonin are specifically linked to impulsive behaviour and recidivist offending. Halperin, Newcorn, Kopstein, McKay et al. (1997) found low levels of cerebrospinal serotonin to be a contributory factor of aggression in boys with ADHD. Low levels of serotonin features strongly in suicidal patients and those with a behavioural disorder that might include aggression. Low serotonin, however, appears to be associated with impulsive aggression and not premeditated violence.

Moffitt, Brammer, Caspi, Fawcett et al. (1998) investigated the hypothesis that serotonergic dysfunction is associated with aggression, but more specifically they considered the effects of high levels of serotonin in the blood. Whilst serotonin in the blood is manufactured by the gut, where it remains separate from cerebrospinal serotonin, it is still a reliable source for measuring serotonin levels. Virkkunen, De Jong, Bartko, Goodwin and Linnoila (1989) predicted that aggressive behaviour in adults is based on low levels of cerebrospinal serotonin. Moffitt *et al.* (1998) found that measures of aggressive behaviour correlated negatively with levels of cerebrospinal serotonin but positively with blood serotonin. This would appear a contradiction but Moffitt *et al.* (1998) claimed that this might not be the case. Based on Cook, Stein, Ellison, Unis and Leventhal's (1995) research this apparent difference could be explained through the increased serotonergic transport by the serotonergic neurons and blood platelets and occurs when there is a deficiency of MAO. Moffitt *et al.* (1998) concluded from their findings that high levels of blood serotonin are characteristic of violent males. Hence low levels of cerebrospinal serotonin and high levels of blood serotonin feature strongly in individuals with behavioural disorders despite their different origins.

Cerebrospinal serotonin is normally inactivated by either being returned to the neuron that released it (process known as **reuptake**) or metabolised by MAO. If MAO is low then **serotonin reuptake inhibitors** (SRIs), such as Prozac, can be used to control aggressive or violent behaviour. Fuller (1996) showed that in humans Prozac can be used to decrease aggressive behaviour as well as feelings of uncontrolled anger and hostility – hence when MAO is low as a consequence of the mutated gene, serotonin levels rise. Morgan (2006) suggested that the mutated gene is rare and other problems, such as developing disabilities and extreme forms of behaviour comparable to a criminal lifestyle, would be expected. Furthermore, according to Marsh, Finger, Buzas, Kamel *et al.* (2006), these behaviours are rarely shown by criminal offenders. In Caspi *et al.*'s (2002) research on MAO depletion and high levels of serotonin, a significant increase in criminal behaviour only occurred when the individual had low MAO and experienced maltreatment as a child. There is support in favour of low MAO and high cerebrospinal serotonin causing violent and antisocial behaviour. At the same time, however, there are many studies suggesting that low cerebrospinal serotonin is indicative of impulsive and aggressive behaviour. What is not appreciated here is that low MAO also increases levels of dopamine and noradrenaline. Furthermore increasing levels of noradrenaline is strongly associated with aggression in violent individuals (Rubin 1987).

Studies investigating the influence of bio-neural chemistry are interesting and certainly contribute towards our understanding of the importance hormones and neurotransmitters play in moderating our behaviour, but the problem of cause and effect prevails in this area of research. It is difficult to fathom whether aggression is the consequence of different levels of hormones or neurotransmitters exerting an effect independently or interdependently, or whether aggression causes high concentrations of these bio-neural chemicals. Furthermore, the impact of hormones and neurotransmitters on aggression and antisocial behaviour provides a **proximate explanation** (i.e. a here and now mechanistic approach) of why some individuals are violent and commit serious crime. Perhaps the contribution of brain studies relying on scanning techniques, such as electroencephalograms (EEGs), functional magnetic resonance imagining (fMRI) and positron emission tomography (PET), might provide further understanding of the biological bases of criminally oriented individuals.

## Brain studies

Researchers are now able to map the different regions of the brain courtesy of new medical technologies. The brain can be scanned whilst engaged in cognitive tasks and in so doing can help researchers identify the function of different regions of the brain.

### Electroencephalogram (EEG) scans

EEG is a method which uses electrodes placed on the scalp via a conducting gel enabling the measurement of electrical impulses in the brain. EEG has aided researchers to differentiate the various brain waves and to understand the structure of these brain waves during states of alertness, relaxation and sleep in normal brains: this therefore provides a normative baseline from which to compare brains that are abnormal. In conjunction with other physiological measures, it has been shown that low heart rate, skin conductance and slow-wave EEG can be used to indicate low arousal – a state that is often found in murderers. Evans and Park (1997) showed that murderers tended to have EEG deficits in the right hemisphere of the brain reflecting the many problems occurring in the right temporal cortex. Yet in the case of repeat violent offenders, there is greater EEG abnormality in the left temporal region (Pillmann, Rohde, Ullrich, Draba et al. 1999). Raine, Venables and Williams (1990) showed that slow theta brain waves as measured by EEG and low resting heart and skin conductance at age 15 could be used to predict later criminality at age 24 – they could classify individuals into criminals and non-criminals based on these measures.

### Positron emission tomography (PET), magnetic resonance imaging (MRI) and functional magnetic resonance imaging (fMRI) scans

Numerous brain imagining studies have consistently demonstrated structural and functional deficits in murderers to two areas of the brain: the frontal and temporal lobes. Many studies have also shown that depressed functioning in these two regions can predispose an individual to violent behaviour and a life of crime. Research on brain imaging of murderers is accredited to Raine, Buchsbaum, Stanley, Lottenberg et al. (1994), the first to publish in this area. In their study, 22 murderers and 22 controls performed a task requiring focused attention and vigilance while their brains underwent a PET scan. PET scans are used to show brain activity rather than mapping its structure. As PET scans use radiation or nuclear imaging to produce 3-dimensional coloured

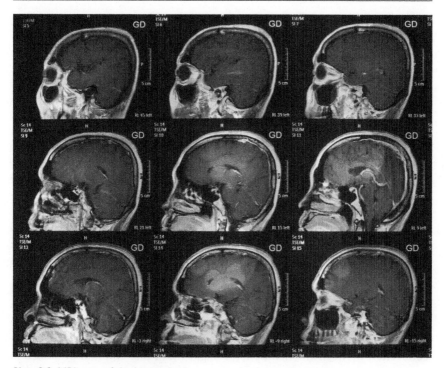

*Plate 3.2* MRI scan of the human brain

© Suthep. Image used under license from Shutterstock.com. Available at http://www.shutterstock.com/pic.mhtml?id=246231835&src=id

images it is possible to 'see' the brain working. Different colours in the images indicate the extent of activity: hence areas that are red indicate hot spots of activity. The murderers in this study had processing deficits to the prefrontal cortex an area of the brain renowned for controlling the more primitive parts of the brain like the amygdala, (responsible for processing fearful and aggressive feelings). Prefrontal deficit or abnormality is responsible for a host of behavioural problems:

- emotional and aggressive outbursts;
- argumentative and hostile social interactions;
- risk taking;
- breaking the rules;
- general irresponsible behaviour.

These behavioural problems can lead individuals to act aggressively and commit violent acts, which was demonstrated in another study by Raine, Meloy, Bihrle, Stoddard *et al.* (1998). They differentiated between murderers based on two types of cognitive styles: kill in the heat of the moment (affective murderers) and bide their time and kill in cold blood (predatory murderers).

Affective murderers showed reduced prefrontal arousal which interfered with their capacity to control and regulate their emotions unlike the predatory murderers. These findings alluded to frontal lobe deficits being associated with impulsive violent criminal acts rather than premeditated violent criminal acts. This is interesting as the dysfunction caused by frontal lobe deficits would prevent an individual from planning a violent crime. The main symptoms of frontal lobe deficits include the inability to perform any foreword planning and/or understanding of connections between action and action consequences. Furthermore, the inability to control impulses often leads to socially deviant behaviour. In 1997 Raine, Buchsbaum and LaCasse found support for previous research findings when 41 murderers and 41 controls were studied but they also showed that murderers had a dysfunctional left angular gyrus. The angular gyrus is considered a junction point between the different lobes of the brain – such that information processed by the temporal, parietal and occipital lobes is integrated. Hence under-activity of the left angular gyrus causes a host of correlated problems linked to learning disabilities, and learning disabilities have been found to feature strongly among violent offenders (see Figure 3.3).

Raine *et al.* (1997) also found problems of function associated with the corpus callosum. The corpus callosum connects the left and right hemispheres of the brain via bundles of nerve fibres which help to associate information across the hemispheres for speedy integration, interpretation and decision making. Poor connection between the hemispheres might mean that emotion processed in

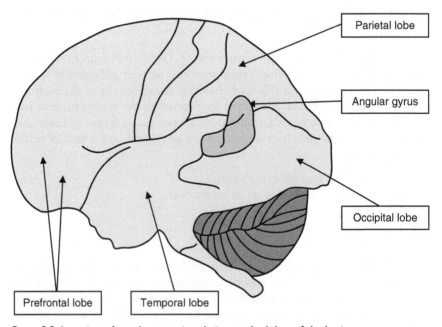

*Figure 3.3* Location of angular gyrus in relation to the lobes of the brain

the right hemisphere is less well regulated due to inadequate control from the left hemisphere (Davidson and Fox 1989). Furthermore, decreased left hemisphere input is argued to be a contributing factor for violent behaviour.

Using MRI scanning, Raine, Lencz, Bihrle, LaCasse and Colletti (2000) submitted 21 community-based males with antisocial personality disorder (APD), 27 substance-dependent males and 34 normal males comprising the control group, to prefrontal grey (neurons) and white matter screening. MRI scans operate by taking pictures of the brain from different angles, which are transmitted to a computer, providing a 3-dimensional static image containing information regarding the health of the brain tissue and the volume of grey matter in the brain. The MRI scans showed there to be reduced volume of prefrontal neurons in the grey matter of APD individuals. Raine et al. (2000) accounted for the difference in prefrontal grey volume as resulting from reduced prefrontal size and not brain size per se. Based on these findings Raine et al. (2000) were able to classify participants according to one of the three groups above using MRI scans, heart rate and skin conductance to an accuracy of 76.9 per cent.

Adopting fMRI scanning, Raine, Park, Lencz, Bihrle *et al.* (2001) were able to differentiate between adults showing serious violence from those refraining from behaving violently despite all having experienced physical abuse as children. fMRI scans are different from MRI scans because unlike MRI scans they provide images of activity within the brain by recording increased blood flow. In this way fMRI scans are similar to PET scans in what they demonstrate (even more magnified), but the way in which they operate differs making them easier and possibly safer to use. In Raine *et al.*'s (2001) study there were four groups of participants all recruited from the community as follows:

1    experienced physical child abuse but not violent;
2    experienced physical abuse but extremely violent;
3    extremely violent;
4    a control group who were neither violent nor had experienced any abuse.

They were all scanned while performing visual/verbal tasks involving memory and therefore activating the temporal and frontal lobes of the brain. Reduced right temporal lobe functioning was shown for the violent and abused individuals. In the case of those abused but refraining from violent behaviour, activity was low in the left but higher in the right temporal lobe. Activity in the left hemisphere was low for both abused groups during the memory task. This study has provided insight as to the protective factor provided from an operable right hemisphere and the risk factor of having a compromised right hemisphere combined with early physical abuse. The latter demonstrates a gene–environment interaction for violent behaviour.

Other researchers have examined brain structural and functional abnormalities of violent criminals who have a personality disorder such as APD. Fazel and Danesh (2002), for instance, estimated that among violent offenders as many as 47 per cent of males and 21 per cent of females have APD. Widiger (1996) and Hobson and Shine (1998) estimated that three-quarters of prisons are filled with prisoners meeting Hare's revised Psychopathy Checklist (PCL-R) of 1991 and a further one-quarter scoring just at the cut-off point for psychopathy (see Chapter 7). It is not surprising therefore that there have been many studies investigating differences of brain structure and function in **criminal psychopaths**.

Blair, Morris, Frith, Perrett and Dolan (1999) focused on the role of the amygdala in processing emotion and interpreting fear – which they claimed might be the key to understanding why individuals with APD lack fear and empathy. Blair *et al.* (1999) connected the research findings together such that the prefrontal area of the brain is responsible in cyphering thought while the amygdala cyphers feeling, both required for socially sound decision making. Yang and Raine (2009) found that there was reduced prefrontal brain structure (using MRI) and function (using fMRI) in antisocial violent and psychopathic individuals. There is an overwhelming abundance of research into psychopaths considered further in Chapter 7. Thus far explanations of criminality discussed have relied on proximate approaches, in other words, factors which provide the mechanisms for violence and antisocial behaviour to occur. Proximate approaches help us to understand why individuals behave in the ways that they do, but they fail to provide an ultimate account. That is, why we, as a species, have the propensity for aggressive, violent and criminal behaviour. Evolutionary psychology has developed in recent years to provide such **ultimate explanations**.

## Evolutionary factors

Charles Darwin introduced the world to his Theory of Evolution by Natural Selection through his writings on *The Origin of the Species* (1859) and his less well-known book *The Descent of Man and Selection in Relation to Sex* (1871). In *The Origin of the Species* Darwin describes natural selection and uses the term fitness, a term first introduced by sociologist Herbert Spencer. When Darwin wrote about natural selection he referred to certain physical and psychological traits of animals and humans that have been inherited from one generation to another because of their value for survival and reproduction. Hence in times of drought a giraffe possessing the longest neck by way of a fluke mutation would be able to reach foliage on the upper most branches of trees that were unattainable to other giraffes. Giraffes with longer necks would therefore be able to feed, survive and live long enough to reproduce and pass on its genes for longer necks to its offspring.

Applying this principle to humans, it might be argued that risk prone and violent males among a population of non-risk prone peaceful males would fertilise more females. They might die younger because of their risk proneness but this could still be selected for if such behaviour enables them to pass on more of their genes to their offspring. If conditions are conducive to such risk-taking behaviour then eventually the genes underlying such behaviour will out-compete those of the risk-aversive males through natural selection. Darwin realised that natural selection could not explain differences of behaviour across the sexes and so introduced his less well-known concept of sexual selection. Although a simple concept, sexual selection has huge ramifications for understanding fundamental behavioural differences across the sexes including aggressive, violent and antisocial behaviour. Put simply, sexual selection refers to characteristics which impress and allow access to the opposite sex and in so doing become selected. For example, males generally compete for females whereas females are choosey in their choice of potential mates. Females are more likely to moderate their sexual behaviour than males and select their mates more carefully as they potentially have more at stake – they are after all the sex that can become pregnant. In humans the duration of pregnancy is about nine months, but the care and nurturing of offspring until fully independent can be longer than 18 years. If the female chooses unwisely she could literally be left holding the baby for a very long time on her own. Furthermore, as each woman has a limited fertility time span (i.e. production of ova), she will want to ensure that a good mate choice has been made (i.e. someone with good genes and is therefore likely to survive, provide protection and support her and their offspring) as the process of procreation is effortful and time consuming.

Darwin realised that female choosiness led to males developing larger bodies, gaudy physical characteristics and a lower threshold for aggression, all features designed for victory arising out of male to male competition. Why males compete for females and females tend to be selective in their mate choice was a problem that Darwin pondered over but never quite solved. This problem was finally solved 100 years later in 1972 by American evolutionist Robert Trivers. In his theory of parental investment, Trivers suggested that males try to impress and in so doing compete for females. Females invest more in their offspring because they become pregnant, carry the foetus for nine months (in the case of humans) and lactate (produce breast milk). Trivers saw female investment as a resource that males compete for – hence this asymmetry of investment across the sexes leads to a lower threshold for aggression in male animals (including humans) and a greater degree of choosiness among females.

Daly and Wilson (1990) considered Trivers' theory of parental investment and used it to explain the high rate of same sex homicides among strangers. Their figures showed that 97.2 per cent of 13,680 same sex homicides involved men and they concluded that same-sex rivalry occurs when the same resources are fought over. In the case of male competitors, the more successful males will get the prized females. According to Daly and Wilson, males might fight over females for both direct and indirect reasons. Fighting on the grounds of reproductive competition is an example of a direct reason for fighting. Examples of indirect reasons for fighting include fighting over resources needed for reproduction or being acceptable to females and fighting over reputation used for obtaining resources and resource maintenance (see Chapter 9 for gender differences in crime). Being less risk averse, according to Quinsey (2002), occurs when males compete for the same resources, which is usually at a time when mate selection is at its optimum – that is during adolescence and early adulthood, referred to by Wilson and Daly (1985) as the 'young male syndrome'. This is reflected in the crime statistics and explains why there is a tenfold increase of males found guilty of violent crimes and about a five-fold increase of males arrested for violent crimes in comparison to females (HO Statistical Bulletin 2003 and 2007, respectively).

Men also murder women and assault their wives, which Daly and Wilson (1990) called sexual conflict. Sexual conflict occurs when males compete against the very resource for which they originally fought. An example of this is when a husband actively deters his wife from pursuing her own interests which conflict with his own, such as an extra-marital relationship. In the words of Daly and Wilson, 'Men have evolved the morphological, physiological and psychological means to be effective users of violence' (cited in Archer, p.274).

Another interesting application of evolutionary psychology to understanding antisocial behaviour is the idea that individuals with personality disorders like antisocial, borderline and narcissistic personality disorders (see Chapter 7) often use a 'cheating' strategy (Raine 1993) where they take advantage of others. This is also known as freeloading, and may be seen in individuals who fail to conform to social convention or engage in reciprocal altruism (i.e. delayed positive 'tit-for-tat' behaviour) (see Chapter 16). Freeloading in this way may have evolved to take advantage of the normally anticipated moderate degree of altruism that people show (see Chapters 7 and 16). Hence whilst biological psychologists have sought to help explain why some individuals turn to violent criminal behaviour through a greater understanding of genes, hormones and brain activity, evolutionary psychologists are now attempting to explain why the males of our species might be particularly susceptible to such patterns of response.

## Summary

- There are many independent and interdependent biological factors that help to explain why some individuals resort to antisocial, violent and aggressive behaviour. These biological factors include genetics and chromosomes; bio-neurochemistry; brain studies, and evolution. Research looking into the influence of genes and chromosomes was considered using familial, twin and adoptee studies and in more detail from gene mutations such as MAOA and chromosome disorders such as XXY and XYY. Twin studies provide partial evidence of there being a genetic basis for criminal behaviour in terms of **pairwise concordance** and hereditability estimates. Such studies also provide evidence of a gene–environment relationship, the extent of which is difficult to determine conclusively.
- Studies that have considered the behaviour of MZ twins separated at birth

have helped us to understand the relative contributions of nature and nurture to criminality. Recent work on variations in genes (and chromosomes) between related individuals has helped to further this knowledge. By studying the lineage of criminal families, it is possible to locate how the propensity for violence for instance is passed on from father to son. Studies of adoptees have helped us to understand the influence of criminal biological and adoptive parents on criminality. Findings suggest that criminal biological parents have more influence on criminality than adoptive parents. There is a combined influence of biological and adoptive parents who are criminal on adoptees, therefore providing evidence of a gene–environment interaction on criminal behaviour.

- Genes identified via markers for set neurological function have provided interesting information regarding the body's bio-neurochemistry. The MAOA gene, for example, is implicated in aggressive and antisocial behaviour in individuals who have this faulty gene. The MAOA gene has been implicated in families with a long history of violence – in particular the male lineage. Other studies have linked high levels of testosterone to violent behaviour and to chromosomal anomalies such as XYY. Chromosomal anomalies, such as XXY and XYY, have been linked to violent prisoners.

- Bio-neurochemical research considers the effects of hormones and neurotransmitters on antisocial and criminal behaviour. Sex hormones, such as androgens, have been researched extensively in relation to aggression. Testosterone in males and oestrogens controlling the menstrual cycle in females have been associated with violent and aggressive behaviour. Most research has focused on testosterone in males and shows that the higher the levels of testosterone the more likely the individual is to be prone to violence. Other hormones, such as insulin, have been found to influence aggressive behaviour also. Effects of neurotransmitters, such as noradrenaline, serotonin and dopamine, on aggressive and antisocial behaviour provide proximate (i.e. a here and now mechanistic approach) explanations. Low levels of cerebrospinal serotonin are implicated in impulsive aggressive behaviour whereas high levels of noradrenaline are implicated in aggressive and violent behaviour.

- Brain imaging studies have provided researchers with a view to the structure and functioning of the brain. Both structural and functional differences in the amygdala, corpus callosum, frontal and temporal lobes have been found in those with antisocial and aggressive behaviour. In the case of individuals with antisocial behaviour, low arousal of the frontal lobes has been observed. The amygdala is important for cyphering fear and interpreting people's feelings under different social situations. This might account for how predatory murderers can be so callous in their killings. Various researchers have alluded to there being different types of murderers: affective who are impulsive killers and predatory who plan their killings. The question posed by Raine *et al.* (1998) was whether these two different cognitive styles of killing could be explained by differences of brain functioning? They found reduced prefrontal activity in affective murderers but not for predatory killers.

- There are many explanations for violence and criminality, however, the evidence is mounting to suggest that violent offending, such as murder, is related to a problem with the workings of the brain and to levels of hormonal and neurotransmitter secretion resulting from neural activity.

- Evolutionary psychologists (by referring to the work of Darwin) provide an **ultimate explanation** of violence and why males are more violent and prone to criminal acts than females. Sexual selection has meant that males have lower thresholds for violence especially during times of mate selection. Male to male competition at this time increases the possibility of violent exchanges between males. Due to the relatively high cost of reproduction for them, females are more likely to be more choosey about romantic partners than males. This choosiness is likely to be based on a number of criteria such as likelihood of provisioning and engaging in parental care. Sexual selection theory predicts that males will more frequently be both the instigators of and the victims of violence – a view that is supported by Home Office recorded crime statistics.

## Questions for discussion

1   Can studies comparing MZ with DZ twins ever provide conclusive evidence of how genes influence criminal behaviour?
2   How reliable are the findings from EEG, MRI, fMRI and PET scans for explaining criminal behaviour? Are there any limitations to these for explaining criminality?
3   To what extent can neurotransmitters and hormones provide reliable explanations of violence and criminality? Is the evidence clear cut or confounded?

# Chapter 4

# Social, learning and developmental approaches to understanding criminality

In Chapter 3, evidence supporting a nature approach to understanding criminality was considered. In this chapter, however, a nurture (environment or upbringing) explanation will be explored by considering aspects of socio-emotional development of the individual throughout the lifespan with a particular focus on childhood. It therefore makes perfect sense to approach this area by considering Urie Bronfenbrenner's **Developmental Ecosystem Model**. In his model, the child sits at the centre, surrounded by social institutions such as the family, education, law, media and culture, which all interact and impact on his or her socio-emotional development. Bronfenbrenner's model can be likened to an onion whereby the child is surrounded by different layers of socialising agents. The child is born with a set of reflexes and abilities to enable and ensure its survival – for instance, the ability to recognise faces (in particular the carer) is an ability that will enable the newborn to bond with the carer thereby ensuring its survival. The first layer from the child is called the microsystem. It is the microsystem that the child first interacts with in the guise of parents, the family and close peers. In this chapter, we explore Bowlby's notion of attachment and how this can influence the individual's future behaviour. We will see how unfortunate childhoods full of parental rejection, neglect and abuse can create a criminally inclined individual (beginning in childhood and progressing into adulthood). Family dynamics impact on the social, emotional, cognitive and developmental functions of an individual. We will explore the dynamic variations and fluctuations that occur within families and how these impact on attachment and the socialisation of children. Of importance also is how parental criminality, family discord, inconsistencies in punishment, family size and economic status impact on the developing child – to what extent these factors encourage a child to embrace criminal ideals and commit crime. As sociologists view the family as an institution that functions within the context of its host society, it is difficult to consider the family in isolation of cultural norms, the law, media, education and politics. Hence in this chapter we will discuss the family in terms of its role within society and therefore the functions it is expected to perform such as teaching offspring to know right from wrong. Teaching children morality occurs through the process of socialisation which itself is constrained by the mores, values and attitudes supported by society. Another important microsystem socialising agent are our peers. Children socialise each other according to the **Group Socialisation Theory** which has repercussions for the development of delinquent/ criminal ideals. Even if parents socialise children appropriately, mixing with delinquent gangs and groups can easily undo their good work, and as we will find, this can occur in school as well as outside of school. The next layer we will consider is the exosystem and how it interacts with the child – in particular the media and law. Media can influence the behaviour of children especially if violence and violent sex scenes are being depicted. Studies have shown that 8–12 year olds are susceptible to the influence of violence on television, and that children model on adult aggressive behaviour as was found in Bandura's 'Bobo' doll experiment. In the case of the law, most individuals will not come into direct contact with it. Nevertheless we are indirectly influenced by the law as it defines what it is to behave appropriately – rules that we follow and a sense of morality that govern our behaviour. We will consider what happens if an individual fails to follow these rules and falls short of the level of morality expected by society and the law. The most outer layer Bronfenbrenner labelled as the macrosystem. This relates to our culture, which is the overarching factor influencing our very societal ideals, values and attitudes. In this chapter we will consider the two types of culture: individualistic and collectivist. Both types of culture influence our behaviour but studies indicate higher rates of criminality in individualistic cultures such as the UK and US – we will explore why this is the case.

## Introduction

Headline examples such as, 'Lives at risk as school arson bill tops £100M' and 'Brutal death of a travelling child' suggest that juvenile criminality is on the rise. In the case of the first headline the explanation for fire-setting was attributed to 'bored and disaffected pupils' of the school who actually put the lives of other children attending the school at risk. The second headline refers to the case of a 15-year-old gypsy boy who was attacked by two boys aged 15 and 16, who were later charged with his murder. Cases such as these have prompted schools to inform parents of their children's truancy and for them to be more proactive in disciplining their children. These offences are relatively rare but there has been increasing concern over juvenile delinquency (see Chapter 10). These explanations of delinquent behaviour are very different from the nature (i.e. gene) and **gene–environment interaction** discussed in Chapter 3. Essentially these explanations are considered to err on the side of nurture (i.e. environment).

During the mid-1990s in England and Wales, 25–35 per cent of **recorded crime** was committed by juveniles under the age of 18. In 2006 the peak age for male offenders was 17 whereas for females this was 15. The offences committed according to the 2006 Home Office records and the British Crime Survey tend to be petty and antisocial but not serious crimes, often involving drinking, speeding, shoplifting and youths congregating in large groups causing noise and disruption. It is rare that juveniles commit serious offences but they sometimes do.

Robert Thompson and Jon Venables murdered the toddler James Bulger, but importantly both were children themselves at the time of committing the murder (see Chapter 1 for discussion on age of criminal responsibility). This of course is not a new revelation, as children have murdered younger children in the past. For example Mary Bell strangled her playmates. At the time it was speculated that because both Thompson and Venables came from families where violence and criminality was the norm, they were unable to separate what was typical behaviour within their family context from what was considered atypical behaviour by society. So why is the family the first to be in the firing line as soon as their children contravene the law? The media would have us believe that children and adolescents who break the law do so because their parents have failed to teach them how to behave appropriately. This sentiment has been embraced by politicians who speak of the 'Big Society' and 'family values' and how the family should be responsible for instilling pro-social behaviour in their children. These are the latest buzz words in politics for which the family plays a central role in ensuring the success of the 'Big Society'. Despite the British Prime Minister's (i.e. David Cameron's) insistence that the 'Big Society' relies on the successful implementation of family values, therefore giving the family high importance, Urie Bronfenbrenner previously encapsulated this in his **Developmental Ecosystem Model** in 1979. This profound model addresses how the family influences the child and how the family is influenced by society and society, in turn, by culture. Bronfenbrenner's perspective can be summarised by the following quote:

> Understanding of human development demands going beyond the direct observation of behaviour on the part of one or two persons in the same place; . . . multi-person systems of interaction not limited to a single setting must take into account aspects of the environment beyond the immediate situation containing the subject (Bronfenbrenner 1977, p.514).

Elements of his observations were clearly incorporated into a model which included multi-levels of socialising agents, varying from primary to more distal ones. These different socialising agents, often termed by sociologists as informal (examples of this being the family and close friends) and formal (examples of this being schools, branches of the law like the police and the media), differ in the amount of direct contact and influence they have on the developing child. Because Bronfenbrenner's model has been influential in the understanding of child development, and offers a structure for which most psychological, sociological and criminological research can be encapsulated, this chapter will be organised according to his model. In the next section, Bronfenbrenner's model will be explored in detail.

## Bronfenbrenner's Developmental Ecosystem Model

Bronfenbrenner's Developmental Ecosystem Model is often represented as concentric layers (see Figure 4.1), which might be likened to the concentric layers of an onion, moving from the centre to the surface of the onion. There are different concentric layers surrounding the development and socialisation of the child which Bronfenbrenner refers to as the microsystem, mesosystem, exosystem and macrosystem. As you can see from Figure 4.1, the child is at the centre surrounded by layers of external factors which influence individual development and the internalisation of morals, values, mores and acceptable behaviour through the process of socialisation. Socialisation, however, is a complex process that involves teaching children the rules and mores of their society – eventually becoming adopted and accepted as the guide to appropriate social behaviour supported by society. It is through the socialisation process that an understanding of moral behaviour and appropriate social conduct develops across a wide range of situations and social contexts. The different sources from which socialisation is taught derives from informal (i.e. personal close contacts) and formal (i.e. institutional distant contacts) socialising agents. In Bronfenbrenner's model both informal and formal socialising agents are accounted for within the microsystem, mesosystem, exosystem and macrosystem. Bronfenbrenner allows for the interaction of informal and formal socialising agents between the microsystem, mesosystem, exosystem and macrosystem. The family is considered to be an informal socialising agent situated within the child's microsystem, which is the powerhouse in the development of family values necessary to the 'Big Society' sentiment embraced by contemporary politicians. The family therefore has a key role in the socialisation of children.

It has been argued that delinquency is represented more frequently among juveniles from certain types of family or social background. The Cambridge Study conducted by West and Farrington (1973) demonstrates this contention well. Participants in West and Farrington's study were young boys aged 8–9 years when first contacted in 1961–62, and lived in working class inner-city areas of South London; 411 boys participated in the research, all attending one of six state primary schools within the radius of the Research Office. Recorded demographics concerning the family included:

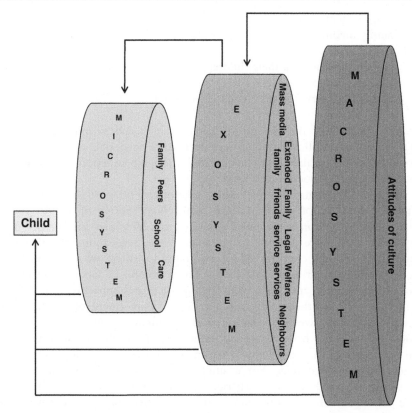

*Figure 4.1* Visual representation of Bronfenbrenner's Developmental Ecosystem Model
Adapted from Bronfenbrenner 1979

- the father being in 94 per cent of cases the breadwinner and employed in a skilled, semi-skilled or unskilled manual job;
- 87 per cent of the boys having White British parents.

The boys were interviewed at school by psychologists and completed numerous tests measuring intelligence, personality, achievement potential and psychomotor impulsivity at the ages of 8, 10 and 14. They were interviewed at the Research Office base when aged 16, 18 and 21, but at ages 25 and 32 interviews took place in their own homes. The interview topics included issues such as employment, relationships, living conditions and leisure pursuits (including questions about drinking consumption, aggressive behaviour and criminal activity). The response rate was high – even at the age of 32 there was a 94 per cent participation rate (378 out of 403 who were still alive at this time).

Parents were also interviewed annually until the boys were 14–15 years old and this provided further demographic information, including:

- employment history
- family income
- family size
- any separations from their children
- child-rearing practices
- nature of supervision their children received.

Further profiles of the boys were provided by teachers and school peers. This information offered insights to performance at school, and any troublesome behaviour, which were corroborated through peer reports of dishonesty, popularity and antisocial behaviours.

West and Farrington (1973) found a relationship between low intelligence and likelihood of offending; a third of the boys scoring up to 90 (100 is the average) for non-verbal intelligence on the Wechsler Intelligence Test by 8–10 years were juvenile delinquents. These boys found it difficult to understand abstract concepts which accounted for their low scores and poor school achievement (see Chapter 5). These combined factors contributed towards a deficit in anticipating the consequences and impact of their offending behaviour for their victims. Cohen's (1955) pertinent observation that parents from a lower class background experiencing relative poverty are more likely to live from day-to-day rather than planning for the future, and to use language in the concrete than in the abstract, adds support to West and Farrington's findings. For example, the use of wording indicated the here and now and described experiences that have happened or are happening at the time of communication, instead of conveying future events in the hypothetical.

West and Farrington (1973) also tested for personality and impulsivity using the Eysenck Personality Inventory (EPI); those who scored high on extroversion and neuroticism tended to self-report offending behaviour as juveniles. The robust factor accounting for this was not derived from family background and upbringing but rather from measures of impulsivity implicit within the EPI. Farrington in a later study (1990a, 1993) found this to be the case; impulsivity as rated by parents and peers predicted convictions at age 32, and restlessness was a key factor in convictions of violent offending (Farrington 1994).

The nature of family functioning is considered a contributory factor for making a child either vulnerable to or protected from criminal pursuit (Rutter and Giller 1983; Farrington 1990a). Why is that? One possible explanation could be related to the number of important roles that the family has to play including:

- parental care and love helps to pre-adjust a child for life;
- family is a strong socialising agent;
- parents are used as role models;

- learning starts in the home;
- parental discipline;
- parental supervision;
- family helps to exert control over 'wild' adolescents;
- siblings can be looked up to and copied.

These different aspects of family role will be considered throughout this chapter; however, it is important to consider the child first given that the child is central in Bronfenbrenner's model and is born with a host of inherited factors which interact with the environment (see Chapter 3).

### The child

Newborns are endowed with a variety of reflexes designed to promote survival. These reflexes become modified as the newborn interacts increasingly with its immediate environment – the parents therefore are the child's microsystem. Jean Piaget, a Swiss developmental psychologist, was one of the first to introduce a universal stage theory of child cognitive development. Piaget believed that to acquire knowledge infants must perform 'experiments' by acting upon the world. He introduced the concept of circular reactions to describe 'organised acts' that lead to stimuli which re-elicit the act. For example, the action of sucking on the mother's breast produces sensations in the infant's mouth which induce further sucking. Eventually such acts become increasingly modified to suit and adapt to the immediate pressures of the environment. This is part of the maturation process and can be argued to comprise the nature element of development. In order for reflexes such as sucking behaviour to develop further, Piaget argued there has to be interaction with the environment (i.e. the gene–environment element).

According to Rene Baillargeon (2004), babies are more capable of understanding the world around them at an earlier age than first considered by Piaget, and argued instead that there is a host of infant competencies which are innate and equip youngsters with the ability to make sense of the world (see Box 4.1). Other researchers, such as Fantz (1963), claimed that humans are essentially social beings and have a predisposition towards identifying and recognising human faces to enhance sociability. Fantz's research findings have been useful in the understanding of human **imprinting**. There are many examples of imprinting in the animal kingdom, but most research has focused on chick behaviour. Lorenz (1935) observed newly hatched goslings and discovered the importance of the mother goose as a role model for the goslings to imitate. This was also observed in chicks who formed an attachment with the mother hen and copied her behaviour (i.e. the chicks imitated the hen's pecking behaviour, an action which is vital to their survival).

## Box 4.1

### The work of Rene Baillargeon

Baillargeon (1994) introduced the violation of expectation model which relies on infants looking at possible and impossible events. Infants spend more time looking at the impossible event which suggests they have some implicit understanding of the laws of physics. Infants are placed in front of a screen projecting different scenarios of possible and impossible events. For instance, if the projected scenario shows an object placed on top of a surface and it does not fall to the floor, then this is consistent with their belief system about how objects should behave. In the case of the impossible event, however, an object placed next to a surface appearing to float unaided that does not fall to the floor, encourages infants to continue looking. They are trying to make sense of what they are viewing. Baillargeon referred to this test as the support phenomena but described three other types of test: collision, unveiling and barrier phenomenon all operating on the same principle of what is possible from what is impossible. Baillargeon found that newborns have limited understanding of these phenomena but within a month or so become competent at comprehending how objects should behave in different situations and circumstances.

In the case of humans, it is important for newborns to attach to the carer who is usually the mother (but does not have to be), so that she will nurture her offspring and in so doing ensure their survival. Knowing which individual to become attached to, however, involves being able to identify and recognise the carer and for this they need to have an innate face recognition system (see face recognition in Chapter 13). Attachment is an important area of child development and is of particular interest to our understanding of criminality. In Chapter 3, the DRD4 gene was discussed in terms of its influence on attachment behaviour and, the implications for Ainsworth's Strange Situation Experiment. Attachment here will be considered in terms of the intergenerational transmission of attachment styles learnt from grandparents to parents then to offspring, and the implications this has on future behaviour (possibly criminal behaviour) especially under circumstances of an absent appropriate attachment model (i.e. mother or other carer). The interaction between the child and microsystem is an important one and is the first to influence the development and learning curve of the infant. It is the family in particular, the mother or other carer, with whom initial communication is made. The main focus in the next section is the family and the impact of nurturance on the developing child's well-being.

## Child and microsystem (the family)

As demonstrated in Figure 4.1, the child is at the centre and is surrounded by different layers of socialising agents beginning with the closest informal socialising agents (the parents and family). The child brings into its social and physical world a survival package consisting of innate, rudimentary infant competencies. The newborn relies on its parents to ensure it is provided for and nurtured so that it can develop into an independent law abiding individual. Before this can occur, however, bonding with the carer increases the likelihood of survival and creates a social environment that is conducive for growth and development into adulthood. This is not always a certainty and in some cases the parent (or carer) child relationship fails to establish itself and social development can go awry.

Kevin Browne's research in the 1980s and 1990s demonstrates this clearly. He has helped to make valuable links between criminal activity in families, parent–child interaction in abusing families, and high and low **risk factors** involved in the initiation of a child into a life of crime. Falshaw, Browne and Hollin (1996) found victimisation during childhood to be a strong contributory factor for delinquency during adolescence. They also pointed out that while most children who have been abused do not resort to delinquency in later years, it is important to consider a host of high and low risk factors for criminality that might leave an individual vulnerable to or protected from becoming an offender. It is difficult to know all the risk factors, let alone weight them according to high or low risk for criminality, but researchers, such as Rutter and Giller (1983), have identified five key adverse factors:

1   parental criminality;
2   problems in family relationships;
3   inconsistencies in discipline;
4   size of family;
5   socio-economic status.

Additionally there are a host of protective factors which will be discussed later in this chapter.

Dixon, Browne and Hamilton-Giachritsis (2005) investigated whether an **intergenerational cycle** of child maltreatment continued from parent to child and the child as an adult to his or her own children. They compared families where at least one of the parents had been physically or sexually abused as a child with parents who had not experienced this form of victimisation. There were 4351 families considered, of which 135 (translating to 3.1 per cent) had a parent who had been abused as a child. A health visitor collected data about these families and assessed any offspring aged 4–6 weeks. Dixon et al. (2005) found that child abuse rates were higher in families where one or both parents had been abused as children – 18 (6.7 per cent) compared with 9 (0.4 per cent) for non-abused parents. Analysis of the assessment information collected by the health visitor, revealed a significantly higher number of risk factors for abusive behaviour in families with an abusive childhood history. The data also showed the presence of three risk factors that helped perpetuate an intergenerational effect of child maltreatment:

1    a history of depression;
2    living with a violent individual;
3    being a parent before 21 years of age.

The presence of the risk factors considered, however, only accounted for 53 per cent of the intergenerational effect leading Dixon *et al.* to conclude that parenting styles might also play an important role.

In an interview with Lance Workman for *The Psychologist* in 2013, Browne reflected on his work at the Glenthorn Treatment Centre where the consequences of neglect and abuse experienced by young offenders in childhood were studied. He found that as many as four out of five offenders experienced child abuse or neglect before their fifth birthday and 80 per cent were troublesome enough to have had eight placements before being admitted at Glenthorn. Browne suggested that as many as 55 per cent had been assaulted many times in their young lives and, because of their abusive childhoods, found it difficult to escape the cycle of violence which they themselves perpetuated by being abusive to their own children. Having a protective factor, such as one non-abusive parent, can help to break this cycle. Browne's research had wider implications for parenting and parent–child interactions within families – it has had implications for childcare institutions in Britain and across Eastern European countries such as Romania. He concluded that positive attachment to parents or carers in childhood is paramount in securing a crime-free individual in the future. Attachment is an important concept used to account for a life-time of mother (carer)–child bonding. This bonding ensures the survival of offspring but also provides evidence of the crucial role it has in nurturance. Attachments begin in the home where the infant is surrounded by family members; the subject of our next section.

### Attachment in the family

#### John Bowlby's Theory of Attachment

Bowlby (1958) in his book *The Nature of the Child's Tie to his Mother* introduced the concept of Attachment Theory. Bowlby showed that emotional and social ties are most apparent in newborns which begged the question of why this should be the case. Human newborns are fairly helpless when it comes to surviving unaided which is why they rely on parents or carers to fulfil their primary drives like, for example, satisfying their hunger and thirst.

It is important therefore that they are assured of non-abandonment – hence an attachment to the mother ensures their survival. Although the mother is the most common attachment figure, if absent, the role can be assumed by a different primary caregiver, such as the father, a sibling or a nanny, as long as there is an enduring relationship based on a reciprocal bond (Papalia, Olds and Feldman 1999). There is little evidence alluding to the attachment figure having to be the birth mother. Provided the caregiver is sensitive to the infant's needs and responds in a consistent caring way, an attachment will form. Furthermore the carer does not have to be female (Hrdy 2011). Findings from numerous studies have shown that fathers make good carers too, and that these attachments are just as effective in terms of the child's future socio-emotional development (Ramchandani, Domoney, Sethna, Psychogiou *et al.* 2013).

According to Bowlby, the infant will show the following attachment behaviours towards the carer: approach behaviour, no fear of parents (or carers), receptive to being cared for, will seek out the carer and maintain close proximity but will show anxiety if separated. Innate attachment behaviours, such as crying when distressed, smiling and gazing at parents, looking cute and helpless and making contact noises, help to ensure that a bond is made between carer and infant. Attachment behaviour, according to Bowlby, is manifested through an emotional tie entwined with dependency and, provided the carer responds to these attachment behaviours, a bond is made and the chances of survival are increased.

### Bowlby's notion of intraorganismic organisation

Before Bowlby's ideas of attachment, theorists, such as Freud, believed that the carer's role was to provide a cupboard love which he defined as a relationship between carer and infant based on provision (i.e. the carer provides food and drink). Harlow's studies of rhesus monkeys in 1962 dispelled this view by providing evidence to show the importance of providing comfort, security, protection and love. In Harlow's experiments, young rhesus monkeys were separated from their mother and encaged with two wired models acting as surrogate mothers: one wired with a feeding bottle attached and the other covered in a cosy cloth providing warmth and comfort. Infant rhesus monkeys would cling to the cloth covered model but when hungry they fed from the wired model, returning to the cloth model once satiated. The cloth covered model simulated the biological mother by providing the infant with a sense of security and comfort. This happens in human infants too where the mother (or carer) provides more than food and water – she provides a bond or emotional tie to reassure the infant that it will not be abandoned. Attachment therefore is not merely a learned or acquired behaviour but rather an internal predisposition which Bowlby referred to as intraorganismic organisation. This means that the infant is biologically organised or ready to form attachments to carers (Ainsworth 1973, Bowlby 1969). Bowlby believed that attachment to others is based on an experience-expectant neurological system. In other words, it makes sense for our neurology to have evolved to expect human contact given that contact with others is a certainty. Organisms who are innately predisposed to form attachments to carers are more likely to survive.

Given that the brain and biological systems of infants are still developing, they find it particularly difficult to manage their stress and emotions experienced. It is not until the age of four that the control of biological mechanisms begins to emerge, but even this has been linked to having a good caregiver who can help soothe the infant from any stress through holding and cuddling (Gerhardt 2004). In the absence of being cared for, high levels of cortisol (the stress hormone) are released which means these infants will have difficulty managing their feelings and could as a consequence become overwhelmed with stress.

### Bowlby's notion of internal working models

After 18 months, attachment becomes more complex and it is during this time that the child begins to form 'internal working models' regarding the relationship held with the primary carer – hence an internal working model is the child's memories of the attachment relationship. These memories are used by infants to make an appraisal of their relationship with their carer enabling them to formulate expectations of their carer's behaviour under different circumstances. Infants begin to understand the type of relationship they have with their carer and will try to modify any plans which do not accommodate their needs. According to Bretherton (1985), children who are rejected or abused when they seek comfort from their parents during stressful situations form negative internal working models signalling that they are unworthy of attention and care. Bowlby claimed that under circumstances of rejection and abuse children often develop multiple models describing the nature of attachment to their carer which can be contradictory or incompatible. For example in the case of the following multiple model, 'I believe that mother is unfailingly loving and has always acted in my best interest/I believe that mother is ridiculing and rejecting and does not consider my interests', both beliefs cannot co-exist harmoniously at the same time. Co-existence of conflicting beliefs causes confusion about the relationship in question.

### Ainsworth's Strange Situation

The nature of attachment has been studied in more detail by Mary Ainsworth's (1967; Ainsworth, Bell, and Stayton 1971) work on the Strange Situation. Ainsworth observed how babies interact with their mother during a set time period which is divided into:

- mother present in the playroom with the infant;
- stranger enters the room;
- mother leaves infant alone with the stranger;
- mother returns and the stranger leaves the room.

From her mother–child observations in the Strange Situation, three categories of infant emerged:

- Anxious/insecure-avoidant (A-dyad) infants ignore the mother; indifferent to her; no distress on her departure and avoid her when she returns; stranger is treated the same as mother.
- **Securely attached** infants (B-dyad) play with mother who is accepted; distressed on her departure; seek contact on her return; stranger is treated differently from mother.
- Anxious/insecure ambivalent/resistant infants (C-dyad) are wary whilst mother is present; distressed on her departure; express anger; actively seek her contact on return but resist her when contact is offered.

Ainsworth's research has been extended to toddlers and adults to see if Bowlby's (1979) contention that, '[a]ttachment behaviour is held to characterize human beings from the cradle to the grave' (p.129) has any evidence to support it. Ainsworth introduced the idea of secure base behaviour based on a child's secure attachment to the carer. She described secure base behaviour in children as originating from having a close bond with the carer who provides a sense of security. Secure base behaviour is shown in the way the child relates to the carer – will want to be near the carer, remain in sight of the carer and will happily return to the carer who is perceived as the secure base. Crowell, Treboux, Gao *et al.* (2002) have demonstrated that Ainsworth's description of the secure base phenomenon provides a cogent perspective on the secure base behaviour of adults. 'Secure base experience in childhood leads to the development of representations that in turn guide secure base behaviour later in life' (Crowell *et al.* 2002, p.2).

These findings suggest that secure relationships in infancy and childhood will influence the way in which future relationships are formed. This is basically down to two factors: the development of a sense of trust in people and their close environment and, the ability to regulate their emotions. The development of these two factors is more likely to be met within the context of a secure attachment. Secure attachments further enable a child to explore its surroundings in the knowledge that the attachment figure will still be there hence providing a secure base. It is through exploring the immediate environment that a child can acquire more skill competency and greater independence. Having childhood experiences such as these is used as a basis for making future attachments which are also likely to be passed on to any offspring. This suggests therefore an intergenerational transmission of attachment patterns – hence the way you are reared is the way you end up rearing your own children.

Research findings have provided support for the notion of intergenerational transmission of attachment patterns. For example, mothers of anxious–avoidant infants respond to their infant's cries and demands only when they are in the mood to do so – ignoring their child at all other times and being less sensitive to their infants' requests and needs (Smith and Pederson 1988). Hence infants behave the way they do because they expect to be rebuffed rather than comforted by their mother. Anxious–resistant infants experience inconsistency from their mother therefore finding it difficult to anticipate how she will behave next. Mothers of **securely attached** infants, however, are accessible, consistent and sensitive, and respond to their infants' cries and signals (Isabella, Belsky and von Eye 1989) which enables these infants to trust and count on their carer (Clarke-Stewart and Hevey 1981). Bowlby argued that internal working models should be stable across generations which makes sense given that individuals draw on their own working models developed in childhood.

There is evidence that mothers with secure babies recall being secure when they were infants. Main (1985) conducted Adult Attachment Interviews (AAI) which included probes for descriptions of:

- close relationships in childhood;
- supportive memories;
- contradictory statements;
- evaluations of the relationships with parents.

Main (1985) asked participants to give five adjectives that best described their relationships with each parent during childhood, qualifying these with supportive episodic (i.e. events) memories. Four patterns of maternal attachment representations were defined: two patterns corresponding closely to their infant's secure attachment to them five years earlier and two patterns corresponding to insecurely attached infants. Main (1985) found that there are adult attachment-types corresponding with Ainsworth's categories (see Table 4.1).

*Table 4.1* Adult attachment-types corresponding with infant attachments

| Adult attachment-types | Type of infant attachment (using the Strange Situation) |
| --- | --- |
| 1  Secure/autonomous with respect to attachment | Secure infants |
| 2  Dismissing of attachment | Avoidant infants |
| 3  Preoccupied by past attachments | Ambivalent infants |
| 4  Unresolved with respect to traumatic attachment related events | Disorganised / disoriented infants |

Main 1985

Insecure-avoidant mothers are more likely to be ambivalent and unsupportive towards their offspring (Crowell and Feldman 1991). It is the fourth point of Table 4.1 which is of particular interest here and relates to Browne's research. The sentiment of point four supports the idea that a child not shown any love and who experiences a traumatic attachment will have difficulty reciprocating love to others. Children who have experienced unconditional love according to Browne (2013) seem to break the cycle of abuse and violence that perhaps their parents experienced when they were young. It is those unfortunate children, however, who experienced conditional love from an abuser who develop inappropriate sexual relationships as adults and fail to reciprocate unconditional love to their own offspring. This belief has led Browne to work closely with WHO, UNICEF and Save the Children UK, in an effort to treat abandoned, neglected and abused children and those who have experienced violence. Identifying children who are of high risk for delinquency in adolescence is difficult despite parental abandonment, rejection, neglect and abuse figuring highly in these cases.

Luntz and Widom (1994) reported a link between abuse and neglect and the onset of psychopathy in later years (see Chapter 7). Marshall and Cooke (1996) studied 105 offenders, 50 of whom were diagnosed as psychopaths. They found that the psychopathic offenders had a childhood history of poor discipline and supervision and continuous rejection by their parents. Van Ijzendoorn, Feldbrugge, Derks, de Ruiter et al. (1997) used the AAI method on 40 male offenders, in different forensic mental institutions, who had committed serious crimes such as murder, child sexual abuse and rape. The prominent attachment classifications in their study were unresolved-disorganised with regard to early abuse/trauma (U/d) and unclassifiable (CC). On a similar note, Fonagy, Target, Steele, Steele et al. (1997) found that 36 per cent of their prisoner sample were classified as U/d of which 82 per cent had been abused or neglected in childhood.

In 2001 Frodi, Dernevik, Sepa, Philipson and Bragesjo used the AAI approach to explore the personal histories of incarcerated psychopaths. The information obtained revealed that offenders with a higher score on the psychopathy scale committed more violent crime, had a higher conviction rate and were more likely to have been physically abused as children. There was a preponderance of dismissive attachment (D), U/d or CC classifications. Those classified as U/d or CC had experienced extreme forms of physical abuse, such as being held upside down in a barrel of water. Frodi et al. (2001) also reported that secure attachments in personality disordered criminal offenders (i.e. psychopaths) were a rarity. It is interesting that Bowlby's concept of the 'affectionless character' conceived in 1944 was used to describe an individual who as a child failed to form an attachment to a carer and continued to have difficulty developing relationships with others that held any meaning or emotional bond. It is interesting that the concept of the affectionless character is still as pertinent now as it was back then.

The impact of having an insecure attachment during childhood has further repercussions for other areas of socio-emotional and cognitive development. Children with secure attachments to their parents, for example, tend to develop a comprehensive understanding of emotions compared with children who had experienced problematic attachments (Thompson 1998). It was also shown that secure attachments help children to develop an advanced comprehension of emotions during pre-school years (de Rosnay and Harris 2002; Ontai and Thompson 2002), which is partly attributed to the open communication encapsulated in secure relationships (Thompson 2000). With openly communicative parents, the mother, in particular, will have conversations about her emotions, how she is feeling and descriptions of emotions that her children can assimilate (Meins, Fernyhough, Wainwright, Das Gupta *et al.* 2002). This communication provides an abundance of information about emotions and the understanding of emotions in others which will ultimately help in the development of a mature **Theory of Mind**.

## Development of Theory of Mind

Theory of Mind (ToM) is important for interpreting the intentions and actions of other people: it is a mechanism enabling us to 'put ourselves into someone else's shoes' and see the world from their perspective. ToM research focuses more on the cognitive element of interpreting people's behaviour but the emotional aspect is equally important. Hence since its introduction the definition of ToM has been expanded to include attention, desires, emotions, beliefs, knowledge, pretence and thinking (Flavell 2004).

ToM has definitions varying from social understanding (Carpendale and Lewis 2004), mental-state understanding (Flavell 2000) and emotion understanding (Harris 1989). It is the understanding of emotion which has received much attention in its link with the mother attachment figure. Denham, Zoller and Couchoud (1994), for example, examined language interaction between mother and child, in particular the frequency of references made to emotion and the number of explanations devoted to emotions (i.e. I am happy because you have eaten all your food). They found that it was the number of explanations to different emotions given that impacted on children's understanding of emotion. It has been argued that this type of communication occurs more often in close relationships such as secure attachments. Ainsworth, Blehar, Waters and Wall (1978) provided evidence of different types of mother–infant attachment and how this ultimately influences future openness of communication between mother and child (Emde, Wolf and Oppenheim 2003). Furthermore, as discussed earlier by Thompson (2000) there is a strong connection between a secure attachment, open communication and advanced socio-emotional and cognitive development. If Thompson (2000) is correct then we can ask what happens to children in insecure attachments who are rejected, neglected or abused.

This was examined by Raikes and Thompson (2006) using a longitudinal study of 42 mothers and 42 children (22 girls and 20 boys) enrolled onto Early Head Start, a programme designed to promote child development among those living in poverty. They found that family dynamics was important. In family conditions where the child was exposed to intense and on-going negativity (i.e. like the mother being depressed), problems of understanding emotions was a common occurrence. This was a consequence of there being reduced, ineffective or no open communication. Dunn and Brown (1994) showed negative emotion in families to be causal in the reduction of understanding emotions among pre-schoolers. Furthermore, Teti, Gelfand, Messinger and Isabella (1995) found children had an increased likelihood of having an insecure attachment if their mother was depressed. Garber and Mardin (2002) argued, however, that having an insecure attachment in addition to the mother being depressed could be causal factors for the development of poor emotional understanding rather than this being a feature of the mother's depression alone.

Raikes and Thompson (2006) considered what happens if the mother–child relationship is secure and the family dynamics are positive yet the mother has depression. How would this impact on the child's understanding of emotions? They found that the family's emotional atmosphere was important to the child's development of understanding emotion but worked independently of the communication between mother and child and a child's attachment status. Their findings are supportive of open communication in association with a secure attachment in promoting the understanding of emotion. These findings extend to other areas of parenting which will be considered next in relation to the socialisation of moral behaviour in children.

## Socialisation of moral behaviour

### Theory of Moral Development

As mentioned earlier in this chapter, parents are the first informal socialising agents that the child comes into contact with and it is their role to teach their children the norms, rules and mores of society through the process of socialisation. In addition to the important roles of carers, parents need to teach their children right from wrong (i.e. moral behaviour). The teaching of moral behaviour is part of what effective parenting is all about, and it goes beyond merely punishing unacceptable behaviour and rewarding acceptable behaviour. As moral understanding and its evaluation for subsequent behaviour has particular significance in explaining transgressions committed by children, adolescents and adults, it will be addressed in detail here. From an early age the child has to learn and incorporate what is unacceptable (wrong) behaviour from what is acceptable (right) behaviour – in other words a morality. Theorists such as Freud, Piaget and Kohlberg have all developed their own versions of how we acquire a sense of morality. The most comprehensive and widely accepted theory, however, is that by Lawrence Kohlberg (1969) who combined a series of levels and stages in his account of moral development. Refer to Table 4.2 for a detailed account of Kohlberg's Theory of Moral Development.

In Kohlberg's levels and stages of moral development, there is an increasing tendency for moral behaviours to be internalised such that they become ingrained and a part of the individual's motive system in the guidance of future behaviour. As individuals progress through the different levels and stages, the advances in their **moral reasoning** reflects increasing intelligence. Young children for example often have to be coaxed into accepting the value of the moral through reward and punishment schedules. At this pre-conventional level they want to avoid the punishment and so behave accordingly without really understanding why the behaviour is wrong. This is a very egocentric (i.e. self-centred) view of the world where their behaviour is motivated by what it can achieve for them. As the child gets older the moderating factor becomes what other people will think of them if they behave inappropriately.

In late adolescence and adulthood the individual's behaviour is driven by ethical standards and human rights. How moral behaviour develops is very much in the hands of the parents as they are responsible for enabling their

*Table 4.2* Kohlberg's Theory of Moral Development

| Levels and stages | | Behaviour and attitudes expected |
|---|---|---|
| *Pre-conventional level* | | *Morality is extremely defined* |
| Stage 1 | Morality of punishment and obedience | Avoidance of punishment |
| Stage 2 | Morality of naïve instrumental hedonism | Egocentric perspective guided by pleasantness or unpleasantness of personal consequences |
| *Conventional Level* | | *Social system where an interest in people's behaviour is shown* |
| Stage 3 | Morality of maintaining good relations | Morality based on approval from others |
| Stage 4 | Morality of maintaining social order | Rules and laws define morality using instruments of social order |
| *Post-conventional level* | | *Realistic moral rules have principles applying to all situations and societies* |
| Stage 5 | Morality of social contracts | Obey societal rules for the common good. Sometimes individual rights outweigh laws |
| Stage 6 | Morality of universal ethical principles | Societal laws and rules are based on ethical values perceived as justified |
| Stage 7 | Morality of cosmic orientation | Adoption of values that transcend societal norms |

Adapted from Kohlberg 1969

children to understand why morals are there and why rules should be obeyed. Smetana (1990) showed that offenders tended to have low levels of moral reasoning – comparable to Kohlberg's pre-conventional level. Previously it was found by Ruma and Mosher (1967) that low levels of moral reasoning related to reduced feelings of guilt. These findings combined suggest that individuals with low moral reasoning ability fail to understand why their behaviour is inappropriate but find it difficult to feel bad about having behaved in this way. This could, in part, be due to their egocentric understanding of the world – a facet of pre-conventional thought. This will be returned to later in this chapter.

Why we, as social beings, are innately endowed with the capacity to embrace the importance of adopting morals, is a challenging question. It would seem that the process of learning right from wrong relies on effective socialisation from our parents but there are other factors which ensure the understanding and adoption of morals: ToM (as discussed earlier) and the emotion called empathy. Empathy is an emotion which normally surfaces when we observe someone in pain – almost as though we are actually experiencing the pain ourselves. Feeling empathy allows us to also sympathise with the other person and possibly to behave altruistically (i.e. helping or pro-social behaviour). Without empathy, an understanding of emotions and being able to interpret the intentions of others would be problematic. This can be clearly seen in psychopaths (see Chapters 7, 10 and 11) whose moral systems are different to most other people (Hare 1980, 1990). Studies reveal that psychopaths are capable of understanding how others might think and feel but are unable to experience this themselves, which might help to explain why **criminal psychopaths** can inflict extreme pain and suffering on their victims. Whether empathy is an innate emotional disposition that psychopaths do not have or whether they fail to develop empathy because of toxic attachments in their childhood are difficult questions to answer. In Chapter 7 this will be debated using the nature–nurture angle; here, however, we will consider different parenting skills and styles to ascertain which are most successful in developing children's understanding of right from wrong. Research addressing children's understanding of shame and guilt will also be considered as this is pinnacle to how the child responds and reacts to having transgressed.

## Influence of parental moral reasoning skills

Researchers have considered the ways that parents resolve conflict, in particular what they say and the actions they take towards their children. Kochanska, Aksan and Nichols (2003), for example, found that the more negative a mother is to her child the greater the likelihood of having a non-compliant child in later years. Hoffman (1975) previously found links between talking about feelings, understanding the effect actions have on others and children's moral development: finding that the more knowledge about their feelings and actions they had the more pro-social behaviour towards others in distress exhibited and the higher the level of compliant behaviour shown (Zahn-Waxler, Radke-Yarrow and King 1979; Maccoby and Martin 1983). Conversely, parental control using power assertion strategies (i.e. physical punishment, rejection and neglect) had short-term but not long-term compliance: power-oriented strategies do little to help facilitate ToM and cooperation. For example, Hughes, Deater-Deckard and Cutting (1999) found a positive correlation between the warmth shown by the mother and a child's ToM but a negative correlation when the mother behaved negatively towards her child. The mother's behaviour (whether warm or showing negative control of her child) was found to influence how her child behaved towards others.

Kochanska (1992) found that a child's interpersonal skills with a peer group reflected the quality of interaction with the mother. Mothers' influence strategies were assessed when their toddlers were five years old, which interestingly predicted their own children's influence style used on their peers. If the mother's influence strategy was to use frequent negative control (equivalent to power-oriented control) then the child's influence style with peers was an unsuccessful aggressive approach. If she used polite guidance then this was adopted by the child. If on the other hand her commands were consistently unclear her child was less likely to behave pro-socially towards peers. In another study Weiss, Dodge, Bates and Pettit (1992) showed that early parental harsh discipline was associated with aggressive behaviour in their children – this aggressive behaviour was primarily directed towards their peers at kindergarten.

In Baumrind's (1972) study, 3–4 year olds were observed at home and at nursery school for the following behaviours:

- self-control;
- tendency to approach new unexpected situations;
- vitality;
- self-reliance;
- competency at expressing warmth towards playmates.

Their behaviours were coded and rated from which three groups emerged:

- Group 1 who were mature/competent;
- Group 2 who were moderately self-reliant and self-controlled but showed little interest in others;
- Group 3 who were immature, showing less self-reliance and self-control but more dependency on adults.

The parents of these children were also assessed for:

- the extent of control they showed and how this influenced their child's activities and behaviour;

- the level of maturity demands they made, such as pressure to perform according to their own degree of competency;
- clearness of their communications with their child, such as reasons for doing what they say;
- the extent of warmth/compassion shown.

Baumrind's findings demonstrated a clear link between the child's behaviour and the parents' style of upbringing:

- children's parents of those in Group 1 were high on all the assessed areas;
- children's parents of those in Group 2 tended to be controlling and lacked warmth or affection;
- children's parents of those in Group 3 were affectionate but failed to control and demand enough from their children.

Baumrind concluded that the best parents were warm and affectionate but showed clarity in the way they communicated and rewarded responsible behaviour.

It is clear that such parents are supportive of their children, who in turn are generally acknowledged by their offspring (East 1989; East and Rook 1992). The extent of support provided within a parent–child relationship and the agreement of this support by the child differed for withdrawn, aggressive and sociable children. Data from 290 sixth graders and their parents revealed that withdrawn girls and aggressive boys perceived less support in their father–child relationships. Mothers of aggressive and withdrawn children, and fathers of aggressive children perceived less support in the relationships with their children. Sociable children, however, were more likely to agree with their parents over the level of support provided (East 1989; East and Rook 1992). It was found by Eisenberg and McNally (1993) that parents who are warm and encouraging, and show sensitive and sympathetic concern for their children, have children who are likely to react in a concerned way towards others in distress. Children who are sociable and assertive are more likely to help, share and comfort others experiencing distressful situations. The opposite is true for angry and punitive parenting which only disrupts the developmental pathway for empathy and sympathy at an early age (Eisenberg, Fabes, Shepard, Murphy et al. 1998).

In addition to parenting styles, the behaviour of parents (who act as role models to their children) can also be a robust factor in influencing the way their children behave towards others.

### Parents as social role models

Parents act as role models. Bandura and Walters emphasised the importance of imitation (or modelling) in the learning of violence. They pointed to considerable evidence demonstrating a link between physically aggressive and punitive parents and physically aggressive children. For example if criminal parents with criminal values behave antisocially, it is highly likely that their children will imitate and use them as role models. According to Bandura, children learn morally relevant behaviours through modelling and reinforcement and learn what is morally wrong or socially acceptable through their parents' reactions. Bandura's Social Learning Theory accounts for this:

- children imitating their parents' behaviour through observation;
- learning what constitutes the difference between moral and conventional transgressions through examples set by their parents.

In other words children learn that moral transgressions break moral codes whereas conventional transgressions violate rules.

Smetana (1981) asked 3–4 year olds to describe and separate a bad from a not so bad act. Putting toys in the wrong place was described as a little bad whereas hitting a child as very bad. The children's ability to appreciate the difference between the two examples illustrated understanding of gradations of seriousness (Davidson, Turiel and Black 1983). It is problematic, however, for children to learn this difference when their parents do not set appropriate standards in both their teachings and as role models. Smetana, Kelly and Twentyman (1984), however, found that understanding of the different types of wrongdoing seems to develop regardless of personal experiences such as having experienced physical abuse or neglect. Toxic attachments in childhood might nevertheless have a hand in causing later problems such as antisocial, delinquent behaviour and criminality per se. Could it, however, be more specifically a result of the rejection often encapsulated within a toxic attachment?

When children are rejected by their parents, they are left with a rejecting parent as a role model from which to imitate. They also miss out on effective guidance on how to manage their emotions in different situations including anger and fear and importantly shame and guilt. These emotions are pertinent for developing moral understanding and a mature ToM but rejecting parents fail to provide children with an awareness of when it is appropriate to show pride and when they should feel shame or guilt. These emotions are known as second higher-order emotions because they are self-conscious emotions involving injury to or enhancement of a sense of self (Tangney and Fischer 1995). In 18–24 month olds, shame and embarrassment is shown by lowering the eyes and head and burying their faces in their hands. Guilt can be shown by returning a snatched toy followed by the patting of a friend's shoulder in a friendly way. Adult instruction, however, is necessary to indicate when it is socially acceptable to experience these self-conscious emotions, which clearly play an important role in the development of moral behaviour. If adult instruction is absent or misguided, as is very often the case in rejecting, neglecting and abusing families, then how can these children be expected to know under which social situations self-conscious emotions should be displayed?

How shame and guilt is experienced by bullies and victims, for example, was addressed in a study by Menesini and Camodeca (2008). They used The Shame and Guilt Questionnaire devised by Olthof, Schouten, Kuiper, Stegge *et al.* (2000) depicting ten situations (five eliciting shame only and five eliciting both shame and guilt). The following example taken from Olthof *et al.* (2000) illustrates a shame only situation: 'You didn't sleep well . . . teacher asked you a question . . . you didn't understand. How do you feel?' An example of a shame and guilt situation is, 'You and your mother . . . sitting at a table . . . move on your chair . . . mother tells you to stop . . . you don't . . . juice . . . spills over the table . . . your mother's letter. How do you feel?'

Using a Likert scale, Menesini and Camodeca (2008) tested 121 children aged 9–11 years for guilt and shame across different situational scenarios. They found that children gave more guilt scores when the perpetrators of the shame and guilt situations caused harm on purpose but if the harm was unintended then children felt less guilt. Menesini and Camodeca also found that children who are bullies expressed lower levels of shame and guilt towards the shame and guilt situations. This was explained by Ciucci and Menesini (2004) as a consequence of bullies being indifferent to any harm caused and proud that they were able to cause harm to their victims. It was suggested that their ego-centric reasoning and inclination to dissociate themselves from the suffering they inflict on their victims were contributory factors. Whether bullies lack feelings of shame and guilt or whether becoming a bully makes them experience less shame and guilt is a 'what came first' question – the chicken or the egg?

What is clear, however, is that parents must take some responsibility in the socialisation of their children: to understand right from wrong and when to feel shame or guilt. Parental rejection, neglect and abuse during childhood clearly influence attachment, understanding of emotion, ToM, moral development and the application of self-conscious emotions. It also encourages a mind-set or a way of perceiving the behaviour of others which can interfere with how cause is attributed to the behaviour of others: the reason why someone behaves the way they do. It has been shown that children who experience rejection, neglect and abuse often give negative reasons (i.e. make a **hostile attribution**) for why someone (i.e. the protagonist) performed a misguided act in situations where the intent is ambiguous. **Securely attached** children, on the other hand, are more likely to give the benefit of the doubt.

### Hostile attribution due to parental rejection, neglect or abuse

Children's cognitive processing skills have been considered in the light of how parenting variables shape the way children interpret the intentions of others, known as social information processing (Hart, Ladd and Burleson 1990;

Strassberg, Dodge, Pettit and Bates 1994). The processing of social information has been explored by using narratives to describe the behaviour of protagonists portraying ambiguous intent. Crick and Dodge (1996) demonstrated a particular type of attribution which portrayed the protagonist's ambiguous intent as negative or hostile which has become known as 'hostile attributional bias' a term coined by Nasby, Hayden and DePaulo in 1979. By this Nasby *et al.* meant an individual who is inclined to interpret people's intentions as negative from their actions observed. It was found by Waldman (1988) that aggressive and rejected children demonstrated hostile attributional bias more often than secure children.

Another interesting connection was found between moral reasoning and social information processing by Speicher (1994) who re-analysed Kohlberg's data with an eye to finding patterns of moral reasoning between parents and offspring. A connection between the level of moral reasoning between parents and offspring was found whereby parents with good levels of moral reasoning had children with similarly good levels of moral reasoning. This supported the findings by Walker and Taylor (1991) of a correlation between higher levels of moral development in children and supportive interactions with their parents. Janssens and Deković (1997) found evidence that children reasoned at an advanced level about pro-social issues when their parents were supportive and used a style of punishment that involved talking and explaining why the behaviour in question was wrong and the implications this behaviour has for others. This style of punishment is known as inductive or authoritative punishment which will be discussed further in the next section on high and low risk factors. Palmer and Hollin (1997) investigated the effects of parental support on the development of moral reasoning. They found university students who perceived their parents as showing warmth and acceptance towards them, tended to have high levels of moral reasoning. Palmer and Hollin (2000) used a self-report method to examine a multitude of inter-relationships between moral reasoning, perceptions of parenting and social information processing, and the impact these had on levels of delinquency. Those adolescents who perceived their father as rejecting had immature moral reasoning skills and showed more hostile attributional bias. Furthermore, they found having a history of parental rejection, low moral reasoning ability and high attribution bias related strongly to higher self-reported delinquency rates. Palmer and Hollin (2000) concluded that a profound interaction between nurturing factors and social-cognitive processes exists.

Thus far the contribution of parenting styles and the socialisation of children by parents have been addressed. This has been examined in the context of socio-emotional and socio-cognitive development in children of varying familial relationships. It is clear that children who have experienced toxic attachments and who are nurtured within rejecting, neglecting and abusing families are more likely to have impaired moral development, ToM, social information processing skills and an immature understanding of emotions. Overall they have problems initiating and maintaining relationships and with understanding and interpreting people's intentions from their actions. Nevertheless despite all the odds there are some children who overcome the adversities experienced in childhood by managing to escape the detrimental effects these can cause. They appear to be protected and resilient but how can this occur? What should psychologists be considering when addressing why some individuals succumb to, while others escape from, the detrimental effects of childhood adversities? Factors of high and low risk are considered to hold the key in explaining this, discussed next.

## High and low risk factors

Childhood factors identified by Farrington (1990b) were divided into six risk factor categories:

- troublesome behaviour and dishonesty;
- convicted family member;
- low intelligence and school attainment;
- poor child rearing;
- impulsiveness;
- economic deprivation.

Those factors considered as adverse included:

- low family income;
- large family;
- a convicted parent;
- poor child rearing;
- a non-verbal IQ score up to 90.

It was found that 63 boys in the study had three or more of these adverse factors and 46 of them were convicted up until the age of 32 which translates to 73 per cent of the original sample of boys. The remaining 17 were considered isolates (i.e. loners) at school which Farrington suggested might have protected them from delinquency. Furthermore, particular life factors, such as unemployment, increased crimes of theft, fraud, robbery and burglary (all considered to provide financial security), while marriage helped to reduce offending (unlike divorce or separation, which increased it) and moving away from London severed ties with delinquent peers. All these factors in varying combinations had differential effects on crime **persistence** and desistence, and on the longevity of criminal careers.

Similar **adverse factors** likely to increase delinquency were outlined by Rutter and Giller (1983) at the same time as considering low risk or what is known as **protective factors** for delinquency. The five adverse factors are:

1   parental criminality;
2   intra-familial discord;
3   inconsistencies in response to unacceptable behaviour;
4   family size and siblings;
5   socio-economic status.

Parents set a social role model for children to follow and socialise their children to adopt socially acceptable attitudes and moral behaviour through appropriate levels of discipline. Hence, parents with deviant attitudes provide their children with deviant models of behaviour which they later identify with. Therefore, deviant parents fail to provide models of normative and pro-social behaviour. The five factors outlined by Rutter and Giller (1983) are often considered to be prerequisites for the development of delinquency. Much research has been focused on parental criminality which we will consider first.

## Parental criminality

There is evidence in support of an increased likelihood of delinquents having criminal parents (McCord 1979; West 1982). West and Farrington (1973) conducted an important longitudinal survey in London known as the Cambridge Study (previously discussed in Chapter 3) which showed that 37.9 per cent of boys who became delinquent had a parent with a criminal record by the time the boy was 10, compared with 14.6 per cent of non-delinquents. Jonsson (1967) previously found that 17 per cent of fathers of delinquent boys were recidivists whereas only 4.5 per cent of fathers of non-delinquents were. According to Robins, West and Herjanic (1975), delinquents are more likely to nurture delinquent children thus creating an intergenerational transmission effect for aggression (Huesmann 1988; Widom 1989a; Widom 1989b). Criminal, antisocial and alcoholic parents are more likely to have criminal sons as found in the St. Louis study by Robins in 1979. Lahey, Piacentini, McBurnett, Stone *et al.* (1988) further found this to extend to conduct disorder where 50 per cent of children exhibiting the clinical symptoms had a parent (usually the father) with an antisocial personality disorder (compared with 11 per cent of children with other disorders). A combined effect of paternal deviance and parental aggressiveness and conflict made the strongest impact on whether children became delinquent (McCord 1986). Of course it should be borne in mind that parental criminality might have a biological basis as was discussed in Chapter 3, but the above findings suggest a nurture impact. When biological and social factors are considered together, a nature–nurture explanation for parental criminality appears highly likely.

## Intra-familial discord

Parental aggressiveness and conflict within families are often responsible for family disruption. Conflict between parents plays a prominent role in the early lives of delinquents and tends to influence the onset of conduct disorder in boys but not girls. West and Farrington's (1973) Cambridge Study found a multitude of family factors causing delinquency in children (including style of parental discipline, passive or neglecting parental attitude, poor supervision and parental conflict). As in later longitudinal studies, such as the Cambridge-Somerville study in the US (McCord 1979) and the Newcastle Thousand Family Study (Kolvin, Miller, Fleeting and Kolvin 1988), they found that separation from one or both parents for one month or more during the first 10 years of life influenced later delinquency. They all found that it made no difference to later delinquency whether the separation was before the age of 6 or between 6–10 years. Farrington (cited in McCord 1992) and the National Survey of Health and Development (Wadsworth 1979) supported findings exempting temporary or permanent separations due to illness or death from causing criminal behaviour, but separations resulting from marital breakdown as a precursor for criminality. What became apparent in all of these surveys was the disruption to a child's development beyond infancy and into schooling, resulting from unresolved, on-going marital issues. Disruption could be caused in many different ways like, for instance, a father's disengagement from his son's leisure pursuits, found by Farrington and West (1990) to be predictive of criminal behaviour persisting beyond 20 years of age. Mothers who had low expectations of their son's future career prospects were shown to constitute a risk factor for later delinquency (Farrington and West 1990).

It has also been found that parents of delinquents tend to hold negative attitudes towards their children and show less affection (Glueck and Glueck 1950). In families where little affection is displayed, the father–son relationship was more likely to be impaired than the mother–son relationship (Bandura and Walters 1959). A lack of affection shown by the mother when her son was 5–13 years old was a significant factor for future property-based offending. Personal crimes (i.e. against the person), however, were associated with parental discord and aggression directed at the child. Self-reports revealed how delinquents:

- experienced high parent–child conflict during childhood;
- were less trusting of their parents;
- experienced less intimate communication with their parents;
- perceived their parents to be rejecting of them (Palmer and Hollin 1997).

Rankin and Kern (1994) showed that forming just one strong attachment to either parent increased the risks of delinquency compared to the protective factor of having two strong parental attachments.

Relating to poor parental relationships is the increased likelihood of inadequate supervisory provision concerning the child's whereabouts, knowledge of who their children's friends are and the nature of activities they perform outside of the home. Inadequate supervision often fosters uncontrollable children with little knowledge and understanding of boundaries and rules. This was shown to be the case by Wilson (1987) who studied boys from deprived inner cities and compared their level of delinquency with the nature of parental supervision received. Interestingly, poor maternal supervision played a more central role for delinquency than did parental criminality per se. Farrington, Loeber, Yin and Anderson (2002) also found a link between poor supervision and high delinquency. Hirschi and Gottfredson (1988) argued that failing to supervise children provided opportunities for crime to occur rather than being causal in developing criminality. McCord (1979), however, suggested it is parental rejection rather than physical abuse or aggression towards children that is significant in delinquency and, that poor supervision is a form of rejection. McCord (1979) found a trend whereby 50 per cent of children who were rejected by their parents, 20 per cent who were neglected and abused by their parents and 11 per cent who had loving parents committed crime. Clearly rejecting parents are more likely to have children who commit crime than are loving parents. Family disruption also involves broken homes but the reason for the broken home is more important than a broken home in its own right. Rutter and Giller (1983) claimed that the association is strongest when absence is through divorce, desertion and separation rather than death. The way parents discipline their children is also connected with rejection, neglect and abuse, and the fact that these parents provide little supervision over their children – inconsistencies in punishment towards unacceptable behaviour will be considered next.

## Inconsistencies in response to unacceptable behaviour

Socialisation also overlaps with consistent responses to unacceptable behaviour in the guise of discipline. If the messages signalled to children are inconsistent then they are less likely to learn and understand the boundaries of what behaviours are permissive or forbidden within and outside of the family. There has been a host of studies considering different parental discipline strategies in relation to encouraging or staving off delinquency. A consensus of findings suggested that harsh and erratic parental discipline predicted later delinquency (West and Farrington 1973). Discipline has been categorised by Glueck and Glueck (1950) and later by West (1982) as harsh, punitive or lax and erratic. Hoffman and Saltzstein (1967) claimed that children who acquired a good grounding in moral behaviour had parents who used induction as their preferred approach to disciplining their children. In the case of children with poor moral behaviour, parents had relied upon power assertion. Hoffman (1977), however, identified three different types of discipline as:

1    Power assertion (physical punishment, criticism, threats and material deprivation).
2    Love withdrawal (non-physical expression of disapproval, withholding affection).

3    Induction (reasoning and a focus on the consequences of a child's actions for others).

Maccoby and Martin (1983) elaborated on Hoffman's and West's classifications of discipline by describing two types of interaction:

1    Affection (acceptance and warmth versus rejection and hostility).
2    Control (demanding and restrictive versus undemanding and permissive – leads to harsh but lax approach).

These combine to produce four distinct parenting styles:

1    *Authoritative*: accepting-demanding (promotes self-control and self-confidence).
2    *Authoritarian*: rejecting-demanding (power assertion has negative consequences: poor moral development, low self-esteem).
3    *Indulgent*: accepting-undemanding (poor socialisation).
4    *Neglecting*: rejecting-undemanding (poor socialisation).

Of course, these styles vary with intensity, frequency and consistency, but it is the element of erratic and inconsistent practices that are often observed in delinquent families.

Patterson (1986) linked deviance with discipline finding that parents of social aggressors (i.e. those who tease and hit siblings and have tantrums) criticised, made unreasonable commands and used coercive interactions with their children. Parents of stealers (i.e. those who lie, steal, are overactive and set fires) were uninvolved with their children and adopted a lax and inconsistent style of punishment. Again, we can see the importance that rejection plays in the upbringing of children. Not paying as much attention and failing to discipline children can occur in large families simply because it is more difficult to monitor all family members at the same time. Hence family size can also put children at risk of criminality.

### Family size and siblings

The issue of supervision and consistent punishment have important ramifications in large families. For instance, West (1982) showed, using data from the Cambridge Study, that delinquents are more likely to come from families with four or more children – the likelihood of juvenile delinquency doubled. Reasons for this include the following:

•    Large families are more likely to live in poor and overcrowded homes.
•    Greater stress and family disorganisation in a large family due to income, social economic status (SES) and parental criminality.

- More difficult to implement discipline in large families.
- Less supervision.
- Less parental attention and affection restricts the development of pro-social behaviour.
- Other siblings might model their behaviour on delinquent siblings.

This last point has been found to be influential in predicting later delinquency especially if members of the family were convicted of crimes before the boys were aged 10.

The point concerning SES will be considered next.

### Social economic status

Social economic status (SES) and relative poverty in families, Rutter and Giller's final key adverse effect, has also been linked to delinquency. This is the most tentative point raised as delinquency occurs across class and levels of economic status. What may differ is the nature of criminal activity as a direct consequence of resource accessibility. Moreover, as demonstrated in Rutter and Giller's fourth key adverse effect, SES and relative poverty are more likely to be associated with larger families. Difficulties arising in larger families, such as discipline and supervision, create opportunities for delinquency which confound any contribution that SES might make. Delinquency will be explored further in Chapter 10. In the next section we will explore factors which help to reduce the likelihood of committing crime but first it is important to separate what is meant by a risk factor, a vulnerability factor and a protective factor.

### Low risk factors: Risk and resilience

Browne and other researchers have suggested that there are risk, vulnerability and protective factors which interactively contribute towards delinquency. These terms are defined as follows:

- a risk factor is something that causes damage to the person or a predictor of a poor outcome;
- a vulnerability factor pertains to the individual in a way that enables a risk factor to have a damaging effect;
- a protective factor, on the other hand, is something that is helpful to the individual and can stave off the detrimental effects of a risk factor (see Box 4.2).

In order to establish the extent of resilience (if any) that an individual has, the processes involved in risk, vulnerability and protective factors need to be unravelled – this is complicated and will vary from one individual to another.

In Box 4.2, protective factors known to aid resilience from delinquency are listed.

## Box 4.2

### Protective factors against delinquency

- Being female.
- Intellectual abilities.
- Cognitive appraisal of situations.
- Social competence.
- Strong achievement motivation.
- Self-esteem.
- Even temperament/self-regulation of emotion.
- Positive outlook/good coping skills.
- Supportive relationships/significant adult in life.
- Maternal affection.
- Inductive/authoritative punishment.
- Non-delinquent siblings and/or peers.
- Family, school and/or hobby involvement.
- Religion.
- New opportunities (i.e. moving home).
- First born.

Research findings are in support of the protective factors in Box 4.2, but as it is difficult to calculate the effectiveness of individual factors without considering the individual and his or her circumstances, cases have to be considered by their own merit. In other words, cases have to be considered in isolation as they are all different. The combination of risk and vulnerability factors is a complex equation which is explored in relation to Thompson and Venables in Box 4.3 (see Chapter 1 for discussion on age of criminal responsibility).

## Box 4.3

### What of Thompson and Venables?

Both Robert Thompson and Jon Venables are responsible for the murder of the toddler James Bulger. How can we account for what Thompson and Venables did to Bulger? Can their acts be adequately explained using a nurture account of criminality? The backgrounds of both Thompson and Venables were considered by social workers and psychologists. At the time it was said that they watched videos of films depicting violence and it was suggested that they were influenced by these films and enacted the scenes on the toddler, Bulger. It is interesting to note that Thompson came from a family background in which his parents and brothers had criminal records. Venables came from a dysfunctional family where he experienced violence. These family backgrounds pose high risk for deviancy and criminal behaviour. Prior to the incident both boys played truant from school and often wandered around the shopping precincts. Their parents were unaware of what their children were doing and provided little or no supervision. There was an absence of appropriate role models to follow, and in the case of Thompson, he had criminal siblings to model his behaviour on as well as his own parents. Both boys appear to have had little discipline in their lives and consequently knew no boundaries of what is acceptable or unacceptable behaviour (hence their profiles very much fitted Rutter and Giller's key adverse points). Additionally, their family roots follow an intergenerational transmission of aggression and violence. For both boys, a culture of violence and deviancy is all they knew. So can we really expect them to behave pro-socially, adopt non-deviant values and respect the norms of society? They do have factors in their lives that are high risk for delinquency. Venables has continued his deviant behaviour and was imprisoned in 2010 for using child pornography. Equally we could argue that murdering a toddler in the gruesome manner that they did defies a nurturance explanation and can only be explained away using nature accounts. Some experts working with Thompson and Venables claimed that they were born evil!

Clearly the parents and family per se have a significant impact on the way their children behave. Given the parental responsibilities of socialising their children to be moral and law abiding citizens, when this process goes wrong it is not surprising that children can become future criminals. This explanation, according to some theorists, is too simplistic and overemphasises the role of parents in the socialisation of their children as our next section, still within Bronfenbrenner's child-microsystem interaction shows.

## Child and microsystem (the influence of peers)

The Cambridge Study showed that delinquent boys were more likely to burgle, rob and steal from vehicles with another peer of the same age and sex; the most common reason for offending offered by delinquents was either a desire to have the stolen item or to seek excitement. Furthermore, by associating with delinquent peers at 14 years, their chances of being convicted as an adult increased. The influence of delinquent peers had a significant impact for the persistence in criminal activity whereas desistence from crime was more likely if bonds with delinquent peers were severed.

According to Judith Harris, peers are paramount in the socialisation of other peers, which in part explains why friendships tend to form among peers of similar background, attitudes, value systems and interests. According to Cognitive Developmental Theory, children first acquire an appreciation of what they wish to be, and the groups they want to be a part of (i.e. self and social categorisation) which they then use as a guide for their behaviour. They observe the behaviour of others who are consistent with their chosen categories and select appropriate behaviours to imitate. What possible factors could be responsible for two friends taking a person's life (i.e. Thompson and Venables)? Close friendships are ubiquitous and tend to last a life-time, so do we select carefully and become close to like-minded people?

Harris (1998) acknowledged the important influential effect that peers have on each other in her **Group Socialisation Theory** (GST). This is where children seek other children who are similar to themselves and the groups that they join have members who are also similar. As social beings we like to be liked by others, and one way of ensuring this is to behave and engage in activities supported by other group members. Children's groups, according to Harris, operate using the majority-rules rule – in other words, whoever comes to the group with behaviour that is different from the majority is the one who has to change. If for example the majority speak in Japanese, then the English girl has to change her language to suit her group or leave and join a different group where they speak English. Children socialise each other, modify each other's personalities, and get their ideas of how to behave by identifying with a group through the acceptance of its attitudes, behaviours, speech, and style of dress. Most of them do this automatically and willingly as they want to be like their peers, and peers will certainly remind them of the penalties for being different.

Other theories have been proposed to explain why the social bond between peers, especially gang members, is so strong. The Social Bond Theory was initially introduced by Travis Hirschi (1969) but revised and renamed as Social Control Theory. Hirschi (1969) defined the Social Bond Theory as, '[e]lements of social bonding include attachment to families, commitment to social norms and institutions (school, employment), involvement in activities, and the belief that these things are important' (p.16). The main emphasis is on attachment. In the cases where there is limited attachment to parents (especially if they are rejecting and provide an environment of insecurity), children often commit delinquent acts. This behaviour, according to Hirschi (1969), can become exacerbated if parents also entertain criminal ideals which are transmitted to their children. Hirschi also focused on the important role that peers and groups of peers play in influencing behaviour. There are four facets to Social Bond Theory:

1    attachment;
2    commitment;
3    involvement in activities;
4    a common value system with the attached society or subgroup fraction.

An attachment to a group can be conventional and therefore conform to society's general norms and values or it can be deviant and criminal – therefore an attachment to a group of peers can be a positive or deviant experience. Commitment to conform to society's norms and values depends largely on the effectiveness of informal socialising agents (i.e. the parents) as appropriate role models. If they fail to be effective role models to their children then the nature of commitment is likely to lie with factions (i.e. subgroups or sub-cultures) within mainstream society. A subculture, for instance, will have its own deviant value system operating outside of mainstream society – often so different from mainstream ideals that members conceal their membership by entering a hidden subterranean world. Hirschi argued that an individual with little attachment and commitment to mainstream society is more motivated to join deviant subgroups. This involves allegiance to the subgroup through the adoption of its value system and norms.

In support of Hirschi's Social Bond Theory, Hindelang (1973) showed that attachment to delinquent peers increased delinquency rather than conformity to mainstream values and norms. Weak social bonds to parents, for example, can facilitate delinquency, while strong social bonds to deviant peers can also lead to delinquency (LaGrange and Raskin White 1985). Attachment to devi-ant parents encourages the acceptance of their values and norms which was found to be the case for individuals with drug abusive parents who in later years followed in their parents' footsteps (Burton, Cullen, Evans, Dunaway *et al.* 1995). Lacourse, Nagin, Vitaro, Côté *et al.* (2006) found that boys raised under adverse low SES family conditions who were also hyperactive and non-pro-social tended to find solace in deviant peer groups.

The Social Bond Theory is considered an advocate of a general theory of crime based on social control. In 1990 Gottfredson and Hirschi further argued that those with low self-control tended to behave in an insensitive, impulsive, short-sighted and risk-taking manner making it difficult to desist from an opportunity to offend. Another perspective of the control approach introduced by Bandura in the 1970s is known as Social Learning Theory. The premise here is that children imitate role models through observation which can be direct (active participation) or indirect (vicarious participation). In relation to understanding crime and deviancy, Akers (1998) applied Social Learning Theory to explain how criminal behaviour is learned through observing devi-ant peers: behaviours are imitated and the justifications for these behaviours provided by peers help reinforce the behaviour. Thus there are two approaches explaining how deviant peer groups influence members to perform delinquent acts: control versus learning theories. Both approaches have empirical evidence supporting the pathway to delinquency (Akers and Jensen 2006; Gottfredson 2006) and, interestingly, more recently the initiation to cybercrime (Holt, Burruss and Bossler 2010; Morris and Higgins 2010).

Do control and learning theories, however, offer efficient explanations of why and how delinquent gang members can kill members from other gangs and innocent bystanders? Do these accounts provide evidence for Le Bon's (1895) law of mental unity? In other words, do learning and control theories explain a crowd becoming one vicious animal whereupon its participants lose all sense of an individual conscience (i.e. de-individuation). Le Bon (1895) claimed that de-individuation enables 'the mob' to be more cruel and impulsive than any individual acting alone, but does this explain how Thompson and Venables could torture and murder a young toddler? Both Thompson and Venables separately looked for another like-minded individual, which is in keeping with Social Learning Theory. It is unfortunate that they were able to find each other, and in each other they found a similar value system, which helped spur them on to commit murder. What of gangs' warfare? Are members of gangs attached, committed, involved and of similar values to each other in keeping with the Social Bond Theory? The Social Bond Theory in this context implies that individuals become 'hooked' by association with deviant peers, and eventually acquire deviant norms, values and behaviours. Alternatively, the Social Learning Theory views individuals as seeking membership of deviant gangs because they are looking for a 'substitute family' – wanting to be part of a subculture. This pathway offers a substitute family where the rewards for deviant behaviour from other gang members reinforce the behaviours to be repeated. Control and learning theories will be explored further in the next section on school and school processes conducive to deviancy, deviant peer formations and subcultures.

### Child and microsystem (school and school processes)

The connection between peers and school is high. It is at school where children make friendships and become involved with other children participating in similar school activities – like playing sport. The importance of having social bonds to family and peers has already been discussed but in this section the influence of schools for fostering strong social bonds will be examined. In particular we will look at how weak social bonds of attachment and commitment to school contribute towards delinquency and the formation of delinquent peer pairings and groupings. The school as a formal socialising agent for teaching children to conform to mainstream culture in society is considered first, followed by the way systems within schools influence delinquency (i.e. school processes).

### Schools

According to Cohen (1955) the education system imposes middle-class (M/C) values and standards on all children attending school. These values and standards imposed, Cohen argued, are often in conflict with working class (W/C) values and standards which create conflict for such children who have difficulty conforming to M/C school ideology. As these children behave differently and in a non-conforming way to M/C teacher expectations, they become

*Plate 4.1* Frightened schoolboy
© Mikael Damkier. Image used under license from Shutterstock.com. Available at http://www.shutterstock.com/pic.mhtml?id=2008063&src=id

labelled as delinquents. Cohen's approach emanates from a conflict perspective (see Chapter 1) which accounts for why some schools have more delinquency problems than other schools (if the school is located near W/C areas then more W/C children attend). Power, Alderson, Phillipson, Schoenberg and Morris (1967) and Power, Benn and Morris (1972), for instance, showed that delinquency ranged in schools from 1–19 per cent, a range remaining consistent over a six year period between surveys. This suggests that some schools have more of a problem with delinquency depending on their location. Power *et al.* (1972), however, concluded that it had nothing to do with the catchment area or rates of delinquency but rather was a consequence of school processes (see next section). Boxford (2006) studied pupils from 20 secondary schools, totalling 3,103 participants, in Cardiff (Wales). Pupils used the method of self-reporting for offences categorised as assault, vandalism, theft, robbery, break-in or other. Boxford (2006) found that just over 20 per cent said they were involved in one of the five categories of offence at school. This study provided information about the high level of offending occurring in schools.

In 2001 and 2008, Neill conducted surveys which divided schools for frequency of and experiences of problematic behaviour by pupils. For the majority of schools there had been little change in the rate of problem behaviour and the carrying of weapons, but for some schools with poor socio-economic status such problems were on the increase. Neill (2005) found that pupils attending schools in the London area who were issued with free school meals were more likely to be carrying weapons. According to Hobbs and Vignoles (2007) being entitled to free school meals was a good indicator of low income family status, intonating that children from low income families were more likely to carry weapons. Why this is so was not made clear but it is possible that these children had difficulty integrating in a system endorsing M/C values.

Since parents have more choice over which school they send their children to, some schools have become more popular than others. Schools which are the least popular are perceived as poor performing schools with problems of delinquency. Not all children are fortunate enough to avoid these schools and, for them, being at a low performing school can create many problems. West and Farrington (1973) attributed this problem of 'good and bad schools' to the increasing admittance of troublesome children (usually boys) to schools that already have a reputation for delinquency. They predicted that later delinquency was attributed to boys who already had behavioural problems and not the school itself. West and Farrington (1973) reported that the best school predictor for juvenile delinquency was the ratings from teachers and peers of the children displaying troublesome behaviour at 8–10 years of age. Of the boys rated as highly troublesome, many attended schools with a high delinquency reputation. The schools' reputations were based on a high or low delinquency intake, and with the exception of this factor, school processes per se were exonerated as explanations for delinquency. It appears that peer group and family characteristics contribute to whether children integrated with the school's academic culture or a delinquent one. In line with West and Farrington's research findings, it appears that pupils who have strong family social bonds are more likely to feel a part of their school and engage in school activities – they experience school membership. Whether these children come from families of low or high economic status makes no difference as it is the strength of family bond that is important. Rutter, Maughan, Mortimore and Ouston (1979), however, argued that what mattered was the nature of pupil intake. They reported in their Fifteen Thousand Hours study of 12 inner London schools that a high delinquency rate was related to the intake of low ability pupils. The four outcome variables that they considered (absenteeism, behaviour in school, academic attainment and delinquency), however, correlated with school processes and not pupil ability.

### School processes

Rutter *et al.* (1979) examined the contribution of school processes to the increasing levels of delinquency in their Fifteen Thousand Hours study. They found that delinquency was associated with:

- high autonomy of the teachers at the school in their planning of courses;
- the tendency of teachers to teach only in their own subject area;

- variation of disciplinary standards;
- frequent use of writing lines;
- giving extra work as a form of punishment;
- failure of teachers to provide positive feedback for pupils' work;
- reduced expectations that pupils will look after their own resources;
- the presence of low pupil peer group stability.

Hirschi (1969) found that academic failure during adolescence increased the risk of delinquency and that certain school processes might be responsible for this. Hirschi (1971) and Patterson (1986) found links between delinquency and inappropriate teaching strategies, special educational need and behaviours originating from the home environment. Hargreaves (1980) discovered that streaming (i.e. putting children of a similar academic ability together in the same class) in schools facilitated the formation of delinquent groupings. Streaming can be flexible where pupils can move up a class or down depending on their academic attainment. This unfortunately created classes where the able and the less able were segregated. Stable streaming on the other hand keeps the same cohort together. It is flexible streaming which can polarise groups into academic subcultures of the 'snobs' and 'swots' and the lower stream subcultures of the 'remedial'. This polarisation applied to staff also, where teachers who taught pupils in the lower streams had lower expectations of their pupils, labelled them as incapable and therefore created a self-fulfilling prophesy among their pupils of 'worthlessness' and/or 'stupidity'. Staff working under these circumstances showed low commitment and were more likely to leave which meant a high staff turnover rate (Hargreaves 1980).

Adult offenders frequently have had a history of low academic attainment at school (Hirschi 1971) attributed to rejection by the school, which only lowered self-esteem even more. Rejection by the school caused defiance, antisocial behaviour and disregard for school rules. These pupils were more likely to associate with similar minded peers who they found rewarding – thus supporting the Social Learning Theory. Deviant peers correlated positively with social skill deficits and academic failure in pre- and early adolescent boys (Patterson 1986), but as suggested by Glueck and Glueck (1950) these individuals are already likely to be delinquent prone. In the next section we address Bronfenbrenner's child-exosystem interaction by looking at how the media and the law influence a child's socialisation and impacts on their future behaviour.

## Child and exosystem (media and law)

The exosystem has a generic influence on individuals who come into direct contact with it but will vary across cultures as the law of the land and the specific laws governing how and what the media reports differs. In July 2011, for instance, the controversial newspaper The *News of the World* came into disrepute because its very own private detectives allegedly hacked into the mobile phones of murder victims and those who died in '7/7' London bombings in 2005 (see Chapter 2). This resulted in job losses, various arrests and the dissolution of the newspaper. Not only this but investigations led to widespread public anger and Rupert Murdoch lost the opportunity to buy out the other shareholders of BSkyB. This type of investigative journalism is illegal and has aroused public anger, which has led to a call for tighter legislation to prevent this from happening again. As discussed in Chapter 1, laws of the land evolve over time, especially laws pertaining to *mala prohibita* (i.e. statutory law defined by rules and regulation). Laws of *mala prohibita* tend to be shrouded in rules that should be obeyed and, if they are not, then there are consequences. Rule breaking results in sanctions against the individual such as fines and short-term incarceration. Cross-culturally, laws of *mala prohibita* vary slightly but individuals living in the same country will be subjected to identical rules under the umbrella of the same *mala prohibita* laws. In this section we will consider how the media and the law influence individuals on a day-to-day basis.

### Media

Media has many guises and different effects on individuals, however, research on how the media influences individuals has mainly focused on violence screened in films and depicted in pornographic magazines. Violence in films has received the most attention especially regarding the certificate rating on films that have violence, sex and violent sex scenes, but research findings are inconsistent and sometimes surprising. Friedrich-Cofer and Huston (1986) found that filmed violence had a small but robust significant effect on levels of subsequent aggression in viewers (although viewers were affected differently). Children of 8–12 years of age were found to be susceptible to the influence of violence depicted on television (Eron and Huesmann 1986). Eron and Huesmann (1986) found that violence on television affected boys more than girls. Factors such as low academic achievement and being unpopular among peers added to the influence of violence on television by increasing the occurrence of subsequent aggressive behaviour. Furthermore they found that children who already have aggressive tendencies were more likely to be influenced by violence broadcast on television.

Hennigan, Del Rosario, Heath, Cook et al. (1982) compared the crime rates between 1949 and 1952 among American cities receiving television broadcasting with those that had not yet been connected. According to their figures the introduction of television did not increase violent crime, such as murder, aggravated assault or burglary, but did increase larceny. Philips (1983), however, reviewed daily homicide figures and found a connection between watching a champion boxing match and a 12.5 per cent increase in murder after it was televised. Philips claimed that this was a direct effect of modelling on the winner of a match especially given that the increase of murder victims represented the same ethnicity as the loser of the match. Wood, Wong and Chachere (1991) considered a number of studies that assessed the effects of exposure to aggressive and non-aggressive films on children and adolescents. Within a school environment, children and adolescents watched either an aggressive or a non-aggressive film. Half of the cohort was told to play with their peers in a room with a one-way mirror from which researchers could observe the behavioural interactions occurring between peers. The remaining cohort was allowed to return to their classroom and interact with peers who had not seen any film. The behaviour of those in the observation room was observed and coded for any spontaneous aggression during their play activities. A marginal but significant effect from viewing aggressive material and behaving aggressively towards others was found. Although a marginal effect was found, Wood *et al.* (1991) concluded that multiple viewings of aggressive films might culminate to have a substantial effect on social behaviour over time. Huesmann and Taylor (2006) demonstrated a direct effect between viewing violent dramatic broadcasts on television or in films and short-term increases of aggressive attitudes (i.e. thoughts, emotions and behaviour) – in some cases this led to the act of actually harming others. Furthermore, Huesmann and Taylor (2006) argued that watching violent music videos causes viewers to become more accepting of a culture of violence.

There has been a debate as to whether children can tell the difference between real (actually reported on the news and documentaries) and make-believe (animations and realistic films) violence and, if being able to differentiate between the two types of presentation had any bearing on the incidence of aggressive behaviour during their social interactions. For example, in the eighteenth century, Goethe's novel *The Sorrows of Young Werther* provoked many young men to commit suicide after having read about Werther who killed himself because his love was unrequited – they too felt the same and copied Werther's actions, known as the 'Werther Effect' (Phillips 1974). Suicide is considered by some psychologists to be an aggressive act against the self (Conner, Meldrum, Wieczorek, Duberstein and Welte 2004; Maiuro, O'Sullivan and Vitaliano 1989; Rustein and Goldberg 1973). Imitation can be one explanation why children and adolescents are influenced by what they perceive as models of behaviour on their screens. After all, Goethe's novel had a strong influence on suicide rates in the eighteenth century: its readers were imitating the character in the book. Bandura, Ross and Ross (1961) discovered the strength of imitation when children were allowed to play with a 'Bobo' doll after watching an adult act aggressively towards the doll by punching it. Children who observed the behaviour later acted more aggressively towards their peers by imitating what they had seen the adult do earlier. It is well established that children imitate others but the 'Bobo' doll experiment demonstrated that they also imitate aggressive role models.

Another approach to understanding how exposure to violence can increase aggressive behaviour comes from Meadows' (2006) application of scripts and working models (see Chapters 13 and 14). Scripts in this context refer to memories of events and how these combine to create a world view of a specific type of experience. In the case of working models discussed by Bowlby, an infant whose mother fails to provide comfort during times of distress will develop memories of an uncaring mother. At the same time, these memories combine to form a script of what happens during times of distress. In this example mother does not care, and it is this interpretation which is generalised to similar situations throughout the lifespan. Scripts, in the same way as working models, explain why an individual interprets a world as a violent place. Furthermore, if an individual's interpretation of the world is one of violence, then it is likely that the scripts and working models will depict antisocial behaviour as well. This suggests that violent media will be influential for individuals who already ascribe to the notion of a violent world. In other words, exposure to violence on television might influence those with an aggressive disposition — hence individuals with an aggressive disposition might be more likely to select any form of media with a violent edge to it.

In relation to the debate concerning the contribution of violent media on behaviour, Brownmiller (1975) suggested that pornography encourages men to rape women through a process of dehumanisation. When the Obscenity Laws during the 1960s were relaxed in Denmark, studies suggested that there was no rise in sex offending. Despite this finding, however, a US Commission in 1986 concluded that pornography did indeed contribute to sexually deviant behaviour. Heavy usage of pornography by sex offenders is not unknown, but, as indicated by Carter, Prentky, Knight, Vanderveer and Boucher (1987), child molesters are more likely than rapists to rely on pornography for arousal both prior and during their paedophilic acts. The contribution of pornography towards violent sexual acts is ambiguous but findings suggest that of the many men who use pornography very few commit rape or acts of paedophilia. It appears therefore that individuals who use pornography and commit rape and/ or acts of paedophilia have a disposition to do so that is independent of reading and viewing such material (see Chapter 8).

## Law

For the most part, individuals only come into contact with the criminal justice system if they break the law: the more seriously they break the law the greater the sanctions. If less serious crimes are committed then the sanctions are greatly reduced (see Chapters 1 and 2). What is important to discuss here is why do some individuals break the law? What is it that stops the majority of us from committing crime? Why do we conform to and obey the rules of society? These questions are challenging and often have a multitude of answers. Consider Thompson and Venables (see Box 4.3). What makes these children different from other children? We know certainly that in the case of Thompson and Venables their upbringing was shrouded in violence and deviant attitudes. Their parents themselves might have had family backgrounds similar to the ones they created for their children. Using the consensus perspective (see Chapter 1), it can be argued that individuals adopt the values and mores of society which they readily accept and adhere to. The criminal justice system therefore is used for punishing those who do not conform to the norms set within society. The criminal justice system is a means to ensuring that those who offend accept that their current behaviour is wrong and needs to change in line with mainstream culture – a last resort to enforcing acceptance of society's norms and values. As discussed previously, the adoption of mainstream norms and values arises out of the socialisation process where children learn what constitutes acceptable behaviour. Parents who have deviant values and adopt a criminal way of life will expose their children to the same value system and lifestyle. Even if children are not directly socialised into thinking this way, they are likely to model their behaviour on their parents, so either way they are exposed to a value system and behaviour that is in conflict with mainstream society.

According to Hirschi, conformity is maintained through having social bonds with the family, peers and school, but it is the process of socialisation that initiates people to conform in the first place. As the parents are the first informal socialising agents a child interacts with, it is very important for parents to socialise children according to the mainstream values and norms endorsed by society. Children such as Thompson and Venables are at an early disadvantage given the families they were born into. Their families were either criminals or violent abusers – both types of behaviour setting the wrong example. Thompson and Venables were not attached to families with mainstream values and norms and so they learnt that it was acceptable to be violent: a mental set enabling them to torture and murder. It is when the law is broken that individuals will come into contact with branches of the criminal justice system in the exosystem.

Bronfenbrenner's outer most layer of his Ecosystem Model is the macrosystem. The macrosystem encapsulates the culture of any one society and has a strong influence over a child's socio-emotional development – discussed next.

## Child and macrosystem (culture)

Cultures can be construed as two types, known as individualistic and collectivist societies (Markus and Kitayama 1991; Moscovici 1984). Societies that are considered to be individualistic place considerable value on autonomy and personal responsibility which drive outcomes based on one's actions. Alternatively, collectivist societies consider interdependence between citizens as important for promoting social ties to larger social groups. Markus and Kitayama (1991), for example, considered the independent self and the interdependent self as a means of differentiating individualistic from collectivist cultures respectively. Numerous researchers have classified the UK and US, Northern Europe,

New Zealand and Australia as having a cultural ethos typifying individualism whereas rural indigenous societies – Asian, African and Latin American countries – embrace collectivism (Rothbaum and Trommsdorf 2007; Tamis-LeMonda, Way, Hughes, Yoshikawa *et al.* 2008).

These differences of ethos influence which values are held in high esteem and promoted through socialisation. For a child brought up in the West, traits such as increased self-esteem, self-determination, autonomy and motivation to fulfil one's full potential are emphasised in the socialisation process. A very different picture is painted for children brought up in a collectivist culture, for here there is importance placed on respect, obedience and integration with their community – thus the good of the community outweighs an individual's needs. In relation to conforming to the values, norms, morals and rules of society, the differences between individualistic and collectivist societies is vast, and this is exemplified in the way obedience and respect for rules is socialised. Moscovici (1988) argued that collective understanding became adopted by the individual person and incorporated into their way of thinking because of a shared social representation (held by a group or society) enabling people to communicate effectively and come to an agreed view of reality – a consensus.

Chen and French (2007) showed how differences such as social initiative (i.e. individualistic) and social control (i.e. collectivist) are reflected in the way parents interact with their children – in keeping with the traits society wants children to develop. In the US, for instance, there is more peer interaction than would occur in countries like China. Chen and French (2007) observed that even the nature of play differed whereby play promoting self-expression and assertion was encouraged in individualistic but discouraged in collectivist cultures. Tamis-LeMonda *et al.* (2008) found more conformity and cooperation in children from collectivist societies where focus on the family, obedience and pro-social behaviour were considered important and virtuous traits. Furthermore, Chen, Chang and He (2003) found evidence in China of parental, peer and school disapproval towards aggressive behaviour. Another way that pro-social behaviour is promoted in collectivist cultures according to Rothbaum and Trommsdorf (2007) is through the indignation portrayed towards individuals who perceive themselves as highly self-important.

These differences of values and expectations of behaviour across cultures are further exemplified in politics. Two different regimes were compared by Bronfenbrenner in 1971: Soviet Union versus the American system. In the time of the Soviet Union (now Russia) there was little crime, children were better behaved and hard-working and felt attached to the Communist (i.e. a political ideology) way of thinking. According to Bronfenbrenner, children were a product of the ethos of the Soviet Union during the 1950s and 1960s. This contrasted considerably with American children who were more likely to cheat and behave antisocially – traits that provided kudos among peers. Bronfenbrenner (1971) stated that England is, 'the home of the Mods and Rockers, the Beatles, the Rolling Stones, and [America's] principle competitor in tabloid sensationalism, juvenile delinquency, and violence' (p.116). The idea that political ethos is responsible for creating individuals within any one society as being similar to each other has been exaggerated (Meadows 2010). While Meadows' point might be construed as fair, denying the influence of cultural ethos and political ideology is difficult given that they are tightly woven into the fabric of society. There are particular personal traits which different societies encourage or discourage that are either reinforced by parents through socialisation or ignored. For some factions within British society, personal traits such as hostility, aggressiveness and non-conformity are in conflict with mainstream values and norms but are nevertheless encouraged by parents or at the very least are not discouraged. This goes against the consensus view of society (see Chapter 1) where such individuals practising these behaviours are perceived as deviant, antisocial and/or criminal. Sociologists and criminologists favouring a conflict perspective of society, however, might perceive such individuals as revolutionists trying to bring about change or those who are marginalised through circumstances beyond their control.

The riots in London (England) and other major cities during August 2011 caused considerable criminal damage to businesses, shops and property and, loss resulting from looting and arson. When the riots first began, police had difficulty controlling and containing the offenders as they only had 6,000 officers operating in the London area; however, this changed when 16,000 police reinforcements from other police forces were assigned. The majority of offenders were described as youths, some as young as 11 years of age. The ex-mayor of London, Ken Livingstone, described the offenders as 'disaffected youths' who are marginalised and without future prospects due to the austere policies introduced by the British Coalition Government to combat the excessive borrowing by the previous Labour Government (Gilligan 2011; Hughes 2011). The politico-economic problems in Britain at the time of the riots coincided with both a crashing share/stock market and global recession. Was the cause of these riots a result of disaffected youths in a macrosystem of uncertainty? The conflict view would certainly advocate this interpretation, however, the British Prime Minister, David Cameron, in his address to Parliament labelled the offenders as criminals who made their own decision to riot. He further emphasised the importance of culture and the 'Big Society' and how the wider picture of the decline of morality, respect, responsibility and discipline cannot be ignored (Hansard Parliamentary Notes 2011). These, with individuals' rights, have to be sensibly balanced and addressed in new policies which complete the circle back to the child-microsystem interaction – where socialisation by the family teaches a child right from wrong. Socialisation continues to be influenced by the exosystem, which itself is partly influenced by the macrosystem.

## Summary

- The nurture approach was used to explain juvenile and adolescent delinquency. There are many factors considered within a nurture approach, but an informative way of categorising the numerous findings from research undertaken in this area is to apply Bronfenbrenner's Developmental Ecosystem Model. This provides a comprehensive multidisciplinary approach to understanding the development of the child: what the child contributes and how it interacts with informal (i.e. parents) and formal (i.e. educators) socialising agents from the microsystem, exosystem and macrosystem. Using Bronfenbrenner's model in this way can help to understand why individuals commit crimes.
- Crime statistics of juvenile delinquency alarmingly show that this age group is increasingly responsible for many acts of delinquency. Current politicians attribute the cause of juvenile delinquency to poor family attachments and faulty socialisation of moral standards and the appreciation of society's values, norms and rules. This assumption has much support from social research findings. For example, there is a catalogue of empirical evidence demonstrating the effects of toxic insecure attachments between parents and child throughout childhood and adolescence. Bowlby's Theory of Attachment and Ainsworth's Strange Situation iterate the detrimental effects to learning appropriate social behaviour and moral development in children who have experienced childhood toxic and insecure attachments.
- Differences in socialisation across families with and without mainstream values and norms of behaviour have been blamed for the rising delinquency rates. Families with deviant values and criminal behaviour tend to perpetuate this through ineffective socialisation of their children. In some cases the children are subjected to rejection, neglect and abuse which ultimately influence the child's understanding of the world – like the negative suspicious interpretations of other people's intent known as attributions of hostile intent.
- Risk factors for children becoming deviant and/or delinquent were considered through Rutter and Giller's five key adverse factors: parental criminality; intra-familial discord; inconsistencies in discipline; size of family and socio-economic status. Parental criminality increases the likelihood of children becoming delinquent – especially the father–son relationship. The Cambridge Study by West and Farrington has provided evidence supporting the criminal parent and delinquent child link. Research from numerous studies (i.e. the Cambridge Study in London; Cambridge-Somerville Study in the US and the Newcastle Thousand Family Study) found evidence of cognitive and socio-emotional problems in children who come from families where there is considerable marital discord (i.e. arguments, domestic violence and non-amicable separation). Discord can contribute

towards children becoming delinquents especially under conditions where they become neglected and in some cases rejected. Research on inconsistencies in response to unacceptable behaviour (i.e. appropriate and effective punishment of transgressions) shows that harsh, punitive or lax and erratic discipline is ineffective and can cause poor socialisation in children. The most effective discipline, induction, uses reasoning and a focus on the consequences of bad behaviour on others. Similarly, Maccoby and Martin refer to authoritative discipline to describe a parenting style that promotes self-control and self-confidence in children. Delinquents were more likely to come from large families for a multitude of reasons such as less supervision, poor overcrowded homes, difficulty of applying discipline, less parental attention and affection and the increased likelihood of modelling on an older delinquent sibling. Low social economic status is often associated with larger families and therefore the aforementioned problems associated with larger families apply. This adverse effect is probably the weakest factor mentioned by Rutter and Giller.

- The deviant nurturance and socialisation experienced by troublesome children expands to other areas within the microsystem (i.e. peers and school), exosystem (i.e. media and law) and macrosystem (i.e. culture). Peers exert a strong effect on a child's behaviour and can lead to actively seeking like-minded peers (i.e. Social Learning Theory) or passively being assimilated by groups and gangs through their continuous exposure (i.e. Subculture Theory). Harris introduced the Group Socialisation Theory to account for why children conform to a 'majority-rules rule' ideology.

- The media has an impact on children's behaviour and has been blamed for causing violent, aggressive and sex-aggressive behaviour in individuals who are already risk prone or have a predisposition towards behaving this way. A direct link between increased crime rates for murder and aggravated assault and television broadcasting was found between 1949 and 1952. In American towns not yet connected to television broadcasting there was no such increase. A link between watching violent broadcasts on television and short-term aggressive behaviour has been explained using findings from Bandura, Ross and Ross' 'Bobo' doll experiment – where children modelled on aggressive behaviour exhibited by an adult. Children clearly imitate images of aggressive behaviour whether seen on television or observed in others.

- Once the rules of society have been undermined then the law plays an active role. The law is a last resort and used in cases where individuals fail to comply with the rules of society – they do not conform to society's consensus of what constitutes appropriate behaviour. Contravening the law is an offence against mainstream culture and reflects the failure of parents to socialise their children appropriately. There are different reasons for this failure but in some cases this is due to deviant values and criminal lifestyles adopted by parents which children later adopt.

- The society an individual experiences has an implicit cultural ethos which is adopted through the process of socialisation. It is implicit because for the most part we are unaware of it. There are differences across cultures for some values and normative behaviour which occasionally come into conflict such as honour killing (see Chapter 1). There are two types of culture – individualistic and collectivist – which emphasise the importance of different traits that parents should instil in their children through socialisation. Markus and Kitayama (1991) perceive the socialisation of an independent self as typical of individualistic cultures while the interdependent self, underlies collectivist cultures.
- The different socialising agents advocated within Bronfenbrenner's Developmental Ecosystem Model are interrelated. Culture influences what is socialised by parents and the value system endorsed by society. Other formal socialising agents ensure that these values are socialised and if an individual fails to conform (i.e. behaves antisocially and commits criminal offences) then the law is used to punish and instigate reform.

## Questions for discussion

1   Many children brought up in a family where violence and aggression is the norm will continue this trend with their own offspring; a few will break the cycle. Discuss the factors which make such children resilient, enabling them to break the mould.

2   How useful is Bronfenbrenner's Developmental Ecosystem Model in explaining delinquency? Consider this in the light of research conducted on the 'child', 'microsystem', 'exosystem' and 'macrosystem'.

3   To what extent is there any truth to the notion that the family is responsible for creating juvenile delinquents?

# Chapter 5

# Decision-making processes by criminals

Chapters 3 and 4 reviewed pertinent issues regarding the underlying causes of criminal behaviour using a nature (Chapter 3) and nurture (Chapter 4) perspective. In this chapter consideration is given to the understanding of cognition in criminals, in particular rational decision-making processes. Historically, the idea that criminals think differently to non-criminals has led to many theories, which have been revisited in current cognitive and neurocognitive research on decision making. Beccaria, in the eighteenth century, made some enlightening social policies concerning the treatment of criminals. He proposed that they could be reformed through the introduction of a series of deterrents, which suggested to him that criminals are capable of rational decision making. This idea was taken further by Sutherland who introduced the term the white-collar criminal to describe a set of criminals who committed often quite complex crimes of deceit and fraud. We will explore how these ideas have been incorporated into current models and theories of decision making. One model that has made a big impact in the area is Cornish and Clarke's (1986) Rational Choice Model. They developed a rounded understanding of criminality which included factors influencing the decision to offend or resist the temptation to commit further crime. As we will see, this model has been influential in the understanding of how individuals decide to become involved with the criminal world and introduced a series of flowcharts indicating factors criminals take into account when deciding to commit an offence. We will also explore the difference between two criminological approaches that of the Rational Choice Model and the Social Control Model (see Chapter 4) advocated by Hirschi to see which accounts best in explaining criminality, criminal decision making and ways of reforming criminal thinking using specially devised training programmes. In this chapter we will also explore the other decision-making models, such as the von Neumann-Morgenstern Expected Utility Model, used by economics (von Neumann-Morgenstern 1944) and, the more popular models introduced by psychologists Kahneman and Tversky in 1979 (Prospect Model) and Payne in 1973 (Simple Contingent Process Model). The problems associated with the Expected

Utility Model (based on the use of probabilities) are compared with the relative simplicity and application of Kahneman and Tversky's Prospect Model (based on the use of **heuristics**). In this chapter all these approaches will be addressed and evaluated for their effectiveness in accounting best for how offenders make decisions. Another area of decision making we will explore is the notion of a typical criminal personality that holds a set style of thinking and decision making introduced by Yochelson and Samenow (1984). Yochelson and Samenow provide a good analysis of the types of thinking and decision-making errors made by offenders that can be applied to different types of criminal. There have been developments in the field of neuropsychology addressing which areas of the brain are more active when we make decisions. With refinements made to scanning techniques of the brain, attention has been directed towards the brain activity of criminals. In this chapter we will explore findings from such research and how our understanding of the criminal mind has progressed. This should also provide some insight as to why certain programmes designed to reform criminal thinking work.

## Introduction

Differences in decision-making strategies utilised by criminal and non-criminal population cohorts were first explored by Beccaria in 1764. How to stop criminals from committing crime was a problem presented to Beccaria in the eighteenth century. Deterrence (ways to stop criminals from committing further crime) figured strongly in Beccaria's way of addressing the problem but in so doing he was making an implicit statement about the 'criminal's state of mind'. If a criminal could be deterred from committing a crime through various legal interventions, then there must be cause to believe that such an individual is capable of weighing the pros and cons of committing or refraining from committing crime. This further implies that decisions are being taken about the risk of successful or non-successful outcomes involved in performing a criminal act – in other words, the rationalisation of options. Cesare Beccaria (1738–1794), who is considered one of the founding fathers of the Classical School of Criminology, introduced, as an alternative to punishments such as torture and hanging, a comprehensive package outlining the merits of deterrence.

This was taken further by Edwin Sutherland (1883–1950), the father of American Criminology, when he introduced the Differential Association Theory. Learning how to commit crime was an important element of Sutherland's Differential Association Theory. Sutherland (1949) proposed that individuals learn how to become criminals which he believed equally applied to the white-collar criminal (see Chapter 6), a label that he introduced to describe the entrepreneur criminal. He proposed, however, that in addition to learning about crime, other associations are made such as the attitudes, motives and the rationalisations used to justify committing crime linked with having a criminal career (Millington and Sutherland Williams 2007).

The idea of the thinking criminal and the notion of free will have spurred other criminologists, such as Cornish and Clarke (1986) and Cusson and Pinsonneault (1986), to entertain the notion of Rational Choice Theory. Furthermore, psychologists such as Kahneman and Tversky (1979) introduced the Prospect Theory to counter some of the more logical probability models used by economists but adapted to explain criminal decision making. More recently Jens-Jacob Sander, in his book *The Criminal Brain: A View from the Bench: Exploring the Criminal Mind*, has considered the question of whether criminals behave the way they do because of their thinking processes and draws upon neuropsychology (i.e. the fMRI and PET scan findings from studies by Raine and colleagues) to argue his case.

In order to assess the nature of rational thought in criminals, it is necessary to have an understanding of how people normally make decisions – are they logical and use a probability formula or do they simply apply a rule of thumb mechanism based on personal experience? According to Sutherland, intelligence is required to commit a white-collar crime (see Chapter 6), which is why in the time of his writings he claimed that the rationalisations of a white-collar criminal would be founded on decision making processes of an intellectual individual. To some extent there is leverage in such an opinion given the complicated nature of **white-collar crime** and the vast legal knowledge required to circumnavigate the law. The difficulty involved with calculating risk and weighing the likely yield from various criminal options can be demonstrated by a problem posed by Lattimore and Witte (1986). The idea is to decide the best decision to make based on a few different outcomes. These are presented as likely probabilities of occurrence (see Figures 5.1 and 5.2). This task is not an easy one and relies on individuals being able to understand probability theory. The task goes as follows:

Imagine that you lead a criminal lifestyle and require money to sustain the standard of lifestyle you have become accustomed to. Your specialism is committing burglary from residential properties. You need to make a series of decisions as to what you should do – whether you should commit the burglary or not. Attached to each option is a probability figure indicating the likelihood of achieving a certain yield if you decided to burgle the house. For instance, there is a probability of 0.3 that you could obtain £500 should you decide to burgle the house for both scenario A and B. There is a probability of 0.4 in scenario A of obtaining £400; however, in scenario B, a 0.4 probability of ending up with nothing cannot be ignored. You need to decide what you would do in both scenario A and B. Your decision should be based on what is the best action to take using the probabilities next to each option. As it might be difficult to visualise these scenarios, Figures 5.1 and 5.2 presents these as diagrams.

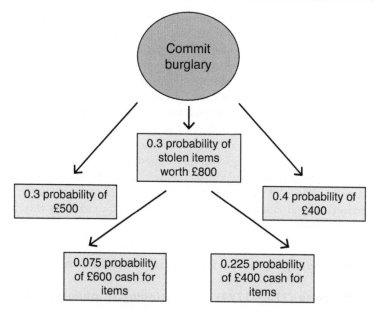

*Figure 5.1* Problem solving task scenario A
Adapted from Lattimore and Witte 1986

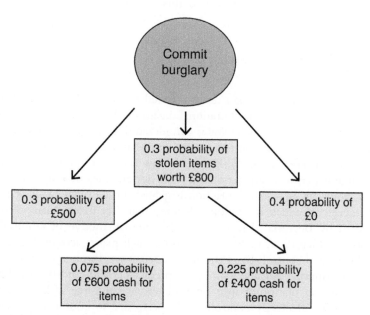

*Figure 5.2* Problem solving task scenario B
Adapted from Lattimore and Witte 1986

Did you consider the amount of potential cash you can make from burgling a particular property? The chances are that as a burglar you will want to make the most profit possible but to also ensure that to burgle a particular property is worth your while. The answers to these problems are not as difficult as they might first appear to be but because we are not used to thinking in probabilities in everyday situations, we find it hard to combine the most profitable option and the most likely outcome and therefore the optimal resolution. Did you work out that for scenario A, it is best to go for the 0.4 probability of stealing £400 and, in scenario B, the option of no burglary given that there is a 0.4 probability of attaining nothing? Another difficulty most of us will have is the inability to isolate gambling and risk elements from the pure logic of the probability figures. This will be returned to later in the chapter, however, in the next section we will consider the history of research examining the thought processes of criminals.

## Historical perspectives of criminal decision making

### Cesare Beccaria (1738–1794) – a criminologist, philosopher and politician

Beccaria was influenced by the **zeitgeist** of his time when the notion of free will was very much in vogue. As part of his approach, Beccaria claimed that all individuals are in possession of three factors:

1    rational manner;
2    manipulability;
3    free will.

Rational manner in Beccarrian terms referred to the need for individuals to attain personal satisfaction using rational measures. Attaining personal satisfaction within the confines of the law is considered to be a positive ambition but becomes obstructive if it contravenes the mores and social rules of society (as discussed in Chapters 1 and 2). Hence the law is there to prevent individuals from gaining personal satisfaction through deviant means. For a few individuals, however, personal satisfaction is gained through licit or illicit means at whatever cost which is a rational decision that they make. Manipulability, considered by Beccaria, describes a 'shared human motive of rational self-interest' (Roshier 1989, p.16) and it is this which makes actions predictable, generalisable and controllable. Preventing deviant acts through legal intervention is less daunting because actions are predictable and controllable. Hence with the implementation of appropriate deterrence and free will, the rational human can be effectively controlled and persuaded to conform to society's social rules and mores.

Beccaria's theory has wider implications concerning the membership of and loyalty to society. He believed that individuals who have free will and can rationalise will have made a choice to be active participants within society; in other words, they chose this option in preference to living alone outside of society's jurisdiction. This means that to participate in the functioning of society and receive the comforts and protection from society, an individual needs to forgo certain personal liberties, which the law helps to enforce. The law also provides a system of ensuring its citizens are protected from individuals and groups who want to reinstate their forfeited personal liberties at the expense of obeying the 'social contract'. In the words of Beccaria in his book, *On Crimes and Punishments* (1764),

> but to have established this deposit was not enough; it had to be defended against private usurpation by individuals each of whom always tries not only to withdraw his own share but also to usurp for himself that of others (p.12).

### Edwin Sutherland (1883–1950) – a sociologist

Sociologist Edward Ross (1866–1951) in 1907 claimed that new criminal opportunities arose as a direct consequence of the growing economy and of the increased social and economic interdependence between individuals mirroring this progression. In response, Ross introduced the term 'criminaloid' to describe an individual who epitomised what later would become known as the white-collar criminal. He claimed that criminaloids could victimise vast numbers of people in a detached, cool but calculating manner. It was Edwin Sutherland in 1949, however, who introduced the term white-collar crime to describe the classification of offending committed by the criminaloid. He readily acknowledged that white-collar crimes could be just as disruptive, if not more, to society as the traditional street crimes of burglary, robbery and homicide. Sutherland's idea of the rationalising criminal was also considered in his writings, where criminal behaviour was learnt through interacting with like-minded individuals. This idea was incorporated into his Interactionist Theory of Deviance which describes how not only the criminal act is learnt in terms of its design and execution but a host of associated behaviours such as attitudes, motives, drives and rationalisations. It is these associated behaviours which make it easier to commit crime than the level of expert knowledge acquired. Sutherland considered white-collar criminals to be the same as other criminals and to learn their craft using similar methods of criminal acquisition (known as differential association). This means that all criminals rationalise.

These two historical approaches of Beccaria and Sutherland have left a lasting legacy in the understanding of how criminals think and, in the case of Sutherland, the addition of a new type of criminal (see Chapter 6). These approaches have made way for new models of decision making in the guise of rational thought. We will next explore the most famous model of decision making arising from criminology known as the Rational Choice Model.

## Rational Choice Model

The Rational Choice Theory, first introduced by Cohen and Felson (1979), was used to account for how criminals make decisions about their criminal career choices. The theory gained momentum when criminologists Cornish and Clarke (1986) wrote about the reasoning criminal which has since become synonymous with Rational Choice Theory. The rational choice perspective houses many micro-models accounting for three different stages of decision making:

- initial involvement;
- event;
- **desistance**.

The different micro-models take account of how the individual became initially involved in criminal activity and the rationalisations that accompanied that decision; the rational choices made concerning the context of the crime and factors promoting the continuation of or desistence from committing further crime. Setting aside descriptions from the three micro-models for a moment, an important question arises. Are we assuming that criminals engage in an intelligent discursive monologue of thought before deciding to commit a crime? Oleson (2002) argued that intelligence and rationality do not necessarily co-vary and to find a criminal with a high IQ is a rarity. Miller, Schreck and Tewksbury (2006) claimed that rationality does not require a high IQ but it does demonstrate the 'human ability to anticipate the consequences of different actions and to calculate the most beneficial outcomes' (Miller et al. 2006). This is one way of considering what rational choice entails but for a more thorough definition using a sociological perspective refer to Box 5.1.

---

## Box 5.1

### Sociological definition of Rational Choice

Simpson (2006) explains the definition of rational choice:

> Rational Choice Theories explain social behaviour via the aggregated actions of rational or purposive actors. The actors are rational in the sense that, given a set of values and beliefs, they calculate the relative costs and benefits of alternative actions and, from these calculations, make a choice that maximizes their expected utility.

Rosenbaum, Bickman, Christenholtz, Chaitin and Roth (1979) demonstrated this in a study where novice and expert shoplifters provided verbal protocols of aspects regarding planning, assessment, and their motivations for shoplifting. Differences between novice and expert shoplifters revealed that experts were more concerned with getting the planning and assessment organised before fulfilling their motivations (time spent, however, decreased as the level of expertise increased). Novice shoplifters were more interested in describing their desires and the goods they wanted at the expense of assessing the shop layout and planning action to prevent detection. Nevertheless, both novice and expert shoplifters showed ability to plan and calculate optimum outcomes.

The Rational Choice Model proposed by Cornish and Clarke (1986) details three components:

- a reasoning offender;
- a crime-specific focus;
- discrete decision models (micro-models of initial involvement, event and desistence).

As can be seen from the definition of rational choice in Box 5.1, offenders seek to benefit themselves by the decisions and choices they make. It is assumed that these decisions and choices are constrained by factors such as the time available to execute an offence, level of expertise and access to relevant information. A crime-specific focus concerns itself with the varying needs that offenders have and the social context in which these decisions are made. This approach focuses on the different types of crime committed rather than the personal aspects of offenders. Therefore it is necessary to separate the offender (initial involvement model) from the crime (event model).

The initial involvement model concerns the processes that impinge on an individual's decision to become involved in committing a particular crime and to continue or desist from committing the same crime. The initial involvement model contains two important decision points: readiness and decision (see Figure 5.3). The factors influencing the readiness to commit an offence are diverse and for each individual the circumstances will be different. For example, background factors are diverse and include psychological, upbringing, social and demographic variables, all considered important in the development of the individual – especially cognitive processes relevant in decision making and the readiness decision element of the model. The decision point in the model indicates the outcome of situations demanding immediate response and action (for example, needing money urgently). Figure 5.3 shows the relationship between all factors impacting on a decision to commit a crime as depicted in the initial involvement model. The event model specifically describes decisions made about the criminal act itself. Cornish and Clarke derived an event model for the crime of burglary and included the possible decisions made concerning the

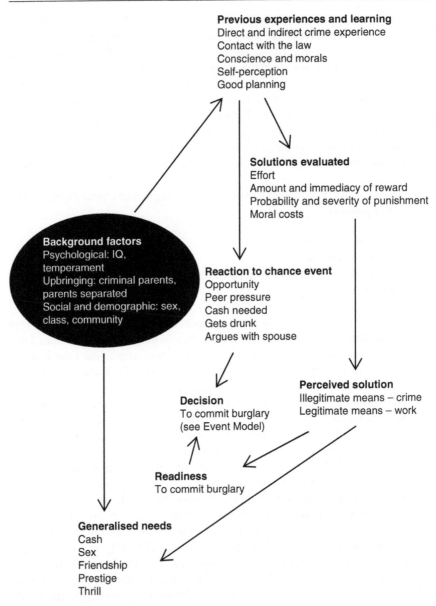

**Previous experiences and learning**
Direct and indirect crime experience
Contact with the law
Conscience and morals
Self-perception
Good planning

**Solutions evaluated**
Effort
Amount and immediacy of reward
Probability and severity of punishment
Moral costs

**Background factors**
Psychological: IQ,
temperament
Upbringing: criminal parents,
parents separated
Social and demographic: sex,
class, community

**Reaction to chance event**
Opportunity
Peer pressure
Cash needed
Gets drunk
Argues with spouse

**Decision**
To commit burglary
(see Event Model)

**Perceived solution**
Illegitimate means – crime
Legitimate means – work

**Readiness**
To commit burglary

**Generalised needs**
Cash
Sex
Friendship
Prestige
Thrill

*Figure 5.3* The Initial Involvement Model
Adapted from Cornish and Clarke 1986

choice of house to burgle. Figure 5.4 provides an example of the sequencing
of decisions made in the event model.

The event model for burglary highlights the deciding factors influencing the
choice of house to burgle or to avoid. This has very important implications

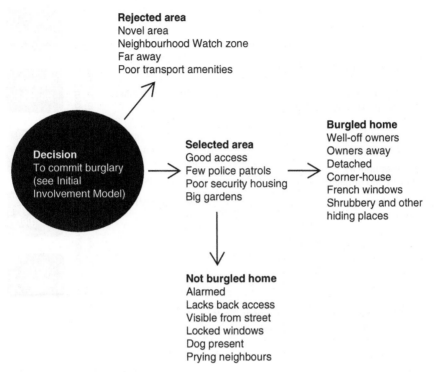

**Rejected area**
Novel area
Neighbourhood Watch zone
Far away
Poor transport amenities

**Decision**
To commit burglary
(see Initial
Involvement Model)

**Selected area**
Good access
Few police patrols
Poor security housing
Big gardens

**Burgled home**
Well-off owners
Owners away
Detached
Corner-house
French windows
Shrubbery and other
hiding places

**Not burgled home**
Alarmed
Lacks back access
Visible from street
Locked windows
Dog present
Prying neighbours

*Figure 5.4* The Event Model
Adapted from Cornish and Clarke 1986

for measures used to protect and secure property in the hope of deterring the would-be burglar. Initiatives like Neighbourhood Watch and the implementation of **CCTV** in potential hot spots for criminal activity like burglary have arisen from Cornish and Clarke's research. They have also considered causes of increased frequency of burglary by introducing the continuing involvement model – see Figure 5.5.

The continuing involvement model shows how the individual becomes more criminalised in attitude, lifestyle and social networking. As the frequency of burglary increases so does the level of professionalism. Professionalism carries with it a multitude of benefits, such as increasing the level of wealth with the minimum amount of effort, which encourages the offender to continue offending – in this case burgling houses. Changes in lifestyle and the experience of prison can alter perceptions towards leading a criminal career, such that imprisonment can lead to desistence from crime.

The desistence model in Figure 5.6 demonstrates the internal and external factors that might make burglary no longer appealing. In this model there are two important decision making points: re-evaluation of readiness and further

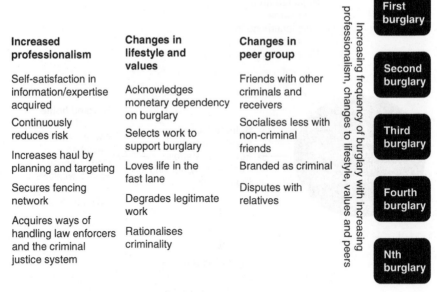

*Figure 5.5* The Continuing Involvement Model
Adapted from Cornish and Clarke 1986

re-evaluation of readiness. The direction of decision – whether to continue or desist – depends on the current situation and if there are any legitimate alternatives to crime.

Cusson and Pinsonneault (1986) developed a more detailed desistence model which takes factors like ageing and 'shock' into account. A surprise attack by a dog could injure the burglar making his escape that more difficult, and it is this narrow escape from being caught that could render the burglar in a state of shock. Difficulty escaping from a crime scene and experiencing shock could be deciding factors in desisting from further involvement in crime. Cusson and Pinsonneault (1986) used the term backsliding to describe circumstances where the offender temporarily desists from involvement in further crime only to be persuaded by peer pressure or the need for urgent cash to do one last 'job'. Hence the decisions of desistence and backsliding are based on the re-evaluation of goals and temptation thus demonstrating that desistence from crime is not a smooth process (see Figure 5.7).

These models are very enlightening and help to see the importance of both internal and external aspects of an individual's life and how these combine to influence a person's decision making. Can the Rational Choice Theory, however, provide us with useful ways of modifying criminal decision-making behaviour? In deciding this, it is often pitted against another criminological approach known as Social Control Theory.

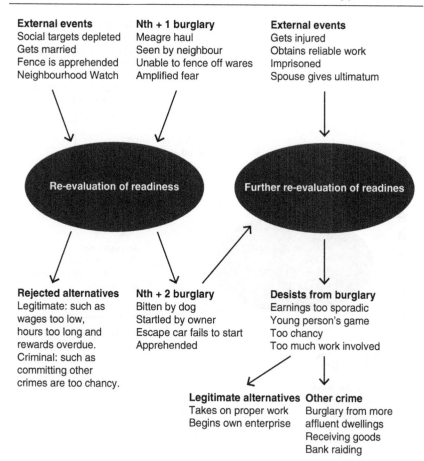

**External events**
Social targets depleted
Gets married
Fence is apprehended
Neighbourhood Watch

**Nth + 1 burglary**
Meagre haul
Seen by neighbour
Unable to fence off wares
Amplified fear

**External events**
Gets injured
Obtains reliable work
Imprisoned
Spouse gives ultimatum

Re-evaluation of readiness

Further re-evaluation of readines

**Rejected alternatives**
Legitimate: such as
wages too low,
hours too long and
rewards overdue.
Criminal: such as
committing other
crimes are too chancy.

**Nth + 2 burglary**
Bitten by dog
Startled by owner
Escape car fails to start
Apprehended

**Desists from burglary**
Earnings too sporadic
Young person's game
Too chancy
Too much work involved

**Legitimate alternatives**
Takes on proper work
Begins own enterprise

**Other crime**
Burglary from more
affluent dwellings
Receiving goods
Bank raiding

*Figure 5.6* Cusson and Pinsonneault's Desistence Model
Adapted from Cornish and Clarke 1986

## Rational Choice Theory or Social Control Theory

Rational Choice Theory assumes that individuals have free will and select options that promote their own profit and pleasure. In the case of Social Control Theory advocated by Travis Hirschi (see Chapters 2 and 4), people consider the costs and benefits of acting legally or illegally. Factors considered for deciding a licit or illicit route of action will depend on the level of attachment, commitment and involvement individuals have with society and the extent to which they believe in the moral validity of norms. If the level of attachment, commitment and involvement in society's norms is high and there is a strong belief in these norms, then an individual will remain a law abiding citizen. Alternatively, if this is low, then they will break the law. Are these two

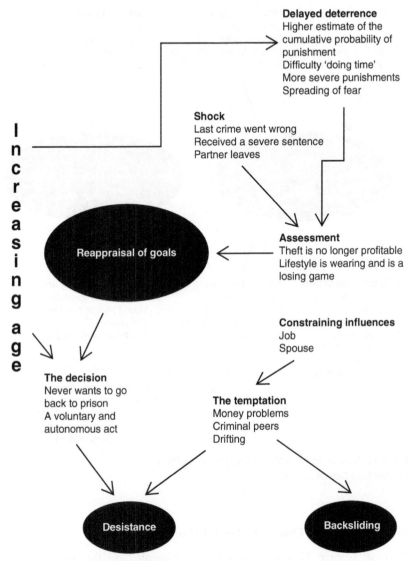

*Figure 5.7* The Decision-Making Process in Desistence from Crime Model
Adapted from Cornish and Clarke 1986.

approaches similar or are they in opposition? According to Hirschi they are not in conflict with each other but instead concentrate on slightly different aspects of criminality: for Rational Choice Theory the focus is on specific crimes which Cornish and Clarke (1986) called events and for Social Control Theory the focus is on criminality itself (i.e. how an individual becomes involved in crime). While Social Control Theory can be considered a theory of criminality, Rational Choice Theory is a theory of crime.

It is the Social Control Theory that is of particular interest here. If, as is argued by Hirschi, society helps to prevent individuals from breaking the law through encouraging social bonds, then can society help to reinstate bonds that have been diminished? One way forward is for the community to create schemes and programmes at a local level to improve the lives of such offenders. The ideology behind this is to promote social bonds, so that not only are offenders taught new skills, they are made to feel a part of their community. This is social control working at its optimum. For instance, DeLisi (2001) described the 'Promoting Alternative Thinking Strategies (PATHS) Curriculum' operating in the US. This is an educational programme that runs for 20 minutes per day three times a week. The emphasis is on learning self-control via the tuition of aspects of executive function (i.e. verbal skills, non-verbal communication, problem solving, and decision making, understanding social cues and the perspectives of others and self-talk used as a strategy for delaying gratification, controlling impulses and being self-aware). The PATHS programme has been successful in reducing the frequency and intensity of conduct problems, anxiety and aggressive behaviour (Greenberg, Kusche and Mihalic 2006). Diamond, Barnett, Thomas and Munro (2007) recently reported the successes of the 'Tools of the Mind Curriculum' which was designed to improve working memory (component of short-term memory involved with processing verbal information) and induce more self-control in pre-school children who were considered to be at risk of developing problem behaviour. The curriculum consists of 40 different activities to improve executive functioning of such pre-schoolers. Activities included a variety of different approaches such as tasks designed to improve memory and attention. Techniques endorsing self-regulatory speech as a means of moderating out-of-control behaviour by telling the 'self' to substitute unruly behaviour for appropriate social behaviour were also taught.

Similar programmes in Britain also address aspects of executive functioning by implementing assertive behaviour training, anger management and relaxation techniques. These programmes are usually implemented by the Probation Service delivered on a client–probation officer basis or as part of a group. Developing and promoting schemes and programmes to improve the often poor level of executive functioning observed in offenders is a step in the right direction. These programmes help offenders develop a sense of self-worth and form a social bond with the society they had previously disengaged from. Further discussion of 'treatment' intervention is considered in Chapter 10 which is explored in the context of preventing delinquency.

While the Rational Choice Model advocated by Cornish and Clarke provides a useful understanding of the processes involved with criminal decision making and offers interventions designed to improve decision-making competency, it is not the only model of rational choice and decision making.

There are different models and perspectives on rational choice and decision making arising from disciplines such as economics and psychology which will be reviewed in the next section.

## Other models of decision making

There are three main approaches accounting for how most people make decisions on a daily basis which can also be extended to offenders making decisions about their criminal pursuits:

- Expected Utility Model
- Prospect Theory
- Simple Contingent Process Model.

### The Expected Utility Model (used by economists)

The Expected Utility Model, also referred to as normative rationality, is an approach used by economists. In particular economists have used the von Neumann-Morgenstern Expected Utility Model since 1968 (based on an article by Gary Becker) and it is this that has been used to model the criminal choice. The premise underlying the von Neumann-Morgenstern approach stipulates that criminals will only contemplate committing a crime if there are gains surpassing any costs that lead to profit and a satisfactory outcome (utility). This approach assumes that an individual knows the probability with which an outcome might occur and that they are logically competent at assigning, maintaining and calculating the overall probability from a number of different possible probabilities: this calculation is rather demanding mathematically and also relies on having reliable information for all possible outcomes (see activity Box 5.2). For an outline of the major criticisms of the expected utility models refer to Box 5.3.

## Box 5.2

### Activity box

To demonstrate how demanding such a calculation is, imagine that probabilities from all possible outcomes must add to a total of 1 and that this standard rule of probability theory is used to determine an overall probability for compound events. To further test how good your understanding of making decisions based on probabilities is, try solving the two tasks in Figures 5.1 and 5.2. Don't forget that by using this logical approach it is important to consider the most likely outcome and that the odds of 0.4 happening is more likely than it is for any of the 0.3 options. It is easy to understand why expected utility models have been criticised (see Box 5.3):

we simply do not think this way and nor would a criminal have time to think of his options using mathematical formulae.

## Box 5.3

### Criticisms of Expected Utility Approaches in human decision making

- Assumes individuals estimate probabilities (p) of a crime leading to punishment or reward (utility).
- If it leads to reward, then what is the probability of a good haul? (For instance they make a decision based on whether they can expect to gain many goods).
- All possible options are considered this way which means the individual's decision is a result of the probability of compound events.
- Little empirical support from laboratory or field research to show that we make decisions this way.
- Model fails to predict individual choices accurately.
- Subjective probabilities are made instead of objective ones.
- Individuals view choices independently and not in multiplicative form (cannot calculate probabilities of compound events).
- Cognitively demanding, and criminals are cognitively limited (Simon 1957).
- People rule things out immediately – rather than holding information in memory for probability calculations – make short-cut decisions (Corbin 1980), and use heuristics (Kahneman and Tversky 1979).
- People use non-compensatory strategies (Johnson and Russo 1984) because criminals are normally specialists in one type of crime.
- Model assumes that people have preferences (for doing things a certain way) but studies show inconsistent preferences from one trial to another.
- Context effects have been observed on preference and loss choices which expected utility models cannot explain.
- People overweigh some outcomes over others because they base their decisions on past experiences and by doing so often fall foul of heuristic errors and biases (Kahneman and Tversky 1979).

Given that individuals are less likely to use the Expected Utility Model for everyday decision making, it is even less likely that a potential burglar would spend time calculating the probability of gaining a good haul by deciding to burgle house A over house B or to steal cash as opposed to goods that could be fenced-off for cash. Psychologists study the way individuals make decisions and have contributed to the arena of decision-making models. The most popularly referred to psychological decision-making theory is the Prospect Theory discussed next.

### Prospect Theory – used by psychologists

Psychologists Kahneman and Tversky (1979) introduced an alternative decision-making account of how decisions and choices are made both under laboratory and field (natural) conditions. They based their Prospect Theory (also known as limited rationality) on the way people use **heuristics** in their everyday life decisions. Heuristics simply refers to a 'rule of thumb' and relies on a simple frequency of occurrence calculation. Consider the likely decision choice of an offender who broke into both residential and commercial properties on numerous occasions in the past. This offender furthermore managed to secure a good haul and evade detection from police only during the occasions that he burgled end of terrace residential properties. On the occasions that commercial properties were burgled, despite attaining a fair haul, the installed security systems made it difficult to effectively steal larger items of worth and nearly prevented his escape. In this case a simple frequency calculation of the number of times the burglary of an end of terrace house versus a commercial property concluded in a fruitful haul relies on a heuristic based on counting the successful events and choosing the dominant option in the future. This is how heuristics work in decision making, especially when making choices about familiar events where previous experience is relied upon. This is not always the case and accounts for why errors are made and biased memory representations occur (i.e. where memory for events are misrepresented).

In relation to the Prospect Theory, Kahneman and Tversky considered the literature on human memory research and the role of cognitive overload in information processing (see Figure 5.8). There is limited short-term memory (STM) retention capacity, and processing availability in working memory (WM). WM relies on a central executive (CE) that directs our attention towards information in our visual field which then sets off a series of processing commands. Once attention is diverted to a specific item in our immediate environment a series of processing occurs that will eventually lead to an interpretation and understanding of what we have just experienced (i.e. the learning, reasoning, language comprehension, and reading of auditory and visual stimuli in our environment (Aronen, Vuontela, Steenari, Salmi and Carlson, 2005)). Furthermore, if we want to remember the information it needs to be rehearsed in what Baddeley and Hitch (1974) referred to as the phonological loop, operating as a go-between WM and long-term memory (LTM). (Figure 5.8). WM enables information to be maintained and manipulated until it is transferred to LTM for indefinite storage (Aronen et al. 2005).

WM enables us to 'shift perspectives on a problem, define goals while considering several parameters of a problem, plan a strategy while anticipating consequences, execute steps of a plan held in memory, monitor progress, detect

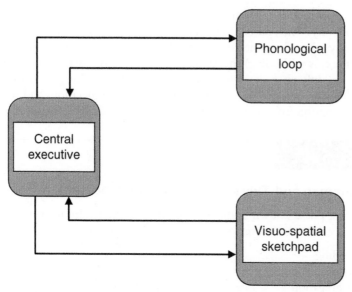

*Figure 5.8* Baddeley and Hitch's Model of Working Memory
Taylor (2015). Reproduced with kind permission from Taylor and Francis.

and correct errors, and accommodate new data while filtering out interference'
(Seguin, Nagin, Assaad and Tremblay 2004, p.604). The limiting factor here is
that only so many items can be held in the phonological loop and processed at
any given time. If there is too much information to attend to, process, rehearse,
decipher, interpret and remember, then cognitive overload is experienced and
cognition (primarily perception and memory) works less efficiently leading to
poor decision making.

The Prospect Theory takes account of many different heuristics but the
most commonly used is that of availability. For instance, when an offender
gauges which type of crime best results in the evasion of detection by police,
one strategy might be to think of the number of criminals who had been
convicted for the crime in question. This is a quick way of making a simple
and basic analysis of the likely outcome for committing a crime of this nature.
The more criminals convicted for committing the crime in question, then
the more challenging it would be to successfully commit this type of offence
and evade capture. The offender can therefore make judgements about which
crime is less likely to result in punishment. The availability heuristic applied in
this way provides a rough guideline as to the most successful crime to commit;
however, it is severely limited as a consequence of biasing factors such as the
misrepresentation of information in memory. Specific information might be
more memorable or is given more credence because of its personal significance
to the individual. Furthermore, there might be external influences such as the

context in which the information is embedded thereby helping to increase its memorability. The context in which information is remembered can promote (especially when the same context is reinstated) or depreciate (especially when the context is misleading) the memory trace therefore making retrieval either simple or difficult respectively. Kahneman and Tversky (1979) proposed a two-phase assessment process involved with making decisions and selecting a less risky option from a series of multifaceted risky alternatives (see Box 5.4).

## Box 5.4

### Kahneman and Tversky's assessment process

The first phase known as the editing phase is where alternatives are edited using six different heuristics:

- coding
- combination
- segregation
- cancellation
- simplification
- detection of dominance.

During the coding operation, outcomes are valued as gains or losses in reference to the offender's current asset situation (or reference point). Any option considered to be below the reference point is a loss and would be ignored; if above, however, the option might prove to be a gain. In the case of the combination operation, compound outcomes are simplified by adding them together. Hence where there is a 30 per cent chance of getting £300 or a 40 per cent chance of getting £300 for stolen goods then this prospect will be a 70 per cent chance of £300. The segregation heuristic accounts for each element of a decision problem separately without due consideration of the wider context in which it is embedded (McDermott 2001). Riskless elements from a decision problem are eliminated when using the segregation operation. In other words, if a set amount of money is guaranteed from a series of options within the decision problem, then the offender will realise that whatever the ultimate outcome this set sum of money will be attained. For example, if the likelihood of gaining £300 is 0.6 and £500 is 0.4 then by using the segregation heuristic, an individual will reduce the odds of gaining the highest amount by increasing the likelihood of gaining a guaranteed set sum – so for example £200: 0.4 with a sure gain of £300 (Lattimore and Witte 1986). Sometimes an offender will commit the crime to avoid a loss rather than to make a gain as would be the odds in this case. Although the money gained is lower than the optimum possible, it is still more money attained than would be the case if the crime were not committed at all. The detection of dominance is simply a matter of choosing the easiest option: breaking into a poorly secured house is easier than breaking into a highly secured house.

The second phase is the evaluation of the edited prospects – the prospect with the highest value is selected. Once all prospects have been evaluated from the editing phase, the prospect that overall provides the highest value is chosen. The decisions are simplified through the substitution of probabilities for weights and utility functions for subjective values placed on options (this also allows for the different and individual needs of offenders).

There are other models of decision making proposed by psychologists which provide an understanding of what motivates criminals to commit offences. The next model considered uses a 'current needs' approach to deciding whether to commit a crime or not. This is called the Simple Contingent Process Model which will be considered next.

### Simple Contingent Process Model – used by psychologists

An alternative to Prospect Theory is the Simple Contingent Process Model proposed by Payne (1973). This is best illustrated by an example provided by Payne depicting a series of judgements (see Figure 5.9).

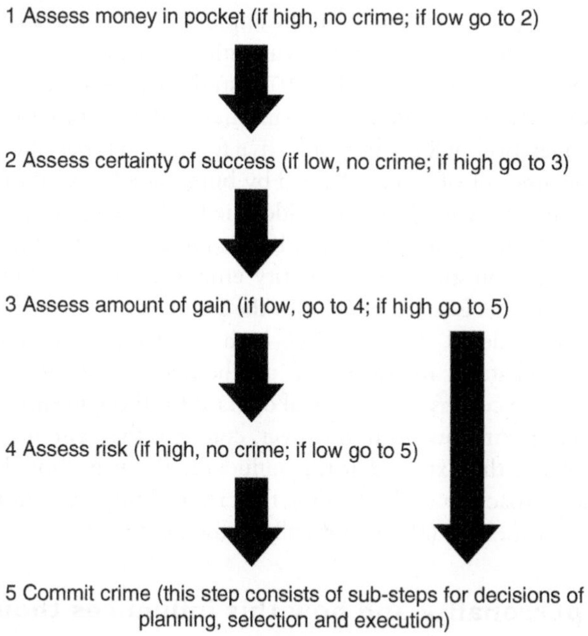

1 Assess money in pocket (if high, no crime; if low go to 2)

2 Assess certainty of success (if low, no crime; if high go to 3)

3 Assess amount of gain (if low, go to 4; if high go to 5)

4 Assess risk (if high, no crime; if low go to 5)

5 Commit crime (this step consists of sub-steps for decisions of planning, selection and execution)

Figure 5.9 The Simple Contingent Process Model
Adapted from Payne 1973

This is a very simple decision making process based on many sub-steps that can be answered quickly and easily. The Simple Contingent Process Model dispenses with any unnecessary calculations or the weighting of probabilities and relies instead on a simple response to the offender's current situation. Despite differences across crimes on a number of factors, the manner in which decisions are made remains constant for all types of crime (Carroll 1978). In support of this model Carroll (1978) found that individuals have robust preferences for particular aspects of a chosen crime, such as how much money will I get or what happens if I get caught? But what are the implications for this model?

### Implications of the Simple Contingent Process Model

As was observed in the Expected Utility Model, people find it difficult to combine multifaceted relevant information in an attempt to make a single judgement. Carroll (1978) presented a hypothetical crime opportunity to incarcerated adults and juveniles and to a control group of non-criminals. They were presented with different types of gambles which varied on dimensions such as the likelihood of loss or gain, the amount of gain and the nature of punishment. It was found that all participants had difficulty combining different dimensions in order to make a single judgement and instead considered the dimensions separately; 41 per cent of participants considered the likelihood of being cap tured, 60 per cent considered success, 67 per cent entertained the severity of punishment whereas the majority at 84 per cent focused on the amount of money available.

Studies like this demonstrate clearly why different deterrents work for some criminals some of the time. Carroll's (1978) study demonstrated how features of a crime vary from one offender to another and accounts for why some deterrents in operation will be more effective for certain types of offender. For instance, if the amount of money hauled by burgling a house is of pertinence to the burglar then they might not consider the level of security the house has. Alternatively, if avoiding detection and imprisonment is valued highly by the burglar, then the sophistication of security employed by a household would take priority in the decision to break into the premises.

All models considered thus far place high emphasis on rational decision making, and by whatever means this occurs the underlying perspective is that offenders make choices based on rational operational thought similar to everyone else. An interesting question, however, concerns the existence of a criminal personality and the extent that this influences the way thought processes operate. This approach to understanding the criminal mind was introduced by Yochelson and Samenow (1976) and will be discussed next.

## Criminal personality and how this influences thought

Based on a longitudinal study (spanning 14 years) of 30 males guilty by insanity, the Criminal Personality Theory was born. Criminal Personality Theory developed by psychiatrist Samuel Yochelson and clinical psychologist Stanton Samenow (1976) enabled them to classify the different errors of thought that offenders make regardless of the type of crime committed. Furthermore, they controversially suggested that criminals have a set thinking process that covaries with the typical **criminal personality**. The criminal personality acts as a template for guiding the behaviour and the cognitive and emotional processes of criminally inclined individuals, which in turn determines and manages their lifestyle. Yochelson and Samenow uncovered factors that appear to be common to all criminals:

- they are fearful;
- they disengage from internal and external deterrents;
- they crave power and control, making them predators;
- they want to be perceived as unique and the best;
- they are egocentric and want their own way but become angry if this is not forthcoming;
- they are determined to get their own way and use whatever means necessary;
- they fail to think in the long term.

According to Yochelson and Samenow, criminals become angry as a consequence of errors in their thinking processes rather than their aspirations and goals being blocked by interfering factors (i.e. high level of police vigilance). Yochelson and Samenow identified 52 different errors of thought housed under three distinct categories:

- criminal thinking patterns;
- automatic thinking errors;
- crime-related thinking errors.

Individuals classified under criminal thinking patterns vie for power and control whilst simultaneously experiencing fear. These individuals lie, have disconnected thinking and no sense of time. Those classified under automatic thinking errors are devoid of empathy, trust no one, are secretive in the manner they communicate with others and see themselves as a victim (see Chapter 7). Crime-related thinking errors pertain specifically to the criminal act itself and involves fantasising over specific details about crimes. This also includes a deluded perception of their invulnerability to capture and punishment (see Box 5.5 for Yochelson and Samenow's examples of crime-related thinking errors).

Individuals with a criminal personality are prone to **cognitive distortions** concerning their own behaviour and that of other people (see Chapters 7 and 8). According to Yochelson and Samenow these cognitive distortions are self-serving cognitive distortions which act as a catalyst for aggressive and criminal behaviour. Gibbs and Potter (1992) classified self-serving cognitive distortions into four classifications:

- self–centred;
- blaming others;
- minimising and mislabelling;
- assuming the worst.

---

## Box 5.5

### Yochelson and Samenow's examples of crime-related thinking errors

- *Loner*: here the criminal feels separate from others and consequently leads a private and secretive life.
- *Lying*: this becomes part of the criminal's way of life and creates a false reality in order to maintain control.
- *Closed channel*: this refers to the closed mindedness of the self-righteous criminal.
- *I can't*: this is said to avoid the need to act responsibly and as a means to escape accountability.
- *Victim stance*: blame for the criminal's actions is attributed to others while they assume victim status when things fail to go their way.
- *Lack of time perspective*: criminals want immediate gratification and want only the best.
- *Failure to put oneself in another's position*: self-centred approach prevents them from considering the effects their actions have on others.
- *Failure to consider injury to others*: criminals fail to acknowledge the injury they cause others and perceive themselves as the injured party.
- *Failure to assume obligation*: criminals find obligations a hindrance and consider it a way of being controlled by others. They respond to obligation with anger.
- *Ownership*: criminals will take what they want owned by others. In their minds they own it and because they perceive themselves as decent individuals, they feel they have the right to do as they please.
- *Fear of fear*: criminals will exploit others who show fear as they frown upon it, but will lose self-esteem if they themselves experience fear.
- *Lack of trust*: criminals have difficulty trusting others and yet they expect to be trusted.
- *Lack of interest in responsible performance*: given criminals find responsibility monotonous, they find responsible tasks uninteresting.
- *Pretentiousness*: criminals inflate their capabilities and always think they are right.

- *Corrosion and cut-off*: in the case of corrosion the criminal eliminates deterrents so that the desire to commit a crime exceeds any deterrent. Cut-off, alternatively, eliminates any deterrent from the equation of committing crime.
- *Deferment*: criminals defer enacting the ultimate crime, quitting crime and performing daily activities such as doing a tax form.
- *Super optimism*: criminals are over-confident in their decisions and entertain little if any doubt. They are confident of their likely success and perceive that a change has taken place as a consequence of making a decision.

A self-centred individual will perceive their own views and rights at the expense of attitudes held by others. By blaming others, such individuals are misattributing blame for their harmful behaviours and refuting any account-ability for their actions. Individuals who minimise or mislabel their antisocial behaviours as acceptable are justifying the continuance of behaving this way. In the case of the 'assuming the worst' category, individuals are attributing hostile intention to others by assuming the worst (see Chapter 4).

The attribution of hostile intention to others, empathy and **Theory of Mind** (ToM) (see Chapters 4 and 10), are pertinent for understanding the criminal personality. According to Baron-Cohen (1995), it is ToM that enables us to understand the intentions underpinning the behaviours of others, a feat achieved through the ability to separate our own beliefs from those of other individuals. There is evidence to suggest that criminal actions are carried out by individuals who have an immature ToM – a finding supported by biological evidence. It has been shown for instance, that psychopaths have damaged con-nections between the frontal lobes and the limbic system (see Chapters 3, 7 and 10). The frontal lobes play an active role in the expression of a conscience and experience of remorse. Many criminals fail to fully develop these important parts of the brain that are so vital to moral development. Empathy also enables the development of morality and ToM (see Chapter 4, 7, 8, 9 and 10), and as seen in Yochelson and Samenow's category of 'automatic thinking errors', criminals are devoid of empathy. Moir and Jessel (1995) address this by con-sidering whether such individuals have positive or negative feelings towards another person's well-being. If low positive feelings or high negative feelings towards others are experienced then this type of individual is unlikely to care whether their actions cause harm to others: little if any empathy is shown by criminals who commit heinous crimes for example.

The criminal personality is important for understanding the initial involve-ment model outlined by Cornish and Clarke (1986) in their Rational Choice Theory which was discussed earlier in this chapter. As part of the initial involvement model, they considered psychological (i.e. temperament, IQ and cognitive style), upbringing (i.e. broken home and parental crime) and social and demographic (i.e. sex, class, education and area) background factors which research has shown to predispose an individual to a life of crime (see Chapters 3 and 4). It is temperament and cognitive style that is robustly implicated in the criminal personality. However, it goes beyond this. Interaction with environmental factors experienced in the home (i.e. socialisation and upbringing for example) can determine the course of direction an individual's personality development will take. Cornish and Clarke's Rational Choice Theory is not only informative but insightful, as it delivers an all-encompassing perspective on how individuals become initiated into a criminal lifestyle and thereafter make the rational decisions that they do. There is nevertheless still the nagging question of whether criminals make rational decisions differently from the rest of us? To answer this, recent neurocognitive and neurobiological research on the criminal brain is necessary – explored in the next section.

## Neurocognitive and neurobiological brain research

Jens-Jacob Sander (2003), a prestigious judge in Norway, was determined to review the neurocognitive/neurobiological literature in the hope of answering his question of whether criminals' brains function in a way that prevents them from processing information in a similar manner to non-criminals. Sander expressed the opinion that unlike non-criminals, criminals are unable to either act responsibly or exert any self-control as demonstrated by their choice of decision – this he argued is a consequence of defected conceptual thought. Using the research of Yochelson and Samenow and linking this with Raine's fMRI and PET scanning techniques, Sander found support for his hypothesis of there being defective conceptual thought in criminals. Yochelson and Samenow considered the inability of criminals to think conceptually, which reduces the number of options and choices available to them. Nevertheless, as discussed previously, they do make choices concerning their criminal activity which Sander argues are limited as a consequence of faulty conceptual thinking. Yochelson and Samenow claimed that criminals experience fear and anger which will eventually interfere with their ability to consider any crime deterrents. In other words, Yochelson and Samenow argued that criminals develop a hyper-optimism that misleads them into perceiving themselves as impervious to harm.

According to Sander, criminals experience these facets differently from the rest of us and concluded that they live in their own personal world driven by inner thoughts, emotions and perceptions. They fail to consider the social world around them and concentrate on their inner drives and thoughts – which might include obsessive thoughts about their criminal fantasies. Interestingly, Sander (2003) stated that the fear generated by criminals, 'seems more a product of their inner generated brain data, thoughts or signals, without contact or reduced contact with the outside world'. In the case of anger, Sander (2003) claimed, 'that anger in the criminal does not stem from outer circumstances'. Sander related his perspective to neurocognitive and neurobiological research on the criminal mind.

The Maxwell Report released by the Department of Trade and Industry in 2001 concludes, 'the most important lesson from all the events is that high ethical and professional standards must always be put before commercial advantage. The reputation of the financial markets depends on it' (Honourable Sir Thomas and Turner 1992). The US has also had its share of white-collar crimes some of which are listed in Box 6.1.

---

## Box 6.1

### Examples of US white-collar crime

It was reported by Shover and Hochstetler (2006) that from 1–4 February 2004 there were 143 reports concerning white-collar crime in America's top 100 newspapers. They found that 43 per cent were high-profile cases and included:

- Martha Stewart, a well-known business executive, for lying about her involvement in an illegal stock sale.
- Larceny and fraud were charges made against an ex-executive working for the Canadian Imperial Bank of Commerce.
- The *Tacoma News Tribune* reported that a bridge construction builder was fined for negligence to control storm water from carrying pollutants downstream despite official notification to solve the problem some four months earlier.
- At a lower level of white-collar crime, it was found that occupational fraud against employers cost them $660 billion (Association of Certified Fraud Examiners, 2004). This supports the idea of white-collar crime no longer being limited to the upper and middle echelons of society.

---

In the US in 1987, a 36-year-old man called John Grambling Jr. defrauded many banks by borrowing millions of dollars without collateral. He appeared as a trustworthy man wearing a suit. His interactive skills rested on using charm, deceit and manipulation; he manipulated his victims so that they had confidence in him. Psychologist Robert Hare likened Grambling to a psychopath (see Chapter 7). The psychopath is an individual who possesses a set of personality traits that enables them to show little warmth and empathy towards others, and a criminal psychopath has these traits which enhance their ability to commit crimes causing harm to others. Hare's distinction between ordinary white-collar criminals and psychopathic white-collar criminals is defined by the extent of deceit and manipulation used towards everyone outside of money making pursuits – hence white-collar criminals like Grambling show the same pattern of behaviour in all aspects of their lives. Grambling, for example, managed to trick his sister into signing a mortgage note for $4.5 million, leaving her liable while he kept the money.

The literature on female crime suggests that fraud-like offences are commonly committed by women (see Chapter 9); hence we would expect more females in high-level finance, accountants or auditor jobs to commit white-collar crimes such as insider trading, price fixing, restraint of trade, toxic waste dumping, fraudulent product production, bribery, official corruption or large-scale governmental crimes. This is not the case. Of course this could be confounded by the fact that very few females occupy these posts. Hence the lack of opportunity helps explain low female involvement in serious white-collar crime (Daly 1989). Serious white-collar crime is a male dominated criminal pursuit, but are there any other defining characteristics separating the white-collar criminal from other types of criminal? This will be examined in the next section.

## Is the white-collar criminal different from other criminals?

Sutherland argued that the main difference between white-collar criminals and the traditional street criminal is the level of contact with victims. Offenders of street crimes such as mugging, robbery, theft and murder typically have face-to-face contact with their victims whereas white-collar criminals operate under the guise of a legitimate transaction which can be performed at a distance. This, according to Sutherland, is what makes the white-collar criminal more deceitful and exploitative. Despite research suggesting similar decision-making processes for street and white-collar criminals, Shover and Hochstetler (2006) viewed the white-collar criminal as behaving more rationally simply because of the social context in which they operate (for example, a working environment that is conducive to rational, calculative decision-making). As we have seen, the type of criminal offence committed by white-collar criminals can be just as dangerous and callous as those of the street criminal. Furthermore, Hare (1993), as we have seen, distinguishes between the ordinary and psychopathic white-collar criminal – claiming that serious high-profile white-collar crimes are more likely to be committed by the latter. Hare's contention holds up very well, as we have seen in the case of Grambling. It might also explain UK-based Robert Maxwell's behaviour. There have been many reports of his callous behaviour towards employees. **Criminal psychopaths** will be discussed further in the next chapter, but in the next section we will consider if there are any structural and functional differences in the brain of white-collar criminals compared with non-criminals.

### Brain structure and function

Interesting findings arise from brain study research on white-collar criminals. Raine, Laufer, Yang, Narr *et al.* (2012) discovered that white-collar criminals have superior executive functioning and enhanced information processing ability courtesy of their structural brain differences. They used the term neurocriminology to account for the brain structural differences found in credit card fraudsters, those issuing stolen cheques and other misdemeanours committed within the financial world – i.e. by the white-collar criminal. In the 21 white-collar criminals who volunteered for their brain to be scanned, the prefrontal cortex was structurally different from the 21 matched controls. This area, as discussed in Chapters 3 and 5, is involved in decision making but also in the moderation of context appropriate social control. The scan revealed that their cortex had thicker grey matter in the ventromedial prefrontal area, the inferior frontal gyrus and at the temporal-parietal junction. This, Raine et al. claimed, gave them specific brain superiorities for processing information over the matched controls. Raine used these differences to account for why they are good at what they do, claiming that, 'They have better executive function, which improves their executive skills like planning, regulation and management'. Ishikawa, Raine, Lencz, Bihrle and LaCasse (2001) found that 'successful psychopaths' have enhanced executive function enabling them to be good liars and to manipulate others – just what we see white-collar criminals do. Raine et al. alluded to white-collar criminals as having 'biological advantages'. Findings concerning the structural difference of the temporal-parietal junction are interesting because this plays a responsible role in decisions of moral content. Furthermore, this demonstrates a link with psychopaths in that white-collar criminals also experience a profound lack of empathy and remorse (see Chapter 7). Figure 7.1 contextualises the connection between psychopaths and white-collar criminals.

There are differences between white-collar criminals and criminal psychopaths per se. Unlike criminal psychopaths, white-collar criminals have an intact amygdala and perform normally on fear conditioning (see Chapter 7). Nevertheless despite an intact amygdala, they do have problems with experiencing cognitive empathy through their failure to recognise fear. As shown in Figure 7.4, the amygdala is structured by a complex series of nuclei (13 in total) which differ in function. It has been shown, for example by Yang et al. (2009), that there are structural aberrations to four nuclei of the amygdala (basolateral, lateral, central and cortical) in psychopaths. A connection between white-collar criminals and specific amygdala impairment has been speculated by Gao and Raine (2010). White-collar criminals have an intact basolateral nuclei which is involved in fear conditioning but other nuclei involved in the processing of fearful facial expression recognition appear to be impaired. Raine (2013) claimed that white-collar criminals in common with serial killers tend to have a well-performing prefrontal cortex. Furthermore, the lack of a conscience rests on structurally deformed amygdala. Raine et al. (2012) demonstrated that white-collar criminals have psychopathic traits but have enhanced attention and good social perspective-taking skills which enable them to function effectively within an organisation. There are clearly some differences in the white-collar criminal's brain from non-criminals, but there are other explanations for their behaviour that are not related to differences in their brains. These will be explored in the next section regarding the criminal personality type.

### Criminal personality type

In Chapter 5, the criminal personality introduced by Yochelson and Samenow (1976) symbolises the nature of the white-collar criminal. They suggested that criminals have a set way of thinking correlating highly with descriptions of the criminal personality such as craving power and control of others and wanting to be seen as the best. The criminal personality also wants his or her own way and will stop at nothing to achieve this. Of particular importance to the white-collar criminal is Yochelson and Samenow's description of autonomic thinking errors. The criminal making these thinking errors is devoid of empathy, secretive in their communication exchanges with others and trusts no one. They perceive themselves as the victim and use deluded perceptions of their own invincibility – in other words they rely on cognitive distortion (see Chapters 5, 7 and 8). As we have seen in Chapter 5 it is these **cognitive distortions** that enable criminals to behave callously, and the white-collar criminal is no exception to this.

## Summary

- White-collar criminals commit crime at a distance from their victims but the impact of their offences is no less harmful than street crime. Sutherland coined the term white-collar criminal as a means of identifying crimes committed by those who are considered respectable and of high social status – these types of crime are connected with the individual's occupation. Despite introducing criminology to this new type of offender, his definition has been criticised and changed slightly. The violation of trust according to Sutherland can be achieved using different methods such as abuse of power violating rules and regulation.
- White-collar crime takes on many guises from bank embezzlement to organisational negligence to all types of fraud such as false benefit claims. Anyone can commit these crimes as long as they have the opportunity to do so – given that the definition now includes illegal acts committed by non-physical means in order to gain money or property. This is probably why more men commit the most serious white-collar crimes than women – women occupy fewer high-brow positions in the financial world. Typical female crime includes fraudulent activity but in the scheme of things these offences are less serious and yield small amounts of money.
- Famous UK examples of white-collar crime includes the Guinness Affair and Robert Maxwell. The Guinness Affair is synonymous with insider trading where the stock market was rigged so that supporters of Guinness bought their shares with the promise of large monetary returns and

indemnity against any loss. Guinness then used the cash and shares to buy the Distillers company. In the case of Maxwell, who owned the Mirror Group and published various newspapers, such as the Daily Mirror and the New York Daily News, his white-collar crime involved moving money from one of his companies to another as a delay tactic for paying back bank loans. He did this by embezzling money from his employees' pension funds: 32,000 employees were affected by this activity and £400 million went missing.

- A famous US example of white-collar crime involved defrauding many banks. John Grambling Jr. borrowed millions of dollars without any collateral. He was a well-presented man, dressed in a suit, and managed to totally convince his victims by using charm and deceit. It has been speculated that Grambling is an example of a psychopath in a suit.

- There are commonalities between white-collar criminals and psychopaths. The psychopath lacks warmth and empathy which enables these individuals to commit crime. Criminal psychopaths tend to commit callous acts against their victims, and it has been argued that the white-collar criminal does just that – the major difference being that the latter operates at a distance from their victims and their offences are occupationally related.

- Psychologist Robert Hare makes the distinction between ordinary white-collar criminals and psychopathic white-collar criminals. They are both defined by their deceit and manipulation of others but in the latter the extent of this is extreme.

- An interesting question is whether white-collar criminals are different from street criminals. According to Sutherland the only difference is that white-collar criminals operate under the misapprehension of a legitimate business exchange – this makes them more deceitful and exploitative than the regular criminal. Some believe that white-collar criminals behave more rationally than other criminals because of the social working context many of them operate under.

- Neurocognitive support for white-collar criminals behaving more rationally than other criminals has been found in relation to executive function (skills such as planning and management). Raine and his colleagues showed that credit card fraudsters and individuals issuing stolen cheques had a structurally different prefrontal cortex – there was thicker grey matter in the ventromedial prefrontal cortex, inferior frontal gyrus and temporal-parietal junction. This gave them advantages in the processing of information which accounted for why they were best suited for committing white-collar crime as opposed to other types of criminal activity. White-collar criminals have also been referred to as successful psychopaths because they have enhanced executive function and therefore are good at manipulating others and good at lying. White-collar criminals tend to have areas within the amygdala that are intact, such as the basolateral nuclei, which plays a role in fear conditioning, but aberrations to other areas of the amygdala responsible for processing fearful facial expression. Raine claimed that a lack of a conscience in white-collar criminals is a consequence of a faulty amygdala.

- There is a criminal personality type defined by thinking patterns and the nature of thinking errors made. This criminal personality has a craving for power and control and will resort to whatever means necessary to achieve them. There are what Yochelson and Samenow refer to as autonomic thinking errors which are devoid of empathy and rely on cognitive distortions. These cognitive distortions play a pivotal role in enabling white-collar criminals to offend in a callous manner towards their victims.

## Questions for discussion

1   Do most white-collar criminals come from the upper echelons of society?
2   To what extent can white-collar criminals be considered as successful psychopaths?
3   Why is it that white-collar crimes are so varied. Is it something to do with how it is defined?

# Chapter 7

# Psychopaths and their crimes

The aim of the chapters in Part III is to present evidence for a nature–nurture contribution towards a selection of criminals: in this case the criminal psychopath. As with all chapters in this part, a multidisciplinary approach will be taken, such that evidence is drawn from a variety of academic subjects which address crime and the criminal. Later, in the concluding chapter of this part, the evidence will be evaluated.

In this chapter we begin by addressing what is meant by the criminal psychopath. A distinction between psychopathy and antisocial personality disorder (APD) is made. Often psychopathy and APD are considered synonymously but there are differences which will be addressed; however, the main focus of attention is the psychopath. The characteristics of the psychopath, as defined both historically and currently, is considered using Robert Hare's (1991) Psychopathy Checklist – Revised (PCL-R). The PCL-R is often used in the assessment of suspected criminal psychopaths, and it is found that for many murderers and serial killers a high score on the PCL-R is attained. Different classifications of criminal psychopaths will be outlined using Millon and Davis (1998) subtypes and Blackburn's (1975) distinction of primary and secondary psychopaths. Social and biological explanations of psychopathy provide insight to why and how psychopaths behave in the way they do. Social explanations consider the role of socialisation in the development of attitudes, morals and social skills used in relationships with other individuals. Attribution theory provides a useful platform in explaining how psychopaths justify their behaviour. We will also consider biological explanations of psychopathy which include: differences in structural and functional areas of the brain as demonstrated by MRI, fMRI and DT-MRI scans; lateralisation studies of information processing; and attention and physiological differences, such as the secretion of cortisol in response to stress. The possibility of a developmental progression of psychopathy in children and adolescents with Disruptive Behaviour Disorders, such as conduct disorder and oppositional defiant disorder, will be considered in association with differences of physiological function. We will explore the contention that adult psychopathy has its origins in childhood, and so providing support for a nature contribution. Treatment prospects for primary and secondary psychopaths will also be examined here. Any treatment success will help to decide whether the symptoms of psychopathy can be turned around and offer another angle towards understanding its causes. All evidence is combined to provide a balanced approach to the aetiology of psychopathy. We will find that there is no one answer in favour of nature or nurture, but rather a nature–nurture interaction.

## Introduction

The depiction of a psychopath has become ubiquitous in crime fiction. Cinematic representation of the psychopath, for instance, is often synonymous with a homicidal criminal. This is far from the truth. The dimension of psychopathy is one dimensional facet of personality and has very little to do with criminality. Psychopathy in DSM-5 (the Diagnostic Statistical Manual) is categorised as APD. So why the confusion? To address this common misconception it is important to consider the literature on personality disorder and the status of APD within the different personality typologies. There are ten different dimensions of personality disorder (APA 2013):

- *Avoidant*: anxious in social situations and overly sensitive to criticism of the self.
- *Dependent*: dependent on others and has little self-confidence or autonomy.
- *Obsessive–compulsive*: following rules and striving for perfection leads to project incompletion – considered a 'control freak' by others.
- *Paranoid*: hostile and suspicious of others' intentions and behaviour and can show intense sexual jealousy.
- *Schizoid*: socially withdrawn and indifferent to others – showing little warmth.
- *Schizotypal*: profound interpersonal difficulties and demonstrates odd beliefs (i.e. attributes causes to magic).
- *Histrionic*: emotionally vacant but demonstrates immense emotion usually for attention.
- *Narcissistic*: opinionated, egocentric and lacks empathy and overestimates own abilities.
- *Borderline*: argumentative and unpredictable, often showing impulsive behaviour and erratic emotions.
- *Antisocial*: lacks empathy, guilt or shame, dishonest, irresponsible, manipulative, destructive and callous towards others' suffering, indifferent to the rights of others and aggressive.

It is possible to assign different dimensions of personality disorder to many types of murder cases; however, the underlying traits of APD are conducive for criminal activity and in many murder cases the individual convicted is assessed and diagnosed with this particular personality disorder. Using the cases in Box 7.1, identifying the traits of APD should be more obvious than for the other personality disorders since the traits and behaviour of individuals with APD have more detrimental effects on other people.

## Box 7.1

### Examples of murder cases

After a brief relationship in 2009, Joshua Davies (16 years old) talked to his friends about killing his ex-girlfriend Rebecca Aylward (15 years old) in exchange for a free breakfast. In October 2010 he lured her to the woods in Maesteg near Bridgend and attacked her by smashing her head with a rock.

On Friday 22 July 2011, Anders Breivik (32 years old) killed 76 people in Norway. Firstly, killing eight people in Oslo in a car bomb attack and then, dressed as a police officer, shooting 68 with a semi-automatic rifle on the island of Utoya at a summer camp for youth leaders of the Labour Party. He wanted to stop the spread of Islam in Norway which he believed the Labour Party was encouraging through their policies.

Jennifer Mills-Westley (60 years old) was stalked, stabbed and beheaded by Deyan Deyanov (28 years old) in a shop in the resort of Los Cristianos, Tenerife in May 2011. It was reported by witnesses that he held his victim's head saying that, 'God is on earth'. Deyanov previously received psychiatric treatment but was released from hospital in February 2011 after his involvement in a violent incident. An arrest order was issued three days before he murdered Mills-Westley on the grounds of fighting and drug usage. His ex-girlfriends informed police that he was a heavy drug user. Rachel Sharpe (22 years of age) said that he told her he wanted to kill someone for the experience and believed he was the Messiah: he became angry when she told him he was not. During a visit to see relatives in Wales in 2010, Deyanov was sectioned under the Mental Health Act and detained in the Ablett Psychiatric Unit at Glan Clwyd hospital – hence it was known that he had a record of mental health issues.

Fiona Donnison (aged 44) murdered her two toddlers, Elsie (aged 2) and Harry (aged 3) on 26 January 2010 in East Sussex. She was admitted to Eastbourne District General Hospital for treatment of injuries sustained through self-harming.

Levi Bellfield (aged 43) murdered Marsha McDonnell (aged 17), Amelie Delagrange (aged 22) and Millie Dowler (aged 15) and attacked at least 20 other women including six attempted date rapes using drugs. He was charged and sentenced for the murders of McDonnell and Delagrange in 2008 and later in 2010 for Dowler. His method of killing was to cause head injury using a hammer and in one case he ran over his victim more than once when she crossed the road to avoid him. He became known as the bus stalker murderer but was also nicknamed 'Hammer Killer Bellfield'.

Thomas Connor and William Paton murdered Dr Guhamhuseinwala in 2009. The victim stopped to answer his mobile phone at which point Connor and Paton hit him with a 10 kg fence post around the head. They then continuously stamped on his head before robbing him. They were reported to have been drinking and taking cocaine at a local pub – once their money ran out they wandered the streets looking for trouble.

Agnes Dupont de Ligonnes (aged 48) and her four children (aged 13, 16, 18 and 20) were murdered in their home in Nantes in France. They were shot dead with a 0.22 calibre rifle and their bodies were severed into pieces and then buried in two pits in the garden. The two family Labradors were also killed in the same manner. The murderer was Xavier Dupont de Ligonnes (aged 50), husband, father and Versailles born marquis. He is wanted by Interpol. Prior to their deaths, suspected to be between 3 and 6 April 2011, Xavier Dupont de Ligonnes had made preparations for their killings and disposal. He also wrote letters to friends saying that he led a double life as a secret agent which is why the family had to move to America. He informed his wife's employer at the school that she was travelling to Australia. He was in debt and owed money to his mistress in Paris but he continued to forge his salary slips to get credit from banks. He still remains a wanted man and a fugitive.

These case examples of murderers are interesting because they all have a personality disorder such as APD or psychopathy. This is often why there is the misconception that psychopaths or individuals with APD are criminals. Not all murderers have a personality disorder, such as APD or psychopathy, just as individuals with APD or psychopathy do not all become criminals and lead a criminal lifestyle. Equally not all criminals are psychopaths but at some point the two dimensions of APD and psychopathy interact with criminality. This interaction between the two dimensions and criminality can be represented diagrammatically (see Figure 7.1).

It is this interaction point between criminality and psychopathy that is of interest and relevancy to our discussion of criminal psychopaths. It is important to note, however, that APD from among all the personality disorders tends to be associated with criminal behaviour and often considered to be the same as psychopathy. With close examination of the traits that cluster together in the APD typology it becomes apparent why – the traits of APD are similar to psychopathy. Consider the description of APD from DSM-5 (2013):

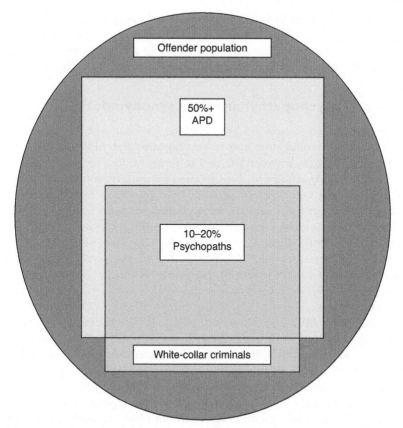

*Figure 7.1* The interaction between the dimensions of APD, psychopathy and criminality
Adapted from Hare 2005

- lacks empathy;
- lacks guilt or shame;
- dishonest;
- irresponsible;
- manipulative;
- destructive and callous towards the suffering of others;
- indifferent to the rights of others and aggressive.

Unfortunately all these traits collectively provide a profile of a selfish and inconsiderate individual whose concerns revolve around self-gain and promotion. As they are indifferent to the feelings of others (in part because they feel little empathy for others and have an immature Theory of Mind – see Chapters 3, 4, 8, 9 and 10), manipulating people and acting deceitful is not perceived as morally wrong, which is why they experience little or no guilt or shame. A mind that is set to work in this way will always be on the periphery of 'normative behaviour' and constantly battling against the inclination to behave in a deviant and socially unacceptable manner. Given this battle of wills, it is easy to see a predisposition towards criminality. But are APD and psychopathy vastly different from one another? An interesting question which we will address next.

## APD and psychopathy: are they synonymous?

Interesting research conducted by Decuyper, De Fruyt and Buschman (2008) questioned the synonymous use of psychopathy and APD and how there might be differences between the two in terms of the Five Factor Model of Personality (FFM). The FFM, used to assess personality, consists of five broad dimensions each with a set of different traits (discussed further in the next section). Decuyper *et al.* claimed that psychopathy is distinct from APD but the behaviour of individuals with APD or psychopathy is consistent. Psychologist Robert Hare (1991) devised the Psychopathy Checklist – Revised (PCL-R) to assess the personality and lifestyle profile of the psychopath (also discussed further in the next section). Hare and Neumann (2006) claimed that the relationship between psychopathy and APD is asymmetric because offenders who scored high on the PCL-R also complied with APD criteria but most individuals with APD scored low on the PCL-R. Blackburn and Coid (1998) and Hildebrand and de Ruiter (2004) previously showed that psychopathy correlated robustly with APD, but that there were also positive correlations with paranoid, narcissistic, borderline and histrionic personality disorders.

Decuyper *et al.* (2008) studied a forensic psychiatric sample, hypothesising that there should be associations between psychopathy and APD. In the case of APD they considered the constructs of FFM, and for psychopathy an expert-based description created by Miller, Lynam, Widiger and Leukefeld (2001) was adopted (see section on classification of psychopaths). They also considered psychopathy in the wider framework of other personality disorders described in DSM-5. Correlations between FFM and psychopathy were disappointing in that only two out of the 18 predictions were supported. Correlations between FFM and APD, however, confirmed previous research. In their sample 27 per cent diagnosed with psychopathy also had a comorbid APD diagnosis, confirming Hare and Neumann's conclusion; 15 per cent of psychopaths were also comorbid for paranoid personality disorder and a further 15 per cent for avoidant and dependent personality disorders. In the case of borderline, histrionic and narcissistic personality disorders, **comorbidity** with psychopathy was 8 per cent, 4 per cent and 0 per cent respectively. These findings provide further support for Millon and Davis' (1998) ten subtypes of psychopath. Although psychopaths are usually comorbid with an APD diagnosis and show many behavioural similarities, not all individuals with APD score high on PCL-R (Hare and Neumann 2006). For the rest of this chapter therefore, the term psychopath will not be used synonymously with APD but as a separate concept overlapping with APD.

In this chapter the psychopath will be described in terms of social behaviour, cognition and difference of brain function throughout the lifespan (i.e. considering children with behaviours consistent with patterns of psychopathic tendencies) to elucidate why a predisposition towards criminality might explain the psychopath's actions. Whether psychopaths are treatable will also be considered. First, however, it is important to define and categorise the psychopath which has a long history, beginning in the nineteenth century. In the next section description and classification of different psychopaths and more specifically criminal psychopaths will be reviewed.

## Definition and classification of the psychopath

### History of defining the psychopath

Benjamin Rush in 1812 wrote of 'innate preternatural moral depravity' in which '. . . defective organisation in those parts of the body which are preoccupied by the moral faculties of the mind' (p.112, cited in Millon, Simonsen, Birket-Smith and Davis 1998). He further claimed that 'the will might be deranged . . . the will becoming the involuntary vehicle of vicious actions through the instrumentality of the passions. Persons thus diseased cannot speak the truth . . .' (p.124, cited in Millon *et al.* 1998). In 1891 the term 'psychopathic inferiority' was introduced by Koch. Kraepelin (1915) further elaborated on the concept of 'psychopath' by describing two types: those who are obsessive/impulsive or sexual deviants, and those who have personality oddities. Those with personality oddities further sub-divided into:

- unstable
- impulsive
- excitable
- eccentric
- liars/swindlers
- argumentative
- antisocial.

The 1913 Mental Deficiency Act, however, maintained the term moral insanity (first used by Prichard in 1835), to describe the psychopath. Cleckley (1941) provided a list of key traits typifying the behaviour of psychopaths:

- impulsivity;
- lack of guilt;
- emotional shallowness;
- inability to feel love;
- superficial charm and social interaction.

The traits associated with Cleckley are also found among the DSM criteria for many types of personality disorder. It is possible therefore to consider psychopathy as a higher order category. Psychopathy can be construed as a single dimension of an interpersonal style so that some psychopaths tend to be social and others withdrawn. This leads to the assumption therefore that some personality disorders, such as narcissism or paranoia, might occupy similar positions on the psychopathy dimension while at the same time having different interpersonal styles (i.e. those reflecting the nature of their personality disorder). Psychopathic personality, for instance, could be considered a superordinate construct that is more consistent with specific types of personality disorder. For example, an individual could typically possess many traits of a psychopath whilst simultaneously entertaining paranoid thoughts that prompt paranoid behaviour – an interpersonal style consistent with a paranoid personality. Blackburn and Coid (1999) claimed that some psychopaths exhibit antisocial and narcissistic disorders whereas others qualify for a diagnosis of Borderline Personality Disorder (BDP). At the same time as Cleckley's list of traits describing the psychopath was introduced, Karpman (1941) differentiated psychopaths into idiopathic and symptomatic classifications which he felt reflected their differences and aetiology:

1   Idiopathic psychopaths experience antisocial behaviour caused by uninhibited instinctual expression that fails to be moderated through feelings of guilt or a conscience.
2   Symptomatic psychopaths experience disturbance resulting from psychosis or neurosis causing their antisocial behaviour – hence they are not true psychopaths.

Blackburn (1975) later substituted the labels idiopathic and symptomatic psychopaths for primary and secondary psychopaths and added that primary psychopaths are non-anxious types whereas secondary psychopaths are anxious deviants (these types will be considered later in the chapter). Probably the most profound personality assessment and lifestyle description of the psychopath, however, can be derived from Robert Hare's Psychopathy Checklist – Revised in 1991 (see Box 7.2).

## Box 7.2

### Hare's traits of the psychopath in the Psychopathy Checklist – Revised (PCL-R)

- Glibness, superficial charm
- Lack of empathy, callous
- Egocentric, grandiose sense of worth

- Commit many types of offence
- Pathological liars
- Lack of realistic plans
- Deception, cunning
- Impulsive
- Lack of sincerity
- Parasitic lifestyle
- Lack of remorse or guilt
- Behaviour problems
- Lack of affect and depth
- Make irresponsible parents
- Fail to accept responsibility for actions
- Promiscuous
- Antisocial behaviour

Hare has devoted a life-time of study towards understanding the psychopath, not just within a criminal framework but APD itself. In his book, *Without Conscience: The disturbing world of the psychopaths among us*, he described how the traits of APD enables individuals with the disorder to weave their way through life behaving in socially unacceptable ways but within the law. He described some of these individuals as rising above the ranks in the workforce to positions of authority by deriding others as a means to gaining promotion. Their personality traits of callousness and ruthlessness, and the ability to charm, enable them to deceive and manipulate their employers to promote them to high positions. Hare (1993) described these individuals as the psychopaths among us but he also provided an in-depth account of criminal psychopaths and why **white-collar crime** (see Chapter 6) and crime per se is the logical choice for the psychopath. In their book, Babiak and Hare (2006) speculated that the traits of a psychopath are conducive to working in a corporate culture – they are thrill seekers, have charm, manipulate and become bored easily. Babiak (2011) explained that within the corporate world there are four times more psychopaths present than in the population. He further added that it is the perfect environment for the psychopath as it is a place that is constantly changing – hence sufficing their need for excitement. This type of working environment creates the temptation to commit white-collar crime (see Chapter 6).

### Classification of psychopaths

Millon and Davis (1998) studied the different types of psychopath in detail by paying particular attention to the slight differences in their behaviour and activity and the motivation and function their behaviour satisfies – why they do what they do. They described ten subtypes of psychopathy. The correlations across other personality disorders found by Blackburn and Coid

(1998) and Hildebrand and de Ruiter (2004) considered earlier in this chapter have significance for these ten subtypes of psychopath, as they help explain the differences in behavioural style across the subtypes. There are, however, two types of psychopath that hold particular significance for understanding homicidal and serial killing psychopaths: malevolent and tyrannical.

- *Malevolent*: This type of psychopath is extremely hostile and vindictive towards others. They are destructive and hateful and take their revenge out on others often in the cruellest of ways. They have a cold-blooded ruthless manner and use this against people to avenge the real or imagined ill-treatment experienced in childhood. They are fearless and experience little guilt, and strongly overlap with the paranoid personality type listed earlier in this chapter and the sadistic personality type. A sadistic personality type, however, is often hostile, cruel, dominating, intimidating, dogmatic and humiliating (Millon 2004). These psychopaths quite often take to murder and serial killing. They have the capacity to understand guilt and remorse, but tend to justify their actions using non-ethical means.
- *Tyrannical*: This type of psychopath is similar to the malevolent type but differs in the selection of victims – they like their victims to cower and be submissive. They are extremely abusive, vulgar, intimidating, inhumane and unmerciful to their victims and the people they interact with. These individuals are the classic psychopaths but also have traits overlapping with negativistic and sadistic personality types. An individual with a negativistic (also referred to as passive–aggressive) personality is often resentful, contrary, moody, irritable, sceptical and emotionally withdrawn. The tyrannical psychopath has inner insecurities and a low self-esteem which explains why they act so aggressively and violently towards others (i.e. to hide their true disposition). As with the malevolent psychopath, the tyrannical psychopath is driven towards murder and serial killing.

The remaining eight subtypes of psychopaths described in Box 7.3 can be aggressive, violent and hostile but rarely commit homicide.

## Box 7.3

### The eight remaining subtypes of psychopath

*Unprincipled*: This type of psychopath overlaps with individuals showing traits that underlie the narcissistic personality type. They live their lives within the boundary of the law but are prone to being con artists and fraudulent. They overestimate their self-worth and are indifferent to the welfare of others. They are unscrupulous, disloyal, and deceptive and lack moral substance. They appear to exalt in a willingness to risk, harm and promote a fearless disposition. They lack guilt and a social conscience which enables them to humiliate and act maliciously towards others. They can be charming and use this to manipulate others.

*Disingenuous*: This type of psychopath can give the impression of being friendly and sociable but beneath this facade they actually harbour deep resentment and can be extremely moody, unreliable and impulsive. Their relationships lack depth of emotion and they are capricious and act impulsively. Often they say nasty things to their partners and base their decisions on limited information, which is why they are likened to the histrionic personality type. They fail to justify their behaviour and be held accountable for problems in their relationships. They want approval but rely on a cunning and manipulative approach for gaining this. Their social facade is replaced with anger and abuse when opposed.

*Risk-taking*: This type of psychopath engages in risk-taking behaviour to satisfy a need for excitement. They act impulsively and have little control, restraint or reflection over their behaviour. As a result of this need for excitement they appear fearless, put themselves in danger and in harm's way which is why their behaviour is seen as foolhardy. They represent both the antisocial and histrionic personality types.

*Covetous*: This type of psychopath feels that they have been deprived of love, support and the rewards due to them. They therefore feel envious and motivated to gain retribution for having been deprived of what should have naturally been theirs. Those who feel limited grievance tend to do minor transgressions but those who feel severely aggrieved will steal from and manipulate others. Despite experiencing limited guilt and empathy for others they are fairly insecure about their position and gains – always feeling that they are still deprived and want more. They have a persona that portrays them as having justified rights over others.

*Spineless*: This type of psychopath is insecure and cowardly. Aggression portrayed in this type is to give signals to others that they are not anxious or weak. Their violence is a means to overriding their fearfulness. They have similar patterns of behaviour to the avoidant and dependent personalities. They perceive their adversaries as powerful, aggressive and sadistic and themselves as vulnerable and undefended, but by acting aggressively towards people they hide their fear and appear as dangerous and 'hard'. They are not motivated by violence but often appear as the tough guy and tend to join militaristic groups.

*Explosive*: This type of psychopath can be unpredictably hostile by demonstrating uncontrollable rage and assault on others. Their explosive behaviour is threatening to others but the underlying motivation is to expel pent up frustration and feelings of humiliation – a kind of catharsis except they have little control over it when it occurs. They are often hypersensitive and over react to a benign event. Their aggressive acts are a consequence of perceived personal failure and serve as a form of release.

*Abrasive*: This type of psychopath acts in a hostile and argumentative way. They perceive others as objects to assault and use for verbal abuse. They are antagonistic and have no second thoughts about demeaning others publicly. This type of psychopath is compared to the negativistic and paranoid personalities primarily because of their irritable, debasing, dogmatic, arrogant, contradictory and corrosive ways. They feel a need to correct people and to put them in their place regardless of whether they themselves are right or wrong and have no remorse or conscience about doing so.

*Malignant*: This type of psychopath has traits that overlap with the paranoid personality as they mistrust, resent and envy others. They abuse others but have found that this only results in further hostility and punishment and so they fantasise their **retribution** instead. They imagine possible plots against them and can become quite deluded about being persecuted. They like to maintain their independence and autonomy and concern themselves with ways of avoiding submission to authority – they fear being forced to conform.

The ten subtypes described by Millon and Davis are specific to the personalities of psychopaths. A different approach, however, designed to highlight the extent of trait deviation of the psychopath's personality from the 'personality norm' is to consider the FFM. The five broad dimensions housing numerous traits (McCrae and Costa 1990) are as follows:

- openness
- agreeableness
- conscientiousness
- extraversion
- neuroticism.

The FFM is commonly used to assess personality; however, by using normative scores for each dimension (based on different population cohorts) comparisons with cohorts of male and female psychopaths have interesting but not surprising results. The standard deviation of scores for psychopaths on dimensions of agreeableness, openness and conscientiousness is striking. Psychopaths score low on the agreeableness and conscientious dimensions of the FFM but high on extroversion and a mixture of low and high on particular traits of the neuroticism dimension (Lynam 2002; Miller and Lynam 2003). In the case of neuroticism, psychopaths score low on traits such as anxiety, vulnerability to stress and depression but high on impulsiveness and angry hostility.

In an effort to determine if the NEO Personality Inventory Revised (NEO-PI-R), which is an FFM assessment tool (Costa and McCrae 1992), could be used to assess psychopathy, Miller and Lynam (2003) screened a group of university students. The NEO-PI-R is a self-report questionnaire derived from dimensions on the FFM which uses a 5-point scale (0, strongly disagree to 4, strongly agree) to answer 240 items. Miller and Lynam (2003) also used an expert-generated prototype of psychopathy which was based on clinical expert knowledge of the prototypical psychopathic characteristics – this information was then entered into the computer. Based on their NEO-PI-R scores for the agreeableness and conscientiousness dimensions, Miller and Lynam (2003) divided participants into four groups:

1   low scores for agreeableness and conscientiousness;
2   high scores for agreeableness and conscientiousness;
3   low score for agreeableness but high score for conscientiousness;
4   high score for agreeableness but low score for conscientiousness.

Participants scoring in the top and bottom third on the agreeableness and conscientiousness dimensions were selected and their data submitted to the expert-generated prototype on computer. They found that individuals closely matching the psychopathy prototype showed increased rates of criminal and delinquent behaviour and APD traits. Miller and Lynam concluded that participants who scored low on agreeableness and conscientiousness and high on extraversion, and high on impulsiveness and angry hostility but low on anxiety (i.e. neuroticism) exhibited psychopathic behaviour. They were more likely to use illicit substances, commit property and violent crime, drink drive, steal and have many sexual partners.

Their findings provided evidence for understanding psychopathy as a constellation of traits from the FFM. They were also able to show that the scores on the FFM can help to predict future criminal behaviour, aggression and substance abuse. Furthermore, response styles helped to explain lifestyle strategies that fitted the descriptions provided by Hare's PCL-R. Research in this area has generally found support for psychopaths scoring low on dimensions of agreeableness and conscientiousness but as yet failed to find conclusive evidence for the overall applicability of the FFM (Edens, Marcus, Lilienfeld and Poythress 2006).

Whether psychopathy should be construed as dimensional or categorical (i.e. subtypes) has been debated for many years. Loranger (1999) has questioned the accuracy and validity of creating subtypes and therefore demarcating one type of psychopath from another on the basis of traits that are not mutually exclusive. Loranger (1999) also questioned the validity of dimensions that are based on poorly defined and agreed clinical criteria. Psychopathy and variants of psychopathy are at the heart of the dimensional-categorical debate. Hare's PCL-R, however, crosses over the debate by separating psychopath from non-psychopath cohorts and distinguishing degrees of psychopathy using a continuous scoring method – the higher the score the more akin to the prototypical psychopath the individual is (Hare 1991). Variants of psychopathy can be gauged as Types 1 or 2 (i.e. Factors 1 – interpersonal/affective element – and 2 – social deviance lifestyle component – on the PCL-R) that are consistent with categorical classification and dimensionally with high or low scores on traits of neuroticism. Hart and Dempster (1997) examined the association between Types 1 and 2 with violent offending and compared features of the offence with Blackburn's (1975) classification of primary and secondary psychopathy. They found that Type 1 was robustly associated with primary psychopathy whereas Type 2 fitted descriptions of the secondary psychopath. In the case of primary psychopathy, the ratings in Type 1 positively correlated with planning, instrumentality and goal directedness whereas for Type 2 with secondary psychopathy – a negative correlation for planning was found. Mealey (1995) considered secondary psychopathy as a dimension and primary psychopathy as a taxon (i.e. a category). The reasoning for this separation relates to the scores on Factors 1 and 2, where primary psychopaths scored high on Factor 1 and either high or low on Factor 2 but secondary psychopaths only attained high scores on Factor 2. For an in-depth account of the category-dimension debate, refer to the paper, 'Psychopathic personality or personalities? Exploring potential variants of psychopathy and their implications for risk assessment' (Skeem, Poythress, Edens, Lilienfeld and Cale 2003).

The definition and classification of psychopaths is largely based on their observed behaviours. The observation of their social behaviours, however, can be very informative in determining the underlying problems experienced by psychopaths such as Theory of Mind (ToM), emotional understanding and moral development. Through understanding the principle problem areas experienced by psychopaths, it might be possible to develop a clearer view of whether nature, nurture or nature–nurture accounts for their condition. The next section, therefore, will explore social behaviour within the context of ToM, emotion and morals.

## Social behaviour of the psychopath

The psychopath demonstrates poor self-control and a high level of impulsivity (Hare 1991; DSM-5 2013). Poor self-control regulation is related to the desire for immediate gratification and might be an important factor in committing a crime. Deficient delay functions in psychopaths are a characteristic that further supports an impulsive profile (Hare 1991; DSM-5 2013). Their preference for immediate gratification gives them a present-oriented time focus which might contribute to their delinquency and criminal pursuit. Their poor self-control and impulsivity is further demonstrated through psychomotor tasks involving the Porteus Maze. This task involves the presentation of a series of visual mazes where participants work their way through solving the mazes by keeping within the lines, starting at 'A' and finishing at 'Z'. Two measures are taken: the Test Quotient (TQ) and the Qualitative Error (Q). TQ correlates robustly with foresight and planning behaviour whereas Q correlates with carelessness, rule breaking and impulsivity. When Porteus (1959) first administered the test he found that workers scoring high on Q often had disciplinary problems.

Psychopaths also score high on Q in comparison to non-psychopaths (Schalling and Rosên 1968). Impulsivity might also play a role in the nature of attitudes held by psychopaths considered next.

### Attitudes

The attitudes, values and beliefs of psychopaths suggest that they endorse sub-terranean values whereby toughness, aggression and excitement are important to them. These values have been corroborated by the scores attained on the FFM (Lynam 2002; Lynam and Widiger 2001). Attribution theory has also been helpful as a means to explaining how psychopaths view their behaviour as being justified (see Chapter 5). Heider (1944) introduced attribution theory to account for how people make decisions about the causes of overt behaviour. He hypothesised that external and internal attributions can be used to explain the causes of people's behaviour. An external attribution used to account for why an individual falls over, for example, might involve a loose paving stone in the street. An internal attribution relies on a variable specific to the individual such as being uncoordinated. Sykes and Matza (1957) modified Heider's approach and defined five attribution techniques that psychopaths use to neutralise the immoral acts that they perform within a criminal setting.

- The first is denial of responsibility where they will blame an external source for their behaviour.
- The second is denial of injury where they conclude that little harm was caused by their actions.
- The third is denial of the victim where they assume that the victim deserved what happened to them.
- The fourth is where they condemn their condemners.
- The fifth is an appeal to higher loyalties by claiming, for example, that the needs of their peers took precedence over the victim.

All of the aforementioned facets of the psychopath have repercussions for their socio-cognitive and interpersonal skills. These attribution techniques resemble the criminal thinking errors discussed by Yochelson and Samenow in their description of the typical criminal personality (see Chapter 5). Attributions made by psychopaths are so different to those made by non-criminals that it begs the question of what underlying processes enable psychopaths to make them. The answer to this might lie within the realm of **moral reasoning** and empathy discussed next.

### Moral reasoning and empathy

Piaget and Kohlberg, for example, hypothesised that role-taking ability is fundamental to moral reasoning. The ability to role-take is indicative of ToM and suggests a competent level of moral maturity (see Chapter 4). Psychopaths, however, are egocentric – they have a selfish point of view and want to satisfy their needs and attain gratification at the expense of others (Hare 1991). Moral maturity, as discussed in Chapter 4, results from appropriate socialisation, empathy, emotional understanding and recognition, all of which are served through good parenting and nurturance. Punishment, for example, plays an important role in good parenting skills and when used appropriately can instil a sense of fear in the child so as to not misbehave again; however, Lykken (1957) found evidence linking the psychopath with reduced anxiety and low levels of fearfulness. Through the application of aversive conditioning, a therapeutic intervention developed from classical conditioning (see Box 8.5), Lykken (1957) established that psychopaths were poor at learning to avoid negative stimuli in the form of punishment (see Box 7.4).

## Box 7.4

### Basic procedure of aversive conditioning

The basic rule in aversive conditioning is to learn that negative or unpleasant stimuli (usually a harmless electric shock in typical aversive conditioning studies) are associated with an event (to be avoided in future if possible). Lykken applied principles of classical conditioning and found the following:

1. An unpleasant event (unconditioned stimulus [US]) such as a painful shock produces sweat (an unconditioned response [UR]).
2. The US is paired with the sound of a buzzer lasting five seconds (conditioned stimulus [CS]).
3. Do psychopaths associate the buzzer with the shock and secrete sweat when the buzzer alone sounded in future trials?
4. Psychopaths in comparison to non-psychopaths showed reduced **electrodermal activity** – they secreted less sweat.

These findings have since been replicated by Flor, Birbaumer, Hermann, Ziegler and Patrick (2002). Interestingly, Lykken (1995) made an important connection between 'attenuated' (i.e. reduced) emotional experiences of fearfulness and anxiety and poor socialisation. The attenuated emotional experiences of fearfulness and anxiety are contributory underlying biological mechanisms preventing these individuals from learning how to behave appropriately through reward and punishment regimes. This idea fits in with Blair's (1995) and his co-researchers' (Blair, Colledge, Murray and Mitchell 2001) work on the Violence Inhibition Mechanism. This describes how emotional deficits in psychopaths result from empathy dysfunction which leads to ineffective moral socialisation. An inability to feel the sadness and fear experienced by others prevents psychopaths from inhibiting behaviour that causes others to feel sad or frightened. Thus the socialisation of society's rules, conventions and morals fail to be acquired, which goes a long way towards explaining the behaviours and belief systems of psychopaths. Blair (2007) found psychopaths to be less responsive to environmental threat which is why they fail to have fearfulness and anxiety responses to punishment. Despite, however, their ability to experience cognitive empathy (i.e. the ability to know what others are feeling) they fail to show emotional empathy (i.e. to feel what others are feeling) (Blair and Blair 2009).

Numerous studies have shown that psychopaths have limited empathy for others and they tend to have parasitic lifestyles where they become dependent on others – these factors are implicit in Hare's PCL-R. Implicit within social interaction is the ability to role take, attend and listen to others. Rimé, Bouvy, Leborgne and Rouillon (1978) found that psychopaths showed significantly more hand gesturing and leaning forward while simultaneously showing little warmth through intimidating eye contact and neutral expression. These social interactions are hostile and corroborate the high score of anger hostility on the neuroticism dimension of the FFM.

It is well established that psychopaths are egocentric, callous, dishonest, experience little guilt or empathy, portray a superficial charm and make external attributions of blame for their behaviour (Hare 1991; Lilienfeld 1998; Sykes and Matza 1957). Further characteristics of the psychopath include extreme risk taking and antisocial and aggressive behaviour (Glenn and Raine 2009; Millon 2011). Despite Blackburn's (1975) classification of psychopaths as primary (i.e. non-anxious types) or secondary (i.e. anxious deviants), recent research by Ali, Amorim and Chamorro-Premuzic (2009) showed a further difference between primary and secondary psychopaths involving abnormal emotional processing of faces. They found that primary psychopaths experienced positive affect (such as happiness) when viewing faces expressing sadness. This supports the previous findings by Cleckley (1988) that primary psychopaths do not experience negative emotions: the implication of this being that sadness will cause little if any distress to them. Coupled with Blair's (1999) research demonstrating reduced autonomic responses to distress and sadness displayed in others and, his research in 1995 showing dysfunction in processing sad and fearful expressions in faces, it would appear that primary psychopaths actually enjoy seeing others in distress, pain or sadness.

These findings go a long way towards explaining why primary psychopaths who murder their victims can commit sadistic atrocities – there is no empathy module to moderate their behaviour. In the case of secondary psychopaths, Ali *et al.* (2009) found that they presented negative affect (such as anger) when shown ambiguous or neutral facial expressions. They compared their findings with a study conducted by Dadds, Perry, Hawes, Merz *et al.* (2006) on a sample of children who previously scored high on psychopathy. These children had difficulty recognising neutral expressions and they rated the faces as having angry expressions. The findings reported by Blair (1999; 1995), Ali

*Plate 7.1* Facial expression of fear

*et al.* (2009) and Dadds *et al.* (2006) are enlightening and provide insight to why both primary and secondary psychopaths typically react in the manner that they do towards their victims. In the case of primary psychopaths there is no empathy switch they can turn on to stop the pleasure they experience in seeing others distressed, frightened or sad – ultimately enabling them to behave callously and ruthlessly towards their victims.

For secondary psychopaths their misinterpretations in reading facial expressions correctly, and the misattribution of neutral expressions as representing negative states of mind, ignite their already anxious disposition to react in a self-defensive mode – which means acting aggressively. Moral reasoning and empathy are closely associated with ToM in that to be able to see yourself from someone else's perspective, you need to understand what they are thinking and feeling and how moral your responses to this actually are.

### Moral development and Theory of Mind

Reading facial expressions is an important element of ToM. ToM is a form of 'mindreading' that enables us to interpret the intentions of others so that we can gauge our own responses to others during social interactions. ToM, however, is more than the cognitive understanding of the situation; it is the emotional feeling experienced, too, and this has a biological foundation in the form of mirror neurons in the brain. These become activated when others experience distress (Jackson, Meltzoff and Decety 2005) and also act to prevent us from causing harm to others; there is significant neurocognitive support for an innate 'module' for empathy (see Chapter 10). The acquisition of morality through socialisation provides a nurture element to moral development (see Chapter 4). The acquisition of morals was considered to be an interaction between learning and maturation whereby children progress through a developmental map of levels and stages (Kohlberg 1969) enabled through the process of socialisation; this occurs courtesy of our parents, in the first instance, followed by formal socialising agents such as education, law and culture (see Chapter 4). Children learn right from wrong through the engagement of reward and punishment schedules, followed by social consensus until it is finally internalised and no reminder of moral principles is necessary (Kohlberg 1969; Piaget 1932, 1965).

Important also for the acquisition of morals are ToM and empathy (see Chapter 4). However, as discussed previously, psychopaths are egocentric and find it difficult to understand and interpret the intentions and feelings of others, especially secondary psychopaths who are misattributing neutral facial expressions for anger. The primary psychopaths' empathy module would appear to be wired in a very different way to the rest of us as they actually gain positive affect from viewing facial expressions of fear and sadness (Ali *et al.* 2009). These findings indicate that the brains of psychopaths might be functioning differently from the rest of us. It is fortunate that science technology has made it possible to visually read the brain activity of psychopaths. In the next section we will concentrate on possible nature related explanations of the differences in structure and function of the psychopath's brain beginning with differences in how their brain operates on various psychological tasks.

## Differences in attention and lateralised function

### Attention

Psychopaths not only exhibit differences in the way that they perceive and interpret social interactions with others and the emotional content of facial expressions, they deploy their attention differently. They pay attention to stimuli and screen-out elements of information that they consider as irrelevant differently to the rest of us. An interesting study demonstrating this ability was conducted by Jutai and Hare (1983). They measured **evoked potentials** in the brain and **electrodermal activity** in the skin among inmates scoring high or low on the PCL-R. There were two conditions:

1   A series of tone pips were broadcast through headphones on their own (known as passive attention).
2   A series of tone pips broadcast at the same time as playing a video game (known as selective attention).

A measure of the attention paid to the tone pips was taken using a component of the auditory evoked potential labelled N100. Attention to playing the video game was measured through their performance. In the passive attention condition where only the tone pips were broadcast, psychopaths had the same N100 reading as non-psychopaths. The difference in N100 arose during the selective attention condition especially for the first trial. Psychopaths displayed small N100 responses for each trial whereas non-psychopaths displayed a large N100 reading for the first trial and smaller responses as trials progressed. According to Jutai and Hare this is an indication of altered deployment of attention in psychopaths: they suppress co-occurring distractor stimuli.

Newman and his team formulated the Response Modulation Hypothesis to account for differences of attention deployment portrayed in psychopaths. This simply involves the ability to shift attention quickly and effortlessly which Newman, Schmitt and Voss (1997) eloquently described as, 'a rapid and relatively automatic (i.e. non-effortful or involuntary) shift of attention from the effortful organisation and implementation of goal-directed behaviour to its evaluation' (p.564). In the case of psychopaths, Newman *et al.* (1997) claimed that they have difficulty self-regulating their attention from one thing to another – it does not come naturally and instead the execution of decisions and actions require effortful processing. According to Lorenz and Newman (2002), 'the impulsivity, poor passive avoidance and emotion-processing deficits of individuals with psychopathy may all be understood as a failure to process the meaning of information that is peripheral or incidental to their deliberate focus of attention' (p.92).

Newman *et al.* (1997) tested prisoners (psychopaths and non-psychopaths) who were divided into low or high scorers on the Welsh Anxiety Scale (WAS) for negative affectivity (NA) such as fear, anger or sadness. There were 160 trials: 80 trials involved comparing two pictures for relatedness and 80 trials involved comparing two words for relatedness. Participants were alerted to focus either on the picture ('P') or word ('W') component prior to being presented with the context display that showed both a picture and word together (see Figures 7.2 and 7.3). Then after a brief interval they were presented with the test display which was either a picture or word depending on whether the 'P' or 'W' alert had been shown. They responded by indicating whether the test display related to either the word or picture shown in the context display. This meant that participants had to switch their focus of attention when presented with the stimulus (i.e. 'W' or 'P') as a pre-warning. This switching of attention is a difficult task to do. Box 7.5 explains their findings.

## Box 7.5

### Evidence for the Response Modulation Hypothesis

The researchers found different levels of interference effects. All prisoners took longer to respond when the contextual cues were related to the test displays than when they were not. There was more interference on picture trials than word trials – in other words, prisoners found it more difficult to ascertain a connection between words embedded in the paired pictures of the picture display and a picture test display. The low-NA non-psychopaths showed significantly more interference effects (comparable to non-incarcerated individuals) than the low–NA psychopaths. High–NA psychopaths experienced more interference effects than high–NA non-psychopaths. Hence the low–NA psychopaths had problems with automatic processing of contextual cues while engaging in the main task (i.e. to decide on the relatedness of the pair), explaining their poor response modulation. This means that unlike controls and high–NA psychopaths (which Newman *et al.* speculated might not be true psychopaths – perhaps secondary psychopaths), low–NA psychopaths might be processing contextual cues to a shallow level because they find it difficult to process such information automatically and rely instead on effortful processing. For most people it is difficult to switch off the automatic processing of contextual cues which is why interference effects are experienced. This study showed that primary psychopaths deploy their attention differently and have a malfunctioning response modulation.

**Picture trial**

*Context display*

**Picture trial**

*Test display*

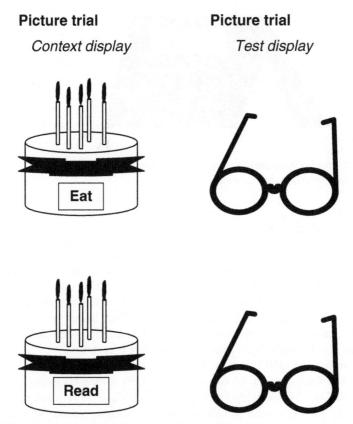

Eat

Read

*Figure 7.2* One example of the picture-word presentation
Adapted from Newman, Schmitt and Voss 1997

**Word trial**                    **Word trial**

*Context display*                  *Test display*

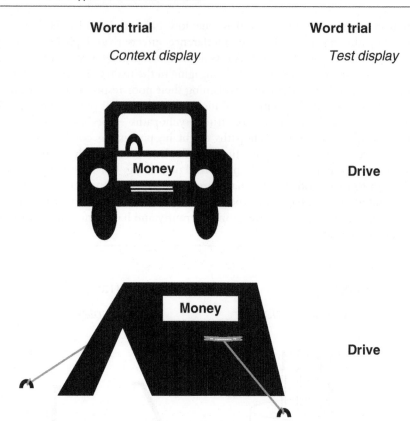

Figure 7.3 Another example of the picture-word presentation
Adapted from Newman, Schmitt and Voss 1997

### Cerebral lateralisation

The two hemispheres of the brain are connected via the corpus callosum which enables the transference of information from one hemisphere to the other. This implies that each cerebral hemisphere is lateralised for function which can be easily seen in fMRI scans: if the left hand moves then this is registered as brain activity in the right hemisphere and vice versa. Each hemisphere is dominant for different cognitive activity where the left hemisphere primarily processes language and the right hemisphere emotion (see Chapter 3).

Research using fMRI to scan the brains of volunteers diagnosed with psychopathy and a control group of non-psychopaths demonstrates the differences in cerebral lateralisation. Cerebral lateralisation research of cognitive processing commonly involves word processing and one such approach, which can be easily set up by broadcasting different messages to the ears using headphones, is known as dichotic listening (see Box 7.6).

## Box 7.6

### Dichotic listening tasks

Dichotic listening tasks are a good way of examining how our attention is deployed and a simple, but effective, method of studying cerebral lateralisation in the context of verbal processing. Models of attention and how we process information were developed by psychologists such as Broadbent (1958), Treisman (1964) and Deutsch and Deutsch (1963). However, it was Cherry's Cocktail Party Effect which highlighted the importance of how easily our focus of attention can be disrupted by unanticipated events.

For instance, Cherry (1953) reported that if you were heavily engrossed in a conversation with a group of friends at a party, as indeed were other groups of people, and suddenly you heard the words 'ballroom dancer' being mentioned in another conversation, you would find it difficult to ignore their further conversation – especially if you are a ballroom dancer or ballroom dancing holds some other significance for you.

Dichotic listening tasks enable researchers to copy the Cocktail Party Effect under controlled laboratory conditions. Here the participant has to pay attention to the message broadcast to the right ear by shadowing what is being said (i.e. saying out loud the message as it is heard). What do you think would happen if while you were doing this task you heard your name and details being said about you in the message broadcast to the left ear? Do you think you would have control over what happened next?

The normal pattern of processing language is in the left hemisphere (LH) of the brain, often considered to be the 'logical' hemisphere, unlike the right hemisphere (RH) which interprets stimuli relating to our emotional life (Borod 1992; Bulman-Fleming and Bryden 1994; Liotti and Tucker 1995). Despite this separation we have a fast track processing system to the RH for negative emotionally laden words. It has been found in numerous studies that psychopaths have problems processing negative emotionally laden words in the RH and shift this function to the LH (Ogloff and Wong 1990). When considering visually presented stimuli researchers refer to the left visual field (LVF) or the right visual field (RVF). Because information in the LVF is processed by the RH and the RVF by the LH, results are often written as LVF-RH or RVF-LH – stimuli are considered to be bilaterally presented. Day and Wong's (1996) research involved bilateral presentation of visually projected emotional words to a group of psychopaths and controls. Controls showed the usual pattern of identifying emotional words when presented in the LVF-RH more quickly than when presented to the RVF-LH. Psychopaths did not show this LVF-RH advantage but tended to be faster and more accurate when emotional words were presented to the RVF-LH.

Using dichotic listening tasks, Hare and Jutai (1988) demonstrated that psychopaths have a reduced LH advantage for categorising nouns but a normal LH advantage for word recognition. In Hare and McPherson's (1984) study they found a small LH advantage for recalling words which was supported by Raine, O'Brien, Smiley, Scerbo and Chan (1990) who found that adolescent psychopaths tended to be more symmetrical (i.e. recalled similar frequency in the LH and RH) than controls on a consonant-vowel dichotic listening task. Hence these findings collectively suggest that psychopaths have a pattern of reduced LH dominance for language. Hiatt, Lorenz and Newman (2002) tested psychopaths and a control group for the processing of emotional tones and words using the dichotic listening task format. In each dichotic listening trial they were presented with either the target word or emotional tone and had to respond by indicating its presence. Hiatt *et al.* used dichotic listening stimuli courtesy of Bryden and MacRae's study in 1988. This was a clever combination of words spoken in a happy, sad or neutral tone. Each word/emotion combination was further paired with another word/emotion combination (totalling 144 pairings). Hiatt *et al.* predicted that psychopaths would have a decreased hemisphere specialisation for recognising words and emotional tones. Psychopaths processed emotion in the RH more effectively than the LH and showed a left ear advantage (i.e. to RH) comparable to the controls but superior processing of emotion targets presented to the right ear (i.e. to LH). Their findings contradicted previous research demonstrating reduced right ear (i.e. to LH) detection for words in psychopaths but supported evidence of there being increased processing of emotional words to the right ear (i.e. to LH).

These differences in brain function of psychopaths, as demonstrated by attention and dichotic listening tasks, might be explained by structural differences in the brain or structural differences causing variations of brain function. This is why neuroimaging might help us to understand what is going on inside the heads of psychopaths – our next topic of discussion.

### Brain neuroimaging in psychopaths

There have been numerous studies examining structural and functional differences in the brains of murderers, violent offenders and offenders with APD using various brain imaging techniques (see Chapters 3, 5, 6 and 8). Neuroimaging studies of the brains of murderers and violent offenders diagnosed as primary psychopaths using Hare's PCL-R are of particular interest here.

Kiehl, Smith, Hare, Mendrek *et al.* (2001) investigated the memory performance of individuals scoring high or low on the PCL-R for neutral and emotional words during an fMRI scan. Reduced amygdala activity was found in the high scoring group (i.e. psychopaths) when negative emotional words were processed. A study by Yang, Raine, Narr, Colletti and Toga (2009) was the first to show structural abnormalities of the amygdala in psychopaths using

MRI. They found volume reduction of the amygdala in the basolateral, lateral, cortical and central nuclei regions of the brain and concluded that this pattern of structural difference of the amygdala was comparable to individuals who had lesion damage to the amygdala – this damage to the amygdala resulted in deficits of emotion and behaviour modulation.

Adolphs, Tranel, Damasio and Damasio (1994) studied amygdala damage in an individual who had Urbach-Wiethe disease. This disease specifically impairs recognition of emotional expression in faces including negative emotions such as fear: this finding is analogous to the typical impairment demonstrated in psychopaths. In support of Yang *et al.*'s (2009) findings, results from a study conducted by Knapska, Radwanska, Werka and Kaczmarek (2007) demonstrate the importance of the basolateral, lateral and central nuclei for emotional processing in the conditioning of fear and the role of autonomic activity in response to emotional stimuli (see Figure 7.4 and Chapter 10). They also found a link between these three nuclei, decision making and the control of behavioural inhibition. Interestingly, Knapska *et al.* found evidence of the cortical nuclei influencing social interaction and parenting skills. Further research has shown a link between reduced volume in the right amygdala with progressive PCL-R scores of psychopathy in violent criminals (Gordon, Baird and End 2004). fMRI findings confirm this connection showing increased abnormal amygdala activity with progressive psychopathy scores during tasks of emotional recognition and moral decision making (Glenn, Raine and Schug 2009; Gordon, Baird and End 2004).

Kiehl *et al.* (2001) administered an fMRI scan to test for activity in the limbic system in response to emotional stimuli on eight psychopathic criminals, eight non-psychopathic criminals and a control group of eight non-criminals. Psychopaths demonstrated reduced activity in numerous areas of the limbic system to negative words but heightened activity in the left frontal-temporal cortex associated normally with semantic processing. Kiehl *et al.* argued it is possible that psychopaths adopt different brain pathways for processing emotional content when the limbic system (particularly the amygdala) is malfunctioning.

Reduced activity in the orbitofrontal cortex region has also been implicated in psychopathy using fMRI. Hu, Vik, Dasher and Fowler (2011) found evidence for this in psychopaths and delinquents. They also demonstrated the important relationship between the orbitofrontal cortex and amygdala (see Chapter 5 for neurocognitive and neurobiological brain research). Craig, Catani, Deeley, Latham *et al.* (2009) previously showed that the white matter connections between the amygdala and orbitofrontal cortex, such as the uncinate fasciculus, underpin the typical behavioural characteristics of psychopaths. Craig *et al.* (2009) demonstrated the important role of the uncinate fasciculus using a different type of MRI technology called diffusion tensor magnetic resonance imaging (DT-MRI) which enabled them to analyse in micro-detail the structure of the uncinate fasciculus. They performed a

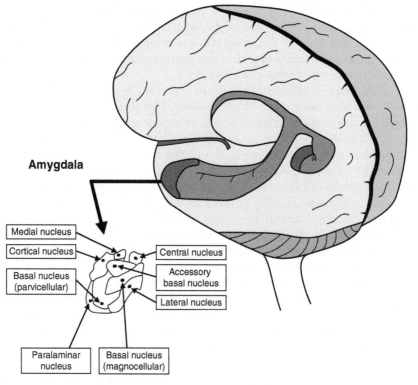

*Figure 7.4* Structural details of the amygdala

DT-MRI scan on psychopaths who were diagnosed using the PCL-R but who were also serious offenders convicted of multiple rapes, manslaughter and attempted murder. The DT-MRI showed that the majority of participants had a weakened or frayed uncinate fasciculus which led Craig *et al.* to conclude that criminal psychopaths have an abnormal amygdala-orbitofrontal pathway. It was further suggested that this faulty pathway could explain why incarcerated criminal psychopaths in the UK (who are 15–25 per cent of the prison population) are responsible for committing 50 per cent more serious offences than non-psychopathic criminals (Dolan 2004).

Further support for abnormal amygdala-orbitofrontal functioning in psychopaths is provided by a study comparing performance for emotion and cognitive based ToM tasks. In 2009 Shamay-Tsoory, Aharon-Peretz and Perry considered the areas of the brain active in emotion and cognitive based ToM tasks. They defined the emotional element as a system which enables us to empathise with others – being able to feel what the other person feels – unlike the cognitive element that allows for empathic perspective taking (De Waal 2007). In this case the cognitive empathy enables us to mentalise about how the person is feeling – being able to understand what the person feels.

As can be seen from most of these standardised behaviours, children and adolescents often portray undesirable behaviours which are nevertheless considered to be the norm. So how can parents and clinicians differentiate normal expected behaviours from abnormal and problematic behaviours? In Box 7.8 are a series of cases of children depicting undesirable behaviours but which of these children are most likely to be problematic adults of the future?

## Box 7.8

### Cases of children with undesirable behaviours – who will become a problem adult?

*Mary* lives on a farm with her parents. Her father is violent towards her and has on occasion hit her so hard that she had bruises on her arms. He became violent towards Mary after he discovered that she is the offspring from an extra-marital relationship five years ago. Her mother is unaware of the physical abuse Mary is experiencing. Mary has become defiant towards her parents and her teachers and has missed classes. She was in trouble for smoking in the toilets at school and was caught kissing and being fondled by boys in her class. Her friends tend to be drop-outs from school and on one occasion they were caught for shoplifting. Mary was cautioned as it was the first time that she was in trouble with the law.

*Mark* comes from an affluent background. Both his parents have decent jobs and earn a lot of money so Mark is well looked after. He has two older brothers who he doesn't see much of, given the ten year gap between them and that they live away. Both brothers are successful and have decent salaries. For most of Mark's life he has been alone and bored. He has friends but finds them boring so he recently started to 'hang out' with older boys who drink and smoke. Recently Mark has had problems concentrating on his school work and has been failing his assignments. In class he often seems dazed and not focused on what is going on around him. His parents were shocked when the police brought him home one evening after having broken into a warehouse with his new friends, causing considerable criminal damage. He was drunk and might have been smoking dope.

*Chris* was increasingly becoming isolated from his friends and was teased by others for being a weirdo. He would say unusual things to his teachers – like they were demons and were persecuting him. This only caused raucous laughter in class but teachers were increasingly concerned for his welfare. It materialised that his father was diagnosed with schizophrenia and was telling his son things that frightened him and brainwashed him into thinking that everyone was out to kill him. Chris, under the orders of his father, let the air out of his neighbour's car tyres and then threw a brick through their kitchen window. Unbeknownst to Chris, the neighbour was hit by the brick and had to go to hospital to have stitches in his head.

*Andrew* was adopted by a married couple who could not have children. Andrew was 3 months old when he was up for adoption and five months by the time he was legally adopted. Everything was fine at first until Andrew started to show cruel behaviour when aged 6 years old. He was seen throwing stones at the local cats and setting fire to the neighbour's dog. His parents were particularly concerned when they caught him putting a hedgehog into a bucket of cold water; the hedge hog drowned and died. When asked to account for this cruel act he said that he was trying to clean the hedgehog and remove the fleas: he was 8 years old. Andrew was caught stealing from his mother's purse and had obviously done this on many occasions. Police had Andrew on CCTV footage kicking a boy in the stomach while the boy was lying unconscious on the ground.

*Kelly* was adopted by a couple: the man had a criminal record for violence and the woman a record for fraud. Nevertheless they did take good care of Kelly who did well at school and was popular and well liked. It was therefore a great shock to discover Kelly beating up another girl in the playground. Kelly who was nine at the time said she was provoked by the girl, who was a bully and who had bullied the other girls; Kelly had taken it upon herself to give this girl a good dressing down and teach her a lesson. She said that her parents taught her to stand up to bullies and her father had shown her a few good fighting moves.

If disruptive home lives are the cause of later criminality, then we could consider Mary and Chris in the equation. If deviant peers or parents are the cause of later criminality then Mark and Kelly can be considered. Andrew, however, appears to have a good home and caring parents, albeit not his natural parents. There is hope for Mary and Chris who can be removed from their disruptive homes or at the very least the disruptive home-life issues can be addressed. As for Mark and Kelly they can change their peers. Andrew is the more worrying case as there appears to be no reactive reason for his behaviour. Furthermore, his behaviour is at odds with the standardised age-related behaviour observed in most children his age. Perhaps his disruptive behaviour fits with descriptions of children with ADHD, CD and ODD whose behaviour breaches the boundaries of normal age-related behaviours studied by bio-psychologists (see Chapter 10). These conditions will be considered next in an effort to establish a link between childhood and adulthood psychopathy.

## Disruptive behaviour disorders (DBDs): ADHD, CD and ODD

Colledge and Blair (2001) found that more than 75 per cent of children with psychopathic traits are highly comorbid with ADHD. Previous research by Biederman, Newcorn and Sprich (1991) showed a high comorbid rate between CD and ADHD.

## Characteristics

ADHD is a frequently referred psychological disorder of childhood (Barkley 2006) and has a host of symptoms like, for example. inattention, hyper-activity–impulsivity and social difficulties with peers. Zametkin, Nordahl, Gross, King et al. (1990) found, using PET scans, reduced cerebral glucose metabolism in the frontal-limbic system of children with ADHD whilst they performed a dichotic listening task: this showed that their brains were less active in these regions. Goodman and Stevenson (1989) studied the herit-ability of ADHD in 127 identical and 111 fraternal twins and found a 51 per cent and 33 per cent concordance rate, respectively. Forsman, Lichtenstein, Andershed and Larsson (2010) considered psychopathy in a Swedish study of 2255 twins from adolescence to adulthood. They found that antisocial behav-iour during adolescence predicted psychopathy in adulthood, supporting the findings of Lynam, Caspi, Moffitt, Loeber and Stouthamer-Loeber in 2007 that showed psychopathy scores at the age of 13 to be predictive of adult psy-chopathy. In the case of children with CD, their parents and teachers found it difficult to control any disruptive outbursts of behaviour. The problem behav-iours associated with CD include aggression and non-compliance, temper tan-trums, stealing, arson and destructiveness, poor moral development and lack of empathy, guilt or a conscience. Their behavioural characteristics can be divided into behavioural excesses (including aggression and non-compliance), behav-ioural deficits (in moral and social behaviour) and poor academic competence.

One possible explanation for their behaviour as suggested by Quay (1988) could be down to an overactive behavioural activation system (BAS) and an underactive behavioural inhibition system (BIS). These systems are part of the septo-hippocampal region of the brain which regulates anxiety and fear (see Figure 7.5). Hence their thrill seeking behaviours and insensitivity to punish-ment could be a consequence of faulty BIS and BAS function (McBurnett 1992). ODD is often regarded as less severe but more common in children than CD. There are differences between the two conditions – the social skills of children with ODD are more impaired compared to children with CD and yet they perform better in school. Furthermore, children with CD are delib-erately more destructive, deceitful and aggressive. Children diagnosed with ODD continuously misbehave and are disobedient towards others and tend to be defiant and hostile for the sake of it. These conditions are sometimes linked to delinquency – and will also be considered in Chapter 10). Common symptoms of ODD include:

- losing their temper;
- arguing;

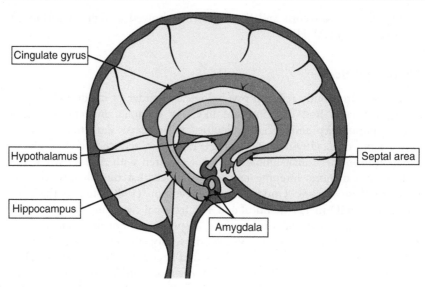

*Figure 7.5* The septo-hippocampal region

- defying and refusing to obey;
- deliberately annoying others;
- acting angry, resentful, spiteful and vindictive towards others.

Despite these symptoms only a proportion of children with ODD progress to CD (Cohen and Flory 1998).

### Progression

It has been argued that, if ignored, ODD in children can progress to CD and CD to APD in adulthood. Robins and Price (1991) found evidence for CD as a robust predictor for APD in adulthood. Findings from Brown, Gleghorn, Schuckit, Myers and Mott's (1996) study suggested that CD often precedes a long-term problem of substance abuse and persistent antisocial behaviour during adolescence. This has been supported further through developmental models, such as that proposed by Moffitt, Caspi, Dickson, Silva and Stanton (1996), which suggest two subtypes of deviant adolescents. The first group showed signs of problem behaviour in adolescence which dissipates at the onset of early adulthood. In the case of the second group, however, their antisocial behaviour continued into adulthood and appeared to stem from a childhood history of hardcore deviant behaviour. Myers, Stewart and Brown (1998) showed that a CD onset age of ten years or earlier predicted future APD in adolescence and adulthood.

There is clearly a relationship between Disruptive Behaviour Disorders (DBD) and later APD, but whether this means they become psychopaths remains unclear. Studies considering the physiological differences between children with DBD and matched control groups for age and sex have found some startling differences. For instance, in various studies conducted by van Goozen, cortisol levels in children with DBD as a measure of defiant behaviour were used.

van Goozen, Matthys, Cohen-Kettenis, Gispen-de Wied et al. (1998) measured salivary cortisol levels in ODD boys (mean age 10.2 years) and controls (mean age 9.6 years) under stressful and non-stressful conditions. These boys were divided into four groups depending on the extent of disruptive, delinquent and aggressive behaviour and level of anxiousness shown using the Child Behaviour Checklist (CBCL). There were four possible combinations:

1  high aggressive-high anxiousness;
2  high aggressive-low anxiousness;
3  low aggressive-low anxiousness;
4  low aggressive-high anxiousness.

Measures of cardiovascular activity were also taken. Cortisol is secreted by the adrenal glands during stressful situations and is monitored by the hypothalamic-pituitary gland – it is the pituitary gland, however, that signals the production of cortisol. van Goozen et al. (1998) predicted that boys with ODD have elevated heart rate and blood pressure during conditions of frustration and provocation which would decrease when baseline measurements were taken. In comparison with the control group, ODD boys excelled in anger (therefore exhibiting increased heart rate and blood pressure) during conditions of provocation and frustration. The prediction that ODD boys would have lower levels of cortisol than the control group during baseline measurements was confirmed. This was found to be the case overall; however, factors such as the level of anxiousness and extent of overt aggressiveness and disruptiveness caused large individual differences. van Goozen et al. (1998) found that cortisol increased under stressful conditions when the child was classified as highly aggressive, disruptive and anxious (as measured by the CBCL) but decreased for children considered highly aggressive and disruptive without being anxious. It has been observed in antisocial adults that low levels of cortisol occur in situations that are stressful. This suggests lifespan continuity between ODD boys low on anxiousness and antisocial adults. Kruesi, Schmidt, Donnelly, Hibbs and Hamburger in 1989 found a relationship between low anxiousness and antisocial adults. They speculated that under-arousal, a higher tolerance for stress or over control of the hypothalamus-pituitary might be the underlying cause. It is possible that this can explain van Goozen et al.'s results.

In 2000, van Goozen, Matthys, Cohen-Kettenis, Buitelaar and van Engeland investigated children with DBD against a matched control group and took baseline physiological measurements, including cortisol levels following stress and non-stress conditions. The DBD children had lower heart rate and blood pressure levels under conditions of non-stress and stress and lower levels of cortisol than the control group. However, within the group of DBD children, those with higher cortisol levels during interpersonal stress were more anxious than those with lower cortisol levels. Cortisol levels in DBD children were investigated further by van de Wiel, van Goozen, Matthys, Snoek and van Engeland (2004). This time cortisol levels were used as an indicator of the severity of disruptive behaviour towards treatment schedules. van de Wiel *et al.* (2004) previously found that low levels of cortisol were related to serious behavioural problems. In this study all the children displayed serious behavioural problems and yet they found that there were differences in levels of cortisol production and behavioural disturbance prior to treatment intervention. Unstressed children who had low levels of cortisol were different to the children who had low levels of cortisol when stressed. It was this latter group who displayed more behavioural problems post treatment. Popma, Jansen, Vermeiren, Steiner, *et al.* (2006) found that male adolescents who had attended a delinquency diversion programme showed decreased cortisol levels while performing a stressful task. Popma *et al.* (2006) suggested that low levels of cortisol could be a useful indicator for delinquent boys with DBD but for delinquent boys without DBD this could be misleading. An interesting study by Finger, Marsh, Mitchell, Reid *et al.* (2008) demonstrated, using fMRI, that children and adolescents with psychopathic traits and ODD or CD had functional abnormalities in the orbital and ventromedial prefrontal cortex comparable to psychopathic adults. As was found in studies using adult psychopaths where it was important to anticipate punishment, the children and adolescents in Finger *et al.*'s (2008) study showed similar poor learning and processing responses to the anticipation of punishment. This was explained through abnormal ventromedial prefrontal cortex activity.

Collectively the studies discussed suggest that delinquent children and adolescents have differences in the way information is processed by the brain and physiological responses to stressful situations. This would further suggest that there is lifespan continuity between DBD and APD and psychopathy. In other words, psychopathic tendencies begin at an early age. In the next section the question of whether psychopathy can be treated will be explored. This is an important question as it helps us to further evaluate the extent of a nature/nurture contribution involved in the making of a criminal psychopath.

## Treatment for psychopaths

Blackburn (1975) defined two types of psychopath – the non-anxious primary psychopath and the anxious secondary psychopath. This important difference can be seen in children and adolescents with DBD – as they too can be separated into groups of low or high anxiety. This is interesting as it appears contiguous with later adult primary and secondary classifications of psychopathy – but why should this be important when considering treatment programmes for psychopaths? High cortisol levels as we have seen are consistent with the human body's physiological response to stressful stimuli, which in effect is a natural physiological response to stress. Most individuals will experience this when they perceive a situation as anxiety provoking. Children and adolescents who have high secretion levels of cortisol during stressful situations generally respond well to treatment interventions such as psychotherapy – an intervention that enables them to understand and adopt new coping strategies and social interaction skills. Those who had low secretion levels of cortisol under the same stressful situations did not react well to treatment programmes as their disruptive behaviour remained the same. The same would be expected of primary psychopaths, but perhaps the secondary psychopaths whose condition is comorbid with underlying neuroticism might show some improvement with treatment intervention.

Different forms of treatment have been used to help alleviate the most disruptive elements of psychopathic behaviour such as aggressive and violent outbursts. These treatments are normally based within an in-patient setting such as high-security psychiatric hospitals (i.e. Broadmoor), regional secure units and psychiatric care units. Psychopaths detained in high-security hospitals are usually dangerous and require nursing under maximum security (see Chapter 11). In the case of regional secure units, difficult and dangerous psychopaths are housed and are offered treatment programmes. Prison is generally not regarded a place for treatment but a few, such as Grendon Prison, do have specialised wings concentrating on treating those with personality disorders. Liebowitz, Stone and Turkat (1986) described how a typical evaluation of a patient should be done (see Figure 7.6). Furthermore, treatment is packaged in different ways:

- use of medication (neuroleptics, anti-depressants, lithium, benzodiazepines, psychostimulants and anti-convulsants);
- physical treatments (electroconvulsive therapy and psychosurgery);
- behavioural therapy (classical conditioning such as aversion therapy and operant conditioning including token economies);
- cognitive (assertiveness, self-control and self-instruction and relaxation training);
- psychotherapy (psychoanalysis and psychodrama).

(These different treatment approaches are discussed further in Chapters 8, 9 and 10).

Secondary psychopaths tend to have high comorbidity with other conditions (Coid 1992) which might be responsive to medication. For instance, those displaying schizotypal and paranoid behaviour respond well to neuroleptic and benzodiazepine drugs (Kalnia 1964). Anti-depressants, such as monoamine oxidase inhibitors, have been helpful in reducing depression in some personality disordered patients; however, Tennent, Tennent, Prins and Bedford (1993)

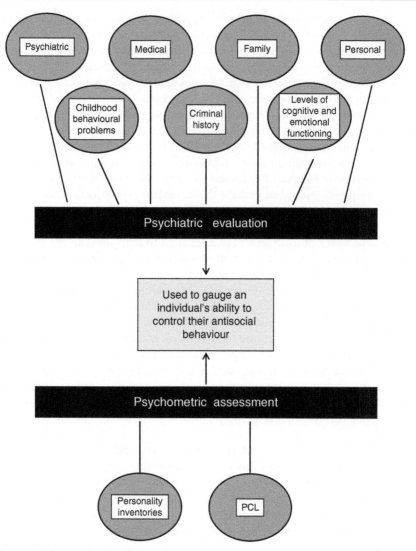

*Figure 7.6* Stages of evaluation
Adapted from Liebowitz, Stone and Turkat 1986

reported that most psychiatrists agree that drug therapy is ineffective when it comes to treating psychopaths.

Behaviour therapy is successful in reducing aggressive and disruptive behaviour among adolescents exhibiting aggressive, self-mutilation and disruptive behaviours when compared to matched groups who received no treatment – a consistent finding even after a two year follow up (Moyes, Tennent and Bedford 1985). Concerns for the effectiveness of behaviour and cognitive therapy, however, lie with the extent of skills learned that can be applied to the outside world. Howells (1986) pointed out that the situations faced in institutions are very different to the nature of social interactions experienced in the home environment and, despite social skills being transferable, patients may become confused. Psychotherapy has its problems too, especially concerning the patient–therapist relationship. Nevertheless, Jew, Clanon and Mattocks (1972) showed that imprisoned personality disordered offenders who had group therapy improved their chances of attaining parole. Using reconviction rates as a measure of success, Cullen (1992) was able to show that patients from Grendon who had been in therapy longer than 18 months were less likely to be reconvicted than non-completers – this was 20 per cent compared to 40 per cent, respectively. It is important to highlight that not all patients considered in these different treatments were primary psychopaths – the majority were not. A major problem with primary psychopaths is that they are deceitful and yet for therapy to be effective there must be trust and honesty between patient and therapist (Blackburn, cited in Howells and Hollin 1993). The findings by Black (1982) are very telling in that the best predictor of low **recidivism** rates rested on a history of fewer criminal convictions. In the case of high recidivism the best predictor was having a diagnosis of psychopathy.

An interesting therapeutic approach adopted by psychiatrist Dr Bob Johnson at Parkhurst Prison was televised on Panorama in 1997 – a programme called *Predators* (Mangold 1997). Dr Johnson presented his recorded interviews of psychopathic murderers and explained the therapy to interviewer Tom Mangold. Dr Johnson was convinced that he could treat and cure these psychopaths of their antisocial and dangerous behaviours (see Box 7.9).

## Box 7.9

### Description of Dr Johnson's therapeutic approach with incarcerated psychopaths

Dr Johnson described a relaxed and informal approach where he would invite psychopathic murderers to sit down and have an informal conversation about their crimes and childhood experience in order to build a rapport. His aim was to attain a trusting relationship, something he believed many of them had never experienced in their lives before. Attaining this trust therefore in some cases took many years. Dr Johnson described how he would discuss their deepest fears from childhood and any childhood traumas that they had experienced. Many of these experiences, he claimed, were difficult for them to talk about, but for his therapeutic approach to be successful, it was imperative that they did.

Dr Johnson claimed that there was terror in childhood that they had buried which he referred to as 'frozen fear' or 'buried terror'. He said it took time for them to reveal this – some would only indirectly discuss it. He believed that within every memory was a 'toxic memory' – the terror.

Dr Johnson claimed that he had to be very persistent to get them talking about this terror as they denied having it. He would say, 'I'm looking for fear and terror from childhood, let's have it'. Dr Johnson admits that it is because he was upfront with them that eventually they trusted him enough to retrieve these memories and to discuss them.

Dr Johnson's main premise was that if you confront psychopaths about their true fears they can be cured. Other forensic psychiatrists, such as Professor Jeremy Coid, are not convinced by this and claimed that it is easy to be duped into believing that psychopaths are telling you the truth when in fact they are telling you what they think you want to hear. However, Professor Coid believes that Dr Johnson may have found something important which needs further examination under controlled conditions – but it is not the cure. Dr Johnson's approach, however, does address the issue of childhood abuse and its effects on the development of psychopathy.

Research findings presented in this chapter, once unpicked, suggest that there is no one nature or nurture-oriented approach which adequately explains the causes of psychopathy. This is also confounded by the two types of psychopath: primary and secondary. This division is important especially when we consider the treatment successes for secondary psychopathy. Treatment is unsuccessful when primary psychopaths are considered. This suggests that primary psychopaths have a different aetiology. As we have seen there are robust gene and brain structural and functional anomalies in criminal psychopaths (especially primary psychopaths) which suggest evidence for the nature side of the debate. However, as we have seen, most criminal psychopaths experienced a toxic childhood – full of rejection, neglect and abuse. This provides evidence for the nurture side of the debate. Clearly both nature and nurture are contributory factors here which suggest a nature–nurture interaction (gene–environment). Professor Fallon's predicament of having the genes and brain structure of a psychopath, but having had a happy childhood and experienced first-hand good parental nurturance, provides an abundance of information about the importance of this nature–nurture interaction. Having this combination has protected him from becoming a criminal psychopath.

## Summary

- Psychopathy and its relationship with APD and other personality disorders, and its cross-over with criminality, can be considered using the FFM and PCL-R. Criminal psychopaths can be subtyped using Millon and Davis' (1998) ten subtypes. The demarcation between psychopathy, APD and criminality is important as the three are interlinked but also independent of each other. Not all criminals are psychopaths nor have APD and not all psychopaths are criminals and not all individuals with APD are psychopaths. Although many personality traits of psychopaths and APD are similar, there are nevertheless differences: there are different views concerning this but the approach adopted in this chapter was to treat them separately.

- Assessment of psychopaths using the PCL-R, indicate that psychopaths are egocentric, impulsive and want immediate gratification often at the expense of others. Primary psychopaths show low levels of fearfulness and poor learning response to classical conditioning tasks. A connection between attenuated emotional experiences of fearfulness and anxiety with ineffective socialisation has been attributed to faulty biological mechanisms (i.e. a nature explanation). These factors contribute towards understanding the greater picture of the psychopath's social behaviour. Their social relationships are very one-sided in that they are not emotionally involved. Their body language differs too. More threatening behaviour, such as leaning forward into another's personal space and staring, little warmth and much hostility, and superficial charm and dishonesty, are all designed to enable psychopaths to get their own way. They are highly egocentric, unreliable and have no true life plan which often leads to shallow and parasitic relationships.

- The Five Factor Model of Personality (FFM) corroborated high scores for toughness, aggression and excitement in psychopaths. Attribution theory was used by Sykes and Matza (1957) to account for how criminal psychopaths neutralise their antisocial and dangerous behaviour. One type of attribution used is to deny any injury or harm incurred to their victims – this also suggests a deficit in feeling empathy, guilt or remorse for their actions.

- Social approaches looking at the socialisation of psychopaths in terms of morality and the nature of their cognitive attributions towards their victims can be further understood through classical and operant conditioning. Poor performance on conditioning tasks was examined as a biological correlate of the psychopathic disorder: evidence suggests an underlying brain deficit, malfunction or abnormality. A similar conclusion accounts for their differences of performance on attention and dichotic listening tasks.

- As criminal psychopaths are renowned for committing crimes such as homicide and serial killing, a connection (although not necessarily causal) between disruptive thought patterns and deficits of empathy, guilt and remorse, might enable them to commit dangerous and serious crimes and to cognitively justify their behaviour. It has been found that psychopaths have abnormal amygdala–orbitofrontal function which disrupts their performance on emotion-based ToM tasks because of deficits of empathy and emotional responsiveness to others. Lateralisation studies, such as dichotic listening and attention switching tasks, have indicated a different pathway for processing emotional content. This also links with studies suggesting that psychopaths deploy their attention differently – they have difficulty in shifting their attention and rely on effortful processing for response modulation.

- Brain neuroimaging provides robust evidence of underlying brain abnormalities in structure and function in adult psychopaths (particularly criminal psychopaths). Psychopaths (in particular primary psychopaths) behave in different ways to most people which might be a consequence of having a brain that is 'wired' differently. Brain neuroimaging provides robust and distinct structural and functional differences in the brains of psychopaths and also between criminal psychopaths and criminal non-psychopaths. Brain neuroimaging has shown distinct problematic areas within the brains of psychopaths.

- The amygdala is pertinent for emotional recognition and moral decision making but in psychopaths fMRI scans have shown abnormal activity and reduced volume. Also the higher the PCL-R scores the more amygdala structural and functional abnormality is apparent during emotional tasks of recognition and moral decision making. Researchers have found reduced activity in the orbitofrontal cortex in psychopaths using fMRI. Abnormal amygdala-orbitofrontal cortex connections via the uncinate fasciculus have also been found. These areas of the brain underlie many of the character and behavioural traits of criminal psychopaths and suggest a problem in prenatal development. Whether these differences of brain structure were genetically, ontologically (i.e. prenatal developmental stages), perinatally (i.e. during birth) or postnatally (i.e. after birth) determined is uncertain but their causes would appear to be nature influenced.

- A lifespan approach of psychopathy beginning in childhood then adolescence and finally adulthood provided an interesting history of the psychopath. ADHD, CD and ODD collectively known as DBD illustrate the problematic, defiant and uncontrollable nature of behaviour parents of such children face. The antecedents of psychopathic traits and behaviour are easy to identify in young children and continue into adolescence. Physiological studies have highlighted differences in autonomic functioning and cortisol production in children and adolescents with DBD. Not all DBD sufferers will become psychopaths but if treatment is unavailable their behaviour can escalate to full-blown psychopathy.

- A multitude of treatments available to psychopaths only help psychopaths who rate high on anxiety. This supports Blackburn's primary and secondary distinction of a causal difference. There are mixed findings regarding the treatability of psychopaths and children and adolescents with DBD. If the premise that psychopathy in adults has its point of origin in childhood (and there is an abundance of evidence to suggest this is the case) and that some individuals with DBD and psychopathy can be treated, then the logical assumption is that there is more than one type of psychopath and their causes derive from different pathways (i.e. more nature, more nurture or an equal contribution of nature–nurture). While both primary and secondary psychopaths have the trademark traits of psychopathy, their aetiology is likely to be different which could explain why secondary psychopaths generally respond well to therapeutic intervention and primary psychopaths do not. This suggests that environmental factors such as an adverse upbringing or child abuse might contribute towards the development of secondary psychopaths. In the case of primary psychopaths, treatment is ineffective suggesting that their experiences are somewhat different and that a nature explanation might be more applicable. For such cases there might be genetic and prenatal causes off-setting their brain development. Care must be taken, however, when assuming such explanations as the brain continues developing postnatally and can be influenced by environmental factors such as physical and sexual abuse and violence (i.e. head trauma). Thus while there might be a predisposition to develop primary psychopathy, it does not necessarily follow that the individual will continue this pathway of development.

## Questions for discussion

1   Not all psychopaths are criminals and not all criminals are psychopaths. Discuss this in relation to personality theory and the classification and assessment of psychopaths.
2   In what way is the amygdala–orbitofrontal cortex connection so important for the processing of social information and moral development? When it goes wrong, as is suspected in psychopaths, what are the repercussions for behaviour?
3   What factors would you consider when judging whether a murderer is a psychopath? Which factors are particularly pertinent to your decision?

# Chapter 8

# Sex offenders and their crimes

The aim of the chapters in Part III is to present evidence for a nature–nurture contribution towards a selection of criminals: in this case the sex offender. As with all chapters in this section, a multidisciplinary approach will be taken such that evidence is drawn from a variety of academic subjects which address crime and the criminal. Later, in the concluding chapter, the evidence will be evaluated.

In this chapter we begin by addressing the prevalence of sexual offences and consider the recorded police figures over the last decade in England and Wales. Self-reporting surveys conducted in England and Wales (the CSEW) and in the US are discussed and considered with the figures estimated using methods of self-reporting from other countries. Surprisingly these figures from self-reporting tell a similar story regarding the prevalence of unreported sexual offending.

In this chapter, different types of sex offender will be considered but the main focus will be on rapists, paedophiles and paraphilics. What is meant by sexual offending, and the reasons why some sexual behaviour is against the law and other sexual behaviours (although they might be regarded as deviating from the norm) are permissible, will be considered in the context of consenting sexual behaviour. The problems with legal definitions of rape are pitted against the deviant sexual behaviours often experienced by victims (which the legal definition falls short of accounting for). Understanding the different underlying motivations for why sex offenders offend in the way that they do has enabled researchers to develop different typologies of sex offender. There are typologies for rapists, paedophiles and paraphilics which we will consider here. These typologies often reflect the theoretical perspectives of the respective researchers, which is why a review of the different theories is important to understanding this area. In this chapter we will discuss the different theoretical perspectives that typify nature and nurture accounts of sexual offending and sex offenders. These will hopefully help to address plausible causal factors explaining the deviant behaviour and affectations shown by sex offenders. There are many different theories, some of which are derived from mainstream psychological and criminological research but have been specifically applied to sexual offending. In this chapter we will consider the more common theories put forward such as behaviourism; neurocognitive, neurobiological and evolutionary approaches; feminist; psychoanalytic; situational and an integrated approach. In the case of the situational approach we will consider and dispel some of the commonly expressed rape myths in society, which are further perpetuated by the media.

Each theoretical stance provides a therapeutic approach aimed at treating and controlling the behaviour of the sex offender. Some of these are more successful than others and might only work with specific types of sex offender and sexual offence. These will be discussed and their level of success considered. Possibly the most successful treatment is from the cognitive-behavioural approach known as cognitive-behavioural therapy. This has proven to be successful at reducing recidivism and can be easily applied to prison populations in the guise of group therapy. The ethics involved with some types of treatment, specifically those derived from behaviourist approaches, will be considered in the light of the effects they have on the sex offender's self-esteem. The ethics involved with some of the methods used to publicly denounce sex offenders in the community will be viewed in the context of measures taken since the introduction of **Megan's Law** in the US. In the UK consideration is given to the type of court orders issued to sex offenders and the impact this has for victims.

## Introduction

The two most commonly recalled examples of sexual offending are rape and paedophilia, and yet there are many more types of sexual behaviours that are prohibited by the law. Sex offenders comprise a miscellaneous group who violate the rights of individuals to refuse sexual engagement: in other words, they behave in an unwanted sexual manner towards an individual who has not consented. Non-consenting sexual behaviour is against the law, as it is considered to be a serious offence and infringement of an individual's right of refusal. It is partly due to these reasons that sexual offences such as rape and paedophilia are good examples of *mala in se* crimes (see Chapters 1 and 2). The nature of sexual behaviour towards a victim varies greatly from one sex offender to another, such that a victim might witness an individual indecently exposing himself (also known as a 'flasher'), causing shock and stress, to a more serious act of violent sexual assault resulting in extensive bodily harm (see Chapter 2).

There is considerable variety in the type of sexual offending committed by sex offenders which in part reflects the rather open definition of what comprises a crime of a sexual nature. This in turn might account for the diversity of sex offenders and their underlying motivations for committing sexual offences. A taster of this diversity can be seen in the case examples provided in Box 8.1.

## Box 8.1

### Selection of case examples of sexual offending

Ian Andrew Elphick used sweets and money to bribe children to his home in Saulkrasti on the Gulf of Riga in Latvia. In his home, he sexually assaulted his victims and later admitted to raping and coercing underage boys to appear in his pornographic films. Elphick admitted to 46 sex attacks on children over a period of three years in Riga. In 2010 he was found guilty and sentenced to eight years in prison and ordered to pay a total of £11,840 in compensation to his victims.

In the Majorcan city of Magaluf, female British tourists were targeted by a serial rapist. His *modus operandi* of punching victims to the ground and rendering them into a semi-conscious state enabled him to rape them repeatedly. Still at large, he is allegedly responsible for six rapes and the possible attack on Cheryl Maddison in 2008 who was throttled until semi-conscious and then raped.

Dr Martin McDonald abused his position of trust by behaving inappropriately towards three of his patients while performing breast examinations. He was charged in Dunklin County, US, in 2011 with non-consensual sexual contact with his patients and performing unrequested and unnecessary breast examinations. Dr McDonald's license to treat female patients was suspended while serving a probation order. Despite an extended probation order until 2017, his license to practice was not suspended.

Clearly in all the examples provided in Box 8.1, the sexual behaviour exhibited is considered to be deviant by society's definition of what constitutes normal sexual behaviour. An additional dimension to the case of Dr McDonald, however, is that he abused his position as a trusted professional. In order to attain an estimate of the extent that sexual offences such as those provided in Box 8.1 occur, criminologists refer to statistics derived from police recorded crime figures presented to the Home Office (HO).

## Prevalence of sexual offending

The following figures provide an indication of the prevalence of sexual offending over a period of at least ten years. During this period it is possible to ascertain any short-term crime fluctuations and long-term crime trends (see Chapter 2). Before considering the more up-to-date recorded figures, the following graphs show a breakdown of the statistical trends based on HO recorded crime figures for sexual offences such as rape and paedophilia (Figures 8.1, 8.2 and 8.3).

Sexual offending is documented widely by the media and is regarded as high profile. It is not surprising, therefore, that it is perceived by people as a

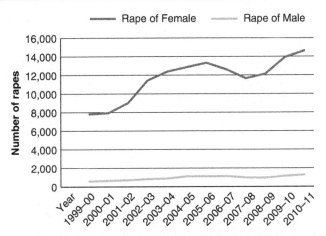

*Figure 8.1* Police recorded crime figures for rape in England and Wales from 1999–2000 to 2010–11

Adapted from '*Criminal Statistics England and Wales*. Her Majesty's Stationary Office' for the years 1999–2011.

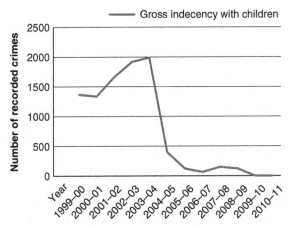

*Figure 8.2* Police recorded crime figures for paedophilia (gross indecency) in England and Wales from 1999–2000 to 2010–11

Adapted from '*Criminal Statistics England and Wales*. Her Majesty's Stationary Office' for the years 1999–2011.

crime that occurs frequently. If we consider the crime statistics, however, it becomes apparent that it is not the most common type of crime but instead comprises a small percentage of 2.6 per cent of all **recorded crime** (based on 2009–10 figures this was 55,169 sex offences – see Chapter 2). In the case of the figures for rape, clearly more females are raped than males (although it is known that males are less likely to report a crime of this nature), and there has been an increase in reporting of rape to the police over the years. The highest recorded figure occurred in 2006–7 which decreased in 2007–8 but has since

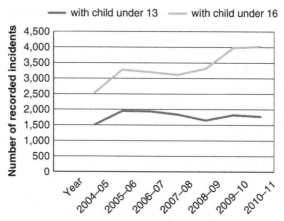

*Figure 8.3* Police recorded crime figures for paedophilia (sexual activity) in England and Wales from 2004–05 to 2010–11

Adapted from 'Criminal Statistics England and Wales. Her Majesty's Stationary Office' for the years 2004–2011.

been rising. The recorded figures considered here for paedophilia are gross indecency with a child and sexual activity with a child under 13 or 16. The rate of recorded crime for gross indecency is at its peak in 2003–4 and plummets in 2004–5. There are no recorded figures for 2009 to 2011, which might reflect a different way of classifying this sexual offence. There has been a rising trend for sexual activity with children under 13 but has remained fairly consistent for sexual activity with children under 16. This might reflect a change in patterns of paedophilic behaviours over the years, where there is an increasing preference for children under 13 (and this is despite the higher baseline for the under 13s). Although these figures may appear alarming their relation to recorded crime figures for other crimes is proportionately small.

In the police recorded figures of 2010–11, Taylor and Chaplin (2011) collated the total number of sex offences for England and Wales at 54,982 with a sanction detection rate of 16,465 which translated to fewer than 30 per cent of sex offenders found guilty. Recorded figures of female rape in 2010–11 totalled 14,624 with 3,468 offenders found guilty and this was 1,310 and 401 respectively for males. Rape for females under 16 was 2,880 (833 found guilty) and 2,235 (915 found guilty) for those under 13. In the case of males this was 247 (93 found guilty) for the under 16 and 671 (257 found guilty) for the under 13.

Other interesting findings indicate a recorded figure of 310 (124 found guilty) offences for sexual **grooming**; 7,202 (2,025 found guilty) for exposure and voyeurism; 153 (102 found guilty) for abuse of children through pornography; and 808 (320 found guilty) for incest or familial sexual offences (Chaplin, Flatley and Smith 2011). Elliott, Browne and Kilcoyne (1995) found that 70 per cent of child sex abusers had 1–9 victims; however they also found that in a few cases there could be as many as 450. Grubin (1998) found that

60–70 per cent of paedophiles targeted girls only, 20–33 per cent boys only and 10 per cent targeted both. Grubin also found that most perpetrators sexually assault children who are familiar to them and 80 per cent of abuse occurs in the offender's or victim's home.

These figures confirm that only a fraction of recorded crime lead to convictions. Furthermore, as discussed in Chapters 1 and 2, recorded crime figures reflect crime that has been reported to the police (and coded for further investigation), again only a fraction of sexual crimes that occur – the dark figure of sexual crimes and crime per se remain incalculable. It appears from the recorded statistics that there has been an increase and decrease over the years for different sexual offences. Furthermore, if the statistics are representative of sexual offences that occur (and this is the best information that we have to go on), then sex offending is relatively low when compared to crime figures per se. Trend data, whether there are obvious differences over the years or not, are useful to governmental agencies for policy making and police investigative strategies.

Statistics, however, are not always representative of the extent of sexual offences occurring. This is primarily because HO statistics are based on police recorded crime figures and, for a crime of a sexual nature to be among these figures, the crime has to be reported. For various reasons victims of sex crimes are reluctant to report what has happened to them to the police – hence the crime goes undetected and becomes part of the dark figure of sexual crimes. There are other ways, however, of measuring the extent of unreported sexual crimes; self-reported crime is an important measure to use. In 2013, the Ministry of Justice documented findings from the Crime Survey for England and Wales (CSEW) combined figures of sexual offences across 2009/10, 2010/11 and 2011/12. Based on figures derived by the CSEW for serious sexual offences, 0.5 per cent of females reported that they were victims of sexual offences of which the majority had been raped and two-fifths had experienced assault by penetration. Males were less forthcoming in reporting their experiences of being a victim of a sexual offence (0.1 per cent). When these percentages were translated into prevalence rates it was estimated over the three surveys that between 430,000 and 517,000 males and females had been victims of sexual offences. Once these figures were broken down, it was estimated that between 366,000 and 442,000 were female and 54,000 and 90,000 were male victims. Breaking these figures down further for serious sexual offences, prevalence estimates between 68,000 and 103,000 for females and 5,000 to 19,000 for males were found. Since the CSEW included questions relating to sexual victimisation in 2004/5, the prevalence levels for this have remained fairly constant for both sexes with only a few statistically significant changes for more minor incidents.

Further information provided by the CSEW shows that females between 16 and 19 had a high risk of being victims of a sexual offence (8.2 per cent), as were single females (5.3 per cent) and those separated from partners (3.7 per cent). Females with disabilities or illness also had an increased risk of becoming victims (3.4 per cent). The CSEW also document victim–offender relationships showing that most serious sexual offences were committed by a partner (56 per cent) while a stranger was more likely to commit other sexual offences (52 per cent). Self-reports by victims who have been sexually assaulted (at all levels of seriousness) helps to provide a more complete, and therefore accurate, indication of the extent of sexual offending. If we compare the police recorded figures for female rape of about 15,000 in 2010/11 (see Figure 8.1), for instance, with the figures derived from CSEW self-reporting of serious sexual offences (between 68,000 and 103,000), it becomes clear how out of synch the two types of crime measurement are. It is important to bear these differences in mind when referring to the HO crime statistics. The HO crime statistics only consider sexual offending that has been reported to the police who then record it as an offence. Rayner and Gardner (2015) reported to *The Telegraph* newspaper, however, that the reporting of sexual offences had increased by 22 per cent. The statistical figures for recorded rape (although there are cross-cultural variations on its definition) in the US in 2010 was 84,767, India 22,172, England and Wales 15,934, Mexico 14,993, Germany 7,724 and Australia 6,378; thus the US had the highest levels of rape during this period (United Nations Office on Drugs and Crime).

Obtaining self-reports from children is often more difficult than it is from adults who have been sexually abused. Therefore estimated child abuse figures are often obtained through self-reporting at a later age (when the child has become an adult). In 1997 a telephone survey, organised by the Gallup Organisation but conducted by Finkelhor, Moore, Hamby and Straus, addressed two questions to a random sample of 1,000 US adults. These questions were about childhood experiences of sexual abuse. Finkelhor *et al.* found that 23 per cent of respondents said they were 'touched' in a sexual manner or had been forced to have sex with either a family member or non-family member before they were 18. Approximately three times more females self-reported child sexual abuse than males. These findings are comparable with other self-report surveys where 20 per cent or more of females and 5–10 per cent of males in the US experienced a form of sexual abuse as children (Finkelhor 1994). Furthermore, these findings have been corroborated by cross-cultural studies using self-reporting methods (Fanslow, Robinson, Crengle and Perese 2007; Gilbert, Widom, Browne, Fergusson *et al.* 2009).

Making the decision as to whether the reported incident is a crime is difficult, especially when the offence is of a sexual nature, and even more so when it involves two people who are in a relationship. There is a further problem, and this refers to our understanding and definition of what constitutes a sexual offence. This will be considered later in this chapter. But first an important question to ask is at what point does sexual behaviour become an illegal act? When we consider deviant sexual behaviour with a consenting adult it is tolerated in a liberal society, but becomes illegal when committed with a non-consenting individual and with an individual who is considered to be underage. There are of course other cases, such as someone considered to be of impaired mind and therefore unable to consent to sexual intercourse.

The harm debate and the notion of victimless crimes are important facets to the discussion of what comprises normal or deviant sexual behaviour and the fine dividing line between what is tolerated by society and what is morally wrong (see Chapter 2). Why this is important very much relates to our understanding of sex offenders – in particular their own ideals and interpretations of the significance of their behaviour towards their victims. In the next section, definitions and classifications of deviant sexual behaviour in relation to violence, are reviewed in connection with breaking the law. This will help us to answer the question above of when does sexual behaviour become an illegal act.

## How is violent sexual behaviour defined and classified?

Sexual violence incorporates many types of sexual behaviour: some behaviour can be considered a part of normal sexual behaviour, while others an extension of normal sexual behaviour that contravenes the law. For example, which of the following sexual behaviours and sexual preferences contravene the norm, the law or both:

- paedophilia,
- incest,
- conservative polyamory,
- monogamy,
- celibacy,
- homosexuality,
- bisexuality,
- sadomasochism,
- bestiality?

There is a fine dividing line between some sexual practices regarded as normal which vary cross-culturally, such as monogamy and polyamory (relationships with multiple consenting partners), or deviant, like, for example, bestiality (sexual intercourse with an animal) and sadomasochism (sado being the element of a relationship where pain is inflicted and masochism where it is received). Furthermore, the prevailing legal **zeitgeist** cannot be ignored, as there are sexual behaviours that were once prohibited by law but are now permissible, like, for example, homosexuality and bisexuality. There are sexual behaviours regarded by many people as deviant that also break the law, such as paedophilia and incest. Other behaviours like celibacy are not considered to be the norm but are perceived as virtuous. Sadomasochism is a sexual practice that is tolerated by society but is on the fringe of normal sexual behaviour. Deviant practices provoke feelings of disgust, and some are illegal in the UK but legal elsewhere; for example, bestiality is legal in Belgium, Denmark, Finland, Germany, Hungary, Japan and Mexico. In Britain, until the Sexual

Offences Act 2003, an offender found guilty of bestiality would be imprisoned for life – but this has since been reduced to two years.

In order to understand the different types of sexual behaviours, particularly those that are legally prohibited, psychologists have profiled sex offenders into five different groups and classified sex offences under three broad categories. In the case of the five profiles, sexual preference for the desired individual is based on age; unlike the three categories which are considered according to variation in the type of sex offences committed – suggesting that sex offenders are different and have diverse needs and motivations that are satisfied through sexual offending.

## Profiles of sex offenders

According to Barbaree (1990) the profiles of sex offenders can be divided into five groups:

- Sex offenders aroused by children and have a clear preference for children demonstrate a child profile.
- Those who have a preference for both children and adults with little arousal to pubescent females comprise the child–adult profile.
- Individuals aroused by females of any age have a non-discriminating pattern of arousal.
- Preference for female teenagers and adults comprise the teen–adult profile.
- The adult profile comprises of those who are aroused by adults (in the case of this profile, sex offenders are rapists rather than paedophiles).

Blanchard and Barbaree (2005) and Abel and Harlow (2001) referred to sex offenders who engage in sexual activities with 13–16 year olds as hebephiles (attraction to females) or ephebophiles (attraction to males), although hebephilia has become a term used to describe both hebephiles and ephebophiles. Hebephiles indulge in reciprocal relationships and have higher levels of social skill competency, which might account for their increased likelihood of having a successful prognosis after treatment intervention. Infantophilia describes sex offenders interested in children under the age of five (Greenberg, Bradford and Curry 1995). Paedophilia describes sex offenders who are sexually interested and attracted to prepubescent children. The term child molester is often confused with paedophile but it is important to understand the difference. Whereas both a paedophile and child molester are interested and attracted to prepubescent children, it is generally the child molester who acts out his or her fantasy and uses the child for sexual stimulation. Therefore not all paedophiles are child molesters as many do not act on their impulses. Interestingly, van Gijseghem (2011) presented in the Parliament of Canada to the Standing Committee on Justice and Human Rights that 'real paedophiles account for only 20 per cent of sexual abusers'. This implies that the majority of child molesters are not paedophiles. In fact van Gijseghem is implying that many individuals who sexually abuse children are not necessarily attracted to them: a point which is difficult to comprehend. The term teleiophilia refers to adults who prefer mature partners therefore fitting the adult profile.

Despite there being different profiles of sex offenders, it is often the case that there is a **multi-paraphilia** element such as exhibitionism and voyeurism discussed later in this chapter (Abel, Mittelman and Becker 1985; Abel, Becker, Cunningham-Rathner, Mittelman and Rouleau 1988). Abel *et al.* (1988) found this to be the case for active paedophiles where 50–70 per cent engaged in voyeurism, exhibitionism, frotteurism or sadism. Furthermore, Cohen and Galynker (2002) found that active paedophiles were more than twice as likely to physically court children as to engage in exhibitionism or voyeurism. Different types of active paedophile are classified according to the motivations and reasoning that their behaviours serve – in other words, their needs which require satiation. Next we will consider how sexual offending behaviours are classified.

## Classification of sexual offending behaviours

The three broad categories used to classify sexual offending are:

- rape, which can involve elements of paraphilic behaviours;
- child molestation, also labelled as paedophilia;
- paraphilias.

These categories are not always mutually exclusive, as there can be a multi-paraphilic element to sex offenders (Abel *et al.* 1985). For instance, Abel *et al.* (1985) found that 50.6 per cent of rapists had also molested children, 29.2 per cent had also exposed themselves, 20.2 per cent had at some point in their lives resorted to voyeurism and 12.4 per cent had previously indulged in frotteurism. We will now consider these three classifications of sexual offender individually, beginning with rapists.

### Definitions and classifications of rapists

#### Definition

Rapists are different from paedophiles not only as regards who they target but in terms of demographical information and their overall intelligence, social and communication skills. Before we can consider what a rapist is and what constitutes rape, a legal definition would help clarify under what circumstances sexual behaviour is classified as rape. Koss (1992) offers the following definition of what rape legally means: 'carnal knowledge of a female forcibly and against her will' (p.61). Carnal knowledge refers to penile–vaginal penetration which given that rape often involves other forms of sexual contact and activity, is a limited definition. A slightly expanded definition is provided in a report to the HO by Myhill and Allen (2002) as rape meaning 'forced to have sexual intercourse (vaginal or anal penetration)'. In the Sexual Offences Act 2003 it states:

> 1-1 A person (A) commits an offence if:
>
> (a) He intentionally penetrates the vagina, anus or mouth of another person (B) with his penis,
> (b) B does not consent to the penetration, and
> (c) A does not reasonably believe that B consents.

In the legal definition it is stipulated that penetration must be penile which again is limiting because it excludes the use of objects for penetration (which is known to happen in some cases). In the UK there have been recent changes to the law and definition of rape. It primarily concerns the issue of consent. It is now possible for a man to be guilty of rape if he cannot prove that his victim had said 'yes' to sex; but it goes beyond this as a man could be guilty if he had agreed to use a condom during sex but then removes or damages it such that he ejaculates during intercourse. Furthermore, if there was an agreement made before intercourse that he will withdraw from her but then fails to do so, he has contravened the level of agreed consent. This has major ramifications for the accused as it is difficult to prove that he has not contravened the agreed level of consent (Perrins 2013). The legal definition of rape as 'penile penetration' excludes the multiple permutations that it can take and, for this reason, falls short of representing the experiences of rape which many women might encounter. Why different permutations of rape exist might be explained by the variations of motive underlying the behaviours of rapists. There has been a considerable amount of research focused on trying to classify rapists according to differences in motivation which we will consider next.

## Classifications

Rapists tend to be classified by the underlying motivations for their behaviours occurring during the act of rape (Cohen, Garfalo, Boucher and Seghorn 1971). For Amir (1971), however, it is the social roles established through sexual offending that can be used to classify rapists. Alternatively, Rada (1978) claimed that clinical criteria should be applied to any form of classification. There have nevertheless been many different classifications of rapists arising from the motivations that the sex offending behaviour gratifies. Cohen, Seghorn and Calmas (1969), Groth and Burgess (1977a) and Knight and Prentky (1990) are key researchers in sex offending behaviour and attempted to develop different subtypes of rapist based on the motivations underlying their behaviour.

Cohen *et al.* (1969) based their classification of rapists on the combination of sexual and aggressive motives and from this deduced four possible subtypes:

1 Displaced aggression is when the rapist is hostile towards women therefore making the rape a hostile act. This behaviour is often initiated through a negative interaction with a woman, such as a disagreement. The sexual act comprises of high aggression and low sexual arousal.
2 Compensatory rape is the opposite in that there is a minimum level of aggression involved but high sexual arousal. In this instance, sexual gratification is surrounded with feelings of sexual inadequacy and incompetency.
3 Sex aggression diffusion is when aggression has become eroticised through the combination of sex with violence. This results in acts of sexual sadism where both aggression and sexual arousal are high and entwined.
4 Impulsive rapists have both low aggression and sexual arousal hence the rape is carried out as an opportunistic act. In many of these cases, rape is a consequence of a different predatory crime.

As far as Groth and Burgess (1977a) are concerned, rape is a disguise for attaining power and off-loading anger rather than achieving sexual gratification. Motives of power and anger tend to be reflected independently or one is more dominantly represented than the other in the two subtypes of power rape or anger rape.

1 Power rape divides further into power-assertive and power-reassurance. Rapists considered as power-assertive perform rape as a means to expressing dominance over the victim thereby acquiring power and control. Those rapists seeking power-reassurance feel doubts about their masculinity and rape to reinstate their masculine status and re-establish their position as an active male.
2 Anger rape is segregated into anger-retaliation and anger-excitation and although both types of rapist express their anger via sexual gratification, the motivations gratified during rape differ. In the case of anger-retaliation, the rape serves as a cathartic outlet for the contempt and hatred of women that they feel which sparks their need for revenge. The motivations of retaliation or punishment describe the anger-retaliation rapist. The motivation for rapists classified under anger-excitation is to inflict pain and suffering to their victim. These rapists are driven by the excitement experienced through their sadistic behaviours performed on their victims.

Knight and Prentky (1990) also developed four subtypes which are very much derived from Cohen *et al.*'s previous work in 1969. The opportunistic rapist overlaps with Cohen *et al.*'s impulsive rapist whereas the pervasively angry rapist is similar to their sex aggression diffusion category. The sexual rapist is similar to the compensatory category as is the vindictive rapist to the displaced aggressive rapist.

One perception of a rapist is someone who impulsively attacks and rapes a female in an obscure place or plans an attack by breaking into her home. It is not unknown for rapists to stalk their potential victim for days or even months before attacking. Stalking refers to behaviours such as watching and following the targeted individual which can escalate to threatening communication intended to intimidate, frighten or cause physical and psychological harm – in some cases leading to rape. Stalking behaviour is not a new phenomenon and yet it has only become recognised as a serious problem during the 1990s when celebrities such as Madonna reported her stalker (Kamphuis and Emmelkamp 2000).

More recently, **cyber-stalking** has become a problem and was classified as a criminal offence in the UK in 1998 by the Malicious Communications Act. Cyber-stalking involves the use of computer aided communication, such as email, aimed at threatening and harassing the intended victim. These communications according to Fisher, Cullen and Turner (2000) are designed to make the targeted victim feel afraid and unsafe. A host of unwanted email activity is intended to harass the victim, such as, for example, sending viruses, subscribing to unwanted list-servers and sending photos to sexually oriented websites (see Box 8.2). Cyber-stalking can also lead to rape (for example in Michigan, Samantha Kelly was cyber-stalked and raped, as was Audrie Pott in California, Rehtaeh Parsons in Canada, and Anna Comrink in Texas). Cyber-stalking can lead to other types of physical attack (Bocij and McFarlane 2002) and even murder (Bocij, Griffiths and McFarlane 2002).

It was suggested by Burgess and Baker (2002) that cyber-stalking can be perceived as 'offline stalking' (p.202) – an extension of stalking. Not everyone agrees with this but consider it as a new type of deviant behaviour arising out of developments in media technology (Thomas and Loader 2002). Reno (1999) associated cyber-stalking with online searching behaviours of paedophiles (see Box 8.4) whereas the editor of the Internet Anti-Fascist online publication believes that fascists use cyber-stalking for political means.

Our next category of sexual offending is paedophilia. As with rapists we will be looking at the definitions and classifications.

## Definitions and classifications of paedophiles

### Definitions

The terms paedophilia and child molestation are often interpreted as being the same thing and used interchangeably by the media in their reporting. A paedophile is different to a child molester in the following ways:

- Paedophilia is a medical diagnosis used to describe an individual who is sexually attracted to a prepubescent child. A paedophile might have thoughts and desires about children but does not necessarily act upon these. In fact as mentioned earlier only 20 per cent of paedophiles actively engage in sexual acts with children. This therefore implies that 80 per cent are not active paedophiles.
- Active paedophiles can be considered as child molesters. A child molester is a term used to describe an individual who attains sexual arousal and gratification through sexually touching a child despite not necessarily being sexually attracted to them.
- In Britain it is specified that an offender must be 5 years older than the child to qualify as a child molester.
- This age difference is applied to allow for the separation between sex-play in children and molestation. This means that a boy of 14 years who fondles a nine year old child is a child molester but not a paedophile. In 40 per cent of cases, 14 years of age was found to be the common age of assaults against children below 12 years (Snyder 2000).
- According to DSM-5, an individual aged 17 to 19 who is currently in a sexual relationship with a 12- or 13-year-old person cannot be diagnosed as a paedophile.
- Abel and Harlow's findings in 2001 showed that 40 per cent of child molesters who had molested a child before they were 15 later had a diagnosis of paedophilia (this implies that these child molesters were sexually attracted to children).

## Box 8.2

### What is the nature of stalking and cyber-stalking?

Fisher, Cullen and Turner (2000) did a study on the sexual victimisation of college women based at an undisclosed college in the US. They found that in four out of five cases the stalker was known to the victim – in 42.5 per cent a boyfriend or ex-boyfriend, 24.5 per cent a classmate, 10.3 per cent an acquaintance and 5.6 per cent a friend. The stalking period typically lasted 60 days and 30 per cent were stalked away from campus. Telephone stalking was common, comprising 77.7 per cent, whereas receiving emails was only 24.7 per cent. Other stalking behaviours included the stalker waiting around (47.9 per cent), following (42 per cent) and watching (44 per cent). Approximately 3 in 10 claimed to have been psychologically harmed whereas 10.3 per cent said the stalker 'forced or attempted sexual contact' (p. 28).

Bocij (2003) conducted an internet survey investigating the nature of cyber-stalking: 56.3 per cent of the sample was female and 43.7 per cent male; 44.6 per cent were married or co-habiting, 41.1 per cent single and 10.8 per cent separated or divorced. The mean age of respondents was 35 (the youngest was 16 and the oldest 84); 45.5 per cent of respondents lived in the UK and 39.5 per cent in the US but in total just over a third considered their ethnicity to be British. Bocij found that receiving threats via email and online 'chat rooms' was the most common format for cyber-stalking. About 40 per cent experienced damage to their computer via 'computer viruses' and almost 27 per cent felt that their actions were monitored and as many as 23.81 per cent were stalked. Respondents were asked to indicate the level of distress suffered as a result of their experiences using a scale from 1 to 10. Distress was high, rated at a mean of 7.16, but was higher for novice than expert computer users. Cyber-stalking occurs over a short period of time – 63 per cent lasting less than six months. For 42 per cent, the cyber-stalker was unknown and for almost 9 per cent it was an ex-partner. Bocij concluded that cyber-stalking is a distinct deviant behaviour but is related to offline stalking.

In the 2004/5 British Crime Survey (Finney 2006) it was estimated that five million people experienced stalking annually but cyber-stalking was unaccounted for. In 2011, a study based at Bedford University revealed that a cyber-stalker was more likely to be a stranger or casual acquaintance and surprisingly that 40 per cent of the victims were men. Many victims were 20–39 years old but those cyber-stalked did include youngsters of 14 and pensioners of 74; 37 per cent of men were targeted by a stranger whereas this was 23 per cent for women. Perpetrators targeted their victims from social networking sites or via blogging forums (16 per cent) and online dating sites (4 per cent). Some of the threats were extreme such as threatening to murder their victims. The co-author of the study psychologist, Dr Emma Short, claimed that such threats gave victims the impression that cyber-stalkers knew where they lived and could therefore potentially carry out their threats (McVeigh 2011).

Paedophilia is defined in DSM-5 as 'recurrent, intense sexually arousing fantasies, sexual urges or behaviours involving sexual activity with a prepubescent child . . . (. . . aged 13 years or younger)' (American Psychiatric Association (APA) 2013). Furthermore, they claimed that these fantasies, sexual urges or behaviour indicate paedophilia only when the level of distress they initiate interferes with their daily routines and activities. In DSM-5, paedophilia and hebephilia are combined and called paedophilic disorder. To clarify the distinction that DSM-5 makes between paedophilia and paedophilic disorder the APA stated the following:

> Pedophilia refers to a sexual orientation or . . . sexual preference devoid of consummation, whereas pedophilic disorder is . . . a compulsion and is used in reference to individuals who act on their sexuality.

This statement has caused outrage by conservative groups, such as the Liberty Counsel and the American Family Association (AFA), who accuse the APA of calling paedophilia a sexual orientation. The AFA's spokesperson, Sandy Rios, stated that, 'now, under pressure from pedophile activists, they [APA] have declared the desire for sex with children an "orientation", too' (cited in Bohon 2013). Since these accusations the APA, in a News Release (2013), defended itself by claiming that sexual orientation in this context was a writing error and has no place in defining paedophilic disorder. They also emphasised that paedophilic disorder belongs under the aetiology of a paraphilia.

The APA offers a clinical rather than legal definition of paedophilia and describes the offender's perspective rather than the victim's. Legally the paedophile has to be 16 years of age or older and at least five years older than the child. This, however, becomes blurred when considering older adolescents, which is why the clinician often reserves the final judgement. Paedophiles are not all the same and there are individual differences in the age and sex of the child to whom they are attracted. These individual differences are informative and help professionals classify paedophiles according to what motivates their sexual attractions. There have been many forms of classification, which despite their semantic differences, describe very similar phenomena discussed next.

## Classifications

Research indicates that paedophiles have a tendency to be attracted to a particular age group and sex of child – paedophiles can be homosexual, heterosexual or bisexual (DSM-5 2013). The figures for homosexual paedophiles in relation to the population statistics for homosexuality, and likewise for heterosexual paedophiles within heterosexual population statistics, suggest that a higher rate of paedophiles arise from the homosexual quarter. For example, findings from numerous studies (Blanchard, Barbaree, Bogaert, Dickey et al. 2000; Cohen and Galynker 2002; Murray 2000) suggest that homosexual paedophiles (at 9–40 per cent) are 4–20 times higher than the prevalence of homosexuality in the wider population (at 2–4 per cent). These figures are not alluding to an increased likelihood of homosexuals being child molesters but rather that there is a tendency for paedophiles to prefer children of their own sex. This finding reinforces the figures attained in a study by Marshall, Barbaree and Butt (1988) showing that men who molested boys had a homosexual orientation and that as many as a third were classified as active homosexual paedophiles. It should be noted that although most active paedophiles are men, women commit a total of between 5–8 per cent of such offences.

Studies show that active female paedophiles tend to have had turbulent childhood histories – often maltreated, exposed to violence and coerced into sexual relationships. They are also more likely than active male paedophiles to abuse younger children, threaten to hurt the child's family, use objects for penetration and to coerce children to perform sexual behaviours on each other

(Araji 2000). Active female paedophiles have been classified into four subtypes based on *modus operandi*: teacher-lover; inter-generationally predisposed; male coerced and experimenter-exploiter (Araji 2000; Matthews, Matthews and Speltz 1991). Despite this, however, most research has been restricted to male paedophiles. Different subtypes of active paedophile based on underlying motivations that drive their behaviour have been devised by Cohen *et al.* (1969), Groth and Burgess (1977b) and Knight and Prentky (1990).

Cohen *et al.* (1969) divided paedophiles into three subtypes: fixated, regressed and aggressive:

1    The fixated paedophile generally feels socially and sexually more comfortable, contented and safe with children and therefore groom children who they are familiar with.
2    Regressed paedophiles tend to show sexual arousal and interest towards adult heterosexuals but regress socially and sexually towards preferring children when they feel their masculinity has been compromised through a perceived threat.
3    Aggressive paedophiles perform sadistic sexual acts using force generally towards boys.

Groth and Burgess (1977b) devised typologies of paedophiles based on the degree of force used: sex pressure and sex force:

• Physical force is absent in paedophiles with the sex pressure typology. As they desire the child and feel safer with children, they resort to using enticement and persuasion or entrapments such as bribes.
• A very different form of behaviour arises when considering the sex force paedophile. Here the offender relies on coercion and physical force. They either approach children in an exploitative way by using them for sexual gratification or for sadistic pleasure involving tactics of physical pain and humiliation towards the child.

Knight and Prentky (1990) divided paedophiles using two dimensions. The first dimension considers the level of fixation and the degree of social competence of the paedophile. The second dimension considers the amount of contact towards the child. The two dimensions form four subtypes of paedophile:

1    Low contact dividing into those causing high or low physical injury.
2    High contact dividing into interpersonal and narcissistic types and sadistic or non-sadistic types.

Active paedophiles operate in many different ways which can often make their detection difficult. This is no more apparent than the case of Jimmy Savile who in 2012 was investigated posthumously after there were many reports of his alleged rape and abuse of underage girls and boys. His celebrity status and figurehead for many children's charities enabled him to have access to children and young adolescents in hospitals, prison hospitals and of course backstage for his own show, 'Jim'll Fix It' and during his hosting of 'Top of the Pops' (see Box 8.3). Since the investigation of Savile, other celebrities have been accused of sexually abusing underage youngsters. While an abundance of evidence exists to convict Savile and Stuart Hall in 2013 and Rolf Harris in 2014 for active paedophilia, other celebrities and politicians in the UK are undergoing further investigation. Although Savile caused extreme psychological harm and distress to his victims he did not murder anyone unlike another paedophile, Robert Black, who was convicted for kidnapping and killing four girls aged between 5–11 years. He sexually abused and murdered Jennifer Cardy in 1981, Susan Maxwell in 1982, Caroline Hogg in 1983 and Sarah Harper in 1986. Black was considered to be extremely dangerous (see Chapters 11 and 12) and in 2009 was given a further life sentence for the abuse and murder of Jennifer Cardy.

## Box 8.3

### Jimmy Savile's dark secret

Operation Yewtree began as a consequence of the ITV documentary *Exposure: The Other Side of Jimmy Savile*, first broadcast on 3 October 2012. In this programme several women claimed Savile had sexually abused them when they were adolescents. Witnesses claimed that they saw Savile French kiss an underage girl who was sat on his lap in his changing room. Another victim claimed she was sexually assaulted in 1970 when she was 14 years old. It was through his television programmes, such as 'Jim'll Fix It', 'Top of the Pops' and 'Clunk, Click' and his many charity works, that Savile attained access to adolescent girls but his activity was not entirely unknown. As Esther Rantzen, the founder of 'ChildLine' said, 'There were always rumours that he [Savile] behaved very inappropriately sexually with children' (Sky News 2012).

After the documentary was broadcast there were a stream of Savile's victims that came forward and accused him of sexual abuse and rape – many of whom were underage and rather vulnerable at the time. For instance, one nurse at Leeds Hospital reported that Savile kissed and molested a recovering brain damaged patient. At Stoke Mandeville Hospital in 1971 he sexually abused a 13 year old and later that day an 8 year old who was recovering from an operation. Staff members were aware of his antics of searching for young patients, so much so that they instructed them to pretend to be asleep when he visited. Savile had access to patients at Broadmoor – even had his own set of keys to their cells allowing him to come and go as he pleased.

Commander Spindler responsible for Operation Yewtree announced that a total of 589 alleged victims of abuse of which 450 claimed to be abused by Savile came forward. The UK and Eire database for sex offences against children, in an article entitled, 'Jimmy Savile – Witch hunt or paedophile?' provides a figure breakdown of Savile's abuse as follows:

- 34 formally recorded rapes;
- 52 female victims aged above 18;
- 63 victims aged between 13 and 16;
- 18 female victims aged below 10;
- 40 male victims – 10 of whom who were under 10 years old;
- 1 offence recorded in 1991 at Broadmoor;
- 22 offences recorded at Stoke Mandeville between 1965 and 1988;
- 16 offences recorded at Leeds General Infirmary between 1965 and 1995;
- 214 crimes recorded and 450 complainants against Savile (three-quarters of these were children at the time);
- 73 per cent of offences were against those aged under 18 (youngest being just 8).

These two cases (Black and Savile) highlight the extremes of behaviour shown by different paedophiles. More recently with the development of the internet and the hosting of online 'chat rooms' and 'instant messaging' (IM), paedophiles have a new and more extensive tool used for the purpose of locating their potential victims. Through online chat rooms and IM, paedophiles can introduce themselves and pretend to be of the same age as the child they are communicating with. Through this relatively new social media paedophiles can 'groom' (i.e. befriend and develop an emotional connection) their potential child victims online (see Box 8.4). By **grooming** their potential child victim, paedophiles are able to prepare the targeted child for sexual activity and exploitation such as prostitution and pornography (Crosson-Tower 2005; Levesque 1999; Wortley and Smallbone 2012). In some extreme cases exploitation can lead to trafficking of children and slavery.

## Box 8.4

### Grooming of children using cyber-technologies and ways of stopping this

Grooming children is a form of manipulation beginning with online communication and building a rapport and ending in sexual exploitation. Active paedophiles try to build a rapport and gain the trust and confidence of their targeted victim before arranging physical contact. In addition to communicating via online chat rooms, paedophiles will make contact using mobile phones by texting messages and actually talking. The way paedophiles gain the confidence and trust of their victims is through flattery and offering emotional support such as providing sympathy and understanding. Once a meeting has been set up, they often shower their victims with gifts and money and provide modelling job opportunities. The showering of gifts can continue over a long period of time and becomes part of the grooming process. The motive behind grooming is to manipulate the victim into believing that they are special in some way to the person and are loved. In reality, however, they are not the only ones being groomed – there are often many children being groomed simultaneously and who are at different stages of the grooming process. Furthermore, as seen in recent cases of paedophilic gangs, underage girls are first groomed and later forced to take drugs and kidnapped to become prostitutes. The use of mobile phones plays a paramount role in harassing these girls by threatening to harm their families if they did not comply with their groomers. In the case of the Oxford child paedophile gang in the UK, seven members (Akhtar Dogar, 32; Anjum Dogar, 31; Mohammed Karrar, 38; Bassam Karrar, 33; Kamar Jamil, 27; Assad Hussain, 32; and Zeeshan Ahmed, 27) were found guilty of organising prostitution, child rape and sex trafficking in 2013. Over a period of eight years girls as young 11 were forced to take cocaine and were raped – in some cases by as many as five men per day. Their first case of grooming is suspected to be in 2004 but over the course of eight years many girls were groomed simultaneously while others were already forced into prostitution (Hall and Rawlinson for *The Independent* 2013).

The use of cyber-technologies in grooming potential child-targets has become a worldwide problem, and in the UK, action has been taken to try and uncover active paedophiles through the Child Exploitation and Online Protection Centre (CEOP) formed in 2006. Although CEOP consists of specialist police officers experienced at finding sex offenders, it works in collaboration with many organisations and businesses (i.e. Childnet Microsoft, The Scout Association, The Football Association, British Telecom, Lycos, AOL and Vodafone), Government Departments (i.e. Home Office, Foreign and Commonwealth Office and Schools) and non-government bodies and charities (i.e. NCH, NSPCC and Barnardos). CEOP police officers have had some success at identifying active paedophiles by going undercover as potential victims for grooming. In 2006, Lee Costi was sentenced for grooming schoolgirls for sex and in 2007 Timothy Cox for online grooming. CEOP is currently investigating 700 new suspected paedophiles.

Operation Chalice led by DCI Edwards (and later by DCI Jamieson) was set up in 2010 as a means of gaining the trust of vulnerable girls being sexually abused and trafficked as prostitutes to many different towns in Britain by predatory sex gangs. West Mercia Police had specially trained officers to gather evidence from the abused girls about the gang operating in the Birmingham area. The girls' experiences of grooming, being forced to drink alcohol and take drugs, being gang raped and hired out as prostitutes led to eight men being sentenced in 2012. In 1999 British police established Operation Ore to investigate and prosecute users of websites showing child pornography. Christopher Williams reporting for the Daily Telegraph in 2011 (Williams 2011) claimed that Operation Ore led the most expansive computer crime investigation where 7,250 suspects were identified, 1,451 convictions passed, 493 cautioned and 140 children rescued from adverse circumstances (Arthur for *The Guardian* 2007). Between 1999 and 2001 Landslide Productions Inc., which provided an online pornography portal, was investigated by the FBI who then provided the UK (police officers involved in Operation Ore) with names of users accessing indecent images. This led to many arrests of people including celebrities, such as Pete Townsend who was cautioned for having a credit card entry to Landslide, which were later proven to be false arrests. This operation proved to be overzealous resulting in many convictions being overturned.

Our final category of sexual offending is known as the paraphilias which we will discover can also overlap with rape and paedophilia in terms of the sexual offending behaviours exhibited by some rapists and active paedophiles. As with rape and paedophilia we will consider the definitions and classifications of paraphilias.

## Definitions and classifications of paraphilias

### Definitions

In the *Diagnostic and Statistical Manual of Mental Disorders*, 4th edition (DSM-IV-TR; American Psychiatric Association 2000) paraphilia is defined in a similar way to paedophilia with the exception that this can involve inanimate objects, animals, children or non-consenting individuals, and can cause pain and humiliation to the self or to a partner (APA 2000). However, in DSM-5 (American Psychiatric Association 2013) a distinction is made between paraphilias and paraphilic disorders, where a paraphilic disorder is considered a psychopathology. A paraphilic disorder is defined as a paraphilia that contributes towards an individual's distress or impairment or causes harm to others. Paraphilias, however, are considered as misplaced attraction directed at an object or living thing other than a human. The descriptions of paraphilias include:

- telephone scatologia or lewdness expressed on the phone (usually heavy breathing and sexual conversations with a stranger);
- necrophilia (sexual attraction to and varying levels of sexual contact with a corpse);

Psychologists have tried to explain these seemingly diverse behaviours which we will explore next.

## Explanations for paraphilic behaviour

Analysis of the type of behaviours associated with an offence, and the needs these behaviours satisfy for the sex offender, have to be considered independently. Interestingly, the concept of courtship behaviour introduced by Freund, Scher and Hucker (1983) has been applied to certain aspects of paraphilic relationships. Freund *et al.* (1983) added that individuals practising paraphilia have distorted thinking about how normal relationships are formed and maintained. They describe four phases of courtship behaviour:

- The first or finding phase, is when a partner is found and appraised.
- The second or affiliative phase, is when non-verbal and verbal communication is instigated.
- The third or tactile phase, is where physical contact is made.
- The fourth or copulative phase, is when sexual intercourse occurs.

The key to understanding Freund *et al.*'s concept of courtship behaviour, involves the application of cognitive distortion. In this context they use distortion to refer to a different way of thinking about someone that bears no resemblance to the information encapsulated within the situation. According to Freund *et al.* (1983) the first or finding phase is distorted in voyeurs, as they believe that their victim wants to be secretly observed, despite no evidence to support this contention. Distortion occurs during the affiliative phase for exhibitionists and callers of obscene telecommunications. Exhibitionists, for instance, seek communication with the desired person regardless of whether it is wanted or not. Due to their distorted cognitions they believe that their desired person wants this type of relationship. In the case of frotteurs, the tactile phase is distorted whereas for rapists distortion occurs at the copulatory phase. Rapists believe that their victims want to have sexual intercourse despite there being no indication of this. Although the stages of courtship proposed by Freund *et al.* (1983) describes and links the behaviours shown in various types of paraphilias, it does not explain effectively why individuals perform these coercive paraphilic acts. To explain the reasoning and motivations underlying the diversity of behaviours demonstrated by individuals practising coercive paraphilias, it is important to refer to the different profiles of sex offenders and micro-level classifications. Considering profiles and classifications help to provide an understanding of behavioural clusters and the needs they serve for the individual.

As can be seen, the classifications of rapists and paedophiles are similar and take account of similar sexual behaviours that co-occur during sexual abuse. Furthermore, the motivations that these behaviours pay lip service to are described in a similar manner. While these descriptions and classifications are useful, they only provide limited insight as to why some sex offenders choose to rape or perform paedophilic acts. To understand the 'psyche' of rapists and paedophiles it is necessary to consider the different theories derived from a diverse set of perspectives which we will discuss next.

## Why do sex offenders become rapists or paedophiles?

There are many theories accounting for the behaviour of rapists and pae-dophiles that reflect different underlying perspectives such as behavioural conditioning; neurocognitive, neurobiological and ultimate (evolutionary)-proximate approaches; feminist analysis, psychoanalysis, situational and an integrated approach. Each approach will be discussed in turn in relation to rapists and paedophiles. Some theories are more applicable and have research evidence supporting their claims in relation to rapists or paedophiles or both.

### Behavioural approach (psychologist John B. Watson)

John Watson is considered the founder of behaviourism after writing an article titled, 'Psychology as a Behaviorist Views it' published in 1913. Behaviourism is also referred to as behavioural psychology and is based on the idea that behaviours are acquired through the process of conditioning (see Box 8.5). Watson claimed that conditioning occurs as a consequence of interacting with our environment and demonstrated this in an experiment on a toddler who became known as 'Little Albert' (Watson and Rayner 1920). The experiment was simple but effective and demonstrated the process of association between stimulus and outcome. The objective of the experiment was to make Albert frightened of white furry rabbits and anything else that resembled something white and furry. This was achieved as follows: on every occasion that Albert stroked a white rabbit, an iron bar was struck to create a loud noise directly behind and above his head. The loud noise frightened Albert and eventually became associated with stroking the rabbit. Watson and Rayner (1920) were responsible for causing Albert to develop a phobia of rabbits and other objects resembling rabbits. This technique involved pairing a neutral stimulus (in this case a rabbit) with a response to an aversive stimulus (fear of a loud noise). Eventually the fear in response to the loud noise will be associated with the rabbit that then becomes the new stimulus evoking fear.

Watson was inspired by the work of Russian physiologist Ivan Pavlov, who studied the salivary reflex responses of dogs in 1927. Pavlov introduced the term classical conditioning to describe a learning process derived through the associa-tion of naturally occurring and environmentally based stimuli. It was through his work on classical conditioning in dogs (see Box 8.5) that Pavlov received the Nobel Prize in 1904. Pavlov's experiment highlights the importance of associative learning and how it can be undone, which has relevant implications for understanding and changing the behaviour of paedophiles and rapists.

---

## Box 8.5

### The stages of classical conditioning

1. Dogs will naturally salivate in anticipation of receiving food – an automated response for which there is little control over. This is known as the Unconditioned Response (UCR) towards an Unconditioned Stimulus (UCS) which in this case is the food.
2. After taking a baseline level of saliva production to food, Pavlov then presented the food at the same time as sounding a bell (the Conditioned Stimulus (CS)).
3. After a few trials the dogs began to associate food with the bell as demonstrated when the dogs salivated at the sound of the bell despite no presence of food (the Conditioned Response (CR)).
4. This can be represented as:   UCS = UCR

$$UCS + CS = UCR$$
$$CS = CR$$

---

Behaviourism also incorporates operant conditioning which was introduced by Burrhus F. Skinner. Skinner (1953) used the term operant to describe any 'active behaviour that operates upon the environment to generate consequences'. Operant conditioning accounts for how learned behaviours are acquired using reinforcement and punishment schedules. Positive reinforcers encourage the repetition of behaviours because of their rewarding outcomes; when a child responds in a positive way in a chat-room forum over the internet, the active paedophile will find this a rewarding experience and is likely to continue grooming the child through further communication (i.e. his behaviour is reinforced). If a child responded in a sarcastic manner that lowered his self-esteem, then it would be very unlikely that the same child would be contacted again. There are two types of punishment schedules that can modify behavioural responses: positive and negative punishment. Punishment schedules are designed to attenuate behaviour by either introducing an unfavourable outcome following the behaviour or removing the favourable outcome after the behaviour has occurred. Punishment therefore reduces the frequency of behaviour in contrast to reinforcement which increases its frequency.

In order to understand how behaviourists explain the behaviour of rapists and paedophiles and the reasons for their actions, it is important to consider the practical applications derived from this approach. Most sexual attractions occur through the process of classical conditioning whereby in the context of sexual offending, violence is associated or bonded with sexual behaviour. McGuire, Carlisle and Young (1965) were able to show that sexual arousal induced by masturbation and sexual fantasies can become associated or paired. This occurs also when a previously neutral stimulus is paired with masturbation which leads to a strong sexual valence for the neutral stimulus. It is this strong preference that ensures the continuation of the newly acquired sexual behaviour. Krafft-Ebing (1886) described a case of a young boy who later in life developed masochistic tendencies; it was argued that while he was spanked across his parent's lap, his penis experienced friction which led to the association between sexual arousal and pain.

Rachman (1966) adopted Pavlovian (classical) conditioning for the development of a sexual fetish. He paired a photographic slide of a pair of black boots (CS) with a photographic slide of an attractive naked woman (US). After showing these pairings a few times, the males in the study did develop penile arousal as measured using penile plethysmography to the boots alone. This laboratory-based experiment demonstrated how classical conditioning could explain associative learning between a stimulus naturally causing sexual arousal (which in the case of a heterosexual male adult would be a picture of a nude woman) and a neutral stimulus which would not normally elicit such feelings (like, for instance, black boots). Rachman's study also shows that the development of sexual deviations is possible through pairing sexual arousal with neutral stimuli. A more recent study in 1999 by Plaud and Martini also demonstrated that it is possible to classically condition males to show sexual arousal towards a 'penny jar' provided it was shown briefly before the sexually explicit visual stimuli (known as short delay conditioning). Conditioned sexual arousal has also been demonstrated experimentally by Hoffman, Janssen and Turner (2004). While these studies have demonstrated sexual arousal to neutral stimuli there remains the question of whether laboratory-based models of sexual arousal can be extrapolated to sexual deviance in the real world.

In order to extinguish inappropriate sexual arousal towards stimuli, classical and operant conditioning procedures commonly use noxious stimuli paired with the sexually deviant behaviour (i.e. paedophilia or rape) – as a measure to replace the behaviour with appropriate sexual behaviour (Quinsey and Earls 1990). Classical conditioning instigated the development of new phallometric techniques for assessing sexual arousal (Marshall 1996, 2005). These included equipment to measure the circumference of an erect penis which enabled researchers to assess when a paedophile was aroused and what elicited the arousal. Phallometric assessment continues to be used in the treatment of sexual offenders like paedophiles (Hanson and Bussière 1998).

According to Ormrod (1999), it was the partnership with social learning (Bandura 1977) that helped develop the oversimplified behaviourist therapeutic approach into a successful treatment intervention known as cognitive-behavioural therapy (CBT). Social Learning Theory describes adolescent sexual offending as originating from internalised definitions favouring deviant sexual behaviours and from the rewards they perceived their abusers as receiving for performing paedophilic acts (Akers 1998). There are many associated reasons why they perceive the need to continue behaving this way but one important factor linking social learning with behaviourist approaches is the conditioning processes underlying sexual orgasm (Marshall and Eccles 1993). Ormrod (1999) reducing deviant sexual urges, CBT, pharmacotherapy and psychotherapy treatment interventions have fared well. Nevertheless, despite psychotherapy and pharmacotherapy administered simultaneously, a cure for sex offending remains wanting. Furthermore, many sex offenders who resist offending have confessed to experiencing on-going deviant sexual desires. It would appear that deviant sexual desires and thoughts remain but for successfully treated perpetrators the behavioural response to these desires and thoughts can be controlled, even extinguished.

- Why it is difficult to 'cure' sex offenders from their deviant thoughts and behaviours has been construed in different ways. For some researchers the behaviours of sex offenders are derived from dysfunctional neuro-cognitive and neurobiological processes in the brain. Others believe that adversity during both prenatal and early childhood development interacts with timelines of brain maturation, and in so doing modifies or disrupts normal neurocognitive and neurobiological processes. Adversity can be anything from mothers taking drugs or being physically abused while pregnant to the child being maltreated, sexually and physically abused or neglected in childhood. Bowlby demonstrated how insecure attachments can foster negative working models of what the mother is like which can be extended to other adults. He further showed that being brought up in institutions where the staff turnover rate was high prevented children from forming any meaningful bonds with adults. This sends the message that no one cares and can in turn provoke hostile beliefs about women for instance. In a similar vein, children who are sexually abused might also develop hostile beliefs about people and can become vulnerable to being sexual abusers themselves in adolescence and adulthood. This is the time when deviant sexual fantasies and cognitive distortions are formed.
- Connections between insecure attachments and personality disorders in sex offenders have been found by numerous researchers. Birtchnell's (1996) interpersonal octagon approach was used by Bogaerts et al. (2005) who found that personality disorders might lead to insecure attachments in sex offenders.
- It is difficult to know whether sex offenders graduate into a life of deviant sexual desires due to their genetic make-up interacting with their upbringing (**gene–environment interaction**), or as a consequence of abnormal brain structure and function resulting from prenatal development or child abuse. This is why the ITSO model of Ward and Beech (2006) is important as it enables research covering different aspects of sex offenders to be integrated and in so doing create a more profound level of understanding.
- Sex offenders have commonalities with other criminals such as psychopaths. While sex offenders rarely commit homicide, criminal psychopaths often have underlying sexual connotations to their murders. Both sex offenders and criminal psychopaths appear to lack empathy for their victims and have immature global empathy. There are certainly neurobiological

anomalies in neurotransmitter production (serotonin, dopamine and nor-epinephrine) which impact on areas of the brain relating to motivation and sexual behaviour in sex offenders. These findings are a facet of addictive behaviour per se but, alone, are not enough to account for deviant sexual behaviour. It is difficult to say whether sex offenders and psychopaths have the same brain deficits for empathy as more empirical evidence is required; however, the strong neurocognitive and neurobiological element to sex offending cannot be ignored.

• There is a robust interrelationship between low self-esteem and feeling shame in most sex offenders. This is believed to be at the heart of cognitive distortion formation which prevents perpetrators from feeling empathy for their victims. Marshall *et al.*'s (2009) model describes the relationship between self-esteem, shame, guilt, cognitive distortion and empathy. It further helps to predict who is likely to seek treatment and successfully change their sexually related cognitions, emotions and behaviour. Marshall *et al.* (2009) also suggested a successful therapist–client relationship that works to change deviant sexual behaviours and boost self-esteem is an important factor in the reduction of recidivism.

• The ethics of Megan's Law and civil court orders on the lives of sex offenders was considered in terms of empirical evidence for their effectiveness in preventing paedophilia and rape. The findings are mixed. While it is important to keep children safe from paedophiles, which Megan's Law and civil court orders do to a point, these measures do not prevent perpetrators from operating. Many go underground and continue to offend using the internet, which makes it difficult to locate their base of operation. In some states of America, individuals on sex offender registers have to make themselves known to their neighbours. In Britain this does not occur but various branches of the criminal justice system know where they live. Many sex offenders experience abuse and harassment once their home address becomes known to the public – they complain that their rights to privacy have been compromised. It could be argued that this is the price they should pay for their crimes. It is a difficult ethical issue to address especially when there is limited evidence to suggest that these rulings work.

## Questions for discussion

1   Which theoretical explanation of sexual offending appears to be most empirically sound? Why?
2   Is there a cure for sex offenders? Discuss this in the light of treatment effectiveness and the underpinning theoretical foundation on which the treatment is based.
3   Is it possible to teach sex offenders how to feel empathy for their victims? If so, would this be truly felt empathy or empathy based on perceptions of expected behaviour?

# Chapter 9

# Female offenders and their crimes

The aim of the chapters in Part III is to present evidence for a nature–nurture contribution towards a selection of criminals: in this case the female offender. As with all chapters in this section, a multidisciplinary approach will be taken such that evidence is drawn from a variety of academic subjects which address crime and the criminal. Later in the concluding chapter, the evidence will be evaluated.

We will begin by exploring the criminal statistics and disseminating the differences in the type and prevalence of crime committed by males and females to highlight the gender divide. There is a robust gender divide for criminality, which cuts across all statistical measurements used by the Home Office (i.e. arrest, sentencing and imprisonment), showing that crime is dominated by males. Different explanations for this gender divide have been put forth by sociologists, criminologists and psychologists. We will see that despite their different approaches, there is overlap in some areas of sociology and psychology as regards to sex-role socialisation, differences in levels of control, and supervision exerted as a mechanism of inducing sex-role conformity across the sexes. Nevertheless, the different theoretical approaches will be considered separately beginning with two traditional theories that of Lombroso (a criminologist) and Freud (a medical doctor and founder of psychoanalysis). The main sociological theories that will be addressed here include: learning theory, strain and control, and Sex-Role Theory. In this chapter we will also focus on feminist accounts, including the impact of the liberation movement on female behaviour and new found career aspirations. This will be further considered in relation to increasing female crime figures. Psychological approaches will be considered primarily using a bio-psychological perspective beginning with evolutionary psychology and leading to a compromise approach of combining evolution with environmental influences such as culture, economical marginalisation and freedom. The biosocial approach binds together genes and the environment in a more obvious way, it has been argued, than outlined by evolutionary psychology. It further acknowledges the importance of androgens, such as testosterone in males, as a factor increasing male aggressiveness. The importance of the role played by a chemical imbalance with respect to **neurotransmitters** such as serotonin will also be considered here. We will also revisit in this chapter the notion and relevance of the **gender paradox** first discussed in Chapter 2. The interesting fact that females who do have conditions such as Attention Deficit Hyperactivity Disorder or conduct disorder (which features more often in males) will show more extreme symptom traits than their male counterparts, and are more likely to express psychopathic tendencies in adulthood, will be discussed as a factor of the gender paradox. We will also consider the differences in the way females are treated by the criminal justice system in comparison to males. In the past male offenders were sentenced more punitively than females for the same crime committed. This difference is less so today. Nevertheless, there is on-going debate concerning the merits of having an equitable approach to sentencing across gender. Some advocate the case for a 'special needs' approach for sentencing female offenders only to find that others believe this would further divide the treatment of male and female offenders by the criminal justice system.

## Introduction

There is a marked gender divide in the nature and frequency of criminal acts committed by males and females. The annual criminal statistics show that males consistently commit more crime than females regardless of the time frame considered. These statistics also show that the nature of criminal activity differs between males and females – males commit more serious and violent crime whereas females gravitate towards shoplifting and fraudulent-based crime. This difference in crime rates between males and females has been explored for many decades by psychologists, sociologists and criminologists. Psychological theories, for instance, can be divided into the more traditional approaches, such as those put forward by Sigmund Freud, and contemporary bio-psychological and evolutionary approaches. A host of sociologically driven explanations, bordering with the social spectrum of psychology, and geared towards explaining the different experiences males and females have of the social world, have been developed. Hence although learning models, sex role, strain and control theories are grouped under sociological theories, it is important to bear in mind that social psychologists have also researched and contributed their findings to these areas. In the case of early criminological thought, Cessare Lombroso, the 'big daddy', developed a theory of criminality that took into account gender differences. Feminist approaches have also provided interesting demographic details that link both political and social ideology with changes in female behaviour. In particular, feminist approaches demonstrate how the liberation of women and the provision of equal opportunities in the workplace and other domains of social life created an ambitious female cohort rather than, as has been argued by some theorists, aspiring criminals. This false accusation that liberation and equal opportunities is responsible for providing a culture of female criminality is refuted by statistical data showing the contrary.

While there has been an increase in female criminality, a gender divide nevertheless exists, clearly showing that males commit more crime than females. The evidence in support of this is robust. For instance, Graham and Bowling (1995) conducted a large-scale self-report survey of randomly selected cohorts of females and males in Britain who, in the survey, admitted committing an offence within the last twelve months. They found that males admitted to committing 50 per cent more crime than females. The Home Office (HO) in 1999 further revealed a number of interesting findings:

- 33 per cent of males have a criminal record before aged 40 compared with fewer than 10 per cent of females;
- 25 per cent of male offenders have a criminal career lasting longer than ten years compared with 3 per cent of females;
- 60 per cent of male offenders have a criminal career lasting less than a year compared with 80 per cent of females;
- Fewer than 10 per cent of female offenders are supervised by probation officers;
- Fewer than 5 per cent of female offenders constitute the prison population;
- 31 per cent of female offenders serving probation orders had no previous convictions compared with 16 per cent of males;
- 60 per cent of female offenders are cautioned or convicted for theft and handling (especially shoplifting) compared with 33 per cent of males.

Mair and May (1997) conducted a study of 1,986 offenders who began their probation in 1994 showing that of the female offenders, theft was the most common offence committed (this was 53 per cent in comparison to 33 per cent for males) and also the first type of offence they were convicted for. While different studies are informative, it is the HO crime statistics published annually in the UK that provide an up-to-date account of **recorded crime**, arrest and conviction figures (see Chapter 2). These statistics are very useful as they also provide details of trends over the years and patterns of crime committed. In the next section, HO statistics will be reviewed and presented as figures so that trends over the years can be examined for both males and females for specific types of crime.

## What do the crime statistics show?

Figures 9.1–9.9 show a striking difference in the number of arrests for males and females – more men commit more crime than women regardless of the type of offence considered. The gender divide is not as vast for crimes of fraud and forgery but in the case of more serious offences the figures rise disproportionately for male offenders. Despite an increase in female arrest figures (including violence against the person) over the years, criminality continues to be male dominated with up to 89 per cent of all offences being committed by men. According to Daly and Wilson (1988), 'The difference between the sexes is immense and it is universal. There is no known society in which the level of lethal violence among women even begins to approach that among men' (p.146).

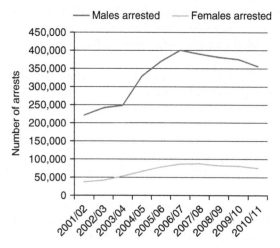

*Figure 9.1* Male and female arrests for recorded violence against the person offences from 2001–02 to 2010–11

Adapted from the Home Office Statistics (2001–2011) for Notifiable Offences

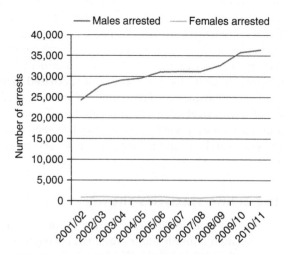

*Figure 9.2* Male and female arrests for recorded sexual offences from 2001–02 to 2010–11

Adapted from the Home Office Statistics (2001–2011) for Notifiable Offences

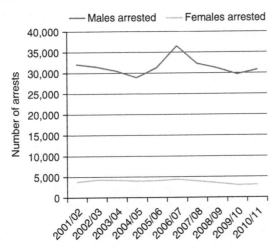

Figure 9.3 Male and female arrests for recorded robbery from 2001–02 to 2010–11
Adapted from the Home Office Statistics (2001–2011) for Notifiable Offences

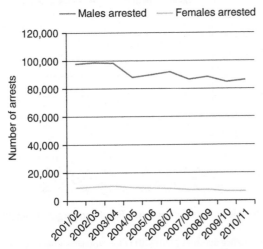

Figure 9.4 Male and female arrests for recorded burglary from 2001–02 to 2010–11
Adapted from the Home Office Statistics (2001–2011) for Notifiable Offences

As discussed previously, the nature of female crime primarily involves acts of theft, whether in the form of shoplifting, fraud or forgery, the outcome is the same – the attainment of monies or goods through illicit means. These criminal acts are regulated crimes and therefore constitute crimes of *mala prohibita*. Crimes committed by men tend to be personal crimes in that they often involve harm towards other individuals and for this reason are considered to be *mala in se* crimes. In other words, these crimes are usually serious and contravene the human moral code (see Chapter 1). The HO also provides a breakdown

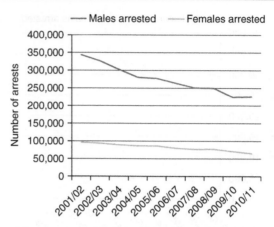

*Figure 9.5* Male and female arrests for theft and handling stolen goods from 2001–02 to 2010–11

Adapted from the Home Office Statistics (2001–2011) for Notifiable Offences

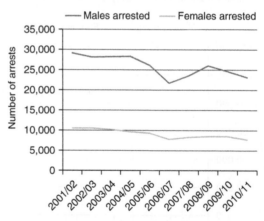

*Figure 9.6* Male and female arrests for recorded fraud and forgery from 2001–02 to 2010–11

Adapted from the Home Office Statistics (2001–2011) for Notifiable Offences

of crime data using age as the defining category, and when age is considered it becomes apparent that most crime is committed by young adult males.

Criminal statistics from the HO further reveal a steady decline in the number of arrests as age increases. For instance, delinquent behaviour declines in frequency and severity after adolescence, and by the age of 40, criminality has reduced to a hard core of male offenders (see Chapter 2 for discussion of criminal careers and Chapter 10 for age and sex differences in delinquency). This tends to suggest that crime arises out of biological constraints such as gender and age (see section on Biological approaches). Wilson and Herrnstein (1985) have eloquently summarised this:

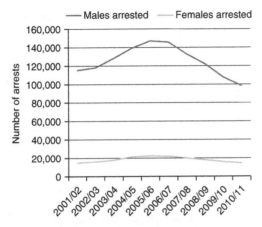

*Figure 9.7* Male and female arrests for recorded criminal damage from 2001–02 to 2010–11

Adapted from the Home Office Statistics (2001–2011) for Notifiable Offences

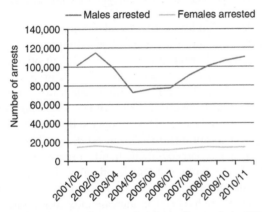

*Figure 9.8* Male and female arrests for recorded drug offences from 2001–02 to 2010–11

Adapted from the Home Office Statistics (2001–2011) for Notifiable Offences

Crime is ... carried out by young men in large cities. There are old criminals and female criminals and rural and small town ones, but to a much greater degree than would be expected by chance the criminals are young urban males... This is true ... in every society that keeps criminal statistics (p.26).

As discussed previously (see Chapter 2), criminal careers can provide insightful information about offenders, in terms of their crime onset and **desistance** age, initiation into a criminal lifestyle (see also Chapter 5) and the motivation to commit crime. Research in this area has, however, been limited to comparing male and female violent offending. What does become apparent when comparing

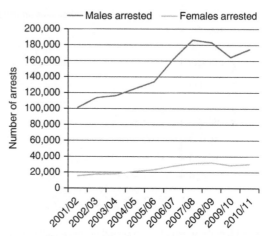

*Figure 9.9* Male and female arrests for recorded other offences from 2001–02 to 2010–11

Adapted from the Home Office Statistics (2001–2011) for Notifiable Offences

the sexes for violent offending is that females commit considerably less acts of violence, and when they do, they begin their criminal careers earlier and peak earlier than males. Female **recidivism** rates for violent offending are far lower than for males, and females are more likely to desist from further violence (Steffensmeier and Ulmer 2005). Hence the research from criminal careers suggests that long-term female involvement in crime is rare. This is further substantiated by the interviews and case studies conducted by Bottcher (1995) suggesting a weak commitment to criminal behaviour. Studies of female crime, however, all suggest that crimes of larceny–theft, fraud, forgery, prostitution and drug/alcohol-related offences typify the female offender. The UK and US recorded crime statistics (and globally) support this, as do studies using self-reporting methods. In the US there has been an increase in what is known as 'pink-collar' crime. Females committing pink-collar crimes are usually from clerical and retail sales, teaching and nursing jobs. In fact 90 per cent of female pink-collar criminals worked as low-level bookkeepers or bank-tellers, which according to Schwartz and Steffensmeier (2008), explains the increased arrests for female embezzlement. Due to the lack of opportunity, females are rarely involved in serious **white-collar crime** (see Chapters 5 and 6). Larceny–theft offences committed by females typically involve shoplifting, use of bad cheques and misuse of credit cards. There have been a few high-profile cases of shoplifting in the celebrity world: Winona Ryder was convicted of shoplifting clothes worth $5,000 in 2001; Megan Fox stole a $7 lip-gloss when she was 15 years old and Lindsay Lohan was convicted of shoplifting a necklace worth $2,500 in 2011.

Despite the existence of a robust gender difference attributing less serious crime to females, the discovery that females are capable of committing violent and dangerous offences, such as murder and serial killing, is still considered to be atypical. There are, nevertheless, many female murderers who have killed for reasons such as jealousy and abandonment (commonly known as crimes of passion), monetary gain or self-defence, but no female murderer has been hated and perceived as evil in the same vain as Myra Hindley. Rosemary West is a close contender but has managed to escape from the public hate campaign. When Myra Hindley died in 2002, one of the newspaper's headlines read, 'At last Myra is where she belongs – HELL'. Hindley was partner in crime with her boyfriend Ian Brady, who is still alive and serving his life prison sentence. Hindley collaborated with Brady to commit crimes against children and young adolescents that included acts of abduction, torture, rape and murder (see Box 9.1).

## Box 9.1

### Female serial killers Myra Hindley and Rosemary West who killed in collaboration with male partners

Hindley and Brady are reported to have had aberrant sexual motivations and behaviours which were role played through dressing in sadistic outfits and using whips to simulate Nazi activities (as was evidenced in their video recordings). Although all their murders were horrific in their manner of execution, the one they are best remembered for is that of ten-year-old Lesley Ann Downey. She was abducted from the Christmas fair and a tape recording of what they did to her was found and played in court and presented as evidence of pornography, assault, rape, torture and murder. This is what the court heard, 'Please take your hands off me a minute, please. Please, Mum, please. I can't tell you. I cannot breathe. Please God. Why? What are you doing with me?' (Igloo Books, 2011, p.28). When the information about what happened to Lesley Ann Downey was released to the public there was an outcry, and Hindley in particular was branded an evil woman. A Sky News' headline in 2002 reported she was an 'Icon of Modern Evil' (p.28). Why was Hindley, more than Brady, regarded as evil and hated so much? The answer lies with the fact that she is a woman, and women are not renowned for killing young children. Similarly, Rosemary West in collaboration with her husband Fred West, raped, tortured and murdered her stepchildren as well as her own. Over the years the Wests tortured and raped boarders, hitch-hikers and nannies to their children, and then murdered and mutilated their bodies, which they buried in the cellar or under the patio. The Wests own children were at risk and subjected to torture, rape and, for some of them, murder. In 1996, Rosemary West was charged with ten murders – at least one murder was committed during the time her husband was serving a prison sentence. Both Rosemary West and Myra Hindley demonstrated behaviour that was atypical of the female stereotype. It could be argued that the nature and manner of killing was

> highly influenced by their male collaborators, which to some extent offers a sound explanation if it could be shown that female serial killers operating alone have different underlying motivations for their behaviour – in other words murdering for money.

The motivations for murder in the cases of lone serial killers, Mary Ann Cotton and Aileen Wuornos, however, are very different. In the case of Mary Ann Cotton, who was born in County Durham in 1832, she murdered members of her family – husbands, stepchildren and her own children. With her first husband she had eight children who would all eventually die of gastric fever caused by the administration of poison. Her second husband and her mother died 13 months after Cotton married. Her third husband had five children from a previous marriage, four of whom died of 'natural causes'. Despite being married, she married again to a man who had two children and provided the Cotton surname. She murdered Fredrick Cotton and later his two children and her 14 month old baby. It was the death of Cotton's baby, considered as suspicious at the time, which led to her capture. Autopsy reports showed that Cotton used arsenic to poison and murder all her victims.

Aileen Wuornos was a prostitute who murdered seven male clients between 1989 and 1990 in Florida, US. Wuornos argued that she shot these men in self-defence as they either raped or attempted to rape her. The men varied in age from 40 to 65 but all were employed and died from bullet wounds (the number of bullets found in the bodies of her victims varied from two to nine). Police traced stolen items belonging to the victims to Wuornos after her fingerprints were identified. Items were exchanged for money by pawnbrokers and money stolen from her victims' wallets was used to support her and girlfriend, Tyria Moore. The motivation for Wuornos' serial killing therefore appears to be motivated for the need of money. Understanding the motives behind serial murder is discussed further in Chapter 12 as part of **offender profiling**. Wuornos was arrested in 1991 and during 1992–3 she received six death sentences and was executed by the State of Florida by lethal injection in 2002 after spending 12 years on Death Row. Despite the extensive press coverage of female murderers and serial killers, however, the extent of homicide convictions in the crime statistics is dominated by male offenders (see Figure 9.10).

Figure 9.10 shows a trend in the number of convictions for homicide in England and Wales from 2000 to 2011. The difference between male and female conviction rates across the years is strikingly vast and reflects the patterns and trends seen for other types of crime. Interestingly, the number of homicide convictions is dropping for both male and female offenders. It is possible that this reflects a true decline in the number of murders committed; however, without taking account of the data for the number of unsolved cases and defendants unable to stand trial that are deployed by some other means, such as institutionalisation, an accurate explanation for the seemingly

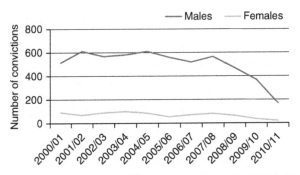

*Figure 9.10* Male and female recorded homicide convictions from 2000–01 to 2010–11
Adapted from the Home Office Statistics (2001–2011) for Notifiable Offences

decreasing homicide convictions cannot be ascertained with certainty. The examples provided are extreme cases of serial murder by women, yet criminologists and psychologists pose the question of whether there is something different about females who commit murder – sociologically or psychologically? In this chapter the reasons why some women commit crime like theft or murder will be considered using traditional theories of Cessare Lombroso and Sigmund Freud, followed by contemporary approaches encapsulated in sociological, criminological and psychological theory.

## How are gender differences in crime explained?

Sociologists, criminologists, feminists, psychologists and biologists have all tried to explain why a difference in the frequency and severity of criminal behaviour exists between males and females. This question was broached and answered by Lombroso as far back as the nineteenth century and Freud in the 1920s. Although both Lombroso and Freud's theories are difficult to substantiate scientifically, they are also impossible to falsify. Despite problems with both Lombroso and Freud's theories, they had some interesting ideas, if not controversial, and it is for this reason that both theories will be considered first. This will be followed by a review of the more popular sociological and psychological, feminist and bio-psychological theories.

### Traditional theories of Cesare Lombroso and Sigmund Freud

Lombroso (1835–1909) was an Italian criminologist and physician. He is accredited with developing the Italian School of Positivist Criminology and established a new way of considering criminals. His promoted anthropological criminology – where he believed that offenders were born criminal (1876) and could be identified by the physical defects exhibited as 'atavistic' characteristics. These atavistic characteristics presented themselves as asymmetry of the face, long arms, excessive hair growth, an enlarged forehead appearing somewhat Neanderthal, low voice pitch, joined eyebrows, ears of unusual size, presence of many moles, being short and having extra fingers. Males who had five or more of these characteristics were considered as born criminals. In the case of females this criteria was reduced to three of these characteristics to be considered a born criminal. Lombroso also claimed that rapists and murderers could be identified via specific characteristics. He made further distinctions between criminals and non-criminals; they were insensitive to pain and touch, lacked morals and remorse, were vain, vindictive, cruel and impulsive. Lombroso further distinguished between criminals and occasional criminals by referring to them as 'criminaloids' but also recognised the existence of criminals by passion and moral imbecility. This is interesting as this was how psychopaths were considered in the early twentieth century (see Chapter 7). His theory was a theory of criminality – male criminality. He failed to adapt his theory to effectively account for female criminality. In fact he applied the same criteria as he used for male criminals. Lombroso did modify his theory during his career such that he claimed a third of criminality was a result of atavistic characteristics and that for the majority it could be explained using environmental factors including sub-standard education and poverty. According to Lombroso 35 per cent of female criminals are born criminals but he did not explain the cause of criminality for female criminals per se. He did, however, consider offences committed by females such as infanticide, murder, poisoning, theft, wounding and prostitution but contrasted these with the majority of crimes being prostitution. He considered the prostitute as a serious criminal type involved in the practice of sexual deviancy. The main thrust of his explanation for female criminality, however, is that females in general are less morally advanced than males and therefore have the propensity to commit crime; and those who do are born criminal and are even more depraved than their male counterpart.

Freud (1856–1939) was an Austrian neurologist who qualified as a medical doctor in 1881 at the University of Vienna. He is renowned for developing a clinical treatment called psychoanalysis used to help improve the symptoms of different psychopathological conditions. Psychoanalysis had theoretical underpinnings – personality and psychosexual development. In explaining personality he introduced three facets – the 'id', 'ego' and 'superego'. Freud considered the id to contain the basic human instinctual drives, such as the libido, which he perceived as the primary force present from birth. The libido is an instinct energy or life force that concentrates on specific regions of the body during different developmental phases which Freud refers to as the erogenous zones (i.e. the oral, anal, phallic, latency and genital stages as part of psychosexual development). The infant passes through these stages and engages in the attainment of pleasure by stimulating these regions through self-controlling actions (i.e. controlling his or her bowels in the anal stage). It is not surprising, therefore, that the id acts according to the pleasure principle which is motivated by the need to avoid pain or any actions causing displeasure (Rycroft 1968). The superego, have positive effects on the individual's health and state of mind. This of course involves selecting among the traditional masculine and feminine traits that best suit their individual temperament and needs. Hence this means that if an individual has a preponderance of masculine and feminine traits then they are psychologically androgynous and this breaks away from culturally defined gender stereotypes. The BSRI is used to measure an individual's gender type of which there are four.

*Table 9.1* The four types of gender category

|  |  | Femininity | |
| --- | --- | --- | --- |
|  |  | High | Low |
| *Masculinity* | High | Androgynous | Masculine |
|  | Low | Feminine | Undifferentiated |

### The Bem Sex Role Inventory (BSRI)

The BSRI was designed by presenting 200 personality traits for the dimensions of masculinity and femininity to 100 students. Two hundred more personality traits that could be rated as desirable or undesirable and applicable to both males and females were considered. All traits were rated using the Likert scale by including the traits within a statement structure like, for example, 'How desirable is it for a woman to be ambitious?' Traits perceived as more desirable for one gender over the other were used as a marker for the identification of gender specific traits. The number of traits used was reduced to 40 (20 masculine and 20 feminine) and participants had to use these to rate themselves. The more masculine traits selected then the outcome was a masculine profile and the more feminine traits selected then a feminine profile was the result. Equal selections of masculine and feminine traits meant an androgynous profile.

### Feminist account

Some feminists believe that there is very little difference in the potential for criminality across the sexes, and that divisions in the frequency and nature of criminal activity have arisen as a consequence of sex role variation (Adler 1975). This is an interesting statement and can be considered empirically by testing the difference in crime rates of women before and after the women's liberation movement. The women's liberation movement initially began in the late nineteenth century but is famous in Britain for the Suffragettes who campaigned for the equal right to cast a political vote. It was not until the 1960s to early 1980s that the women's liberation movement became more active and campaigned for further equal rights with men such as social and cultural equality. The 'burning of the bra' came to symbolise a new sense of female freedom. The liberation movement was integral to the changes in attitude and legal legislation concerning all legitimate spheres of society for women, such that women received recognition and elevated social position.

Liberation has opened doors for women to enter legitimate as well as illegitimate areas of social and economic opportunity, which begs the question of whether there has been an increase in female criminal activity commonly associated with men. Simon (1975), however, believed that women who are employed were more likely to commit crimes related to their occupations. Furthermore, she claimed that the frustrations women felt in the past, due to economic marginalisation and dependency on the breadwinner of the family (who was usually male), have been removed because liberation has reduced the need for women to vent their frustrations using violence.

There are two points of view here: that liberation has increased female crime rates or it has reduced the need for women to resort to criminal pursuits. Criminal statistics and trends over a period of years are useful in ascertaining whether there is an increase, decrease or no difference in female crime rate. Smart (1979) reviewed the number of indictable offences (across classes of crime 1, 2 and 3) committed by men and women in England and Wales between 1965 and 1975 (see Figure 9.11), a time frame considered relevant to when the liberation movement was most active.

Considering these figures it would appear that there has been a great increase in female crime. These figures, according to Smart (1979), are very misleading,

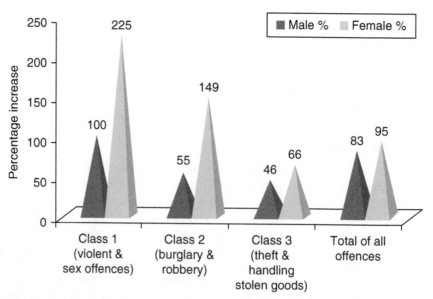

*Figure 9.11* Proportionate increases in indictable offences by males and females between 1965 and 1975

Adapted from Smart 1979

and nurture. The sociological research considered in this chapter focuses mainly on the theory of social control. This considers studies examining the influence of subcultures, **contra-cultures** and **youth culture**s for gang formation. A historical account of the cycle of violence will also be considered using the impact of slavery on some aspects of Black culture. We will also consider the differential effectiveness of social, therapeutic and treatment measures used in crime prevention strategies. Many therapeutic and treatment interventions geared towards reforming individual delinquents have been devised, each with varying successes – but for some delinquents nothing works. Why this is so is a difficult question to answer.

## Introduction

**Delinquency** is a general term used to refer to petty crime, and a juvenile delinquent is a young person who commits petty crime. The most common delinquent crimes committed, however, include a wide span of criminal acts such as theft, like shoplifting and petty burglary, criminal damage, vandalism, the handling of stolen goods and occasionally manslaughter. The following examples demonstrate the vast nature of what comprises delinquency. As far back in time as 1922, Baby Face Nelson caused havoc on the streets of Chicago with his gang of juvenile hoodlums. He was involved in stealing car tyres and bootlegging and was an accomplished car thief, for which he would be convicted for in 1922 at the age of 14. He would eventually go on to commit more serious crimes like armed robbery. In a slightly different vein, BBC News reporter, Peter Gould in 2005 commented about a 'yob culture' in Britain arising out of young people leaving pubs drunk and fighting each other and any other innocent person who happens to be in their way. It was claimed that the yob culture consists of lager louts, teenagers loitering on the streets and soccer hooligans. It has been argued that such young people disregard and show no respect for the law and what constitutes orderly behaviour. The yob culture is associated with young people but is generalised across age, class and different social groups. The BBC reported that restaurant owners complained about the disrespectful behaviour from professionals like lawyers and bankers who also get drunk and make sexist and racist remarks to their staff.

Problems on the streets occurred again in August 2011 (see Chapter 4) when large groups of rioters, in London and other major cities in England, caused criminal damage to residential and commercial properties by setting them alight and smashing windows and looting shops. There were criticisms of the police in terms of their sparse presence and ineffectiveness at controlling the rioters, but, later, arrests and court hearings ran more swiftly. *The Guardian News* reported on 6 October 2011 on a 17-year-old rioter, Joshua Penney, whose sentence was eventually halved. He entered a Sainsbury's store in Manchester, looted cigarettes and alcohol and was caught by police with the stolen goods on his person. He was sentenced to eight months detention which was later reduced to four months by Judge Michael Henshell at the appeal hearing, given this was Penney's first offence. He was described by his head teacher as a 'polite, respectful, conscientious and an absolute pleasure'. Despite this type of looting being typical of many of the rioters (i.e. four other defendants were charged on the same day for looting, two aged 17, one 15 and one 18), Penney appears to be an exception to the rule, if his defence is to be believed.

Ben Leapman, Home Affairs Correspondent (2008), claimed that there was a rise of 37 per cent in the number of violent offences committed by those under 18 between 2007 and 2008 (17,590 to 24,102). A crime such as the murder of Garry Newlove in 2007, who was beaten to death by a street gang, caused a moral panic in British society. The gang leader was 18 and was a repeat violent offender – he and two other teenagers were arrested for Newlove's murder. The youth crime statistics show a steady rise in the number of offences committed by 10–17 year olds. In 2003 this was 184,474 which rose to 222,750 in 2006 (Ministry of Justice 2008 cited in Leapman 2008). A breakdown of the figures reveals that the number of violent offences has risen more steeply than any other type of crime. Convictions for the under-18s carrying knives and other weapons doubled from 1,909 in 1997 to 4,181 in 2006.

The youth crime figures for 10–17 year olds in 2003 and the increase of violent offences, such as carrying and using knives in the under-18s in 2006, led the Association of Chief Police Officers to publish a youth strategy to **crime prevention** in a report titled, 'It's Never Too Early . . . It's Never Too Late'. This report identified 24 **risk factors** – including family breakdown, drug-abusing parents and failing to achieve at school – all of which could contribute towards children entering a criminal career. The underlying sentiment of the report was to introduce vulnerable families to appropriate Social Services to prevent their children from being cuckolded into a life of crime. According to findings from sociological research most juvenile delinquents are boys and their peak age for criminal activity is 14–15 years. Delinquents tend to be from a low social class who experience poor education and come from large families or broken homes (see Chapter 4). They usually live in bad or impoverished neighbourhoods that are rife for the formation of deviant gangs and/or small deviant peer groups. In a report by James Slack of the *Daily Mail* (2009) an increase in youth robbery and violence was confirmed by Home Office Statistics. Juvenile delinquency increased among the 10–17 year olds such that there was more than one offence committed every two minutes. The Youth Justice Board 2009 presented figures showing a 29 per cent increase between 2005 and 2008 (House of Commons Home Affairs Committee 2009). Drug crime and criminal damage increased by 12 per cent. In 2004/5, 18.4 per cent of youth offences were committed by girls, which increased to 20.9 per cent in 2007/08. Common crimes committed by females were handling stolen goods and theft and drunkenness (see Chapter 9). Further findings by the Youth Justice Board 2009 revealed that one in six young people have used their mobile phones to take photos of the victims they attacked through slapping – a new trend called 'happy slapping'. Of the young pupils questioned by the Mori poll for the Youth Justice Board, 22 per cent revealed that they had used their mobile phone to send nasty voicemail or text messages, and of this percentage, 26 per cent were young girls (House of Commons Home Affairs Committee 2009). Frances Done, the Youth Justice Board's chairperson said, 'Many of these young women have had difficult childhoods, have been abused or seen violence in the home'.

Rutter and Giller (1983) and West and Farrington (1973) revealed a series of life factors considered to either put individuals at risk of delinquency or protect them from committing delinquent acts (see Chapter 4). One of the most renowned studies of delinquency, however, was conducted by West and Farrington (1973) known as the Cambridge Study in Delinquent Development (1961–81). This prospective longitudinal study unearthed important antecedents of delinquency which were discussed in detail in Chapter 4. We will therefore consider antisocial behaviour and other psychological explanations in the next section.

## Psychological explanations of delinquency

### Antisocial behaviour

Delinquent behaviour is antisocial and contravenes the law for which it is punishable by the endorsement of curfews, Acceptable Behaviour Contract (ABC), Dispersal Order (DO) or Parenting Order (PO) – see Situational Crime Prevention Measures (p. 414). Antisocial behaviour is generic to all ages but in the guise of delinquency it is considered a childhood and adolescent problem. When the onset of antisocial behaviour in children occurs, their behaviour is investigated further for likely progression into adolescence and adulthood. In order to investigate this various psychobiological measures are used which examine differences between delinquent and non-delinquent children. Any psychobiological differences are often linked to explanations for these children's poor socialisation of moral acquisition.

It is through the consideration of biological evidence of delinquent prone behaviour in childhood that a more informed understanding of future antisocial behaviour can be found. Raine, speaking in an interview in 2011, claimed that it is important to study children with developmental disorders that result in poor control and management of aggressive impulses in adulthood. It is through the study and understanding of childhood developmental disorders that early detection and appropriate intervention can be made. Children with conduct disorder (CD) and oppositional defiant disorder (ODD), for instance, have a high risk for delinquency later in adolescence and adulthood (50–60 per cent). One factor that Raine (cited in Lerner 2011) investigated in 1,800 three year olds was autonomic fear conditioning (see also Chapter 7 for fear conditioning in adults). This approach rested on the measurement of skin conductance response towards the anticipation of punishment. In 1998 Raine, Reynolds, Venables, Mednick and Farrington tested these children, now aged 11, and found that poor fear conditioning at age three predicted aggressive behaviour. Twenty years later in 2010, Raine, Liu, Venables, Mednick and Dalais examined court records pertaining to the participants of the study. The striking and robust finding was that poor fear conditioning at the age of three predicted criminal offending at 23 years. Other evidence of pathology included underdevelopment of emotion in the limbic system before six months of age (which can lead to antisocial personality disorder and psychopathy and future convictions); smaller amygdala (crucial for fear conditioning) and lower activity in the amygdala when given moral dilemmas (psychopaths, for instance, fail to feel what is right or wrong – see Chapter 7).

Fearlessness in children with behavioural problems, such as CD and ODD, has also been investigated using the startle reflex (van Goozen, Snoek, Matthys, van Rossum and van Engeland 2004). In their study twenty-one 7–12 year olds with ODD or CD were psychologically assessed and shown a series of 27 slides (9 positive, 9 neutral and 9 negative objects or scenes). Their blink responses to the slides were measured using electrodes placed around the eye – which enabled van Goozen et al. (2004) to calculate the mean startle amplitude response to the positive, neutral and negative slides. In comparison to the control group, the ODD and CD children had lower startle responses on all three types of emotional slides. The ODD and CD children were also assessed using the delinquency sub-scale of the Child Behavioural Checklist (CBCL) devised by Achenbach (1991). van Goozen et al. (2004) found that the more delinquent these children were the lower the blink amplitudes during the viewing of negative slides. They were able to rule out other possible contributory factors like anxiety. Additional physiological measures such as heart rate, skin conductance and cortisol levels have also been found to be lower in children with ODD and CD as compared with controls (see Chapter 7 for more details of such studies).

All these factors combined have led to the 'fearlessness theory of antisocial behaviour' (Raine 1993). The underlying assumption of the fearlessness theory is that reduced activity of the autonomic nervous system (as found in heart rate and skin conductance) reflects low levels of fear. Furthermore, children who are fearless are more likely to initiate and become involved in fights because their fear of punishment is subdued. van Goozen et al. (2004), however, concluded that as the ODD and CD children in their study had low startle responses to the positive, neutral and negative emotional content on the slides, they are likely to have a general brainstem problem involving the amygdala. This finding is not consistent with adult psychopaths whose lowered startle response is specific to negatively laden stimuli. It is important to note here that not all ODD and CD children will become offenders, which is why the revelation that children with ODD and CD who scored high on the delinquency scale had lowered startle response to negatively laden stimuli was of interest.

Interesting research has been conducted on children with ODD, CD or ODD comorbid with ADHD to ascertain differences in executive function (EF) measures such as planning, working memory (WM) inhibition and impulsivity (see Chapter 5 and Box 10.1 for the influence of EF and WM in antisocial youths). Research designed to investigate differences between cognitive and motivational impulsivity among the three disorders was conducted by Kindlon, Mezzakappa and Earls (1995). They used a variety of neuropsychological tests of executive frontal lobe function and discovered strong evidence to support a differentiation between cognitive and motivational impulsivity. Cognitive impulsivity can be defined as the suppression of behaviour or thought in relation to a future goal (i.e. this can be seen by the ability to control the need for immediate gratification and therefore delay its course). Motivational impulsivity, on the other hand, is the suppression of behaviour directed at immediate gratification. In the case of children with CD, it would appear that they are driven by reward but at the same time are insensitive to punishment (Daugherty and Quay 1991). Daugherty and Quay (1991) subjected children with CD to three conditions: reward only; punishment only; and reward/punishment. Under the reward/punishment condition, CD children scored poorly on tasks that measured motivational inhibition as their focus of attention was geared towards attaining rewards only. In other words, they found it difficult to wait for rewards and attained rewards at the expense of being punished for their actions.

## Box 10.1

### The influence of EF and WM in antisocial youths

Moffitt and Caspi (2001) found a link between antisocial youths and impaired WM caused by neurological deficits in the prefrontal cortex. Researchers have been spurred on to investigate this connection by testing specifically for executive dysfunction in WM. Seguin, Boulerice, Harden, Tremblay and Pihl (1999) found that physically aggressive boys performed poorly on tests of WM as compared to their non-aggressive counterparts. As WM is important for evaluating prospective outcomes (a cost–benefit analysis), which according to Dunn, Dalgleish and Lawrence (2006) is an important aspect of rational choice decision making, it is not surprising that physically aggressive boys make poor decisions. It was previously found in a study by London, Ernst, Grant, Bonson and Weinstein (2000) that young offenders presenting symptoms of substance abuse have problems with decision making and demonstrated poor orbitofrontal cortex functioning. These young offenders had problems with WM, particularly executive functions like planning, decision making and risk assessment. This was further exemplified by extreme betting behaviour as portrayed in the Cambridge Gambling Task, a finding very similar to patients with ventromedial prefrontal cortex lesions (Clark, Bechara, Damasio, Aitken *et al.* 2008). Syngelaki, Moore, Savage, Fairchild and van Goozen (2009) found similar problems of WM and planning behaviour in their study of young offenders who made more risky decisions than their control counterparts. Syngelaki *et al.* (2009) also suspected deficits of ventromedial prefrontal processing.

The Cambridge Gambling Task is a simple but effective measure of an individual's decision-making and risk-taking behaviour. It also provides information about the impulsive nature of the individual's decision to place a bet. Participants are presented with a series of 10 squares – some are red (represented in grey in the illustration below) and some are blue (represented in white) – appearing at the top of a screen. The number of red to blue squares varies across different trials. The objective is to make a calculated guess as to whether a yellow token resides in one of the red or blue squares. At the bottom of the screen are two responses (red or blue) and the participant has to select one. At the same time there is a number representing the bet which increments slowly and the participant has to indicate one of the two possible responses as the bet increases (but has to wait for this to happen – hence the measure of impulsivity). Once the betting is completed, the participant is informed as to whether they have won or lost the bet.

*Plate 10.1* The Cambridge Gambling Task
Adapted from the original. Permission of use granted by Cambridge Gambling Task, CANTAB, © Cambridge Cognition Ltd.

Research conducted by van Goozen, Cohen-Kettenis, Snoek, Matthys *et al.* (2004) extended the cognitive-motivational impulsivity divide further but with children who had ODD or ODD with ADHD. Children aged 7–12 years were subjected to a number of assessments including the CBCL (the delinquency scale in particular) and tests of EF. The ODD children did not show any evidence of deficits in EF but children with ODD/ADHD performed poorly on one of the tests for EF. Results for motivational inhibition, however, told a different story. The ODD and ODD/ADHD children in comparison to the controls demonstrated poor performance – they continued seeking rewards even when punished through diminished returns. van Goozen *et al.*

(2004) concluded that ODD children in common with CD children do not exhibit problems of EF but instead have an inhibition deficit relating to monetary rewards – hence motivational impulsivity. No deficits of EF in children with CD and ODD might be an anomaly given that other researchers such as Moffitt (1993) showed that EF dysfunction can impact on aggressive behaviour and poor rational decision making choices.

The Dunedin Multidisciplinary Health and Development Study is a longitudinal project covering all aspects of life and development of 1,000 individuals born in 1972–3, and assessed at ages 3, 5, 7, 9, 11, 13, 15, 18 and 21 (Moffitt, Caspi, Rutter and Silva 2001). The participants were all born in Dunedin, the capital of New Zealand's South Island, and were assessed in eight modules. Each module contained a variety of areas of assessment such as delinquency, mental health and a physical examination. Diagnosis of CD was made for some of the children on the basis of a self-report, parent and teacher reports using a checklist. At 10–11 years, parents and teachers of the children with CD and a self-report documented that physical fights, destroying property, lying, truancy and stealing were typical traits. Numerous risk factors for CD, delinquency and violence were identified in the Dunedin Study but of relevance here are the neurocognitive and behavioural risk predictors.

Previously Moffitt (1990) studied IQ as a neurocognitive risk factor for delinquency in 3–13 year olds and found a robust relationship. Assessment of IQ was derived from a host of cognitive tests such as those testing for neuropsychological memory and reading ability and a battery of neurological measures including reflexes, heart rate, motility, facial musculature and gait. In the case of behavioural measures, Moffitt (1990) rated temperament and hyperactivity and emotional functioning. Of the eight neurocognitive risk predictors/modules in the Dunedin Multidisciplinary Health and Development Study (including neurocognitive risk predictors such as EF measures), seven correlated with male antisocial behaviour (for females this was five) with the data from Moffitt's 1990 study. In addition it was found that low resting heart rates correlated with antisocial behaviour in adolescents. The measures for behavioural risk prediction for antisocial behaviour showed that having a difficult temperament with hyperactivity featured strongly. Furthermore, as discussed in Chapter 7, Quay (1988) argued that children with CD might have a faulty behavioural inhibition system (BIS) and behavioural activation system (BAS). An overactive BAS will compel children to seek rewards and thrills whereas an underactive BIS reduces their fear and anxiety levels which could also explain the behavioural traits demonstrated in children with CD.

Another area of interest for antisocial behaviour as shown by delinquents is **moral reasoning** with empathy and Theory of Mind (ToM). As we have seen in Chapter 4, theorists considering moral reasoning, such as Piaget (1932, 1965) and Kohlberg (1969), emphasised the transition in children from an egocentric perspective of the world to one that encompasses the perspectives of others. Not considered in Chapter 4 is the theory of moral development by Selman (1971). Selman introduced a five stage perspective-taking approach (see Box 10.2).

---

## Box 10.2

### Selman's five stage perspective-taking approach

- Stage 1, called undifferentiated perspective taking, occurs from 3–6 years. Children should be able to recognise that the self and others can entertain different feelings and thoughts.
- Stage 2, called social-informational perspective taking, occurs from 5–9 years. Children should be able to understand that different perspectives arise from having different information.
- Stage 3, called self-reflective perspective taking, occurs from 7–12 years. Children should be able to perceive their own feelings, thoughts and actions from someone else's perspective.
- Stage 4, called third-party perspective, occurs from 10–15 years. This is a more sophisticated stage in that children/adolescents can imagine how one's point of view is considered by a third party.
- Stage 5, called societal perspective taking, occurs from 14 years to adulthood. This stage embellishes third-party perspective taking using societal values.

The earlier stages can be surmised as concrete perspective taking and the later stages as more conceptual and influenced by cultural and social values.

---

Chandler (1973) found links between egocentrism and delinquency in 11–13-year-old delinquents who scored high on egocentricity in comparison to a matched control group, providing support for Selman's stage approach. Other researchers, such as Lee and Prentice (1988), found differences between delinquents and non-delinquents in other facets of perspective-taking ability. Blackburn (1995), however, pointed out that the acquisition of mature perspective-taking skills does not ensure the acceptance of appropriate socialised behaviour. He further claimed that while perspective-taking skill is associated with compliance, it can just as easily be used in a manipulative way.

Hollin (1992) speculated that moral reasoning might be delayed in delinquents, explaining why they have difficulty resisting and controlling their temptations to break the law. Interestingly, differences in level of moral judgement were implicated in different types of crime. For instance, only in acquisitive crimes, such as theft, robbery, burglary and fraud, did young offenders show poor moral reasoning and judgement skill (Thorton and Reid 1982). Gurucharri, Phelps and Selman (1984) interestingly found delayed performance in the interpersonal stages for children with CD. Differences in level of moral reasoning are found between delinquents and non-delinquents (see Box 10.3) but it has been argued that the emotion of empathy underpins the poor moral reasoning ability acquired.

## Box 10.3

### Differences of moral reasoning in delinquents

In 1998 Palmer and Hollin conducted a survey measuring differences in the level of moral reasoning between 13–22-year-old controls and 13–21-year-old convicted offenders. They found that the convicted offenders were operating at Kohlberg's pre-conventional level of moral reasoning whereas the control group were a level above – the conventional level. Deficits of moral reasoning in delinquents in part might be symptomatic of being nurtured by parents who do little to encourage participation in solving family issues or fail to use inductive discipline to explain why a behaviour is wrong within a moral reasoning context (Hoffman 1971). Ineffective discipline, which fails to use moral reasoning can lead to poor socialisation. If socialisation can be restored (through appropriate educational input), then cognitive views towards offending might be altered and a greater understanding of why it is wrong to offend achieved. Many multifaceted intervention programmes address this and have had varying levels of success.

As discussed in Chapter 4, empathy is a feeling of distress expressed when another person experiences discomfort such that if they are hurt and in pain, you feel sympathy and want to help them. In many cases delinquents fail to experience or at the very least to acknowledge another person's distress. Inability of delinquents to feel their victims' distress makes it easy for them to commit criminal acts. There are sex differences in the extent empathy is experienced – where females are considered more empathy driven than males, which goes a long way towards explaining the male domination in the crime statistics (see Chapters 2 and 9).

There are different measures and interpretations of empathy but a useful understanding is that of Hogan (1969). He defined empathy as the ability to imagine another person's state of mind, and considered it to be a 'dispositional skill' (i.e. part of temperament/personality that is inborn) influenced by socialisation. Parents socialise children about morality and moral rules and concepts which are applied in conjunction with the feeling of empathy. Empathy (Em) as measured by Hogan has been useful in differentiating delinquents from non-delinquents, and furthermore aggressive from non-aggressive delinquents (Ellis 1982). Damon (1988), however, provided a stage account of the nature of empathy as it progresses from early infancy to the age of 12:

- *early infancy* – the empathic response is generalised and cannot separate the needs of the self from other people;
- *two years* – experiences genuine feelings of concern at someone else's distress;
- *early childhood* – children become informed of different reactions to situations that others might have which enables an appropriate response to the distress of others;
- *older children of 12 years* – development of higher-ordered and conceptually driven empathy responses (capable of feeling empathy for the poor living in a developing country thus provoking a humanitarian outlook to life).

Hoffman (1982) considered guilt to be a facet of empathic distress at having caused harm to another person. Delinquents whose moral understanding is at a higher level of functioning (i.e. the conventional level) are more likely to experience and self-report guilt reactions to their offending behaviour than are those at the pre-conventional level (Ruma and Mosher 1967). This suggests that empathy and moral reasoning are strongly connected. In relation to Selman's perspective taking in others, two important elements were outlined:

1    the emotion comprising the feeling;
2    the cognition comprising the understanding.

Hence, if empathy is the emotion, then ToM is the cognition.

As discussed in Chapter 4, ToM is the cognitive understanding of another person's perspective. Delinquents are considered to have poor social skills but this in part might be a consequence of impoverished skills at mindreading the social situation or ToM of another individual's perspective of the situation. The acquisition of perspective taking relies on the ability to theorise about people's behaviour, but having an understanding of why people behave the way they do (i.e. ToM) is not enough to prevent individuals from causing distress to others. There has to be some experience or feeling of what it is like to cause distress in others. This has been partly addressed by research on mirror neurons, correctly known as sensorimotor neurons, located in the brain (see Box 10.4).

## Box 10.4

### The role of mirror neurons in empathy

Specific mirror neurons become activated when the 'self' experiences distress but slightly different mirror neurons of these regions are stimulated when another person experiences distress (Jackson, Meltzoff and Decety 2005). The result is the emotion of empathy which is a major factor controlling and preventing us from causing undue distress to others.

There is an abundance of neurocognitive evidence supporting an innate 'brain hardware' for the development of empathy in the guise of mirror neurons. It is worth describing mirror neurons in more detail given their significance for empathy and ToM, and consequently moral development. fMRI scans have shown that when we observe actions carried out by another person, the premotor cortex and superior temporal sulcus become active. An area of the premotor cortex (F5 area) contains mirror neurons that code for the interpretation of actions. The same occurs for the interpretation of emotion and pain experienced by the self or by others which is so important for ToM. Levenson and Ruef (1992) found that when people feel the same emotion, they are more accurate at gauging each other's intentions and this was supported by the fMRI scans. Recognising the pain experienced by others underlies empathy and it appears that mirror neurons are involved here too (Morrison, Lloyd, di Pellegrino and Roberts 2004). Morrison *et al.* (2004) and Jackson *et al.* (2005) found using fMRI that mirror neurons fire in the anterior cingulated cortex (ACC) and the anterior insula. There are qualitative differences of firing pattern in the ACC but this is to enable us to differentiate between our own and someone else's pain and therefore empathise accordingly.

Blakemore and Frith (2003) also showed that mirror neurons fire in the right inferior parietal cortex which enables us to identify our own actions from actions initiated by others and furthermore, to understand actions from another individual's perspective. Saxe and Wexler (2005) argued that this region is specifically involved in ToM, and Jackson *et al.* (2005) claimed that this enables us to imagine what it would feel like for another person in a difficult situation. Delinquents who fail to experience empathy often have an immature ToM and limited moral reasoning ability.

Instilling a sense of moral reasoning and empathy are key components in many different treatment interventions designed to re-socialise delinquents into accepting that their antisocial behaviours are wrong. Delinquent behaviour, however, comprises a multitude of deviant and antisocial acts and there are just as many different acts as there are different types of delinquent. Furthermore, added to the mix are the different **risk** and **protective factors** (see Chapter 4). These interact and influence the motivations and purpose served by the delinquent acts performed. Hence different delinquents will have different needs, which is why one particular crime prevention strategy might work for some but not all (discussed later). An interesting question arising from psychological findings (including research on criminal careers discussed in Chapter 2) is the extent to which juvenile delinquency and adult offending are connected? Juvenile delinquency if it develops in the first place begins early; the earlier it begins the more problematic it is and the longer lasting the criminal career. We have to be careful, however, when making a connection between juvenile delinquency and offending in adulthood because as stated above there are many types of delinquent acts as there are delinquents. Studies on childhood progression suggesting a robust connection between children who have ADHD, CD and ODD conditions and problematic antisocial behaviour, with continuous criminal behaviour in childhood through to adolescence and adulthood, are very convincing. There appears to be a robust neurocognitive and neurobiological similarity between these children and adults with criminal psychopathy. The same social and biological problems spurring their antisocial behaviour remains a constant feature of adult criminal psychopaths. In other words, the same areas of the brain with functional and structural deficits underpinning problems of self-control, moral reasoning, empathy and ToM.

A childhood progression from delinquency to adult offending for these cases appears very likely. But not all children have ADHD, CD or ODD. For many their antisocial acts are spurred on by other peers – a sense of wanting to belong to a group or gang and wanting to be accepted and perceived as the same. Under these circumstances the possibility of altering behaviour can be achieved through a change of lifestyle and peer affiliation. With the right intervention a criminal career might be short lived. There are treatment interventions that focus on enhancing social communication skills and delivering the type of help that will boost self-confidence and self-esteem – discussed later (see also Chapters 4 and 8). There are also ways of improving empathy skills for delinquent children and adolescents who have experienced poor parental attachment and rejection from family and friends. For some children these interventions will help them to desist from further crime and opt out of a criminal career (see Chapter 2). For others this might not be possible. Depending on the nature of their delinquency, delinquents might continue to commit the same types of crime or progress to more serious offending. For the most part, delinquent acts, despite being antisocial, are less serious than many types of adult offending. Delinquency by definition (i.e. petty crime) can be regarded as different to adult offending but if delinquents continue to be involved in crime and establish a criminal career their delinquency can progress to other forms of adult offending (perhaps into serious crime).

Findings from sociological research have also contributed towards understanding delinquency and have helped inform criminologists, law enforcers and politicians of the causes of delinquency and how problems of delinquency can be tackled at a government level. The main sociological theories will be considered in the next section.

## Sociological explanations of delinquency

According to sociologists delinquency arose out of the social problems associated with urbanisation. Furthermore, as urbanisation increased, so did delinquency, vandalism, suicide, prostitution and drug addiction. These breakdowns are referred to as social disorganisation of which juvenile delinquency is an example of an ineffective urban social infrastructure. There are many different reasons why delinquents commit delinquent acts; however, one sociological approach which appears to dominate is the Social Control Theory which we will explore next.

## Social control

Social control refers to the methods used in society, and by groups within society, to influence the behaviour of its members so that they conform to set norms, mores and attitudes (see Chapters 1, 2 and 4). Social control can be said to operate at two levels – the level of the individual and of large organisations in society.

Social control at the level of the individual conforms to Bronfenbrenner's **Developmental Ecosystem Model** (see Figure 4.1). For instance, at the centre of society's control over individuals is the formation of appropriate attitudes determined through the process of socialisation, which is the most powerful form of social control. The next level is the effect that close friends and people with important ties have on our own self-perception. Sociologists refer to this level as the sphere of the intimate (Gillies, Ribbens McCarthy and Holland 2001; Jamieson 1998), and it is towards people in our intimate zone that we try most to sustain a positive self-image. Primary groups in the next level will have subtle but effective methods of controlling an individual's behaviour. Primary groups rely on concepts such as personal loyalty, persuasion, gossip, disapproval and ridicule to exert a controlling influence over an individual. For example, the work environment can be made unbearable by colleagues who become unhelpful and disruptive if they believe that a new work colleague is ignoring the rules. Economic and occupational award comprises the next level of exerting control over an individual. This is important as it directly influences an individual's livelihood. Demands specified by an employer are adhered to by the employee as the benefits for conforming outweigh the costs of rebelling. Rebelling against the demands made by one's employer could be costly such as demotion or unemployment. In all occupations there are unwritten codes dictating an individual's conduct and these are powerful social controlling agents. The extreme level of control is that used by law enforcing agents such as the police and military. At this level physical restraint is the last option of gaining social control over an individual.

Some sociologists, such as Nikolas Rose (1989, 1996), have questioned the extent of influence those in the sphere of the intimate wield over our development of the self. This is especially so given the changes to Western society values where there has been an increasing tendency towards individualisation (i.e. material gain and self-achievement) at the expense of close-knit community bonds. Rose (1996) claimed more focus should be placed on processes of how individuals become citizens in society and asked, 'to what extent, and in what ways, are persons understood and managed, by themselves and others, in relation to values that are accorded to an internal self?' (p.305). Rose believed that power and political systems are responsible for controlling and governing the behaviour of individuals and the nature of their social relationships. This suggests that the balance of how the self is developed and represented favours a more organisational and institutional facet of the public sphere (Habermas 1989).

As delinquents conform to deviant norms, mores and attitudes, sociologists argue that different levels of social control throughout an individual's journey to becoming a delinquent have failed to be effective deterrents (see Box 10.5). It is clear that delinquents aspire to different norms, mores and attitudes used by mainstream culture, which explains in part why social control measures such as punishment have little influence over their behaviour. Sociologists, however, proposed that another route towards the attainment of delinquent values and behaviour might in part stem from **youth cultures**. Many sociologists argued that there is a difference between the next generation and their parents in terms of attitudes, values, beliefs and lifestyle towards issues such as drug taking, sex before marriage, fashion sense and general lifestyle. There are different interpretations of youth culture such as the generation gap (i.e. those with values and attitudes that differ from the previous generation), **contra-culture** (i.e. those with values and attitudes in conflict with the dominant culture) and Matza's three forms of youth culture (Bohemian, Radical and Delinquents). Of relevancy here is Matza's delinquent youth culture.

## Box 10.5

### Deviants, deviance and crime

#### What is deviance?

Members of society share expectations of society known as norms. Norms control all social interactions but vary from one society to another (although there are more similarities than differences). A slight stray from norms is tolerated but there is a point where non-conformity to norms becomes obvious and the non-conforming individual becomes depicted as different. Sociologists refer to non-conformists as deviants. Deviants could be perceived as individuals whose behaviour sidesteps the norms and exceeds the limit of tolerance that society is prepared to accept.

#### Deviance and Crime

Deviance overarches crime, although criminals are a type of deviant. Crime is breaking the law whereas some other types of deviant behaviour are not against the law and therefore do not warrant legal punishment. There is a difference between deviance and crime. Deviance embraces all types of non-conforming behaviour whereas crime is one type of deviance. Society labels what behaviours are deviant whereas the law defines criminal behaviour. The response by society to deviants varies with the type of deviance portrayed – sometimes welcomed, indifferent, requiring treatment, disapproved of or threatened – whereas crime is deviance met with punishment. There are many different types of deviant such as tramps, transvestites and gypsies but there are also many less obvious examples.

### Explanations of deviants

Merton (1949) argued that all societies have certain basic values which are widely accepted. In the US, Merton argued, one basic value is to have financial success which is why Americans are expected to attain financial success through a well-paid career and hard work. American society, however, has an unequal distribution of opportunity and advantage but for those who are disadvantaged a state of anomie is experienced. This means that they are unable to achieve that which is considered normal and become labelled as deviants. Merton classified deviants into four types depending on whether they can achieve financial success through career advancement.

|  | General goal (financial success) | General method (career success) |
| --- | --- | --- |
| Innovation | Yes | No |
| Ritualism | No | Yes |
| Retreatism | No | No |
| Rebellion | No | No |

1 *Innovation*: this individual searches for means to achieving the norm of financial success through alternative methods such as crime (fraud, robbery or gambling).
2 *Ritualism*: this individual is not interested in pursuit of financial success but continues in a ritualistic involvement using accepted means such as having a career (this person may be a timid bureaucrat who follows the rules).
3 *Retreatism*: this individual abandons the pursuit of financial success and the ways to achieving it, and refuses to engage with society (people falling into this category are tramps, alcoholics and drug addicts).
4 *Rebellion*: this individual also abandons the pursuit of financial success and the ways to achieving it but refuses to retreat from society, and instead tries to change it to his or her satisfaction (this person may be a left wing guerrilla using terrorist tactics).

Matza (1964, 1969) claimed that delinquent gangs usually form and congregate in areas where adult culture is slightly deviant, such as a family member who did time in prison or follows criminal ideals. Matza (1969) outlined how a family member could be involved in criminal activity and have active social/business criminal networks. It is these networks and/or gangs who emphasise bravery and toughness, and prove to each other their deviant delinquent loyalties to the gang by behaving badly. Football hooligans can be perceived as a form of delinquent gang who have their own subcultural values, albeit closely tied and specific to the sport. In the 1970s and 1980s football hooligans plagued the reputation of British football fans, despite their being the minority. An unintended consequence of the development of all-seater stadiums during the 1990s (as a health and safety precaution to reduce crushing of fans against barriers) was the reduction of football hooliganism.

In modern Britain, the delinquent gang problem reinstates itself in the form of knife and gun crime: gang murders (and murders of innocent bystanders) through knifing is rising. In Salford during December 2011, Anuj Bidve was murdered while walking with a group of friends. It was reported that two men approached and shot Bidve at close range in an unprovoked attack. Five people had been arrested of which three were under the age of 18. In Sunderland in 2011, two male youths (an 18 and a 16 year old) were arrested for slashing three teenagers in a knife attack. A 14-year-old boy, Leroy James, was stabbed to death in Enfield by two boys aged 14 and 15 during August 2011 (two nights after the Enfield riots and looting of 7 August 2011). In a report by *The Guardian*, it was estimated that knife crime involving youths had risen by 10 per cent in London, according to the Scotland Yard figures (Topping 2011). Topping (2011) reported that Scotland Yard figures indicated a rise from 941 to 1,070 knife crime injuries in London between February and April in 2011. Furthermore, between 2008/9 and 2010/11, there was a 30 per cent rise in the number of victims for knife injuries for people aged 13 to 24 years. In 2010–11 the Metropolitan Police reported a total of 1,157 knife crimes in London alone. In a Standard Notes document compiled for Members of Parliament by Gavin Berman (2011) titled 'Knife Crime Statistics', it was reported that at the end of September 2011 in England and Wales there were 21,034 disposals for possession of a knife (in 54 per cent of cases) or an offensive weapon of which juveniles (aged 10–17) comprised 18 per cent of cases (i.e. 3,786 disposals). The juvenile custody figure was 9 per cent but 28 per cent for cautions and 56 per cent for community service.

When crimes committed by youths are examined, an interesting question arises – do they commit crime alone, with another peer, or as part of a delinquent gang? Of course it is a combination of all three; however, much research has focused on gang membership and in particular their delinquent subcultural origins. Delinquent gangs and subcultures will be considered within a context of **delinquent subculture**s and the cycle of violence.

### Delinquent subcultures

A classic study of adolescent gangs was conducted by Thrasher in 1927. In his study of 1,313 delinquent and non-delinquent Chicago gangs, Thrasher reported that gangs were formed in slum areas marked by physical deterioration and social disorganisation. According to Thrasher, the gangs he studied did not form with the motive to commit delinquent acts but rather they emerged incidentally through unsupervised and spontaneous play. These gangs, Thrasher argued, offered a sense of order, prestige, security and relief of boredom by providing excitement – something that was missing from conventional social institutions.

It was not until Albert Cohen's work in the 1950s that delinquent gangs were systematically investigated within the context of a **delinquent subculture**. Cohen (1955) observed that middle-class parents emphasised self-discipline, the need for ambition and the constructive use of free time. This, he believed, paved the way to instilling an educational success ethos in their children, and with educational success follows occupational advancement. The repercussions of an educational success ethos using conventional means, such as securing a well-paid job and a successful career, is status gain. Working class parents, however, did not instruct their children in this way and instead their children were less disciplined and ambitious, and consequently failed within an educational setting – this spiralled into limited career success and a reduced probability of attaining a well-paid job. As working class children were less likely to gain status through conventional means, they used non-conventional strategies. Thus Cohen considered delinquent boys as failures within the education system who struggled for status but experienced frustration instead (this forms the basis for his status frustration theory). Their socialisation was typical of the working classes which inadequately prepared them for status competition in schools. Cohen argued a delinquent subculture, provided through gang membership, offered these youngsters an alternative source of status and a legitimate pathway to violence. Cohen also studied one type of delinquency – vandalism – in detail (see Box 10.6).

## Box 10.6

### Vandalism, an example of delinquency

Although the word vandalism denotes the senseless destruction of property and is associated with public places in urban areas, Cohen published an article called, 'Property Destruction, Motives and Meanings' in which he explained four types of vandalism:

1   Acquisitive vandalism where money or materials are taken from coin boxes in telephone booths as a consequence of having caused damage.

2    Vindictive vandalism is a reaction against someone who or something that is disliked. A vandal might have a dislike of teachers working at their school but will cause criminal damage to school property instead as this is more likely to go undetected than a physical attack on a person.
3    Play vandalism often results from street games that cause unintended damage to windows or signposts.
4    Malicious vandalism is an expression of frustration, resentment or anger against society and the vandal has a 'me' against 'them' attitude. Examples of this type of vandalism include slashing car tyres and smashing train fittings.

Downes (1966a, 1966b) studied delinquency in the East End of London and concluded that it was not a reaction to mainstream values but rather a consequence of economic inequality and perceived failure at school. This was supported by Hargreaves (1967) who found that bad behaviour was linked to boys attending lower stream classes at school (see Chapter 4). Willmott (1966) researched adolescent boys living in East London and found that for some, there is a pattern of behaviour and attitude enveloping a violent and law breaking subculture. With a dislike of school and resentment towards any form of discipline, these boys attained failing grades and reputations as rebels. They were disinterested in joining youth clubs but for those who did, trouble soon followed and they were expelled. Furthermore, delinquent boys had poorer quality relationships with their parents, in particular their father, compared to non-delinquent boys. Willmott concluded that these boys were discontented inside and outside of the home and had a history of parental rejection (see Chapter 4). It is this history of rejection that caused the boys to respond with aggression – in effect, they were hitting out at an unsympathetic society through delinquency. Other British studies, such as Phil Cohen's (1972) observations of 'mods' and 'skinheads' in London's East End, suggested that these two conspicuous subcultures emerged in response to a problem society.

Albert Cohen's interpretation of delinquent subcultures has received praise but also criticism. Cloward and Ohlin (1960) in 'Delinquency and Opportunity', argued that in American society, individuals desire economic and financial success, but as working class boys have unequal access to legitimate opportunities for attaining this, they feel cheated by the system. Alternatively, Cohen observed that working class boys blamed themselves rather than feeling cheated and angry. Cloward and Ohlin further argued that these working class boys indulged in illegitimate activities within their community comfort zone as a means to achieving status. They claimed that within a neighbourhood there were three patterns of delinquent subculture: criminal, conflict violent and retreatist drug subcultures. In the case of criminal subcultures, juvenile delinquents living in stable working class areas graduated into organised crime. Conflict violent and retreatist drug subcultures escalate in disorganised neighbourhoods where both legitimate and illegitimate opportunities are scarce (Cloward and Ohlin 1960).

Cloward and Ohlin's point that juvenile delinquents living in stable working class areas become involved with criminal subcultures and later to organised crime supports a study conducted by Miller in 1958. Miller (1958) claimed that the lower class valued a set of traits that included a sense of toughness, excitement and autonomy. The boys studied by Miller came from working class households held together by one or more adult females prompting them to seek masculine status by joining street gangs and fighting on the streets. According to Sutherland (1939) whether a young individual becomes a delinquent or a law abiding citizen depends upon their social environment and peer group. Hence a youngster from a bad school and neighbourhood is more likely to come into contact with older delinquent children entertaining deviant attitudes. The consequence of such contact is to learn to reject law abiding principles and adopt delinquent ones – he refers to this as Differential Association Theory where delinquency as a way of life has to be learned (see Chapters 5 and 6). Miller's findings appear to be in agreeance with Sutherland.

Matza (1964) unlike Miller, however, proposed that young offenders 'drift' into delinquency as a matter of choice. They support the norms of society but because they drift into delinquency they adopt 'techniques of neutralisation' for their behaviour: in other words, they shift the responsibility for their actions to being labelled a delinquent. Techniques of neutralisation also involve:

- the denial of injury to their victims;
- denial of there being any victims;
- the condemnation of their condemners;
- appeal to higher loyalties (i.e. they did it for their peers), a technique often adopted by antisocial individuals such as psychopaths (see Chapter 7).

Researchers have focused on delinquent gangs but some sociologists have their reservations about the extent of delinquent acts occurring within a gang or group context. For instance, Kitsuse and Dietrick (1959) believed that most delinquency occurs in pairs or individuals working alone. Evidence of this has been found in a study by Johnstone (1981) where only 13 per cent and 8 per cent of Black males and females respectively in Chicago reported being in a gang. The formation of gangs and acceptance of subcultural deviant values and attitudes has been associated with the notion of a cycle of violence. A cycle of violence is believed to be perpetuated across generations of families with specific characteristics and demographics that increase their vulnerability to a lifestyle of violence. This will be considered in the next section in more detail.

### Cycle of violence

According to the cycle of violence, delinquent acts are carried out by youths who have been socialised into a subculture of violence and have adopted the violent attitudes and values of their parents. Bullock (1961a, 1961b) alluded to there being a constellation of life circumstances attached to certain groups of people that trigger violence. These life circumstances underlie a set subculture of violence which encourages individuals to use force for settling their interpersonal disputes. Subcultures of violence tend to be located in urban slum areas where poverty, disorganised family life and unstable communities are prevalent and foster specific lower class values that justify the use of violence. Miller (1958) claimed that values such as 'trouble, toughness, smartness, excitement, fate and autonomy' in individuals from areas renowned for violence heightens their potential for committing violent acts. Yinger (1960) distinguished between subcultures and contra-cultures:

- subcultures have values that are different from the dominant culture but are not in conflict;
- contra-cultures have different values from the dominant culture which are in conflict.

A further distinction is made between tolerant concordant values and untolerated discordant values (Wolfgang and Ferracuti 1967). In the former case the differences cause no harm or disruption to the dominant culture, whereas the latter acts as a potential threat because it is in conflict. Given that dominant culture gravitates towards older White middle-class males, then ethnic minorities will be perceived as different and this was certainly the case for Black Americans living in urban poverty zones (Ladner 1973). In many cases, the transportation of slaves from Africa to America resulted in a loss of African heritage and identity which they reclaimed via a Black ethno-genesis after the Civil War. Ladner (1971, 1973) added that a non-materialistic Black culture had its origins in African culture, but the adaptations later made to this were in response to racism and poverty caused through slavery. The urban Black man, according to Pettigrew and Spier (1962), might have resolved issues through homicide due to a history of violent tradition arising from a past of slavery. This history can be represented as Figure 10.1.

Prior to emancipation, three types of contra-culture arose, according to Blassingame (1972): Sambo, Jack and Nat. The Sambo figure was considered to be faithful and submissive to their masters, whereas the Jacks worked faithfully until mistreated by their masters. Of interest here is the Nat named after Nat Turner who was a rebel. The Nat character retaliates against the slave owners and runs away and causes rebellions. After the abolition of slavery many Blacks migrated to the cities as part of the urbanisation of America only to end up in urban ghettos and slum areas. This resulted in the development of a contra-

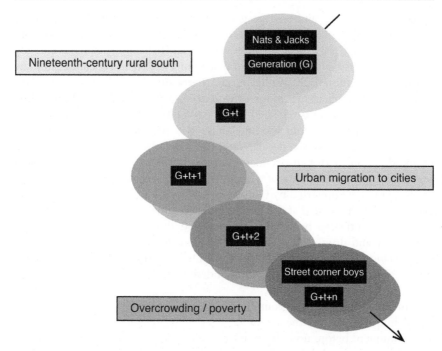

*Figure 10.1* History and violent reinforcers outside of the Black community (where G refers to generation, t refers to time and n refers to any number of generations down the line)

Adapted from Blauner 1972

culture evolving from one generation to the next. With overcrowded living conditions and poverty, and prevailing institutional racism, contra-cultures undermining the dominant American culture became increasingly robust.

Hannerz (1969) claimed that clusters of behaviour, attitudes and values resulted in two emerging types of person – the street corner men and the swingers. The street corner men were usually drifters in low paid jobs who tended to drink and gamble, whereas their teenage counterparts joined gangs. Swingers are mobile and go out with friends and although they might not be in long-term employment, they do have money to spend on women, entertainment and clothes. It is the street corner males and teenage gangs that seem to encourage violence. Sociologists believe that this could be a consequence of their short-term and undefined relationships with women which cultivates a sense of distrust and disagreement concerning the sexual faithfulness of their partner. Taken further, this aroused jealousy and male competitiveness which often resulted in violent fights and homicide. Alcohol and drugs, in particular cannabis and opiates, were often implicated in reprisal assaults on drug dealers who had cheated them. Drugs played an important role in arrests for aggravated assault, more so among barbiturate users, followed closely by those using amphetamines (Blum 1969).

Street corner men and teenage gang members were a part of an on-going subculture of violence. Individuals were strongly integrated into this subculture and conformed to the expected conduct norms and behaviours which eventually shaped their personality structure – so that a tendency to be violent became the norm and commonplace. Wolfgang and Ferracuti (1967) hypothesised that, 'overt (and often illicit) expression of violence is part of a subcultural normative system and this system is reflected in the psychological traits of the subculture participants' (p.158). Drug use and abuse was prevalent among delinquent groups and gangs of young people. James and D'Orban (1970) stated that, '[h] eroin addiction in Britain occurs predominantly in young people of marked sociopathic personality, most of whom were delinquent prior to their addiction' (p.19). This was supported by Gordon in 1973 who reported that most of the young addicts he treated at the London Clinic came from a delinquent population with antisocial behaviour. He believed that the connection between criminality and drug addiction was robust and that these were facets of general deviancy. In Burr's (1987) 'Chasing the Dragon' study of North Southwark, typical social profiles of participants included:

- an adverse family background;
- delinquency before the age of 9;
- delinquent before using heroin;
- truancy from school;
- had delinquent peers;
- affiliations to gangs;
- illicit drug use as part of the gang's norm;
- acquisitive crime to fund drug habits;
- loss of employment;
- 'chasing the dragon'.

Chasing the dragon developed into a skag subculture of stealing for drugs, scoring (using the drug) and serving (dealing the drug). The skag culture became more problematic as it spiralled into heavy criminal activity and injecting heroin. Burr's explanation of how chasing the dragon readily infiltrated North Southwark relied on a well-established deviant subculture of criminal values that led to delinquency followed by heroin use. Obtaining heroin within the confines of an established criminal economy was easy and stolen goods for heroin were an acceptable and readily available commodity (Burr 1987). The onset age for trying heroin was 16–17 years in the Wirral (England) area and this coincided with committing acquisitive crime to fund the drug habit (Parker, Bakx and Newcombe 1986). Delinquency and truancy, however, began earlier than this, suggesting that heroin use is an epiphenomenon of increasing delinquency.

An interesting question arising from research on subcultural ideology is whether delinquency and violence occur as responses to constant life adversities such as poverty, marginalisation and racism – responses which become engrained in a set way of thinking or a deviant mental set which is passed on from one generation to the next. Of importance here is the socialisation of moral understanding and the connections this holds with empathy and ToM, which clearly have a role in delinquency and are very much in the forefront of therapeutic and treatment programmes. Before describing different therapeutic and treatment interventions, however, it is useful to contextualise where such interventions lie in the scheme of **crime prevention**, but to do this crime prevention requires explanation first.

## Crime prevention and treatment interventions

The ex-British Prime Minister, Tony Blair, when he was in office, considered different ways of tackling yob behaviour through measures of 'zero tolerance'. It was discussed in the Criminal Justice and Police Bill before Parliament in 2005 that a night-time curfew after 9pm should be used for children under 16. Of course there were criticisms of this from the Conservatives regarding the impracticality of implementing curfews, and from the Liberal Democrats of the problems this would cause police among the law abiding youth. Deborah Clarke of Liberty said, 'Children have a right to be on the streets. If they are not causing any trouble then that is absolutely fine. If they are causing trouble, the police should be stopping them with the powers they have already' (Gould 2005). Another measure considered by Tony Blair was on the spot fines but this was immediately dropped as images of drunken louts getting cash out of cash machines to pay their fines caused concern. The Labour Government, however, considered the idea of a fixed fine for 'acts of drunkenness and disorder in public places'. Charles Clarke, the Home Office Minister in 2005 said, 'The government is determined to tackle the problem of alcohol-related crime by giving the police and local authorities the support and powers they need to deal with unacceptable, loutish behaviour. This includes legislation where necessary' (Gould 2005).

Night-time curfews and on the spot fines are impractical for police to enforce and could be considered as draconian measures used to control a minority of troublesome juveniles and adolescents. Other measures of controlling delinquency were discussed by Government which placed nurture approaches towards understanding delinquency and the delinquent very much in the forefront of treatment interventions. Crime prevention and treatment interventions used to tackle delinquency can be directed at the individual and/ or situational circumstances. These two levels of approach bring with them a variety of programmes and governmental directives aimed at reducing youth offending (see Chapter 5 for Cornish and Clarke's work on crime initiation and rational decision making). Crawford (1998) put forward a 'Process/ Target Two-Dimensional Typology of Crime Prevention' (see Figure 10.2). Crawford (1998) proposed a primary, secondary and tertiary approach to social

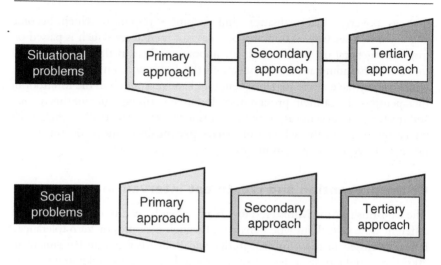

*Figure 10.2* Process/Target two-dimensional typology of crime prevention
Adapted from Crawford 1998

and situational oriented problems. For example, a primary approach to a social problem might entail programmes of education and socialisation whereas secondary approaches involve closer working with individuals who are at risk of offending such as youths and the unemployed. Alternatively, a tertiary approach might focus on the rehabilitation and aftercare of the offender. Primary, secondary and tertiary approaches can be applied differentially depending on the nature of the problem. A situational problem, such as criminal damage to shop windows, might best be considered using a primary approach like target hardening and increased surveillance. Secondary measures could be used in the case of target hardening towards identified high-risk groups of individuals for predicting their future behaviour. In the case of a tertiary approach, individual deterrence and assessment of dangerousness might be appropriate for specific individuals. A primary approach is often adopted to monitor and deter situational crime – hence the use of technology and local legislation to permit the use of technology such as **CCTV** in public places and spaces. This is commonly referred to as situational crime prevention – considered next.

### Situational crime prevention measures

Situational crime prevention involves a host of implementations designed to make it difficult for criminals to offend, and this includes delinquent behaviour. By introducing deterrence measures such as property protection using locks, screens and fences, specific crimes like burglary become more difficult to commit. Other measures such as using humps in the road prevent cars from speeding – hence reducing the use of cars as 'getaways'. Increasing the risk of detection is another situational crime prevention pathway that can be taken when designing community layout. CCTV cameras are very popular in urban areas and can offer good continuity surveillance of shopping districts and main road areas to public buildings and services. It was through the use of CCTV in Liverpool that Venables and Thompson were detected kidnapping James Bulgar, which eventually led to their capture, conviction and incarceration.

The use of alarms is another example of situational crime prevention aimed at deterring would-be burglars from breaking in to commercial and residential properties – their success as deterrents rests on the amount of effort and time needed to disarm alarms and therefore reduce the incentive to burgle a well alarmed property. Natural surveillance can be used in a way to ensure that 'places' can be seen by observers. This relates to the notion of defensible space where good street lighting deters potential criminals. Employees can also deter potential criminals by performing roles that require vigilance such as guards and concierges to man premises. Neighbourhood watch is another example where members of the community take turns to keep vigilance over their immediate neighbourhood.

Situational crime prevention measures seek to deter potential criminals by making crime difficult for them and by increasing the risk of their detection, but another strategy is to reduce the rewards and possible gain achieved from committing crime. An obvious method is the use of invisible and visible marking of goods to devalue the items' worth and increase the chance of detection. Target removal is another course of action. This involves the replacement of telephone coin boxes with card swipes and radios in cars that can be easily disconnected and taken indoors to reduce the possibility of acquisitive crime (i.e. opportunistic crime). Situational crime prevention strategies can have direct effects on the behaviour of the offender but also implicit advantages and benefits for victims of crime and the community as a whole. The use of CCTV for instance, can be used for collecting evidence against delinquents accused of antisocial behaviour and to justify awarding a curfew, ABC, DO, PO or until recently an antisocial behaviour order (ASBO). ASBOs were introduced as a punishment and deterrence measure in the 1998 Crime and Disorder Act and were used to prevent antisocial delinquents from entering areas where they have caused problems for residents and commercial outlets. Although ASBOs were frequently used to prevent problem youths from entering 'no go areas', they are now phased out in favour of other orders mentioned above. In their time, however, ASBOs were regarded as situational rather than a social crime prevention measure because they were designed to keep antisocial individuals away from specified areas.

Situational crime prevention has been influenced by Rational Choice Theory (Clarke and Cornish 1985). Rational choice theory describes the decision-making process in relation to the choices that criminals make (see Chapter 5). These choices may be as simple as choosing whether or not to commit a criminal act and how to execute it. If the decision is to burgle a house, then further choices and evaluations have to be made regarding the rewards versus the effort and risk of detection. Situational crime prevention strategies rest on the notion of whether an offender will find it worth his time and effort of burgling a well-secured house (i.e. a house with a variety of deterrent measures like an alarm, security lighting, a guard dog and a Neighbourhood Watch patrol).

There is a cost, however, to the many situational crime prevention strategies endorsed – which is crime displacement. According to Hakim and Rengert (1981) there are five types of crime displacement:

1   Spatial or graphical displacement is when an identical crime is committed elsewhere.
2   Temporal displacement occurs when the same victim endures the same crime committed at a different time of day.
3   Tactical displacement is when the same victim is targeted for the same crime but the way it is executed is different.
4   Target displacement involves a different victim but the nature of the crime is the same.
5   Type of crime displacement occurs when the nature of the initial crime changes: robbing from a petrol service station to mugging a pensioner.

Perpetrator displacement was added to the list above by Barr and Pease (1990). This means that a niche for a particular type of crime becomes available to other perpetrators once the 'kingpin perpetrator' has left the area. Successful crime prevention can also be achieved using a secondary approach referred to as social oriented interventions (Crawford 1998) which will be covered next.

### Social crime prevention measures

Crime prevention and treatment interventions at the level of the individual or social oriented interventions (Crawford 1998) are varied but often address issues of poor socialisation and family dynamics. According to Crawford many of the social crime prevention strategies derive from control theory outlined by Hirschi (1969). As far as Hirschi is concerned, what we have to explain is not why individuals commit crimes but rather what prevents them from offending. Considering criminal behaviour from this perspective, Hirschi was able to argue that people conform to society's values and mores through the development and maintenance of social bonds which ultimately prevent most individuals from acting selfishly in pursuit of hedonistic desires and motivations. These social bonds arise out of attachment, commitment, involvement and belief through the process of socialisation (see Chapters 1 and 4 for how social bonds arise at a societal and individual level respectively).

Gottfredson and Hirschi (1990) considered self-control as key to understanding why some individuals offend and others do not. They believed low

*Plate 10.2* Car crime
© Dudarev Mikhail. Image used under license from Shutterstock.com. Available at http://www.
shutterstock.com/pic.mhtml?id=46736902&src=dt_back_to_image

self-control to be a consequence of deviant or poor socialisation – juvenile delinquents are subjected to ineffective socialisation and are therefore at risk of offending. Informal and formal socialising agents, such as parents and schools respectively (see Chapter 4), have been ineffective at socialising delinquents and therefore instilling appropriate and socially acceptable behaviour. Informal and formal socialising agents become the focus for social crime prevention strategies where social bonds to the dominant culture are re-established (Crawford 1998). Herrnstein and Murray (1994) introduced the term 'underclass' to describe a group of people who are morally and culturally separate from the dominant culture. This, according to Hernstein and Murray, is a consequence of poor socialisation skills by the family and school – in effect, these institutions have failed to instil self-control in children and adolescents from the underclass.

A slightly different approach adopted by social crime prevention interventions is to identify possible risk factors for delinquency (see also Chapter 4). Criminologists have identified seven risk factors which feature consistently in delinquent profiles:

1    gender
2    personality and behaviour
3    family influences
4    living standards
5    schooling
6    peer affiliations and pressure
7    employability.

The crime statistics provide robust evidence of males committing more crime (across all types of offence) than females (see Chapters 2 and 9). Personality and behaviour contribute to delinquency as described previously in the literature on ADHD, CD, ODD, APD and psychopathy (see Chapter 7). A host of family factors such as family size and class, ineffective parenting and socialisation, abuse and parental discord have been identified (see Chapter 4). Living standards refers to housing conditions and the stability of living conditions. In the case of schooling, risk factors can vary from the standard of education and level of achievement to the school experience such as bullying and truancy (see Chapter 4). Furthermore, school achievement is bound to employability as under-qualification will result in fewer job opportunities. Also the saying 'birds of a feather flock together' is pertinent for peer affiliations because delinquent prone individuals will seek like-minded individuals who then indulge in unlawful acts together (see Chapter 4). There is often a combination of more than one type of risk factor giving rise to different levels of risk for delinquency. Graham and Bowling (1995) found that 81 per cent of boys who had delinquent peers, records of truancy and exclusion from school, poor parental supervision and delinquent siblings were offenders.

Risk factors have good predictive quality, however, identifying **protective factors** against delinquency is equally important and can be used to prevent the onset of offending behaviour. Graham and Bowling (1995) suggested a number of protective factors that can help prevent delinquency from occurring. For example, by strengthening the family situation and encouraging effective parenting, the prevention of family breakdown and enhancement of psychological well-being can be attained. Services such as Home-Start are designed to do just that but because they are responding to crisis families there is little input for the prevention of future criminality. This in part is due to the lateness of intervention and the fact that the nature of intervention does little to prevent their crisis situation from occurring in the first place. Graham and Bowling also referred to the importance of parental supervision as a protective factor against delinquency and demonstrated the effect of adequate and inadequate supervision through self-reported offending. The figures obtained revealed that 53 per cent of males receiving poor supervision admitted to offending versus 32 per cent whose supervision was adequate. They further claimed that by strengthening schools to increase pupil motivation for learning, attendance might also improve. Improved attendance, they argued, reduces truancy thereby decreasing opportunities for delinquent acts away from the school environment. Graham and Bowling suggested that effective socialisation can be improved by a two-prong approach of partnerships between parents and school.

Some examples of successful implementation of programmes designed to prevent crime among the young include the High/Scope Perry Pre-School Project and the Dalston Youth Project. The High/Scope Perry Pre-School Project originally began in Ypsilanti, Michigan and was designed as a social crime prevention scheme aimed to help children of 3–5 years in deprived areas. These children were identified as being at risk of school failure due to impaired cognitive development, and also at risk of future involvement in a delinquent lifestyle as a consequence of their family background. A pre-school programme of 'cognitive enrichment' was provided for these children while parents received child-rearing advice and input. Children on the programme in comparison to a control group of matched children had fewer criminal records – one-fifth of the rate found in the control group (Schweinhart, Barnes and Weikart 1993). The Dalston Youth Project supported by the Youth at Risk organisation began in East London in 1990 (Benioff 1997). This organisation concentrated on 15–18 year olds who were considered to be at high risk of offending. The aim was to help young people change their deviant ways and have a sense of purpose and direction in their lives. An educational slant focused on career and personal development which provided opportunities for self-improvement, both educational and social, to increase self-esteem and empower individuals to live a crime-free lifestyle. This has been a successful project as demonstrated through increased employment and training among youngsters and reduced crime figures.

Therapeutic oriented approaches (i.e. a tertiary approach) have had varying degrees of success with crime prevention. As a consequence of a diverse number of considered factors such as the content of the therapy and the individual's level of comprehension, varying degrees of success at reducing a criminogenic mind-set has resulted in reduced crime levels and criminality. In the next section a sample of these therapeutic approaches will be discussed.

### Treatment and therapeutic interventions

Therapeutic approaches such as Carkhuff's Human Resources Development (HRD) model involve expert counsellors teaching delinquents how to problem solve, relate to people and develop their career and person skills (Carkhuff 1993). As delinquents have a variety of deficits, the programme is geared towards their needs but its success depends on the ability of delinquents to communicate and demonstrate empathy skills. Nevertheless, this approach has had some success in the US where **recidivism** was 10 per cent for those on the programme versus 50 per cent for matched controls. A similar approach of improving problem solving – more specifically interpersonal problem solving, social skills, social perspective taking (akin to ToM and Selman's model), reasoning and development of values (i.e. moral reasoning) and self-control have been packaged in Ross, Fabiano and Ewles' (1988) Reasoning and Rehabilitation Project. Social skills training is poorly defined but often includes the advancement in verbal and non-verbal communication, ability to be appropriately assertive without being aggressive, self-esteem enhancement and negotiation skills. Self-instructional training has been used as a form of self-control. Initially this begins as a modelling exercise where the juvenile delinquent practices the therapist's verbal instructions of appropriate behaviour as a substitute for impulsive inappropriate behaviour. This verbal instruction is repeated aloud to control impulsive behaviour until eventually the child can say the verbal instruction covertly. This approach has had success with children exhibiting behavioural problems in class. Although there is little robust evidence to show that this works for antisocial behaviour per se, the use of rational-emotive therapy which is similar to self-instructional training has proven effective in the treatment of shoplifters. Soloman and Ray (1984) studied 94 shoplifters who entertained irrational beliefs about shoplifting which helped them to justify their behaviour. When their beliefs were challenged using rational-emotive therapy, only one had reoffended a year later.

Moral reasoning and perspective-taking strategies have been implemented to reduce egocentric behaviour in delinquents. In one study delinquents were taught perspective-taking skills indirectly through their participation in film making. Those who had played a role in the film demonstrated less self-centred behaviour, which was believed to have contributed towards reducing their offending by half in an 18 month follow up (Chandler 1973). As most delinquents were operating at the pre-conventional level of moral reasoning, the aim of moral reasoning and perspective-taking strategies is to progress their moral development to the next level – the conventional level (see Chapter 4). Hence, by improving moral reasoning to the conventional level, it is hoped that delinquents will respect society's mores and behave appropriately in accordance with set expectations stipulated by society rather than following rules for self-interest purposes only.

Findings from many studies corroborate the view that delinquents operate at a much lower level of moral reasoning than non-delinquents (Gibbs 2003; Nelson, Smith and Dodd 1990; Palmer 2003a; Stamms, Brugman, Dekovic, van Rosmalen *et al.* 2006). Furthermore, egocentrism, a main trait of the pre-conventional level of moral reasoning, might be a pre requisite for delinquency in late adolescence/early adulthood. An interesting question, however, is whether aspects of moral reasoning develop differentially. For instance, Brugman and Aleva (2004) found that delayed moral reasoning in delinquents is contributory to the problems they have in obeying the law. Chen and Howitt (2007) extended the question of differential moral reasoning across many types of crime committed by offenders such as drug related, violence and theft. They found that moral development was of a similar level across offenders despite having committed different types of crime. There was one moral value that differentiated the level of moral reasoning of offenders committing one out of the three types of offence, and this was the value of 'life'. The question posed for this moral value was, 'How important is it for a person to live even if that person doesn't want to?' (cited in Howitt 2011, p.94). The direction of difference suggested that delinquents who committed violent crimes had poorer moral reasoning ability and this was linked to their age.

In another intervention, known as The Just Community Model (Power, Higgins and Kohlberg 1989), offenders were encouraged to discuss issues in a morally mature and enlightened way. Often endorsed within prison settings, prisoners are invited to discuss moral issues that influence their everyday lives in prison and to participate in decisions that may concern them. There has been mixed success with this model in terms of mobility within Kohlberg's levels and stages of moral reasoning. A few studies have shown progression, at the very most, from one stage to the next (Gibbs, Arnold, Ahlborn and Cheesman 1984; Gordon and Arbuthnot 1987; Hickey 1972; Scharf and Hickey 1976), while other studies found no change (Copeland and Parish 1979; Gendreau and Ross 1987). The ideology behind improving moral reasoning is a just one, but successful advancement might be impeded by other factors like cognitive immaturity and poor role-taking skills of the delinquents taking part. Researchers such as Gordon and Arbuthnot (1987) advocated instead a multi-skill training approach that takes account of numerous social and cognitive deficits experienced by many delinquents. The content of different programmes used is important but, more significantly, the nature of the relationship between the young offender and the practitioner is key to the success of any intervention adopted. The Social Exclusion Unit reported to the Office of the Deputy Prime Minister in 2005 that there are four important facets for effective intervention with delinquents:

1 a holistic approach;
2 having a trusted person;
3 operate on an individual's needs basis rather than age;
4 the development of useful skills (i.e. critical thinking).

Various initiatives have been introduced in England and Wales run by the Probation Service, such as Aggression Replacement Training (ART) which originated in the US in 1981. An adapted form of the ART programme, used in a one year trial study in Britain, has been successful at reducing the reconviction rate for those on probation who completed the programme (Sugg 2000). Since Sugg's study, the ART programme has been fully implemented by the Probation Service throughout England and Wales. The ART programme offers a multi-skill training approach where personal, interpersonal and socio-cognitive skills are provided and practiced in a safe environment. Approaches to controlling impulsive and aggressive behaviours are taught and moral reasoning deficits addressed. The effectiveness of the ART programme was further investigated by Hatcher, Palmer, McGuire, Housome *et al.* (2008) using two groups matched for risk score on the Offender Group Reoffending Scale Version 2 (OGRS2). The group receiving ART showed a 13 per cent reduction in reconviction rates, and the ART completers were less likely to reoffend than those failing to complete the programme. The ART programme is a good example of a multi-skill training approach but, unfortunately, tends to be a generic approach where one glove fits all.

As suggested by Gordon and Arbuthnot in 1987, a multi-skill training approach is needed which also caters for the individual needs of offenders. Such an approach was included in the Violence Prevention Program run in New Zealand. This consisted of eight 'modules':

1   emotion regulation
2   moral reasoning
3   victim empathy
4   interpersonal skills
5   cognitive restructuring
6   recognising triggers for offending behaviour
7   problem solving
8   relapse prevention.

Overall the success of this programme in comparison to comparable programmes was the same; however, reconviction rates for those treated were significantly lower than for the controls (Polaschek, Wilson, Townsend and Daly 2005). It appears that programmes addressing similar issues while adopting a multifaceted approach have comparable success rates and reconviction figures regardless of whether they use a generic or offender specific-needs model.

Situational crime preventions are successful to a degree but will not deter the hard-core offender. Social strategies when properly organised, such as programmes concentrating on skill development, are successful for some but not all delinquents. What is important is that each delinquent is risk assessed and a personalised programme of therapeutic intervention is devised based on the needs of the individual. This approach enables the offender to engage in learning and improving their basic socio-cognitive life skills which tend to be impaired.

The big question is why does recidivism reduce and desistence increase for some delinquents as a consequence of crime prevention strategies and therapeutic intervention but not for others? Would it be a fair assumption to make that in cases where recidivism reduces and **desistance** increases, an essentially nurture-oriented problem may be at the heart of the offending behaviour? Under circumstances where delinquency continues could it be that an essentially nature oriented problem exists? Perhaps this is too simplistic a breakdown of the available information regarding delinquents and the information yet to be discovered. If we consider the **gene–environment interaction** and its implications then it makes more sense to work backwards from the available evidence of what strategy worked in combination with the delinquent's personal profile (including prominent **risk** and **protective factors**). This stepwise backward regression of information might be more elucidating, providing key causal factors in the delinquent's offending career.

It may be more informative to evaluate psychological evidence from research characterising how deficits in many behaviours first arise. For instance, a delinquent who comes from a background where there is little or no effective supervision is more likely to get involved with the wrong crowd and get into trouble with the law. By relinquishing ties with delinquent peers and helping parents with child-rearing through education programmes, the problem behaviour might be resolved. Providing adolescent delinquents with realistic goals and education to increase their opportunities for employment might resolve low self-esteem issues and elevate their income, such that they no longer feel it necessary to burgle, thieve or shoplift.

Empathy is more difficult to develop in offenders who have very little. Evidence suggests that empathy develops from a very young age but is rudimentary. Workman (pers. comm. 2012) argued that newborns crying on hearing other newborns cry might be a social facilitation effect where it is more a matter of imitation without truly understanding their reaction than it being empathy. If so, then does empathy develop gradually by shaping behaviour through learning and interacting with other social beings? If the social beings (i.e. the family) are uncaring, neglecting, abusive and/or rejecting, does this mean that appropriate socialisation fails to develop a child's predisposition for empathy? Or is this failure to develop empathy inherited from parents who have empathy deficits themselves and generations before them? A difficult one to answer!

## Summary

- Delinquency refers to petty crime and a juvenile delinquent is a young person who commits petty crime. A diversity of delinquent crimes exist spanning across theft (i.e. shoplifting), petty burglary, criminal damage, vandalism and the handling of stolen goods. Reports suggest that delinquency is increasing but it has always existed – in the 1920s, for instance, there were gangs of juvenile hoodlums in the streets of Chicago who were involved in stealing, thieving and bootlegging. In the 1970–80s, football hooligans caused many problems and in 2005, the BBC reported the rise of a yob culture. In 2011, rioting in many English cities was yet another example of delinquent behaviour. Delinquency, nevertheless, is rising – in particular, violent offences involving knives and other weapons committed by those less than 18. This type of crime has doubled between 1997 and 2006.

- Questions have been asked concerning the nature of demographical factors contributing towards a delinquency prone culture. Psychologists and sociologists have researched the causes of delinquency and factors which contribute towards creating the delinquent. An important psychological study known as the Cambridge Study in Delinquent Development (1961–81), conducted by West and Farrington and discussed in Chapter 4, provided clues to the antecedents of delinquency.

- Other psychological research has unearthed a biological component of delinquent behaviour. First, through research by Raine (2002a, 2002b) and his colleagues, children with behavioural problems such as CD and ODD have a high risk for delinquency in later adolescence which they attribute to poor fear conditioning in anticipation of punishment. They also found evidence of pathology in the limbic system, smaller amygdala and reduced activity in the amygdala during the solution of moral dilemmas (performance in common with psychopaths). van Goozen and her colleagues showed that children with CD and ODD had startle reflex anomalies. These children had lower startle responses to emotional content and the more delinquent they were the lower their startle response to negative emotional content. Other physiological responses, such as, for instance, levels of cortisol were found to be lower in ODD and CD children. Anomalies of amygdala function were considered to be causal. Problems of EF and WM function appeared in ADHD, CD and ODD children where they found it difficult to suppress their impulsive behaviour due to problems with the frontal lobe.

- Problems and delayed development of moral reasoning, empathy and ToM have been found in delinquents. Young offenders show poor moral reasoning and tend to be at the first level of Kohlberg's time frame for moral development – the pre-conventional level. This is on a par with young children who Kohlberg considers to be egocentric and unconcerned about the fate of others. Empathy is limited in delinquents who fail to feel guilt or remorse for their actions towards their victims. ToM is the ability to understand another person's perspective – being able to put yourself into another person's shoes. This links strongly with empathy but as there is a deficit in empathy, ToM is immature in delinquents. Mirror neurons or sensorimotor neurons found in the ACC, anterior insula cortex, premotor cortex (i.e. the F5 area) and superior temporal sulcus of the brain, are responsible for the perception of pain experienced by the self or by other selves. Mirror neurons play a vital role in being able to experience empathy, which research indicates might be malfunctioning in delinquents who have little or no empathy for their victims. As empathy is important to ToM and ToM is immature in delinquents, this might explain their poor acquisition of moral understanding. This coupled with inadequate socialisation, increases the likelihood of delinquency (another risk factor identified by psychologists and sociologists).

- It is clear that nurture has an important hand to play in the development of antisocial behaviour and delinquency. Research findings indicate that deviant families and problem backgrounds put children at risk of becoming delinquent. The problem, however, goes beyond the family to extended families, peers and local gangs. The calibre of the neighbourhood and community per se impacts on the richness of resources available to youths.

- Neighbourhoods and communities with a history of poverty tend to develop their own subcultural values that separate them from the dominant culture, and these values are transmitted from one generation to the next, perpetuating a cycle of poverty and violence. Environments such as these provide a niche for criminal gangs to operate and to recruit youngsters into a career of delinquency. Sociologists have identified characteristics of particular neighbourhoods as potential crime-spots. Where neighbourhoods and communities have their own subculture, there are divides in the nature of values and mores from the dominant culture which exaggerate differences in the socialisation process.

- Dominant culture, through the process of socialisation, ensures that the same moral values and rules are instilled in its citizens: an implicit social contract is made where citizens reap the benefits society has to offer provided they conform to its rules and moral values. If children receive ineffective socialisation then these rules and moral values will not be instilled and their behaviour is more likely to be in conflict with the dominant culture. This is seen within the educational system where delinquents do not conform to school rules, have attitudes in conflict with essentially middle-class educational values and behaviour considered deviant and troublesome. This continues in other contexts where their behaviour fails to conform to expected social values, mores and attitudes.

- Inappropriate and deviant socialisation makes it difficult to 'retrain' delinquents to accept society's rules and moral values, and to behave in a socially appropriate way. Achieving these outcomes is the aim of multifaceted social interventions. Multifaceted social interventions prove to be more effective than programmes concentrating on one aspect of offending behaviour or crime prevention. The importance of identifying different risk and protective factors contributing towards delinquency help local government and practitioners devise effective, comprehensive situational and social crime prevention strategies and other levels of intervention.

Social research regarding the causes of delinquency provides an important frame from which government initiatives for reducing crime are derived, and it is risk and protective factors which are vital for the success of these initiatives. Nevertheless, it would appear that for some delinquents, intervention (whatever the format) will be ineffective. For these delinquents it might be a case of immature moral reasoning arising out of ToM and empathy deficits that have a biological causation.

## Questions for discussion

1    Are delinquents the victims or the perpetrators of society?
2    Do risk factors stigmatise delinquents and therefore bias society's approach towards changing their behaviour?
3    Do situational crime prevention strategies work?

# Prediction of criminal behaviour

# Prediction of criminal behaviour

# Dangerousness risk assessment and the mentally and personality-disordered offender

Part IV is about predicting future criminal behaviour. In this chapter we will explore ways of predicting future criminal behaviour on the basis of assessing dangerousness and risk of reoffending. Although in this chapter we will focus on how dangerous behaviour can be predicted, we also consider dangerous offenders and their actions, thereby forging links with Part III.

We will begin by considering the problems associated with the **concept of dangerousness** – how it is ambiguous and often misunderstood. This is partly a consequence of a definition which fails to distinguish between a dangerous individual and an act considered to be dangerous. The assessment procedures used to assess an individual as being a danger to themselves and society is also questionable – especially as the conclusions drawn from such assessments underlie predictions of future behaviour. In the context of the law, the assessment of an offender as dangerous has poignant implications for the type and length of sentence given. These are important issues which will be addressed in this chapter. We will also examine the link between mental disorders, violence and dangerousness using demographical information to demonstrate who is most responsible for committing dangerous offences (as defined by the Mental Health Act). Attempts to unravel the ambiguity of the definition of dangerousness by referring to the Mental Health Act (2007) will help provide clarity and a consensus understanding of this. References will be made throughout this chapter to the Mental Health Act; the Criminal Justice Act 2003; Sentencing Guidelines Council for Dangerous Offenders 2008; and to proposed legislation for sentencing dangerous offenders. Knowledge of how the dangerous offender is understood by these different legislations is important because they each have their own definitions which can cause confusion amongst clinicians. We will explore the Offender Assessment System (OASys) introduced by the Criminal Justice Act of 2003 to provide a care package for the dangerous offender, with input from a multitude of professionals. Youth Offending Teams will also be considered in relation to the use of ASSET, which is a clinically based interview assessment for children. Different approaches to assessing dangerous offenders and the risk of their reoffending will be evaluated for effectiveness and accuracy. In this chapter the two main approaches to risk assessment of dangerousness, risk of harm and reoffending will be discussed: clinical and actuarial, or statistical, methods. The use of examples will help to highlight the difficulty clinicians have in assessing who is a danger to themselves and society, and who is most at risk of reoffending. We will also consider the topical issue of terrorism and ways of understanding terrorists. Additionally, we will focus on suicide bombers and war crime offenders in terms of their dangerousness and the underlying causes of their behaviour. In the case of war crime offenders we will see how personality disorders (for example, psychopathy) play a strong hand in determining their behaviour and ability to commit atrocities on other ethnic groups.

## Introduction

The definition of dangerousness is ambiguous and problematic. Whether the term dangerousness refers to a personality trait of the individual or to the criminal act itself remains unqualified. This means that there is confusion over the violent element of the crime committed – was it committed because the person is inherently violent and therefore dangerous, or, even though the criminal act was violent, the individual is not dangerous? Violence and dangerousness are considered to co-exist together. Furthermore, violence and dangerousness are often linked with the mental health of an individual. The association between mental disorder and violence for instance has a long history (Howitt 1998), but the extent to which a relationship exists between the two is in need of empirical evidence and clarity of what constitutes a mental disorder. Is a psychopath to be considered in the same way as an individual with schizophrenia for instance? The Mental Health Act (MHA) of 1983 considers psychopathy to be a mental disorder and yet an individual diagnosed as a psychopath who commits a dangerous criminal act would almost certainly be imprisoned in a high-security prison. High-security psychiatric hospitals, such as Broadmoor, are normally reserved for schizophrenic offenders like Peter Sutcliffe, alias the Yorkshire Ripper, for instance. The association between mental disorder and violence therefore needs to be clarified – in terms of which mental disorders are being considered and how they relate to violent behaviour. There is disagreement among some researchers of whether a robust link between mental disorder and violent behaviour exists (Bonta, Law and Hanson 1998) but strong evidence suggests that the two co-occur (Hodgins 2004). By referring to three sources of empirical evidence (i.e. the discharged in-patient; convicted offender studies and follow-up studies of birth cohorts), Hodgins (2004) concluded that there is a robust association between mental disorder and violent behaviour. Hodgins and Côté (1993) for example, found that from a fifth to over a half of murderers had a mental disorder – this would frequently be depression (Howitt 2012).

Whilst there is evidence for an association between mental disorder and violence, there needs to be information to demonstrate a relationship between mental disorder and offending – in particular, offending considered as dangerous. The evidence for this is mixed because it depends on the mental disorder being considered, and yet jurors are required to make judgement about a defendant diagnosed with a mental disorder. According to Pilgrim (2000), a defendant might be described as having a mental disorder but the term is not legally defined; hence jurors rely on their common knowledge of what is meant by a mental disorder. As there are differences between legal and psychological interpretations of the link between dangerous offenders and mental disorder, the jurors' task is made even more complicated. One cause of this might relate to there being a failure in cross-cultural consistency concerning definitions of mental disorder and its relationship with dangerous offending behaviour. There are further problems relating to the 'etiological and diagnostic clarity' of disorder classifications (Hodgins and Müller-Isberner 2004). In other words, the causes of mental disorders and how they are diagnosed remains unclear and uncertain. To complicate matters further, Blackburn, Donnelly, Logan and Renwick (2004) stated that there might be some offenders exhibiting symptoms from more than one category of mental disorder – making a clear diagnosis based on descriptions and classifications derived from the MHA or Diagnostic Statistical Manual (DSM) difficult.

There are many factors, outside of having a mental disorder, which induce violent and dangerous behaviour, such as provocation and having criminogenic needs (i.e. which cause or promote crime). Extreme violence can be construed as dangerous behaviour that contravenes the law, for example, thereby classifying the individual as a dangerous offender. Under these circumstances, a dangerous offender does not exhibit symptoms of a mental disorder but rather a criminal mind-set or a casualty of unfortunate circumstances. Alternatively, there are dangerous offenders who exhibit symptoms of a mental disorder which practitioners sometimes have difficulty diagnosing and, in the case of murder trials, a *mens rea* (i.e. guilty mind). Mental disorders sometimes go unrecognised and it is only when an individual has been brought to the attention of the criminal justice system that a diagnosis is made.

Although links between violence, dangerousness and mental disorder have been made, and we understand that an offence considered as dangerous will involve different degrees of violence, what dangerousness means remains undefined. It is important therefore to address what dangerousness means by considering the definition used in law. In the next section we will explore different aspects of the legal definition and link this with assessment guidelines used by the courts.

## What is dangerousness?

### Legal definition

Dangerousness can be defined as the danger that individuals convicted of violent serious crime pose to society and its citizens. Bottoms and Brownsword (1982) stated that, 'Dangerousness has three constituent elements of the predicted act, viz. (i) seriousness; (ii) temporality, with two ingredients of frequency and immediacy (or recency); and (iii) degree of certainty about the future conduct' (p. 240). Their second point refers to an individual who poses a constant and continuous danger to society – if the individual continues to be dangerous then this information can be used to help satisfy the third point raised by Bottoms and Brownsword.

Under the dangerous offender provisions ruling of the Criminal Justice Act 2003, 'the court must first decide whether there is a significant risk to members of the public of serious harm caused by the offender committing further specified offences' (Section 229(1)(b)). There are two criteria which must be met: 'there must be a significant risk of the offender committing further specified offences (whether serious or not), and there must be a significant risk of serious harm to members of the public being caused by such offences'.

The assessment of dangerousness, based on clauses from the Criminal Justice Act 2003 (CJA), divide into the following sections:

- General relevant factors (see Box 11.1).
- Relevant factors regarding significant risk of further specified offences (see Box 11.2).
- Relevant factors regarding significant risk of serious harm (see Box 11.3).

General relevant factors taken into consideration by the court include the nature of the offence committed and the context in which it occurred. Interestingly, however, information about other offences committed is permissible when assessing the offender's level of dangerousness. A history of an offender's patterns of behaviour is important and can be construed as symptomatic of their condition. This helps inform the court of why the offender behaved violently and dangerously and provides a contextual framework for the circumstances of the offence (see Box 11.1).

## Box 11.1

### General relevant factors for the assessment of dangerousness

The court:

- Must take into account all available information about the nature and circumstances of the offence (Section 229(2)(a));

- May take into account all available information about the nature and circumstances of any other offence(s) of which the offender has been convicted by a court anywhere in the world (Section 229(2)(aa));
- May take into account any information about any pattern of behaviour of which the offence is part (Section 229(2)(b));
- May take into account any information about the offender (Section 229(2)(c)).

Any information that may have been put before the court to prove that the offender was guilty of the offence for which he or she is to be sentenced may be relevant to the assessment of dangerousness, regardless of whether the information actually was before the court prior to conviction, unless that information would have been excluded from a trial.

Source: Sentencing Guidelines Council Manual for Dangerous Offenders: Guide for Sentencers and Practitioners 2008, http://sentencingcouncil.judiciary.gov.uk/guidelines/guidelines-to-download.htm.

Assessing the risk of likely reoccurrence of offending is an important element in the assessment of dangerousness. Life circumstances of the offender, such as the social and economic circumstances and how these impact on the emotional well-being of the offender, are taken seriously when making risk assessments. An offender's history of offending and the nature of previous convictions, help to evaluate whether the offender is a danger to society and will commit similar offences in the future. Also taken into consideration is the offender's state of mind and whether there are indicators of emotional disturbance that allude to being a danger to society (see Box 11.2).

## Box 11.2

### Relevant factors regarding significant risk of further specified offences for dangerous offenders

The offender's 'offending history':

- The existence (or non-existence) of previous convictions does not determine whether an offender is a dangerous offender; an offender with no previous convictions may be a dangerous offender, whilst an offender with previous convictions may not.
- Any previous conviction may be relevant in the assessment of whether an offender is a dangerous offender; offences may be considered whether or not they are specified offences.
- For these purposes, a conviction could have occurred anywhere in the world (Section 229(2)(aa)). Also included are findings of guilt in service

disciplinary proceedings or conviction of a service offence (Section 229(2A)).

- The offender's offending history includes the facts of any previous offence and the sentence passed, as well as the type of offence.
- Any information which formed the basis for the imposition of an Anti-Social Behaviour Order may be considered in assessing whether the offender is a dangerous offender.

The offender's emotional state:

- An offender's inadequacy, suggestibility or vulnerability may mitigate his or her culpability. However, such features may also produce or reinforce a conclusion that he or she is a dangerous offender.

Source: Sentencing Guidelines Council Manual for Dangerous Offenders: Guide for Sentencers and Practitioners 2008, http://sentencingcouncil.judiciary.gov.uk/guidelines/guidelines-to-download.htm.

The risk of serious harm in future offending is graded according to four categories – low, medium, high and very high (see Box 11.3) and the level of risk to society an offender poses is based on the likely level of serious harm they might potentially cause in future offending. The assessment of this will prove difficult under circumstances where offenders have committed serious offences in the past that have caused low levels of serious harm. Previous serious offending does not necessarily imply a risk of causing serious harm in future offending. Alternatively, the absence of serious harm in previous offending might be a consequence of fortunate coincidences rather than through judgement, in so much that such an offender cannot be precluded from causing serious harm in future offending.

## Box 11.3

### Relevant factors regarding significant risk of serious harm by dangerous offenders

- The court should not assume automatically that there is a significant risk of serious harm because the foreseen specified offence is a serious offence; many serious offences can be committed in ways which do not give rise to a significant risk of serious harm.
- If the foreseen offence is a specified offence other than a serious offence, it is unlikely that there will be a significant risk of serious harm. Repetitive offending at a relatively low level without serious harm does not give rise of itself to a significant risk of serious harm in future.
- The absence of actual harm caused by the offender in the instant offence or any offence previously committed by the offender does not lead automatically to a conclusion that there is a negligible risk that

he or she will cause serious harm in future. In some cases it may be entirely by chance that no harm actually was caused by the offender; in such cases the court should consider the offender's likely response if the circumstances had been different, such as if the victim attempted to defend himself or herself.

- The pre-sentence report will contain an assessment of the level of risk of serious harm posed by the offender. Serious harm is defined, for the purposes of a pre-sentence report, as 'an event which is life-threatening and/or traumatic and from which recovery, whether physical or psychological, can be expected to be difficult or impossible'. This differs from the definition of serious harm in Section 224(3) (death or serious physical or psychological injury). However, the two definitions are compatible.

- The pre-sentence report will assess the risk of serious harm as being low, medium, high or very high. The principles which determine the level of risk are whether the foreseen behaviour meets the pre-sentence report definition of serious harm, the likelihood of the behaviour occurring and the impact of such behaviour. The levels of risk are defined as follows:

a. *Low*: current evidence does not indicate any likelihood of causing serious harm.

b. *Medium*: some risk has been identified but the offender is unlikely to cause serious harm unless circumstances change.

c. *High*: a risk of harm has been identified. The potential event could occur at any time and the impact would be serious.

d. *Very high*: there is an imminent risk of serious harm. The potential event is more likely than not to happen imminently and the impact would be serious.

Source: Sentencing Guidelines Council Manual for Dangerous Offenders: Guide for Sentencers and Practitioners 2008, http://sentencingcouncil.judiciary.gov.uk/guidelines/guidelines-to-download.htm.

From the Sentencing Guidelines Council Manual for Dangerous Offenders (2008) it appears that the legal definition and references to the assessment of dangerous offenders are closely entwined. The assessment helps the criminal justice system to decide whether there is a high probability of the offender reoffending in the same way in the future, which then determines the nature of incarceration or sentence given. Dangerousness also has implications for other aspects of the law, such as **retribution** and **public safety**, which will be considered next.

## Dangerousness and the law

The law operates on the premise that if an individual intentionally harms or murders another person, then that individual should be punished using a just deserts model of **retribution** (i.e. get what is deserved). Furthermore, individuals who commit serious offences that involve harming or murdering others are segregated from the rest of society for the protection of its citizens. Hence, the functions of the law include: the protection and safety of its citizens; retribution; **rehabilitation**; **deterrence**; and reparation (see Chapter 16 for discussion of these factors). Both *actus reus* (i.e. guilty act) and *mens rea* (see Chapter 1), once established in a Crown Court, are weighted in terms of offence seriousness. As an example, homicide is a serious and dangerous *mala in se* (i.e. crime against the human moral code) offence that warrants severe punishment. Punishments for serious offences in the UK include high tariff sentences of detainment in prison; however, there are other options some of which have caused concern by Human Right Campaigners.

In England and Wales those, for example, who have committed serious offences, such as murder, can volunteer to go to Grendon Underwood which is a unique prison offering a highly structured form of rehabilitation and, as Professor David Wilson in 2011 explained to the BBC News, 'a therapeutic community is a 24-hour, seven-days-a-week, 52-weeks-a-year commitment to analysing your behaviour in the context of a prison to try and gain insight and understanding into why you ended up in that prison' (McClatchey 2011). Furthermore, it is the only prison in Europe which surrounds inmates in a community of therapy. Broadmoor Hospital on the other hand, is a high-security psychiatric hospital housing male patients who have a severe mental illness or personality disorder: many have been convicted of committing serious crimes or assessed as being unfit to stand trial in court. There are other high-security hospitals such as Rampton, Ashworth and Carstairs. A new unit called the Paddock Centre based at Broadmoor in 2005 was designed to house and treat individuals with a severe personality disorder but who were also assessed as being dangerous. To be admitted at Paddock, two criteria had to be sufficed: an assessment of dangerousness where the individual was considered a 'grave and immediate danger' to the public; and considered to suffer from more than two severe personality disorders as stipulated in DSM-5 and a significant score on the Hare Psychopathy Check List-Revised (see Chapter 7). Despite much controversy over the Paddock Centre and the opening of only four of 12 wards and its closure in 2012 (Department of Health and Ministry of Justice National Personality Disorder Strategy 2011), in 2013 it still housed a few individuals with a mental illness or personality disorder issues.

The opening of the Paddock Centre has provoked an ethical debate concerning the notions of 'preventive detention' and 'extreme rendition' also known as 'extraordinary rendition'. In the case of preventive detention, the idea behind this is to incarcerate an individual who has the propensity to be dangerous (whether in the form of self-harm or criminal behaviour) but has not as yet committed a dangerous act – preventive detention is therefore justified for non-punitive purposes. This means that under preventive detention, an individual can be imprisoned without a criminal charge. Furthermore, if the government considers an individual to be a threat to the law or the integrity of the nation, then it is justified in detaining the individual. The type of individual who might be incarcerated using this criterion is an individual with a mental disorder (i.e. schizophrenia) or personality disorder (i.e. APD or psychopathy (see Chapter 7 for differentiation between the two)). The use of preventive detention can also be used in the detention of individuals previously sentenced for having committed a serious offence. Preventive detention has been criticised for contravening the human rights of those detained and has been likened, by Michael Ratner president of the Centre for Constitutional Rights, to the film *Minority Report*, produced by Steven Spielberg. Ratner further said that, '[Obama] is re-wrapping a preventive detention scheme and giving it some more due process. In the end, it still comes down to holding people – much like *Minority Report* or pre-crime stuff – for being dangerous, and that is not something that I think is constitutional or this country should be engaged in' (Stein 2009).

Glenn Greenwald, a former Constitutional and Civil Rights litigator, stated in response to Obama's speech in 2009 that,

> It's important to be clear about what 'preventive detention' authorizes. It does not merely allow the US Government to imprison people alleged to have committed terrorist acts . . . 'preventive detention' allows indefinite imprisonment not based on proven crimes and or past violations of law, but of those deemed . . . 'dangerous' by the Government.

Although preventive detention is used in the UK, it is more limited to dangerous individuals who have previously committed serious and dangerous offences. As we have seen, however, with the opening and continued use of the Paddock Centre at Broadmoor until 2012–13, dangerous individuals who have personality disorders can be detained without having committed a dangerous offence – based on the criterion that they have the propensity to do so in the future if their liberty is not curtailed. The question is should the justice system be allowed to make decisions of incarceration based on future prediction?

Equally concerning is the use of extreme or extraordinary rendition, introduced by President George W. Bush. This refers to the practice of extraditing terrorist suspects to other countries where they are imprisoned indefinitely and highly likely to be subjected to torture. Extreme rendition was introduced as a reaction to the 2001 terrorist attacks ordered by Al Qaeda, in what has become known as 9/11 (Jacobson 2012). Obama in 2008 promised to 'eliminate the practice of extreme rendition, where we outsource our torture to other countries' (Jacobson 2012). Detainees under extreme rendition are known as 'ghost detainees' because they remain outside of the judicial process and are usually detained in another country awaiting to be transferred into US custody. This does not necessary occur, in which case they remain imprisoned in a foreign detention facility (Mayer 2005). Extreme rendition is an unethical form of detention because the individuals suspected of terrorist activity have not been taken to trial and undergone prosecution through the legal system. This means that the status of these detainees is innocent until proven guilty, which is seemingly and conveniently forgotten.

A mandatory sentence of life imprisonment is the maximum tariff a judge in the UK can give, which is reserved for murders committed by individuals of 18 and over. In murder trials, judges have no choice but to give a life sentence as murder automatically receives the maximum sentence tariff in recognition of its seriousness and implied dangerousness. Prior to the 2003 CJA, the life sentence was the only indeterminate sentence available to judges but they could award discretionary life sentences where release of a prisoner was based on demonstrating to the Parole Board that they were of no danger to the public. In 2005, a new type of mandatory sentence called Imprisonment for the Public Protection (IPP) was introduced to enable judges to sentence dangerous offenders who had committed a serious violent or sexual offence to an indeterminate prison sentence that carried a maximum tariff of at least 10 years (see Chapter 1). Offences such as aggravated burglary; grievous bodily harm; manslaughter; rape and paedophilia; kidnapping; and the use of explosives to cause damage and harm could warrant an IPP. Judges now had the judicial power to either pass a determinate sentence using sentencing guidelines of maximum sentence tariff based on the seriousness of the offence, or award a mandatory IPP to dangerous offenders.

The IPP sentence has brought much controversy and was considered to be an infringement on the rights of offenders by Strasbourg Judges in the European Court of Human Rights. This prompted a change in the sentencing of dangerous offenders by the Ministry of Justice who set the date for the abolition of IPPs at 3 December 2012 in accordance with the Legal Aid, Sentencing and Punishment of Offenders Act of 1 May 2012. Although IPPs will no longer be used, its abolition is not retrospective which means that existing offenders serving an IPP will continue to do so. It is interesting how the history of sentencing dangerous offenders resulted in the IPP. The history of proposed legislations for dangerous offenders in the UK will be considered next.

### Legislations proposed for dangerous offenders

The IPP was a relatively new form of sentence legislation for dangerous offenders, which arose from debates of how to punish the dangerous offender. Numerous legislations have been proposed over the last 35 years which led to the IPP. A short history of these proposed legislations is described below:

- Butler Committee (Home Office and Department of Health and Social Security 1975) proposed a reviewable open-ended indeterminate sentence. The Butler Committee made four recommendations relating to the issue of dangerousness.

  1   A new form of sentence should be introduced specifically for offenders considered to be dangerous. Their release would depend entirely on issues of dangerousness so that their detainment period would be unspecified. Normally such offenders would present with a history of mental disorder that could not be dealt with appropriately under mental health (MH) legislation and for whom a life sentence would be considered unjust. This sentence would be subject to review once every two years and the offender following discharge would undergo statutory supervision.

  2   The use of this sentence would be restricted for offenders convicted of offences causing serious harm to others and includes the following offences: murder, manslaughter, sexual offences, arson, intended grievous bodily harm, robbery and aggravated burglary.

  3   The Home Secretary reserves the right to transfer prisoners to hospital under MH legislation.

  4   The review is conducted by the Parole Board and offenders' release would be subject to licence of unlimited duration.

- In 1976 the Howard League for Penal Reform convened a working party led by Jean Floud. The report became known as the Floud Report which put forward the double-track sentence similar to an extended sentence of four years on top of the time served. They concluded in 1981 that, 'the public should be entitled to the protection of a special sentence only against grave harm' (Floud and Young 1981, p.154).

- In the Criminal Justice Act of 1991 it states that, 'A dangerous offender may be sentenced in the same manner as any other offender in accordance with the "just deserts" philosophy expressed in Section 2(2)(a).' In Section 2(2)(b), however, where the offender has committed a violent or sexual act, it is in the court's jurisdiction to impose a 'longer than commensurate determinate sentence' provided this does not exceed the maximum sentence stipulated under the sentencing guidelines for that offence. For example, if the maximum tariff for a particular offence is 10 years, the normal commensurate determinate sentence might be something like eight years with a minimum of six years. The judge can increase this to the maximum guideline tariff of 10 years, but not beyond, if the offence contains further disturbing elements.

- According to the Crime Sentences Act of 1997, courts are obliged to give long minimum sentences for serious crimes and can impose a mandatory life sentence for a second serious offence committed. The ideology behind this is very similar to the 'three strikes and you're out' legislation adopted in the US. Interestingly, the Act also proposed a sentence of imprisonment with a Hospital and Limitation Direction for psychopaths. This is a measure taken to ensure that if psychopaths do not respond to hospital treatment (and they usually do not – see Chapter 7) then they can be legally transferred to prison.

- Imprisonment for the Public Protection (IPP)

    1   The content of past legislation for the sentencing of dangerous offenders influenced the development of the IPP. The Home Office, however, had not anticipated a major problem with the guideline use of IPPs – that of prison overpopulation caused by the high numbers of prisoners meeting the criteria of a mandatory IPP. The Criminal Justice and Immigration Act of 2008 amended the use of the IPP, where the mandatory use of IPP for cases meeting the dangerousness criteria was removed and its use restricted to offences that warranted a sentence tariff of more than two years. According to the Ministry of Justice this had reduced the number of offenders sentenced to an IPP, but the prison population serving an IPP in 2010 was 5,828.

    2   Another major problem pointed out by Jacobson and Hough (2010), in a report on behalf of the Prison Reform Trust, is the discrepancy between the number of prisoners serving a mandatory IPP prior to 2008 who have surpassed serving their sentence tariff but have failed to convince the Parole Board that they no longer pose a danger to society, and the number of IPP prisoners post 2008 who have been given a determinate sentence and know their release date. Of course in both cases, prisoners have to demonstrate to the Parole Board that they are safe to be released into the community. According to Jacobson and Hough (2010), only 4 per cent of prisoners serving on IPPs are released back into the community on expiry of their sentence tariff.

    3   There are many reasons for this low release of prisoners but a major problem is that decisions by the Parole Board rely on prisoners completing an offending behaviour programme to signal their readiness for release. This programme, however, is difficult for many prisoners serving an IPP to complete, as they often failed to understand the content delivered – due to their low level of intelligence, experience of a mental disorder or both. It is also very difficult to demonstrate whether a prisoner on an IPP would constitute a low risk to the community when there is no way of putting this to the test within a prison environment.

It is not surprising given the release date discrepancy between offenders on an IPP prior to 2008 with those on an IPP post 2008 that the IPP sentence has been abolished. The IPP sentence was simply unfair (see Box 11.4).

# Box 11.4

## The unfairness of the IPP sentence

The Sentencing Guidelines Council (2008) provides a manual based on clauses from the 2003 CJA for the sentencing of dangerous offenders. The sentencing guidelines are divided into 'serious violent offences', 'specified violent offences which are not serious offences', 'serious sexual offences' and 'specified sexual offences which are not serious offences'. For instance, a crime such as wounding with intent to cause grievous bodily harm that is categorised as a serious violent offence would be fixed at the maximum penalty of life imprisonment. Threats to kill, however (Section 16 of the Offences against the Person Act 1861), is fixed at the maximum penalty of 10 years even though this is also classified as a serious violent offence. In the case of genocide, crime against humanity and war crimes (other than murder) under Section 51 or 52 of the International Criminal Court Act of 2001, a maximum of 30 years is set. Malicious wounding and abandoning children, which are both specified violent offences (Section 20 of the Offences against the Person Act 1861 and Section 27 of the Offences Against the Persons Act 1861 respectively), are set at a maximum of five years imprisonment. Rape (Section 1 of the Sexual Offences Act 2003) and assault by penetration (Section 2 of the Sexual Offences Act 2003), classified as serious sexual offences, have a maximum penalty of life imprisonment. Section 33 of the Sexual Offences Act 2003 stipulates that a maximum penalty of 10 years could be awarded for 'causing a person with a mental disorder impeding choice to watch a sexual act' and likewise for a 'care worker causing or inciting sexual activity' under Section 39 of the Sexual Offences Act 2003. In the case of specified sexual offences which are not regarded as serious offences, such as exposure, voyeurism, bestiality and necrophilia (under Sections 66, 67, 69 and 70 respectively of the Sexual Offences Act 2003) have maximum penalties set at 2 years.

Despite the sentencing guidelines and the set maximum penalties for the different offences, judges can also pass a life sentence when the offence is serious and the offender is perceived as mentally unstable and very likely to repeat the same crime or other types of crime causing harm to others. Hence, when a *mala in se* offence is committed, the IPP implicitly gave recognition to an individual constituting a danger to society and posing a high risk of reoffending. Judges could legally use their own powers of sentencing discretion (with the exception of a mandatory life sentence for murder) without the consultation of a professional expert's evidence regarding the assessment of dangerousness, if they considered it to be unnecessary. Where advice was required, a pre-sentence report was presented to the court (Section 156(3) and (4)). On the basis of the pre-sentence report regarding the assessment of dangerousness, the judge could decide whether a determinate sentence or an IPP was appropriate. An IPP sentence could have a set tariff but the offender was normally detained at Her Majesty's Pleasure until demonstrating that they no longer posed a danger to society. IPPs were generally reserved for offenders who had a mental disorder.

In the case of a determinate sentence, a release date is based on the judge's recommendation of a minimum period that should be served by the offender before any decisions are made. This recommendation is passed on to the Lord Chief Justice who informs the Home Secretary. If the Home Secretary is satisfied that time for the crime has been served and clinical assessment indicates he or she no longer poses a danger to society, then the case will be reviewed by the Local Review Committee (LRC) three years before the end of the tariff or after 17 years had lapsed (whichever is first). This means it is the LRC's decision to approve the case and provide the Home Secretary with the information to give to the Parole Board. If the Parole Board does not recommend release then the prisoner is detained for a further two years until the next review. The Parole Board's decision to detain the prisoner should be based on issues of public safety and dangerousness. In the case of IPPs, the Parole Board consisted of a Chair who represented the judiciary, a psychiatrist and one other member, all of whom decided whether to release or detain prisoners. It is clear that the IPP was an unfair sentence which, unlike a determinate sentence, failed to have any precise and definitive criteria stipulating the length of detainment a dangerous offender should endure. In the case of determinate sentences, judges have sentencing guidelines for different types of offence which the offender serves as punishment.

Considering the history of legislation for dangerous offenders and the IPP sentence, it would appear that the criminal justice system does not know what to do with offenders assessed as being dangerous. Moreover, offenders who are assessed as being dangerous will have the label for the rest of their life. It is an interesting question of what happens to the offender with the 'dangerous' label. We will next explore the impact a 'dangerous' label has for an offender.

### What happens to offenders labelled as dangerous?

Once an offender has been labelled dangerous, a catalogue of events follows and remains with the individual throughout their life-time. Dangerous offenders are released on licence where they have a supervision order, and are under the ward of a probation officer or a psychiatrist to whom they report on a daily basis. If they contravene the conditions of their licence then they can be sent back to prison or a hospital prison. Hence, being labelled as dangerous has serious consequences for the individual concerned, which is one reason why it is important to assess dangerousness correctly. Assessing for dangerousness depends on the definition used and the factors constituting dangerous behaviour. In Boxes 11.1, 11.2 and 11.3, the way dangerousness is considered in law and **jurisprudence** provided a legal perspective: for legal purposes the term dangerousness refers to the person. Describing a person as dangerous loses sight of the context in which the behaviour occurred and becomes lost in bureaucracy. In effect, the term dangerous is a misunderstood adjective that often causes ambiguity concerning the judgements made about such individuals.

Whereas the use of the term danger denotes the risk of harmful consequences, dangerousness might refer to a host of acts, situations or persons. Professionals try to avoid this ambiguity by describing the behaviour as dangerous especially when referring to violent acts of *mala in se*. Even with this modification, however, there are problems with the definition. A violent act, for example, can be dangerous but not all dangerous acts are violent such as drink driving. According to Mulvey and Lidz (1984), dangerousness, dangerous behaviour and violence are not to be used interchangeably as they derive from separate constructs. Instead for the prediction of dangerousness they proposed a two-fold evaluation: the criminal act and the probability of the offender committing the same act in the future. This is why an assessment of whether the offender constitutes a high or low risk of reoffending is just as important and informative as one that focuses on dangerousness. Before assessment procedures can be reviewed, it is important first to have an understanding of the relationship between dangerousness and mental disorder, given that they are closely interlinked. The criteria used to assess dangerousness and **risk factors** for violence and **recidivism** can be traced to the symptoms displayed by the offender and to the aetiology of their mental disorder, but how this is defined in law and psychiatry needs explanation.

## Dangerousness and its relationship with mental disorders

### Definition of mental disorder: referring to the law

To address this question it is necessary to understand what is said in the MHA of 1983. The MHA 1983 made three distinctions as regards to the state of an individual's mind: mental illness; learning disability and psychopathic disorder. Mental illness includes a range of categories such as psychosis, affective disorders and exceptional anxiety states. Learning disability as defined by the MHA refers to arrested or incomplete development of mind, such as the impairment of intelligence and social functioning. The MHA stipulated that a psychopathic disorder is a persistent disability of the mind that induces abnormally aggressive or seriously irresponsible conduct. With the introduction of the MHA in 2007, the main change concerned the diagnostic categories and substitutions of certain wordings such as 'medical practitioner' for 'clinician'. For example in Section 1(2) it now reads:

For the definitions of 'mental disorder' and 'mentally disordered' substitute:

> 'mental disorder' means any disorder or disability of the mind; and 'mentally disordered' shall be construed accordingly.

> The following definitions are omitted: (a) those of 'severe mental impairment' and 'severely mentally impaired', (b) those of 'mental impairment' and 'mentally impaired', and (c) that of 'psychopathic disorder'.

In other words, under the MHA of 2007, the diagnostic categories are no longer explicitly stated and instead a vague reference to any disorder or disability of the mind suffices. The same definition of learning disability is used in both the 1983 and 2007 MHA. The Department of Health (2011) considered personality disorders as common in society – between 5–13 per cent living in the community; 40–50 per cent as psychiatric in-patients and 78 per cent residing in prisons. Clusters of physical, social and mental health problems help to identify the type of personality disorder exhibited; however, the most commonly diagnosed are borderline and antisocial (see Chapter 7). In the MHA (2007) a section on victims' rights has been added and under Section 1(5) it states that:

> specific rights for victims of offenders who are made subject to the 1983 Act. These apply to patients who have committed one of the specified sexual or violent offences and who are then detained in hospital under:
>
> - a hospital order (Section 37);
> - a Hospital and Limitation Direction (if the associated prison sentence is for 12 months or more) (Section 45A); or
> - a transfer direction (if the associated prison sentence is for 12 months or more) (Section 47).

When a serious offence has been committed, there is cross referencing with other Acts such as Sexual Offences Act (2003); Domestic Violence, Crime and Victims Act (2004) and the Criminal Justice Act (2003). In Britain, offenders can be placed under probation on the proviso they refer to psychiatric treatment, and that failure to do so will mean submitting to criminal court proceedings. It is the role of the courts to decide whether the defendant is sane enough to stand trial or insane as decreed by clinicians and therefore hospitalised without prosecution. It is also possible that, during the trial, circumstances change such that the defendant is considered unfit to plead and is therefore sent to a psychiatric hospital without a criminal record. According to Grubin (1996b), the majority of defendants considered unfit to plead suffer from schizophrenia. As a criterion of defence, the defendant can plead insanity and is given a 'special verdict' of 'not guilty by reason of insanity'. Defendants found guilty but who clearly have a mental disorder can receive a sentence involving treatment rather than punishment – this would also lead to incarceration in high-security psychiatric hospitals like Rampton and Broadmoor, and prisons practising treatments like Grendon Underwood.

The problem for the courts regarding defendants with a mental disorder is the necessity to present evidence of *actus reus* and *mens rea* (see Chapter 1). Evidence of *actus reus* might be more straight forward to ascertain provided there is forensic proof placing the defendant at the crime scene and in connection with the victim's body, and that their own confessions are reliable and genuine. Establishing the individual's state of mind before, during and after the offence, however, is difficult if there is a mental disorder involved. To establish evidence of *mens rea*, the courts have to be satisfied that the defendant understands the difference between right and wrong and that they behaved inappropriately and recklessly. This is where clinicians are important in the assessment of the defendant's level of understanding, cognition, emotional stability and temperament. Furthermore, when police interview suspects with a mental disorder, it is important that procedures under PACE (Police and Criminal Evidence) 1984 are followed, such as having an appropriate adult present to explain and ensure the suspect understands what they are being accused of (see Chapters 14 and 15 for discussion of police interviews of witnesses and suspects respectively).

The concept of blameworthiness or how responsible the defendant is for his or her actions is important in determining the extent of guilt. In the case of defendants with a mental disorder, they can be fully exempted from blame depending on the severity of their illness as decreed under the McNaughton Rules of 1843. They could be partially exempted if diminished responsibility is decided, in which case the charge would be manslaughter instead of murder in the first degree. **McNaughton Rules** are based on a case in 1843, where Daniel McNaughton shot Edward Drummond, the Prime Minister Robert Peel's private secretary. Five days later Drummond died and McNaughton was convicted of his murder. His defence counsel argued that McNaughton felt persecuted by the Tories in his town of Glasgow and this 'compelled' him to act by attempting to assassinate the Prime Minister – but he missed and shot Drummond instead. His defence counsel further argued that McNaughton experienced delusions which prevented him from controlling his behaviour. The prosecution also had medical evidence suggesting he was insane. The trial was stopped by Lord Chief Justice Tindal and a 'special verdict' was given by the jury whereupon McNaughton was moved from Newgate Prison to the State Criminal Lunatic Asylum at Bethlem Hospital under the 1800 Act for the Safe Custody of Insane Persons Charged with Offences. Medical doctors at this time had expanded the concept of insanity and they now were at the helm in determining criminal responsibility. Addressed in the McNaughton Rules and to this very day is the following:

To establish a defence on the ground of insanity it must be clearly proved, that, at the time of committing the act, the party accused was labouring under such a defect of reason from disease of the mind, as not to know the nature and quality of the act he was doing, or if he did know it, that he did not know that what he was doing was wrong.

The House of Lords and the Judges' 'Rules' 1843

Another important organisation is the charity run by the National Association for the Care and Resettlement of Offenders (NACRO). NACRO's main objective is to help offenders accommodate to life outside of prison and to prevent them from reoffending. The help provided is wide ranging depending on a needs basis and this includes the mentally disordered. NACRO (1993) state that:

- those offenders who may be acutely or chronically ill;
- those with neuroses, behavioural or personality disorders;
- those with learning difficulties;
- some who as a function of alcohol and or substance misuse have a mental health problem; and
- any who are suspected of falling into one or other of these groups.

In effect NACRO have similar criteria of mental illness to that stipulated in the MHA of 1983. NACRO have been successful in reducing crime through implementing programmes ranging from the resettlement of ex-prisoners and offenders with mental illness issues, to enabling employment for offenders. NACRO boasted that in 2010–11, over 73,000 people were helped via one of their service provisions. They claimed that over 24,000 children and adolescents stayed crime-free due to their services and that more than 19,000 prisoners were resettled.

Whilst the legal definition of a mental disorder is important for the criminal justice system, it is to psychological assessment that the court defers to. Therefore the psychological definition of a mental disorder is not only informative but often required by the criminal justice system. In the next section we will consider the definition of mental disorder used in psychology and referred to by clinicians.

### Definition of mental disorder: referring to psychology

Clinical psychologists and psychiatrists commonly use the Diagnostic Statistical Manual (DSM-5), which until recently was the DSM-IV-TR that categorised different clinical problems according to five different sections: axis I; II; III; IV and V. Axis I included clinical disorders, such as schizophrenia, whereas axis II housed the personality disorders and mental retardation. This of course has changed since the introduction of DSM-5 in 2013 as the multiaxial system of diagnosis has been discarded, the subdivisions of schizophrenia collapsed and the term mental retardation replaced with intellectual developmental disorder. The International Classification of Diseases (ICD) by the World Health Organization (2011) also adopts a subcategory approach based on defined diagnostic categories. They have a subcategory of mental and behavioural disorders which lists 11 sub-categories such as schizophrenia, schizotypal and delusional disorder, mental retardation and adult personality and behavioural disorders. The DSM-IV-TR and ICD are very similar and DSM-5 less so, but nevertheless still contains more detail regarding the nature of mental disorders than the MHA and NACRO. The clinicians assessing offenders with mental issues for the courts will continue to use ICD and the new DSM-5 but for guidelines within the law reference to the MHA will be made. It is clear that there are some prisoners who have mental illness issues but 78 per cent of prisoners have a personality disorder – in particular APD (see Chapter 7).

There are ten different dimensions of personality disorder (DSM-5 2013): avoidant, dependent, obsessive–compulsive, paranoid, schizoid, schizotypal, histrionic, narcissistic, borderline and antisocial (see Chapter 7). Of particular relevance to criminality is APD (i.e. an individual who lacks empathy, shame or guilt and is destructive, irresponsible, dishonest and manipulative). The underlying traits of an individual diagnosed with antisocial personality disorder (APD) are conducive for criminal activity and in many murder cases the individual convicted has APD. As discussed previously in Chapter 7, psychopathy is categorised as APD in DSM-5 due to the similarity of trait clustering. The most in-depth assessment of the psychopath, however, can be derived from Robert Hare's Psychopathy Checklist – Revised (PCL-R) in 1991. The PCL-R is the standard assessment tool for psychopathy and the trait descriptions used are very similar to those stipulated in DSM-5 (see Chapter 7).

Symptoms of mental disorder can also be confounded by drug use as Eaves, Tien and Wilson (2000) found. Complications derived from substance abuse, such as heavy cannabis or cocaine use, can increase the risk of causing symptoms similar to schizophrenia and mania respectively. This approach arises from a pharmacological model positing that certain drugs have the property to induce paranoia and encourage violent behaviour (Fagan 1990). As there are subgroups of offenders abusing substances to accommodate their criminal lifestyles (Farrington, cited in McCord 1992; Levi 1993; Shover and Honaker 1992), they might be at risk of exhibiting symptoms of mental disorder. Levi (1993) reported that just over a third of drug agency users admitted to committing crime before they initially used drugs compared with 62 per cent and 72 per cent responses from probationers and prisoners respectively. Drug misuse, however, did not significantly increase their frequency of criminality, but instead was an activity undertaken as part of a criminal lifestyle. These findings support a criminal or subculture model (see Chapter 10) stating that drug users tend to be criminally inclined. Alternatively, Hodgins (2008) highlighted the problem of **mentally disordered offenders** using substances such as illicit drugs and alcohol to 'self-medicate' their symptoms which can often lead to further symptoms of schizophrenia for instance. Hence, there are other factors which might complicate the relationship between mental disorder and offending, such as violence expressed as a consequence of drug misuse.

The important question is whether those presenting a mental disorder (even if drug induced) are more likely to commit serious and dangerous offences or is it a subgroup of personality disordered individuals who are responsible for most of these crimes? The next section will consider this in the light of the 'mad, sad or bad' debate addressed by Bottoms (1977).

## Who is represented in prisons: the mad, sad or bad?

If 'mad' refers to offenders with a serious mental disorder, then 'sad' refers to severely depressed and anxious offenders and 'bad' to those with personality disorders. The question is, which of the three are most represented in prison and other forensic institutions? Many researchers have compared different groups of dangerous offenders: the two prominent categories being mental illness and psychopathic disorder. In 1978 a study by Gunn, Robertson, Dell and Way was conducted in two English prisons on 149 prisoners who were assessed for psychiatric problems. They found that 34 per cent (about 51 prisoners) had moderate to severe psychiatric disturbance. Robertson (1981) separated individuals according to whether they were diagnosed as having a psychopathic disorder, a mental illness or a learning disability. Robertson (1981) found that psychopaths committed more offences, received more sentences and spent more time in prison than any of the other cohorts, thus suggesting a criminal predisposition.

Spry (1984) had a slightly different approach by focusing on the rate of offenders referred for psychiatric treatment. Offenders who had committed serious violent crimes among his cohort tended to suffer from schizophrenia: this number was higher than the 1 per cent in the general population for this time. Taylor (1986) reported that two-thirds of lifers in London had a psychiatric disturbance: 9 per cent had schizophrenia, 13 per cent had depression and 33 per cent had a personality disorder. Modestin, and Ammann (1996) studied a cohort of 282 male offenders with schizophrenia and concluded that they were five times more likely to have committed a violent crime than the control group. Häfner and Böker (1982) estimated that five in every 10,000 sufferers with schizophrenia are likely to show violent tendencies. While schizophrenia tends to be high among the mental disorders for violence, the problem lies with individuals failing to take their medication. This is supported by evidence of increased violent behaviour that coincides with acute psychotic episodes and experiences of delusions (Häfner and Böker 1982). Clinicians also claimed that psychotic episodes prevent those with schizophrenia from functioning coherently and being organised and able to plan acts of violence (Krakowsky, Volavka and Brizer 1986).

Studies by Taylor and Gunn (1999) and Singleton, Meltzer and Gatward (1998) suggest that offenders with mental disorders, who commit serious crimes such as homicide, comprise a small number of criminals. Taylor and Gunn (1999) found that the majority of homicides over a 38 year period were not committed by individuals with a mental disturbance. Furthermore, Singleton *et al.* (1998), after interviewing 3,142 prisoners, found that 7 per cent of male prisoners, 10 per cent of males on remand and 14 per cent of female prisoners had a psychotic illness. These figures were small in comparison to the 49 per cent, 63 per cent and 31 per cent respectively who had an antisocial personality disorder. Appleby, Shaw, Ames and McDonnell (1999) found that of the 500 homicides in England and Wales between 1996 and 1997, 44 per cent of the perpetrators responsible had a record of mental disorder, 8 per cent had contact with mental health providers before the offence and 14 per cent were experiencing mental health symptoms during their offences. Added together these figures indicate that 66 per cent of the 500 homicide cases (translating to 330 homicides – of course it must be borne in mind that one murderer might have committed a multitude of murders) were committed by people who had mental health issues, whether active or dormant.

A different approach in Finland was adopted where psychiatric statements taken from offenders were based on the four categories in DSM-III-R: schizophrenic; substance abusers; personality disordered and unconfirmed diagnoses. In terms of planning their crimes, interesting differences of *modus operandi* (i.e. method of operating) existed between schizophrenics and those with a personality disorder. The schizophrenic cohort was more likely to murder using the first thing that comes to hand, i.e. sharp and blunt weapons, which is consistent with an impulsive act with limited planning. They are also more likely to injure relatives during a heightened psychotic episode. Those with a personality disorder (usually APD) were more likely to use guns and resort to violent physical actions like kicking and hitting their victims (Häkkänen and Laajasalo 2006). The use of a gun indicates an element of planning behaviour and their *modus operandi* illustrates an intention to harm someone who is usually a stranger (Häkkänen-Nyholm and Hare 2009). By comparing these two examples it becomes apparent that a guilty mind or *mens rea* is easier to ascertain for offenders exhibiting a personality disorder.

Among the prison population, as many as 50–80 per cent of prisoners have APD (Fine and Kennett 2004). It has been argued that APD is different (although there is much overlap) from psychopathy (see Chapter 7) as measured using Hare's Psychopathy Checklist Revised (PCL-R). Fine and Kennett (2004) claimed that psychopaths represent 30 per cent of inmates in prisons. A 30 per cent prevalence of psychopaths in prison is still high and deserves special consideration. More recently Häkkänen-Nyholm, Repo-Tiihonen, Lindberg, Salenius and Weizmann-Henelius (2009) connected high scores of 26+ on the PCL-R with 56 per cent of 19 sexual homicide offenders. In particular, their scores on the interpersonal and affective dimensions typified the classic psychopath, suggesting they were more prone to lying, and showing superficial charm, manipulative behaviour and deficits of empathy than non-sexual homicide offenders (see Chapter 12).

An important question to ask is whether a mad–bad distinction can be made between offenders with a mental or personality disorder. If those with specific types of mental disorder causing confused thought, such as schizophrenia, are considered to be 'mad', then surely psychopaths who demonstrate *mens rea* can be considered as 'bad'? This distinction is not straight forward as Blackburn (1995) and Fine and Kennett (2004) pointed out. Blackburn (1995) believes that psychopaths can be 'bad' or 'mad' or 'bad and mad'. Fine and Kennett (2004), however, based their acceptance of psychopaths not being 'bad' on the assumption that they do not develop an understanding of what is morally acceptable from what is morally unacceptable. Of relevance to this is the fact that they also fail to develop empathy and it is questionable as to whether they acquire a Theory of Mind (ToM) (see Chapters 4 and 7). Perhaps neurocognitive and brain scan technology can help to clarify the debate.

Using MRI scans, Gordon, Baird and End (2004) were able to demonstrate a significant relationship between reduced volume in the right amygdala of violent criminals and increasing psychopathy scores. Glenn, Raine and Schug (2009) were able to show abnormal amygdala activity using fMRI scanning while psychopaths performed tasks of emotional recognition and moral decision making. Reduced activity in the orbitofrontal cortex region has also been demonstrated in psychopaths (Hu, Vik, Dasher and Fowler 2011). Hu *et al.* (2011) also found the orbitofrontal cortex and amygdala in psychopaths to be impaired. Craig, Catani, Deeley, Latham, *et al.* (2009) concluded that this explains why incarcerated criminal psychopaths in the UK are responsible for committing 50 per cent of serious and dangerous offences. Impaired orbitofrontal cortex and amygdala function explains why psychopaths experience empathy deficits and accounts for their lack of emotional responsiveness towards others (Shamay-Tsoory, Harari, Aharon-Peretz and Levkovitz 2010).

Fine and Kennett (2004) questioned whether we can be so certain that psychopaths are in full control over their behaviour, especially as there is a deficit of moral understanding. The MRI and fMRI scans suggest that there are both structural and functional differences in the brains of criminal psychopaths which are likely factors accounting for their behaviour. Considering their actions from this perspective, it would be difficult to ascertain *mens rea*, just as is the case for those with other mental disorders. Could this potentially mean that criminal psychopaths are 'mad' also? This is a convincing argument were it not for the fact that psychopaths and those with APD tend to plan their actions in advance, suggesting an organised and determined personality that is intact with the exception of not being able to feel what is right from wrong. This in itself does not mean that they are 'bad' but rather that they are different from offenders exhibiting other mental disorders such as schizophrenia.

Offenders with schizophrenia experience delusions courtesy of their condition, which can cause violent tendencies and encourage violent and dangerous behaviours. Academics are increasingly interested in the brains of violent offenders suffering from schizophrenia and have used scanning techniques such as MRI and fMRI to ascertain differences between seriously violent and non-violent schizophrenic offenders. There have been interesting findings – unfortunately, however, many of the studies have methodological flaws. One consistent finding was the reduced volume of the amygdala in schizophrenics who were less violent (committed only one offence as opposed to having a history of offending) had the smallest amygdalae. Those schizophrenics with a history of violence had intermediate amygdalae volumes (Wong, Lumsden, Fenton and Fenwick 1997) and an increased volume of the amygdala was observed in violent offenders (Barkataki, Kumari, Das, Taylor and Sharma 2006). Larger left orbitofrontal grey matter volumes were reported by Hoptman, Volavka, Weiss, Czobor *et al.* in 2005, which were associated with increased levels of aggression. Puri, Counsell, Saeed, Bustos *et al.* (2008) overcame many methodological concerns seen in past studies through the inclusion of patients with confirmed diagnoses of schizophrenia. They used MRI scanning to compare two cohorts of schizophrenic in-patients: serious violent offenders and non-violent non-offenders. Puri *et al.* (2008) found reduced grey matter volume in the cerebellum and supramarginal gyrus regions among the violent offending group. They claimed the supramarginal gyrus might be involved in the processing of language and that the abnormal neural circuiting in this region is responsible for problems of verbal working memory among violent schizophrenic offenders.

Based on brain scanning techniques, it appears that there are fundamental differences in the brain structure and function between criminal psychopaths and violent offenders with schizophrenia. There are common findings concerning the volume of the amygdala and the orbitofrontal cortex between criminal psychopaths and violent offenders exhibiting schizophrenia (although these findings are from studies with methodological concerns – in particular the diagnostic contamination across participants). The differences between criminal psychopaths and violent schizophrenic offenders, however, are distinct and might explain the differences in the nature of the two disorders. Psychopaths, for example, are not deluded as a consequence of their condition but instead in their interpretation of the world – a world where empathy does not figure in their calculation of what is appropriate behaviour. Does this imply that they are **'mad' or 'bad'**? Blackburn might be correct in assuming that they can be 'mad', 'bad' or 'mad and bad'. In Box 11.5 are some examples of murderers who have killed their victims in different ways – but are they 'mad', 'bad' or 'bad and mad'?

## Box 11.5

### Examples of murderers – who is 'mad', 'bad' or 'mad and bad'?

- John Wayne Gacy worked for the Chamber of Commerce but in his spare time entertained at children's birthday parties as Pogo the Clown. He raped, tortured and murdered 32 young boys at his home, who were then buried in the cellar. He was considered an intelligent and popular man who socialised in political circles.
- 'Moors Murderer' Ian Brady, in collaboration with his accomplice, Myra Hindley, murdered five children between 10 and 17 years of age during 1963 to 1965. He humiliated, tortured, raped and murdered his victims in his home in the Greater Manchester area. He made tape recordings of his victims' ordeals. He showed no remorse at his trial. He tortured animals and had a past history of criminal behaviour.
- Rahan Arshad murdered his wife Uzma and three children by beating them to death using a rounders bat. In court his defence claimed he was motivated by jealousy after discovering his wife had an affair. He told the court, however, that his wife had bludgeoned their children and on discovering this he had killed her. The jury did not believe this story and he was found guilty of murdering four people in 2007. He beat his wife to death in the bedroom and then took his sleeping children downstairs and killed them. The Judge said, 'There is no suggestion of mental illness on your part. Life imprisonment in your case means life.'
- Mark Martin, known as the 'Sneinton Strangler', killed three homeless women between December 2004 and January 2005 by strangulation and then set fire to the buildings where he had left his victims. He was found guilty in 2006. Mr. Justice Butterfield told the 26 year old: 'The facts of these crimes are so horrific and the level of offending is so serious, you must be kept in prison for the rest of your life. These matters were committed by you because you positively enjoyed killing, taking the wholly innocent lives of these three young women for your own perverted gratification. You have not shown a moment of remorse. You have revelled in what you did, glorifying the macabre details of these senseless, brutal and callous killings.'
- Mark Hobson was convicted in 2005 for killing two twins and an elderly couple. These murders were shown to be premeditated as revealed from notes he had made detailing how he planned to commit the murders. These notes included details such as a shopping list for big bin liners, tape, tie-wraps, fly spray and air freshener. He pleaded guilty and was sentenced to life imprisonment with a proviso that he should

never be released. It was revealed at his trial that he was a heroin addict and an alcoholic, consuming as many as 20 pints per day.

- Dennis Nilsen, also known as the 'Muswell Hill Murderer' and the 'Kindly Killer', killed at least 15 men in his North London home. He strangled and drowned his victims in buckets of water during the night. The corpses of his victims were kept for several months, usually under the floorboards where he would later relive his sexual experiences through necrophilia.
- Peter Sutcliffe, known as the 'Yorkshire Ripper', murdered 13 prostitutes during the 1970s. He killed his victims by a blow to the head using hammers taken from the crime scenes. There was no evidence to suggest that the motive for killing was sexual. When in court, he claimed he was 'on a mission from God' to kill prostitutes. He was sentenced in 1981 to life imprisonment but was later transferred to Broadmoor on the grounds of a schizophrenic diagnosis.
- Anthony Arkwright was convicted in 1989 for three murders. He mutilated his victims during a two day killing spree in 1988. Arkwright stabbed one of his victims 70 times as a punishment for trying to scrounge cigarettes from him. Arkwright 'gouged out his eyeballs and placed unlit cigarettes in the sockets, in his ears, up his nostril and in his mouth'. Arkwright was considered to be an evil fantasist claiming that he will be as infamous as Jack the Ripper one day.
- Gu Kailai murdered British businessman Neil Heywood using poison in 2011 after Heywood demanded payment for an unsuccessful business venture. Kailai took him to Chongqing and poisoned him when he was in a drunken stupor. Kailai was found guilty of his murder in 2012 but escaped the death penalty. Kailai claimed she suffered from a variety of problems including anxiety and depression, insomnia and paranoia for which she was taking a cocktail of medications (Patranobis 2012).

Despite the difficulties of defining dangerousness and distinguishing dangerous offenders as 'mad' or 'bad', it is possible to make intuitive distinctions. Of the examples in Box 11.5, it is possible to separate offenders with a mental disorder such as schizophrenia from those with a personality disorder such as criminal psychopathy. Offenders clearly meeting the criteria for psychopathy are John Wayne Gacy, Ian Brady, Rahan Arshad and Mark Martin, unlike Peter Sutcliffe who suffers from schizophrenia and Mark Hobson who is drug and alcohol addicted. It could be argued that Dennis Nilsen and Anthony Arkwright have other mental issues given the nature of Nilsen's sexual activities and Arkwright's deluded beliefs. Gu Kailai suffered from depression and anxiety and took a cocktail of drugs to treat these symptoms – all contributory factors to her experiences of paranoia.

Dangerousness and mental disorders are assessed by clinical practitioners who have experience of diagnosing forensic and non-forensic in- and out-patients.

There are different approaches of assessing dangerous offenders who exhibit mental disorders and some of these approaches are more successful than others. In the next section assessment of dangerousness and the risk of violence and reoffending will be evaluated in terms of accurate prediction.

## How is dangerousness and risk of reoffending assessed?

Predicting which offenders will pose a danger to society, and therefore labelling them as dangerous, involves two considerations: deciding who will behave violently or aggressively and identifying situations and triggers that incite violent behaviour in specific individuals (Hodgins 1997). This equates to the identification of an individual with a dangerous predisposition and the external factors that trigger the individual to behave dangerously towards others.

NHS England (2013) described the multidisciplinary approach adopted in the UK (albeit with slight variations across Scotland, Wales and Northern Ireland) where professionals from different backgrounds contribute towards the management of secure services. This enables mental nursing staff, forensic psychologists and psychiatrists, clinical psychologists and other relevant professionals to provide a 'care pathway' for offenders considered to be dangerous and at risk. This operates under the Care Programme Approach and involves all stages within the criminal justice system such as referral, assessment and pre-assessment, admission, care and treatment, a forensic care pathway (which facilitates discharge) and a transition care plan (i.e. in prison or back in the community). As we have seen earlier the CJA 2003 defines dangerousness within a legal frame, but has also introduced legislation directing clinical practice. This legislation involves the provision of evidence to the courts regarding an offender's level of risk and future dangerousness. For example, a range of professionals (the same, most likely, as those mentioned above) are a part of the Offender Assessment System (OASys). The OASys uses a variety of assessments and measures to categorise offenders according to different levels of reconviction risk: low, medium or high. A similar scale is used in the assessment of risk of serious harm (i.e. dangerousness): low, medium, high or very high. There is ambiguity, however, as to how these levels of risk translate to categories of dangerousness used by the CJA.

In England and Wales special teams known as Youth Offending Teams (YOTs) help children who are in trouble with the law. These children often have a multitude of needs and difficulties which YOTs assess using ASSET. ASSET is a structured assessment tool designed to obtain information which can be used to inform court reports and appropriate treatment interventions. This also provides information concerning the risk of a young offender reoffending in the future; risk of serious harm and their current needs. The National Standards for Youth Justice (2000) stipulated that ASSET be used on all young offenders whether this be to inform a court report, bail, supervision, community disposal, review, custodial sentencing or transference to the community (Youth Justice Board 2000). ASSET involves interviewing the young offender (and family members) using a set of guidelines. Once all the information is collected, it is rated by considering the extent of relatedness occurring between issues raised and the probability of reoffending. A scale from 0–4 is used where '0' means 'not associated at all' and '4' means 'very strongly associated'. It is hoped by YOTs that ASSET will provide long-term information about different types of young offender thereby increasing our knowledge of all young offenders from all types of background and ethnicity.

Assessment of dangerousness and risk of reoffending is normally undertaken by a clinician (who could be a forensic psychologist, forensic psychiatrist or forensic nurse) using primarily one of two approaches: clinical prediction and statistical or actuarial data.

## Clinical prediction

Clinicians are usually qualified psychiatrists or psychologists specialising in the forensic field. They assess and treat offenders and provide tailored intervention programmes for individuals to follow. These programmes are based on the individual and situational factors that influence dangerous behaviour and how such individual and situational factors impact on one another (Megargee 1976). In addition to following clinical protocol, the clinician makes use of acquired knowledge and experience from years of dealing with similar cases – 'a clinical lore'. Clinicians also refer to information concerning the offender's current offence, criminal record and history of criminality and other factors including social and family background and any childhood anomalies. Cooper and Werner (1990) found that clinicians use information about the nature of the offence (i.e. was there any violence?) and any other relevant details as reliable predictors of dangerousness.

As the relationship between clinician and offender is subject to confidentiality in the same way as it is between therapist and client generally, there are no stipulations in law stating that the clinician is obliged to inform police or service providers of an offender's intention to cause harm to a targeted person. This remains the case in the UK, although in the US since the **Tarasoff Decision Rules** of 1976, clinicians are obliged to detain their clients if they suspect they might behave violently at a future date. Failure to detain their client, who then subsequently commits a violent act towards another individual, will result in the clinician's liability. The Tarasoff Decision Rules came about because of the murder of Tatiana Tarasoff by Prosenjit Poddar. Poddar was infatuated with Tarasoff but his feelings were unrequited so he told his therapist he was going to kill her. The therapist informed the police of Poddar's intention and said the following:

> been threatening to kill an unnamed girl . . . intends to . . . buy a gun and
> . . . to kill the girl. He . . . has alluded strongly to the compulsion to 'get
> even with', and 'hurt' the girl . . . Mr. Poddar should be committed for

observation in a mental hospital. I request the assistance of your department in this matter (Winslade and Ross, 1983 p. 53).

The police did interview Poddar but were reassured that he would stay away from Tarasoff. This promise was not kept and Poddar purchased a gun and murdered Tarasoff. Monahan (1981) stated the importance of having the client's and society's interests balanced, and ensuring that this occurs should be part of the clinician's job description. In the UK there is no equivalent of the **Tarasoff Decision Rules**; however, Dolan (2004) noted that despite disclosure of confidential information being a breach of confidence, there are three circumstances where release of information is upheld: client gives consent; law requests it via a court order; or it is of public interest. The nature of information a client can consent to disclosing, however, is limited to physical health issues. No statute law exists demanding that confidential client information be passed to the police even if it were to help the investigation of a serious crime. If, however, a clinician was privy to confidential information that would facilitate police investigation and be in the public interest, then breaching their confidentiality obligation to their client is acceptable.

Court orders can subpoena clinicians to disclose and present confidential client information without litigation for breaching their obligation to their clients. Confidential information deemed to be in the public interest can be disclosed provided it is disclosed to the appropriate person and is necessary for the prevention of any danger or serious harm to others. Disclosure of confidential information under such circumstances is permitted by the UK General Medical Council Guidelines (GMCG) when public interest demands it. Hence, this implies that the disclosure of information is in the interest of society per se rather than any identifiable individual(s). In Box 11.6 is the interesting case of W v. Edgell, which highlights the latter point regarding confidential disclosure of information.

## Box 11.6

### W v. Edgell 1990

Dr Edgell, a psychiatrist, was treating a detained patient known as W. He was asked to prepare a report for a Mental Health Tribunal regarding the release of W. Dr Edgell included confidential information regarding his patient's level of dangerousness that was damning but which he felt the team treating W should be privy to. This information was passed on to W's Medical Officer, but W had not been asked if he consented to the disclosure of such personal information which he had told Dr Edgell in confidence. W took Dr Edgell to the Court of Appeal but his claim was dismissed on the grounds that Dr Edgell had acted in accordance with the

GMCG and weighed the issue of client confidentiality versus public interest in a professional manner. Furthermore, Dr Edgell was aware of information that would be withheld at the tribunal hearing which could result in W's freedom even though he was still a danger to society. W had been convicted of manslaughter of five of his neighbours. He was diagnosed as having paranoid schizophrenia, hence why he was detained in a special hospital under a restriction order. After serving ten years his solicitor approached Dr Edgell to write a report supporting his release. His report was initially suppressed but eventually Dr Edgell managed to submit it to the Home Office.

In 1993 the GMC issued guidelines on the issue of confidentiality concerning child abuse. In their guidelines they stated concern for cases of child abuse where the client might be incapable of providing or withholding consent of disclosure. In a situation where the doctor believes the client might be experiencing abuse, it is important to prioritise the client's interest and disclose information to an appropriate person such as a police officer or social worker. Clinical decision making can be dependent upon a progression of simple questions that inform the clinician of the appropriate action to take. Questions can pertain to the immediacy and urgency of threat or serious danger the client poses to a targeted individual, group of individuals or to a system or process within society. Depending on the answers to these questions, the clinician can decide whether to inform the police or if involuntary hospitalisation is necessary. This method of approach arms the clinician with a risk assessment based on years of experience and clinical subjectivity.

Assessing dangerousness is difficult when an individual has not yet committed a crime; however, assessing an offender can be just as tricky. In the case of dangerous offenders, clinicians take account of past criminal conduct and perform a personal assessment based on interviews. Sometimes clinicians make use of assessment scales and inventories to ascertain the level of dangerousness and the state of mental health and personality disposition in their clients. This information is used to help clinicians make decisions about their clients' state of mind which can ultimately be informative to police and social workers if deemed to be of public interest. Often this link implies a relationship between mental disorder and an inclination towards criminality. While this should not be assumed, statistics do suggest that a third of dangerous offenders have mental issues. For instance, in a survey conducted in England and Wales in 2005/6, it was shown that of 1,435 prisoners, 12 per cent had a mental disorder and 20 per cent needed help with emotional and mental health issues (Ministry of Justice 2010). On the basis of their assessment, clinicians can make decisions regarding the best direction of approach for their clients – whether treatment will be effective or if incarceration is necessary for the protection of the public.

Clinicians, however, do not always make correct judgements about their clients' future likelihood of dangerous behaviour and therefore being a threat to the public (Monahan, Steadman, Silver, Appelbaum *et al.* 2001). This has serious legal, political and moral implications, such as what level of risk justifies freedom or detainment? More importantly what is being predicted in assessments of dangerousness by clinicians? As long as this remains a vague concept, clinicians will make mistakes. Peay (2002) claimed that accurate prediction of dangerousness is a myth of the scientific expert – 65 per cent of dangerous offenders have been predicted falsely. Peay noted that there are two types of error commonly made by clinicians – false positives (FPs) and false negatives (FNs). A FP error occurs when an offender is detained but does not demonstrate any behavioural indicators of dangerousness or which could be used to predict future dangerous behaviour. FNs are a more serious type of error where offenders considered to be harmless are released into the community but later reoffend. If professionals detain offenders for the purpose of protecting the public when they have served their time in prison, and the evidence suggests they are no longer a danger, then surely this contravenes the offender's Civil Rights. Alternatively, once an offender serves his sentence and is released on the grounds of posing no danger to society but then commits another murder, then this FN error of judgement has cost someone their life. Good assessment strategies lower the likelihood of FN and FP errors while increasing the frequency of true-negative (TN) and true-positive (TP) hits.

The difficulties involved with predicting who is at risk of committing a dangerous act is best illustrated through the use of case examples (see Box 11.7). To demonstrate the scale of difficulty involved with predicting future dangerous behaviour, consider the following cases in Box 11.7. Do these individuals pose any danger to society? Should they be allowed to reside in the community?

## Box 11.7

### Case studies of individuals who might be dangerous

Case A was sent to Broadmoor in 1962 for poisoning his father. He also poisoned his stepmother who died. Eight years later he was conditionally discharged. Is he likely to kill anyone?

Case B ran a series of boys clubs but these were in decline because he was suspected of being a paedophile – this discouraged parents from sending their children to his boy clubs. He always had a fascination with firearms and the desire to control others, especially boys. Is he likely to kill anyone?

Case C was detained for arson and assault and released from Broadmoor in 1983. Previous offences included indecent phone calls and indecent assault on a female. Is he likely to kill anyone?

Case D worked in an old people's nursing home. She would often say to her colleague that many of these people do not know whether it's night or day and putting them out of their misery would be an act of mercy. Is she likely to kill anyone?

In 1978, Case E attempted to murder his girlfriend, Kim Hill, after she wanted to end their relationship. He was sentenced to seven years imprisonment but served less than half for grievous bodily harm to Hill's mother and the attempted murder of Kim Hill. He married Pamela Lomax in 1986 with whom he had children – she later claimed he was controlling and was glad when he left her. In 1991 he was given a conditional discharge for head-butting a colleague. Is he likely to kill anyone?

What of the five cases in Box 11.7? The correct answer is that all five cases commit murder. In the case of Graham Young (Case A) he found employment in a warehouse storing chemicals for photographic development. Despite supervision by a probation officer and a psychiatrist, he murders three colleagues using thallium. Professionals missed his obsession with poison. Thomas Hamilton (Case B) became infamously known as the 'Dunblane Primary School Killer'. He shot dead 16 children and one teacher and wounded a further 10 children and three teachers. His obsession with guns was missed but predicting his violence would have been difficult because he was unknown to the police and had no prior criminal record. There were, however, indications of paedophilia which might explain his target choice of children at school. In 1986 (three years after his release from Broadmoor), Daniel Mudd (Case C) killed a resident at the mental aftercare hostel where he resided. At the time of his release it was the opinion of medical professionals that he remained a danger to society and would reoffend.

Beverly Allitt (Case D) left her job at the old people's nursing home and was employed by Grantham and Kesteven General Hospital in the children's ward. While in her care as a nurse between February and April 1991, three children and a baby died. Medical staff at the children's ward found these deaths inexplicable as all patients were recovering successfully from their illnesses. Investigation of the staff working at the time of these deaths (and nine other attempted murders) alluded to Allitt who was the nurse in charge. Allitt's past employment background had been inappropriately vetted. Case E was that of Mick Philpott who murdered six of his children in a fire he started in 2012, and was charged with murder. He (and his wife and neighbour) deliberately started a fire in their home using petrol and igniting it, resulting in the deaths of his children who were asleep in bed. Philpott hatched a plan whereby he would save his children and be acclaimed status as a hero, but it went wrong when he failed to evacuate the children who consequently died in the blaze. He lied about arson and appealed to the public to help police find the culprit. This pretence was maintained even after police became suspicious of his faked emotions. According to Glenn Wilson (2013), Mick Philpott is a 'psychopath and exhibitionist with an anti-social personality disorder'. Clearly he is a dangerous man and, although he served time in prison, his level of dangerousness and likelihood of recidivism was high but remained undetected. Other factors indicative of a psychopath are lifestyle choices such as having many children (17 from different women), being controlling of them by use of violence, and living off state benefits and in a council house – very much a parasitic lifestyle often seen in psychopaths. It is likely that he would offend again if released from prison, which makes him a dangerous individual.

These cases demonstrate the difficulty of predicting who is likely to be a danger to society and at risk of committing murder. It is not surprising that it is difficult to predict dangerousness given that the concept is riddled with misinterpretation and is ambiguously defined. An important question to ask is 'what are professionals assessing?' Is the person dangerous or is the act that they committed dangerous?

Steadman and Cocozza (1974) provided clinical experimental evidence highlighting the unreliability of predicting dangerousness. A legal case known as Baxstrom v. Herold (1966) became key in showing the frequency with which FP errors are made. Baxstrom was sentenced to three years in prison for committing an assault. Whilst in prison, he and many others were assessed as mentally disordered and were transferred to a civilian psychiatric hospital. What followed was a moral outcry and a panicked response from the public who were concerned about these offenders being released from maximum security mental hospitals to civilian psychiatric institutions. In total 1,000 prisoners were transferred to civilian psychiatric hospitals and out of the 101 who were released into the community only three returned to a high-security prison. Of the remaining 98 who were released into the community, only 14 behaved violently. Cocozza and Steadman (1978) did a three year follow up of 257 patients considered incompetent to attend court, 154 of whom were assessed as dangerous by psychiatrists and 103 who were not. Cocozza and Steadman found that 14 per cent of those considered dangerous and 16 per cent not declared as dangerous were arrested for committing violent crime: there was no significant difference in recidivism rates between the two groups. According to Monahan (1981) psychiatrists tend to over-predict dangerousness and their accuracy is low – they get it right for one in three predictions. With the advent of the ideology of 'normalisation' in the 1980s where patients were transferred from institutions to half-way houses and then the community, predicting dangerousness became an important issue. Glover (1999) reminds us that while the rights of individuals should be valued, we should never oversee the public's right to protection.

Away from the subjective clinical assessments, clinical prediction based on scale and inventory testing and the use of actuarial or statistical methods can be more effective in predicting future dangerous behaviour. Different scales and inventories used help practitioners predict recidivism rates for particular offences. The Psychopathy Checklist (PCL-R) introduced by Hare (1991) is an effective measure for the prediction of violent reoffending and in the assessment of psychopaths, whereas Andrews and Bonta's (2006) revised Level of Service Inventory (LSI–R) offers a reliable assessment of deviancy and rule violation in the prediction of criminality. Other measures such as the Static–2002 devised by Hanson and Thornton (2003), uses factors about the offender which cannot be changed through therapeutic intervention (such as age, sex and criminal background) to produce a total score. This score is judged against five standardised categories of risk for reoffending found to be effective in the prediction of violent and sexual crimes (see Chapters 4, 7 and 8).

The Historical-Clinical-Risk Management-20 (HCR-20) is used to assess the risk of violence in individuals from forensic and civil, institutional or community-based settings. The HCR-20 was designed by Webster, Douglas, Eaves and Hart (1997) as part of the Structured Professional Judgement (SPJ) model of violence risk assessment, and has since been translated into 16 languages and used widely in many countries by forensic, mental health and criminal justice agencies (i.e. the UK, Australia, Canada, New Zealand and the US). Based on 20 risk factors spanning three sub-scales – historical, clinical and risk management – the HCR-20 is used to inform practitioners of appropriate management strategies and treatments for reducing the risk of violent behaviour (see Box 11.8).

---

## Box 11.8

### Sub-Scales' Items in the HCR-20 Risk Assessment Scheme

**Historical Scale**

1 Previous Violence
2 Young Age at First Violent Incident
3 Relationship Instability
4 Employment Problems
5 Substance Use Problems
6 Major Mental Illness
7 Psychopathy
8 Early Maladjustment
9 Personality Disorder
10 Prior Supervision Failure

**Clinical Scale**

1 Lack of Insight
2 Negative Attitudes
3 Active Symptoms of Major Mental Illness
4 Impulsivity
5 Unresponsive to Treatment

**Risk Management Scale**

1 Plans Lack Feasibility
2 Exposure to Destabilisers
3 Lack of Personal Support
4 Noncompliance with Remediation Attempts
5 Stress

Most clinical effectiveness studies of the HCR-20 were conducted in the US; however, more recently there have been numerous small-scale studies undertaken in the UK (Doyle and Dolan 2006; Grevatt, Thomas-Peter and Hughes 2004). The prediction of future violent behaviour and the probability of reoffending among 887 male offenders two years after release from medium secure units were investigated using the HCR-20 (Gray, Taylor and Snowden 2008). Gray *et al.* (2008) found the risk management and historical sub-scales to be particularly effective predictors, and concluded that the HCR-20 is a useful assessment tool in ascertaining the likelihood of recidivism: however, the clinical sub-scale fared less well.

Risk assessments have also been carried out by the Probation Service using the Offender Group Reconviction Scale (OGRS) by Copas and Marshall (1998). This uses seven items of information to generate a risk score of reconviction: gender; present age; age of first conviction; number of previous offences; number of previous custodial sentences; presence or absence of a custodial sentence as a youth; and the type of current offence. A total score is obtained which represents the percentage of offenders with any given characteristic who are likely to be reconvicted within two years. OGRS-2, introduced in 1999, only slightly improved risk calculation by including social background factors.

Even though these scales and inventories have reasonably good success rates of prediction, they fail to predict all types of crime. Pfohl (1978, 1979) claimed that psychiatric models on the whole have a poor record for the successful assessment and prediction of dangerousness and that instead the employment of behavioural approaches emphasising an individual's past would fare better. It is, in part, for this reason that actuarial or statistical predictions are used as reliable indicators for dangerousness and recidivism.

### Actuarial or statistical methods

Actuarial or statistical methods are used for the identification of factors that reliably predict dangerous individuals. Factors that successfully and reliably predict dangerousness tend to relate to an individual's past behaviour. The methodological approach involves grouping individuals according to their similarities, such as for example, the nature of crime committed or the onset of criminal behaviour. By considering different groups and the factors these have in common, it is possible to determine the factors responsible in the prediction of high and low risk reoffenders that pose a danger to society. In Chapter 4 the different **risk** and **protective factors** that either encourage or prevent criminal behaviour were considered. Of particular importance to actuarial or statistical methods is the need to find risk factors that are common to dangerous and violent offenders. Statistical prediction therefore is based on the premise that an offender who has the same factors as other offenders is likely to behave in the same way.

According to Palmer (2001), there are two types of factors that can be used to predict recidivism: static and dynamic. Static factors refer to a multitude of variables that cannot be changed in any way like for example, an individual's offence record and history, family background and age. Alternatively, dynamic factors can be changed through different means of intervention. An individual's social and psychological circumstances can be altered through intervention and life experiences such that changes occur to attitudes held, friendships made, self-control and maintaining legitimate employment, all of which are effective variables for reducing the need to offend. Blackburn (2000) classified **risk factors** into four types:

- Historical risk factors relate to offence history and any life-time patterns of violent behaviours.
- Dispositional risk factors, cognitive and emotional attributes of the individual are highlighted as important indices of how an offender reacts to social situations and tries to solve problems.
- Clinical risk factors include a host of mental disorders that could effectively be linked to violent behaviour – the problem here of course is that mental disorder can only be used as a measure of co-variance and not necessarily a predictor of violent behaviour.
- Personality disorder is separated from mental disorder and of particular interest to criminal conduct would be APD (see Chapter 7).

Further factors and classifications have been considered by Gannon, Beech and Ward (2008). They referred to functional assessments used for the identification of 'dynamic risk factors' that led to the offence – these include decisions made and the contributing thoughts and feelings and actions that follow as a consequence (see Chapter 5).

Whereas actuarial assessments focus on statistical analysis of offence history and risk of reconviction, dynamic risk assessments consider factors open to change as a consequence of life experience and therapeutic intervention. Gendreau, Little and Goggin (1996) grouped both social and psychological factors in a meta-analysis using data from 131 studies – this produced a total of 1,141 correlations with recidivism. They found that robust predictors were criminal history, criminogenic needs and antisocial behaviour and, static factors like age (see Chapter 10) and gender (see also Chapter 9) and family background (see Chapter 4). Factors such as intelligence and socio-economic status were less effective as predictors. Andrews and Bonta (2003) argued that criminogenic needs, involving a criminal lifestyle, lend itself to criminal social networks and antisocial attitudes (see Chapter 5). These present as successful measures in the determination of treatment intervention. Howells and Day (2007) agree that successful interventions are those based on the needs and characteristics of each individual offender. The reason why interventions which address criminogenic needs are more successful at reforming an offender relates to the fact that these are a part of dynamic factors that lend themselves to change. It is easier to alter an offender's antisocial attitudes and antisocial peer associations than it is to change a static factor. Moreover, criminogenic needs are highly correlated with criminal behaviour. Latessa and Lowenkamp (2005) demonstrated the importance of addressing criminogenic needs in treatment programmes. If four to six criminogenic needs are targeted in treatment programmes, recidivism can be reduced by 30 per cent. They argued that a combination of criminogenic needs have a cumulative effect on the risk of offending which is why it is important to target more than one factor. Latessa and Lowenkamp (2005) said, 'Remember, "what" you target for change is important, as is the density of those targets around crime producing needs' (p. 16).

The underlying ethos of prediction studies is to find the more reliable and effective risk factors that minimise errors and maximise the number of hits. The assessment and identification of criminogenic needs, for instance, in many ways leads to more successful outcomes in terms of both error reduction and helping an offender turn his or her life round. By achieving a reduction in the number of errors made and an increase in the frequency of correct evaluations, then issues of Civil Rights of the offender and public safety are addressed in a balanced way. The best way of illustrating how predictor factors operate is by the following example. Suppose the predictor factor when present correlates with committing a serious offence (its presence is denoted by '+') but when absent correlates with not committing a serious offence (its absence is denoted by '-'). As regards to the decision of detainment or release, those who exhibit the predictor are more likely to be detained than those who do not have the predictor. A desirable predictor is one which maximises the number of correct hits and minimises the frequency of errors. This translates to a TP being correctly predicted by the predictor – in other words, making the right decision. A TN is also a correct prediction that occurs as a consequence of the absence of the predictor coinciding with the absence of recidivism. A FP, however, is to be avoided as the presence of the predictor in this case coincides with an absence of recidivism (the Baxstrom case illustrates this type of error). The most costly error made by the predictor variable is the FN. As the predictor is absent, the offender is released into the community and reoffends.

It would seem that a high FN rate is undesirable from society's point of view, as many potentially dangerous offenders are released, and a FP is undesirable from a civil liberties perspective since many potentially safe offenders are detained unfairly. A good predictor variable predicts beyond chance level alone. Meehl and Rosen (1955) elaborated by saying that the predictor must not only correlate highly with the criterion (i.e. recidivism and committing a serious offence) but with the base rate (i.e. the frequency of the criterion in the population considered). Blackburn (1997) explained this well, by supposing that a predictor is present in 40 out of 50 recidivists but absent in 40 out of 50 non-recidivists – this would mean that the base rate of reoffending is 50 per cent and the predictor would perform at an accuracy of 80 per cent.

The 50 per cent figure is calculated by the fact that 50 out of 100 reoffend and for the 80 per cent accuracy value, the predictor in its presence and absence is getting it right in 40 + 40 times out of 100 respectively. Furthermore, the FP is calculated at 20 per cent using the equation $(10 \div 40) + 10$ and the FN at 20 per cent using $(10 \div 40) + 10$. Hence, it can be said that there is a probability of 0.8 of recidivism when the predictor is present and likewise the same for non-recidivism. In effect the base rate figure can be different depending on the number of times the presence and absence of the predictor correctly predicts the criterion (recidivism versus non-recidivism).

Predicting dangerousness is difficult and this is borne out by the errors of judgement in clinical assessment. Often dangerousness is used as a criterion in the assessment of murderers and serial killers (see Chapter 12) and other forms of violent behaviour, but is rarely used as a factor in assessing terrorists. Terrorism is classified as a dangerous criminal act using violence and terror to force governments into submission. But what of the individuals carrying out terrorist acts – are they more likely to be 'bad' or 'mad' (see Box 11.9)?

## Box 11.9

### Terrorism and suicide bombings are dangerous: are the perpetrators 'bad' or 'mad'?

Despite the view that acts of terrorism are evil there is little research to suggest that terrorists are psychologically disturbed, although Horgan (2003) alluded to there being a parallel between terrorist and psychopathic behaviour (i.e. apparent lack of empathy for victims). This makes sense when the extent of planning and organisation involved in the execution of terrorist operations is considered – an individual who is mentally disturbed would be a liability (Horgan 2005; Taylor 1988). Taylor and Quayle (1994) stated that, 'it may be inappropriate to think of the terrorist as mentally ill in conventional terms' (p.92). Taylor and Quayle (1994) claimed that terrorists have no specific psychological qualities separating them from the general population – after all terrorists are recruited from the general population. They pointed out that terrorists can be compared to people sharing the same career but not necessarily having common psychological traits. The acts of terrorism are perceived as dangerous and of extreme violence which is why they are considered as 'mad' by some researchers; however, McCauley (1991) claimed that terrorists are no more likely to suffer from a psychopathology or personality disorder. But the remaining question is, if they are no different from non-terrorists then why do they commit multi-murder? One explanation comes from the notion of group allegiance, which is suggested in what the lifestyle of a terrorist entails –

a dutiful soldier who is part of a group (McCauley and Moskalenko 2008). This allows the terrorist to alienate themselves from mainstream values and norms, and to rationalise their behaviour as legitimate (Lyons and Harbinson 1979), thereby serving a 'nationalistic duty rather than as freelancing criminals' (Bandura 2003, p.130). Hence, Wood and Alleyne (2010) considered terrorists as being driven by rational forces instead of psychopathology which fitted well with group membership ideology.

Long (1990) suggested that terrorists tend to have common traits such as risk taking, low self-esteem and engaging in fast-paced activity. According to Long (1990), terrorists tend to be 'stimulus hunters who are attracted to situations involving stress and who quickly become bored with inactivity'. Long (1990) further stated that for some researchers, terrorists are neurotic or psychopathic and yet for others they can be understood by their cultural, political and economic environment. Freedman (2002) compared the mentality of serial killers with terrorists and noted an obvious difference – serial killers stalked and selected victims on a one-by-one basis whereas terrorists targeted governments and chosen nations to make their philosophy known to as many people as possible by threatening only a few. Although serial killers often experience childhood abuse, brain trauma and a host of other biological factors, there is no evidence available to suggest that terrorists were also subjected to these experiences. In 2013, Vincent Egan reviewed Roger Griffin's book *Terrorist's Creed: Fanatical Violence and the Human Need for Meaning* for *The Psychologist*, which made it clear that to understand the terrorist, psychologists need to avoid the oversimplification of cognitive, neuroscientific and personality analysis. Griffin (2012) perceives terrorists as 'idealist conservatives reacting violently to their way of life (and/or ideology) being threatened by the forces of modernisation' (Egan 2013, p. 226). Terrorists refuse to conform and succumb to change and would rather defend their existing cultural and ideological ways. They perceive individuals who conform to the new ways as traitors, which explains why bombs are often targeted at communal areas where 'traitors' operate – hence shopping precincts and train stations (Griffin 2012).

What of the suicide bomber? Grimland, Apter and Kerkhof (2006) considered non-psychological and psychological approaches to understanding the suicide bomber – this involved historical and cultural approaches. They claimed that to understand and prevent suicide bombing, group dynamic indoctrination coupled with political ideology and religion, nationalism and cultural traditions are crucial factors. Grimland *et al.* perceived suicide as an instrument of war and not a facet of psychopathology. Suicide bombing is used as a weapon to achieve the objective of killing as many people as possible, and for this reason the mission is accomplished. Pape (2003) described the suicide bomber as being part of a strategy to coerce and force a government to change national policy. In the case of Palestinian suicide bombers, Pape argued that by killing Israeli citizens the Government will concede the rights to the West Bank and Gaza Strip. Pape also argued that suicide attacks are strategically and logically planned as they take note of the exact timing of events and the staging of political events – hence, this is more a sign of an organised individual rather than a psychopathological one. Huson (1999) alluded to a number of factors having a contributory effect on why an individual chooses to become a suicide bomber: political, economic, social and biological. Some psychologists, however, believe that they have a personality disorder, but again as is the case with terrorists, there is no evidence to substantiate this. A common factor linking suicide bombers, however, is their need to be involved in a group which suggests a desire to be accepted. This fits with a low self-esteem and a mentality to be persuaded by the group's norms and values and the group leader (Bell 2013). Bell (2013) also alluded to there being an intense hatred towards the targeted enemy.

As rightly pointed out by criminologists, Sandra Walklate (2011), 'terrorism itself is not a singular, coherent concept' (p. 209). One way to envisage terrorism is to consider a continuum of terrorism, beginning with national problems progressing to extremism (i.e. animal rights) followed by global threats. In the case of the UK, national problems could be in the guise of problems occurring in Northern Ireland. Criminologists have focused on old and new forms of terrorism, helping to provide some insight to the organisations involved, who they are, what they want and the weaponry used to achieve their objectives (Walklate 2011). Walklate claims that despite the simplicity of the categorisation of terrorism, it does provide a quick reference to the ways in which terrorism has modernised in keeping with technological advancement. Walklate (2011) further asks why criminologists should be interested in terrorism and provides a series of issues impacting on the definition of terrorism:

- What is crime? (Does it include international law breaking?)
- Who can be a criminal? (Individuals or governments?)
- By what processes are they identified as criminal? (. . . powerful . . . exempt?)
- Who is the victim (Individuals or states?)
- What does the 'fear of crime' mean? What are people afraid of and when?' (p.210).

These questions are important and link back to issues addressed in Chapters 1 and 2. In common with dangerousness, the focus has become levelled at how to detect and prevent a terrorist attack – risk-oriented thinking. O'Malley (2010) focuses on risk by adopting the notions of structural regulation and self-management (macroform and microform respectively). Both macroform and microform assessments of risk influence the lives of many people – even on personal decisions concerning travel. Hence, risk–oriented thinking is an important impact terrorism has had on society and the individual.

The US Psychology of Terrorism Initiative Director Randy Borum (2004) outlined the many different explanations of the terrorist drawn from psychological theory:

- Instinct theory (psychoanalytic and ethological (i.e. attachment)) – see Chapters 8 and 4 respectively;
- Drive theory (frustration–aggression hypothesis proposes that aggression always follows the experience of being thwarted in one's aims or goals);
- Social Learning Theory (behavioural patterns learned through associating behaviour and consequences – see Chapters 4, 6, 7, 8, 9 and 10);
- Cognitive theory (internal/external factors affecting perceptions of provocation);
- Biological theories (neurochemical, hormonal, psychophysiological and neuropsychological – see Chapters 3, 6, 7 and 8).

Whilst these theories might explain some behaviours of terrorists, they do not really address the right questions we should be asking, such as 'How and why do people enter, stay in, and leave terrorist organizations?' (Borum 2004, p. 23). Interestingly, Horgan and Taylor (2001) claimed that, 'What we know of actual terrorists suggests that there is rarely a conscious decision made to become a terrorist. Most involvement in terrorism results from gradual exposure and socialisation towards extreme behaviour' (p. 23) (see Box 11.9). This argument has been used to explain the recent spate of young Muslim girls leaving the UK to join Islamic extremists in Syria. In 2014 as many as 20 teenage girls left Britain to become part of the Islamic State of Iraq and Syria (ISIS) group in Syria (Robson 2015). A latest report claims that a further two teenage girls have fled the UK to join ISIS (Macfarlane 2015). This has become a problem. The current explanations are very close to what Horgan and Taylor (2001) claim and the discussion of group allegiance in Box 11.9.

Terrorism can be understood from a historical perspective as the justification for fighting 'just wars' (i.e. warfare and the treatment of civilians that are governed by rules of armed conflict sometimes referred to as international humanitarian law) – but is this really a form of terrorism? Discussion regarding the moral foundation for 'just wars' and the nature of combat, are relevant to contemporary Britain. For example, there has been increasing dialogue regarding the use and 'appropriate' type of arms deemed acceptable in 'just wars'. This has been weighed against the number of civilian casualties and the concept of 'arms mala in se' (see Box 11.10). While it may be disputed that 'just wars' are a form of terrorism, it is the war crimes committed by the victorious leaders and governments that could be conceived as constituting terrorism (see Box 11.11).

# Box 11.10

## Concept of *arms mala in se*

Archer (2007) has argued for a moratorium on the use of cluster munitions on the grounds that they are indiscriminate weapons that cause many fatalities and injuries to non-combatants of war. The use of these weapons (or *arms mala in se*), Archer argued, causes threats to civilians after fighting has ceased in the same way that un-exploded mines do. While government officials argue strongly against their use on legal terms, Archer considers the banning of cluster munitions on moral grounds. Orend (2000) and Walzer (2000) contended that both moral and legal discourse is relevant to understanding when and how wars should be fought. To engage in such a discussion Archer claims it is important to retrace history, and in particular, to the Christian 'Just War' doctrine first conceived in the fifth century by Augustine of Hippo.

In this doctrine the Church strives to keep a balance between the 'proscription against violence and the need for the Roman Empire to defend its people and holdings from invasion' (Johnson 1984, 2011). Augustine established two concepts of Just War Theory (JWT): *jus ad bellum* (i.e. the right to go to war) and *jus in bello* (i.e. what is acceptable in using such force). *Jus ad bellum* defines the circumstances under which a community can justly resort to armed violence. Thus *jus in bello* works on the principle of limiting the potential harm caused to civilians by ensuring the methods of combat are as discriminate as possible – that is, they target the fighting force only (Archer 2007; Johnson 2011). Two further concepts emerged from *jus in bello*: non-combat immunity and proportionality (Johnson 1984, 2011). The 'Just War' doctrine continued to be modified throughout the Middle Ages and is still referred to as a moral guide for how war should be fought and the strategy used (Johnson 1984, 2011). Methods of combat such as mass rape, genocide, and disguising soldiers as Red Cross workers to administer poison to civilians as medical treatment, are considered to be immoral (Orend 2005).

The United Nations Charter and The Hague and Geneva Conventions have adopted the 'Just War' doctrine as a means of governing contemporary international laws on how armed conflict should be conducted (Orend 2005). Orend (2005) outlined six *jus ad bellum* principles that should be fulfilled before waging war: just cause, right intention, proper authority, last resort, probability of success and proportionality. In the case of *jus in bello*, Orend (2005) outlined six principles. Three of these include, for example, 'discrimination and non-combatant immunity' (i.e. weapons should target those who are engaged in combat and avoid the civilian population: deliberate targeting of civilians is morally wrong); 'proportionality' (i.e. the extent of force required to achieve aims); and 'no means *mala in se*' (i.e.

avoiding the use of weapons considered to be *arms mala in se* and therefore evil in themselves).

## Box 11.11

### War criminals and psychopathy

Häkkänen-Nyholm and Nyholm (2012) defined war crimes as, 'acts and practices committed in times of international armed conflict' (p. 193). These acts and practices committed are not in keeping with The United Nations Charter and The Hague and Geneva Conventions rules and regulations surrounding the 'Just War' doctrine governing international laws on how armed conflict should be conducted (Orend 2005). They further stated that only the leaders and policy makers should be prosecuted at an international level. The purpose of international prosecution is to deter other leaders from committing acts constituting war crimes. Despite research findings failing to find evidence of there being personality disorders (i.e. primarily psychopathy) among terrorists, Häkkänen-Nyholm and Nyholm (2012) proposed that this might not be the case for fallen war heroes accused of war crimes. They cited Babiak and Hare's (2006) finding of psychopaths in the business world and suspect it is just as rife in the military. The typical traits of psychopaths, such as limited empathy, guilt and remorse and manipulativeness and superficial charm, they argued, might prove advantageous traits in a leader. One study by Glicksohn, Ben-Shalom and Lazar (2004) demonstrated how Israeli military conscripts engaging in risky behaviours using weapons were more likely to point loaded weapons at their fellow soldiers. They speculated that this behaviour might be a consequence of boredom or motivated by the desire to show off. These soldiers were more likely to have traits deemed to be psychopathic. Acts of genocide, for example, are motivated by the desire to instil fear and to humiliate victims (Jones 2010) and, as argued by Häkkänen-Nyholm and Nyholm (2012), leaders who instigate genocide usually have pathological personality traits that are very similar to those held by psychopaths. Past examples include Adolf Hitler, Joseph Stalin and Pol Pot and more recently, Kim Il Sung, Robert Mugabe, Saddam Hussein, Slobodan Milosevic, Muammar-al-Gaddafi and Ratko Mladic. All these leaders introduced policies of genocide by waging war on ethnic minorities, who in their opinion, were inconveniently residing in their country. This led to the massacre of thousands of men, women and children based on their ethnic origin (i.e. the Kurds in Iraq by Saddam Hussein; Albanians in Kosovo and Muslims in Croatia and Bosnia by Slobodan Milosevic and the Jews in Germany by Adolf Hitler). What they all have in common is the need for power, control and status and the ability to scapegoat (i.e. single out people to blame for a country's problems) individuals and encourage public support so that they develop a 'them' and 'us' mentality (Häkkänen-Nyholm and Nyholm 2012). They dehumanise scapegoated individuals and by doing so can justify their policies of genocide, which become accepted. Häkkänen-Nyholm and Nyholm (2012) have argued that these types of atrocities occur when a psychopath is at the helm of leadership.

## Summary

- The difficulty in defining dangerousness was considered in relation to crime and the individual. The concept of dangerousness is not clear and is poorly understood because of misconceptions derived from ambiguous definitions. Assessing dangerousness in terms of violence and harm committed to others can be done through clinical tests and guidance from the law (especially in relation to the seriousness of the offence and the sentence tariffs stipulated for such crimes); however, it is difficult to predict future dangerousness based on clinical assessment. Poor prediction outcomes derive from clinical judgement but statistical models of predicting future dangerous behaviours are more reliable since they are based on factors such as history of offending and the type of offending and other static variables such as upbringing and background. Other means of predicting the likelihood of future offending can be derived from risk assessments of recidivism – typically the Probation Service use OGRS for this task.

- While it is possible to assess dangerousness and risk of reoffending on the basis of previous criminal history and the nature of the offence, it is difficult to predict whether an offender will always be a threat to society and likely to commit another serious offence. Using the law to assess the dangerousness of the crime committed can be done through the gradient of crime seriousness and concepts of *mala in se* and *mala prohibita*. Assessing whether the offender is dangerous, however, must rely on clinical judgement using guidelines from the MHA (2007) and CJA (2003) and diagnosis based on DSM-5 and ICD specifications. Through the use of these sources clinicians can make diagnoses but the difficulty of predicting future behaviour remains an issue.

- How to sentence dangerous offenders can be equally problematic and has been debated in law for many decades. Different types of sentences such as a reviewable open-ended indeterminate sentence was proposed by the Butler Committee in 1975; a double-track sentence by the Floud Committee in 1981; a longer than commensurate determinate sentence by the CJA of 1991 and the Crime Sentences Act of 1997 proposed a long minimum sentence. The CJA of 2003 introduced the IPP which came into being in 2005, but this sentence was increasingly overused and amendments were made in 2008 with the introduction of the Criminal Justice and Immigration Act. In December 2012 the IPP was abolished.

- It is best to consider dangerousness from the offender-offence perspective – in other words, the type of crime committed and the seriousness of violence involved. The situational circumstance of provocation is clearly important but if, as in many of these cases, there was no external source causing the dangerous criminal act, then the individual is considered culpable. As has been seen from studies examining the composition of prison populations, three major cohorts exist: those with drug/alcohol addictions, personality and mental disorders (specifically schizophrenia). In this chapter, personality and mental disorders were primarily considered. Schizophrenia disrupts the individual's normal cognitive functioning through invasive hallucinations and delusions occurring during psychotic episodes. Clearly, the source of the problem lies with the individual (a neurotransmitter imbalance for instance) and not an external factor such as living in poverty – although this will not help matters. Evidence suggests that it is during psychotic episodes that individuals with schizophrenia are most likely to be violent and dangerous towards others such as relatives and carers. Most schizophrenics, however, can control these outbursts of violent behaviour through the regimented application of medication.
- Offenders with personality disorders, usually APD or psychopathy, are difficult to treat and respond less well to therapeutic intervention. Offenders with APD tend not to overtly experience psychosis or neurosis and for this reason can function relatively normally. Criminal psychopaths are very similar to offenders with APD but are assessed using Hare's PCL-R, in particular, Factor 4, labelled the antisocial dimension.
- Appropriate sentencing for dangerous offenders is difficult given the problems of predicting future dangerousness and the risk of reoffending. Determining an appropriate sentence for dangerous offenders exhibiting a mental disorder is more problematic for law legislators. The MHA provides some guidance but it is medical opinion that has the power to detain a dangerous offender diagnosed with a mental disorder and to advise the type of detainment – prison, high-security psychiatric hospital or other psychiatric institution for example. This advice also rests on perceptions of an offender's fit or unfit state of mind to plead prior to or during court proceedings. While it might be easier to assess offenders who have a mental disorder such as schizophrenia and psychopathy, it is more problematic to sentence offenders with mental disorders appropriately and, in the case of psychopaths, to provide effective treatment.
- There has been a long debate of whether criminal psychopaths are 'bad' or 'mad'. Some researchers believe that because there is a deficit in the psychopath's moral development, it would be unfair to consider them as 'bad'. Evidence from fMRI scans and other physiological measures indicate that the orbitofrontal cortex and amygdala operate differently in psychopaths to non-psychopaths. Deficits in the processing and experiencing of empathy have been found in criminal psychopaths which enable them to

commit serious and dangerous offences (see Chapter 7). Hence, the fMRI brain patterns of criminal psychopaths function differently from offenders with other types of mental disorder such as schizophrenia. Whether they are 'bad' or 'mad', however, is a philosophical debate. For some researchers such as Blackburn psychopaths can be 'bad', 'mad' or 'bad-mad'.

- What can be assumed is that the criminal behaviour of offenders with a mental disorder is influenced by their condition. The level of responsibility and blameworthiness are dictates of symptom severity and manifestation beyond their conscious control. This tends towards a nature interpretation of dangerous and violent offenders but this does not preclude any contribution from environmental factors such as brain damage incurred in childhood, rejecting parents and/or failure to make an attachment (see Chapter 4).

- Terrorist acts are dangerous. Terrorists are regarded as either 'bad' or 'mad' but there is little empirical evidence suggesting that they are. Suicide bombers use suicide as a weapon of war and, as with terrorists, there is little evidence to suggest they are 'mad'. It appears that terrorists and suicide bombers have a political agenda and are organised and logical planners in the execution of their objectives. Criminologists tend to consider risk-oriented thinking as a good way of dealing with terrorists. Psychological approaches also outline risk factors for identifying the terrorist profile. There seems to be an understanding, however, that most involvement in terrorism is due to exposure to, and socialisation of, extreme attitudes in line with terrorist organisations. Another way of considering the profile of terrorists is to study fallen leaders accused of committing war crimes; in particular, genocide. The personality traits of war criminals demonstrate commonalities to individuals with psychopathy. There is also some support for this in the behaviour of individuals who take risks in the way they use weapons such as pointing loaded guns at their fellow soldiers.

## Questions for discussion

1  Why might it be more productive to concentrate on dangerous acts than dangerous individuals?
2  Is it morally justifiable to detain a potentially dangerous offender indefinitely? What are the problems associated with this?
3  Why is the Baxstrom case highlighted as a particularly important case to the issue of Civil Rights versus the protection of the public?

# Chapter 12

# Offender profiling: serial killers

Part IV is about predicting future criminal behaviour. In this chapter we will explore ways of identifying serial killers on the basis of **offender profiling**. Although, in this chapter, we will focus on the behaviours of serial killers and how they can be identified and incarcerated to prevent future reoffending, we also consider serial killers and their actions thereby forging links with Part III.

First, the birth of offender profiling will be considered within a historical context, outlining the development of fingerprinting and the struggle for acceptance against the prevailing dominant culture of psychological thought – that favouring the study of positive human behaviour. In this chapter we will explore the work of the Federal Bureau of Investigation (FBI), in particular Robert Ressler, who introduced the term serial killer, and with other colleagues founded the FBI classification of serial killers: organised and disorganised. The traits of the organised and disorganised typologies will be described in detail and applied to a famous serial killer, Albert Fish. We will also explore other approaches such as the typologies introduced by Holmes and DeBurger and the Model of Personal Violence. These are described and considered in relation to examples of different serial killers to understand the underlying motivations for their crime scene behaviours.

The US offender profiling approach of the FBI and typologies devised by Holmes and DeBurger will be considered in terms of their success rate at predicting who the perpetrator is and where he or she can be found. Furthermore, we will consider success rate in relation to the attitudes towards profiling held by police. It will be shown that expert profilers have a higher level of success than non-trained police profilers and non-profilers. Serious flaws, however, in the reliability and validity of the FBI classifications and Holmes and DeBurger's typologies have been uncovered by empirical research. In this chapter we will consider these flaws in detail and refer to the work of leading profilers in the UK, such as Canter. These flaws, identified using statistical methods of analyses, show that all serial killing has organised elements, explaining why these offenders escape capture often for very long periods of time.

In this chapter the alternative approach commonly used in the UK, known as geographical profiling, will be considered. Geographical profiling is proven to be a successful method of describing the boundaries covering an offender's likely area of operation and residence.

## Introduction

The notion of being able to classify people based on their behaviour is not a new concept. There are many examples to illustrate that, as humans, we find it difficult not to try and package other people's behaviours and actions into concrete categories. In the late eighteenth century, Austrian craniologist Franz Joseph Gall introduced his theory of phrenology which was a system of classifying people according to the bumps and raised or flat areas on the head (Gall and Spurzheim 1810). These areas corresponded to attributes of personality and intelligence – even questions of whether a woman would make a good mother were answered using phrenology. This tradition of classifying people was also used in the quest for identifying criminals and predicting who had committed a crime and why. The ability to predict who is most likely to be culpable of committing a particular crime belongs to an area of investigative psychology known as offender profiling. Offender profiling is a relatively new approach to policing and investigation; however, its objective of providing police with a profile of a likely culprit derives from the field of forensic science and the use of manual fingerprinting.

The development of fingerprinting is of relevance here as it provides insight to how the step from physical to psychological assessment of crime scene information occurred. Two British officials, William Herschel (1880, 1894) in India and Henry Faulds (1880) in Japan, both independently realised that handprints and fingerprints are unique to all individuals and could therefore be used to detect fraudulent claims. In the case of Herschel, who was appointed magistrate in Hooghly, Calcutta, one of his roles was to pay out government pensions and to ensure that the deceased were not being impersonated. He did this by recording people's first and middle fingers of the right hand as a signature equivalent. At Tsukiji Hospital in Tokyo, Faulds noticed that those who were illiterate signed documents using their hand print and wondered whether handprints varied across races. He managed to solve a crime on the basis of a handprint left by a thief.

Extending the concept of unique physical differences amongst individuals, Alphonse Bertillon continued his father's (the statistician Louis-Adolphe Bertillon) work on people's physical measurements and noted that no two people shared the same physical profile. Armed with this knowledge, in 1882–3 Bertillon devised a card system of 1600 records based on measurements taken from arrested criminals. Using this card system, Bertillon identified 50 repeat offenders in 1883 and 300 more the following year. There was an air of excitement and expectation for the 'bertillonage' method as it could be used to predict

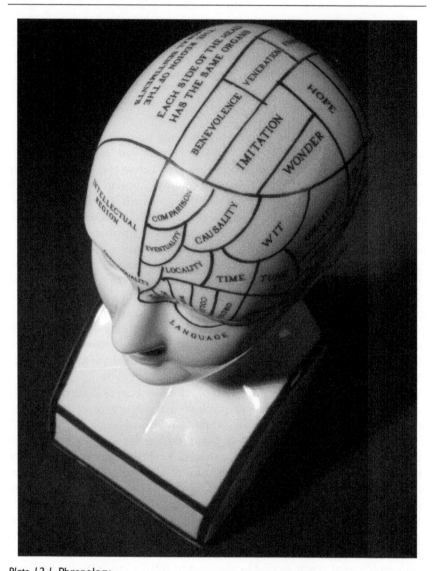

*Plate 12.1* Phrenology

culpability (Bertillon 1886). Unfortunately, the bertillonage method was over-taken by Sir Francis Galton, who in 1888 popularised the use of fingerprinting based on Johann Purkinje's publication in 1823 on skin patterns. Galton found more than 60,000 classes of fingerprint based on all 10 fingerprints which he published in 1892 in his book, *Finger Prints*. This method was developed further using computer technology and continues to thrive in police detective work

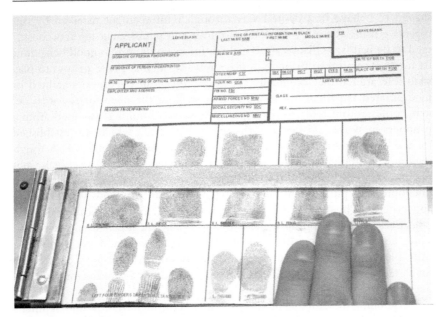

*Plate 12.2* Taking fingerprints
© kilukilu. Image used under license from Shutterstock.com. Available at http://www.shutterstock.com/pic.mhtml?id=65234224&src=dt_back_to_image

today: in England and Wales fingerprint technology is admissible evidence in court provided there are at least 16 matching fingerprint elements.

Although technological advances in forensic science were made, profiling criminals was restricted to Gall's phrenology and Cesare Lombroso's 'atavism' during the eighteenth and nineteenth centuries, and, in the twentieth century, to psychiatrist James Brussel's 1950s approach of examining the behaviour and actions of criminals to deduce their character typology (Brussel 1968). Brussel's approach, however, remained hidden for 20 years for two reasons – two influential approaches to understanding the behaviour of individuals took precedence. In psychology there were two popular approaches to studying individuals which dominated mainstream thinking: Abraham Maslow's hierarchy of needs (1954) and Burrhus Frederic Skinner's operant conditioning (1953).

Maslow popularised positive psychology where the pursuit of self-fulfilment and happiness was the mantra of the hierarchy of needs approach. Positive psychology lends itself to studying that which is essentially 'good' and provides us with a sense of well-being, thus accounting for why negative aspects of humanity such as criminal behaviour and prisoners were of no interest. Maslow claimed that once our basic drives for survival have been sufficed, such as food, shelter and status, we can then concentrate on self-improvement and the activities in life that make us self-fulfilled (which has a spiritual mantra). Skinner, alternatively, claimed that we as individuals are shaped to behave in a desired way through reinforcement received by our parents – using rewards for good behaviour and punishment for acts considered to be bad (see Chapter 4). If a child, for example, shows good behaviour then this is reinforced through positive rewards such as praise or toys to play with. He argued that eventually the good behaviour becomes engrained or incorporated as part of our moral system without the need for rewards (i.e. it becomes automated). An example of how conditioning was used among prisoners in Wakefield Prison is the segregation wing which was established for the experimental set-up of the 'Special Control Unit' in 1974. A tough regime was implemented to subdue the most dangerous of criminals, and designed to 'break the spirit of defiance'. Prisoners were subjected to strict discipline and punishment that included a regime of sensory deprivation and cruelty. The Special Control Unit was designed specifically with the objectives of psychological regression, and a sense of learned helplessness to cause depersonalisation (Bowden 2010). Here, they would use Skinnerian principles of shaping behaviour towards the desired behaviour of conformity for instance. Prisoners were deprived of their clothes and other simple daily necessities until they showed 'good behaviour'.

Researching the criminal mind was hindered through Maslow and Skinner's psychological doctrines; however, Ressler, who was working for the Federal Bureau of Investigation (FBI), established a method of making the study of criminals and criminal minds acceptable and worthy of investigation – now known as **offender profiling**.

## Offender profiling in serial killings

The FBI Behavioural Science Unit, based at Quantico in the state of Virginia under the authority of Ressler, gave offender profiling a structure and a method of gathering information. Through interviewing infamous serial killers, Ressler attained information regarding the covert nature of the criminal's mind. Information included personal accounts of these criminals' lives and motivations for committing their crimes. This information was put on to a computer database and cross-referenced with documented evidence such as crime scene victim and forensic evidence and personal details. This led to the FBI approach to offender profiling which will be returned to later in this chapter. Offender profiling is normally used to identify and locate criminals who commit the same crime repeatedly, such as burglars, arsonists, paedophiles, rapists, cult murderers and serial killers. It is easier to look for patterns of behaviour that are commonly associated with offending than to consider a single crime event. Given that offenders have their own styles and motivations for offending, they are highly likely to offend in a consistent manner. Therefore, as many crimes are likely to have been committed, there is more chance of a profiler identifying similarities across offences committed by a specific individual. Consider the differences in offending style and motivation outlined for burglary in Box 12.1.

Ressler's FBI approach, however, is normally associated with serial killing which we will explore next.

---

## Box 12.1

### Profile of burglary style

Fox, Farrington, Chitwood and Janes (2013) created a profile for burglary by analysing burglary data for 405 solved but randomly selected burglaries that occurred in Volusia County, Florida during 2008–9. Criminal histories of the burglars and offence details were analysed using a statistical method. From this they identified four styles of burglar: organised; disorganised; opportunistic; and interpersonal. Organised burglaries demonstrated planning and were professionally executed such that no physical evidence could be found. Fox *et al.* (2013) found the motivation for organised burglars was financial reward. Alternatively, disorganised burglaries had a ransacked crime scene where windows were smashed to enable entry. In many cases of disorganised burglary, no items are stolen suggesting that the motivation for the offence is not property linked. There is an abundance of physical evidence left at the crime scene which Fox *et al.* allude to as a consequence of a disorganised lifestyle. Their targets live close by as such burglars rarely have a car. Opportunistic burglaries occur when the offender sees an open window or unlocked door and enters easily without causing any disruption. These burglaries occur spontaneously and often occur as a social activity among a group of adolescents. Stolen items tend to be for personal use and those easy to hand. These burglars might also have a previous record for shoplifting. Interpersonal burglaries (paralleling aggravated burglary) occur when the victim is present. For this type of burglar the victim is the object of desire and not items belonging to the victim. Causing fear in the victim gives this burglar a sense of power and control. Any items stolen will signify a connection to the victim, such as underwear, and remind them of their prowess over the victim. If interpersonal burglars have a criminal record it is likely to be for stalking, voyeurism, domestic violence and sometimes rape. This type of research can be useful for police investigations.

---

### What is meant by the term 'serial killers'?

FBI agents such as Ressler coined the term serial killers to describe murderers who have killed in 'three or more separate events in three or more separate locations with an emotional cooling off period in between homicides' (Douglas, Burgess, Burgess and Ressler 1992, p.21). Controversy and disagreement over this definition has highlighted the problems of standardised and reliable offender profiling. For example, Holmes and Holmes (1998; 2001) claimed that serial murder is a form of multiple murders committed with another person or alone in two or more separate events (Egger 1990; Geberth 1996). Despite differences in the definition of what constitutes serial killing, profilers agree on the importance offending behaviours have for the serial murderer. These behaviours are underpinned by a host of cognitions and interpretations which only have meaning for the serial killer and therefore are repeatedly performed in every homicide committed (Canter and Wentink 2004; Hickey 2002; Wright, Pratt and DeLisi 2008). These behaviours and their significance are consistent across murders committed by the same serial killer – each serial killer therefore has his or her own set of offence behaviours and interpretations. Killing many people does not necessarily define serial murder and could in fact be described as mass or spree killing. There is a difference between the three types of murderers as explained in Box 12.2.

## Box 12.2

### Difference between mass, spree and serial murderers

#### Mass murderers

Examples of mass murderers include the following:

- Columbine High School shootings in US in 1999;
- Tempe Military Base in Bloemfontein murders in South Africa in 1999;
- Dunblane School shootings in UK in 1996.

In all these cases, a single individual killed many people in the same location over a short time period in what Leyton (1986) described as 'one explosive event' (p.18).

#### Spree murderers

According to Holmes and Holmes (2001), three different locations are used to kill people implying that these are separate events where there might also be other opportunistic crimes occurring simultaneously, such as armed robbery. Lane and Gregg (1992, p.1) claimed that spree killing occurs over a 'longer period of time hours or days' compared to mass murder. For example, in South Africa two spree partners in crime, Peter Grundling and Charmaine Philips, murdered many people over a three week period in 1981 – places included Durban, Secunda, Bloemfontein and Melmoth.

#### Serial murderers

As far as Del Fabbro (2006) was concerned, the defining factors separating mass, spree and serial murderers pertain to spatial and temporal dimensions.

She further alluded to there being a 'continuum with respect to distance in space and time' (p.15) for all multiple murders. Ressler, Burgess, Douglas, Hartman and D'Agnostino (1986) separated serial from mass and spree murder by claiming there must be at least three separate murders in different places with a defined emotional cooling off period between murders.

Over the years there has been an interesting evolution of the many modifications to the definition of serial killers. From Ressler *et al.*'s (1986) definition, Holmes and De Burger (1988) added that the victims of serial murderers tend to be strangers and that motives derive from internal factors relating only to the killer and not from extrinsic variables like provocation. They further suggested that in the majority of cases there was an underlying sexual motivation driving the serial killer's actions during the crime. Pistorius (1996) commented on South African serial killers – defining them as individuals murdering several victims, usually strangers, at different times and locations. They are driven intrinsically by an irrepressible compulsion to murder underpinned by fantasy which can lead to torture and mutilation. Holmes and Holmes (1998) defined serial killers as repeat homicide offenders who continue to prey on victims unknown to them until they are stopped. Their motives are usually intrinsically driven and of a sexual nature. Hickey (2002) claimed there should be three or four victims to qualify as a serial killer and that with each murder typical patterns should emerge such as the nature of victims selected, the *modus operandi* and **crime signature** (see Box 12.3).

## Box 12.3

### Definition of *modus operandi* and crime signatures

Crime scene characteristics are very informative and add objective credence to any patterns emerging through profiling. The presence of crime scene evidence can be used in the determination of the offender's method for committing crime, known as the *modus operandi* (MO) (Jackson and Bekerian 1997). This also implies that the behaviour occurring during the criminal act is necessary for its successful completion – as stated by Douglas and Olshaker (1998), 'What an offender has to do to accomplish a crime' (p.90). Keppel, Weis, Brown and Welch (2005) defined the MO as 'the offender's actions during the commission of a crime that are necessary to complete the crime' (p.14).

The signature can be determined in the same way as the MO but is generally regarded as idiosyncratic to the serial killer and captures the characteristics of the killer. According to Neitzel (1979), 'Crime is the result of some personality attribute uniquely possessed or possessed to a certain degree, by the potential criminal' (p.350). While it is possible for the MO to evolve as a consequence of situational circumstance and through learning more efficient ways of evading capture, the signature is more static and unchanging. This is because the signature serves as a fundamental core element of the serial killer's psyche. According to Woodworth and Porter (2001), a signature defines what satisfies the offender's psychological needs by committing the crime. Geberth (1995; 1996) claimed that the signature highlights a distinctive aspect of the serial killer's personality especially as their fantasies are acted out through committing their crimes. Douglas and Olshaker (1998) claimed it is 'something the offender has to do to fulfil himself emotionally . . . it is not needed to successfully accomplish a crime, but it is the reason he undertakes the particular crime in the first place' (p.90). Hence the signature is reflected in the crime scene and can often be deduced from the MO. According to Canter (2007), not all serial killers have a signature but will have a MO. Canter (2007) stated that 'it is as rare for any criminal to have a unique and distinct way of committing a crime as it is for anyone else to have a unique and distinct way of doing anything' (p.35).

While the MO of Ted Bundy, the infamous American serial killer, relied upon a planned set of actions including the selection of his victims and how he enticed them to his car and the manner in which he killed them, his signature was not clearly defined. What does stand out, however, is the similarity of his selected victims to his ex-girlfriend who had snubbed him many years prior to his killings. His desire to prove himself to his ex-girlfriend and demonstrate his control, power and status to her might have been enveloped in his fantasy to sexually dominate his victims. This is reflected in the way Bundy committed his crimes (the MO) but also the details in which he killed his victims and the purpose this served for him psychologically. For example, the authoritative disguises (i.e. dressed as a policeman) he used as a means to controlling his victims and the domination shown through the use of restraints and torture could potentially be his signature.

The FBI in 2005 defined serial murder as 'the unlawful killing of two or more victims by the same offender(s) in separate events' (p.9). Furthermore, serial killers can be either geographically stable (i.e. murder in the same place) or transient (i.e. murder in different locations), and although they tend to be sexually driven they also desire power and control over their victims. Furthermore, most victims are strangers (Hickey 2002).

The findings do not always support key elements of these definitions. A good illustration of this are the findings from Gorby's (2000) and Hodgskiss' (2004) studies showing that other non-North American countries and South Africa, in particular, have a total of 25 per cent of serial killers targeting strangers which means in 75 per cent of cases victims are known. This contrasts with Hickey's (2002) assertion that known victims are in the minority. Pakhomou

(2004) found that approximately 27 per cent of North American serial killers knew their victims implying that 73 per cent did not. Another contradiction is the definition introduced by Holmes and Holmes (1998) stating that murders are committed in three different places. Not all serial killers murder in different locations – Jeffrey Dahmer, for instance, enticed his victims back to his flat where he murdered them and disposed of their bodies. In 2005 the FBI claimed that the notion of serial killers travelling across the US is a mere fallacy. This was supported by Hickey's (2002) concept of the comfort zone where serial killers operate in familiar surroundings thereby boosting their levels of confidence and providing a sense of safety.

Pistorius (1996) claimed that the motives of serial killers are underpinned by fantasy. This was found to be the case for 80 per cent of serial killers in North America who reported experiences of violent sexual fantasies. This was considered by Schlesinger (2004) as a subtype of compulsive sexual offending. The problem here, however, concerns clarity between murder associated with sexual behaviour and sexually motivated murder. For this reason the FBI in 2005 believed it appropriate to assume that some serial murders are sexually motivated. A more definitive understanding of serial murder considered the behaviours occurring during the murder as being on a continuum rather than discrete clusters representing distinctive categories (Hodgskiss 2004). This is also the viewpoint of Canter (2000) who adapted the **Radex Model** (i.e. a radex can be visually represented as a circular disk with two continuums on which variables can be located) as a means to understanding the criminal behaviours assessed at the crime scene which, despite a continuum, consisted of dominant themes (this will be discussed further in the section on Empirical research testing on the reliability of offender profiling).

### What is the FBI Approach to offender profiling?

Research at the Behavioural Science Unit studied the personality and offence behaviours of serial killers by focusing on the crimes committed and the motivations that these crimes endeavoured to gratify. Given that serial killers and serial rapists were of particular interest to the FBI, it is of no surprise that sexual motivation featured strongly in their profiling ideology. Burgess, Hartman, Ressler, Douglas and McCormack (1986) were funded by the FBI to investigate whether a motivational model could explain serial sexual murder. Through informal but intensive interviewing they obtained narratives from 36 sexual murderers. These murderers remained incarcerated while they free-recalled information about their background, upbringing and thoughts underlying their motivations for killing – this tapped into their fantasy world of sadism, violence and sex. Burgess et al. (1986) formulated two different classifications or typologies of serial killers based on the information from the narratives: organised non-social and disorganised asocial (referred to as 'organised' and disorganised' henceforth). These typologies are aptly

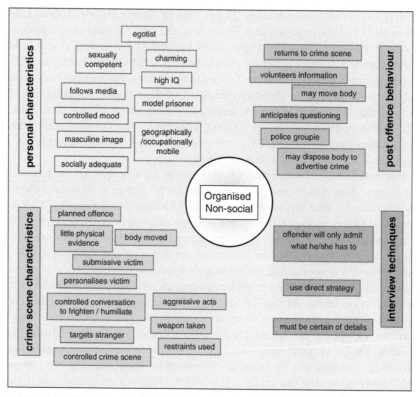

*Figure 12.1* Scene and profile characteristics of organised serial killers
Ressler and Burgess 1985

labelled as they imply that an organised serial killer, for instance, plans his or her murders in advance and that the MO is clearly defined and executed. In the case of disorganised serial killers the opposite is true – there is no planning, killing is spontaneous and weaponry is improvised at the location of the attack.

Offenders' actions during a crime and their characteristics are connected (Hodge 2000), which is how Burgess *et al.* (1986) were able to forge links between offence, behaviour and personality characteristics through the examination of the crime scene. Figures 12.1 and 12.2 list the different personal characteristics (including personality traits), crime scene and victim factors, behaviours shown after the offence (i.e. post offence behaviour) and interview techniques police should adopt when dealing with organised and disorganised serial killers respectively.

Reliable and valid profiles ascribe serial killers to either organised or disorganised classifications but not to both – hence these classifications are supposed to be mutually exclusive. To illustrate the problem of mutual exclusivity in

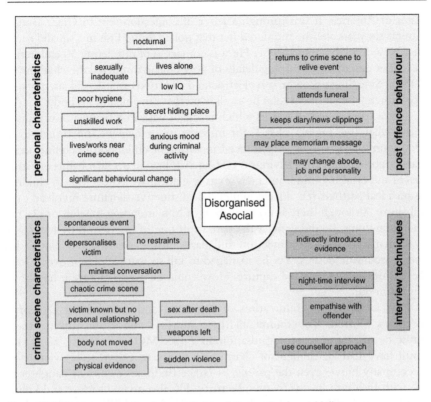

*Figure 12.2* Scene and profile characteristics of disorganised serial killers
Ressler and Burgess 1985

the profiling of serial killers, the following example of Albert Howard Fish (renowned as the 'Thrill Vulture' and 'Vampire Man') is reviewed next.

Fish was born in Washington, DC, in the year 1870 and was brought up in an orphanage, therefore not knowing his parentage. At the orphanage he witnessed young boys being whipped on a daily basis as a form of punishment. The experience of watching boys being whipped influenced his later sadomasochistic urges which were manifested in an unusual way such as the cannibalism of children who he cooked in stews or roasted. He also behaved oddly: dancing naked under the moon, sticking needles into his genitalia, eating excrement, drinking urine and soaking cotton wool in lighter fuel which he inserted into his rectum and ignited. He was married and had six children but his wife left him for a younger man when he started to hear voices, experience hallucinations and became obsessed with pain and sacrifice. In 1928 he killed 10-year-old Grace Budd by strangulation, and, using a butcher's knife and cleaver, he dismembered her body and retained some flesh for his consumption. He was geographically mobile through his job as a house painter, which provided him with access to cellars. It is in these cellars that he abused and killed children across different states of America. It was through a letter of confession sent to Grace Budd's parents six years after he murdered her that police found Fish in a squalid room in a New York boarding house. He was convicted of murdering 30 children, a year after describing disturbing details of how he had murdered the children. In 1936 at Sing Sing prison he was electrocuted after two unsuccessful attempts – a consequence of all the needles he swallowed that remained in his body.

There are a couple of factors which resonate with Fish being a disorganised serial killer (see Figure 12.2) – for instance, poor hygiene, nocturnal, lived alone, unskilled worker, experienced inconsistent childhood discipline and a harsh upbringing. His behaviour is odd, such as having peculiar habits of eating faeces and drinking urine, and he is sexually inadequate as he resorts to children as his ideal partners (i.e. a paedophile). His distinctive signature involved cannibalism. Although there is no indication of him attending funerals or placing memorandums, he did contact the parents of one of his victims by letter. He was unaffected by his conviction and happy to be electrocuted due to his sadomasochistic desires. Yet he managed to kill so many children over a long period of time and evaded capture. How could he evade capture if he was so disorganised?

This is where the bifurcation of organised and disorganised categories becomes blurred. To commit all these murders and evade capture there must be an element of organisation in Fish's MO (see Figure 12.1). He must have had an element of charm and ability to convince his victims to accompany him – even the parents of Grace Budd allowed their daughter to go with Fish into his car to attend a party. He also owned torture and killing implements and knew exactly how he was going to kill his victims, where and what parts of their body he was going to dismember and consume. His job enabled him to travel across states, so he was geographically mobile and was able to dispose of his victims' bodies in different places – none associated with where he lived. The crime scenes left little physical evidence that could be used to help police identify Fish – all these factors indicate an organised crime scene.

From this analysis it appears that Fish is a 'mixed' serial killer. The mixed serial killer typology was introduced by Douglas, Burgess, Burgess and Ressler (1992) to account for cases where circumstances beyond the killer's control intervened such as:

- the occurrence of unanticipated events not originally accounted for in the plan;
- the victim responds differently to expectations;
- the killer changes the pattern of killing during the event or over a series of events.

The need for the mixed serial killer highlights just one of the many problems for the FBI offender profiling approach which will be returned to later in this chapter. The FBI categories of organised and disorganised serial killers is not the only typology approach that has been used by profilers in the US and UK – there is also Holmes and Holmes' (1998) classification scheme consisting of four typologies: visionary; mission, hedonistic (lust, thrill and comfort-oriented); and power/control.

## The Holmes and DeBurger's typology approach

This approach rests on the assumption that individuals behave differently from each other as a consequence of social and psychological experiences that underpin the motivations for behaving in a particular way (Holmes and Holmes 2001). The four typologies first developed by Holmes and DeBurger in 1985, based on interviews of incarcerated serial murderers in US prisons, will be discussed in turn.

### Visionary serial killers

These killers are compelled to murder due to the hallucinations that they see and voices they hear which emanate from inside their minds. Serial killers hearing voices are often instructed by these voices to murder specific victims, such as prostitutes or homosexuals. They can see apparitions of the devil or demons in animate objects such as animals. David Berkowitz is an example: he claimed his neighbour's dog instructed him to kill people. In 1976 Flora-Rheta Schreiber interviewed Joseph Kallinger, a shoemaker, who killed three people in Pennsylvania and New Jersey. She wrote a book titled *The Shoemaker* and revealed a serial murderer who was seriously mentally ill; a murderer who the justice system refused to acknowledge as suffering from paranoid schizophrenia and dangerous delusions.

Kallinger was married and had five children and it was his 12-year-old son, Joey, with whom he committed burglaries and robberies often using a knife or pistol. In 1972 his own children had complained about their father to the police that he had abused and threatened them with a gun. They later retracted their accusations when Kallinger was imprisoned. Doctors assessed Kallinger and found that his IQ was 84 and that he had had a history of psychiatric problems since the age of 15. His son Joey had been in trouble and confessed his role as his father's accomplice and was sent to a reformatory. After his release in 1974 Joey was drowned by Kallinger. Kallinger claimed that, 'God communicated with him by touching his arm and conveying specific feelings . . . he was the son of God and that for 961 years he had existed as a butterfly'. When Kallinger was accused of his son's murder he said that was the day when 'Charlie' the ghost showed up. Schreiber concluded that the ghost was his son Joey which he saw as a face in a bubble, and was the hallucination that instructed him to continue murdering.

## Mission serial killers

The mission serial killer's goal is to eliminate a particular group or category of individuals – a mission to eradicate the world of undesirables. There have been many mission serial killers who, like visionary serial killers, also target particular victims. Mission serial killers, however, are *compos mentis* (i.e. have a clear mind) and do not suffer from psychosis, experience delusions or auditory and visual hallucinations like the visionary killer. Albert DeSalvo, known as the Boston Strangler, murdered women from 1962 to 1964 out of hatred: he felt his mission was to free the world of women.

Joseph Paul Franklin is another example of a mission killer who during the 1980s tried to restore his form of justice by killing young Black males who had White partners. Beoria Simmons was a social worker in Louisville and campaigned against immoral women who were in the sex trade. In 1984 he murdered a prostitute and continued killing or 'cleansing' the city until he was caught. Charles Manson is also considered to be a mission serial killer even though he never actually murdered anyone. He was dangerous as he convinced others to do his bidding through what became known as his 'Family'. His aim was to create a race war between Whites and Blacks so that his Family could rise as rulers. It is common for mission serial killers to use a weapon such as a gun for a quick kill (i.e. also referred to as act focus which occurs when the motivation of gratification is the act itself). This can entail a quick kill such as the case of shooting or can be savage involving over-kill.

## Hedonistic serial killers: lust, thrill and comfort-oriented

For this type of serial killer, murder is a form of pleasure and provides self-gratification – hence the term hedonism. In the case of the lust serial killer, pleasure is achieved through murder serving as a form of sexual gratification. Erotophonophilia is the act of sadistically killing to attain sexual hedonism and is considered the most extreme form of a paraphilia as it results in a victim's death (see Chapter 8). According to David Rumbelow (2004) in his book, *The Complete Jack the Ripper*, Jack the Ripper attained sexual pleasure and gratification through the mutilation of his victims and the extirpation of body organs. John Wayne Gacy is another example of a lust serial killer who molested and murdered 33 males during the 1970s and buried their bodies in a cellar beneath his house.

Thrill serial killers are similar to lust killers in that the content and nature of their crime and the crime scene can overlap. It is not the sexual component that provides pleasure and gratification for the thrill killer but rather the process of murdering to satisfy thrill seeking motivations. Christopher Wilder in 1984 murdered eight females through strangulation and knifing but only after a long process of torture by rape and bondage. Ken Bianchi and Angelo Buono murdered women but not before torturing them for prolonged periods through asphyxiation followed by resuscitation. In the case of lust and thrill serial killers, gratification is derived through a long drawn-out process of torture and murder. Their killing is not quick or act-focused as it is for the mission serial killer and in many cases the visionary serial killer, it is instead process-focused. Gratification derives from the whole process of killing, and this involves the planning, the torturing and the actual murder. In this case the act of killing is not as fulfilling as the processes involved with killing someone.

The third type of hedonistic killer is the comfort-oriented serial murderer. Murder in this case is perceived as a means to an end – a way of achieving a goal. Often this type of killer murders to attain money, goods or inheritance. A rather bizarre example is Joe Ball, who in the 1930s owned a tavern and employed many waitresses and other employees. There was a high staff turnover rate as Ball used his employees as fodder for his pet alligators – in total murdering 20 of his employees. Killers such as James Watson in 1910 and George Howard Putt in 1969 murdered people to attain money. Harold Shipman, a doctor, is alleged to have murdered 218 of his elderly female patients but was only found guilty for the murder of 15. In many of these cases Shipman gained money by altering the wills of his patients but in one case a daughter and her children were excluded from her mother's will leaving £386,000 to Shipman, which aroused suspicion.

### Power/control serial killers

Power/control serial killers are motivated and gratified through the complete domination over their victims – in life and death. Their fundamental pleasure is not derived through sexual activity but being in control and exerting power over their submissive and helpless victims. Ted Bundy is a prime example of a controlling serial killer and admitted this in an interview by claiming that, 'Violence was never an end in itself, sex was almost perfunctory. . . . Gratification lay not in assault but in the possession of the victim' (Michaud and Aynesworth, 1999, p.21).

Randal Brent Woodfield, known as the 'I-5' killer murdered from 1980 to 1981. He was known as the I-5 killer because the bodies of his victims were found on Interstate Five in Oregon and Washington. His motive was to prove to others that he was the best and wanted to be a hero. As is the case for lust and thrill killers, power/control serial killers are process focused. Furthermore, power/control serial killers often fulfil the stipulated criteria of Hare's Psychopathy Checklist (see Chapter 7).

In all of Holmes and DeBurger's typologies, victims played an essential role in the serial killer's fantasy world whether their role is short lived or has longevity (it is when the victim has served the serial killer's purpose that they are disposed of). Gratification once achieved means that the serial killer has no further purpose or use for the victim who now becomes a liability and must be disposed of. Holmes and Holmes (2002) stated, 'once a serial killer's violence has run its course, providing the desired self-fulfilment, his battered victim is of no more use to him than a soggy, used-up paper cup' (p.124). An interesting question to ask is why serial killers need to find a victim to torture and kill when they do, and what makes them stop? Holmes and Holmes attempted to answer this by referring to the psyche of a serial killer in their Model of Personal Violence.

### Model of Personal Violence

In this model there are five stages of serial murder that a serial killer will experience:

1   distorted thinking;
2   the fall;
3   negative inward response;
4   negative outward response;
5   restoration.

Holmes and Holmes (2002) argued that there is a process of violence initiated by external stimuli which can be imagined or real but is very real and of significance to the serial killer. The first stage is known as distorted thinking and describes a serial killer as being in a positive psychologically balanced state. While in this psychological state of mind, serial killers avoid the consideration of negative repercussions of deviant behaviour and instead focus on the rewards for such behaviour. They are able to convince others of their normality through charm and by maintaining their level of distorted thought so that it remains concealed from public scrutiny. This does not last, and the second stage known as the fall occurs. What initiates the fall can be an accumulation of events (real or imagined; trivial or important) which are taken personally. These events are stored in the serial killer's psyche until eventually a reaction which is disproportionate to the events occurs. The reaction might be delayed through a cathartic release in the way of masturbating to violent pornography, but this is a short-term solution and eventually stage three the negative inward response is activated.

While in this stage the serial killer must deal with a deflated self-esteem and self-concept which triggers feelings of inadequacy. Inward negative messages become thwarted through confronting them head-on with responses like, 'I don't have to take this lying down as I'm better than this.' This form of mental hyping maps out the response that serial killers next take. Stage four is the negative outward response and is the time when serial killers murder their victims. They no longer can control their compulsion to kill as it is this that drives their reinstatement of self-superiority and self-importance. The act of murder is a form of self-affirmation of their inflated beliefs of worthiness and importance. On successful completion of stage four they transgress to stage five known as restoration. During this stage the focus is on victim body disposal and the reduction of personal risk, such as being apprehended by police. Once the victim's body has been effectively disposed of the serial killer can revert back to the distorted thinking captured in stage one.

The period between stage one and stage four can be months or years but Holmes and Holmes noticed that as serial killers progress through their killing career, the time between each cycle reduces until their compulsion to kill can be a matter of days or hours. This is often how serial killers are discovered – this increasing compulsion to kill heightens their risk prone behaviour that causes them to make errors of judgement and poor body disposal decisions. A good example of this is Jeffrey Dahmer whose method of body disposal relied on a vat of acid kept in his own home. About ten years had elapsed between his first and second murder but towards the end of his killing career he was murdering as many as two a week and as a consequence found it difficult to effectively dispose of the increasing number of victims' bodies housed in his flat, alerting neighbours to the putrid odours emitted from his flat. He also became careless in administering the correct drug dosage to comatose his later victims which enabled one of his victims to escape and inform the police.

In all of the profiling addressed thus far, the correct decisions from the sources of information considered is important; however, there are two different methods of decision making used when profiling known as inductive and deductive. Methods of decision making are important for profiling regardless of whether this be for the FBI and Holmes and DeBurger's approaches or stages in the Model of Personal Violence (also based on the information available to the profiler). We will consider these two types of decision making next.

### Inductive and deductive profiling

Inductive profiling makes use of information regarding the personality traits of offenders who have committed similar crimes and left a similar crime scene. The idea is to draw upon information that links offenders together and the most obvious way to do this is by considering the crime scene evidence. This approach is labour saving and does not require any basic skills of understanding human behaviour. Alternatively, deductive profiling requires profilers to analyse the crime scene and any remaining evidence which can help construct a mental image of the offender. This involves analysis of the victim's body and who the victim was. Holmes and Holmes (2002) believed that optimum information regarding the victim will provide more clarity as to the nature of the offender. As well as the physical evidence, the crime scene and victim can provide unspoken clues about the assailant's state of mind and the motivating factors that led to the crime. The disadvantage with deductive over inductive approaches is the length of time it takes to produce a profile report for the police.

Furthermore, given that the goals of profiling for the criminal justice system include:

- a social and psychological assessment of the offender,
- a psychological evaluation of belongings found on the offender,
- advice on interviewing techniques and strategies.

it is important that the profiler pays particular attention to the evidence and details of the crime scene. Police and law enforcers, especially in the US, rely as part of their investigation on offender profiling which makes it even more imperative that profilers are as accurate as possible. According to Geberth (1981), however, offender profiling is 'an educated attempt to provide investigative agencies with specific information as to the type of individual who committed a certain crime' (p.46). Offender profiling, therefore, is not a science but an educated guess at interpreting the available crime scene evidence and other relevant information from psychologists, psychiatrists, sociologists and criminologists. Armed, however, with psychological theory of how people behave, it is possible for profilers to use the following assumptions:

- the crime scene reflects the personality of the offender;
- the central core of personality does not change – a criminal lifestyle does not happen overnight;
- the crime scene holds the clues, which are like an offender's signature.

All information helps in the production of a report to the police. Despite inductive and deductive reasoning used by profilers to provide an accurate offender profile for the police, the reliability and validity of offender profiling as an effective investigative tool has not been without its critics. In the next section criticisms of the FBI and Holmes and DeBurger's offender profiling strategy will be evaluated.

## Evaluation of offender profiling

There has been an abundance of research undertaken to show how unreliable the FBI approach to offender profiling is as a tool for predicting an offender's identity and location. One major criticism of the FBI approach is the limited empirical evidence in support of the organised–disorganised classification. Initially based on interviews with 36 serial sexual murderers, FBI profiling has continued to rely upon information derived from these interviews which has been used time and time again to generate new profiles. Howitt (2011) argued that there is some merit to the FBI approach and the typologies of Holmes and DeBurger but further empirical study is required to clarify and modify the concepts they used. In order to evaluate offender profiling fairly, it is important to present the evidence for and against and to have a baseline measure of success rate – in other words, the number of profiles generated that have helped the police in their investigations culminating in arrest.

### Does offender profiling successfully predict culpability?

Psychiatrist James Brussel in the 1950s and 1960s successfully profiled George Metesky, known as the Mad Bomber of New York and Albert DeSalvo, the Boston Strangler, which led to their arrest and conviction. Metesky bombed different areas of New York over a 16 year period by leaving his homemade bombs to detonate. He left bombs in busy areas used by many people such as the New York Public Library, Grand Central Terminal and the Radio City Music Hall. Metesky sent a letter to the police openly describing his annoyance with the Consolidated Edison Company. Brussel read this letter and was able to extract information that the police had failed to notice. Brussel (1968) said, 'by studying a man's deeds, I have deduced what kind of man he might be' (p.4). The profiled details provided were accurate but did not, in fact, lead to Metesky's arrest. A clerk working for the Consolidated Edison Company assumed that an ex-employee who was dismissed on ill-health grounds was responsible for the bombings. The clerk investigated the files and by comparing the writing style in the file with the letter police had received deduced that the bomber was indeed the ex-employee Metesky.

Despite the clerk's research leading to Metesky's arrest, Brussel's profile was compared with the facts about Metesky and a strong overlap was found, even down to the details of attire. Brussel also profiled DeSalvo who had violently raped and murdered 13 women between 1962 and 1964. A panel of experts and police concluded that they were looking for two murderers based on the differences across the crime scenes and victim ages. Brussel, however, disagreed claiming that it was one killer who had modified his MO over time and experience. DeSalvo was a known rapist with a string of previous convictions for assault and was later incarcerated in a psychiatric hospital where he confessed to being the Boston Strangler. The profile Brussel provided overlapped with the facts of DeSalvo to the extent that police were convinced and satisfied that he was the Boston Strangler – hence a success.

There have been other successful profilers such as Dr Patrick Tooley who, in England, helped police find the murderer of Susan Stevenson. Tooley had made descriptions of her killer that were informative and led to the conviction of Peter Stout who fitted the profile well (Tullett 1987). Unfortunately the police in England did not acknowledge the potential of profiling in the investigative process until at least a decade later when they approached Professor David Canter, now a key academic in the study of offender profiling and instigator of investigative psychology.

The question of how successful FBI profiling has been in predicting culpability was addressed by Pinizzotto and Finkel (1990) who presented evidence to show that profilers have an accuracy rate of 67 per cent compared to other experts who averaged 57 per cent. They gave profiling experts and non-experts, such as students, transcripts of a criminal case to read who then made predictions of the offender's traits. These predictions were compared with the actual characteristics possessed by the offender in a bid to test the assumption that profilers have a more sophisticated understanding of criminal behaviour. Although evaluating existing profile transcripts and using a checklist is an interesting approach, the study misses the crucial element of deductive profiling – which is to generate a profile using deductive analysis based on crime scene and victim characteristics. Nevertheless this approach has been useful and many researchers have adopted it. A meta-analysis (comparing results of similar studies) has shown profilers to be more accurate overall than non-profilers (Kocsis, Middledorp and Karpin 2008). The difference in overall accuracy by profilers is 66 per cent compared with 34 per cent accuracy for non-profilers. This margin of difference in accuracy is fairly consistent for other characteristics of offenders such as cognitive, physical and social history – the exception, however, is in the prediction of offence behaviour (53 per cent for profilers and 48 per cent for non-profilers).

Kocsis *et al.* (2008) argued that this presents evidence of profilers being able to make more accurate predictions about offenders than non-experts. This has been disputed by researchers such as Snook, Eastwood, Gendreau and Bennell (2010) who analysed the same data but concluded the opposite. Howitt (2011) accounted for this difference of opinion as a consequence of disparate definitions of what comprises expertise in offender profiling. He claimed that, 'If we exclusively define an expert profiler to include those who have clear training and expertise in the FBI style of profiling then the evidence that profiling experts are better than non-profilers at producing accurate profiles is stronger' (p.272). When police officers, regarded as the experts but who have not been trained to profile, are compared with non-profilers, there is little difference in their profiling competency. Howitt considered which of the two is correct and concluded neither because there is no clarity of what constitutes an expert profiler. It is also important to consider police attitudes towards any generated profiles in terms of helpfulness even if they did not lead to an arrest – discussed next.

## Police opinion of profile usefulness

Another way of considering the usefulness of profiles is to ask police if they find the profile generated helpful even if it does not lead to the capture of the offender. The findings here are interesting and demonstrated that police believe profiles to be helpful even when the generated profile was fictitious and had no bearing on the true offender characteristics. This is important because as well as hopefully leading to the apprehension of an offender, profilers aim to provide useful information for the database to expand the theoretical knowledge and understanding of different types of criminal behaviour. If police find profiles helpful then this can be regarded as one measure of success. In one study by Alison, Smith and Morgan (2003) police were given a FBI profile to evaluate for its accuracy as measured against the facts for a convicted offender. Descriptions depicted in the profile included statements relating to age, IQ, mental health and sexual tendencies. Police were positive about the profile and believed it would be an asset in future criminal investigation. The police, however, made the same positive claims when a fictitious profile depicting inaccurate information about the offender was substituted for the profile based on facts. Regardless of accuracy therefore police found profiles useful – a sentiment not shared by many academics. This finding questions the reliability of police opinions of profile usefulness as a measure of profiling success. Another route to examining the accuracy of offender profiling is to look for similarities of application in cross-cultural studies.

## Cross-cultural comparisons in the application of offender profiling

It is possible to compare the application of offender profiling used in different countries and determine whether the same typologies occur to those ascertained by the FBI. Comparisons between US and South African serial killers have shown partial similarity in the application of FBI and Holmes and DeBurger's offender profiling. US serial killers are often diagnosed with personality and mood disorders, substance abuse, paranoid and schizoid traits (Hickey 2002; Pakhomou 2004), and autistic spectrum disorders (Silva, Leong and Ferrari 2004). Studies in South Africa showed comparable findings (Labuschagne 2001). Del Fabbro's (2006) study of two South African families of serial killers' also found a history of childhood abuse, rejection, cruelty and family dysfunction in the background of these killers, hence supporting previous research by Hickey (2002) and Kurtz and Hunter (2004). Similar to the descriptions of inadequacy, loneliness and helplessness reported by many US serial killers, South African serial killers also echoed these feelings (Labuschagne 2001). The trauma-control model proposed by Hickey has received much support from research on serial killers in the US. In particular, the self-experienced trauma in childhood that many serial killers described resurfaces in adulthood in the guise of offence behaviour which often imitates and recreates these experiences: offence behaviours in this context resemble process-focused behaviours that are concerned with the whole offence and not just the act of killing. Research in South Africa, however, only provides partial support for this as murderers there tended to be act-focused and typically depersonalised their victims (Hodgskiss 2001). As is the case with Hickey's analysis, the role of sexual fantasy is minimised and this is true of South African serial killers who lack what Hodgskiss (2004) referred to as sexually violent conscious fantasy. Furthermore, sexual fetishes, fire-setting and cruelty to animals are rarely seen in South African serial killers unlike the US (Hodgskiss 2004). Other research findings showed:

- There is limited support for lust, mission and thrill serial killers in the US (Canter and Wentink 2004).
- A similar pattern of typology for South African serial killers who were primarily act-focused was found by Hodgskiss (2001).

- The typologies of US serial killers might be irrelevant to what Hodgskiss (2004) referred to as non–North American serial killers. This is in part due to cultural differences that impact on people's beliefs and daily life, supported by Hickey's (2002) comment regarding how profiles compiled in the US often contradict those in other countries. There is more overlap with other developing countries such as South and Central America, Asia, the Middle East and the rest of Africa than there is with US serial killers (Gorby 2000; Hodgskiss 2004).
- There are similarities that are shared across cultures, some of which have already been discussed, such as crime scene behaviours showing different coherent structures (Hodgskiss 2001); sense of inadequacy and helplessness (Hickey 2002); elements of psychiatric disorder (Labuschagne 2001); application of Hickey's trauma–control model similar for both Germany and the US (Harbort and Mokros 2001); motivating factors of control (Hodgskiss 2001) and the progression of more distinctive behaviours (signatures) expressed as killings continue (Hodgskiss 2001; Wentlink 2001).

These findings suggest that there is an element of reliability and validity to the FBI method and typology approach of Holmes and DeBurger. Despite differences across countries relating to their individual cultural climate, there also appears to be evidence showing some support for FBI and Holmes and DeBurger's profiling that needs unpicking and further investigation. Empirical research has been conducted to make sense of these findings within a more scientific framework – the topic of our next section.

### Empirical research testing on the reliability of offender profiling

The FBI approach to offender profiling has been criticised for relying upon a poor database of 36 cases of serial murder. In response to this, however, the FBI developed a system of a computerised database designed to link unsolved and unusual homicides. This system is known as the Violent Criminal Apprehension Program (VICAP) and records similarities of crime scene and victim characteristics of unsolved homicides throughout the US. Its purpose is to link crimes that might not have been considered to be associated in any way (Howlett, Hanfland and Ressler 1986). This helps investigators to think outside the box of their jurisdiction area, as many serial killers are geographically transient and will cross counties to continue killing. Despite being conceptually good, VICAP is only as effective as the content it contains. VICAP relies upon questionnaire completion from local law enforcers, which is time consuming, and explains why the rate of return is disappointing. Nevertheless, this system has proven to be successful in cases of multiple murders, where different crime scenes and victims across the US has helped increase the extent of data amassed and analysed using technology like VICAP. This has helped to improve the odds of successful profiling by the FBI.

1    Empirical research conducted by Canter and his team have uncovered conceptual and structural flaws in the organised–disorganised dichotomy and the four typologies (visionary, mission, hedonistic and power/control) using statistical analysis of crime scenes and victim characteristics. Through the use of the dataset of over 3,000 files of serial killers operating in the US since 1960 (known as the Missen Corpus), Canter and colleagues were able to derive a subset for statistical analysis consisting of crime scenes, behaviours during crimes and characteristics of victims.

- Canter, Alison, Alison, and Wentink (2004) were interested in whether crime scene behaviours included in their subset would divide into two mutually exclusive categories: organised or disorganised. There were three stages to their analysis but first they performed a frequency of occurrence count of 39 crime scene behaviours from a cohort of 100 serial murders: representing the FBI's organised and disorganised categories. Frequency counts were then converted to percentages which clearly showed that the majority of murders had crime scene behaviours belonging to the organised category. They concluded that most serial murder was organised and that many crime scene behaviours were generic to most serial murders. This can be demonstrated through the following examples: in 67 per cent of all serial murders the organised trait of 'the murder weapon missing' was the case. In the case of 'victim alive for sex', this occurred in 91 per cent of serial murders. Crime scene behaviours that were more idiosyncratic occurred in fewer serial murders like, for instance, 'decapitation' and 'dismemberment' appearing in 5 per cent and 3 per cent of all serial murders respectively. The frequency of occurrence percentages provided little empirical support for the organised/disorganised dichotomy and instead alluded to most serial murder being organised or having organised elements while a few having an additional disorganised hallmark.

- The first stage of their analysis addressed 'within-type consistency'. They analysed the co-occurrence of pairs of crime scene behaviours stipulated within the organised and disorganised categories using Jaccard's coefficient, but found this to be low even among the six highly placed crime scene behaviours for each category. This, they concluded, provided little evidence for the placement of crime scene behaviours in the organised and disorganised classifications. The co-occurrence for many of these pairings was below 50 per cent per cent; however, Canter and Youngs (2009) stated that for the four top crime scene behaviours in the organised classification, co-occurrence reached as high as 71 per cent (this, for instance, being the case for the crime scene traits of 'victim alive for sex' and 'body positioned').

- The second stage of their analysis addressed 'between-type discrimination'. For this analysis, crime scene behaviours from organised and disorganised categories were pair-cross-compared for co-occurrence. The assumption was that these pairings should have poor co-occurrence in order to support the mutual exclusivity of the organised and disorganised classifications. These pairings, however, co-occurred to the same magnitude as the within-type pairings. This suggested that the crime scene behaviours could be just as representative of organised as disorganised categories.

- The third stage of their analysis involved using the Multi-Dimensional Scaling technique known as Smallest Space Analysis (SSA) to ascertain the overall patterns of crime scene behaviour co-occurrence. The 39 crime scene behaviours were analysed using SSA to formulate a figure plot (see Figure 12.3) showing the most strongly associated crime scene behaviours together and the least associated further apart. This provided a visual of the relationship between organised and disorganised crime scene behaviours – demonstrating that crime scene behaviours associated with the disorganised category appearing across the plot while those linked with the organised category as residing at the centre of the plot. This meant that crime scene behaviours associated with the organised classification permeated most serial murders, and that organised behaviour encapsulated what it is to be a serial killer. These three stages demonstrated conclusively that empirical evidence supporting the FBI's organised–disorganised dichotomy is very limited. What is most apparent from this visual map (Figure 12.3) is the distribution of organised and disorganised crime scene criteria. The organised crime scene criteria are in the centre, unlike those of the disorganised category which are peripheral and less generic of serial crime per se. In the case of 'ransacking', its occurrence is in less than 10 per cent of serial murder, unlike 'victim alive for sex' whose occurrence is in 50 per cent of serial killings.

2   Taylor, Lambeth, Green, Bone and Cahillane (2012) conducted a study to investigate the FBI organised–disorganised categories using a 'bottom-up approach' where crime scene behavioural and victim characteristics (i.e. crime scene criteria) were analysed using a Multi-Dimensional Scaling technique known as agglomerate hierarchical cluster analysis.

- The aim of this study was to ascertain whether 50 crime scene criteria extracted from a sample of 40 (20 female and 20 male) serial killers would co-occur as clusters representing the FBI traits of organised or disorganised classifications. By considering crime scene criteria in this way it was hoped that the clusters would support the theory and form mutually exclusive categories of organised and disorganised typologies – hence, the 'bottom-up approach' where the data builds a narrative and not the theory informing the data (i.e. a top-down approach). Using the Wards statistic, four clusters were formulated for the male serial killer sample showing some support for the organised

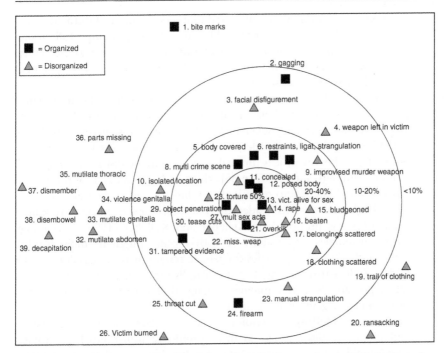

*Figure 12.3* SSA visual map of organised-disorganised crime scene criteria behaviours for serial killers

Canter *et al.* 2004. Reproduced with kind permission from David Canter and the APA.

and disorganised classifications. In all four clusters there were rogue crime scene criteria. In the case of female serial killers three clusters were formed which showed organised and disorganised crime scene criteria in all of the clusters.

- Differences in the preponderance of crime scene criteria within clusters for male and female serial killers cannot be easily explained through the FBI interpretation. Clusters suggesting a disorganised typology have other organised crime scene criteria present supporting an organised MO. These findings could be explained using a mixed offender typology but this does not further the empirical evidence for the FBI approach. Canter *et al.*'s (2004) conclusion that most serial killings have an organised element is supported by Taylor *et al.*'s (2012) findings. For instance, when the frequency of occurrence for crime scene criteria was examined, Taylor *et al.* found a strong element of organised traits even in clusters suggesting a disorganised typology. The same trend was found for female serial killers. In cluster 1 for example, there were fewer organised traits but their frequency of occurrence was 80–95 per cent. These findings are in support of a generic organised element to serial murder but also highlight the possibility of differentiating serial murders on merit of distinctive disorganised crime scene criteria. Hence, in future, an empirically sound approach might be to assess serial murders based on disorganised crime scene criteria given that there appears to be a core organised element to the MO in most serial killings.

3   Another potential problem for the FBI classification is the importance of offenders leaving evidence at the crime scene so that the MO can be ascertained (Jackson and Bekerian 1997). An obvious signature can also be helpful in assessing the offender as organised or disorganised. As previously pointed out, however, it is unusual to see 'uniquely distinct actions in all of their crimes' (Canter 2007, p.35) which makes it difficult for profilers to separate serial killers into organised and disorganised categories.

4   The FBI dichotomy fails to adequately account for the female serial killer's behaviours. As proposed by Kelleher and Kelleher (1998), a typology based on females acting alone or with another might be more fruitful. They outlined five typologies for female serial killers acting alone: black widow (kills partners), angel of death (kills the vulnerable in their care), sexual predator (sexual homicide), revenge (kills for hate and jealousy) and profit (kills for gain or incidentally).

5   Holmes and DeBurger's typologies have also been criticised. Gresswell and Hollin (1994) alluded to three problems: non-mutual exclusivity; there could be more unaccounted for typologies; and the interactions between the environment, victim and murderer are not considered as possible factors for killers changing their motives across time.

6   Non-mutual exclusivity of these typology traits was investigated by Canter and Wentink (2004). Using SSA and crime scene variables from the Missen Corpus representing the four typologies, they found a generic contribution of power/control variables to serial murder. There were some clustering of traits under the mission and hedonistic typologies but too few to resonate with the content of these typologies. Some support was found for the visionary typology but limited support for psychosis or any compulsions to kill.

   •   Canter and Wentink (2004) re-organised crime scene criteria of the four typologies along the FBI disorganised to organised dimension. As the typologies overlapped suggesting non-mutual exclusivity of the typologies, Canter and Wentink (2004) concluded that the typologies were a mere modification of the organised–disorganised dichotomy.

7   Holmes and DeBurger's typologies also fail to account for female serial killing. According to Frei, Vollom, Graf and Dittmann (2006) this is because female serial killers are a rarity comprising 20 per cent of all serial murderers. Frei et al. showed that the most common covert method for killing is the use of poison but other methods include drowning (5 per cent), stabbing (11 per cent), suffocation (16 per cent) and shooting (20 per cent). Frei et al.'s research of 86 female serial killers in the US showed

that victims were often the vulnerable such as the elderly, their own and other children, but also their spouse. Despite much research looking at the usefulness of the organised–disorganised classifications in female serial killing, the application of the typologies to female motives for killing has received very little empirical investigation.

8   Taylor *et al.* (2012) investigated whether there are differences between male and female serial killers in terms of the Holmes and DeBurger's typologies. By adopting ten of the traits from Holmes and DeBurger's typologies and a further 48 crime scene criteria taken from their first study investigating the FBI classification, a total of 58 crime scene criteria were used. All crime scene criteria used were relevant to the typology categories.

- Four clusters were identified for male serial killers and three for female serial killers. A difference in the preponderance of crime scene criteria within clusters for female and male serial killers was found; however, these could not be explained using Holmes and DeBurger's typologies. Despite there being some semblance to Holmes and DeBurger's classifications, Kelleher and Kelleher's (1998) typologies proposed for female serial killers offered a better fit.

- Taylor *et al.*'s (2012) distribution of crime scene criteria patterning resembled that found in Canter and Wentink's (2004) study. If the crime scene criteria were collapsed using a disorganised to organised dimension, the origins of the typologies would clearly derive from the FBI classification.

9   The **Radex Model** used by Canter offers further criticism of American offender profiling.

- Using the SSA approach Canter has shown that discrete clusters of offences that congregate into distinct types of offending simply do not occur. He further claimed that typology classification is simplistic and misleading. When using SSA, visual mappings demonstrate the most ubiquitous of crime scene criteria as co-occurring in the centre suggesting that these criminal actions are at the core of criminality. This means that in the case of murder, there are common attributes of the crime scene and victim that tend to occur together – likewise for other types of offence. There are also more peripheral crime scene criteria which reside further away from the central core of criminal actions. Canter claimed that it makes more sense to concentrate on themes that make up offending than to entertain the notion of 'primary types', which comprise all offences. Themes are useful as they not only describe any type of offence they also enable inferences to be made about different offences. From this it is possible to derive different themes or, as it is often referred to as, different 'facets'. A facet as defined by Shye and Elizur (1994) is, 'A set playing the role of a component set of a Cartesian set' (p.179). Put simply, this means that it is possible to devise a series of visual maps that represent an object or person in a two-dimensional physical space. Applying this to serial killers, Howitt (2011) has provided the examples of the 'amount of effort by offender to hide own identity' versus 'amount of effort by offender to hide the identity of victim' (p.281), both of which are rated from high to low. Hence, these are examples of two facets which can be visually mapped using SSA to show the extent of co-occurrence between inputted crime scene criteria. To illustrate the worth of this approach, consider the closeness of similarity between aggravated burglary (see Box 12.1) and a street mugging versus the distance of similarity between aggravated burglary and breaking into a commercial property with no employee on site at the time.

• The thematic approach is derived from Guttman's (1982) **Radex Model** which he used to differentiate between individuals by using a variety of facets (also known as **Facet Theory**). In relation to criminals, the facet of 'specificity', for instance, explains the centrality of many crime scene criteria shared by all offences which then radiates out towards the peripheral crime scene criteria that are more specific to certain crimes. The 'thematic' facet describes how qualitative aspects of behaviour differ. Hence it is possible to focus on themes of crime targets such as people or property. A radex can formulate a measure of the different attributes of crimes ranging from the more common to rarer aspects of a crime and to the psychological implications of these crime scene behaviours. Further information is provided by the radex such as what or who the targets are and the levels of aggression portrayed through the nature of crime scene criteria. The Radex Model has shown how criminals can simultaneously be generalists and have a crime focus (see Figure 12.4 and Box 12.4).

10  The statistical profiling approach used by Canter relies on the compilation of salient crime scene criteria from crime scene records held by police. The SSA approach is then applied to establish any patterns among the different data sets. While there is overlap in ideology between statistical and FBI approaches to profiling, the manner in which they are executed differs in terms of empirical saliency. For both statistical and FBI profiling, the assumption holds that crime scene criteria have vital clues about the nature of behaviours committed by the offender during the crime. These clues inform profilers of offender characteristics which can be used by police to help their investigations. The ideology may be the same but the methodology differs from a top-down approach (FBI) to a bottom-up approach (statistical). Thus the interpretations using the FBI approach is theory-driven unlike the data-driven interpretations resulting from statistical examination using SSA (Canter et al. 2004) or agglomerate hierarchical cluster analysis (Taylor et al. 2012). Both of these statistical analyses are examples of Multi-Dimensional Scaling (MDS) techniques differing in the statistical quotient used (Jaccards and Wards respectively). The aim of

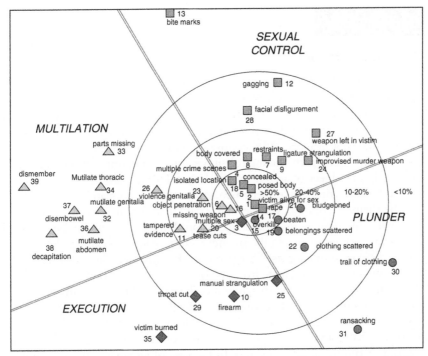

*Figure 12.4* Demonstrates through SSA the distinct subsets of behaviours by serial killers Canter *et al.* 2004. Reproduced with kind permission from David Canter and the APA.

both statistical analyses is to consider the crime scene criteria that co–occur together.

- Canter, Alison, Alison and Wentink (2004) using SSA devised an interesting visual map of the crime scene criteria for serial killers. There were distinct subsets of behaviours that fitted mutilation, sexual control, plunder and execution. Figure 12.4 displays these subsets quite distinctly.

  Another angle to profiling is geographical profiling which Canter originally used in his early investigations of serial rapist and murderer John Duffy in 1986 (Canter 1994).

### Geographical profiling

Police wanted to know if a single offender was responsible for the 'railway murders' or were there two culprits working together. Through the use of geographical profiling, Canter was able to advise police on the nature of the culprit they should be looking for. Box 12.5 describes Canter's first profile based on painstaking and meticulous examination of crime scene details and the adaptation of geographical profiling.

# Box 12.4

## The Radex Model

It is possible that by using different themes (i.e. of object, vehicle and person), crime scene criteria can be mapped according to the victim as an object, victim as a person or victim as a vehicle. In the case of a victim as an object, the offender does not perceive the victim as having any human significance nor feelings, and therefore shows no feelings towards his victim. The victim has no participating role in what happens during the offence and is simply the object of action for the killer. This in part enables offenders to perform horrific crime scene behaviour, such as mutilation. In the case of the theme victim as a vehicle, the serial killer uses the victim as a means of expressing desires, anger and aggression. Under these circumstances the victim is very important to the offender and provides a meaningful context from which the offence itself arises out of. For instance, the anger directed at the victim might originate from the offender's life experiences – a person who the victim has come to symbolise. There is acknowledgement of the victim's humanity which satisfies the offender's needs even more and it is this that can lead to extreme killing. The victim symbolises all that the offender hates and is used as a means for venting anger, which explains why a victim is carefully targeted. In the case of victim as a person theme, the victim is perceived as a human being who has feelings. The interaction between offender and victim is one of manipulation, abuse and violence – all of which are methods of achieving goal satisfaction. The victim is the target of the offender as the victim has something that the offender wants. The nature of crime emerging from this relationship includes, for example, domestic arguments leading to murder or opportunistic rape. This type of interaction with victims is the offender's normative behavioural style arising out of a criminal background (Canter 1994; Canter and Youngs 2009).

Further research has concentrated on the victim as vehicle and victim as a person, referred to as the expressive-instrumental divide. As the expression of desires, aggression and anger are sub-facets of the victim as a vehicle, and being instrumental and manipulative sub-facets of the victim as a person, Salfati and Canter (1999) have considered this in their exploration of homicidal behaviours using the crime scene. They found that the expressive-instrumental divide successfully described and accounted for their data. Since adopting this research approach, numerous cross-cultural studies have looked at single homicides in Greece (Salfati and Haratsis 2001), Finland (Santtila, Canter, Elfgren and Häkkänen 2001), Belgium (Thijssen and de Ruiter 2011) and Canada (Salfati and Dupont 2006) and have provided credence to the expressive-instrumental divide. Studies by Salfati and Bateman (2005), and later Field, Johnson, Kim and Salfati (2006), used cohorts of US serial killers and found that the expressive-instrumental explanation can be equally used for multiple murders. Sorochinski and Salfati (2010) also reported offender-victim interactions that influenced the cognitive strategies used by serial killers. These findings suggest that crime scene behaviours for single and multiple homicides have common underlying themes reflected in the MO – even cross-culturally.

# Box 12.5

## Canter's first profile based primarily on geographical profiling

As part of his investigation of the railway murderer in 1986, Canter collated information that could be analysed quantitatively. This involved endless searching through crime scene details such as the different locations of murder sites, the order that the murders occurred (i.e. chronology) and the estimated times these murders were committed (i.e. temporal). Using the locations, chronology and temporal factors, Canter was able to ascertain a geographical profile. Typically with each murder, crime scene criteria were coded and inputted into a computer for analysis of similarity and difference. A high degree of similarity was found for some of the murders, in particular, the nature of rape performed before victims were killed. Analytical skills of interpreting multi-layered maps of crime scenes and timings enabled Canter to conclude that there was a long time gap of murder, suggesting that the offender might have been apprehended. From all information inputted, the offender's abode was suggested by Canter to be near to the locations of the first three murders. Furthermore Canter suggested that an offender's mental map of an area influences where they commit their crimes. With this in mind the railway murders signalled a clue to the area the murderer lived and worked. Canter successfully profiled the murderer on the basis of the similar cases of rape using 17 discreet factors. All his assumptions led to the arrest of John Duffy, who later revealed his partner in crime to be David Mulcahy – responsible for the rapes and murders that had different features from the crime scene criteria of Duffy's crimes. Duffy had a profound knowledge of the railway network because, as was revealed, Duffy was employed as a carpenter for British Rail.

Geographical profiling works on the premise that the environment of the offender is tangible with where he chooses to operate. This is corroborated by what is known as crime hot spots – areas where an offender is likely to commit his crimes. Offenders work in areas in which they feel comfortable and familiar with, which is why the distribution of their crimes is often skewed or biased towards specific areas of a city, town or even rural country spots. Geographical profiling has similarities with the Routine Activities Theory based on research by Cohen and Felson (1979). The underlying assumption of the Routine Activity Theory is that in the absence of effective controls, offenders will seize the opportunity to commit offences against attractive targets. The offender and attractive target need to meet at the same place. In the case of personal crimes such as serial murder, the target is a person but if there is no convergence between the two then no crime occurs. As is the case with Hirschi's social bond (aka Social Control Theory), Cohen and Felson referred to offenders having social bonds with others but also to having 'social handlers' who are the controllers and whose presence can prevent a crime from occurring in the first place. Handlers can be a host of people such as parents and the family or peers who constitute informal guardians unlike the police who are formal guardians. Handlers can control offender behaviour but can also protect potential victims by having a presence, especially if present when the offender and victim co-habit the same place. They also suggested that offenders use tools to aid in accomplishing their crimes but without these tools they are more likely to have problems of escaping handlers and consequently over-powering their victims.

Although there are similarities with FBI profiling, geographical profiling is argued to have begun in the 1980s in the UK. Others attributed the introduction of geographical profiling to Detective Rossmo (2000) who used a computer programme called RIGEL. Whoever is responsible, the ideology remains the same – different crime hot spots, chronology of murder and timings are analysed to ascertain the most likely address of the offender. Furthermore, the consideration of crime scene criteria of each case can help geographical profilers decide the likelihood of the same, different or more than one offender being accountable. This is due to crime scene criteria holding clues as to how long it would have taken to complete the murder, and the co-occurrence of specific details. Dragnet is a computerised system enabling profilers to establish the likely residence of an offender based on the locations of the crime scenes. Dragnet was trialled in Las Vegas where information linking numerous rapes was inputted into the system. This produced a map of the probable areas the offender operated, and eventually this led to a single apartment block where Duffy was arrested (Canter 2003). Geographical profiling provides useful visual maps (see Figure 12.5) of the possible home locations of offenders.

Dragnet revealed that many offenders live and work close to where they commit their crimes. Armed with this finding, Canter and Larkin (1993) introduced the circle theory of environmental range. The notion of a circle theory of environmental range implies that if a circle is drawn that includes all the linked crimes the offender's residence is likely to be located somewhere within this circle (see Figure 12.5). This was also suggested by Rossmo (2000) who claimed that offenders operate close to home and that their offending declines with increasing distance from their home-base. This is supported by the figures showing that 85 per cent of offenders did indeed live within the circle (Godwin and Canter 1997; Kocsis and Irwin 1997), and in Germany 63 per

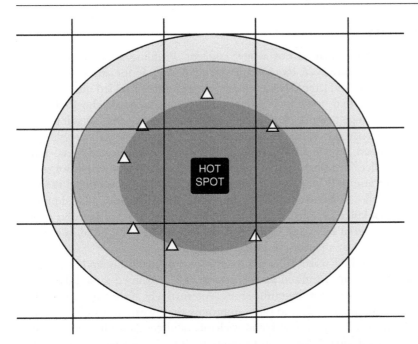

*Figure 12.5* Representation of visual map provided through Dragnet Triangles represent crime locations. Lighter shading denotes increased distance from the likely residence of the perpetrator.

cent of 53 serial murderers lived within a six mile zone from where their crime scenes were discovered (Snook, Cullen, Mokros and Harbort 2005). There are age and intelligence factors that can be informative in ascertaining the extent of offence dispersal and the nature of offenders. For example, murderers who travelled away from their area of residence tended to have higher IQs, while younger offenders remained closer to home (which could be related to limited criminal experience than to IQ per se).

Geographical data, when coupled with temporal information, is even more robust (Ainsworth 2001). Ainsworth described how burglaries occurring between 3 pm and 4 pm are committed by teenagers as this tends to be when they are on the move, heading for home after a day at school. The Routine Activity Theory predicted that street robberies increase at the beginning of the new academic year when new student arrivals settled on campus. Burglary increased when student residences became vacant during marked holiday periods such as Christmas and the summer. Geographical profiling is a useful investigative tool proving to be an asset for police detective work. It is, however, only as good as the information inputted into the system, such as crime scene criteria and victim location details.

## Summary

- Profiling criminals is not a new concept. Profiling criminals for a very long time, however, focused on objective forensic measures such as fingerprinting and later DNA testing: these measures provided more concrete evidence of an individual's presence at a crime scene. In the 1970s there was a change towards profiling offenders' personality and behaviour based on evidence left at the crime scene. This form of offender profiling was progressed by the FBI who had interviewed incarcerated serial rapists and killers to obtain narratives which led to the organised–disorganised classifications. It was Ressler (working for the FBI) who coined the term serial killer to mean a murderer who kills more than once. The definition of serial killer has been revised in terms of the number of murders constituting a serial killer and whether murders must be committed in different locations over a period of time.

- The organised serial killer plans his crime meticulously and as a consequence has an organised *modus operandi*. The organised serial killer leaves few clues, if any, at the crime scene. Alternatively, disorganised serial killers act spontaneously and often improvise their weapon from the location of the attack. The crime scene is chaotic and contains physical evidence. Organised serial killers tend to enjoy the process of their crime – which includes the *modus operandi* and the behaviours associated with killing (i.e. process-focused) unlike disorganised serial killers who tend to focus and enjoy the act of killing itself which is often quick (i.e. act-focused).

- Other typologies were introduced such as Holmes and DeBurger's visionary, mission, hedonistic and power/control. Both visionary and mission serial killers target specific victims but in the former case, killings are led by delusions and hallucinations. Hedonistic serial killers can be one of three types: lust, thrill and comfort-oriented. Although there are slight differences in what these serial killers focus on, the common denominator is the pleasure principle, hence the label hedonism. For power/control serial killers, the complete domination of their victims motivates them to murder but not until they have tortured their victims (i.e. process-focused killing).

- Whilst these classifications and typologies appeared interesting there was little empirical support of their reliability. Studies by Canter, Alison, Alison, and Wentink's (2004) and Taylor, Lambeth, Green, Bone and Cahillane's (2012) showed robust patterns of organised crime scene criteria prevailing across many murders committed by serial killers. This suggests that disorganised crime scene criteria might be more informative as they tend to be less frequent, more distinctive and idiosyncratic in their dispersal among the spectrum of serial murder. The organised–disorganised classifications are not mutually exclusive and the need to introduce the mixed offender exemplifies this. Empirical research suggests Holmes and DeBurger's typologies originate from the FBI organised–disorganised dimension.

- The Model of Personal Violence was introduced as a five stage description of the different states of mind a serial killer cycles through. During the first stage, the serial killer is in a 'balanced' state of mind and whose deviance is concealed, covert and under control. The second stage is the beginning of feeling the need to commit a crime which is exacerbated in stage three by negative inward thoughts. Stage four is when the criminal act is committed known as the negative outward response. Once the crime has been committed, the serial killer is concerned with body disposal in stage five. This model outlines the psyche of serial killers prior to, during and post killing.

- The geographical profiling method tends to have higher success rates in terms of locating the whereabouts of the offender, but this is limited by the extent of accurate and reliable crime scene reporting and the detailing of crime scene criteria. This is important for the circle theory of environmental range, where an offender's residence can be pinpointed to a reasonable degree of precision provided the reporting of crime scene locations are correct. The estimation of time of death of the victim is important too, especially for ascertaining chronological sequencing of murders and for calculating the possibility of manoeuvring between points A and B within a set time period. Integrating geographical profiling with temporal information increases the likelihood of defining a precise circle in which to locate the offender's base of operation.

- The important question is whether offender profiling and, to some extent, geographical profiling are methods that can be reliably used by police in their investigations of serial killings for the identification and location of perpetrators. The US approach tends to rely on the FBI classifications and the typologies of Holmes and DeBurger; while in Britain, although concepts of organised and disorganised killers are often referred to, an offence oriented stance is taken when profiling. Focusing on offence details rather than the offender lends itself towards statistical analyses and geographical profiling. These methods have proven to be more successful in locating offenders and estimating their comfort zone of operation.

## Questions for discussion

1 What are the main criticisms of the FBI organised–disorganised classification and the typologies of Holmes and DeBurger?

2 In what ways are statistical and geographical profiling approaches more reliable in predicting who offenders are?

3 What did Canter do to accurately profile the 'railway murderer'? How was this different from the FBI approach?

# Reliability of investigative processes

Part V

# Reliability of investigative processes

# Chapter 13

# Eyewitness testimony and extra-legal defendant characteristics

The three chapters in Part V will explore different aspects of the investigative process. These aspects of the investigative process are important in the gathering of evidence by police, which in turn is submitted to the courts. It is, therefore, important that these methods are effective and offer reliable evidence to the court, so that the defendant gets a fair trial. In this chapter we will explore the first of these investigative processes – eyewitness testimony.

Despite research findings demonstrating the fallible nature of human memory, eyewitness testimony continues to be a valued form of evidence in the courtroom. Why this should be the case will be explored in this chapter by tracing the historical antecedents of how evidence was presented in the past. Eyewitness testimony was, and still is, based on providing verbal accounts of criminal events to the court. Given that, in the past, most people could not read and write, providing a verbal account became an important way of transferring information. The UK and US have a different legal system to mainland Europe, known as adversarial law. In Europe the inquisitorial legal system is used which, unlike the adversarial system, does not rely on a jury. We will see in this chapter that there are major implications for having a jury system – there are advantages but at the same time jurors making decisions of a defendant's guilt can be problematic. They have to assess factual information for its reliability and likelihood of proving the case. Furthermore, jurors have to take account of eyewitness evidence in the form of a testimony given under oath in the courtroom. The reliability of this testimony has been questioned since a spate of cases of falsely accused and imprisoned individuals has come to light. We will see how easy it is to be convinced of an eyewitness's identification of the suspect, and later in court, the accused, given our good track record at recognising and identifying familiar faces. We are naturally good at remembering faces. This has empirical support, as research shows that faces are processed automatically and holistically, and that familiar faces are easier to identify than unfamiliar faces. This accounts for why we rarely misidentify people we know but can incorrectly identify an unfamiliar person as someone else. Different psychological theories specifically concerned with the retrieval of verbal information will also be considered here. Wells (1978) has pointed out that there are many internal and external factors influencing the reliability of eyewitness testimony per se. He referred to these as estimator and system variables respectively. In this chapter we will explore both estimator and system variables in detail and show how these can impede the recall of information and the recognition of a face. Estimator variables can impair an individual's ability to process, encode and retrieve information from memory, while system variables can obstruct the methods used by police to attain evidence – in other words, one aspect of the investigative process. We will consider problems associated with older methods of facial composite construction and identity parades and discuss the new technologies introduced to help eyewitnesses improve their information retrieval of criminal events. In this chapter we will also consider the impact of non-evidential information (also known as **extra-legal defendant characteristics**) on juror decision making. We will see how jurors, like the rest of the population, use an Implicit Personality Theory, guiding our understanding and interpretation of people's behaviour. This includes the use of stereotypes which very often are biased and have no empirical evidence to substantiate their truthfulness. Physical attractiveness and ethnicity are two extra-legal defendant characteristics found to influence jurors' decisions of guilt. The findings, however, are mixed.

## Introduction

Eyewitness testimony is based on a special form of memory that relates directly to the events perceived, encoded and retained by the person witnessing them. It is different to other aspects of daily memory, not so much in the way it functions, but because accuracy of event recollection is of the utmost importance in a court of law. Eyewitness testimony has an important role in court proceedings since the retrieved information about a sequence of criminal events by a witness might influence the jury deliberation process. Research addressing eyewitness accuracy has found that witnesses often make errors of judgement about what they thought they saw and had actually seen. It was Hugo Münsterberg who claimed in 1908 in his book *On the Witness Stand* that different psychological factors can alter a trial's outcome. Taylor (1982) said:

> We can all recall situations where we remembered having seen an individual at . . . a cocktail party, only to subsequently discover that he was never there and that what we had remembered was an earlier party at which the individual was present. This is an example of the . . . phenomenon of unconscious transference (p.39).

The point Taylor is making here was addressed by Lawrence and Kubie in 1959 when they made the statement that

People quite often do not see or hear things which are presented clearly to their senses, but do see and hear things which are not there. . . What is more people frequently do not remember things which did happen to them but do remember things which did not happen to them.

A good example of where the testimony of one eyewitness led to an arrest and conviction is the case of Sam Hallam, who was accused of murdering trainee chef Essayas Kassahun in 2004. He was 17 years old when arrested but despite pleading not guilty and proclaiming his innocence he was imprisoned. The prosecution presented two witnesses who said that they saw Hallam at the murder scene, even though there was no forensic evidence to corroborate their account. One of the witnesses withdrew her statement saying that, 'I was just looking for someone on the spot to blame' (Evans 2012). Hallam said, after his conviction was quashed and having spent seven years in prison that, 'I don't want anyone else ever to suffer what I've been through since 2004. The identification evidence against me was so unreliable that it should never have been put to the jury' (Evans 2012). QC Henry Blaxland claimed that Hallam was the victim of a 'serious miscarriage of justice'. QC Henry Blaxland went on to say that

appellant Sam Hallam . . . has been the victim of a serious miscarriage of justice brought about by a combination of manifestly unreliable identification evidence, the apparent failure of his own alibi, failure by police properly to investigate his alibi and non-disclosure by the prosecution of material that could have supported his case (*Mirror News*, 17 May 2012).

There are problems with eyewitness testimony as the above case demonstrates. Many studies focusing on memory for faces and factors influencing how well eyewitnesses can recall information and identify perpetrators in mug shots and line-ups have found that while we are exceptionally good at remembering familiar faces, the memories of eyewitnesses can be fallible. Wells (1978) introduced estimator and system variables to eyewitness research, which has enabled researchers to concentrate on various aspects of the eyewitness process – factors focusing on the encoding process to those concerned with identity line-up structure. In the case of estimator variables, the focus of research is very much concerned with how eyewitnesses perceive, encode and retrieve information from memory. System variables relate to the techniques devised to help eyewitnesses remember, recall and recognise information. The construction of facial composites is an example of an aid to reconstructing the face of the perpetrator from the eyewitness' memory, whereas the viewing of mug shots are used to see if the perpetrator can be recognised from a database of convicted criminals. Identity line-ups are another example police use as a means to identifying the culprit.

The contribution of research addressing estimator and system variables have resulted in major changes to understanding how memory operates and to the techniques used by police to attain information from witnesses. Research findings on estimator and system variables will be discussed and evaluated later in this chapter. First, it is important to establish why eyewitness testimony is given such high esteem by the criminal justice system and why, despite research demonstrating the fallible nature of memory, it continues to be perceived as important and prestigious evidence. The answer to this is partly rooted in the history of how the law courts operated in medieval times which will be addressed in the next section.

## The law and eyewitness testimony

The importance of eyewitness testimony in court proceedings originates from the beginning of criminal law; relying on what people saw and said they had seen. Prior to the Industrial Revolution (1750–1850), most people in Britain lived in rural areas in small villages; travel was limited and, given these geographical demographics, villagers knew all the other villagers making it difficult for strangers to go unnoticed. Furthermore, the concept of physical evidence was unknown and, with formal education a privilege reserved for the elite, most of the populace remained illiterate. These factors combined accounted for why many local hearings and tribunals relied on the verbal testimonies of events witnessed by people. The fundamental operation of the judicial system therefore, was as it is to this day, based on the transfer of information obtained through perceptual processing. In Box 13.1 the task of jurors to deduce facts that can be used in deciding a verdict is described.

## Box 13.1

### Jurors assessment of factual information in court

Before information is heard in court, it is the role of the police to gather and ascertain the merits of available facts. They do this by looking for evidential facts based on constitutive facts. What is considered to be an evidential fact has been defined by Hohfeld (1923) as 'one which on being ascertained affords some logical basis – not conclusive – for inferring some other facts. The latter may be either a constitutive fact or an intermediate evidential fact.' Thayer (1898) differentiated between these two types of facts, claiming that constitutive facts are those taken to mean events and beliefs to which the law attaches some consequence. An example of this would be an individual who intentionally broke into someone's house to burgle the owners and is therefore guilty of burglary. Evidential facts are presented in the courtroom to establish the truth of constitutive facts and where constitutive facts can be inferred. For example, if the accused's hands tested positive for the precipitation of Semtex then this evidential fact could be used to infer that the suspect had previously handled explosives. This coupled with the police finding the accused at the scene of the explosion could provide substantial evidence to prove the constitutive fact of the accused was using explosives and therefore involved in the crime.

It is assumed that jurors are capable of making decisions based on deductive inference and that they can differentiate between relevant and irrelevant evidential facts. Jurors are expected to be able to make deductive inferences following syllogistic logic, such that only one possible conclusion can be derived. This is further linked with the application of probabilities. Hence in the courtroom when evidence is presented by the prosecution and defence lawyers, jurors are expected to draw inferences and assess the probability of truth. The role of jurors therefore is to disseminate these facts in order to prove or disprove the case put forward. The following example demonstrates the difficulty involved. If the accused is charged with burglary, the fact that he put his arm through the window is not proof of entry but rather the means of entry – a constitutive fact. Putting his arm through the window does not conclude the constitutive fact of entry in order to burgle. According to Thayer (1898) this would be of relevance to the case and the juror would have to decide whether it is enough to count as entering to burgle.

There are two elements of law known as substantive and **adjectival**, and it is adjectival law that is of particular relevance to eyewitness testimony. **Substantive law** influences the way we behave and interact with other people on a daily basis. Knowledge of these aspects of law is learnt informally through socialisation within the family and formally through, for example, the state education system (see Chapter 4). As citizens we behave according to the defined mores of the society we represent, although not everyone aspires to these social conventions and might decide to contravene the rules (see Chapters 1, 4 and 16). Those citizens who contravene the rules are more likely to come into contact with **adjectival law** which is the system that enforces all substantive rules (i.e. the various branches of the criminal justice system).

For adjectival law to function effectively there are defined rules of procedure and evidence in place to ensure defendants are safeguarded against vigilantes and those with vendettas. These rules are set to standardise judicial practice and enforce a 'just deserts' model (i.e. receive appropriate punishment or retribution) for fair treatment of both defendants and victims. In the UK and US the rules of evidence are founded on the adversarial system, whereas for most of Europe the inquisitorial system is endorsed (see Box 13.2). Whichever system adopted – adversarial or inquisitorial – witnesses are important and their evidence provided is given considerable credence which, as discussed previously, is a legacy from medieval times. In the case of the adversarial system, however, the rules of evidence aid in arriving at the truth by using deduction. This is important as the rules of evidence are derived by the rules of relevancy and admissibility, and it is the evidence presented in the legal process which leads to proof.

Eyewitness evidence is regarded as direct evidence and is the only direct evidence on which the facts can be proven. Hence, eyewitness reports cannot be taken as proving the facts directly because they violate the purpose of the definition which is to prove the facts. Yet eyewitness testimony can be valuable in furthering the facts of a case and never more so than in the identification of a perpetrator. The question still remains of why we consider eyewitness memories to be reliable. This, according to Cutler, Penrod and Dexter (1990), is because jurors give high weighting to eyewitness testimony. From a psychologist's perspective this is problematic given that errors in memory processing can be disrupted during any three stages of criminal identification:

1   witnessing of events (i.e. attention paid and perception of information);
2   recounting the person's appearance using PhotoFit or E-Fit and artist impressions;
3   identification of perpetrators using mug shots or identity parades.

Errors in any of these stages might have dire consequences for a potentially innocent defendant who is found guilty by the jury.

## Box 13.2

### Differences between the adversarial and inquisitorial systems of law

Prior to the Medieval Inquisition in the twelfth century, Britain and Europe resorted to the adversarial system of law. During Pope Innocent III's reign in 1198, however, changes to the court system in most of Europe were made. Pope Innocent introduced a series of decretals that reformed the ecclesiastical court system (see Chapter 1). It is to this point in legal history that the origins of the inquisitorial system can be traced. In England the adversarial system remained intact although the **ecclesiastical courts** adopted the inquisitorial system. This was allowed because King Henry II had established during the 1160s a separate secular court system. This enabled the use of the inquisitorial system for ecclesiastical courts and the adversarial for common law courts; usage which was further cemented in the Magna Carta. The main difference between the two systems rests on how the court is run and the manner in which a case comes to court. Under the adversarial system there are two advocates representing their party's position – the prosecutor has the victim's interests at heart and the defence defends his client or defendant who is accused of a felony (see Figure 1.2). The case is brought to court and the positions of both the prosecutor and defence are made clear to an impartial group of people (the judge and jury in the case of criminal courts or a group of judges in the magistrate's court). Lawyers working on behalf of the prosecution or in defence of the defendant present evidential information to determine the truth of the case (Hale 2004). The adversarial system is prevalent in common law countries such as the UK and the US (however, even in Scotland and the US, for minor traffic offences, the inquisitorial system is often used).

The inquisitorial system often has court officials investigating the facts – in other words, they can be directly involved in gathering evidence unlike in the adversarial system where this is left to the police. Police, under the adversarial system, write a report of their investigation which is reviewed by the Crown Prosecution Service (CPS) who decides whether evidence for the prosecution meets the 50 per cent chance of conviction criteria. If it does not, then the case is thrown out and no formal charges are made against the suspect. If there is substantial evidence, the suspect is arrested and remains on remand (in prison but not yet tried) until the court hearing. When a date is set, the person on remand (who is still innocent until proven guilty) attends court and the evidence against and in favour of the defendant is presented by the prosecution and defence respectively. In the inquisitorial system a public procurator manages the case which includes the investigation, evidence gathering, any enquiries and the court hearing (i.e. operating in countries such as the Ukraine, Russia, China and Japan). Whereas the inquisitorial system is strongly influenced by criminal procedure, the adversarial system refers to substantive law. In other words, the adversarial system relies on people contravening the social conventions and legal rules and for this to be reported by a witness or victim.

A formal accusation against the person who offends against the substantive laws has to be made first before it can be investigated. This is the major change that Pope Innocent made when he proposed *processus per inquisitionem* (inquisitional procedure). This meant that formal accusations to summon a defendant were unrequired for ecclesiastical magistrates to investigate a case. The repercussion of this new ruling was the increased power of the ecclesiastical courts to summon and question their witnesses and suspects without any accountability. Many witnesses were summoned privately which made it easier to accuse a targeted individual. This new ruling was cemented in law in 1215 by the Fourth Council of the Lateran which also confirmed the inquisitorial system as a writ. This became the dominant system in most of continental Europe.

The divide between the adoption of the adversarial and inquisitorial systems is confounded by a few countries and states using a mixed civil law system such as Scotland, Quebec and Louisiana. In these cases, substantive law is very much in operation but their procedural codes based on the inquisitorial system are used: although increasingly their procedural codes have slowly gravitated towards the adversarial system.

The inquisitorial system has been criticised for monopolising the court proceedings and enabling biases against the defendant to arise. Proponents of the inquisitorial system claim that under the adversarial system many cases resort to plea bargaining and settling out of court, which means that unless the defendant has a good lawyer there could be injustices arising and defendants confessing to allegations they are not guilty of. Those in favour of the inquisitorial system claim that under the adversarial system the judge has little power to preside over decisions made by a panel of lay people (the jury) of limited understanding of legal procedure. Hence it might be the case that a jury presiding over a court case outcome is no less biased than many judges under the inquisitorial system.

Why eyewitness memories are considered reliable in court appears to have origins in the way courts were managed historically. Whether eyewitness testimony is reliable needs to be reconsidered using empirical evidence from forensic science and forensic psychology. In the next section we will consider psychological theory regarding how our memory works, and the type of memory specifically used by eyewitnesses.

## Is eyewitness testimony reliable?

Many convictions based on eyewitness testimony alone – in some cases a single uncorroborated eyewitness account – lead to convictions of innocent individuals. The death penalty prevails in 33 states of the US which means convicted criminals imprisoned on Death Row could be waiting many years for their state execution. For example, Tony Ford was accused and found guilty of murder based on evidence from one uncertain eyewitness identification and was sentenced to death. Cases like Ford have been reopened under the Innocence Project which uses current **DNA** technology to prove an offender's innocence. Based on the number of 'DNA acquittals', it would appear that a high number of misidentifications have been made by eyewitnesses. This makes eyewitness misidentification a major contributory factor for the incarceration of innocent individuals like Tony Ford who was wrongly convicted of murder (see Box 13.3).

## Box 13.3

### Tony Ford – wrongly convicted of murder

Tony Ford gave two brothers (Van and Victor Belton) a lift in his car to the home of Armando Murillo. He remained in his car while the Belton brothers went inside to resolve a debt owed by Murillo. They came out and were driven home by Ford. The next day Ford was arrested for murder.

Both the Belton brothers were arrested too. In order to save his brother from execution, Van Belton alleged that Ford had shot and killed Murillo and shot a further three occupants of the house (Murillo's mother and two sisters). Ford was threatened with the death penalty by detectives and was refused a lawyer but continued protesting his innocence. A photo spread, excluding Victor Belton, was shown to Murillo's sisters. The first sister had selected a different person in the photo spread from Ford but this number was crossed out and changed to number 4 (Ford's position number). The other sister selected Ford's picture from the same photo spread after seeing Ford's picture in the news and the newspapers depicting him as the prime suspect. Many errors surrounding the police investigation were made including how the eyewitness evidence was obtained. Despite no physical evidence linking Ford to the crime scene, he was formally charged with murder. Police failed to pursue evidence linking Victor Belton to the crime scene, such as blood on his clothing and the discovery of identical ammunition, found at his home to that used to murder Murillo. Ford was also denied an expert witness to represent him. A court journalist overheard police discussing rumours that another man was responsible for the shootings and were surprised that Ford was found guilty. Further still, at a pre-trial Murillo's sisters were asked directly if Ford 'looked like the man from that night' to which they responded 'maybe'. Ford was convicted on a 'maybe' and a biased line-up. Since Ford's incarceration there have been witnesses reporting to the police that Victor Belton had admitted he got away with murder. Ford has been in prison for 16 years for a crime he did not commit but has recently been granted the right to have Victor Belton's clothing tested for Murillo's **DNA** eight days before his execution date in December 2005. The Innocence Project passed Ford's case on to a lawyer on the grounds of a clear miscarriage of justice.

The Innocence Project is a non-profit legal organisation based in the US, Australia, New Zealand, Canada and the UK, whose mission statement is to save innocent prisoners on Death Row from execution and those who are victims of miscarriages of justice. Since the establishment of the Innocence Project in 1992, as many as 283 wrongfully convicted prisoners from Death Row have been exonerated and freed as a consequence of DNA testing (Innocence Project 2012). Paul Hildwin was convicted of raping and murdering Vronzettie Cox whose body was found in the boot of her car in 1985 in Florida. The Innocence Project was responsible for reopening Hildwin's case, and using DNA testing eliminated Hildwin of raping Cox. Semen and saliva found on the victim's underwear indicated a rapist who was a non-secretor (this is when the blood-type of the perpetrator cannot be traced through bodily fluids – only 11 per cent of the world's population are non-secretors) and Hildwin was a non-secretor. Since 1985, DNA technology had advanced and in 2003, Hildwin's DNA was compared to the seminal fluid on the victim's underwear and the saliva on a washcloth found in her car. The results were negative, ruling out Hildwin as the rapist. Hildwin spent 25 years on Death Row before his acquittal in 2011.

The reliability of eyewitness testimony has been questioned by psychologists like Elizabeth Loftus, who devised experiments to test the fallible and malleable nature of human memory. It is through valuable social research like this that judges can keep up-to-date with recent findings relating to important aspects of the legal system: such social research is communicated by submitting briefs to the court known as *amicus curiae* or friend of the court briefs. Findings from mainstream psychological memory research have been included in many *amicus curiae* and have been invaluable for understanding the problems associated with eyewitness accounts. There are many theories of how human memory operates, but we will focus on those which have relevancy to eyewitness testimony – discussed next (for further theories of memory see Chapter 14).

### Memory involved in eye witnessing

The common structure of memory used in psychology is the model introduced by Atkinson and Shiffrin (1968) – a multi-store model consisting of sensory, short-term and long-term memory. Information is described as flowing from sensory to short-term and, once rehearsed, into long-term memory. Later additions to the model by Baddeley and Hitch (1974) included working memory, considered as short-term memory (see Figure 5.8). For further discussion of the relevance of working memory see Chapter 5. Information detected by the sensory organs enters sensory memory and, if attended to, will be passed into short-term memory. Information here resides between 0–18 seconds if it is not rehearsed in any way. If information is rehearsed using auditory encoding strategies, it will progress to long-term memory where it is permanently stored. Alternatively, we can consider memory in terms of whether it is content to be remembered from the past (retrospective memory) or in the future (prospective memory). Prospective memory is concerned with remembering to remember and is relevant to eyewitness recall of events as it is involves event- and time-based prospective remembering.

### Prospective memory

Monitoring and 'keeping track' of on-going actions and actions yet to be performed is a part of prospective memory (Cohen 1998). Prospective memory is similar to having a record of past events which includes storage of intentions and plans and remembering to perform intended actions. Prospective memory is important for processing information that provides feedback regarding the current status of planned actions – whether an action had been successfully accomplished. The memory of an action and the memory of an intention to perform an action is known as reality monitoring. It is this aspect of prospective memory that has significance for eyewitness testimony, as errors in remembering if an event had occurred or not could lead to wrongful convictions. As stated earlier by Lawrence and Kubie (1959), people can see or hear things that clearly did not happen or fail to remember things that did. Cohen and Faulkner (1989) demonstrated that as people age their reality monitoring ability deteriorates, which can be problematic in the courtroom if the main source of evidence is from an elderly eyewitness. Schnitzspahn and Kliegel (2009) found that young adults generally have superior prospective memory than older adults while Smith, Bayen and Martin (2010) found that children's (7–10 years) prospective memory was less efficient than young adults. These findings suggest there is differential prospective memory efficiency across the lifespan, where optimum performance occurs during early adulthood. Does this imply that children and elderly adults might be less reliable as eyewitnesses than young adults?

This has been partially answered by one of the most commonly known theories of prospective memory – the Preparatory Attentional and Memory (PAM) theory. PAM consists of two types of processes that function interdependently to optimise memory performance (Baddeley and Eysenck 2007):

1   Reality monitoring ensures that a constructed intention is stored in memory until it has been performed. This relies on the allocation of optimal attention to the newly formed intention to do something, as this is needed to maintain and store the intention in memory until it has been performed.
2   There are retrospective memory processes that help separate the newly acquired intention from distracting thoughts (Smith and Bayen 2004), which is accomplished by allocating attention towards the intended goal. While retrospective memory heightens the recollection of intentions waiting action, reality monitoring ensures that we remember to perform the action when appropriate to do so (Smith and Bayen 2004). PAM therefore assumes that our full attention should be allocated to intentions formed. This was supported by McDaniel, Robinson and Einstein's study in 1998, showing superior prospective memory performance in conditions of full attention.

Stress has also been found to reduce the efficiency of prospective memory. Landsinger (2002) compared the effective workings of prospective memory under conditions of high and low workload stress. Workload and stress were shown to independently depreciate prospective memory performance but had more of an impact when they occurred simultaneously. Given that eyewitnesses experience potentially stressful events, their focus of attention is more likely to be restricted to selected aspects of the event, such as the weapon, at the expense of encoding other aspects like the perpetrator's face – the result being a weak memory trace. (The effects of stress will be returned to later in this chapter.) Another important aspect of memory which is relevant to our discussion of eyewitness memory is the notion of schemata and scripts.

### Schemata and scripts

When a criminal event is perceived, encoded and committed to long-term memory, post-event information (introduced after the event) can interfere with the memory trace of the event (see estimator variables). It is not only external information that can interfere with memory traces of events, but also the way information is encoded and stored can modify the original perception of the event (Baddeley 1990; Craik and Tulving 1975). Long-term memory can store information as schemata and scripts (Baddeley 1990; Bartlett 1932; Rumelhart 1975 and Schank and Abelson 1977). Schemata can best be considered as modified neural pathways arising out of experienced-based learning. They are often described as mappings of previous interactions with our environment, which enable us to remember and to re-experience life events. Schemata can be networked with other schemata so that different factual and experiential information can be interconnected. They can be modified through the addition of new information or the extraction of existing information (Rumelhart and Norman 1983). While this enables us to use hypothetical constructions as a way of making optimal decisions, they can also lead to memories that did not occur.

Alternatively, scripts are considered to be organised sequences of events that define the actions, actors and props present. We all utilise scripts which are similar to schemata but on a smaller scale – they can be considered as sub-schemata. Students have scripts about lectures for instance. A typical script defining a lecture is likely to stipulate what should happen during the lecture – the lecturer (i.e. the actor) stands in the front of the lecture theatre using a lectern (i.e. the prop) to support any material that will be referred to while he or she gives the lecture (i.e. the action). Such scripts provide a guidance of what to expect in different situations, and if events occur that are not in the script then they are considered to be script-inconsistent.

The use of script-consistent and script-inconsistent information has been explored by Milne and Bull (2003) in the ability of children to resist suggestive questioning using the cognitive interview approach (see Chapter 14). They found that children gave more incorrect responses to script-consistent than script-inconsistent questions and were less able to resist script-consistent than script-inconsistent misleading questions. Pezdek and Roe (1997) found that script-consistent suggestive information is only influential under circumstances where the original memory trace of the event was weak or lost. This is because memories of similar content across many individual events can become lost in separation. This is particularly so in cases of constant sexual abuse where the ability to distinguish details of multi-events becomes blurred.

Scripts therefore can interfere with how the perceived event is remembered – especially criminal events where preconceived expectations can bias, alter or substitute the original memory of what had occurred. Schemata and scripts are internalised means of structuring our knowledge which can facilitate, modify, attenuate or bias memory for events.

Also relevant and very important to eyewitness memory is the ability to provide information about the perpetrator's face. Processing faces has received much attention in psychology as it is regarded as a special case of memory. The research literature on facial memory will be examined by referring to our exceptionally good memory for familiar faces and the hand played by an innate face processing package.

### Memory for processing faces

Most studies demonstrate that we are very good at recognising familiar faces – we rarely misidentify people we know. Bahrick, Bahrick and Wittlinger (1975) used an experimental approach to see how well ex-students, who graduated 50 years previously, could identify students in their own year-book. Ex-students identified photos taken randomly from their year-book presented with five other photos taken from different year-books to an accuracy of 90 per cent. In many cases photos from year-books had not been viewed for at least two to five years. Despite not seeing friends for many years, and allowing for age transformation, we are good at recognising familiar faces. Bahrick *et al.* (1975) further showed that people are better at remembering faces long after a lapse of 35 years, which exceeds the time limit of 20 years for recalling the names of people. Our ability to recognise faces appears to stem from birth and continues to be good throughout the lifespan. Findings from laboratory-based face recognition research, for example, has shown a 70 per cent correct recognition score when there are changes to the original facial pose (Bruce 1982); the original context (Watkins, Ho and Tulving 1976); and to the target face at recognition test (Patterson and Baddeley 1977). This might not be as high as 90 per cent but it is important to note that unfamiliar faces are normally presented in laboratory experiments. It is difficult to undermine our ability to recognise faces, whether familiar or unfamiliar, which might be explained by our innate fascination with looking at faces as shown in studies of brain development in infants (see Box 13.4) and a preference towards seeing intact faces or holistic processing.

In 1991, Johnson and Morton suggested there are two processes – conspec and conlearn – which enable infants to develop an efficient level of facial processing. Conspec, they argued, is an innate immature facial processing mechanism enabling newborns to identify the facial configuration of their caregiver as a means to forming an attachment. While conspec has its origins in the subcortex of the brain, conlearn is processed in the cortex: the most recent part of the human brain to have evolved, which is largely responsible for cognitive processing. Conlearn extracts information from the 'primitive' representation of the face, first initiated by conspec, and modifies it. This more realistic representation of a face relies on previous experiences within the social environment. It is conspec that enables a newborn 30 minutes after birth to attend and track a schematic representation of a face moving across their field of view in preference to a jumbled face or blank stimulus (Johnson, Dziurawiec, Ellis and Morton 1991). Conspec is also responsible for other face recognition competencies shown in infants, such as attending preferentially to the mother's face at two days old (Bushnell, Sai and Mullin 1989), showing visual preference for a photo of the carer than a stranger (Barrera and Maurer 1981) and preferring to look at patterns with curves that resemble the outer contour of a face (Fantz and Miranda 1975). This research therefore implies that the recognition of faces by eyewitnesses is not a forced or deliberate method of conscious rehearsal. Recognition of faces is based on an evolved innate system which operates automatically.

## Box 13.4

### Newborns' brain patterns for processing faces differs

Brain imaging research using infants younger than 12 months has shown that a variety of brain regions across the left and right hemispheres become active when processing facial stimuli. By the time they reach the age of one year, brain activity is restricted to the right hemisphere in the same way it is in adults (Neville 1995). De Haan (2001) and De Haan, Humphreys and Johnson (2002) found widespread brain activity in young infants under 12 months. They observed that brain activity to facial stimuli becomes more selective with age and increasing experience of interacting with faces. This suggests that parts of a newborn's brain are involved in recognising faces which continue developing as they engage increasingly with the social world.

Another factor that appears to be innate is our preference for holistic processing. Many studies have shown that we prefer to process a fully intact face, and to encode and store memory traces of faces in this way (Baenninger 1994; Bartlett and Searcy 1993; Carey and Diamond 1994; Tanaka, Kay, Grinnell, Stansfield and Szechter 1998). These studies further demonstrate that preference for processing whole faces over isolated features is prevalent from a young age and continues throughout the lifespan. This makes perfect sense and explains findings from other studies showing that rehearsal methods do not improve face recognition (see Box 13.5) – and depending on the nature of rehearsal used it can actively disadvantage the retrieval of face memory traces (Chance and Goldstein 1981; Taylor 1990 and Winograd 1981). Repetition of facial stimuli does improve recognition especially when the number of other faces presented between the first and second presentation of the to-be-re-membered (or target) face increases by lag (Mantyla and Cornoldi 2002: Mammarella, Russo and Avons 2002; Russo, Parkin, Taylor and Wilks 1998). Again no intentional rehearsal is required for this improvement in recognition barring the repeated exposure.

## Box 13.5

### Our bias towards holistic processing

The bias towards processing faces holistically can be further exemplified through studies that compare different training schemes for improving face recognition. Malpass, Lavigueur and Weldon (1973) considered and compared four learning strategies:

- Feature analysis;
- Global personality sorting;
- Global facial judgements;
- Repeated face recognition tests.

Baseline levels of recognition performance were established for all participants before each strategy was tested. Feature analysis involved familiarity with separate facial features commonly used by PhotoFit. Global personality sorting required participants to classify faces using personality dimensions like trustworthy/untrustworthy, whereas global facial judgements involved the categorisation of faces based on the similarity to four target faces. The repeated face recognition condition consisted of a sequence of target faces later shown at test. In this condition non-target faces (or distractors) were distributed among target faces. Malpass et al. (1973) found little evidence of effortful learning strategies improving recognition performance. They concluded that learning strategies encourage participants to focus on faces in a way that conflict with an innate tendency to process faces automatically. This provides support for Johnson and Morton's (1991) conspec/conlearn differentiation. Encouraging participants to adopt a specific learning strategy causes conflict for the automatic innate processing mechanism (i.e. conspec) and the activation of the conlearn mechanism based on experiencing faces. Alternatively, other studies demonstrated the effectiveness of focusing on facial features when using IdentiKit to construct facial composites (Laughery, Duval and Wogalter 1986). Laughery et al. suggested that feature analysis is a superior approach for remembering faces provided the recall aid used relies on the reconstruction of faces. This involves a *bottom-up* processing strategy where features are combined to reconstruct the whole face. As we naturally use *top-down* processing to remember fully intact faces, the best recognition aid is one relying on the identification of a face as a mug-shot. In the case of faces, the features make up the whole, but it is more than remembering the features (i.e. componential processing) that help comprise the whole face – there are the spatial properties between features (i.e. configurational processing). Hence automatic processing of faces involves a combination of configurational and componential processing (Taylor 1990).

The significance of these findings is important for the retrieval of memories that lead to the successful identification of the perpetrator. It is for this reason that investigators must avoid post-event contamination of memory during questioning. Interestingly, in relation to holistic processing, Ellis, Davies and Shepherd (1975) demonstrated that it is more difficult to construct a facial composite using PhotoFit than to identify a face from a series of mug shots. Unlike mug shots, PhotoFit involves the construction of a facial composite, using individual facial features – the antithesis of holistic processing. Wells and Hryciw (1984) added that while learning strategies adopted might be useful for recalling verbal information, this is not the case for a recognition system such as face memory retrieval.

Extracting eyewitness memories yet avoiding contamination of the original memory trace has been considered by Wells (1978) using the notion of estimator and system variables. Estimator and system variables will be discussed in the next section as another factor influencing the reliability of eyewitness memory.

### Estimator variables influencing eyewitness memory

Estimator variables are individual factors that impact on the way events are perceived, encoded and stored. They influence an individual's ability to encode and retrieve event information effectively and accurately. There are a multitude of estimator variables that have been studied by psychologists over the years such as:

- Leading and misleading post-event information;
- Stress levels during witnessed events;
- Consequentiality on witness accuracy;
- Accuracy and confidence;
- Accuracy and age;
- Accuracy and suggestibility.

#### Leading and misleading post-event information

Elizabeth Loftus was the first to seriously study the effects of leading and misleading information on witnesses' memories of events, and in so doing, introduced an experimental paradigm designed to isolate factors responsible for changing, modifying or supplanting the original event memory trace. Loftus and Palmer (1974) demonstrated how easily witness judgements could be influenced by substituting a word embedded in a leading question. They showed participants film footage of a car accident which was followed by a series of questions. For half of the participants the question posed was, 'How fast were the cars going when they hit each other?' The remaining participants were asked, 'How fast were the cars going when they smashed into each other?' Substituting the word 'hit' for 'smashed' elicited a higher estimate of speed (40.8 mph versus 34 mph). One week later participants returned to answer a series of further questions about the accident such as, 'Did you see any broken glass?' (the original film footage showed no broken glass). Loftus was interested in why the substituted word 'smashed' had changed memories of the original accident – encouraging participants to recall that they had seen broken glass. When the key question contained the word 'smashed', 32 per cent (16) responded that they had seen broken glass compared with 14 per cent (7) who were originally asked the question using the word 'hit'. Loftus and Palmer concluded that two bytes of information become stored for the event: the original perception and the information supplied after the event, known as post-event information. This implies that leading or misleading information can easily supplant the original perception of an event if introduced during police questioning.

Loftus, Miller and Burns (1978), using the same experimental paradigm, showed a succession of slides depicting the different stages of a car–pedestrian accident. The scenario involved a red Datsun, approaching an intersection from a side street, which had stopped but knocked a pedestrian over. Participants were allocated to one of two conditions where either a stop sign or a yield sign was presented. The question posed to all participants was, 'Did another car pass the red Datsun while it stopped at the stop sign?' Hence, for half of the sample the question content was consistent with the slides of the accident, but for the other half this was a misleading question. This was followed by a series of paired slides: where for both groups one slide from each pair was previously viewed. When the misleading question was asked, correct slide selection was 41 per cent – down by 34 per cent from the non-misled group. The misleading information reduced accuracy below the expected 50 per cent chance level. Why misleading information reduces accuracy of response by a large margin was explained by Loftus using the concept of substitution.

According to Loftus the substitution hypothesis best explains how information transforms or displaces the original memory trace which becomes irreplaceably lost. Misleading post-event information therefore can be a 'destructive updating mechanism'. Leading questions on the other hand, encourage a biased way of considering the response to a question which might not have occurred if the format of the question were neutral. For example, 'How fast was the yellow car going when it smashed into the black car?' is a leading question as opposed to, 'How fast was each car travelling when the incident occurred?' which is neutral. Both leading and misleading questions can affect the original memory of an event, but it is misleading questions that are more problematic as they can cause memory traces to be irreplaceably lost.

The underlying problem of misleading post-event information arises out of Bartlett's notion of reconstructive memory. Here, he referred to memories that are distorted by our very own expectations and knowledge. Bartlett (1932) argued that when we try to reconstruct past events we do so by trying to incorporate information into existing schemata of the world – hence our memories are imaginative reconstructions rather than definitive recordings that can be played back. It is inevitable according to Bartlett that we 'fill in the gaps' about events using preconceptions stored by our schemata and scripts. Tuckey and Brewer (2003) demonstrated this using the bank robber schema. It is difficult to stop ourselves from imagining a masked gunman with a sack of money once our bank robber schema is activated. This phenomenon can be explained using source misattribution where witnesses believe an object was at the crime scene because such an object is commonly present at crime scenes (hence, expected to be there). This could also be the source of misidentifications in a line-up. Post-event misleading information is also referred to as the misinformation effect (Loftus 2005; Robinson-Riegler and Robinson-Riegler 2004; Weiten 2010). According to Robinson-Riegler and Robinson-Riegler (2004) the underlying causal problem for the misinformation effect is retroactive interference, where new information tampers with the previously encoded event information causing distorted, substituted or lost memory traces of the original event.

### Stress levels during witnessed events

Using the Yerkes–Dodson Law, information can be plotted to form a normal distribution curve (see Figure 13.1) where the highest point of the curve indicates the optimum level of performance (Yerkes and Dodson 1908). When applied to memory recall, this curve illustrates the impact of low and high levels of stress; where both low and high levels of stress reduce memory recall efficiency. It appears that some stress is required to motivate performance but if it goes beyond one standard deviation either way of the optimum level, stress can interfere with the formation of effective memory traces.

Using the Yerkes–Dodson Law in relation to eyewitness memory, findings support the prediction that too much stress is detrimental for effective memory retrieval of faces. Stressful situations, such as witnessing a serious criminal event, might increase attention towards specific information. A good example of this is weapon focus. Stanny and Johnson (2000) compared police and citizen recall of stressful events using simulated training scenarios of shootings. They took measures of stress induced by the scenarios for both police and citizen witnesses, and tested recall accuracy for details of the event. They found that retrieval of weapon details outweighed that of the perpetrator's face.

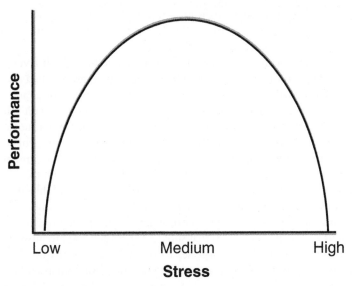

*Figure 13.1* The Yerkes-Dodson normal distribution curve
Yerkes and Dodson 1908

Kassin, Ellsworth and Smith (1989) found that low levels of arousal resulted in poor memory performance and high levels interfered with recall but moderate levels of stress produced optimum recall. Buckhout (1982) claimed that a dramatic event can increase attention paid to the event but when it is stressful and frightening, recall becomes unreliable (this is compatible with the effects of weapon focus). Kramer, Buckhout, Fox, Widman and Tusche (1991) showed participants coloured slides of traumatic autopsies which were distributed among neutral slides of travel scenes. The slides of autopsies were labelled as property of the New York Police Department (NYPD) or the MGM studio. The source of slide ownership affected stress levels differentially: higher stress levels resulted from the NYPD slides which interfered with recall of the neutral travel slides. These results suggest that as stress levels increase memory recall decreases significantly.

The detrimental effect of stress on memory performance is consistently found across many studies including applied research investigating how stressful military 'survival training' can interfere with memory recall. Morgan, Hazlett, Doran, Garrett *et al.* (2004) tested 500 active-duty military personnel for memory recall using stressful and non-stressful interrogation room scenarios. In the stressful interrogation scenario they were in a room for 40 minutes face-to-face with the interrogator. When asked to identify the interrogator, only 34 per cent correctly selected the interrogator from a photo line-up compared with 76 per cent in the non-stressful condition. In a follow-up study, 68 per cent of those in the high stress condition made a misidentification compared with 12 per cent in the low stress group. This suggests that high stress levels actively prevent memory from working effectively by preventing witnesses from focusing attention to event details.

Aharonian and Bornstein (2008), however, claimed that high levels of stress can focus attention to central details which when tested are recalled exceptionally well. They made a distinction between remembering central and peripheral details during a highly stressful event, and used this to explain why some memories of stressful events are considerably robust. They did a meta-analysis of studies testing eyewitness memories under low and high stressful situations and found that stress generally has a negative impact on recall and recognition. Aharonian and Bornstein's meta-analysis also revealed that eyewitnesses are less likely to identify a perpetrator in a line-up when highly stressed. In suspect-present line-ups, they are more likely to identify an innocent person. When witnesses are asked to free recall what had happened during a stressful event, their recollection exceeds that shown when they tried to answer specific questions. Free recall allows witnesses to report information they are certain of while excluding details they are uncertain about (Aharonian and Bornstein 2008).

Christianson (1992) argued that there is little evidence to suggest that emotional stress can have detrimental effects on memory. He concluded that memory for central details of negative emotional events are superior to neutral events: memory for general details is more impaired for negative emotional events than for neutral ones. This difference was explained by the increased attention given to negative emotional events which heightens witness ability to recall and elaborate on central details. Christianson and Hubinette (1993) demonstrated how high stress levels increased accuracy, detailed recall and longevity of memory among 110 witnesses who between them had witnessed 22 bank robberies. They answered questions about their experiences and rated their own emotions during the event. Despite there being no correlation between emotionality ratings and recall, they remembered vast amounts of information describing their ordeal. Christianson and Hubinette concluded that good recall of highly stressful situations is representative of real-life experiences and not contrived laboratory experiments.

High stress, however, has been found to impair other areas of eyewitness testing such as face composite reconstruction. It was suggested by Frowd, Bruce, Ness, Thomson-Bogner et al. (2007) that this is because we encode faces holistically rather than processing individual features. The Evolving Facial Identification Technique (EvoFIT) enables witnesses to select and 'breed' complete faces repeatedly until a composite likeness to the suspect is achieved (Frowd, Bruce and Hancock 2008). EvoFIT has been tried by several police forces in Britain and is tested for reliability under conditions of high and low stress. High levels of stress were predicted to impair face composite construction as measured by poor likeness to the perpetrator. This prediction confirmed and supported previous findings demonstrating the negative effects of stress (Brigham, Maass, Martinez and Whittenberge 1983) and Post Traumatic Stress Disorder on face perception (Islam-Zwart, Heath and Vik 2005) and eyewitness testimony per se (Deffenbacher, Bornstein, Penrod and McGorty 2004). Valentine and Mesout (2009) showed that under high levels of stress, correct identifications from line-ups also decreases as does the quantity and quality of recalled information.

## Consequentiality on witness accuracy

When people make judgements which have consequences for the individual concerned, then consequentiality will be perceived as high. It has been shown in eyewitness laboratory-based studies that high consequentiality has serious consequences for an individual, which is why eyewitness recollections of events need to be accurate. For instance, in laboratory experiments participants know that an individual's life or freedom is not at risk – hence consequentiality is low. Foster, Libkuman, Schooler and Loftus (1994) showed that consequentiality can have an effect even in laboratory-based research. Participants were shown a video of a bank robbery and were later asked to identify one of the robbers in a line-up. Half of the participants, however, were told that they were observing a real robbery and that their responses would influence the direction of the trial as a consequence of their information. The remaining participants were not informed of this. They found that male participants were more influenced by consequentiality, where memories recalled were more accurate under these high consequentiality conditions.

## Accuracy and confidence

People believe there to be a robust relationship between accuracy of memory recall and the level of confidence projected by a witness. Intuitively this makes sense as we would expect a person with specialised knowledge to be confident and certain of their facts (i.e. an expert witness or consultant). Gruneberg and Sykes (1993) found a robust relationship between confidence and accuracy that depended on the perceived saliency of the event. For example, a woman can be certain that her dog was run-over by a car at 5 pm because it is her dog and therefore is important to her. The presence of external cues, such as the chime of the town clock, can further corroborate her account. Event saliency and external factors help contextualise event content in real-life situations. Under experimental conditions, variables are manipulated in a way that allows researchers to investigate isolated effects, and this can mean that the context of a real life event is lost.

Nevertheless, laboratory-based research can be informative. Cutler and Penrod (1989) measured the level of confidence shown by witnesses before they identified a suspect from a line-up; the number of correct identifications was used as a measure of accuracy. The correlation between confidence and accuracy was low (0.20), suggesting that confident and non-confident witnesses can be equally as accurate. Other studies put this correlation at 0.40, so it very much depends on the figures of inclusion. Are all witnesses, for example, included or just the witnesses who make identifications? Furthermore, it depends on the measures of memory used in studies – recall or recognition. Recall tends to correlate higher with confidence than does recognition for instance (Krug 2007). A difference in the level of difficulty for remembering some aspects of an event might also explain why some questions are easier to answer (Kebbell, Wagstaff and Covey 1996). This can be illustrated by the level of difficulty in recalling information about the suspect's height versus the presence of freckles. Kebbell *et al.* (1996) showed participants film footage of a murder followed by 33 open-ended questions about what they had just observed. The level of difficulty across the questions was controlled so that some questions were easy to answer while others required more thought. The relationship between confidence and question difficulty was robust; confidence was higher for easier questions and this was confirmed by the 97 per cent accuracy score given to answers that participants felt most confident about.

Another way of considering accuracy is to ask people how confident they feel about their response. If they gauge this to be at 80 per cent, then there is an 80 per cent likelihood that they will be correct. This measure was adopted by Luna and Martin-Luengo (2010) who showed participants footage of a bank robbery. After asking questions regarding the content of the footage, participants rated how certain they were of each answer. They showed an incremental scale between percentage accuracy and percentage confidence estimation, such that a low percentage confidence rating matched a low accuracy percentage. Confidence estimations provide a more informed index of an individual's accuracy and confidence score than does a global correlation such as 0.20.

The relationship between confidence and accuracy can be analysed using the 10–12 second rule, introduced by Dunning and Perretta (2002) to gauge the length of time it takes eyewitnesses to select a suspect from a line-up. The rule predicts that suspects selected from a line-up within 10–12 seconds are usually the correct choice. Findings, however, are not clear cut. The rule is considered by some to be a good indicator of accuracy and eyewitness confidence, but Weber, Brewer and Wells (2004) are less positive about the suggestion that spontaneous identifications are more likely to be correct. Under circumstances where the original memory trace of the suspect is robust and the suspect is present in the line-up, a spontaneous identification might be possible given that faces are compared one at a time with the original memory trace of the suspect – known as the relative judgement decision process (Wells 1984; 1993). This would make sense, but the relationship between confidence and spontaneous selection does not.

## Accuracy and age

Children, the elderly and mentally disordered were often considered to make incompetent and unreliable witnesses. According to Quinn (1986), this view rested on the opinion that they were unable to fully appreciate the intricacies of taking an oath. This meant that many cases were thrown out of court because the only witness was too young, too old or mentally incapable. Opinions have changed as children are now permitted to provide an unsworn statement to the court if they are considered competent to do so. According to Myers (1987), 'a child must possess certain characteristics, including the capacity to observe, sufficient intelligence, adequate memory, the ability to communicate, an awareness of the difference between truth and falsehood, and an appreciation of the obligation to speak the truth' (p.5).

Davies and Flin (1988) compared the accuracy of event information (i.e. a verbal report) and identity information (i.e. physical appearance of perpetrators) in child witnesses, and found that although younger children recalled less information than older children and adults, there were no differences found in the level of accuracy. Their findings showed that children had more difficulty identifying someone from a line-up, but any differences in recall of event information between children and adults were grossly exaggerated. Flin, Boon, Knox and Bull (1992) also compared recall in children aged 5–6 and 9–10 years of age with adults, using interviews either one day or five months after they had witnessed an event. No differences in the amount of recalled information were found after a one day delay; however, more forgetting in children than adults resulted after a five months delay.

There is evidence showing that the greatest effects of misleading information on memory performance occurs in children of 5–10 years and older adults of 65 years plus. Cohen and Faulkner (1989), for example, found that the proportion of older adults who made errors in conditions of false misleading information was significantly higher than the number of middle-aged adults who made similar errors. This difference was generalised to errors of false identification (Searcy, Bartlett and Memon 1999). In 2000, Searcy, Bartlett and Memon found that older adults made more identification errors under target-absent line-ups than younger adults. They extended this study by including narratives which contained either misinformation or an unrelated control narrative that participants heard while viewing footage of a crime event. Younger adults were unaffected by the misleading narrative; however, the older adults made more false identifications when they heard the misleading narrative. It appears that misleading narratives about a perpetrator's appearance (despite watching footage that is to the contrary), will increase the odds of selecting an innocent person in a line-up who has similar facial features to the narrative's description.

## Accuracy and suggestibility

Suggestibility is one reason why children might make incompetent witnesses (Ceci and Bruck 1993). They proposed that child witnesses can be easily influenced by leading questions because of their vulnerability towards accepting information suggested to them during an interview. A study in 1987 by Goodman, Aman and Hirschman, however, showed how resilient to suggestion children actually are. After visiting a medical centre, children were asked leading questions such as, 'Did the man kiss you?' Despite leading questions, they nevertheless provided accurate reports of their visit. Davies and Flin (1988) claimed that suggestibility in children arises out of social conformity rather than the original memory undergoing restructuring as a consequence of leading questions. In other words, children want to be seen as helpful and respond in a way that is expected of them.

Myers, Saywitz and Goodman (1996) proposed that question style also influences suggestibility. Myers *et al.* (1996) classified question style using a continuum of absent to increasing suggestiveness:

- open-ended;
- focused questions;
- specific questions;
- leading questions.

An open-ended style of questioning in relation to the cognitive interview (see Chapter 14) provides robust evidence for enhanced recall and recognition. Focused questions can be useful in phase 7 of the cognitive interview where interviewees are asked to focus on a particular aspect of the event, like for example a shop layout. Focusing in this way encourages the activation of a specific picture about the shop, which is then probed by the interviewer. Focused questions therefore encourage the child to attend to a particular issue – such as the shop layout. This type of question does not implicitly suggest anything to the child but encourages attention towards issues of interest to the interviewer. Specific questions focus more specifically on issues and can involve simple direct answers that require little elaboration to questions like for example, 'What was the colour of his coat?' Loftus' research, as previously discussed, provides insight of how misleading questions can disrupt the original memory for the event. A leading style of questioning can also disrupt the original memory for an event (Loftus 1975).

Sternberg, Lamb, Hershkowitz, Yudilevitch *et al.* (1997) investigated the quality and quantity of information provided by child witnesses who were interviewed using different types of encouragement to invite further comments. For example, interviewers used:

- open-ended and feedback responses (i.e. feedback to what the child had said);

- direction to comment further on specific issues;
- leading utterances (i.e. encouraging comment about things the child has not talked about);
- suggestive utterances (i.e. encouraging the child to respond in a certain way).

They showed that open-ended questions increased the child's engagement in communication such that their responses were four times longer and three times more likely to contain additional information. Horrowitz (2009) also demonstrated that open-ended questioning rather than direct questioning styles, resulted in longer responses. Horrowitz considered the nature of errors made by children: omission and commission. In the case of omission errors, children simply failed to recall the information unlike commission errors where spurious information was recalled. In Horrowitz's study, younger children were likely to make more errors of omission and commission when interviewers used a direct questioning style as opposed to open-ended questioning which produced the least number of both types of error. Despite research demonstrating the effectiveness of an open-ended style of questioning, four-fifths of interviewers continue to use focused or closed questions.

Despite the interview style adopted, there are still numerous studies indicating that both child and adult witnesses can have high levels of suggestibility, confabulation and acquiescence; where they agree with the sentiment of the question content (Bender, Wallsten and Ornstein 1996; Clare and Gudjonsson 1993; Priestley and Pipe 1997 and Valenti-Hein and Schwartz 1993). Flin (1995) claimed that, historically, people considered to be of low intellectual capacity, or too young to have a level of developed mental capacity required for cross-examination in the courtroom, were excluded from giving evidence. To aid the assessment of an individual's capability to provide evidence in court, Gudjonsson (1997) formulated a test known as the Gudjonsson Suggestibility Scale (GSS). This provides a measure of vulnerability to suggested information and could be used further to separate vulnerable individuals from malingerers (see Chapter 15).

The GSS is used by police to establish the extent to which a person is prone to accepting the content embedded in leading questions. If an individual scores high on the GSS, then under PACE (1984) rules, an appropriate adult can be present during police interrogation to explain what is being said. The argument that children's mental capacity is also under-developed, and would pose a problem in understanding legal concepts in the courtroom, has been investigated by focusing on whether children can distinguish between truth and lies (Bussey 1992). This is particularly pertinent to understanding the purpose of an unsworn statement – the equivalent of the oath that demands they tell the truth. Bussey (1992) found that pre-schoolers could tell the difference between lies and truths beyond the level of chance. This was investigated further by

Siegal and Peterson (1998) who showed that 3-year-olds were capable of differentiating between lies and genuine mistakes.

The legal system, however, requires that children can separate intentional false statements or lies from intentional true ones or truths. According to Myers (1987), child witnesses need to, 'understand the difference between truth and falsity, and appreciate the duty to tell the truth' (p.66). In Bussey and Grimbeek's study in 2000, children were asked to allocate different statements to two categories: prototypic lies or prototypic truths. In the case of prototypic lies statements have elements of false facts, false belief and false intent. This means that the statement is false and the person speaking believes it is false but intends to deceive the recipient. Young children were able to separate prototypical lies from prototypical truths, although there was a developmental difference between 7–10 year olds (who were better at this) and 4 year olds. From four years onwards, children are very knowledgeable about what constitutes lies and truths (Cashmore and Bussey 1996). This fits in with the developmental time frame for developing a Theory of Mind (Baron-Cohen 1995) (see Chapter 4), and also an understanding of epistemic mental states such as believing, thinking, pretending, wishing and wanting (Baron-Cohen 1995; Flavell 2004; Leslie 1991). Children are very good at understanding pantomime story telling because they can suspend the normal truth relations of propositions – an ability known as referential opacity (Leslie 1991). Hence children can understand that while they can see events behind the actor on stage, the actor can remain unaware.

Given these findings it appears that children are more capable of understanding legal concepts than was originally thought. Children are capable of differentiating truths and lies which suggests they have the required level of mental capacity needed in court. But are they suggestible? London, Bruck and Melnyk (2009) studied the effects of post-event information during an interview with children of 4–6 years of age who had witnessed a magician falling over and then asked a child for assistance. Children were asked questions about what they had seen and were asked specific questions which contained correct or incorrect information – this was done by adding true or false reminders of what had happened. They found that children were influenced by post-event information when they immediately free-recalled details about the event. For delayed recall more than 15 months later, however, they recounted events accurately. Incorrect responses remained constant during the 15 month period, where 75 per cent of these were based on misleading post-event reminders during questioning: after 15 months these had reduced to 0 per cent. Any errors made after 15 months were genuine errors of recollection and not due to misleading information. Correct information recalled, when correct reminders were provided during questioning, reduced after 15 months had lapsed, whereas correctly recalled information that did not rely on reminders remained constant. These findings suggest that the misinformation effect lacks longevity.

Unlike estimator variables, system variables focus on how memories are retrieved for investigation purposes by the police. System variables, for example, include the reconstruction of a face using PhotoFit, IdentiKit or E-Fit; viewing mug shots and identifying the culprit from an identity parade (commonly referred to as a line-up) – discussed next.

### System variables influencing eyewitness memory

System variables refer to the techniques investigators use to attain information from witnesses such as the use of different face composite construction tools (i.e. PhotoFit, IdentiKit, Mac-A-Mug Pro, Compusketch, FaceKit, E-Fit, CD-Fit and EvoFIT), viewing mug shots (photos of faces) and identity parades, known as line-ups. Although system variables are not concerned with factors influencing the perception and encoding of events in the same way that estimator variables are, the tools used by investigators to attain information from witnesses can still interfere with the original memory trace. Methods used by police in the identification process include:

- facial composite construction;
- mug shots and line-ups.

#### Facial composite construction

The use of PhotoFit is shown to be disruptive to the processes involved with remembering faces and the way they are retrieved. As we do not remember faces as separate features, it is difficult to construct a facial composite from memory in this way. This would involve deconstruction of the original memory trace of the face and then reconstructing it from an array of individual features. Since faces are processed holistically, deconstructing memory traces of faces in to their component features is contrary to how facial encoding mechanisms normally operate. For this reason, methods used by police that involve face deconstruction and reconstruction are counter-intuitive to the retrieval mechanism of recognition. When we describe faces verbally, for instance, a recall pathway is used, but this is not what normally occurs since we use recognition for the identification of people we know. The recognition pathway makes more sense for a number of reasons listed below:

- faces are pictorial stimuli and are easier to recognise because we see them;
- conspec and conlearn are automatic processes;
- faces are processed holistically;
- deconstructing faces serves no purpose;
- interpreting emotional expression in faces involves both configurational (i.e. the spatial relations between facial features) and componential (i.e. individual facial features) properties of the face which are difficult to separate.

Taylor, Turner, Groome and Gardner (2011) addressed the role of holistic cognitive style in the construction of facial composites. Using Peterson, Deary and Austin's (2005) Extended Cognitive Styles Analysis-Wholistic/Analytic (E-CSA-W/A) test, participants were categorised as having 'holistic', 'analytic' or 'neither' of the cognitive styles. Holistic cognitive styles involved learning faces intact, unlike analytic styles that encouraged the learning of individual facial components. Participants were shown faces from the Psychological Image Collection (devised at the University of Sterling) and were then asked to complete a facial composite, from memory, using E-Fit. Taylor *et al.* (2011) found that participants using holistic cognitive styles out-performed both the 'analytic' and 'neither' groups, when using facial composite accuracy construction as a measure of success. They concluded that even though the production of facial composites relies on selecting features of a face, features are selected within a holistic facial framework and it is for this reason that holistic cognitive styles might be advantageous.

## Mug shots and line-ups

Traditionally witnesses were invited by police to select who they think might be the suspect from a line-up consisting of 5–7 volunteers (that included the suspect). The line-up was structured so that witnesses could view members of the line-up simultaneously or sequentially. The modern approach to line-ups is the use of the Video Identification Parade Electronic Recording (VIPER), where faces are presented sequentially on a computer screen. The use of mug shots and line-ups is more compatible with how we perceive and encode faces; however, even these techniques have their problems. The structure of line-ups for instance has been criticised. The analysis of how line-ups were conducted in the past has identified a multitude of problems such as a biased selection of volunteers – all too short or too tall so that the police suspect stands out as fitting descriptions provided by witnesses. Furthermore, eyewitnesses might feel pressure to identify someone, given that the police believe they have apprehended the perpetrator. Eyewitnesses might also believe that the suspect is present in the line-up and it is their duty to identify the perpetrator and support the police in their investigation.

Wells (1984) established another problem of the line-up format that directly influences the mental processes involved when viewing members of a line-up simultaneously. Wells (1984) was aware that when eyewitnesses selected a suspect from a line-up they chose the individual on the basis of closest resemblance to their memory of the perpetrator. He referred to this as relative judgement decision processing. Relative judgement decision processing works best under simultaneous line-up structures (all individuals are seen together) when the suspect is present in the line-up. Under circumstances of suspect-absent line-ups, the closest lookalike is more likely to be selected instead of voiding the line-up completely. This begs the question of how similar to the descriptions of the perpetrator should line-up members be?

Whether members of a line-up should all closely resemble the perpetrator was examined by Luus and Wells (1991). They found that it depends on whether the suspect is present or absent in the line-up. For example, under conditions of suspect-absent line-ups, innocent members are protected from being misidentified provided they all look similar to the descriptions of the suspect. If there is only one member of the line-up resembling eyewitness descriptions, then the probability of mistaken identification increases. When the suspect is present in the line-up then the number of inaccurate identifications made reduces. Increased resemblance of a line-up member to the descriptions provided by eyewitnesses can be problematic and result in mistaken identifications (Clark and Tunnicliff 2001). Wogalter, Malpass and McQuiston (2004) studied police planning of line-up structure in 200 North American police jurisdictions, and found a host of good and bad practices. Good practices involved the selection of lookalikes for line-ups based more on upper facial features (i.e. eyes, hairline and colour of hair and face shape consistent with race and ethnic characteristics) than lower features (i.e. chin and mouth). This is consistent with research showing that we more readily recall the upper facial features of faces. Furthermore, only in a few cases were eyewitness told that they did not have to make an identification if they believed the perpetrator was absent from the line-up. In these cases, there was no pressure to make a selection, but there were many more cases where eyewitnesses would have felt pressured to do so.

Wogalter et al. (2004) further discovered that the majority of mock (pretend) eyewitness misidentifications (83 per cent) were based on the level of likeness to the perpetrator as opposed to verbal descriptions provided by eyewitnesses (7 per cent). This suggests that physical similarity to the perpetrator increases the probability of being selected. Intuitively, it makes sense to have similar lookalikes in a line-up to increase the discernibility of eyewitnesses, but in practice this does not occur. It is more a practical problem of how similarity is manipulated than the issue of similarity itself. Similarity is usually manipulated by selecting individuals on the basis of their similarity with the perpetrator instead of to each other. The latter encourages eyewitnesses to give weights of similarity to each member of the line-up instead of with memories of the perpetrator. This therefore increases the distinctiveness of the perpetrator who is in effect the 'exemplar'.

In line-ups where the structure is such that suspects are presented simultaneously to eyewitnesses, Lindsay and Wells (1985) have argued that misidentifications are more likely to occur. Wells (1993) found a misidentification rate of 46 per cent in suspect-present line-ups which increased to 68 per cent in suspect-absent line-ups under the system of simultaneous line-up structure. Wells (1993) instead has advocated that the sequential line-up structure should be used where one suspect is shown at a time (Steblay and Dysart 2003).

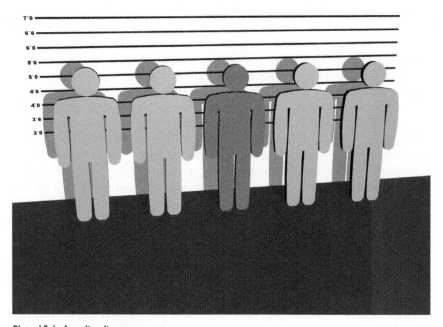

*Plate 13.1* A police line-up

© Darren Whittingham. Image used under license from Shutterstock.com. Available at http://www.
shutterstock.com/pic.mhtml?id=11569537&src=id

The sequential line-up structure disenables eyewitnesses from relying on the relative judgement decision process and encourages them to compare each 'suspect' individually with their memory of the perpetrator. By considering 25 studies in a meta-analysis, Steblay, Dysart, Fulero and Lindsay (2001) were able to show a reduction of mistaken identifications in suspect-absent line-ups using a sequential structure and a rise in correct identification in suspect-present line-ups.

Despite the sequential line-up overcoming to a large degree the problem of relative judgement decision processes, Clark and Davey (2005) have shown that the suspect in a line-up most resembling the perpetrator is more likely to be selected when presented later in a line-up sequence (i.e. the fourth position versus the second position). They explained that when a suspect who most resembles the memory of the perpetrator is shown early in the line-up sequence, eyewitnesses tend to wait for a more suitable alternative and will reject the line-up if one fails to appear. Ebbesen and Flowe (2002) claimed that eyewitnesses have thresholds of response where they raise their threshold for making a selection regardless of having seen the face previously or not. Thus when a similar-looking suspect occurs late in the line-up sequence, eyewitnesses will lower their decision criteria and make an identification – a problem which has yet to be resolved.

Brewer and Palmer (2010) described a series of guidelines for investigators to use when planning the structure of line-ups – a measure to help prevent biased eyewitness identifications summarised as follows:

- one suspect per line-up;
- members of the line-up should be based on eyewitness descriptions;
- members should be similar but not overly similar;
- a double-blind procedure should be followed where the person organising the line-up has no prior knowledge of who the suspect is;
- previous viewing of mug shots by eyewitnesses should preclude them from line-up suspect selection;
- eyewitnesses should be informed that the suspect might not be present in the line-up;
- simultaneous or sequential line-up structures are permissible;
- identifications, certainty of selection, time lapse between witnessing the event and providing information and witness comments should be recorded;
- no feedback concerning a misidentification should be given;
- exclusion of eyewitness confidence reports in court.

These guidelines help investigators meet the CPS criteria and prevent their case from being thrown out by the CPS on grounds of poor police investigative policy. The new system VIPER, has been introduced to British police forces. VIPER line-ups consist of five to eight faces that match eyewitness descriptions of the perpetrator. Eyewitnesses are presented with footage of a person for 15 seconds showing a full-face head and shoulder pose followed by a three-quarters profile and then returning to a full-face pose. They are also permitted to observe the line-up sequence twice after all faces have been presented. VIPER was tested for reliability by comparing eyewitness identification accuracy with mug shots (Darling, Valentine and Memon 2008). Darling *et al.* (2008) were unable to find a difference between simultaneous and sequential presentation formats for the number of correct identifications – hence viewing a video or a series of mug shots did not appear to compromise identification accuracy. VIPER has other advantages over identity parades such as:

- they are ten times less likely to be cancelled;
- planning is more time efficient as video footage can be taken of the suspect at any time and the other faces can be easily retrieved from the database;
- more cost effective;
- causes less stress for eyewitnesses (Brace, Pike, Kemp and Turner 2009).

Findings thus far are promising and show that correct identifications can be increased while misidentifications reduced. What these procedures cannot eliminate are the stereotypes that eyewitnesses apply to people. We all have an Implicit Personality Theory (IPT) providing us with a theory of which personality traits co–occur, and stereotypes, schemata and scripts about people. The application of IPT can result in misrepresentations of people, which can cause problems for some defendants. For example, a physically unattractive defendant might be considered as threatening and therefore likely to be guilty of a crime. Factors like physical attractiveness are known as **extra–legal defendant characteristics** discussed next.

## Extra-legal defendant characteristics

Extra-legal defendant characteristics include social and physical informa-tion about the defendant that has nothing to do with the facts of the case against them – which is why the term non–evidential information is sometimes used. In the courtroom jurors are expected to consider evidential information (i.e. the facts of the case) and decide whether these facts are founded. Non-evidential information should be excluded from the deliberation process as it is biased and subjective. An example of this can be seen in the stereotyping applied to physically unattractive defendants. The more physically unattractive a person, the more threatening that person appears to be. The application of such stereotyping is often used without reference to its source, likelihood, reli-ability and validity.

It is difficult to avoid the use of IPT, stereotypes, schemata and scripts, as these are ways of organising information and forming categories for the inter-pretation of people's characters. Furthermore, as jurors are representative of the population, they too will be influenced by these factors. Many studies have demonstrated the impact of 'prior knowledge' to the way we perceive others and more importantly our memories of other people's behaviour (Berman, Read and Kenny 1983; Cohen 1981; Taylor and Crocker 1980). Prior knowl-edge and IPT can influence the **Just World Hypothesis** and our understand-ing of **Equity Theory** used by jurors (see Box 13.6).

Epstein (1985) studied the Just World Hypothesis in relation to the **Cognitive Experiential Self Theory**. Epstein argued that there are two dif-ferent pathways influencing juror verdicts: rational and experiential information processing. The rational route is founded on analytical and logical processing of factual information which can be regarded as equivalent to evidential infor-mation. The experiential approach uses intuition and pre-conscious thought connected with emotions and prior knowledge (i.e. IPT, stereotypes, schemata and scripts): analogous to non-evidential information. Van den Bos and Maas (2009) studied the connection between having a just world belief of people and justice and the Cognitive Experiential Self Theory. They found that people who had a strong belief in a just world were less sympathetic towards the victim and believed they were partly to blame – a position described in the victim precipitation theory (see Chapter 8).

The underlying reasoning for this relates to people having a belief in the world being a just place – an equitable playing-field – where logically it follows that the victim deserved what happened to them. This was demonstrated in a mock jury study by Feild (1979) who investigated interactions between defendant and victim race, victim physical attractiveness and sexual experience, the nature of rape and the strength of evidence on jurors' verdicts. A significant interaction of defendant and victim race and physical attractiveness led to the conclusion that defendant–victim racial differences in sentencing rested in part on the level of physical attractiveness of the victim.

## Box 13.6

### Just World Hypothesis and Equity Theory used by jurors

Lerner (1966) suggested that many people entertain the belief in a 'just world' where people's actions and the consequences following their actions occur together. Lerner elaborated by suggesting that we all have an understanding of our deservingness and a belief in the idea that others get what they deserve pending on what they have done. Applying this to a legal context for example, if someone commits a crime then they should be punished accordingly. Lerner claimed that when we have been wronged against, we will try to equilibrate the situation by compensating the victim and punishing the offender. We re-establish a sense of justice by ensuring the offending person receives their 'just deserts'. The extent to which we believe in a just world can be measured using a scale devised for differentiating individuals on the need for restorative justice (Rubin and Peplau 1973). Individuals scoring high on this scale endorse the just world belief and have an intense need to perceive their environment as a place where an appropriate fit between behaviour and consequences occurs (see Chapter 16). The Just Deserts Hypothesis is linked to **Equity Theory**, which stipulates that social interaction is a reciprocal exchange guided by a norm of distributive justice. In other words, individuals will try to optimise their rewards from any social interaction. Equity arises out of a socialised belief that we should behave equitably. This means that rewards are given to members of our society who treat others equitably and punishments to those who do not. Leventhal, Weiss and Long (1969) stated that the socialisation process ensures we experience distress when in an inequitable relationship. Hence, the greater the inequity the greater the distress experienced and the greater the need to restore equity to the situation.

Equity Theory and restorative justice are important to the way jurors interpret the relationship between defendant and victim. If the victim loses a large amount of money which the defendant then attains, jurors will perceive an inequitable situation that heightens their distress – distress that they will want to off-load, and an inequitable situation which they will want to correct. Outside of the courtroom, people may experience a situation that they feel perpetrated against but do nothing to restore fair play. This begs the question why? Two major factors considered important in the equation are the locus of causation and degree of intentionality. For instance, in the case of locus of causation, if the person was acting under external constraints the distress experienced will be reduced. When inequities are caused by intentional actions, the distress experienced is higher than would be under unintentional actions. Individually or combined these factors influence whether any action is taken against the wrongdoer. Equity Theory accounts for many of the findings concerning extra-legal defendant characteristics and how such information is used in the decision-making process. Kaplan and Kemmerick (1974) examined how information such as physical attractiveness can be used to make complex social judgements in the absence of other concrete information. They proposed that juror decisions of guilt or innocence can be conceptualised using information processing where evidential and non-evidential information is evaluated and integrated. Using mock jurors in a simulated mock jury task, it is possible to investigate the individual impact of evidential and non-evidential information. Kaplan and Kemmerick (1974), for example, had participants rate the guilt of defendants depicted in a series of fictitious transcripts that varied in the level of incriminating evidential information and non-evidential personality descriptions (i.e. positive, negative or neutral). All participants used both evidential and non-evidential information to help with their verdicts. Highly incriminating evidence and a negative personality description conspired to produce the highest guilt and sentence ratings.

Linking non-evidential information such as physical attractiveness to IPT, Lampel and Anderson (1968) found that participants shown a photograph of an attractive person were more likely to infer that they had a 'nice' personality. Dion, Berscheid and Walster (1972) supported this finding and suggested that attractive traits are attributed to attractive people and called this the Halo Effect.

When the rape victim was physically unattractive there was no difference in sentencing for a Black or White defendant regardless of the victim's race. However, when the victim was physically attractive, Black defendants were sentenced more harshly if the victim was White. Furthermore, there was no difference in sentence for raping a sexually experienced victim but for Black defendants raping a sexually inexperienced, physically unattractive victim, the sentence received was the most punitive of all possible variable combinations. These findings suggest that non-evidential information about the victim is taken into account when deciding a sentence. Even though the victim was 'crimed' against, information about appearance and personality was being processed subconsciously, thus explaining van den Bos and Maas' previous findings.

Epstein's Cognitive Experiential Self Theory has particular relevance in jury decision making, and has proven to be a valuable source for understanding how mock jurors are influenced by non-evidential information such as physical attractiveness (see Box 13.7). The rational and experiential pathways of processing information can help to differentiate under what circumstances evidential and non-evidential information takes precedence. It was suggested by Gunnell and Ceci (2010) that non-evidential information is processed via the experiential pathway. After participants were classified according to information processing style using the Rational Experiential Inventory, Gunnell and Ceci (2010) presented a trial transcript including an attached photo of the defendant (i.e. of high or low physical attractiveness) for participants to read and decide a verdict and sentence. As predicted, experiential processers made more convictions than rational processers; however, the rate of conviction was the same when the defendant was attractive. When the defendant was unattractive, experiential processers convicted in 89 per cent of cases compared to 67 per cent of rational processers. Evidential information was standardised; however, non-evidential information varied in the level of defendant physical attractiveness and it was this information that experiential processers used to determine the case outcome (Gunnell and Ceci 2010).

Physical attractiveness is just one example of non-evidential information or extra-legal defendant characteristics. There are a multitude of extra-legal defendant characteristics categorised along physical and social dimensions. The physical dimension pertains to characteristics that can be seen and heard – physical attractiveness and dress sense can be seen whereas a person's voice and the language used can be heard. Social dimensions include factors relating to the person that are not immediately noticeable but can be inferred from information about them such as being employed versus being unemployed. There are many physical and social factors that constitute extra-legal defendant characteristics such as:

- scruffy versus clean shaven;
- bruising and cuts to the face;
- poorly dressed versus presentable;
- clearly spoken versus poor diction;
- respect versus disrespect in the community;
- positive versus negative personality;
- involved in charity work;
- churchgoer;
- employed versus unemployed;
- professional career versus manual work;
- educated versus uneducated;
- handsome versus homely looking;
- settled versus unsettled lifestyle;
- conformist versus non-conformist;

- eccentric;
- political activist;
- distinguishing facial mark such as a scar;
- friendly versus unfriendly demeanour;
- ethnic origin.

These are some examples of extra-legal defendant characteristics shown to influence decision making in mock jury studies. It is physical attractiveness and ethnicity, however, that have received the most attention in mock jury studies and produced the most conflicting findings (see Box 13.7).

## Box 13.7

### Mock jury studies investigating defendant physical attractiveness and ethnicity on ratings of guilt and sentence

Smith and Hed (1969) considered physical attractiveness with the age of the defendant, hypothesising that young physically attractive defendants would be sentenced for burglary more leniently than old unattractive defendants, but the reverse would be the case for crimes where victims are swindled. The hypothesis was confirmed. Sigall and Ostrove (1975) described two different crimes in a fictitious transcript that were rated for length of sentence by mock jurors. In the case of burglary, physically attractive defendants received shorter sentences than unattractive defendants but the reversal occurred for crimes involving swindle – supporting Smith and Hed's findings. One explanation is that in crimes involving swindle, physical attractiveness of the perpetrator can be entwined with the criminal act such that they are using their attractiveness to take advantage of the victim. Leventhal and Krate (1977) had two independent groups where participants either sentenced the defendant or rated defendant physical attractiveness. The ratings of sentence correlated with the ratings of attractiveness, such that those rated as attractive were given more lenient sentences and vice versa for unattractive defendants. This suggests that even when participants rated for sentence only, they were inadvertently influenced by the defendant's level of physical attractiveness. Stewart (1980) reviewed real-life court cases varying in level of crime seriousness. Physical attractiveness and crime seriousness were found to be significant predictors of lenient and punitive sentencing. Conviction and acquittal rates, however, were not significant, suggesting that juries are no more likely to acquit physically attractive than unattractive defendants. Rector and Bagby (1993) and Stewart (2001) demonstrated the attraction–leniency effect, finding that defendant attractiveness correlated negatively with punitive sentencing.

Taylor and Butcher (2007) tested the hypotheses that physically attractive defendants will be rated leniently for extent of guilt and sentence; that Black defendants will receive punitive extent of guilt and sentence scores, and that an interaction between ethnicity of the defendant and mock juror will be influenced by the defendant's attractiveness. Previous research by Abwender and Hough (2001), Foley and Chamblin (1982) and Ugwuegbu (1979) found a significant interaction between defendant and mock juror ethnicity. They found that both Black and Hispanic mock jurors were lenient towards White defendants but this was not reciprocated by White mock jurors. Support for these findings was shown by Pfeifer and Ogloff's (2003) study where defendants with different racial heritage to the mock jurors' received higher ratings of guilt. In Taylor and Butcher's study an interaction between defendant and mock juror ethnicity was not supported; however, a significant interaction was found for attractiveness and defendant ethnicity for sentencing. Unattractive Black defendants were rated punitively on the sentence scale but this occurred once jurors had decided that a defendant was guilty – hence attractiveness was not found to influence ratings of guilt. This suggests the attractive defendant experiences the attractive-leniency effect before deliberation. A defendant's ethnicity had more influence once a guilty verdict was determined. Hence they are more likely to receive a harsh sentence once they are found to be guilty. The combination of defendant ethnicity and attractiveness summate to have a robust effect at a secondary level of decision making (i.e. sentencing rather than the determination of guilt). In interpreting the tendency for physically attractive defendants to be treated leniently compared to their unattractive counterparts, physical attractiveness can be regarded as one of many defendant inputs in the equity formulation. Often there are other extra-legal defendant characteristics operating concurrently which can compound findings as seen in the study by Taylor and Butcher (2007).

## Summary

- Eyewitness testimony has its roots in medieval law where evidential information (such as eyewitness evidence) was used to prove the facts of the case. In contemporary Britain, eyewitness testimony still has an important role in the courtroom, but is only considered to be robust and reliable when it can be corroborated with other sources of information such as forensic and medical evidence.
- The reliability of eyewitness testimony has been questioned for most part of the twentieth century and concerns have arisen out of empirical research showing the fallible nature of human memory. Face recognition research has shown that we are exceptionally good at recognising familiar faces which explains why misidentification of people we know is typically low. Laboratory-based research using unfamiliar faces also indicates that

we are good at recognising faces (albeit recognition performance decreases from 90 per cent to 75 per cent), provided that the automatic processing mechanism for remembering faces is not inhibited. Findings suggest that faces are processed automatically and holistically; thus explaining why methods of remembering faces that encourage deconstruction are unsuccessful strategies for encoding faces.

- Despite being good at recognising familiar faces, the identification of suspects in a line-up is not consistently reliable. There are many reasons for this. Wells (1978), however, divided factors which impair memory retrieval of events and recognition of faces in to estimator and system variables. Estimator variables have an effect on an individual's perceptual, encoding and retrieval processes, like for example, high stress levels impairing information retrieval or misleading information displacing memory traces of an event. System variables are concerned with the investigative approaches used to extract information from eyewitnesses, such as, tools of facial composite construction, viewing mug shots and selecting suspects from line-ups. There are different ways of improving the retrieval of information from eyewitnesses which have been documented by psychologists in *amicus curiae* for court judges to review. Forensic psychologists have helped police develop effective techniques to achieve eyewitness accuracy free from the influences of post-event contamination and biased line-ups. There are new techniques of structuring line-ups that are currently being tested such as VIPER.

- The judicial system expects jurors to base their verdicts on the evidence presented by the prosecution and defence and to weigh this information for reliability and factual content using probabilities. They are expected to use deductive logic to help ascertain the reliability of the case facts presented. Decisions, however, are based on rational thought (i.e. making deductions from the facts) and, importantly, subconscious processing of experiential information (i.e. prior knowledge from IPT, stereotypes, schemata and scripts). It is the subconscious processing of experiential information that is irrelevant for verdict deliberation and can lead to misinformed decisions. It is difficult to separate the rational from experiential information pathways but rational processing will dominate as long as evidence (other than eyewitness accounts) presented in court is robust, reliable, corroborated and triangulated using other sources. Under these circumstances the evidential information is less likely to be disputed, any ambiguity minimalised and the reliance on experiential information processing reduced.

- Understanding how jurors make decisions in the courtroom has been researched using simulated mock jury studies. While mock jury research has been criticised for not being ecologically valid, they do offer insight to the nature of how information is processed and the weightings given to evidential and non-evidential information. As an academic exercise, the use of mock jurors in such studies has provided insight to how decisions are made.

- Research on extra-legal defendant characteristics, in particular physical attractiveness and ethnicity, has been investigated using mock juror studies. Mock jurors are typically presented with a fictitious transcript with a photograph attached (previously rated for level of physical attractiveness in a pilot study) to read and assign extent of guilt and sentencing ratings. The findings from these studies are mixed – some attain robust effects of physical attractiveness (i.e. attractive defendants receive lenient ratings), whereas other studies have null effects. Extra-legal defendant characteristics comprise of non-evidential information that is non-factually based. Despite extra-legal defendant characteristics relying on IPT, stereotypes, schemata and scripts, it is difficult to disengage from using these in decision making. The evaluation of evidential information is more likely to result in an equitable verdict in accordance with the just deserts philosophy. Alternatively, non-evidential information will lead to unreliable decisions based on unfounded suppositions.

## Questions for discussion

1   Why do we believe eyewitness testimony to be accurate and reliable?
2   To what extent can the effects of estimator and system variables be controlled and changed?
3   How can Epstein's Cognitive Experiential Self Theory be applied to jury decision making?

# Chapter 14

# Cognitive interview

The three chapters in Part V will explore different aspects of the investigative process. These aspects of the investigative process are important in the gathering of evidence by police which in turn is submitted to the courts. It is therefore important that these methods are effective and offer reliable evidence to the court, so that the defendant gets a fair trial. In this chapter we will explore the second of these investigative processes – the cognitive interview.

In this chapter we will explore the importance of having an interview format that is conducive to extracting information from eyewitnesses. During the investigative process, police interview victims, eyewitnesses and suspects. These interviews are mostly conducted at police stations but at times they might have to interview at the crime scene or at the homes of victims or eyewitnesses. Despite the location, they tend to use the standard police interview. The standard police interview format requires little training but frequently obstructs optimum retrieval of information about witnessed criminal events. Why the standard police interview can be obstructive will be explained in relation to psychological research of how human memory operates. Different memory theories relevant to eyewitness memory are described, and in particular, theories for which the principles of the cognitive interview are founded. The principles of the cognitive interview are derived from psychological memory research, which is why it is a successful investigative tool. The cognitive interview is increasingly used by different police forces in the UK because of its successful approach to attaining information from witnesses, victims and suspects. We will explore the modifications made to the cognitive interview format over the years – in particular the enhanced cognitive interview, which draws upon 13 types of interview skills and consists of 11 phases. In this chapter, evidence of how effective the cognitive interview actually is will be explored in the context of case examples where perpetrators were apprehended and arrested on the basis of valuable information presented by victims and witnesses using this method of interview. Furthermore, there have been many successes with the enhanced format, especially with young children, senior adults and those with learning difficulties. The empirical evidence presented in this chapter demonstrates the success rate of the cognitive interview (regardless of modification) versus the standard police interview in the increase of information retrieval. This success extends to facial composite construction using systems encouraging holistic processing. The evidence supporting the use of the cognitive interview (including its modifications) will be reviewed, and how police training in Britain now incorporates the cognitive interview into the Professionalising Investigation Programme of 2009.

## Introduction

The cognitive interview (CI) is a successful and useful method of attaining information from eyewitnesses, victims and suspects. This interview technique was recently introduced to police forces across Britain and is steadily overtaking the standard police interview as a successful investigative tool. It is successful because the underlying principles of the CI are founded on sound psychological research of how memory operates. The CI was first introduced by Geiselman, Fisher, MacKinnon and Holland (1986) as an effective working method for enhancing information retrieval. The CI follows a fixed sequence based on four mnemonic (a device like a rhyme or formula used to help learn and remember information) principles. Using these principles, witnesses are able to supply investigators with a narrative report (the structure of the CI will be discussed in more detail later). The CI strategy is very different from the standard police interview where eyewitnesses would be interrupted by the police interviewer at the commencement of information recall (Fisher, Geiselman and Raymond 1987). During the standard police interview three open-ended questions are normally asked such as, 'Describe what your attacker did?' When the interviewee responded to a question, the police interviewer would intervene on average 7.5 seconds after they started to answer the question. This time-frame was repeated for all questions asked. The interviewer would interrupt on average 11 times per question answered. Interruptions are not conducive for effective retrieval of information because it not only disrupts the continuity and flow of information recall but it impairs witness concentration (the structure of the standard police interview will also be discussed in more detail later).

Despite the successes of the cognitive interview, not all police forces in Britain and other countries use this approach to interviewing. Regardless of all its faults, the standard police interview format is still the prime interview strategy used by police. The effectiveness of interview strategies used by police has received attention dating back to the early twentieth century. In 1900 for instance, Alfred Binet in France was studying the effects of suggestibility in child eyewitnesses, whereas in Germany in 1904, William Stern considered the strategy of interrogation techniques used on eyewitnesses. It is clear that Elizabeth Loftus paved the way for research on post-event misleading

information and has initiated a string of studies looking at post-event interviews and how this might influence the nature of information recalled. Loftus'
work has become the inspiration for many different theoretical explanations
of how eyewitness memory can be easily manipulated through misinformation (see Chapter 13). There have been many different eyewitness studies
conducted in both the UK and US. Even the BBC in collaboration with
the Greater Manchester Police broadcasted a programme called *Eyewitness*
in 2010, comprising three episodes which set out to investigate the accuracy
of eyewitness memory and the effectiveness of the cognitive interview (The
OpenLearn Team 2010). The details of this broadcasted study are described
in Box 14.1.

Before the successes of the cognitive interview can be fully appreciated, and
the reasons why it works well as a method of eyewitness memory retrieval, it
is important to trace its development from psychological research on memory
and the many theories explaining different memory phenomena.

## Theoretical explanations explaining memory relevant to eyewitnessing

From experimental, clinical and applied psychological research many different
theories of memory have arisen. There are six theoretical approaches, however, relevant to our understanding of how eyewitness memory operates and
the way knowledge is structured and stored in memory:

1   fuzzy-trace theory (Miller and Bjorklund 1998);
2   source-monitoring (Lindsay and Johnson 1991; Johnson, Hashtroudi and
    Lindsay 1993);
3   activation-based memory (Ayers and Reder 1998);
4   retrieval-induced forgetting (MacLeod 2002);
5   multi-component faceted (Bower 1967) and encoding specificity (Tulving
    and Thompson 1973).

These will be discussed in turn beginning with the fuzzy-trace theory by Miller
and Bjorklund.

### Fuzzy-trace theory

The fuzzy-trace theory has relevance for decision making and the formation of
judgements. It stipulates that there are two memory representations encoded in
parallel, referred to as verbatim and gist. Miller and Bjorklund (1998) claimed
that verbatim representations contain detailed information, whereas gist traces
extract the meaning from this information. Gist traces are inaccurate and lack
longevity and yet people prefer to think and reason using gist representations.
The fuzzy-trace theory has been used to explain how false memories occur.

# Box 14.1

## Eyewitness broadcast by the BBC

Each episode explored different aspects of eyewitness memory and the best strategies for eyewitness information retrieval. Three expert psychologists in the field were responsible for different aspects of the 'eyewitness experience'. Professor Pike concentrated on the eyewitness experience of viewing a crime and identifying faces using E-Fit (see also Chapter 13) while Professor Conway focused on flashbulb memories and Dr Milne on the structure of the cognitive interview.

The outcome of this research demonstrated how effective the cognitive interview format is as an investigative procedure for police interviewers to follow. In one episode the volunteers were informed that they would be participating in a study about memory and would be subjected to a batch of memory tests. The main purpose of the study was therefore disguised by subjecting the volunteers to these different memory tests. They were unaware of their second role as emerging eyewitnesses to a series of criminal events. In the first experiment they became key eyewitnesses to a staged pub brawl resulting in a fatality (this was faked, of course, but they did not know this). Police detectives investigated the crime and treated the pub as the crime scene – resulting in the detainment of witnesses for questioning. They were asked individually to give accounts of what had happened and what they could remember of the event using the cognitive interview format.

As part of their memory tests some of the volunteers had to wear tracking glasses which recorded the sciatic movements of the eyes using a memory chip built into the framework. This enabled information regarding what the eyes were focusing on to be stored and downloaded onto computer for later analysis. Unbeknownst to the volunteers, one volunteer was an actress who was informed that an armed robbery of a security van will occur, and her role was to play the hostage. Two of the volunteers remained at base while the others went for a walk – two of whom were wearing the tracking glasses. During the robbery, one of the security guards was hit to the ground and one robber was unmasked and looked directly at the 'eyewitnesses'. The getaway car arrived and the hostage and robbers left with the getaway driver. Police interviewers used the cognitive interview approach to extract as much information from these eyewitnesses as possible. The police were able to piece together the information from all the eyewitnesses and from this were able to reconstruct what had happened. The two volunteers who were absent from the walk instead saw the event footage second hand. They were allowed to discuss what they were seeing and share their thoughts and interpretations, which were recorded to enable researchers to trace the source of perceptual and memory errors made when they too were later interviewed individually.

As a means to identifying the unmasked robber, volunteers (including the two who were absent from the scene but watched video footage of the event) were asked to choose the unmasked robber from a sequential line-up computer presentation very similar to VIPER (see Chapter 13). The two volunteers viewing the incident on video together made misidentifications, and their recollections of the event were contaminated by their shared discussions and interpretations (as seen from the recordings made) – errors in their accounts were identical. The results of the tracking glasses showed that, despite the eyes looking and moving around the crime scene event, what the eyes actually witnessed did not always corroborate what they recalled and reported to the police. Information downloaded from the tracking glasses provided embellished details of what had been witnessed. This demonstrated that what we perceive is not necessarily encoded in a way that is subject to easy retrieval. To tap into this information requires a technique of interview encouraging conscious analysis and examination of every stored memory trace relating to the event on a frame-by-frame basis. The cognitive interview enabled just that.

Errors of omission and commission, for example, can be explained using gist representations where false memories (i.e. errors of commission) are consistent with gist memories or the meaning of experiences.

Younger children have been found to be sensitive to gist-consistent false information (Brainerd and Reyna 2004). In other words, when a child has experienced sexual abuse where the content of these memories are very similar, they will draw upon gist memories of these events (i.e. meanings are derived from their experiences of abuse). It is under circumstances where false memories consistent with gist memory that gist-consistent false information can replace true memories (Brainerd and Reyna 2002). It is important therefore that when child witnesses are interviewed (especially in cases of sexual abuse), they are allowed to free recall – precisely what the cognitive interview encourages.

### Source-monitoring theory

In the case of source-monitoring theory memories can be located to a particular event experience such that when a source-monitoring error is made, the memory is mistakenly identified as having occurred at a particular time and place. Source-monitoring errors are problematic and can result in the misidentifications of innocent people – simply because eyewitnesses have attributed the source of their information incorrectly. According to Johnson, Hashtroudi and Lindsay (1993), if the contextual details of an event are ineffectively encoded at the time of the event, then relevant information will not be completely recovered. This is because the memory records of an event have been ineffectively activated. There are two types of cognitive processes pertaining to source-monitoring: heuristic and systematic (Lindsay and Johnson 1991). Judgements that are of a heuristic nature (see Chapter 5) occur automatically without conscious awareness of implicit perceptual and contextual information contained in the event. Alternatively, systematic judgements are based on effortful conscious processing used to examine the specific source of relevant memories. Three types of source-monitoring exist:

1   External source-monitoring – this involves keeping track of different events occurring around the individual and being able to discriminate between them. An example of this would be who said what at a party.
2   Internal source-monitoring – this is used to discriminate between the different memories an individual has stored over the years.
3   Reality monitoring – this focuses on the discrimination between externally and internally retrieved sources of information (see Chapter 13). Johnson et al. (1993) used the example of being able to separate a real-life experience of a plane crashing into a building from having merely read about it in a newspaper.

Relating the source-monitoring theory to eyewitness retrieval, Johnson (1997) said, 'People sometimes confuse what they inferred or imagined and what actually happened, what they saw and what was suggested to them, one person's actions and another's what they heard and what they previously knew and fiction and fact' (p.1733).

### Activation-based memory

Ayers and Reder (1998) adopted an activation-based framework to account for the misinformation effect (see Chapter 13). The activation-based semantic network model of memory first introduced by Anderson (1976; 1983), assumes that memories are linked conceptually through a series of nodes of varying distance – the closer the node the more conceptually similar the information. Information is retrieved more quickly if it is encoded and stored in the node encapsulating the relevant concept. If, for example, the colour 'red' is stored in the node that houses other colours, then this is conceptually congruent and therefore easier to retrieve. If, alternatively, it is stored in the node housing the concept 'cars', then it might take longer to retrieve information relating to the colour red. Another example is information about a robbery. It makes sense to store this memory event under the concept of crime instead of a bank where the route to memory retrieval is more explicit than implied. Ayers and Reder (1998) introduced the term 'source of activation confusion' to explain how memory errors occur as a consequence of misinterpreting the source of activation. In other words, eyewitnesses fail to identify the source of activation because the memory event was encoded and stored in a conceptually incongruent node. Hence the spread of activation in a conceptually incongruent node will be slower and more difficult to locate than the memories stored in a conceptually congruent node – in this case there will be a mismatch between the event source of activation and the correct memory representation. According to Ayers and Reder (1998) the model assumes that:

- activation spreads from concept to associated concepts;
- context is represented as a collection of concepts with distinct features reflecting the event encoded;
- there is conscious access to concepts with their associations;
- errors occur when inferring the activation source.

### Retrieval-induced forgetting

Retrieval-induced forgetting enables us to remember and recall even more information about an event. This sounds contradictory but the underlying assumption is that the accumulation of related memories increases the difficulty of information retrieval. This occurs because the information we wish to retrieve is in direct competition with other related information that we do not want to retrieve. Thus if related but irrelevant information were inhibited, retrieval of targeted information would be easier (Saunders and MacLeod 2006). This was demonstrated by MacLeod (2002) when eyewitness retrieval of competing information was inhibited. According to Anderson and Spellman (1995), forgetting competing memories so that they can no longer be accessed consciously is what retrieval inhibition does. The inverse of this, however, is that selective retrieval of information can cause eyewitnesses to forget related and potentially relevant information about an event. During questioning, for instance, eyewitnesses might only be able to retrieve selected information at the expense of retrieving other related and relevant information – hence they can forget potentially relevant information.

### Multi-component and encoding-specificity approaches

While the above memory approaches account well for how the misinformation effect can occur, it is on two memory principles that the cognitive interview is primarily founded. The first principle is that memory traces are multi-component faceted (Bower 1967); hence a memory trace is not just visual in nature but comprises information from other sense modalities such as smell (Cann and Ross 1989), sound, taste and touch. This view of how memory traces are encoded further suggests that aspects of established memory traces might respond more effectively to different types of retrieval probe. Questions enabling an eyewitness to explore other aspects of a memory for an event, such as the smell of the crime scene area, could help provoke further details about the location.

skills and rapport building, interviewers are in a better position to respond appropriately to interviewees who might be nervous, unsure of what to expect or have poor articulation and communication skills. The 13 basic skills that interviewers use in ECI include:

1  building a rapport;
2  key listening skills;
3  encouraging spontaneous recall;
4  using open-ended question format;
5  pausing after responses to questions;
6  no interrupting;
7  asking for detailed accounts;
8  enabling intense concentration;
9  encouraging the use of imagery;
10  enabling the recreation of the original context;
11  adopting the witness' perspective;
12  asking compatible questions;
13  referring to and following the sequence of the CI.

The ECI method enables witnesses to take control, be more active during questioning and take as much time as they need to respond to questions. Police interviewers are taught relevant skills of communication such as building a rapport and using the appropriate level of dialogue; unintimidating body language; effective question structure and the use of pausing (see evaluation of CI).

ECI is divided into 11 phases, all designed to increase the likelihood of an effective rapport between interviewer and interviewee but also to elicit optimal information retrieval. The phases are as follows:

• Phase 1 involves greetings, personalising the interview and an introduction.
• Phase 2 is all about establishing a rapport with the interviewee. During this phase a relaxed and secure atmosphere is created by asking neutral questions about the person such as their hobbies and interests. A meaningful interaction is necessary so the interviewer might self-disclose details about him or herself.
• Phase 3 is where the interviewer explains the purpose of the interview. It is here that the interviewee's attention is directed towards the event and they are encouraged to describe everything about the event that they can remember without resorting to guessing or confabulation.
• Phase 4 is about context reinstatement where the interviewee is encouraged to think about the context of the event. For example, they might be asked to visualise the layout of the shop including the number of isles using as much time to do this as they need. Any questions asked are delivered slowly with pauses to allow interviewee elaboration.
• Phase 5 is about initiating a free report. Interviewees are encouraged

to free recall descriptions and details of the event in narrative style. It is important that there are no interruptions made while interviewees make their recollections.

- Phase 6 is when questions are asked but interviewees are reminded again that they should describe everything that comes to mind in response to the questions.
- Phase 7 is when the interviewer asks compatible questions. In other words, only questions are asked which are consistent with the interviewee's current focus of attention. The interviewee is encouraged to activate a mental picture of one aspect of the event while the interviewer asks questions about this until no more information is forthcoming. Once this mental picture is exhausted the next mental picture is subjected to the same format of information extraction. In order to activate a mental picture, the interviewee is encouraged to recreate the psychological and environmental context by referring to a specific moment in the event based on the interviewee's previous free reporting. By asking questions relevant to the activated mental picture the interviewer is probing for further information.
- Phase 8 is when the interviewee recalls information from different perspectives. They might be asked to visualise the position of another eyewitness and describe what they possibly could have seen. This procedure is designed to facilitate further retrieval from memory and not to encourage speculation or induce confabulation.
- Phase 9 involves recalling information in the reverse order as a means of inducing further recall. When we recall information in the order of occurrence we might be influenced by our expectations of what should follow and what should normally occur during such an event, courtesy of our schemata (i.e. which are organised sets of information about events and items and influences how we perceive and interpret our experiences) and scripts (i.e. which are specific schemata consisting of a set order or sequence of occurrence – such as getting ready to go to work). Recalling event information in a different time sequence (or out of temporal order) might help induce retrieval memories that are unusual and therefore script-inconsistent (see Chapter 13).
- Phase 10 is when the interviewer summarises (using the interviewee's own words) the account of the event provided. This offers another opportunity for the interviewee to elaborate further should any additional retrieval pathways be activated.
- Phase 11 provides closure to the interview. This is designed to reduce any tensions experienced by the interviewee during the interview. The intention is for the interviewee to leave on a positive note, which is why the conversation is gradually directed towards neutral topics.

## Example of a CI questioning format

Dando and Milne (2009) described the cognitive interview in detail and provided examples of question phrasing for each of the four mnemonic principles. The first principle of 'reinstating the context' is designed around encoding specificity (Tulving and Thompson 1973) and should help trigger memories of the event. The following is a hypothetical example of how typically such an interview might go:

> I want you to try and think back to the event and tell me as much as you can remember about it. Try and relax and clear your mind of other things and concentrate only on that day. Remember all details about that day including where you were and why; try to get an image of the place in your mind's eye; what and who was there; what did the place smell like and how did it feel? Focus on what happened and when ready re-tell everything.

The second principle of 'reporting everything', reminds interviewees that all information is useful even if they think it to be irrelevant. The following is a hypothetical example of how this might go:

> It is possible that you might feel some information is irrelevant or that this information is already documented. It would be helpful to us if you include everything in your account. I would like to hear all details whether you think they are important or not.

The third principle of 'changing the temporal order of accessing event information' is derived from the multi-component approach (Bower 1967). The multi-component approach stipulates that memory traces are encoded in a variety of ways and can therefore be accessed using a multitude of probing techniques. Recalling event information using different temporal orders provides another technique of accessing the encrypted information encoded in the memory trace previously irretrievable through free recall. Recalling event information in reverse order, or beginning at mid-point, reduces interference from schemata or scripts. Research by Geiselman et al. (1986) and Geiselman and Callot (1990) demonstrated the advantages of recalling information in reverse order – one being an increase in the volume of information retrieved. The following is a hypothetical example of how this might go:

> It makes perfect sense to remember details of the event in the order of occurrence. I find that it can help if you try to remember things by beginning with what happened last and then slowly working your way back to the start. Try and remember what the last thing that happened was, then the thing before that and before that, until we are at the beginning of the event.

The fourth principle of 'a change of perspective' is another technique introduced to access previously irretrievable information. The idea behind changing the perspective of the witness derives from research showing how a deviation from the individual's personal perspective can help unlock additional information encoded in the memory trace (Anderson and Pichert 1978). Anderson and Pichert (1978) found that reading a narrative from a burglar's and house purchaser's perspective combined increased the amount of recalled information – this exceeded the amount of information recalled from the reading of either the burglar's or house purchaser's perspective. The following is a hypothetical example of how this might go:

> Everyone will have their own take on what happened. I want you to try and remember the event using another person's perspective who also witnessed what happened. Concentrate on this person by singling them out and tell me all details you can remember about them. Focus on what they saw.

CI and ECI are effective interviewing techniques and have been particularly successful in promoting the retrieval of sensitive information from vulnerable adults, the old and very young, and female victims of sexual attacks. ECI is especially successful for obtaining information from young children who have been victimised, abused and traumatised. Hence it is not surprising that much of the evaluative research on ECI has involved interviewing children and vulnerable adults. In the next section, studies investigating the effectiveness of ECI and CI will be considered. One important measure of success rate is the extent information gathered is correct or incorrect.

## Evaluation of CI and ECI

Numerous measures of CI and ECI success are considered – the most obvious being eyewitness retrieval of information during cognitive interviewing that led to the capture of a perpetrator. An example of a less obvious measure of success relates to whether police decide to adopt the CI format. To encourage police to use the CI approach as a form of good practice, empirical evidence showing how ineffective the standard police interview must first be presented. The standard police interview, previously described, has numerous problems and yet many police forces across Britain rely on this format of obtaining information from witnesses and suspects. Evidence from studies shows the standard police interview to be ineffective and in many cases obstructive to the process of recalling information. We will consider the ineffectiveness of the standard police interview by considering the following:

- correct and incorrect responses across CI and the standard police interview;
- successful resolution of cases based on CI;
- use of CI/ECI for recall in children, senior adults and the mentally impaired;

- police training of CI/ECI;
- applications of CI for facial composite construction.

### Correct and incorrect responses across CI and the standard police interview

In a study by Geiselman, Fisher, MacKinnon and Holland (1985), effectiveness of the CI was tested and compared with the standard police interview. Eighty-nine students were interviewed by police officers (using CI or the standard police interview) two days after viewing police training films of simulated crimes provided by the Los Angeles Police Department (LAPD). The number of correct responses, errors and confabulated information were compared across the two interviewing strategies (see Figure 14.1). Significantly more correct information was recalled using the CI approach, and despite the increase in the number of errors and confabulations made, this failed to reach significance.

Geiselman, Fisher, MacKinnon and Holland (1986) recruited 51 non-student volunteers from a variety of occupational backgrounds such as laboratory assistants, administrative staff and maintenance workers. They were informed that they will be shown a four minute audio-visual film of a violent bank robbery or a 'liquor' store robbery; both resulting in a fatality. Two days later they were interviewed by police detectives from various South Californian Police Departments and randomly allocated to either the standard police interview or CI condition (see Figure 14.2). On average 6.09 more correct information was recalled by eyewitnesses in the CI condition which translates to an increase in recall of more than 17 per cent.

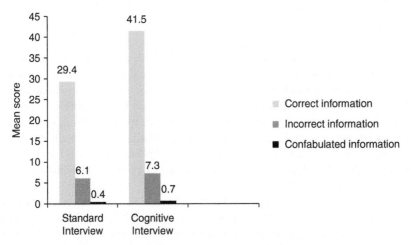

Figure 14.1 Mean score of correct and incorrect responses and confabulated information obtained using the standard police interview and CI
Adapted from Geiselman 1985

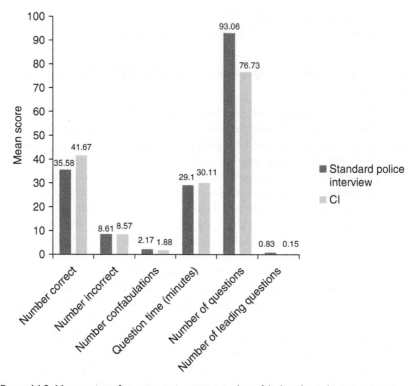

*Figure 14.2* Mean scores for correct, incorrect and confabulated results, interview time, number of questions asked and number of leading questions asked using the standard police interview and CI

Adapted from Geiselman 1986

In 1987 Fisher, Geiselman, Raymond, Jurkevich and Warhaftig compared recall effectiveness using the ECI with the original CI. Student participants viewed the same LAPD police training film as that used in Geiselman *et al.*'s (1985) study and were allocated to either the CI or ECI condition. The ECI elicited 45 per cent more correct information than the CI although errors and confabulations remained consistent. They calculated that ECI elicits 75 per cent more correct information than the standard police interview based on the premise that CI is about 30 per cent more effective than the standard police interview.

Fisher, Geiselman and Amador (1989) compared the amount of information retrieved using both the standard police interview and CI and found that up to 25–35 per cent more accurate information was extracted using the CI format. Fisher *et al.* (1989), in collaboration with the Miami Police Department, tested the effectiveness of CI using 16 police officers from the Robbery Division. A total of 88 standard police interviews were recorded over a four month period after which the 16 officers were divided into two groups: a control group who continued using the standard police interview and a group who were trained to use CI. After training in CI, further interviews over a seven month period were recorded and analysed blindly by an independent team based at the University of California. A significant difference was found in the quantity of information recalled by witnesses interviewed by police officers using CI. Police officers using CI enabled witnesses to recall 47 per cent more information and 63 per cent more than their untrained colleagues in the control group. Furthermore, 94 per cent of the information recalled using CI was corroborated – thus demonstrating a high accuracy rate.

In support of Geiselman's findings, Köhnken, Milne, Memon and Bull (1999) considered 53 studies in a meta-analysis (i.e. comparison of studies with similar objectives, method and controlled variables) of CI effectiveness and found that CI elicited 34 per cent more accurate detail than the standard police interview. Using a meta-analysis approach, significant improvements to recall were revealed when using two or more principles of the CI approach in tandem and, furthermore, when applying the first two principles of CI (Milne and Bull 2002). There are variations in Britain on the usage of the 'reinstating context' instruction – the Merseyside and the Greater Manchester Police Forces adopt the original CI template whereas Thames Valley Police tended to dispense with the 'reinstating the context' instruction. CI tends to be criticised for taking longer to conduct (mean of 39.70 minutes) as opposed to the standard police interview (mean of 32.10 minutes). Hypnosis style interview takes the least amount of time to conduct (mean of 28.20 minutes) but induces fewer correct responses than CI but more than the standard police interview (mean number of 38) and fewer incorrect responses than both CI and the standard police interview (mean number of 5.90).

The CI/ECI approaches have been tested cross-culturally, attaining similar successes to those achieved in Britain. For example, Stein and Memon (2006) compared the standard police interview with CI in Brazil and found correct recall rates to be consistent with previous research. In countries such as Canada (Turtle, Lawrence and Leslie 1994), Spain (Campos and Alonso-Quecuty 1999), Germany (Köhnken, Thurer and Zoberbier 1994), US (Brock, Fisher and Cutler 1999) and the UK (Clifford and Gwyer 1999), findings compatible with previous research demonstrated the advantages of using the CI approach to the standard police interview, and ECI to CI. Furthermore, these findings have extended to interviews with children (Akehurst, Milne and Köhnken, 2003), senior adults (Wright and Holliday, 2007) and those with learning impairments (Robinson and McGuire 2006).

### Successful resolution of cases based on CI

The effectiveness of CI can also be judged by the number of cases solved as a consequence of good quality information and an increase in the quantity of information retrieved by eyewitnesses which can be corroborated using other forms of evidence (see Box 14.2 for case examples)

## Box 14.2

### Examples of three cases solved using CI

In 1991, Fisher was asked to help a Miami, US, woman who was a witness to a murder case. She was having difficulty remembering details of two men who were standing together in an office building. These men murdered a man, who was an employee, only minutes after the woman had walked past. She only had a fleeting glance at these men and therefore had difficulty remembering anything specific about them. The case rested on her testimony as she was the only witness; therefore it was imperative that police interviewed her. They used the standard police interview but had little success; however, Fisher used the CI approach which helped the woman recall that one of the men brushed his hair from his eyes and revealed a silver earring. This crucial information helped police capture the men and solve the case.

In 1992 Stephanie Slater, an estate agent, was showing a prospective buyer a house in the Great Barr area of Birmingham, UK. He attacked her using knives in the bathroom of the empty house and bound, gagged and blindfolded her. He transported her to his workshop in Newark, Nottinghamshire where she was put into a makeshift coffin, her hands handcuffed and electrodes attached to her legs, which was then sealed inside a wheelie bin. This is where she was left for eight days until a ransom of £175,000 was paid by her boss. During this time, her kidnapper would let her out in the morning to eat breakfast and go to the toilet. Despite being terrified and threatened with electrocution by her kidnapper should she try to escape and being tortured and raped, she tried to make conversation with him to form a rapport, which surprisingly he reciprocated. This rapport building was an effort to attain details about the man she could not see, and the smells and sounds of the place where she was imprisoned. Slater asked her kidnapper for a hug as a means of attaining details of his build, face structure and smell, and to hear his voice. At night, when Slater was on her own, she could hear distant sounds of trains and rats running around what sounded and smelled like a garage workshop. All this information proved to be very useful when Slater was interviewed by the West Midland's Police using the CI method after the ransom was paid and she was released. As she was blindfolded there was no visual information encoded in her memories of her ordeal; however, her memory traces were embellished with rich multi-modal sensory information which helped police locate the workshop in question and lead to her kidnapper, Michael Sams. Sams was arrested and sentenced to prison in 1993 for the murder of Julie Dart in 1991 and the kidnap and rape of Stephanie Slater. He is due for release in 2017 and since 2008 has resided in Whitemoor Prison, Cambridgeshire (Weathers 2011).

In 2007 Casey Miller, disguised as a postman, forced his way into the Aird's home in Cheshire, UK, after Louise Aird opened the front door while holding her two year old daughter. Miller threatened to kill her daughter with a 10-inch chef's knife and forced them both to the floor. He repeatedly said, 'Don't look at me, don't look at me', but despite this Aird scrutinised his face. There were three other accomplices who helped Miller steal LS Lowry paintings worth £1.7 million. Aird said she had watched the robbers stealing paintings from one room to the next. Aird, despite being frightened, was able to provide detailed information of the event when interviewed using CI, and provide an E-Fit that was immediately obvious to police who the man was. She was also '99 per cent sure' that the man she identified in the line-up was the robber who threatened her with the knife. Police recordings of her CI showed how the procedure enabled Aird to retrieve detailed event information and descriptions of her attacker (Carter 2009).

### Use of CI/ECI for recall in children, senior adults and the mentally impaired

Implementation of CI and ECI has proven to be successful in enhancing children's recall of events. Children recalled significantly more correct information when subjected to the CI/ECI format than the standard police interview (Chapman and Perry 1995; Memon, Wark, Bull and Köhnken 1997). Granhag and Spjut (2001) contrasted the effects of ECI with structured interviewing formats (where closed questions were asked in a set order) and the standard police interview. They hypothesised that the error rate across the three types of interview format would be the same but the amount of correct information retrieval would be superior under the ECI. In total 32 children (equal number of boys and girls) aged between 9–10 years of age participated. The results were positive for the ECI approach where 56 per cent more correct information was retrieved than recorded for children subjected to the structured interview (which resulted in 133 per cent more correct recall than the standard police interview, making the standard police interview the worst interview format to use with children). Granhag and Spjut's hypotheses were supported and added further consensus with previous research findings by Chapman and Perry (1995) and Memon et al. (1997). Granhag and Spjut (2001) also reported children's testimony to be no less unreliable than that of adults and their errors were errors of omission rather than commission (see fuzzy-trace theory).

Milne and Bull (2003) investigated whether children were any more likely to make more errors of commission resulting from the effects of suggestive questioning. They found that children recalled significantly more correct information pertaining to people and actions per se when the CI format was used rather than a structured interview. Erroneous information reported, however, remained consistent across the two types of interview structure. It was also found that children subjected to the CI format were resistant to suggestive questioning, especially so to misleading script-consistent questions (see Chapter 13). The percentage resistance to misleading questions as a consequence of the CI was 50 per cent (prior to the CI interview this was 34 per cent) and 36 per cent for the structured interview (which was 35 per cent prior to the structured interview). This demonstrated that prior to either interview type, children succumbed to misleading questions equally, but after the interviews there was a significant difference. The effect of asking misleading and non-misleading, leading and non-leading questions had a profound effect on retrieval which depended on whether these questions were script-consistent (i.e. questions that favoured the time and order sequence of the original memory for the event) or script-inconsistent (i.e. questions that deviated from the time and order sequence of the original memory for the event). Children provided more errors of commission when misleading questions were script-consistent (64 per cent). In other words, the misleading information contained in the questions would have been similar to the original content contained in the memory of the event and therefore plausible. A misleading script-inconsistent question would obviously be in conflict with the original memory of the event and considered an implausible possibility; as reflected in the 18 per cent score of acceptance. The children were less resistant to script-consistent than script-inconsistent misleading questions thus supporting Milne and Bull's (2003) hypothesis that children show resilience to misleading script-inconsistent questions and, furthermore, that the CI increases resistance to misleading questions per se. Milne and Bull's findings provided insight to why individuals of physical or sexual abuse have difficulty distinguishing the details from one event occurrence to another, and how details can become confused and the person vulnerable to suggestibility (which unfortunately is often mistaken as an indicator of an unreliable witness).

Although the CI and ECI have been successful, there have been a series of next generation modifications to the CI format known collectively as the modified cognitive interview (MCI). MCI is particularly useful for vulnerable witnesses such as children, the mentally impaired and senior adults (Memon, Meissner and Fraser 2010), and it was for this reason that changes to the CI format were made (Memon, Cronin, Eaves and Bull 1996). Studies comparing the effectiveness of the MCI and ECI with the CI structure showed similar information retrieval advantages – of which 45 per cent of these studies used child witnesses and 10 per cent senior adult witnesses. One version of the MCI geared towards children between 7–12 years of age encouraged them to say, 'I don't know' if they felt unable to answer the question. Also as the change of perspective instruction is difficult to understand this was rephrased to make it more child friendly (Saywitz, Geiselman and Bornstein 1992). In the case of Memon, Holley, Wark, Bull and Köhnken's (1996) MCI version aimed at children between 8–9 years of age, principles 3 and 4 were excluded;

nevertheless both versions of the MCI had successes with child witnesses. Holliday (2003) also changed the CI version to make it more understandable for children as young as 4, while a study by Searcy, Bartlett, Memon and Swanson (2001) attained similar successes with senior adults. Senior adults particularly benefitted from the CI format, as context reinstatement provided an external cued template which aided their memory and compensated for age-related cognitive deficits.

Wright and Holliday (2007) investigated the effectiveness of the ECI and MCI for memory recall in 75–96 year olds who were previously tested for cognitive function using the Mini-Mental State Examination (MMSE). They were shown footage of a crime event and asked to retrieve as much information about it that they could. Those who had low scores on the MMSE retrieved less accurate information than high scorers; however, both high and low scorers retrieved significantly more information under the ECI and MCI conditions than the control group, who were subjected to the structured interview. Wright and Holliday suggested that senior adults with reduced cognitive ability can perform more efficiently under the ECI and MCI formats.

Bull (1995) defined people with communicative disabilities as those, 'whose intelligence is within the normal range but who may have, for example, speech or hearing impediments, and people with learning disability, who could be described as having lower intelligence (i.e. what used to be termed "mental handicap")' (p.248). People with communicative disabilities are often disadvantaged in an interview situation as they have difficulty understanding the questions asked by the interviewer, which Turk and Brown (1992) argued can expose them to risk of abuse. This is why it is stipulated in the Police Codes of Practice modified under the Police and Criminal Evidence Act 1984 (PACE), that an 'appropriate adult' should be present during an interview. The appropriate adult (usually a relative) is present to ensure that questions asked during an interview are fully comprehended and the implications and repercussions of any responses they provide are understood. Therefore the appropriate adult's role is to act as mediator between the interviewer and interviewee.

Previous research findings highlight how vulnerable those with a mental illness or mental handicap actually are. They are easily misled and have a tendency for acquiescence where they respond 'yes' to a yes–no question (Sigelman, Budd, Spanhel and Schoenrock 1981). Sigelman et al. (1981) also found that the lower the IQ of the individual the more likely that they will be influenced by, and to agree with, the propositions stated in the interview questions. Police interviewers have a difficult task of balancing the right amount of external cues to help the mentally impaired retrieve information and providing the correct cues to prevent their memories from bias and contamination. Dent (1986), for example, compared free recall, and the use of general and specific question formats on the retrieval of information in children with a mean IQ of 62. After viewing a staged incident they were asked questions in one of the three formats. Children asked specific questions such as, 'What was the man's hair colour?' recalled the most information but made more errors (i.e. 30 per cent of responses were incorrect). Free recall, however, provided the most accurate information with the least number of errors (i.e. 20 per cent of responses were incorrect). It has been argued by Milne and Bull (1999) and Nathanson, Crank and Saywitz (2002) that free recall can be accurate but the amount of information recalled tends to be incomplete. Furthermore, individuals with various disabilities have problems retrieving specific event details (Milne, Clare and Bull 1999).

Using CI on mentally impaired individuals increased information recall by 32 per cent but unfortunately the number of confabulations also increased (Brown and Geiselman 1990). Milne, Clare and Bull (1999) showed a recording of an accident to 47 adults with mild intellectual disabilities and 38 adults comprising the control group; all were interviewed 24 hours later either by the CI or structured interview format. The control group overall retrieved more correct information than adults with intellectual impairment; there was, however, a further significant performance enhancement due to the use of CI. Both the control group and adults with intellectual impairment recalled significantly more information when subjected to the CI format, but consistent with other findings, the number of confabulations made also increased. Milne and Bull (2001) believed that when conducted appropriately, CI can produce accurate information retrieval from the learning disabled. Given the advantages of CI/ECI over the standard police interview, training police how to use CI/ECI effectively is important. The effectiveness of police training in this area has received much attention and research.

### Police training of CI/ECI

The role of police is diverse but a substantial amount of their workload involves communicating with the public to help with any problems experienced (Newburn 2003). The nature of communication varies and can include hostage negotiation, talking down someone threatening suicide, answering questions by the public, interviewing potential new recruits and interviewing eyewitnesses, victims and suspects. Nevertheless, it is the interviewing of eyewitnesses, victims and suspects that is part of investigative interviewing because of the requirement to acquire information of what had occurred (Ord, Shaw and Green 2004). The acquisition of event information using CI was intended for witnesses and victims but Bull and Cherryman (1995) suggested that suspects can be interviewed in this way as long as they are co-operative and willing to assist police inquiries.

It is assumed that police officers can be trained to interview witnesses, victims and suspects alike using the CI approach but their training should provide adequate instruction (Memon, Milne, Holley, Bull and Köhnken 1994; Ord et al. 2004). For Milne and Bull (1999), however, if the appropriate training is not forthcoming then research suggests that their interviewing skills will be poor and they will continue to be bad interviewers. Despite the robust evidence showing that CI is a superior interview format to the standard police interview and increases the quantity and quality of witness information retrieval, many police officers remain reluctant to use it. There are various reasons for this reluctance but not wanting to change the way they work is a fundamental factor in the equation (Memon et al.1994). The CI method takes longer to administer and employs techniques which are difficult to perform effectively without understanding the psychological concepts behind their use. Additionally the CI method requires police interviewers to 'think on their feet' as predetermined questions are to be avoided. This increases the demand for effective social and listening skills and the ability to home these skills appropriately to the needs of different types of witness (i.e. those who are vulnerable), victim (i.e. those traumatised by their ordeal) and co-operative suspects (i.e. those who want to conscience off-load). Before the necessary skills needed for CI can be acquired the basic skills of interviewing must be attained (Dando and Milne 2009; Dando, Wilcock, Milne and Henry 2009).

A survey asking British police officers about their use of CI showed that 83 per cent employ the standard police interview (Clarke and Milne 2005) and of those who do use CI many exclude principles 3 and 4 but use the report everything instruction (Dando, Wilcock and Milne 2008; Dando et al. 2009). The exclusion of principles 3 and 4 is partly to do with their complexity but also to the time issue: the interview time is considerably lengthened by their use. It is for this reason that Gabbert, Hope and Fisher (2009) introduced the self-administered CI which has undergone tests of reliability (Gabbert, Hope and Jamieson 2010). Dando, Wilcock and Milne (2009b) have also devised an alternative MCI that encourages witnesses to draw detailed sketches of what they observed while recalling the event simultaneously – this helps to reinstate the context. The concept behind the use of sketches is to formulate self-induced cues instead of relying on directed cues initiated by the interviewer.

Although CI has been incorporated into the training of most UK police forces, the amount of training designated for developing interview skills is limited. This training has been called the National Interviewing Package and is sometimes known as the PEACE approach standing for: planning, engage and explain, account, closure and evaluation (see Chapter 15). The training normally lasts for five days of which two days are spent on CI for witnesses and three days on interviewing suspects. Dando et al. (2009) commented on how the CI training occurs too early in their career and that more emphasis should be placed on interviewing witnesses than on suspects (Dando, Wilcock and Milne 2009a). As a response to the problems of engaging police to embrace CI, PEACE training was incorporated into the Professionalising Investigation Programme (PIP) in 2009. This stipulated a standardised level of interviewing skill required for interviewing witnesses and victims in less serious and serious crime events (PIP Level 1). It also provides a pre-requisite for the next level that involves specialist interview skills (National Investigative Interviewing Strategy

2009). In cases of interviewing unwilling suspects the interview strategy is different from CI (see Box 14.3). In Chapter 15 interrogation techniques and methods to attain confessions will be discussed.

## Box 14.3

### Interviewing unwilling suspects

The aim of interviewing suspects is not entirely agreed upon within the police community: some believe it is for obtaining a confession whereas others claim it is for reaching the truth. According to Baldwin (1993; 2003), the aim is to construct a case built on evidentiary fact, and if there is no case to be had then to demonstrate this by insubstantial evidence. Interviewing suspects in England and Wales has been reviewed under the three stage approach outlined by Ede and Shepherd (2000): suspect's agenda, police agenda and challenge. In the suspect agenda the suspect is given opportunity to discuss whatever he or she wants to, whereas the police agenda relates to informing and questioning the suspect. During the challenge stage, police confront suspects with any incongruences of information provided earlier and address any deception. The three stage approach is part of the 'account' element stipulated under PEACE. This is similar to suspect interviewing in the US outlined by Walters (2002). Walters described the narration phase as listening to what the suspect has to say and asking appropriate questions for clarification purposes. The cross-examination phase provides police with an opportunity to ask in-depth questions about the suspect's narration. The idea behind both approaches is to ensure the suspect knows that the interviewer is listening and is focusing on their account given. By asking questions police hope to identify those who are evading specific issues and who might be lying. It is anticipated that by interviewing suspects in this way those telling the truth can be differentiated from those who are lying. Interviews of suspects are carried out quickly – often lasting just over seven minutes (Evans and Webb 1993). Evans and Webb (1993) listened to 60 taped interviews of suspects conducted by the Merseyside Police, UK, in 1990. Up to 25 per cent of the interview content comprised of police stating the facts especially for juveniles aged 10-13 years of age, and the conversation was very much one-sided with police directing what was said. Furthermore, Evans (1993) found that interviews with young suspects lasted less time than with adult suspects and also led to an early admission in 77 per cent of cases versus 68 per cent respectively. This suggests that police were more inclined to be persuasive with juvenile suspects as 12 per cent of the 23 per cent who did not make an early admission did so by the end of the interview. When suspects showed resistance to questioning, however, perhaps by responding 'no comment', police needed to have appropriate strategies acquired through training in conversational and interpersonal skills – best attained through psychological knowledge of human nature (Milne and Bull 1999). Shepherd (1993) summed this up well as:

> rejection of a 'win-lose' mentality; detailed knowledge; forethought ... detailed planning ... detailed preparation ... balance of assertion and listening consistent with finding out facts and minding feelings i.e. respect for the person, empathy, supportiveness, positiveness, openness, a non-judgemental attitude, straightforward talk and a conversational style signalling a commitment to talk across as equals (p.7).

The effectiveness of CI/ECI can also be evaluated by generalising their use to the construction of facial composites. Research in this area is limited but has shown some success in the development of good composite likeness of the perpetrator.

### Applications of CI for facial composite construction

Police investigations draw upon different methods such as obtaining verbal descriptions of events, identification in a line-up or from mug shots and the construction of facial composites. There are many different composite production systems currently in operation (see Chapter 13):

- PhotoFit
- Identi-Kit
- Mac-A-Mug Pro
- Compusketch
- FaceKit
- E-Fit
- CD-Fit
- Field Identification System (FIS).

Davies and Milne (1985) found that the quality and likeness of the facial composite to the target face from memory improved significantly when the mental reinstatement of the context instruction was used (as used in CI). Only a few studies have explored the use of CI in facial composite construction using one of the composite production systems listed above. A comprehensive investigation using the CI technique was conducted by Luu and Geiselman (1993) who used the FIS and instructed participants to construct a facial composite from one of two techniques:

- thinking about the face of the culprit (as would be done in the standard police interview);
- adopting elements of the CI such as reconstructing the original context, recalling events in reverse order, alternating across perspectives and reporting everything that came to mind.

Two approaches to constructing composites were used:

- adding features one at a time to a developing composite – hence it was partially constructed and relied on holistic processing (see Chapter 13);
- selection of features in isolation so that there was no partial construction – hence relying on featural processing (see Chapter 13).

The CI approach increased the standard and likeness of the facial composite of the culprit in the 'partially constructed faces' condition only. This finding alludes to the importance of a holistic approach to remembering faces – a strategy consistent with how we naturally remember faces (see Chapter 13). Thinking about a face or using elements from CI resembles a holistic processing strategy. Featural processing is inconsistent with how we normally remember faces and encourages attention towards individual features such as the eyes or mouth at the expense of encoding the whole face. Koehn, Fisher and Cutler (1999) investigated whether CI elicits more accurate and detailed composites using Mac-A-Mug Pro. Participants observed a target culprit and were asked to compose a facial composite two days later but the quality of composites generated was poor. As a consequence it was difficult to detect any advantages of using CI over the standard police interview.

The findings in this area are inconsistent and more research is clearly needed. There are many composite production systems that emphasise different aspects of facial processing. It appears, however, that those systems encouraging holistic processing tend to be consistent with CI approaches.

## Summary

- Police interviews for the most part are conducted using the standard police interview regardless of who is being questioned: witnesses, victims or suspects. This strategy of interviewing has many problems for vulnerable individuals such as children, senior adults and those with mental impairment. Due to the type of questioning and the interruptions made by the interviewer during the course of the standard police interview, retrieval of information especially by witnesses is limited. Police investigators using the standard police interview apply questioning styles that actively interfere with effective retrieval. For example, they ask few open questions and interrupt witnesses during their recall of events – encouraging succinct and brief responding.
- CI, ECI and MCI have proven to be effective interview strategies as witnesses, victims and co-operative suspects retrieve much more information than they would using the standard police interview. These interview formats are also effective for interviewing vulnerable individuals, the very young and old and female victims of sex attacks. There are four principles of CI directly relating to how memory works:

1    mental reinstatement of context;
2    report everything;
3    recalling of the event in a different order;
4    change the perspective.

The first two principles are designed to elicit more cues encoded originally with memories of the event while principles 3 and 4 encourage witnesses to construct a new description of the event.

- All three interview formats are based on psychological memory theory – the principles of these interviews are grounded in elements of memory research that are known to account for how our memory best works. Memory research focusing on the retrieval mechanisms involved in recalling information, such as those of encoding specificity and the multi-component model, are encapsulated in cognitive interview formats, which explains why the CI, ECI and MCI are successful at inducing recall.
- Despite empirical evidence showing the advantages of using CI, ECI and MCI, many police interviewers continue using the standard police interview. Surveys have found that the majority of police do not use any form of cognitive interviewing because it is time consuming, difficult to master the intricacies of the technique and they believe that less serious crimes do not warrant the time and effort involved with the CI. The ECI, for instance, requires training in 13 basic interview skills: building a rapport; key listening skills; encouraging spontaneous recall, using open-ended question format; pausing after responses to questions; no interrupting; asking for detailed accounts; enabling intense concentration; encouraging the use of imagery; enabling the recreation of the original context; adopting the witness's perspective; asking compatible questions and referring to and following the sequence of the CI. In addition to these skills, police investigators must be proficient in administering the 11 phases of ECI.
- CI interviews are on average 30 minutes long but the number of correct information attained averages 41.67 versus 35.58 attained when using the standard police interview. The ECI, however, elicits 45 per cent more correct information than the CI format but 75 per cent more than the standard police interview. This is a consistent finding across many studies and in different countries. The MCI has also been successful especially with children. One version of MCI allows children to answer, 'I don't know' whereas other versions exclude principles 3 and 4, which are often difficult for children to understand. Both ECI and MCI have helped senior adults (75–96) with reduced cognitive ability to recall more information than they would have to other structured interview formats.
- CI is incorporated into the training of most UK police forces under the National Interviewing Package known as the PEACE approach – planning, engage and explain, account, closure and evaluation – but there is little

training designated to developing interview skills. Work is underway to encourage police to adopt any form of CI and this includes the way they are trained and the introduction of a two-stage interview training strategy (the first stage for acquiring basic interview skills (PIP Level 1) and the second for specialised interviewing). This was introduced in 2009 into the Professionalising Investigation Programme (PIP).

- The CI format can be used to help in the formation of facial composites. By adopting one of the composite production systems that has a holistic leaning towards developing facial composites, such as FIS, Mac-A-Mug Pro or E-Fit, the CI can induce superior composite likeness of the perpetrator's face. Findings in this area, however, lack consistency.

## Questions for discussion

1   Describe how each principle of the CI method is founded on the way memory works.
2   Describe the advantages and disadvantages of using any form of CI and compare these to the standard police interview.
3   Why are CI, ECI and MCI effective for interviewing vulnerable individuals?

When the appeal tactic is used, police try to engage the suspect's 'good' nature to cooperate with them and to confess their crime. Manipulation is a step from the appeal tactic where police will try to minimise the seriousness of the offence committed, and reduce the suspect's accountability in the hope of a confession. In the case of intimidation police use the opposite tactic from manipulation. By increasing the suspect's anxiety level, emphasising the seriousness of the offence and asking questions without providing enough time to respond, the interrogator hopes to lower the suspect's self-esteem and 'break' their defiance to obtain a confession.

How police operate, including the collection of evidence and police interrogation, is important in understanding the police approach to interviewing suspects (particularly non-cooperating suspects) – discussed next.

## Police procedure

### Gathering evidence

Skolnick (1966) referred to a police culture where through training, or by virtue of having a personality that is conducive to the police way of thinking, its members embrace police values and adopt specific cognitive and behavioural styles (see Box 15.1). Skolnick (1966) further claimed that when police apprehend a suspect and are convinced of the suspect's guilt, they will look for evidence to confirm this. This mind set is reflected in the way interrogations of suspects are performed, and when a confession is obtained it further reinforces police beliefs that feed into the police culture. It is believed by scholars like Skolnick (1966) that the type of police training cadets undergo helps to create and maintain a police subculture embracing a specific cognitive and behavioural style: a style which tends to look for confirmatory rather than disconfirmatory evidence to support their suspicions. If this is true then their beliefs of evidence will undoubtedly influence the direction of investigation and the gathering of information, especially within an adversarial context of law. Their role is not an impartial one and police have views which reflect their prosecutorial role (Stephenson 1992).

According to Skolnick (1966) and Balch (1972) police have similar personality and cognitive traits that bind them together to form a close working unit. Hence, if they apprehend a suspect and have reasons to believe their suspect is guilty, then they are likely to adopt the position that their suspect is guilty beyond reasonable doubt and will find evidence to confirm this. Walsh and Milne (2007) found interviewers with poor interviewing skills were more inclined to presume suspects were guilty before the interview had begun. This biases the interview procedure by encouraging questioning styles primed to confirm hypotheses of a suspect's guilt (known as confirmation bias) at the expense of any other relevant and contradictory information (Hill, Memon and McGeorge 2008). This was supported in Walsh and Milne's (2007) study where 66 per cent of interviewers investigating benefit fraud claimed they felt the suspect to be guilty.

Skolnick's views on police culture, if true (although Walsh and Milne's study suggests this to be the case), might be damning to the way police operationalise their investigations. The law, however, requires impartiality and review of the facts only. Police by law must follow stipulated guidelines and a breach of these can lead to disciplinary action. Given these restrictions, surely the police as a professional body are more likely to be governed by the facts. Moston, Stephenson and Williamson (1990) found from analysing 1067 cases that the strength of evidence was determined largely by predictors such as police interviewers' beliefs and attitudes about the suspect's guilt or innocence. When the evidence, however, was weak, the police interviewer was sure of the suspect's guilt in 31 per cent of cases. When evidence was moderate this changed to 74 per cent and to 99 per cent when evidence was strong. Without previous convictions, police interviewers were sure of the suspect's guilt in 69 per cent of cases, changing to 76 per cent when there had been arrests for previous convictions. This suggests that police belief of a suspect's guilt hangs on the balance of the evidence. Obtaining a confession helps to increase the balance of evidence towards a guilty verdict. It also means that the case is more likely to be approved by the CPS and processed in a court of law.

As police have many discretionary powers that they are free to enforce during the investigative process, they can decide which facts to pursue, how to piece the evidence together in order to ascertain a viable case, and whether to continue investigating once the suspect makes a confession. Police discretion is exercised throughout their role within the criminal justice system:

- reporting and recording crime;
- decreeing caution;
- investigating crime;
- collating evidence;
- deciding whether or not to arrest a suspect.

Once a crime has been recognised and a suspect identified, various deployment options are available to the police. These include:

- arrest or summons;
- charge;
- bail;
- legal aid and advice;
- caution (Williams 1982).

Of course police power is bound within confinements of written law, thus ensuring rules and procedures predicate the investigative process stipulated in the PACE of 1984 (Zander 1990). This is not only for the protection of potentially innocent suspects but for police accountability. Even so the discretion exercised by police plays a strong part in determining who comes to court and is eventually judged to be a criminal (La Fave 1965).

As police are the first law enforcing body suspects come into contact with, it is important at this early stage of legal proceedings that police investigations conform to stipulations outlined in PACE 1984. Furthermore, police understanding of evidence reliability, validity and its *res gestae* (or facts that may be admitted as evidence in court) is crucial to successful outcomes. Although adversarial law is such that the judge leaves the jury to deliberate judgement over the defendant after the defence and prosecution have presented their arguments, it is the police who initially provide evidence to the Crown Prosecution Service (CPS) to state a case. On the basis of this evidence the CPS decide whether there is a more than 50 per cent chance of winning the case. If there is not, then the case is thrown out and further legal proceedings are dropped until more substantive evidence is found. In fact under inquisitorial criminal law, it is the police who investigate and review the facts of a case to determine whether the suspect committed the crime. If criminal charges are made, it is the court which then audits and tests the reliability of police findings and determines the sentence (Anderson 1999; Malsch and Freckelton 2005). The police therefore have great power in determining the direction of a case under the inquisitorial system. Under the adversarial system police also have great power in determining the direction of the CPS decision (see Box 15.1).

Police gather evidence through a variety of means but it is the questioning of suspects that forms a major part of police interrogation which will be considered in more detail next.

### Police interrogation

Forensic psychologists and police officers, all who were experienced at investigative interviewing, assessed audio-taped police interviews using an assessment form listing 28 interviewing skills. Psychologists were consistent in their answers and police officers in theirs, but the differences across the two professions rested on whether a confession was obtained. Police officers were more likely to rate an interview as executed well when a suspect confessed (Bull and Cherryman 1995). Morgan and Stephenson (1994) acknowledged the desire for police to obtain confessions:

> If there exists some, . . . evidence against the individual, and the interviewing officer has been unable to find more evidence, yet 'feels sure' that the suspect is guilty of the offence, . . . with the . . . belief that individuals will not confess to something that they have not done, may lead to . . . taking the risk of being oppressive (cited in Schollum 2005, p.18).

This was further substantiated by research which considered the attitude of the police interviewer during questioning and how this influenced the elicitation of a confession by the suspect. In a study by Holmberg and Christianson in 2002, prisoners of serious crime revealed how the interviewer's attitude during interrogation determined whether they confessed or not. They found that more confessions were obtained under interrogations where interviewers were empathic, ethical in their means of execution and formed a rapport. This was not the only approach, however, as other prisoners claimed dominant interview styles using coercion, aggression and confrontation made them more determined to deny than to confess. Similar findings by Kebbell, Hurren and Mazerolle (2006) also linked interview style with confessing, and identified six types:

- compassionate
- understanding
- non-aggressive
- honest
- non-judgemental
- explanation of procedure.

## Box 15.1

### Police discretion and piecing the facts using story telling

The whole process of evidence gathering is not as straightforward as it may first seem. Setting aside practical issues, police require constitutive facts (see Box 13.1) before they are in a position to acquire evidential facts. In other words, evidential facts can only be presented in support of case events provided there is a belief that an event had taken place: also that the suspect was possibly involved with determining the outcome of the event in question in such a way that he or she can be held responsible. Knowing what is relevant and how facts interrelate is crucial to police investigative work. Any investigative work, even within science, often involves following up certain clues which are believed to relate to the case in question. How clues are followed up is also a matter for police decision. Who would make relevant witnesses and why? What type of expert witnesses will help to unfold the significance of certain clues or clarify issues relating to the case? Although it is not up to the police to decide whether the evidence from the forensic expert witness is reliable or not, it is important for the police to obtain uncontaminated evidence. There is therefore an argument to be made in favour of police having superior understanding of evidence reliability and validity compared to members of the jury.

In Pennington and Hastie's (1981) generic model of jury decision-making, seven conceptually distinct elements of processing information that jurors should try to achieve are outlined: assimilation of information during the trial; continuation of a causal-sequential representation of the factual information; evaluation of evidence reliability; differentiation of admissible from inadmissible evidence; knowledge of legal categories; application of legal categories to evidence; and, finally, to use the legal standard of proof (i.e. beyond reasonable doubt). These points have been incorporated into their Story Model (Hastie and Pennington 2000). Ellsworth (1989) previously found that jurors concentrate on understanding trial events, putting facts into a time and sequence frame, evaluating reliability and relating evidence to a legal category. There are stages they omit to do, and when deciding a verdict they base their judgement on self-perceptions of crime severity using a simple, 'dumbed down' appraisal of what happened. Once jurors have identified what they consider to be the best story, they select the verdict that offers the most likely match accounting for the criminal events. The 'Story Model' therefore asserts that jurors reach verdicts through actively interpreting and evaluating the evidence provided (Hastie and Pennington 2000). Stages of story construction and the evaluation of evidence credibility are important for jurors but also in police investigations. It might be argued that story construction is analogous to the process of developing a sequence of constitutive facts. Unlike the jurors' passive role of assimilating information and constructing a story, police are actively involved in initiating the nature of information required to develop the constitutive facts – in other words, develop the story. This is where their role in evaluating information differs. Police are active in their search for evidence whereas jurors are recipients of information. Furthermore, police go through the court trial procedure before any court sitting has taken place, as they must present their case to the CPS. Before the CPS agrees to start any court proceedings, a strong body of reliable and valid constitutive and evidential facts is required to guarantee a more than 50 per cent chance of conviction.

A further three types were identified for denial:

- aggression
- dishonesty
- imposed guilt bias.

Interview style clearly influences suspects to confess or deny committing an offence, and has been taken seriously in the US by way of documented advice on how to attain confessions from suspects (known as the Reid model). The Reid model consists of two phases: phase one is directed towards attaining information and evidence relevant to the case, whereas phase two is the interrogation itself consisting of nine steps. If in phase one there is enough evidence to convince police of the suspect's guilt, then an interrogation will commence as follows:

- *Step 1:* The suspect is presented with a statement containing the interrogator's belief of the suspect's guilt but questioning will allow them to tell the truth.
- *Step 2:* The suspect is given an explanation for events that had occurred. In the case of suspects who are considered emotional, the explanation provided tends to angle for a moral excuse of their actions. Non-emotional suspects are persuaded to confess using tactics of reasoning.
- *Step 3:* If presented with a denial the interrogator will reassert their belief of the suspect's guilt using the step 2 protocol.
- *Step 4:* The interrogator effectively deals with suspect objections or any reasons given as to why they would not commit the act they are accused of.
- *Step 5:* The interrogator employs tactics to maintain the suspect's attention such as increased physical proximity.
- *Step 6:* The interrogator employs sympathetic tactics to disengage suspects from passivity and depressed affect so as to encourage suspects to confess to the truth.
- *Step 7:* Two possible explanations based on the proposition expressed in Step 2 are provided. One is designed to provide an element of dignity, or a face-saving measure, unlike the other which is reprehensible.
- *Step 8:* The suspect is given an opportunity to describe event details once they have confessed.
- *Step 9:* A written confession is provided and witnessed.

In addition to the stages stipulated in the Reid model, other more peripheral, and yet effective, factors include the type and layout of the interview room (i.e. small and empty); lighting controlled by the interrogator; one-way mirror to observe non-verbal communication of the suspect for readiness to confess, and the suspect's invasion of space. The Reid model and police interview tactics are designed to make the suspect believe that the evidence against them is substantial, thereby increasing their sense of helplessness and likelihood of compliance. Police interrogators use different strategies to gain the confidence of the suspect such as claiming they have more evidence against the suspect than they have, and that admission might lead to reduced punishments.

In the UK, forensic psychologists have concentrated on elements of the interrogation process such as police tactics used during questioning. Bull and Soukara (2010) focused on interviewer tactics used just before a confession was given. From the cases they examined they found that the common tactics used were:

- disclosure of evidence;
- open, leading and repetitive questioning;
- focus on contradictions made by the suspect;
- challenging the suspect's account in a positive way;
- effective handling of the suspect's mood.

Prior to the PEACE model (see Box 15.2), Bull and Soukara (2010) considered a confession following initial denial to be unknown especially in ethically driven interviewing. The PEACE model emphasises the importance of interviewing using methods that are ethical and even if this does not lead to a confession, there is a degree of solace in that the interview procedure was conducted fairly. Griffiths (2008) stated: 'any interview that probes a suspect's account, and explores possible motives and defences should be viewed as being just as effective as one that gains a confession' (p.72). Despite this, however, Walsh and Bull (2010) found that interviews with a confession outcome also included tactics such as leading questions that are not recommended under the PEACE model.

## Box 15.2

### PEACE model for interviewing

Prior to the 1980s there were limited interviewing guidelines for police to follow (Milne and Bull 1999), but this changed in 1991 when the Home Office steering group was established to form guidelines for investigative interviewing. They devised an interview model based on an ethical approach known as PEACE. PEACE stands for:

- Planning and preparation;
- Engage and explain;
- Account;
- Closure;
- Evaluation.

The PEACE model of interviewing was designed to be generic to suit any type of interviewee.

#### Planning and preparation

Planning can be regarded as a process for getting everything ready for the interview. Ord, Shaw and Green (2004) used the adage 'investigate then interview' rather than 'interview then investigate' (p.3–5). It is important to prepare in order to avoid missing potentially important evidence, signs of contradictions and losing the interview direction.

#### Engage and explain

It is essential for a good interview to have an interviewee who is not unduly stressed by the prospect of being interviewed; therefore efforts to establish a rapport will increase interview outcome success (Ord, Shaw and Green 2004). PEACE training plays lip service to this aspect of the interview and stresses how important it is to communicate in plain English. There are points that interviewers have to make to ensure that interviewees understand what will happen during the course of the interview such as feeling free to say if they did not understand a question or if the interviewer has misinterpreted what they had said. Allowing interviewees to say they did not understand the question offers opportunity for the interviewer to evaluate their level of comprehension.

### Account

The interviewer obtains a full account of events from the interviewee: an uninterrupted account. Their account can then be expanded and clarification asked if needed while a suspect's account can also be challenged. Milne and Bull (1999) pointed out that it is important to have an accurate account at this stage of the interview. Interviewers are advised to continue asking relevant questions despite no comment responses, so that the defence cannot accuse police of not asking the right questions. Once details are complete the interviewer might need to challenge the account provided by the suspect if there are any inconsistencies.

### Closure

This stage needs to be just as thorough as previous stages, and there should be a mutual understanding of the interview intricacies. The account needs to be summarised and points made verified. The interviewee needs to be informed of what happens next – whether they will have to attend court and in what capacity.

### Evaluation

This is the conclusion of the interview and where the interviewer assesses whether objectives have been achieved. The investigation is then reviewed in relation to the information attained and the interviewer reflects on how the interview was conducted and if it could have been more effective.

Since the introduction of the PEACE model in the UK, evaluations of police interview performance have shown mixed findings despite their own perceptions being positive. Police interviewers, for example, tend to overestimate their interview skills and overall interview performance; 90 per cent claimed they were skilled interviewers (Bull and Cherryman 1996), while many claimed to be good at detecting lies (Mann, Vrij and Bull 2004). Clarke and Milne (2005) found that 19 per cent of police interviewers demonstrated limited planning and none showed a profound knowledge of what they were trying to do. The engage and explain element of the PEACE interview had areas for improvement because only 16 per cent introduced themselves with clarity and 26 per cent did not. As many as 32 per cent gave no explanation of what the purpose of the interview was. They failed to build a rapport or show any signs of empathy. The rapport element is more important than police believe it to be as it can elicit further information from suspects and help recognise inconsistencies in their accounts (Colwell, Hiscock-Anisman, Memon, Taylor and Prewett 2007). Also displays of empathy can encourage a confession (Holmberg and Christianson 2002). Furthermore, 53 per cent omitted to say that it was an opportunity for interviewees to give their account of events. In the case of the account element of the PEACE interview, only 38 per cent of interviewers made any effort to allow interviewees give their own account; 47 per cent made no effort in developing content arising from accounts given, and in 43 per cent of cases the points made in the interview were not effectively authenticated for proof. As many as 59 per cent of interviewers failed to provide any closure; 62 per cent failed to ask interviewees if they had any more details to add and 83 per cent omitted to inform interviewees of the next stage in the legal process. Evaluation was also limited and police interviewers were found to restrict this stage to the typical format of the standard police interview. Walsh and Bull (2010b) demonstrated that police interviewers following the PEACE model and applying appropriate skills of interviewing as required when using the PEACE format were more likely to obtain reliable accounts and a comprehensible confession. In Box 15.3 failures of police interviewing techniques have been noted by Walsh and Bull (2010a, 2011).

## Box 15.3

### Failures of police interviewing techniques

A study by Walsh and Bull (2010a) showed that police interviewers were deficient in their ability to build a rapport with life benefit fraudsters. They found that only 20 per cent of interviews were skilfully managed:

- problems with the planning and summarising stages;
- only 66 per cent completed three facets of the engage and explain stage (informing suspects of the reason for being interviewed, informing suspects that they can provide their own account and signposting where the interview was going);
- signposting where the interview was going occurred in less than 5 per cent of the 142 interviews;
- caution was explained less than 20 per cent of the time and, of these, 80 per cent of the time interviewers asked if interviewees understood the caution read to them.

Walsh and Bull (2011) addressed the question of how effective police are at adapting the PEACE model when interviewing fraudsters. They found discrepancies regarding what constitute good interviewing skills (which went up to the level of supervising managers). This failure to recognise poor interviewing skills links with the evaluation stage of the PEACE model where interviewer self-reflections of their performances are at odds with their actual levels of interviewing skills.

One of the problems with implementing the PEACE approach in the UK is the amount of time given towards training police in effective interviewing skills. Training lasted only five days, where two days were spent on cognitive interviewing for witnesses and three for suspects. This has changed with the introduction of the Investigative Interviewing Strategy formed by ACPO in 2003. The Central Police Training and Development Authority, commonly known as Centrex, was introduced as part of the Criminal Justice and Police Act of 2001 to oversee police training in England and Wales. Centrex was replaced by the National Policing Improvement Agency (NPIA) in 2007 which has itself been replaced in 2012 by the College of Policing. The College of Policing takes on the responsibility of training police in all skills and knowledge required to improve their policing and investigative abilities (which includes interviewing skills). Police training now includes residential, distance and workplace courses, lasting between one and three weeks, which are based on national guidelines. All operations by the West Yorkshire Police, for instance, devote three weeks of training to suspect interviewing.

In the UK, the PEACE model is designed to provide guidance for ethical interviewing techniques so as to help avoid innocent suspects from making false confessions. This is different in the US. The US has a Constitutional law consisting of 27 Amendments, some of which have a direct influence over police procedure. Of relevance here, however, is the Fifth Amendment. The Fifth Amendment states that: 'No person shall be held to answer for a capital, or otherwise infamous crime, unless on a presentment or indictment of a grand jury . . . nor shall be compelled in any criminal case to be a witness against himself, nor be deprived of life, liberty, or property, without due process of law. . . .' (US Constitutional Amendment, 5).

The Fifth Amendment provides a guideline of the constitutional limits concerning police procedure. In so doing it is preserving the rights of suspects from receiving a biased trial and from submitting coerced confessions. The inclusion of the Grand Juries Clause and the Due Process Clause can be traced back to the Magna Carta of 1215. Of relevancy to this discussion, the Fifth Amendment covers the following constitutional rights: grand juries; prohibition against the request for self-incrimination; and the guarantee of a fair trial. In the case of grand juries, the suspect charged has the right to challenge members of the selected jury. By this is meant that a juror can be removed if for some reason the suspect feels that the juror might be biased against him or her in some way. Grand juries are allowed to see testimonies and documents in advance in order to make a presentment. Furthermore, during the presentment they can inform the court if they have a reasonable suspicion indicating the suspect's guilt. Defendants are protected by the Fifth Amendment from incriminating themselves through testifying in court. The full implications of this aspect of the Fifth Amendment is that when police take a suspect into custody, then the suspect must be made aware of his/her right to remain silent, to have legal representation during questioning and to legally be provided one if the suspect cannot afford to do so. (When a suspect is arrested the police procedure first used is to recite his/her Miranda rights – see earlier) If any of these aspects are ignored then the courts can suppress statements made by the suspect by claiming that they violate the Fifth Amendment and therefore the protection it offers against self-incrimination. In order for police to use any statements made by the suspect, he/she must voluntarily waive those rights. If the suspect during police interrogation indicates that he/she wants to remain silent then, by law, the interrogation must cease. Furthermore, any questioning must cease if the suspect wishes to have an attorney present. If an interrogation occurs without the presence of an attorney because the suspect waived his/her right to counsel representation then this must be proven. The suspect has the right to remain silent after having responded to some questions during police interrogation (Constitution of the United States, Amendment 5).

The Fifth Amendment also makes reference to the Due Process Clause. This refers to the Bill of Rights which promises protection to all citizens against the federal government. This means that the right to a jury trial and how it is run will be standardised across the US. Due process also entails equal protection of the law to all citizens (Constitution of the United States, Amendment 14) by ensuring that procedures are properly in place and are followed. This involves legislatures for the police as well as the judiciary. Hence the government is responsible for ensuring that the procedures used by police, for example, are fair and constitutional. Other amendments, such as the Fourth Amendment, disallow police from performing unreasonable searches and seizures without a search warrant; obtained through showing probable cause (Constitution of the United States, Amendment 4).

Despite the differences in police procedure across the UK and US, the interrogation process still involves the ability of police to detect when a suspect is lying. But are police able to detect when a suspect is lying about the information they provide and, importantly, a confession they submit? The next section will explore this question in relation to police competency at recognising lies using verbal and non-verbal communication and written admissions of guilt.

## Police detection of lies during interrogation

One of the important tasks that police perform is the detection of suspects who are telling the truth from those who are lying. This is no easy feat, as psychological evidence suggests we generally find the identification of liars a challenging task. Research findings of police attitudes concerning their ability to identify a liar during interrogation were at odds with their actual performance (Garrido and Masip 1999). Garrido and Masip (1999) further showed that novice police officers were on a par with the more experienced officers at identifying suspects who were lying from those telling the truth, but neither was any better than the general public at teasing the two types of suspect apart – they all performed at chance level. We may ask just how true is this and how accurate is police perception per se? In order to answer this it is necessary to review the literature concerning people's ability to identify lies and truths.

The nature of knowing when someone is lying derives in part from a well-established Theory of Mind (ToM). As discussed previously, ToM is a skill used for making assumptions about an individual's thoughts and beliefs during social interactions – once the situational circumstances and constraints have been accounted for (see Chapter 4).

We have all been socialised to behave in a prescribed way (i.e. socially acceptable) under many different social situations, and therefore have a model of another person's likely behaviour for specific situations. Hence if a person kneels and searches the floor during a social dinner, others will interpret this behaviour as the person looking for a dropped item. The psychology of lying, however, is more complicated than this scenario as it relies on two assumptions: intention to mislead and absence of any notification to do so (Ekman 1996). This is an important distinction and helps rule out a number of possibilities such as:

- informing others of the intention to mislead;
- maintaining secrets;
- unintentional provision of false information.

There is a potential problem with this definition, however, which is that the accuracy of information provided goes unchallenged if the intention to deceive is absent. There are further problems concerning what is communicated non-verbally to the recipient or to the police in this case. According to Ekman (1992), there are numerous observable non-verbal communications that are underpinned by specific emotions which we find difficult to consciously manipulate. These emotions are difficult to control and simulate and their behavioural manifestations are also challenging. For instance, Ekman has identified a number of these behaviours which could be considered as evidence of lying:

- Evidence of increased sympathetic neural activity (i.e. faster breathing, more swallowing, blinking and sweating and pupil dilation). When we experience emotions (whether this be any of the six universal emotions of anger, fear, sadness, happiness, disgust or surprise [and later, contempt was added by Ekman and Friesen 1986]) they are underpinned by the activity of the sympathetic nervous system (SNS). The SNS and parasympathetic nervous system are both branches of the autonomic nervous system (ANS). The ANS is beyond our conscious control, which is why it is called autonomic because it operates autonomously. This means that the SNS is normally beyond our conscious control which is why under interrogation an individual will not be able to subdue their tell-tale signs of arousal. The interpretation of the actual emotion experienced is very much dependent on the situation and aspects of the interaction (i.e. a guilty suspect might experience fear of being caught for lying). The SNS is designed to kick-in during stressful situations thereby invoking activity in preparation of 'fight or flight' (Cannon 1927).

- Evidence of raising ones voice depicting anger.
- Evidence of fear of being caught for lying might be manifested in a poorly prepared verbal communication which is littered with errors of literacy and frequent pausing. A high pitched voice may also be an indicator of fear.
- A pale face due to the drainage of blood from the skin surface which is redirected by the SNS to the muscles in preparation of fight or flight (i.e. anger or fear).
- Faking an emotion (i.e. suspect lying and trying to simulate an appropriate emotion during the interview) can be detected through observable expressions and behaviours which the suspect believes to be appropriate. The problem is that faking an emotion is difficult to do and for most part the emotion is automatically and not consciously driven. Ekman pointed out that an asymmetrical facial expression is an indicator of deceit. An emotion that occurs too abruptly is faked as is an emotional expression that is inconsistent with the verbal account.
- Emotions of strong negative valence (i.e. anger and fear) that occur in isolation of ANS activity are also considered to be false.
- People often misconstrue the feature of the face responsible for the emotional expression in question. Hence when someone smiles they mistakenly attribute the mouth as the central feature depicting the emotional expression of happiness. Ekman demonstrated that the muscles around the eyes have a major part in establishing a genuine smile – without this the smile is a fake, also known as the Duchenne smile. Likewise, to create the expression of fear and anger the forehead and eyebrows are key features – in the case of fear the eyebrows are raised and the eyes are open whereas for anger the eyebrows are lowered and the eyes are bulging.

Faking the expression of anger is difficult to do because of the complex interaction of the facial muscles involved, and yet it is one of the most commonly faked negative emotions by deceitful individuals. It has been posited that the genuine expression of anger is more likely shown in innocent suspects simply because of the difficulty involved with simulating muscular contraction of facial muscles used when expressing anger. If this is so, then the inverse can be considered true where the faked expressions of anger are committed by guilty suspects. A study by Hatz and Bourgeois (2010) found support for this when they arranged for students to independently solve a mathematical problem followed by a period of collective resolution with another student. The other student was a confederate of the researcher and was instructed to ask for help with solving the problems set even though this was against the rules. In a different condition the confederate announced that he was working with the researcher and that it was okay to cheat. When confronted by the researcher about cheating, the students in the first condition who had not cheated showed more anger, which was difficult to fake, compared with the liars who claimed they did not cheat but had. In the second condition the innocent and guilty students expressed the same amount of anger when accused of cheating – demonstrating the difficulty involved with telling the guilty apart from the innocent. But can police detect liars more accurately than the general population?

Dutch police officers looked at British police press conference recordings of relatives appealing to the public and potential killers to return their loved ones unharmed. Their task was to identify from these recordings whether the relatives making the appeals were genuine or not and whether the emotion expressed was genuine or faked. This study was conducted using Dutch police officers who made judgements of these British cases – done this way to ensure that they were unlikely to be influenced by any previous press coverage. Vrij and Mann (2001) found that these officers were performing at chance level translating to a 50 per cent hit rate. They claimed using cues, such as judging how genuine the emotions depicted were, and whether eye gaze was diverted or focused, helped them decide the guilt or innocence of the person(s). These findings do not bode well for police competency at detecting liars.

In a study by Kassin, Meissner and Norwick (2005) students and police participants watched or listened to ten prisoners confessing to crimes of which only half were true accounts. Students were more accurate than police, and accuracy rates increased overall under audio-taped confessions. Police investigators in this study were more confident in their decisions and had a higher rate of guilty judgements than the student participants. In a second study, when participants were informed that half of the confessions were true and the other half false, the response bias shown by police was effectively eliminated but accuracy did not increase despite confidence levels remaining high. Strömwall and Granhag (2003) compared police officers with judges and prosecutors for their beliefs of what effective behavioural measures can be used to help identify liars. Their beliefs were compared with the literature evidence provided by forensic psychologists that revealed a number of interesting congruencies and incongruencies. First, the literature suggests that fewer body movements are made by liars; however, police believed that liars made more. Judges and prosecutors assumed that this is not a good measure for lie detection. Second, the literature and the police, judges and prosecutors all agreed that sparse detail in statements tended to include false information. Third, the literature suggests no robust relationship between gaze aversions and lying, but the police insisted that liars avoid eye gaze; judges and prosecutors maintained there is no obvious difference between innocent and guilty suspects. Fourth, the literature suggests that the pitch of voice and lying are linked; however, this was not considered to be a tell-tale feature of lying by police, judges and prosecutors alike. Fifth, the literature suggests some support for the view that inconsistency of statements throughout an interrogation is a sign of it being untrue; a view held by police, judges and prosecutors.

More promising findings of police competency at identifying deception occurred in a study by Bond (2008). Bond (2008) found that there are some police officers who are exceptionally good at detecting lies, and referred to them as detection wizards. There were four lie detection tests given. Officers who performed at an accuracy rate of 80 per cent or above continued with the battery of lie detection tests the next day. Their task was to ascertain who from a series of ex-prisoners were lying when interviewed under four different conditions:

1  a mock crime interrogation;
2  work relevant history for an employment interview;
3  discussion of people most influential in their lives (positive or negative);
4  description of videos they had seen.

The interviews were diverse and provided opportunity to consider non-verbal and verbal communication across many types of interview situations. The ex-prisoners were instructed to either lie or be truthful in their four different accounts. There was an accuracy of between 31–94 per cent for police participants but only between 34–63 per cent for the student controls. Those police participants scoring more than 80 per cent continued with the tasks of ascertaining which ex-prisoner' accounts were fallacious. The high accuracy scoring police officers were required to wear eye-tracking sensors. Their gaze was monitored using eye-tracking sensors which revealed an immediate focused attention to non-verbal behaviours that helped them to make rapid decisions of who were lying or telling the truth. This attention to non-verbal behaviours not only enabled rapid decisions but accurate ones. Given that increased attention to non-verbal communications helped to detect liars, it follows that police could be trained to become efficient detection wizards. Researchers have considered ways in which suspects under interrogation can be forced implicitly to lower their guard and betray their true disposition.

Vrij (2004) suggested that through the use of cognitive overloading, the suspect will eventually find it difficult to orchestrate their lies and control their non-verbal behaviours which override any façades. Telling the truth is a simple act of communicating the facts of a situation. Fabrication of the truth, however, is more difficult as various assumptions have to be made about the recipient's mental state – what he or she knows and understands and how they will interpret the information. Whitten and Byrne (1988) labelled the ability to manipulate others as Machiavellian intelligence. The Theory of Mind Mechanism (ToMM) outlined by Leslie (1994) is a system for inferring all mental states from behaviour including epistemic states which Baron-Cohen listed as pretending, thinking, knowing, believing, imagining, dreaming, guessing and deceiving (see Chapter 4). If suspects are cognitively overloaded then monitoring Machiavellian intelligence becomes a challenging feat resulting in non-verbal behaviours indicative of deception. Police officers were more successful at detecting liars under interviews of cognitive overload using the cognitive interview principle three of recalling in reverse order (Vrij, Mann, Fisher, Leal *et al.* 2008). It appears that detecting liars is possible when the interviewer knows what to look for and how to create circumstances where non-verbal behaviour betrays the liar. At the moment, however, police detection of lying suspects remains challenging. Equally problematic for police is the detection of innocent suspects who provide a false confession. Suspects make confessions for a variety of reasons which will be covered in the next section on who is likely to confess.

## Why do individuals confess?

Three main reasons why people confess to crimes they committed was established by Gudjonsson and Sigurdsson (1999):

1 Suspects weight the evidence against them, and if there is substantial robust evidence then they confess to their crime.
2 A fear of further custody during interrogation puts external pressure on suspects to confess.
3 Suspects are compelled to clear their conscience adding internal pressure to confess.

Gudjonsson and Sigurdsson (1999) suggested that the extent of evidence against the suspect is the most influential factor in providing police with a confession. The reasons for submitting false confessions, however, is more complicated and puzzling but Wrightsman and Kassin (1993) found three psychologically defined types of false confessor:

1 voluntary – confesses without any pressure to do so;
2 coerced-compliant – confesses to avoid further interrogation and/or a police promise of lenient treatment;
3 coerced-internalised – confesses as a consequence of self-belief in having committed the crime in question.

In 1996 Kassin and Kiechel devised an experiment testing the reliability of the three psychological types of false confessor. Eliciting the help from a confederate, Kassin and Kiechel had participants working as a pairing. The participant typed (at high or low speeds) letters onto a computer which were read out by the confederate. The participant was previously informed not to hit the ALT key as this would cause the computer to crash and the data to be lost. The researcher informed participants that they were testing for reaction time. Participants, however, were not privy to the staging of a computer crash which meant that they could be accused of hitting the ALT button. A further variable introduced was whether evidence provided by the confederate confirmed that the ALT button was pressed or not pressed by the participant. The experiment was designed to introduce typing errors in the fast-paced conditions and to induce uncertainty over pressing the ALT key in conditions where the confederate had witnessed the action. As expected, when accused of hitting the ALT key, those in conditions of high speed typing and confederate confirmation of the action believed that they had done so. The experimenter prepared a confession for participants to sign, and if they agreed to do so then this was considered to be compliance. Admissions to hitting the ALT key, when asked what had happened, were considered as internalisation. All told, 69 per cent had falsely confessed due to their vulnerability and the false information that they were presented with. In the case of confabulation, the experimenter asked if the participant could recall details matching the accusation – the occurrence of this option, however, were rare but when it occurred it was most likely under the high speed condition and confirmatory confederate testimony. The findings of this study have been confirmed by numerous researchers including a study by Candel, Merckelbach, Loyen and Reyskens (2005) using children aged between 6–9 years of age; a study looking at gender (Abboud, Wadkins, Forrest, Lange and Alavi 2002); a study investigating the impact of stress (Forrest, Wadkins and Miller 2002) and the consequences of confessing (Horselenberg, Merckelbach and Josephs 2003).

A slight modification to Kassin and Kiechel's design was achieved by changing an accidental action to an intentional action using an exam fraud paradigm. Participants were required to solve logical problems either on their own or working with a confederate and were informed that they were not allowed to cheat. For half the time confederates asked for help in solving the problems and some participants obligingly provided confederates with the solutions. Under these circumstances participants could be accused of cheating as they intentionally, of their own volition, provided confederates with the answers to the problems (Russano, Meissner, Narchet and Kassin 2005). True and false confessions were obtained when participants were interrogated, demonstrating that the use of the exam fraud paradigm can induce individuals to provide both true and false confessions to an intentional rather than a potentially accidental act.

A 12 per cent rate of false confessions among prison inmates was found by Sigurdsson and Gudjonsson in 1996, and the three main reasons for these confessions were to protect someone else, avoid police pressure and to escape police detention. Sigurdsson and Gudjonsson (2001) compared the type of person who makes a false confession with other prison inmates, finding that they were more involved in criminal activity and tended to have a personality disorder such as an antisocial personality (see Chapter 7). Investigating personality disorders further, Gudjonsson, Sigurdsson, Bragason, Einarsson and Valdimarsdottir (2004) studied suspects who had made denials or confessions during police interrogation. In this case 1,080 students (461 males and 619 females) known to the researchers as having previously disclosed a high level of self-reported offending and who were in trouble with the police, completed the Eysenck Personality Questionnaire (EPQ); The Adult Impulsivity, Venturesomeness and Empathy Questionnaire; Gough Socialisation Scale; Gudjonsson Compliance Scale; The Rosenberg Self-Esteem Scale; Self-Reported Delinquency Scale; and the Background, Interrogation and Confession Questionnaire.

Gudjonsson et al. (2004) hypothesised that individuals who provide police with a false confession were more likely than true confessors and true deniers to have an antisocial personality and an extensive career of offending. There were three main reasons for confessing to the offence: perception of robust proof (52 per cent); wanting to escape the police or police pressure (38 per cent) and a desire to clear their conscience (24 per cent). High scores of psychoticism were associated with confessing as a consequence of robust evidence whereas scoring high on empathy related to confessions based on clearing one's conscience.

Alternatively, denials were based on the suspect's perception of police having limited evidence hence enabling them to go undetected if they continued denying the accusations. Furthermore, of the false confessions made (6.5 per cent), 60 per cent were to protect someone else. Of the remaining false confessions, reasons for doing so included: feeling pressured by the police; persuaded that they had committed the crime; or simply 'playing' with the police. Results from the psychometric tests depicted false confessors as being more extraverts but with a personality disorder unlike true confessors. High scores of psychoticism derived from the EPQ and poor socialisation scores from the Gough Socialisation Scale provided a reliable indicator of who was likely to make false confessions and false denials. Those with a history of offending and who were still actively engaged in criminal pursuits tended to deny their accusations.

These findings support Inbau, Reid, Buckley and Jayne's (2001) contention that emotional offenders (i.e. suspects with high levels of empathy) can be reached by appealing to their conscience during interrogation. Appealing to a suspect's conscience, however, does not work with non-emotional offenders (i.e. suspects with high scores of psychoticism and diagnosed with an antisocial personality disorder) who are best approached using a rational strategy of reasoning about the evidence. Gudjonsson (2003) argued that providing false confessions is strongly linked with antisocial personality factors and a persistent criminal lifestyle. Many who make false confessions do so to protect another person; nevertheless, there are those who falsely confess as a consequence of external pressure from police coercion. These individuals tend to be psychologically vulnerable, often with a low IQ, and can be easily influenced into believing they are guilty of a crime they did not commit. Our attention now continues with individuals who are suggestible and fall prey of what is called **interrogative suggestibility**.

### Interrogative suggestibility

Gudjonsson and Clark (1986) defined interrogative suggestibility as, 'the extent to which within a closed social interaction, people come to accept messages communicated during formal questioning, as a result of which their subsequent behavioural response is affected' (p.84). This is what had happened to Michael Crowe who, after hours of interrogation, confessed to a murder he did not commit (see Box 15.4).

According to Milne and Bull (1999) attempts should be made to prevent investigating officers from unwittingly suggesting expectancies or revealing details that might distort a suspect's (or even a witness') recollection of events. It is important during the interrogation of suspects that their memories are uncontaminated with what is already known about the case, especially if the suspect is vulnerable to suggestion. The question of why people accept suggested information, therefore heightening their vulnerability to suggestion, has been addressed by many researchers. Gudjonsson (1988) for instance found that IQ negatively correlated with interrogative suggestibility. This was explained by the finding that average IQs did not significantly correlate with interrogative suggestibility but IQs below the average did.

## Box 15.4

### The case of Michael Crowe

In 1998, the body of 12-year-old Stephanie Crowe was found, in her bedroom, stabbed nine times. It was her brother, Michael Crowe, and two of his friends who were interrogated by police. In the case of Crowe, he was questioned for 27 hours over three days (Smith 2003) but all three boys were accused of murder and all three submitted confessions to that effect. According to Humes (2004) of the Knight Ridder/Tribune Service, the police were satisfied with the evidence obtained in particular the incriminating evidence from one of the friends. Humes reported that the police used lies, fake promises and threats in order to obtain confessions. There were concerns that all three boys had been coerced by the police into confessing a crime they had not committed. The videotaped interrogations were analysed by a false confession expert who concluded that the interrogations were classic examples of how not to question suspects. The videotapes also revealed how the boys were subjected to psychological torture forcing them to fabricate a description of events and the planning of the murder. Police were suspicious of Crowe because of his behaviour and some of the things he said. For instance, the prosecutor Summer Stephan observed that Crowe was playing with a game and appeared to be distant while the rest of the family grieved. Furthermore, Crowe said that he woke up with a headache and went to the kitchen to get some milk. Police assumed that as his sister's room is opposite his and her body was found blocking the doorway; it is very likely that he would have seen her body and yet he failed to raise the alarm to the rest of the family. In the early stages of Crowe's interrogation he denied murdering his sister but after long hours of questioning he said that he was positive that he had killed her. Leung (2009) in her report quoted Crowe saying, 'She was like a threat to me. Everything I did she could match. That wasn't right . . . she made me feel worthless.' Police concluded it was a case of sibling rivalry and that Crowe had recruited his friends to help him murder her. His friend Josh Treadway was questioned for 12 hours and it was not until his second interview that he confessed to planning the murder. Treadway informed police that Crowe had the motive but his other friend Aaron Hauser had a collection of knives. When Hauser was questioned he described how you could murder someone using a knife to inflict similar wounds to those on the victim. The descriptions provided by all three boys did not reflect the crime scene and the wounds of the victim, so Vic Caloca an investigator for the San Diego Sheriff's Department examined the original interrogation tapes and claimed that all three boys were subjected to external pressure by the police and consequently coerced into confessing. Caloca noted that there were no lawyers appointed to the three boys and they were very much kept in isolation for long periods of time from their families. Furthermore, the police lied to the boys by promising leniency. From the tapes it was apparent that Crowe never confessed, but provided police with a story that they wanted to hear. The accusations against the three boys were dropped and instead attention was directed towards a felon who was a drifter suffering from schizophrenia known as Richard Tuite who was seen at the outside of the Crowe's house on the night of the murder. He was in search of another girl who the victim had resembled. **DNA** tests revealed he was the murderer and in May 2004 he was found guilty of manslaughter and sentenced to 13 years in prison.

The works by Loftus on leading questions showed the impact this has in contaminating eyewitness memories and how misinformation becomes intricately confused with the original memory trace (see Chapter 13). Situational factors have been considered as causal influences for the uptake of suggestible information. Orne (1959), for example, outlined situational factors such as interviewee perceptions regarding police beliefs and expectancies of how they should behave; trustworthiness of the interrogator and demand characteristics of the situation, as influential in the acceptance or refusal of information. McCloskey and Zaragoza (1985) claimed that interviewees believe the interrogator must be correct and, therefore, try to be good witnesses/suspects by providing answers that they assume the interrogator wants to hear (Gudjonsson 1989). It has also been highlighted by Gudjonsson and Lister (1984) that increasing the psychological distance between interviewer and interviewee leads to suggestibility. This was supported by Baxter and Boon (2000) and Bain and Baxter (2000) who showed that perceived differences of status and prestige can encourage suggestibility. They examined the effects of two interview styles – abrupt or friendly demeanour. In the abrupt condition the likelihood of suggestibility increased as shown in the scores using the Gudjonsson Suggestibility Scale (GSS) – see Box 15.5.

Boon and Baxter (2000) studied the contributions of the cognitive and situational factors implicit in interrogative suggestibility. Undergraduate students in their study played the role of interviewer and interviewee, and it was when they were acting as interviewees that they were divided in to three groups:

1    warned of misinformation in the questions – without negative feedback;
2    negative feedback was given;
3    the standard procedure adopted in the normal GSS format (see Box 15.5).

They hypothesised that when a warning was given, students would be able to resist suggestibility, which was found to be the case. Boon and Baxter concluded that interrogative suggestibility is caused in part by the interview style, intonating that two-thirds of the variance in interrogative suggestibility might be under the control of the interviewer.

The GSS has been an informative instrument in the detection of those who are vulnerable to interrogative suggestibility. But who are they most likely to be? Children (Westcott, Davies and Bull 2002), the elderly (Mueller-Johnson 2009) and people with learning disabilities (Gudjonsson, Murphy and Clare 2000) were shown to be the most likely candidates for vulnerability to interrogative suggestibility.

## Box 15.5

### The Gudjonsson Suggestibility Scale

The Gudjonsson Suggestibility Scale (GSS) was designed as a tool to test for an individual's suggestibility and their acceptance of misinformation. It provides a good indicator of the individual's susceptibility to interrogative pressure by the police. The procedure of its use operates as follows:

A spoken narrative is presented to interviewees who are then asked to recall immediately and after 50 minutes had elapsed what the narrative content they had heard contained. They are asked 20 questions about the narrative of which 15 are leading questions. The number of suggestions accepted in the leading questions provides an initial score called 'Yield 1'. Negative feedback is then given whereby the interviewee is told, 'You have made a number of errors. It is necessary to go through the questions once again, and this time, try to be more accurate.' The questions are therefore repeated and three scores pending on the responses are calculated: 'Yield 2', 'Shift' and 'Total Suggestibility'.

Yield 2 represents the number of suggestions accepted from the leading questions post negative feedback (i.e. a score out of 15). Hence Yield 2 is a measure of the extent interviewees give in to (yield) leading questions. The shift score reflects the number of changed responses to questions post negative feedback (i.e. difference between Yield 1 and Yield 2). Shift represents the interviewee's ability to cope with the pressures of interrogation (i.e. the negative feedback and continuous questioning). The total suggestibility score is the sum of Yield 1 and shift.

Gudjonsson (1984) considered the negative feedback as having two effects: to increase susceptibility to future leading questions or cause a change (shift) to the previous responses given. Of course negative feedback can be accepted or rejected and for those who reject it there is no susceptibility to suggestions. In some cases negative feedback can cause interviewees to become resilient to suggestions and instil a sense of suspicion. However, by accepting negative feedback interviewees become uncertain of their memories and more readily accept other versions of events.

Testimonies provided by witnesses and victims are assumed to be honest and less self-serving than those given by defendants (Gudjonsson 1999). This of course does not necessarily mean that their accounts are reliable given that evidence presented in the courtroom is dependent on an individual's ability to communicate their memories of events when questioned (Kebbell and Hatton 1999). This can be difficult for children and adults with learning disabilities whether they are witnesses, victims or suspects (see Chapters 13 and 14). Whether a witness, victim or suspect, the underlying impairments to intelligence and ability to effectively socially interact and communicate are the same but manifested differently from one individual to another – including the level of suggestibility (Ceci, Bruck and Battin 2000). The reason why such impairments are more likely to induce suggestibility hinges on the nature of problems to memory capacity and coping strategies used during intense police questioning. Low intelligence and impaired memory collectively and separately contribute towards a predisposition to accepting misinformation (Sharrock and Gudjonsson 1993).

Kassin and Gudjonsson (2004) discussed dispositional and situational factors that can induce a false confession, summarised as follows:

# Discussion about the function of law, its impact on antisocial behaviour and its origins

# Part VI

# Discussion about the function of law, its impact on antisocial behaviour and its origins

# Chapter 16

# 'Big 5' legal concepts

In Part VI, we explore the importance of the law and why we have law. The function law serves is considered in relation to what happens if it is disobeyed – individuals who disobey the law behave in an antisocial way and are labelled as being criminal. The purpose of law is considered in terms of why it originated in the first place. In this chapter we explore why law is important and what happens to those who contravene the law.

When individuals contravene the law they are punished by the criminal justice system based on the 'Big 5' legal concepts of **retribution**, **deterrence**, **public safety**, **punishment** and **rehabilitation**. These important concepts are dynamic in that they are not necessarily equally represented in government policies and legislations – it depends on the current political leanings. In this chapter we will explore what is meant by each of the 'Big 5' and how these are interconnected. We will further examine how the criminal justice system draws upon these concepts in order to do the right thing for the victim but also decide what is appropriate for the offender. Retribution is what the victim wishes to have, as indeed does society, but this has to be in keeping with what is fair and justified. The punishment therefore should fit the crime – this is why the Indeterminate Sentences for Public Protection was consider unfair and abolished. There is another reason for punishment and that is to ensure the safety of the public. In this chapter we also consider the important role played by deterrence as a means to preventing other potential criminals from offending. It has been argued that deterrence can indirectly be considered a form of rehabilitation. If a deterrent inhibits an offender from committing further crime then it has worked to increase **desistance** – therefore has a rehabilitation effect. In this chapter we consider rehabilitation in terms of its success at changing the offender's criminal mind-set and behaviour. This is examined further by linking why rehabilitation only works for some offenders with a nature–nurture continuum. We will explore the different levels of rehabilitation defined by Palmer as macro, micro and **multi-modal interventions**. Examples of each type will be considered here in relation to their success rate of non-recidivism.

## Introduction

Retribution, deterrence, public safety, punishment and rehabilitation are five important factors taken into consideration in social policy reformation and when making amendments to legislation. Maintaining an equal balance between all five factors depends to some extent on the current political **zeitgeist** (or the prevailing spirit of the time) and the social climate created and expressed by citizens of the society in question. If people, for example, feel that the criminal justice system is too lenient towards defendants found guilty at the expense of their victims, then the consensus might be that there is little reparation paid to victims and punishment should therefore be harsher. The knife gang culture is an example of this, where pressure groups campaigning for more to be done to apprehend gang leaders, and to punish them harshly, featured strongly in Britain during the early to mid-2000s. Equally the criminal courts responded quickly to prosecute individuals causing criminal damage and unrest on the streets of many major cities in England during the summer riots and protests of 2011. Dangerous offenders released before serving their full sentence who then murder more victims cause social concern which could lead to campaigns for tighter controls on release and more accountability to those responsible for these decisions. The social climate felt among citizens therefore can influence the political zeitgeist and visa-versa. The social climate and the political zeitgeist play an interactive role in social policy and amendments to law. The criminal justice system takes into consideration the 'Big 5' legal five factors of retribution, deterrence, public safety, punishment and rehabilitation when deciding an appropriate sentence for a defendant found guilty. These five legal factors and how they impact on decision making will be the focus of this chapter. The first of these to be considered is retribution.

## Retribution

Retribution implies that when a crime has been committed against a person, it therefore follows that they should be punished in accordance with the just deserts philosophy (see Chapters 1, 2 and 11). When we perceive a situation to be inequitable, as is the case of a victim of crime, we will try to equilibrate the situation by resorting to the law for help in apprehending, sentencing and punishing the perpetrator accordingly (Lerner 1966) – in effect for offenders to receive their just deserts. In this way the inequitable situation has been restored (McGuire 2008).

In Chapter 13 the differences between individuals in their need for restorative justice was established using a scale devised by Rubin and Peplau (1973) where a high score indicated a strong belief in the just deserts philosophy (see Box 13.6) – meaning that behaviour and the consequences are positively correlated. In general terms this implies that individuals will persevere to gain optimum rewards from any social interaction. Therefore individuals across different situations expect an **equitable reciprocal exchange** but if they perceive an unfair exchange then they will seek to restore this injustice. Individuals scoring high on the need for restorative justice are likely to take a strong stance on punishing those who deviate from the norm of distributive justice. It is through the process of socialisation that we learn to experience distress during inequitable relationships (Leventhal, Weiss and Long 1969) which then motivates us to restore equity and seek retribution. The two factors influencing the necessity for and extent of retribution pursued are known as locus of causation and intentionality. A person constrained by external factors such as acting out of duress is perceived as less blameworthy in the same way as an individual who accidently causes harm to another. When these two factors are combined, the necessity to restore equity to a situation will either be pursued or ignored. In relation to punishment, the restoration of equity will be a matter of administering punishment that fits the crime (Andrews and Bonta 2006; Cavadino and Digman 2007).

The concept of retribution stems from the classical school of criminology and favours the mantra of 'the punishment should fit the crime' (see Chapters 5, 11 and 13). Lacey (1994) has interpreted extreme classical retributivism as reinforcing the idea that the state has 'both a right and a duty to punish, in the sense of inflicting unpleasant consequences upon an offender in response to her offence to the extent that, and by reason of the fact that, she deserves that punishment' (p.16).

Classical retributivism appears to rely on restoring a moral equilibrium that arises out of a perceived inequitable situation by using some form of punishment. An offender therefore will be deprived of rights that are proportionate to the violation of rights incurred to the victim, which is more likely to happen if the state perceives a need for social protection. There are two different perspectives of classical retributivism discussed in Box 16.1. According to Siegel (1992) 'Retributionists argue that punishments are fair and necessary in a just society' (p.148). A less extreme form of retribution in sentencing practice is that which relies on a tariff system where the punishment should be done fairly and proportionately. A tariff system sets the standard within a guided range where, for example, house burglary might be two years and shop burglary 20 months; theft 18 months; and murder 10 years. There are also tariffs within tariffs. Judges, however, often use their own guidelines as tariffs tend to be implicit rather than explicitly recorded. Wilson (1975) argued that tariffs should be explicit and based on the just deserts model where offenders do time for the crime (see Chapters 1 and 2). In California there is a mandatory tariff system where the judge has no discretion as there are set years for different crimes but this approach is considered an extreme form of the just deserts model. In the UK the Judge has much discretion and access to mandatory life and indeterminate sentences for dangerous offenders (see Chapter 11).

Lacey (1994) argued that punishment must serve some other function besides attaining moral equilibrium, and suggests that the answer comes from looking at other justifications for punishment such as those arising out of classical utilitarian philosophy (i.e. deterrence, public safety and rehabilitation). Supporters of a utilitarian philosophy base their views on concepts of rationality and the adherence to society's social contract (i.e. following values, mores and morals of society). Therefore punishment for behaviours causing harm to others and society should be based on a reasonable and measured response. The aim of punishment is to prevent crime not just for the perpetrator but for potential perpetrators.

## Box 16.1

### Perspectives of Classical Retributivism

#### Lex talionis

Implicit in the **lex talionis** is the notion 'an eye for an eye' and 'a life for a life'. The problem with the *lex talionis* is that it fails to give practical guidance on measures of punishment for most crimes. While it stipulates that murder should be punished by state execution or theft through maiming a hand for instance, there is no guidance on appropriate punishment for crimes such as fraud or joy-riding. Furthermore, it fails to consider the important principle of responsibility. The fact that a perpetrator might have a mental disorder that impairs judgement, understanding and full knowledge and control over their actions is not accounted for in the *lex talionis*. Other important factors such as intentionality, deliberateness, causation and culpability are ignored.

#### Culpability

This is linked with blameworthiness: in other words the extent to which an offender is causal in the harm caused to a victim by way of his behaviour. **Culpability** is considered in relation to the extent of responsibility attributed to the perpetrator (i.e. was the behaviour intended to cause harm to the victim or could the harm have been avoided given less reckless behaviour?). The extent of culpability can be used to ascertain the most appropriate punishment – that which is in accordance with the proportionality between offence and punishment given. The notion of culpability also has problems:

- Is an offender morally blameworthy in all cases of law breaking? (i.e. parking in the wrong place).
- Does responsibility (or criminal liability) imply moral blameworthiness? (i.e. having a heart attack while driving into a pedestrian causing death).
- How is it decided which wrongs are punishable by the state?
- How is it decided that a punishment is proportionate to the offence committed?

- Rawls (1971) advocated that culpability should rest on the concept of a comparative instead of an absolute just deserts philosophy. This means that while it is difficult to ascertain that 20 years in prison corresponds directly with the nature of culpability for murder, it does give an indication that this is a more appropriate punishment for murder than it would be for robbery. This still has the problem of deciding which crime deserves a longer prison sentence, aggregate burglary or rape for instance.

Retribution can be avoided if the crime can be prevented in the first place. The judiciary try to encourage other potential offenders to abstain from committing crime through the use of deterrence measures in their sentencing of criminals found guilty. This is known as deterrence which can also be used outside of the courts – discussed next.

## Deterrence

According to classical utilitarian philosophy, deterrence is another justification for the use of punishment (Bentham 1781). There are two types of deterrence: general (or indirect) and specific (or individual). In the case of general deterrence, a sentence for an individual is usually severe as it is designed to send a message to other potential offenders thinking of committing a similar crime that 'crime does not pay'.

Under these circumstances the offender is often used as a scapegoat to deter others from committing a similar crime. Severe sentencing such as this, while serving as a general deterrent, is sometimes difficult to justify under the terms of the just deserts model (i.e. the sentence fitting the nature and severity of the crime). Furthermore, Cavadino and Digman (2007) argued that punishment is ineffective as a general deterrent because would-be offenders are ill-informed of the different forms of punishment and have the mind-set of evading capture and punishment. General deterrence is used as a means of achieving a social goal – it sends a message to potential offenders that this is the consequence of offending (Lacey 1994). The purpose of general deterrence, therefore, is to reduce undesirable behaviour that contravenes the law, which means that offenders are sacrificed in order to achieve this goal (Lacey 1994).

General deterrence works on the assumption that individuals engage in criminal acts if they have no fear of punishment. The law makes it clear that if rules are broken then negative consequences will occur such as prison for manslaughter. General deterrence is designed to focus on reducing the likelihood of criminal behaviour in the general population. Good examples of this are notices such as, 'Shoplifters will be prosecuted' or 'Trespassers will be shot'. The death penalty is another form of general deterrent practised in some states of the US for instance but there is debate over the extent of truth this contention holds. Radelet and Lacock (2009) did a survey asking criminologists if they believed the death penalty is a good deterrent to which 88 per cent responded that it is not. Furthermore, 87 per cent believed that the abolition of the death penalty would not have an effect on homicide rates.

Alternatively, specific deterrence is designed to prevent the offender from **recidivism** (i.e. repeating a crime). Prison, for example, is used to deter the offender from recommitting the same crime, simply because incarceration and the loss of liberty are unpleasant experiences. Theories of conditioning are of relevance here, especially classical conditioning (see Chapters 7 and 8). It is assumed that offenders will learn to make the association between committing crime and the resulting consequence of freedom loss; which for most individuals would be an unpleasant situation. Some criminologists consider incapacitation as a form of specific deterrence as it aims to prevent the offender from repeating the crime by ensuring that the opportunity of doing so is stopped (McGuire 2008). It has been argued that incapacitation through the confinement of offenders will decrease the rate of crime (Andrews and Bonta 2006). This association is too simplistic, and as pointed out by Cavadino and Digman (2007), those who are imprisoned are replaced by the next generation of criminals waiting to occupy the empty niche. Hence offenders are imprisoned to prevent them from doing further crime rather than learning from the consequences of their actions (seemingly the antithesis of what classical conditioning in the context of deterrence tries to achieve). Rehabilitation (where classical conditioning as a treatment intervention can be used) will be discussed later in the context of learning about the consequences of actions and a means to initiating change.

Another problem with specific deterrence is that the reasons motivating criminal behaviour are difficult to pinpoint, which is why the punishment focuses on stopping the problem behaviour from occurring again (i.e. through a life sentence for a serious crime or corporal punishment). Incapacitation through imprisonment, however, is not an effective specific deterrent, as statistics show a 57 per cent reoffending rate for adults in prison for less than a year and 38 per cent for those imprisoned between one and four years. The reconviction figure for those on community punishments do not fare much better at 34 per cent (Travis 2011). In the UK, the Prisons and Probation Minister Crispin Blunt claimed that the reconviction figures were high and said:

> That is why we are introducing tougher sentences that properly punish offenders while addressing the root causes of their behaviour. We are also exploring the use of payment by results in both prison and the community, targeting improved reductions in reoffending and paying for what works (Travis 2011).

This viewpoint is in line with the contention that while punishment in its own right does not change offenders' future criminal behaviour, it will reduce the opportunity for engaging in crime. Incarceration not only has a double role of being a punishment and a deterrent but provides the public with a

7    there must be rewards for virtue;
8    education for all;
9    the legal system must follow the laws and avoid temptation to corruption.

There would be fewer requirements for trials and punishments if these nine principles were adhered to claimed Beccaria.

Bentham (1781), a British philosopher, was instrumental in ensuring political accountability and transparency to protect citizens from government corruption. Bentham adopted the utilitarian (i.e. the philosophical doctrine aspiring to the use of morally correct action benefitting the greatest number of people) euphemism that punishment in its own right is evil but its use is justified if it averts a greater evil. Bentham supported the view that if punishments were made known to citizens and actually used against criminals then this would deter further criminal behaviour.

It is to Émile Durkheim (1858–1917), however, that our attention is now focused. Durkheim (1925), unlike Bentham, did not believe that individuals were deterred from behaving immorally out of fearing punishment. Durkheim had a more positive approach to human nature, claiming that when an individual behaves immorally, people experience emotions, usually anger towards that person. For Durkheim, punishment was merely a defined measure used against an individual who contravened the moral code and order in society. Therefore punishment was perceived by Durkheim as a measure of society's values and not something metered out to induce obedience or conformity. Put another way, punishment represents the moral disapproval expressed by society or groups within society against those who have rejected the moral code or order therein. Punishment therefore becomes an important mechanism for enforcing law by using specific and general deterrence, and by fulfilling the requirement of retribution and the just deserts philosophy to ensure public safety and protection. Punishment can be considered in different ways but in a fair and just society the punishment assigned to offenders should be proportionate to the seriousness of the crime committed. However, other factors should be considered like the mental health of the individual, the likelihood of recidivism, the dangerousness of the individual and any factors that comprise a case for mitigation in the reduction of the sentence tariff (see Chapter 11).

In Britain, in the Green Paper, 'Breaking the Cycle: Effective Punishment, Rehabilitation and Sentencing of Offenders' presented to Parliament by the Ministry of Justice in 2010, a clause read:

We plan to transform the administration of punishment in this country to make it more robust and credible. Prisons will become places of hard work and industry, instead of enforced idleness. There will be greater use of strenuous, unpaid work as part of a community sentence alongside tagging and curfews, delivered swiftly after sentencing. When fines are a sensible sentence, we will place a greater focus on enforcement and collection. We will put a much stronger emphasis on compensation for victims of crime (p.1).

In this Green Paper, which was reviewed in May 2011, the coalition government in Britain were very much favouring a 'payment back to victims and society' approach in its deployment of punishment. The phrase, for example, 'Criminals should face the robust and demanding punishments which the public expects' (p.9) was used. References to consequences being in situ for breaking the law were made in addition to 'hard work' being at the centre of punishment regimes. There were further references to prisoners experiencing 'tough discipline of regular working hours'. The Green Paper also asserted that community-based sentences will become more intensive. The idea of 'working prisons' and the implementation of the Prisoners' Earnings Act (as a means of paying the costs of services for victims) were put forward for discussion as well as tougher curfews and electronic tagging and immediate Community Payback schemes. The Green Paper also addressed issues relating to the sentencing of adults committing knife crimes – such knife crimes are considered as serious crimes and automatically warrant a prison sentence. There were further suggestions of:

- long prison sentences for serious offending (including crimes committed by juveniles);
- Indeterminate sentences such as Imprisonment for Public Protection (IPP) to be reserved for serious offenders (see Box 16.3);
- the release test used by the Parole Board is to be tightened up;
- punishments involving financial payback are to be monitored more effectively by ensuring payments are collected (Ministry of Justice 2010).

These proposals are in support of a public safety and reparation to victims and society ideology. In the Ministry of Justice, 'Breaking the Cycle: Government Response' of June 2011, many of the aforementioned points were supported and the public safety and reparation ideology was retained.

## Box 16.3

### Changes to IPP sentencing taken from 'Breaking the Cycle: Government Response'

We are conducting the IPP review with a view to replacing the current IPP regime with a much tougher determinate sentencing framework which includes:

- an increased number of serious offenders would receive life sentences – with mandatory life sentences for the most serious repeat offenders;

- it would be less open to challenge in the courts than the IPP system;
- serious sexual and violent offenders would spend at least two-thirds of their sentence in prison, where they cannot pose a risk to the public, rather than being automatically released half-way through their sentence – and they would only ever be released before the end of their sentence if the Parole Board are satisfied that it is safe to do so;
- there would be compulsory programmes for dangerous offenders while they are in prison, to make them change their ways and not just commit more crimes when they are released.

We will also review the Parole Board arrangements for the rehabilitation of those with IPPs, to ensure that real work is done to reform offenders while in prison. Following the conclusion of our review, we will bring forward government amendments to the Bill in the autumn. In the meantime, IPPs will continue to be available to the courts as they are now.

Ministry of Justice, Breaking the Cycle: Government Response, HMSO, June 2011 (p.11).

The Ministry of Justice, however, set the date for the abolition of IPPs at 3 December 2012 as a response to the many problems of IPP sentencing. For in-depth discussion of the IPP refer to Chapters 1 and 11. The unfairness and ethics revolving around the use of IPPs was the main reason for its abolition (see Box 11.4).

Although the ideology of the Government's response is one of public safety and reparation, there is emphasis on reducing reoffending through rehabilitation schemes. There has been an increase in reoffending by prisoners receiving sentences of less than one year from 58 per cent in 2000 to 61 per cent in 2008 (Ministry of Justice 2011). Furthermore, figures for 2009–10 suggested that about 50 per cent of offenders reoffend within a year of release from prison. Further analysis of figures from 2009–10 suggested that 16,000 offenders are active at any one time, each having about 75 previous convictions and 14 stints in prison (HMSO 2011). These figures prompted the previous coalition government to include policies for rehabilitation as a means of changing offenders' thinking, lifestyle and options. They proposed that dangerous offenders, for example, should receive compulsory programmes that help to reform them. In the next section rehabilitation and the different forms it takes will be examined.

## Rehabilitation

Both utilitarian and retribution ideologies focus on the crime in different ways rather than the individual. Utilitarians perceive proportionate punishment to the crime as a means to specific and general deterrence without consideration to notions of reformation and rehabilitation. It was not until the end of the nineteenth century, however, that the notion of rehabilitation arose

(Martin, Sechrest and Redner 1981). Through modified legislation in the UK deriving from government, such as the Gladstone Committee (Departmental Committee on Prisons 1895), imprisonment was perceived as punishment but also an opportunity for offenders to improve their moral standards. This came about through education, work opportunities within prison and instilling moral understanding through instruction – all very similar to the current efforts taking place within the penology system. Rehabilitation is not considered to be a replacement for punishment although it is often perceived this way by the general public. It is instead a form of specific deterrence designed to change the offender so that the desire for criminal pursuit is reduced or eliminated. In this way it is hoped that reoffending rates can be effectively reduced.

Rehabilitation and treatment programmes, especially in prison, are aimed at reducing further reoffending but do they work? This has been an ongoing debate in criminology and many have concluded that 'nothing works'. Martinson (1974) published an article that was negative about the effectiveness of different treatments for reducing recidivism, only later in 1979 to retract this. Martinson's retraction was ignored and his original stance continued to drive policies away from rehabilitation towards hard-liner legislations. The 'traditional' therapies, such as those based on psychoanalysis, have largely failed, but with the rise of cognitive-behavioural approaches, there has been some success. Redondo, Sanchez-Meca and Garrido (1999) examined the effectiveness of prison treatment initiatives in Europe and found a 10 per cent reduction in reoffending for those who had received some kind of treatment intervention. In 2002, adopting a meta-analysis design, Redondo *et al.* compared recidivism figures for British, German and Dutch studies of offenders who had received treatment with those who had not. A difference of 22 per cent was found between treatment and non-treatment cohorts. Further breakdown analyses revealed that educational programmes had the highest success rates in terms of reduced recidivism followed by cognitive-behavioural interventions.

It is interesting that treatment intervention, albeit in the form of educational programmes, appears to work for some offenders. Without actual details of the types of crime committed and the nature of offenders receiving treatment interventions, we can only speculate that there might be a relationship between the offender and the nature–nurture continuum. As we have seen from previous evaluations of the effectiveness of treatment programmes for violent and dangerous offenders, such as criminal psychopaths and sex offenders, it is difficult to find an intervention which successfully rehabilitates them (see Chapters 7, 8 and 11). This suggests that the possible underlying causes of their criminality are nature determined, in that a change of lifestyle and methods of social interaction are not enough to extinguish a criminal mind-set nor criminal behaviour. For some types of offender, however, it has been shown that change is forthcoming. Successful change in mind-set and behaviour has been demonstrated in some types of young offender (see Chapter 10) and to females committing crime due to their marginalisation (see Chapter 9). These successes suggest that the underlying motivations for committing crime are nurture determined – change their social and economic circumstances and so too will the need for offending. This might be too simplistic an analysis, but it is interesting how some offenders manage to successfully turn their lives around when given rehabilitation (see the concluding chapter).

Rehabilitation therefore has a measure of credence and can be used as a form of deterrence despite the utilitarian approach to imprisonment. Utilitarians believed that prison could be used as a deterrence, thereby reducing recidivism; however, there is little empirical evidence to suggest that prison on its own reduces reoffending. A meta-analysis of studies in the last 40 years by Smith, Goggin and Grendreau (2002) indicated that prison and longer prison sentences do not reduce or increase reoffending figures (including subsections of the prison community such as juveniles, females and ethnic groups). In Canada, Nunes, Firestone, Wexler, Jenson and Bradford (2007) studied a cohort of imprisoned sex offenders who were assessed for risk of reoffending using an assessment devised by Hanson in 1997 called the Rapid Risk Assessment for Sexual Offence Recidivism (RRASOR). They concluded that:

1    sexual and violent recidivism were unrelated to being confined, and being confined for a long time;
2    offenders who scored high on RRASOR correlated with violent recidivism.

The hard-liner policies are returning since the British Coalition Government took power in 2010; however, rehabilitation and treatment interventions are still taken seriously. The Home Office in 2007 introduced 40 accredited offender treatment programmes which despite criticisms are still in operation. For rehabilitation and treatment programmes to be effective, McGuire (2004) highlighted that they need to incorporate and focus on:

•    sound empirical and theoretical infrastructure;
•    the level of offender risk (i.e. the mid-high end of risk);
•    dynamic **risk factors** that are prone to change with circumstances unlike the offender's history or family background which are static risk factors;
•    treatments known to be effective (i.e. social and cognitive-behavioural approaches);
•    an appropriate environment to increase offender response to treatment.

Behaviour programmes can be divided into those that tackle general offending behaviour and those concentrating on specific behavioural problems. Palmer (2003b) introduced three levels of programme intervention: macro, micro and multi-modal. In the case of a multi-modal approach both general (e.g. Reasoning and Rehabilitation; Enhanced Thinking Skills and Think First) and specific (e.g. Aggression Replacement Training) behavioural problems can be addressed. These approaches will be considered in turn.

### Macro-interventions (also called 'Just Community')

**Macro-intervention**-style programmes, or 'Just Community' programmes, are normally set within an educational setting but can occur inside prisons also. This programme works using a consensus among members (i.e. prisoners and prison officers) that they all have equal rights and can each cast a vote on issues requiring a decision. Issues considered could include mundane activities such as how rotas are devised to important factors including the way discipline is used. Just Community programmes have been successful in improving the moral development of prisoners (Scharf and Hickey 1976). Scharf and Hickey (1976) found that **moral reasoning** had improved in female prisoners by a third of a stage of Kohlberg's Theory of Moral Development (see Chapter 4) in comparison to those subjected to a standard prison regime. The success of this programme was further cemented by the 15 per cent recidivism rate versus 35 per cent for those under the standard prison regime (Hickey and Scharf 1980).

### Micro-interventions

**Micro-interventions** operate on a small group basis and address the immature level of moral reasoning often seen in offenders by using moral dilemmas and scenarios of problematic social circumstances. In groups, participants discuss the different moral dilemmas posed while the group leader guides the direction of interaction. Gibbs, Arnold, Ahlborn and Cheesman (1984) showed a progression from stage 2 to stage 3 on Kohlberg's levels of moral development (see Chapter 4) in 87.5 per cent of participants who completed the eight week programme of moral reasoning. The male and female participants had effectively moved from the pre-conventional to the conventional level of moral reasoning (this was only 14.3 per cent for the control group). Disappointingly, however, there was little empirical evidence to show that behaviour changes as a consequence of moral reasoning enhancement (Niles 1986). Assuming that immature moral development is responsible for offenders committing crime, it is still too simplistic and excludes a multitude of integrated factors which will be considered next.

### Multi-modal interventions

These can be divided into the following approaches:

- Reasoning and Rehabilitation;
- Enhanced Thinking Skills;
- Think First;

- Priestley One-to-One;
- Aggression Replacement Training.

*Reasoning and Rehabilitation*   Ross, Fabiano and Ewles (1988) developed the Reasoning and Rehabilitation (R&R) programme as a package to enhance the cognitive deficits observed in many offenders. This included a series of cognitive skills that normally help to control our behaviour and lead us to make the right decisions. Cognitive skills such as moral and critical reasoning; control of anger and the ability to monitor and regulate emotions; empathy training; solving problems using appropriate interpersonal skills; less rigid cognitive styles of thought and more self-control were implemented. In the 1990s a programme called Straight Thinking on Probation (STOP) was piloted in Wales which showed some success with reconviction dropping to 35 per cent from projected figures of 42 per cent. This fall in reconviction rate, however, was short lived as revealed two years later in a follow-up study. Nevertheless, an R&R approach has been implemented for use in the Prison Service in Wales and England.

*Enhanced Thinking Skills (ETS)*   was designed within the Prison Service and resembles R&R programmes. Offenders are required to complete psychometric tests for the identification of specific cognitive and skills deficits. ETS was developed to complement R&R, and like R&R, attention is given to interpersonal skills, problem solving and moral reasoning. Both R&R and ETS programmes have been evaluated simultaneously finding that the most successful changes incurred have been in self-control, impulsivity and using cognitive skills to think problems through (Blud, Travers, Nugent and Thornton 2003). A reduction in reconviction rates of 11 per cent and 14 per cent among medium-high risk and medium-low risk offenders respectively were found in those who participated in R&R and ETS programmes (Friendship, Blud, Erikson, Travers and Thornton 2003).

*The Think First programme*   is used by the Probation Service and has a crime centred focus. A battery of psychometric tests is used both pre- and post-programme intervention to identify specific cognitive deficits that offenders might have. Think First is designed to change offenders' attitudes towards crime while the psychometric tests help identify areas that require attention. The Think First programme managed to reduce the extent of criminal attitudes and increased self-esteem (McGuire and Hatcher 2001).

*The Priestley One-to-One*   is an alternative version to all three aforementioned programmes for offenders considered inappropriate for group session participation. These offenders have a tailor-made programme delivered on an individual basis that is designed to address cognitive deficits found using psychometric testing. Content and approach of the Priestley One-to-One programme mimics the R&R, ETS and Think First interventions.

*Aggression Replacement Training (ART)*   is essentially designed for offenders posing medium to high risk for reoffending. The primary objective of ART is to reduce aggressive behaviour by focusing on moral reasoning, self-control and awareness (and other social and interpersonal skills) and managing anger (Palmer 2005). In the case of social and interpersonal skills training, methods such as role play, modelling and feedback on tasks set are used in the hope of replacing inappropriate aggressive styles of interaction. Anger management activities are designed to help offenders increase their self-control and use alternative coping strategies to anger. According to Hatcher (2008) this is achieved through identifying the triggers that initiate an aggressive reaction to situations, and learning to replace this with pro-social coping alternatives. In the case of moral reasoning training, the focus is on discussions of moral dilemmas. Here, offenders have the opportunity of integrating what they have learnt from their social and interpersonal skills and anger management training. Palmer (2003b) pointed out that the way these different skills are integrated is through considering 'what to do . . . how to do it . . . and why to do it' (p.170). In other words, the 'what to do' relies on social and interpersonal skills, the 'how to do it' on anger management and the 'why to do it' on moral reasoning. Sugg (2000) evaluated the success of ART on 153 ex-probationers. The reconviction rate for those who had completed the ART programme was 20.4 per cent in comparison with the figure of 65 per cent for ART non-completers. The control group had a reconviction rate of 60 per cent per cent, which is similar to those who failed to complete the ART programme. The 20.4 per cent reconviction rate for ART completers can be regarded as a successful reduction of recidivism.

There are mixed findings supporting the use of rehabilitation and treatment interventions in both prison and community settings; however, **multimodal interventions** like the ART programme address the many aspects of offenders' lives. Clearly, retribution, deterrence, public safety, punishment and rehabilitation are considered simultaneously when formulating policies and criminal justice legislation but their extent of representation will alter depending on the political and economic zeitgeist.

## Summary

- Penalties for contravening the law if harm is caused to society and its citizens are decided by the criminal justice system such that the more harm caused the greater the penalties incurred. Decisions of penalty by the criminal justice system are based on the 'Big 5' legal concepts of law: retribution, deterrence, public safety, punishment and rehabilitation. These factors combine to determine the offender's fate in terms of whether they receive a custodial sentence or a community order – the more serious the crime committed the more likely it is that the offender will be imprisoned.

- *Mala in se* crimes are serious crimes that break the human moral code and are therefore punished more severely to ensure:
  - reparation to the victim;
  - public safety in knowing that the offender is in prison;
  - other potential criminals are deterred from committing the same crime;
  - the balance of injustice has been restored by punishing the perpetrator;
  - a change in the perpetrator's attitude and lifestyle via rehabilitation.

- Retribution is a term used to weigh the seriousness of the crime committed against a person and the level of punishment deserved. This operates on the just deserts philosophy. Individuals expect an **equitable reciprocal exchange** but if this is not forthcoming then they feel aggrieved and want the situation to be corrected – this applies in criminal justice also. Retribution stems from the classical criminology mantra that the punishment should fit the crime. Furthermore, a moral equilibrium should be restored through the use of punishment.

- Deterrence according to classical utilitarian philosophy justifies the use of punishment. There are two types of deterrence: general (indirect) and specific (individual). The reason for deterrence is to stop offenders from reoffending and to give the message out to potential offenders that if you get caught you will be punished. Conditioning provides a link between committing crime and the consequences which follow. Such an association has to be learnt.

- Public safety is one factor considered in the National Offender Management Service. It also provides the opportunity for correctional services to integrate information about offenders to aid in their rehabilitation. Fear of crime is closely associated with the public's need for offenders to be incarcerated. Studies have shown that fear of certain types of crime is actually higher than what the true figures for these crimes are. Crime television has been shown to increase fear of crime scores fitting in with the Cultivation Thesis by Gerbner and Gross. The public also have their concerns with the use of Electronic House Arrest as an alternative to prison because of the problems associated with the way it is implemented and controlled.

- Punishment is a way of dealing with an offender – the more serious the crime committed, the higher the sentence tariff (hence imprisonment). Figure heads of the Enlightenment period believed that deterrence is more important but for those who do commit crime then they should be punished to protect the public. Indeterminate Sentences for Public Protection was considered an unfair punishment and was abolished in 2012.

- Rehabilitation is designed to help offenders change their ways of thinking and behaving such that they no longer want to commit crime. In the UK, with the Gladstone Committee (Departmental Committee on Prisons 1895), the opportunity for offenders to alter their poor moral standards was introduced. Not all offenders can be successfully rehabilitated. It was speculated that perhaps there is a nature–nurture element involved whereby those who can be rehabilitated change because the underlying reasons for their offending is derived from circumstances of nurture – quite the antithesis of those who cannot be changed.

## Questions for discussion

1   Is deterrence the key to crime reduction?
2   To what extent should the public's safety be put ahead of alternative forms of sentencing?
3   In what ways do the 'Big 5' legal concepts influence the way offenders are treated?

# Chapter 17

# Law drives criminality

In Part VI, we explore the importance of the law and why we have law. The function law serves is considered in relation to what happens if it is disobeyed – individuals who disobey the law behave in an antisocial way and are labelled as being criminal. The purpose of law is considered in terms of why it originated in the first place. In this chapter we explore the possible origins of law.

In this chapter an attempt to understand how law was conceived will be considered using three speculative interpretations: criminality occurs because of the way we define crime; law arises out of morality, and socialisation drives law abiding behaviour but can also cause criminality. The first interpretation uses concepts of cooperation and reciprocal altruism as key factors in the detection of individuals who fail to comply with the rules held by early humans. Examples of modern day Stone Age cultures highlight the very nature of relationships and dependency these people living in small groups have. The second interpretation views laws as depending on what is regarded as moral behaviour. Again reference is made to cooperation and reciprocal altruism and how these led to a sense of what it is to be fair and moral. With reference to early humans, this approach sees morality as having an innate basis (which is supported by studies looking at the brain and differences in activity for different types of moral decision making). In the third interpretation we will consider nurturance and socialisation as being at the heart of instilling appropriate behaviour and developing **moral reasoning**. Furthermore, we will consider the literature which shows that children who have been rejected or socialised to have deviant criminal attitudes and values are more likely to contravene the law.

## Introduction

'Law drives criminality' is a bold declaration but is there any truth to this statement? This statement appears to be simple but its implications are rather profound. We can speculate the truthfulness of this statement by using three different levels of approach.

First, we can speculate that criminality occurs out of the way we define crime (see Chapters 1 and 2). There is much evidence for this as we have seen in Chapters 1 and 2. An interesting way of approaching this is to consider the antithesis of this approach. If for, example, there was no law dictating that it is wrong to murder, would we still find the act of killing someone abhorrent? Would we find it difficult to kill another human being despite there being no ruling or sanctions against committing such an act? Second, we can speculate that laws arise out of morality. Humans, for example, might define laws based on what is perceived to be the right way to behave, so as to protect citizens from being harmed by individuals who refuse to follow these laws. This implies that we are essentially pro-social beings. An obvious question to ask if this is the case is 'why should this be so'. This might be explained using an evolutionary approach where in our evolutionary past various adaptations were made to enable us to live co-operatively together. Third, we can speculate that socialisation drives law abiding behaviour but can also cause criminality. Through the process of socialisation we develop our understanding of morality and how to distinguish between right and wrong. This understanding guides the way we behave which encourages us to embrace the law. Equally, however, inappropriate socialisation can cause an individual to reject the law and follow a path of immoral and criminal ideals.

These three levels of speculation will be considered separately each with its own underlying theoretical assumptions. Furthermore, these theoretical assumptions derive from different perspectives which err on the side of a nature or nurture approach.

## Criminality occurs out of the way we define crime

As was discussed in Chapters 1 and 2, crime and what constitutes criminal behaviour derive from social definitions of law. British law goes back a long way but there is evidence of laws ruling the Sumerians in the twenty-first and twentieth centuries BC, as stipulated in the 57 articles by King Ur-Nammu and the 50 articles of the code of Lipit-Istar respectively. These laws encapsulated personal rights and protection of its citizens and the codes listed penalties for contravening rules (functionally very similar to what English law tries to accomplish even today). The Babylonians also had laws written in the Code of Hammurabi which included penalties in the form of corporal punishment and confinement. It stipulated punishments in accordance with the seriousness of the offence and was the first to consider placements for juvenile delinquents from families considered dysfunctional. There were Hebrew laws based on the Bible and the Ten Commandments. But it was the Roman occupation of Britain that made an impact on how English law developed. With their system of *pater familias*, property matters were in the hands of the *pater* who dealt with theft and misbehaving slaves but were compensated by law enforcers who also ensured appropriate punishments for perpetrators. Teutonic laws of Germanic tribes also had a system of compensation which very much influenced English law during the wave of Saxon invasions (see Chapter 1). Law, it appears, has been the infrastructure for civilisations over many millennia, but why do human cultures need to have rules and agreed social definitions of what law should involve?

To answer this we need to refer to evolutionary psychology and our understanding of how our ancestors developed their own rules and systems of order. Current evidence suggests that with the advent of bipedalism (i.e. walking upright) in our hominid ancestors, *Ardipithecus ramidus* inhabited woodlands some 4.4 million years ago and *Australopithecus* came down from the trees and lived in the savannah plains some 4.2 million years ago. It is believed that humans (*Homo sapiens*) evolved from the gracile Australopithecine line that existed some 2.5 million years ago. In the case of *Homo sapiens*, fossil records suggest they have been around for about 150,000 years but there is still controversy concerning exact dates of descent from *Australopithecus* (Workman and Reader 2014).

Why the short history lesson of human evolution is crucial to our understanding of how society and laws first developed among small dwellings of individuals relates to the adaptations made to survive the adverse environmental conditions. The fossil and artefact record suggests that our ancestors lived in small groups of 20 to 200 individuals, who were mainly related, but friends resided together also. The harsh environmental conditions meant that it was difficult for individuals to survive on their own, but in groups hunting and gathering food sources would increase the success of the yield. Hunting and gathering food in groups would mean that individual members needed to cooperate with each other. Furthermore, members of the group would need to be of the understanding that if they failed to find food on one occasion they would not starve, as others in the group would share their yield on the premise that this favour would be returned in future. Trivers (1972) introduced the term reciprocal altruism to explain this. He claimed that reciprocal altruism was crucial for hominid evolution and explained how it operated as follows:

> We routinely share food, we help the sick, the wounded and the very young. We routinely share our tools and we share our knowledge in a very complex way. Often these forms of behaviour meet the criterion of small cost to the giver and great benefit to the recipient (Trivers 1985, p.386).

Trivers is making a series of important revelations about reciprocal altruism:

- the cost of altruistic acts is less than the benefits;
- it enables the detection of cheats;
- it allows for reciprocation;
- give aid to friends to encourage reciprocation;

- out of the above arises an emotional system (i.e. empathy and morality) that underpins reciprocal altruism.

Alexander (1987) further elaborated by saying that: 'Complex sociality should be expected to arise only when confluences of interest produce benefits that override the costs of conflicting interest' (p.65). This means that under situations where everyone is to benefit from having common goals, it makes perfect sense to cooperate. The operation of reciprocal altruism can be seen in modern day Stone Age cultures such as the !Kung San and Yanomamö despite differences in their foraging styles (see Box 17.1).

For early hominids, it would appear, cooperation was important but some have argued this might not necessarily be the case. John Nash introduced the notion of **Game Theory** which he devised as a means of predicting how people make decisions about their investments. This idea was later used to explain behaviour and evolution by John Maynard-Smith. In Box 17.2, Game Theory is explained using the prisoner's dilemma example.

Cooperation and reciprocal altruism appear to underlie the development of human laws. Some evolutionary psychologists would argue that our moral codes arose from the pressures of the open savannah, and the cooperation that followed from that created the possibility of **free-riders** who exploited this system (Trivers 1985). Moral codes are clearly entwined in laws that were socially defined by humans: a form of social order would have been necessary even during the days of early hominids. It is almost as though we need to have social order – 'laws' – so that we can live together harmoniously. As we have seen, however, there will always be individuals who are non-conformists or **free-riders** – in other words, those who take without giving (Trivers 1985). According to Workman and Reader (2008), many free-riders might be kept in the population (providing they occur at a relatively low level) because they reap the benefits without paying the costs of behaving altruistically. Those with antisocial personality disorder (at around 1 in 50 of the population), for example, are renowned as free-riding non-reciprocators, and, when other non-reciprocating personality disorders, such as histrionic personality disorder, are taken into account, then the proportion of free-riders in the population is likely to increase to 1 in 20 (Workman pers. comm. 2013). Hence, to evolutionary psychologists, laws and moral codes arose in order to negate the effects of free-riders (Krebs 1998).

## Box 17.1

### Modern day Stone Age cultures: the !Kung San and Yanomamö

The !Kung San are a monogamous (i.e. having one sexual partner at one time) nomadic people living in the savannah of the Kalahari traversing some

87,000 miles over Namibia and Botswana. According to Wells (2003) they have inhabited these parts for over 22,000 years. Even though agriculture was introduced approximately 10,000 years ago they have maintained their hunter-gatherer strategy of foraging for food (Lee 1979). They share their food with their kin and offer gifts of food to others which is considered the norm; however, loss of prestige and status occurs to an individual who fails to share food sources with others (Lee 1979). This is particularly the case when living in harsh environmental conditions where the sharing of food among relatives would help increase their inclusive fitness (i.e. fitness of an individual as measured by reproductive success). Note that this would also encourage reciprocation and the development of allies outside of the family (Harris 1985).

Alternatively, the Yanomamö have a different approach to foraging – they have a slash-burn approach to agriculture which has meant they live in permanent villages in the rainforest of the Amazon basin. They are polygynous (i.e. having more than one wife at one time) and have well established trading systems operating both within and outside of their village. They too have a gift system but they expect to receive gifts of similar worth. Different villages have different areas of expertise – such as one village might be good at producing jewellery and another at making pottery. They are of the understanding that exchanging goods and reciprocation can be delayed but a tab is nevertheless kept.

Clearly there is a difference in the nature of food sharing which Diamond (1997) attributed to the method of foraging and need for storing food. In the case of the !Kung San it is difficult to store food in the heat of the savannah, so it makes sense to share it with relatives and friends. For the Yanomamö, having agriculture and hunting abilities are perceived as measures of success by females. This, therefore, attracts the females as it is a good indicator that they will be well provided for and that the male would have good genes. From the male's perspective this increases his reproduction output as more access to females is gained. Hence, giving food away as gifts did not necessarily make sense for Yanomamö men, but the Yanomamö people still relied on reciprocal altruism. How reciprocal altruism is manifested in different cultures to some extent revolves around the nature of economic factors operating. It still makes sense to cooperate.

## Box 17.2

### Nash's Game Theory

**Game Theory** is used to explain how people make decisions without the need for Theory of Mind (ToM). John Nash (1950a,b,c; 1951 and 1953) introduced this as a mathematical solution to predicting the decision strategies that people adopt. It has been applied to animal, including human, behaviour as a means of understanding reciprocal altruism, and one example of how to test its application is the prisoner's dilemma problem. This basically goes as follows: if two suspects committing crime together are caught and held in two separate interrogation rooms, and promised freedom if they implicate the other who would then receive a harsher sentence, what would they do? One possible outcome is that if neither implicates the other then they both receive light sentences. Game Theory uses specific terminology such as cooperation and defection. Hence, the question is do they cooperate or defect? The payoff each individual gets depends on whether they cooperate or defect. 'T' represents the temptation to defect; 'R' the reward for cooperation; 'P' the punishment both receive for defecting and 'S' the 'sucker's payoff' where one defects and the other cooperates. In the case of the suspects, it pays to defect; hence, if there is a one-off decision then defecting is the optimal decision. The problem in real-life situations is that it is difficult to know for certain that the encounter is a singular one. If there are many encounters it makes sense to cooperate as both individuals gain rewards and benefits. This is in fact what happens in real life – most individuals cooperate most of the time (Rapoport and Chummah 1965), meaning that even when it does not make any sense to cooperate people do. To explain this, it is important to point out that the prisoner's dilemma does not reflect real-life interactions with other people on a daily basis. We generally have many encounters with the same people or could potentially meet the same individual in the future which in Game Theory language is known as iterated prisoner's dilemma. An example of where we could potentially meet the same individual is a restaurant scenario: if you fail to give the waiter a tip, this will be remembered so that the next encounter with the same waiter might lead to a tit-for-tat approach where you receive poor service or are left waiting. Therefore a co-operative strategy is best (Axelrod and Hamilton 1981) and this was realised by our hominid ancestors who were aware that there are no come backs for cooperating with others but there are repercussions for defecting. According to Maynard-Smith (1974) this is an evolutionary stable strategy. Furthermore, Axelrod (1984) pointed out that it is 'nice' to be first to cooperate as it encourages further cooperation; defection encourages a retaliatory response so that defection follows on from a previous defection. The situation can be righted by providing a cooperation response – a previous defection can be forgiven if cooperation is the current response. Price, Cosmides and Tooby (2002) viewed the detection of non-cooperators or free-riders as an evolved mechanism deriving from cooperation, where punishment is the consequence of defection. Wilson (1975) supposed that: '**Xenophobia** (i.e. dislike or prejudice against people from other countries) becomes a political virtue. The treatment of non-conformists within the group grows harsher. History is replete with the escalation of this process to the point that the society breaks down or goes to war. No nation has been completely immune' (p.290).

The question is do humans need to have state controlled rules and laws in order to prevent some individuals in society from behaving badly? Some people subscribe to the view that it is part of human nature that we will gravitate towards moral codes without state intervention – this is generally the view held by anarchists (i.e. people who believe laws are unnecessary). The views of those who subscribe to anarchy presume that people will gravitate to a harmonious social order and that it is the state's intervention that leads to problems. This is in contrast to the view of Thomas Hobbes (1588–1679) who argued that the natural human state is one of selfish ruthless conflict, which is why state intervention is necessary – as a tool for curbing these tendencies. Hobbes (1651) subscribed to the view that due to our natural selfish tendencies, human life is likely to be short and brutish. Nayef Al-Rodham (2008) argued in his theory of 'Emotional Amoral Egoism' that human behaviour is guided by emotional self-interest arising out of 'genetically coded survival instincts' that have become 'modified by the totality of our environment and expressed as neurochemically-mediated emotions and actions' (p.16). In other words, like Hobbes, he sees our behaviour as resembling the early hominids known to have behaved selfishly and out of self-interest as a means of aiding their survival. It is as a consequence of this that some kind of social order (relying on cooperation) was required to encourage us to live together in a conformist and 'harmonious' way.

This begs the question of whether humans ultimately make laws to create social order because:

- they are selfish but at the same time realise that through cooperation they can benefit themselves optimally;
- they are moral beings and recognise fair play and free-riders, and so have laws as a measure of controlling these non-conformists;
- through cooperation and reciprocal altruism as adaptations to challenging environmental conditions, humans evolved a series of 'moral modules' used as a foundation for the establishment of law and punishment.

What can be said is that most individuals behave morally and obey socially defined rules and laws (a nature–nurture approach). There are, however, a few individuals who, for whatever reason, fail to cooperate with other members of their society. In the second supposition, law is considered to have arisen out of morality. This has strong links with altruism and cooperation discussed above but also with religion. The fact that religion considers some behaviours to be immoral in common with the legal notion of crimes of *mala in se* is interesting and worth exploring further.

## Laws arise out of morality

When human laws are considered superficially, it appears that they arise out of human morality and indeed in Chapter 1 there was discussion of the relationship between laws and religion. Furthermore in Chapter 1, behaviours labelled as deviant, antisocial, immoral and criminal, or any combination of these, were considered in the light of society's perception of what is appropriate behaviour counterbalanced by how the law should intervene to exert control over individuals exhibiting inappropriate behaviour (see also Chapter 16). What becomes apparent immediately is that some behaviour is considered to be more immoral than others – especially *mala in se* crimes that contravene the human moral code. It is difficult to ascertain whether religion preceded laws but what can be assumed is that some form of social order pre-existed religion. What can also be assumed is that written laws pre-existed many religions practised today such as the articles by King Ur-Nammu and the code of Lipit-Istar governing the Sumerians in the twenty-first and twentieth centuries BC. An interesting question is whether morality pre-existed law and possibly religion. We can speculate to a large extent and base our response on what evolutionary psychology has to say about how humans evolved brain mechanisms for processing moral decisions.

An interesting point of view was proposed by Ruse and Wilson in 1985, who suggested that we are born with innate dispositions (i.e. we are not an empty blank slate known as *tabulae rasae*) which are shaped by our genes. Ultimately our compliment of genes is designed to increase our inclusive fitness (see Box 17.1) – in other words, the proportion of our genes passed on to future generations demonstrating reproductive success. With this in mind, we can see, for example, that inbreeding would not be a good reproductive strategy as it suppresses the viability of offspring. Incest therefore does not make sense genetically, which is why Ruse and Wilson (1985) have argued we have specific **epigenetic rules** (i.e. channelled learning due to genetic constraints – see Workman and Reader 2014) that make us unlikely to develop incestuous relationships. These epigenetic rules are gene-driven and influence behaviour in tandem with our environmental interactions. Ruse and Wilson also argued that epigenetic rules, such as the avoidance of incestuous relationships, are there to increase long-term inclusive fitness and decrease illicit behaviours. Epigenetic rules, they argued, will also ensure that morally correct behaviour is followed as long as it increases inclusive fitness, which might explain why incest is considered by many cultures to be an immoral act.

Evolutionary psychologist Denis Krebs (1998) expanded on these views by suggesting that the evolution of morality derived from three pathways:

1    reciprocity that led to altruism;
2    devotion;
3    deference to authority.

As mentioned in the previous section, reciprocal altruism played an important role in the development of law and the detection of cheats. Reciprocity and cooperation in the early hominids together helped create a culture of sharing with and helping others. At the same time it helped cultivate a sense of injustice towards individuals who took advantage of what was on offer without reciprocating (i.e. the defectors). This can be seen in other great apes who like humans also take retribution on defectors (Rossano 2003). In the case of devotion, Krebs explained that males, just like females, would form strong bonds to their partner as a way of ensuring their paternity. Out of these strong bonds devotion to their partner developed. Strong bonds and devotion, leading to relationship longevity, are mechanisms that help to increase the likelihood of passing one's genes to offspring and offspring survival. Krebs (1998) asked the important question of why we accept the Ten Commandments or other religious scripture. His response to this question is that in modern day society we embrace institutions, such as law and religion, as a replacement of the 'alpha male'. According to Krebs early hominids had a system of social hierarchy where there were dominant hominids (i.e. alpha males) to whom others showed deference. Showing deference, Kreb's argued was a way of surviving, because to challenge an individual would have involved fighting and possible death through wounding. That is not to say that the dominant males in our hominid past never challenged one another but that it made more sense not to. Reciprocity, devotion and defence have influenced the development of laws but there also appears to be an underlying moral default mechanism that is reliant on our ability to feel emotions which will be considered next.

### Moral decision making and emotion

When we make decisions about what is moral or immoral behaviour, we often feel specific types of emotion such as pride or disgust respectively. However, it is empathy and having a ToM, as discussed in Chapter 4, that underlies moral development. Hoffman (1982) claimed, for example, that when another baby cries, the pain shown in the face of the crying baby elicits an empathic distress response in the non-crying baby who finds the painful facial expressions stressful. In this study babies definitely experienced stress. This was demonstrated in Radke-Yarrow and Zahn-Waxler's (1986) research when babies attached to equipment measuring their stress levels responded negatively to pictures of faces portraying expressions of pain were shown to them. Thus happy faces were found to be pleasurable, while expressions depicting pain elicited stress. This suggested to Radke-Yarrow and Zahn-Waxler that the development of moral universals begins at a very young age. Moral universals, however, still fail to account for cross-cultural variations, such as in India where the cow is a sacred animal and its consumption would be regarded as morally wrong. *Mala in se* crimes as discussed in Chapters 1 and 2, however, are considered to be morally wrong cross-culturally. When someone commits an immoral act, the associated emotion is one of anger or disgust (Wright 1994), which changes to embarrassment, shame or guilt if we commit the immoral act ourselves. Hence, when we make decisions about our own and other people's immoral behaviours different emotions are activated. As argued in Chapter 4, however, it is the emotion of empathy which helps regulate behaviours that are guided by moral judgement. This appears to be deficient in psychopaths, which enables them to commit *mala in se* crimes (see Chapter 7).

Emotions of anger and disgust are not limited to *mala in se* crimes. Individuals experience these emotions to behaviours that they feel are immoral but do not know why they are. For example, Haidt, Koller and Dias (1993) introduced the term moral illusions to explain circumstances that cause anger or disgust without really understanding why they do – they know they are immoral but find it difficult to ascertain exactly what it is about the behaviour that causes offence. A good example of a moral illusion is Gunther von Hagens' 'Bodyworlds' exhibition which toured across Europe during the late 1990s. Corpses preserved using a plastic substance enabled him to stage the bodies in particular postures with areas that were dissected so as to show internal organs of particular interest. Of course the permission of the deceased to display their bodies in this way was granted prior to death so that he was not acting illegally. Many thought this was morally wrong but could not find Gunther von Hagens accountable. Many found the whole concept and exhibition disgusting or they felt outraged – emotions accompanying what they perceived as immoral behaviour by Gunther von Hagens. Understanding the important connection between moral decision making and emotions has been investigated by Greene and Haidt (2002) using fMRI scans in relation to how the brain operates which we will discuss next.

### Moral decision making and the brain

The idea of moral universals has been considered in the light of research considering moral dilemmas and the areas of the brain that become activated when specific moral-linked decisions are being made. From the findings of such research it would appear that our brains have evolved to encourage moral behaviour. In a study by Greene, Sommerville, Nystrom, Darley and Cohen (2001) the areas of the brain that became activated during moral decision-making were investigated using fMRI scanning. They looked at the areas of the brain activated when two types of moral decisions were made: moral-personal and moral-impersonal (see Box 17.3 and Plate 17.1).

## Box 17.3

### Moral-personal and moral-impersonal decision making

Hauser, Cushman, Young, Kang-Xing and Mikhail (2007) used moral dilemmas involving a runaway train that is likely to kill people if something is not done to change its course. Participants are presented with pictures depicting the different scenarios.

1   In one case dilemma the train driver faints but Denise is a passenger who can make a decision about which course the now runaway train will take. She could veer the train off into a left-hand track thereby killing one person who is on this track or she could let the train continue its course resulting in the death of five people on the track. The key question asked by Hauser *et al.* is, 'Is it morally permissible for Denise to turn the train?'

2   In another scenario Frank is standing on a footbridge towering over the tracks. The runaway train is on route to killing five people on the track but he could stop it by throwing something heavy from the footbridge. The only thing available is a fat man who is standing with him on the footbridge. 'Is it morally permissible for Frank to shove the man?'

3   In the case of Ned who is walking near the track, the death of five people can be avoided if he diverts the train onto a side track by throwing a switch. There is a man on the side track. Ned can switch the train to the side track in which case one man will die or he can leave the train to continue its route thereby killing five people. 'Is it morally permissible for Ned to throw the switch?'

4   In the final scenario, Oscar is also standing next to a switch which he can throw in order to divert the train away from five people thereby saving their lives. On the side track is an object which will slow the train down; however, behind the object is a man who would be hit by the runaway train. 'Is it morally permissible for Oscar to throw the switch?'

Hauser, Young and Cushman (2008) presented the scenarios in Box 17.3 to participants who then decided if it was morally permissible to do the actions suggested in the dilemmas. They found that in the case of Denise in scenario 1, 85 per cent decided that it was morally permissible to veer the train to the left track. In the case of Frank in scenario 2, 12 per cent considered it morally permissible to throw the fat man off the footbridge. In scenario 3, 56 per cent decided it was morally permissible for Ned to throw the switch directing the train into a side track killing one man. In the fourth scenario, 72 per cent considered it morally permissible for Oscar to do the same action as Ned, also killing one man but in this case the man was behind a heavy object. These findings beg the question of why there were differences across the four moral dilemmas. The difference between Denise and Frank are reasonably obvious, in that Denise saves five people at the expense of one and is making a decision that is a step removed from personal contact. In the case of Frank's action he too could save five people at the expense of one man, but the action involves personal contact. The situation between Ned and Oscar again is very similar

*Plate 17.1* A moral dilemma
Adapted from Hauser 2008

in that they both can save five people at the expense of one, but in Ned's case there appears to be more personal contact unlike Oscar's situation where the man is a step removed from personal contact.

When people make decisions of moral permissiveness they rely on a rule which they find difficult to define, but the rule is known as the principle of double effect. This means that it is permissible to cause harm to the few for the greater good of the many. In effect it is permitted to kill one person, if it is a consequence of an action that saves others, which explains why Frank's action is not morally permissible. In Frank's dilemma a new threat is introduced which people judge more harshly than a threat which is being redirected, as is the case of the runaway train. To confound this further, people find decisions involving personal contact even more threatening such as the action of physically touching the fat man in order to throw him off the footbridge. This particular scenario has three interacting principles:

- double effect;
- introduction of a new threat;
- increased personal contact.

It is intriguing that Greene *et al.* (2001) found a difference in brain activation for moral-personal and moral-impersonal decisions. Using fMRI scans they were able to observe areas of the brain activated during displays of emotion.

More specifically they pinpointed areas of the brain that were increasingly more active during moral-personal than moral-impersonal decision making (i.e. the medial frontal gyrus, the posterior cingulate gyrus and the angular gyrus). This suggests that there is more emotion spent when making moral-personal decisions than moral-impersonal ones. This makes perfect sense if we consider how much more difficult it would have been for early hominids to make moral-personal decisions concerning those they know and live in close proximity to. Deciding on whether to come to the aid of a friend who is pursued by aggressors from another tribe, for example, could be a serious dilemma and cause much angst given that providing assistance could result in one's own death but refusing aid could contribute towards the death of the friend. Again refusal of aid to a stranger from a different tribe will not be as emotionally challenging a moral decision to make because there is more distance between the two individuals. It would appear that the brain has evolved different mechanisms for moral-personal decisions, suggesting that humans evolved to acquire the ability to be moral (a nature approach). In the next section, the third speculation makes a connection between socialisation or learning to behave morally with the development of laws. This approach presents a circular argument where morality has helped to develop laws which are followed by ensuring the next generation are socialised into being moral and law abiding citizens – perpetuating the cycle of socialisation (a nurture approach).

## Socialisation drives law abiding behaviour but can also cause criminality

One of the important roles of the family is to teach children right from wrong by socialising them to accept and conform to society's norms, mores, values and rules. Norms, mores, values and rules of society, as we have seen in Chapters 1 and 2, stipulate how citizens in society should behave and what happens to individuals who reject these stipulations (i.e. those who break the law are punished by the different branches of the criminal justice system – see Chapters 1, 2 and 16). Behaviours considered to be morally correct are stipulated in law, and behaviours that contravene the law are perceived as criminal, deviant, antisocial, immoral or a combination of these. Of interest to this discussion, however, is the cross-over between behaviour considered as immoral and that which breaks the law.

The importance of socialising children to accept what is morally correct behaviour and to obey the law has been encapsulated in Bronfenbrenner's **Developmental Ecosystem Model**. He interlinked the relationships between child and the microsystem; child and the exosystem and child and the macrosystem (see Figure 4.1), and stressed the importance different informal and formal socialising agents cast across these systems. In the case of the microsystem, the first informal socialising agents are the parents (or the carers) – discussed next.

### Parents

As Bowlby outlined in his Attachment Theory, the infant forms a bond with parents (or carer substitute) that become his or her first point of contact. Not only do parents provide subsistence, security and love, they act as mentors and guide their children directly (i.e. through overt teaching) and indirectly (i.e. through acting as role models) to develop moral understanding – understanding the difference between right and wrong (see Chapter 4).

It could be argued in points one and two that we have an innate predisposition, courtesy of our hominid ancestors, to be moral beings but despite the hardware for developing moral understanding, it requires adjustment through learning and nurturance. In Chapter 4, moral development was discussed using Kohlberg's levels and stages approach to understanding the acquisition of moral reasoning skills. Kohlberg argued that punishment schedules in the early stages of the pre-conventional level helped children learn what acceptable behaviour is. Essentially young children are considered to be egocentric and so assimilate moral rules through the avoidance of punishment and unpleasant personal consequences of their actions (i.e. receiving a good telling off). Personal consequences of their actions that are considered to be pleasant become reinforced and therefore are repeated (i.e. being praised for sharing their toys).

Children in the early stages of development refer to their parents (or carers) for guidance but if this guidance is not forthcoming then their socio-emotional understanding might be compromised. Much research has compared the parents' level of moral understanding and reasoning with their children's acquisition of morality. Researchers have considered the ways parents resolve conflict – as shown in Kochanska, Aksan and Nichols' (2003) findings of a relationship between a negative mother and a non-compliant child. Hoffman (1975) demonstrated that the more communication there is between parents and their child about feelings and the consequences their actions have for others, then the more pro-social behaviour the child will show towards those experiencing distress (Zahn-Waxler, Radke-Yarrow and King 1979). Hughes, Deater-Deckard and Cutting (1999) showed the importance of a warm relationship between mother and child for the development of ToM (see Chapter 4). This link was further supported by Kochanska et al.'s work on mother and child interpersonal skills. Kochanska et al. (2003) found that if the mother's approach was to use polite guidance then this is what was seen in the child's interactions with his/her peers. Harsh discipline has also been associated with a child's aggressive behaviour towards children at kindergarten (Weiss, Dodge, Bates and Pettit 1992).

Baumrind (1972) also found connections between the nurturing approach used by parents and their children's level of maturity. The best parents were warm, affectionate, had clear boundaries and provided rewards for responsible behaviour. Eisenberg and McNally (1993) further showed that parents who are warm, sensitive and sympathetic have children who are more likely to show concern for others and demonstrate pro-social behaviour towards those in distress. What is more, the opposite is true where punitive parenting disrupts the development of empathy and sympathy (Eisenberg, Fabes, Shepard, Murphy et al. 1998).

Having punitive parents can cause problems for moral development, but as we have seen in Chapter 4, equally as problematic are rejecting parents. Children who are rejected fail to have an effective role model from which to imitate. Children under these circumstances receive poor guidance on how to manage their emotions such as anger and fear, and when they should feel shame and guilt. It is the experience of guilt and shame that are important for moral understanding, and without effective instruction from rejecting, neglecting and abusing parents there will be deficits in these emotions. Rejected children will learn to process information differently especially social information as was found by Nasby, Hayden and DePaulo (1979). Nasby et al. (1979) coined the term hostile attributional bias where people's intentions are interpreted as having negative intent despite it being to the contrary (see Chapter 4). Rejected children were found to use hostile attributional bias more often than secure children (Waldman 1988).

Patterns of moral reasoning between parents and their children therefore indicate that parents with good moral reasoning and who are supportive had children with good moral reasoning skills (Janssens and Deković 1997; Palmer and Hollin 2000; Speicher 1994; Walker and Taylor 1991). These studies suggested an **intergenerational cycle** of socialisation quality relating to the way morality is acquired. If a child, for example, is rejected or maltreated by parents, it is likely that they will have received poor quality socialisation (including moral guidance of what is right and wrong). This cycle of poor socialisation is likely to continue as was found by Dixon, Browne and Hamilton-Giachritsis (2005). Children in their study who were abused had parents who had an abusive childhood. They acknowledged other **risk factors** too and argued that parenting styles must be key elements in the continuation of poor socialisation skills. Palmer (2000) commented on how good supervision of young children leads to parent–child bonds which enable their children to internalise parental values and the norms of society. In later years this supervision can be reduced as the child, now an adolescent, has internalised the values and norms of society. This works well in non-criminal families but becomes problematic when the supervision is absent, the parent–child bond fails to form, and a criminal subcultural ideology envelops the child.

The link between moral development and risk of criminality is an important one. Researchers have considered the outcome of various risk factors on the likelihood of delinquency. Farrington's (1990b) six childhood risk factor categories, for example, highlight how these can influence a child's behaviour. The six categories include troublesome behaviour and dishonesty, impulsiveness and low intelligence as well as having a convicted family member, poor child rearing and economic deprivation. The notion of high-risk factors for criminality as discussed in Chapter 4 was taken further by Rutter and

Giller's (1983) five adverse factor approach for delinquency, which showed that any combination of these will impact on the child's behaviour. This becomes confounded by protective and vulnerability factors. In the case of **protective factors**, the impact of risk factors can be minimalised or cancelled out. Vulnerability factors, however, leave the child more open to the damaging effects of risk factors. Resilience to the effects of risk factors can be increased if the number of protective factors outweighs the number of risk and vulnerability factors.

Risk factors such as poor child rearing and a convicted family member have been shown to influence moral reasoning. The link between the level and nature of moral reasoning of parents and children is an important one. Criminal parents have criminal ideals and therefore will socialise their children according to the values that they hold. Furthermore, they are their children's role models. Numerous studies have demonstrated a link between criminal parents having delinquent children (Glueck and Glueck 1950; McCord 1979; West 1982). According to Robins (1974) delinquent parents are likely to nurture delinquent children, and this socialisation process continues across generations leaving a legacy of aggressive offspring (Huesmann 1988; Widom 1989b). It would be a fair assumption to make that criminal parents who disagree with the law are less likely to abide by it and more likely to refuse to teach their children the values of the law. We must be conservative, however, when making connections between attitudes and behaviour as they are not always consistent (Eagly and Chaiken 1993). There are likely to be other factors such as the constraints of a situation, emotions, motives and consequences of action for self and others, which will also conspire to drive behaviour (Ajzen 1991). Also important here, is the interaction between risk factors and protective factors for criminality (see Chapter 4).

A different take on Kohlberg's Theory of Moral Development, however, has been applied to the mentality of criminal families which they use as a template to socialise their children. Palmer (2003, p.100) outlined five stages of moral reasoning for the offender:

> offending is justified . . . (1) if punishment can be avoided . . . (2) if the rewards are judged to outweigh the risks. . . . (3) if it maintains relationships . . . (4) if it is in the interests of society or is sanctioned by a social institution . . . (5) if it maintains basic human rights or furthers social justice.

Stages (4) and (5) can be perceived in the light of offending for the benefit of society. Particular rules and laws are perceived as damaging to society and its citizens and therefore needs to be changed – hence the need for protest for which an arrested protestor receives a public order offence. This can be seen to link with Kohlberg's post-conventional level of morality where the law at times comes into conflict with specific moral principles. In the case of stages (1) and (2), the individual is operating at an egocentric level of thought and justifies criminal activity by being told it is okay, and that the evasion of punishment makes it acceptable. Although the individual in stage (3) might be trying to help a friend, he/she is doing so at the expense of someone else who ultimately is victimised. Stages (1), (2) and (3) certainly can be the result of poor moral socialisation, whereas stages (4) and (5) are debatable. Parents are not the only influential informal socialising agents; peers also play a major role. If they are delinquent they too can be classified as a risk factor for criminality – considered next.

### Peers

Piaget (1932) emphasised the importance peers play in facilitating moral development through social perspective taking with other children, particularly during play. In other words, children learn to be less egocentric through the realisation that other children have different points of view to their own (see Chapter 4). It is through social interactions with peers that moral reasoning develops further. Peer popularity gained through being a member of a club and having a leadership role, for example, can relate to the stage of moral reasoning acquired (Keasey 1971; Sedikides 1989). It is peer interaction, however, that plays a dominant role here (Sedikides 1989). Peers have been found to have a greater impact on moral reasoning than parental interactions (Kruger 1992). Kruger (1992) found that adult–child or peer–peer pairings had a different impact on discussions about moral issues: the peer–peer pairings initiated more active reasoning about moral issues than adult–child pairings where the child remained passive and deferential. It is possible, argued Palmer (2003b), that the balance of power between adult and child favours the adult whereas peers perceive themselves more equally matched. Another explanation could be that peers perceive other peers as more credible models to emulate and will be more inclined to do so even if there is initial disagreement – and this is even more so if they perceive the other peer as having higher social status (Taylor and Walker 1997).

According to Harris (1995), peers are very influential when considering social behaviour and attitudes. In her **Group Socialisation Theory** (GST) children look for children and groups to join that they perceive as similar to themselves. Members of these groups will behave in a similar way and expect other members to do the same. According to Harris (1998), group norms operate on a majority-rules rule basis where newcomers will have to conform to the majority behaviour of the group – it is a matter of change to be the same as other group members or find an alternative group to join. This is the mechanism by which children socialise each other and modify their personality characteristics to conform to the group – including attitudes, behaviours and dress sense. There are penalties for not conforming to the group's norms, such as being ostracised (see Chapter 4). Peer influence on moral reasoning is paramount when contextualised within deviant or delinquent groups where the majority-rule would be to accept a criminal morality, similar possibly to that outlined by Palmer (2003b) in the previous section on how parents influence moral development. The contribution of socialisation clearly has an important role in the relationship between morality and the law which is explored further in the next section.

### Summary of the relationship between morality and law

Moral reasoning and morality are important facets in law; after all, laws, it would appear, are founded on moral understanding of what is right and wrong (see Chapters 1 and 2). Referring back to the initial premise that 'socialisation drives law abiding behaviour but can also cause criminality', if we assume that law is founded primarily on moral issues (for which there is much evidence to show that crimes considered to be *mala in se* contravene the human moral code), and morality is taught through socialisation, then an individual who is socialised by criminal parents with criminal ideals that contravene the law, is highly likely to acquire a criminal mentality (Cohen 1955; Matza 1964; Sutherland 1939; Willmott 1966; Wolfgang and Ferracuti 1967). This criminal mentality rejects the norms and values of the dominant culture which often causes conflict with the law. Hence individuals with a criminal mind-set have different moral values to those encapsulated in the dominant culture (see Chapter 10). They therefore follow their own deviant moral values that have been instilled through socialisation by criminal parents. Citizens of a society, in exchange for protection from potential harm, will accept the social contract to obey the law and all the social norms, values, mores and rules. Individuals within a society who refuse to obey the law are also refuting the stipulations of the social contract, and it is this behaviour and attitude that is driven by inappropriate socialisation espousing deviant social norms, values, mores and rules. The fact that these individuals are rejecting the norms, values, mores and rules of dominant culture, which enable them to break the law, is in part a consequence of the law itself. If the law were based on a different set of 'moral values' such as the criminal mentality, then individuals subscribing to these values would not be breaking the law. Thus it could be argued that the law is driving criminality by virtue of its definition (supporting the first and second speculations). If the current definition did not exist then 'criminals' would not be breaking the law and nor would they be considered as having a criminal mentality developed through deviant socialisation processes. The law therefore drives criminality because its definition enables criminality to exist.

## Summary

- 'Law drives criminality' was explored using three different speculations: criminality occurs out of the way we define crime; laws arise out of morality and socialisation drives law abiding behaviour but can also cause criminality. The first explored our prehistoric ancestry and how laws became defined as a consequence of cooperation and reciprocal altruism. The link between cooperation and reciprocal altruism for the development of rules and 'law' is an important one that might have had the purpose of identifying **free-riders** who were non-reciprocators living among reciprocators (i.e. expecting to take from reciprocators without giving anything in return).

- The relationship between morality and law was explored from the perspective of laws having arisen as a duty to protect citizens from individuals failing to abide by the norms and values of society – in effect breaking the social contract. These norms and values guiding what is considered to be appropriate behaviour are rooted in morals that are driven by epigenetic rules. Moral decision making is closely linked with emotion, especially empathy, and there is evidence supporting the view that moral decision making is processed differently in the brain depending on whether a moral-personal or moral-impersonal decision has to be made.

- In the case of 'socialisation drives law abiding behaviour but can also cause criminality', it was argued that individuals who contravene the law have attitudes and lifestyles that deviate from mainstream culture. These deviant attitudes and lifestyles originate from inappropriate socialisation by parents and peers. Despite having an innate predisposition to be moral beings, it is through learning and nurturance that morality develops further. Research suggests a link between parents' and their children's level of socio-emotional understanding and moral reasoning. Rejecting parents, for example, can influence the way their children perceive others known as hostile attributional bias. Hence children who have been rejected perceive others as having negative intent. Risk factors play an important role in the socialisation of criminality. Many risk factors have been identified but of relevance here are those influencing the upbringing of the child. If children are rejected, neglected or abused by their parents, they have no appropriate role models or someone to teach them right from wrong. Furthermore, if they have criminal parents, then they are likely to receive inappropriate socialisation which can enable delinquent behaviour. Protective factors, if present, can negate the potentially disastrous effects of risk factors and increase resilience from adopting criminal ways.

- The first approach that 'criminality occurs out of the way we define crime' errs towards a nature–nurture evaluation; the second, a nature evaluation; and the third, a nurture evaluation.

## Questions for discussion

1 Why did laws develop in the first place?
2 In what ways can inappropriate socialisation lead to criminality?
3 Why is it the norm to be moral?

# Concluding comments

A main aim of this text has been to understand crime and criminality using a multidisciplinary approach. This was undertaken by presenting research evidence from relevant disciplines such as psychology, criminology, sociology and law. The presentation of multidisciplinary theory and research (Chapters 3, 4 and 5) provided a basis for understanding crime and criminality using a nature–nurture framework. It is through this nature–nurture framework that different types of offender were discussed (Chapters 6, 7, 8, 9, 10, 11 and 12). Furthermore an attempt was made to ascertain which of the two assumptions (i.e. **nature drives nurture** or **nurture drives nature**) is more applicable to understanding criminality. In Chapter 16 this was further debated in relation to the 'Big 5' legal concepts, where the contention is that these legal concepts influence how offenders should be treated by the criminal justice system. Attitudes towards offenders, especially on issues of retribution, punishment and **public safety**, it was argued, depend strongly on beliefs of whether the offender can be reformed and desist from further criminal behaviour. Therefore the exercise of discussing different explanations of criminality in relation to offenders helps us understand the attitudes held by society towards those who contravene the law. In Chapter 17 an understanding of how law drives criminality was also considered using three speculative interpretations (that are not necessarily independent of each other). These three speculations underlie how laws might have developed and the purpose they served. They also offered an understanding of why some individuals fail to conform, and instead continue to lead a lifestyle in conflict with the law.

## Where do laws come from?

Chapter 17 explored the speculation that criminality results from the way in which crime is defined – which can be traced back to the twenty-first and twentieth centuries BC. Why our ancestors developed laws is telling and can, arguably, be best accounted for using an evolutionary analysis (relying on information from the disciplines of evolution and evolutionary psychology). It appears that in order to survive under extreme environmental conditions, humans needed to live together altruistically. However, there were always individuals (**free-riders**) who took advantage of this arrangement which is why laws were developed – to make it difficult for such individuals to live non-cooperatively. Those who failed to abide by these laws forfeited their rights of freedom or were punished in some way. The development of such laws can be seen in modern day Stone Age cultures such as the !Kung San and the Yanomamö.

The second speculation that laws arise out of morality leads to definitions of criminality from religious perspectives. Indeed there is a strong connection between laws and religion. Religion over the centuries has provided a doctrine of how we should live our lives – what is considered to be immoral, deviant and antisocial, and therefore a transgression against religious belief. In Chapters 1 and 2 the interface between the disciplines of law and religious studies was explored by considering the history of religious doctrine in the development of laws cross-culturally; using the concepts of *mala in se* and *mala prohibita*. Crimes considered to be *mala in se* contravene the human moral code. These crimes cause harm to others and are identified as serious acts warranting severe punishment. Interestingly such crimes are perceived as abhorrent cross-culturally. This implies that for most humans, causing harm to others is not the natural course of action. For some individuals, however, this is the natural course of action, and it is for the purpose of identifying and in some way punishing these individuals that laws based on moral principles were developed. The development of moral behaviour has been researched from both a nature and nurture perspective. The viewpoint that we have channelled learning as a consequence of genetic constraints, known as epigenetic rules, is an example of a nature perspective. A good example of an epigenetic rule is the avoidance of incestuous relationships. As epigenetic rules are gene governed, it is not surprising then that incestuous relationships are to be avoided given the possibility of pregnancy and of bringing together deleterious genes; consequently, in many cultures incest is immoral and illegal. Other evolutionary concepts offer an explanation of morality and its connection with the development of laws, including Denis Krebs' three pathways of reciprocity (leading to altruism), devotion and deference to authority. As previously discussed, these contribute towards detecting uncooperative individuals, strong bonding and survival respectively.

Closely involved with morality is the development of specific types of emotion and a Theory of Mind (this relationship was discussed in Chapter 4 and further in Chapter 16). We seem to be wired with the ability to 'feel' another person's pain and, as a consequence, 'are able to' empathise with others who have been wronged in times of travesty. Babies can even do this, which suggests it occurs early in development. It is through the process of socialisation that the understanding of what is morally right and wrong is learned, but emotions such as empathy, disgust, anger and pride are necessarily for this to work effectively. Research has also shown that our brains have evolved to support moral behaviour. fMRI scans reveal that specific areas of the brain become active during moral decision-making. Interestingly, fMRI scans also reveal that psychopaths in particular have structural and functional brain anomalies including areas of the brain concerned with emotion processing (see Chapters 3, 5, 6, 7 and 8).

The third speculation that socialisation drives law abiding behaviour but can also cause criminality is very much concerned with behaviour considered to be immoral and which breaks the law (see Chapters 1 and 2). What constitutes immoral behaviour is instilled through socialisation, not just by our parents, family and peers but by institutions such as school, church and the community (see Chapter 4). This understanding is very much a nurture oriented one as socialisation contains information about how we should behave and what behaviour is deemed as socially appropriate by our society. It therefore involves teaching children to conform to the mores, beliefs and values stipulated by society. It is a method of ensuring that, from one generation to the next, citizens know how to behave appropriately in society and understand what is expected of them. Antisocial, immoral and criminal behaviour are considered inappropriate, and if pushed to their extreme are punishable either by the legal system (as is the case for criminal behaviour – see Chapter 16) or by others shunning the individuals concerned (as would be the case for an individual who behaves in a crass way, for instance). If, for some reason, the socialisation process goes awry, then an individual's mores, values and beliefs are likely to be in conflict with society. As outlined by Palmer in Chapter 17, offenders could have a different type of moral reasoning based on the experience of socialisation by parents who do not conform to society's values. The contribution of socialisation to criminality lies with the way in which morality is developed. Without appropriate guidance of what is morally right and wrong, a child has an increased likelihood of developing a criminal lifestyle. Criminal lifestyles will have inherent rewards that further motivate offenders to continue with a life of crime. Longevity of offending is often the result of an extended period of such rewards. Therefore individuals socialised by criminal parents will acquire a criminal mentality that rejects the norms, values, mores and rules of society which consequentially leads to conflict with the law. If a criminal mentality were the norm, then it could be argued that criminals would not be breaking the law – hence socialisation can also be the cause of criminality.

In Chapter 17, the 'how' of why laws were developed was entertained using three speculations, whereas in Chapters 1 and 2 ways of defining crime and criminality were introduced from the disciplines of law, sociology, criminology and psychology. In particular four different approaches to understanding how crime can be considered and criminality examined, provided by sociology and criminology, offered an alternative perspective to the legal definition. By using social constructionism as a method of understanding how we define crime and the criminal, the four approaches developed by sociologists and criminologists alike were: consensus, conflict and critical criminology, symbolic interactionism and labelling and **discourse analysis** (also referred to as a contemporary approach). While the consensus approach offered the viewpoint of a harmonious functioning society, conflict and critical criminology are the antithesis believing society to be fragmented with different factions disputing power and control. Symbolic interactionism or labelling examined the social processes involved with becoming a criminal and discourse analysis (or the contemporary approach) provided a means of understanding crime and criminality through what is said and written and how this influence people's attitude and consequently their behaviour. A psychological perspective is more concerned with what constitutes criminal behaviour and the motivations for it. Antecedents of criminality from a psychological perspective help to provide an analysis of why an individual behaves the way they do and what spurs them on to commit specific types of crime. Throughout this textbook, many different theories and research findings have been entertained from a multitude of disciplines (see Introduction).

## Problems with the theories

Many theories from a multitude of disciplines have been developed in an attempt to explain why individuals commit crime. These theories tend to be either more social/environmental or more biological/evolutionary oriented. As we have seen, explaining criminality using only one type of theory does not explain all. Individuals become involved in crime for many different reasons (see Chapters 5 and 10). We should bear in mind that one important explanation of such differences is the fact that each individual will have their own personality profile. Given these factors, it is not surprising that there may be more than one approach required for the development of an all-embracing integrated theory of criminality. This would be a difficult feat to accomplish as researchers from different disciplines have their own research dogma and theoretical underpinnings. Furthermore, different types of criminal should not be considered and understood as one generic type. This becomes very clear when reviewing different types of crime and the individuals who commit these crimes. From the literature presented in Chapters 6–12, it is apparent that different types of crime attract different types of individual. Alternatively, it may be suggested that different types of individual feel comfortable committing specific types of crime. In Chapters 5 and 6, white-collar criminals were addressed within the context of cognition and decision making. Here, Cornish and Clarke's work on rational decision-making introduced us to models outlining the decision processes involved in becoming a criminal and continuing a criminal lifestyle. The initial involvement model stipulated the different persuasive factors involved in leading an individual to a life of crime. Many of the factors introduced social/environmental reasons for committing criminal acts but there was acknowledgement of background factors such as psychological, upbringing and social and demographic traits. There is evidence, for example, to suggest a genetic/biological involvement in some psychological traits such as temperament, IQ and cognitive style. This genetic/biological contribution is further amplified by upbringing and other social factors. Cornish and Clarke were acknowledging the complicated nature/nurture interface. Once involved in crime, a set of criminal attitudes (whether already present or developed afterwards) justify the illicit activity that provides the rewards and further reinforces the criminal behaviour.

In Chapters 6–12, the research findings were presented using a multidisciplinary approach to examine these theories in a balanced way. For some types of criminal, such as serial killers (see Chapter 12), more biologically oriented research evidence is available. In the case of delinquents (see Chapter 10), however, research has focused primarily on issues related to family background. Nevertheless, even here there is research suggesting biological causes in serious cases of delinquency such as where a youngster had committed murder. van Goozen and her colleagues studied children with behavioural problems, such as oppositional defiant disorder (ODD) or conduct disorder (CD), both considered to be a pre-requisite condition of adult psychopathy. They found a host of biological differences for children with ODD or CD ranging from heart rate, skin conductance and circulating cortisol (all very much lower in these children than is the norm). This led to the 'fearlessness theory of antisocial behaviour' by Raine in 1993. This means that a lack of fear observed in these children, demonstrated through psychological testing, was a consequence of reduced activity of the autonomic nervous system (which controls heart rate and skin conductance for instance). This, in turn, leads to an increased likelihood of committing certain crimes. Even in the area of delinquency, where there is a large body of literature suggesting that an abusive and rejecting upbringing is a causal factor for juveniles to 'kick off' at society and the people around them, there is confusion concerning the interface between nature and nurture as causal effects (see Chapter 10). Brain damage sustained by physical abuse in childhood has been put forward as a causal influence for psychopathy and extremely antisocial delinquent behaviour. Does this constitute a nature or nurture causal effect? Should we consider structural and functional brain damage incurred in childhood as a factor of nature? Given that this was a consequence of physical abuse experienced in childhood, is this not then in the realm of nurture (a biological change caused by an environmental factor)? Furthermore, would it be correct to say that all criminal psychopaths have been abused or had an unfortunate childhood? Another question we might ask is how do these nature–nurture findings relate to the differential pattern of brain function observed from fMRI scans of criminal psychopaths? The evidence might be taken as suggesting that criminal psychopaths behave in the way they do because of these brain differences, particularly when considering the amygdala-orbitofrontal cortex. Whether they are born with these differences of brain function or have sustained some form of brain damage through violent physical abuse is difficult to determine. Thus there are shades of grey between which factors constitute a nature or nurture explanation. Furthermore, as Karmiloff-Smith (1996, 1998) claims, the path of brain development is influenced by continuous feedback from the environment, and when there is violent physical abuse in that environment then the brain can develop along an 'abnormal' or damaged path. This has to be put into perspective, however, because not all psychopaths have such experiences in childhood, so how can their different fMRI scan findings and behaviour be accounted for? Does psychopathy run in families? And if so does this suggest a genetic link?

Professor James Fallon alluded to criminal psychopaths and serial murderers having different and distinctive PET scans (PET scan activity patterns) from controls, and proposed that this and the possession of the MAOA or 'warrior' gene (see Chapters 3 and 7) predisposes an individual to be violent. This failed, however, to fully account for why Fallon, who had both these features, did not become a violent criminal. He claimed that nurturance makes an additive impact on these high-risk biological predispositions such that good childhood experiences protect the individual from becoming a violent criminal. Fallon's case presents robust evidence for a gene–environment interactionist perspective and supports Karmiloff-Smith's (1996, 1998) assertion of development occurring from interactions between genes, the brain, behaviour and an individual's experience of their environment.

Most crime is committed by men (this is borne out by criminal statistics). Hence most theories of crime tend to be based on male cohorts. The point raised by Karmiloff-Smith can equally be applied to female criminals – implying that those who commit crime might be genetically predisposed to behave violently which develops when environmental factors such as an abusive childhood are thrown into the mix. The Biosocial Theory (see Chapter 9), used to explain female criminality, identifies a combination of sex differences, age-graded developmental processes and cultural influences in a similar vein to Karmiloff-Smith's assertion. Explanations of female criminality came from a variety of disciplines. Disciplines such as sociology, criminology, feminist studies, political science and social psychology largely defended a nurture approach whereas biology/physiology, evolutionary and biological psychology, psychiatry, neuroscience and genetics/biochemistry largely supported a nature–nurture interaction airing more so on the side of nature. In the case of sex offenders (see Chapter 8) different perspectives were used to explain rape and paedophilia. Situational and behavioural perspectives, deriving from psychology and feminist and psychoanalytic approaches, tend to support nurture-based explanations of why individuals commit sexual offences. In contrast, neuroscience-based (such as neurocognitive and neurobiology) and evolutionary approaches tend to support nature-driven explanations. Even here the findings are not straight forward and an interaction between nature and nurture has been proposed in an integrated approach by triangulating these different theories. Treatment interventions derived from these approaches tend to suggest that nothing 'cures' the paedophile but there are methods of controlling their behaviours; a similar outcome can be found for specific types of rapist. This further suggests that changing life circumstances might aid in controlling their behaviour but the addictive element of their condition (e.g. the sexual orientation towards children) might be nature-driven.

Alternatively, dangerous offenders were primarily considered using the mental/behavioural and personality disorder divide. There are primarily two perspectives concerning mental disorders such as schizophrenia – they are either biologically based or socially defined. This is a separate debate not addressed here. The understanding of mental disorders was considered using the Diagnostic and Statistical Manual (DSM-IV-TR and DSM-5). This was also used for our understanding of personality disorders. There is much evidence to suggest that mental disorders like schizophrenia have biological foundations, but interestingly it is offenders with personality disorders (particularly APD) who are more likely to commit dangerous crimes. As discussed previously those with APD who commit violent and dangerous crimes tend to be classified as psychopaths (as they exhibit traits at the extreme end of APD). There are differences in the *modus operandi* of those with schizophrenia (who do commit crime) and criminal psychopaths. Criminals with paranoid schizophrenia tend to use sharp and blunt weapons indicating impulsivity and limited planning unlike criminal psychopaths who plan their crimes and are more likely to obtain guns. Furthermore, most violence committed by criminals with schizophrenia occurs during a psychotic episode suggesting that they often have no *mens rea* (i.e. the intent to commit a criminal act). Criminal psychopaths, alternatively, have both *actus reus* (i.e. the criminal act) and *mens rea*. We could argue, therefore, that criminal psychopaths interpret the world using calculations of how to interact and behave towards others – often devoid of any empathy which makes them 'bad'. Offenders with a mental disorder often have a deluded interpretation of the world based on their psychosis which makes them 'mad'.

## Where does all this leave us in terms of the nature–nurture divide?

Clearly the closer the literature is examined from a multidisciplinary perspective, the more difficult it is to fractionate the level of interaction between nature and nurture (i.e. gene and environment). With the aid of technological developments in scanning techniques, however, it is possible to demonstrate the differences in brain structure and function of criminals, especially violent criminals. Unfortunately this is all scans can tell us. There is no indication of whether the individual was born with these brain anomalies or developed them post birth. Although neuroscientists can 'map' the brain of a criminal, they cannot be certain that these brain anomalies cause an individual to commit criminal acts. Having a gene responsible for impulsive and violent behaviour as is the case of the 'warrior' gene, is easier to detect now with the developments in modern genetic coding – especially since the Human Genome Project. Neurochemistry has also advanced our understanding of how androgens and other hormones affect our behaviour. With careful monitoring and control using organic interventions, the effects of under-or over-production of these hormones can help to regulate certain behaviours. This, with the control of aspects within an individual's immediate environment such as reducing contact with triggers causing violent outbursts, means that nature- and nurture-based solutions can work in tandem to reduce problem behaviour.

It is possible, however, that the continuance of a criminal lifestyle relates to the motivation and drives for committing crime in the first place.

### Nature–nurture of motivation and drives for committing crime

Why serial killers (see Chapter 12), psychopaths (see Chapter 7) and sex offenders (see Chapter 8) are difficult to reform might be linked to innate factors, such as biological, genetic and brain structural, and functional anomalies (all considered to be driven by nature). As we have seen from neuroscience there is evidence that these perpetrators have different brains to the rest of us, both structurally and functionally. In many cases there are clear deficits derived from particular brain structural anomalies which defence attorneys in the US have used as evidence to justify their client's criminal behaviour. It might be argued that nurture-based explanations of these types of criminal are influential only because of there being an initial criminal predisposition (i.e. brought about by way of genes, anomalies of brain structure and brain neurochemistry). There are cases, however, where individuals born with normal brain structure and function later develop 'brain problems' as a consequence of violent abuse during their childhood, which could be used as a potential explanation for their future criminal behaviours. Hence in this case it could be argued that an environmental factor such as abuse is causing structural and functional brain problems leading to criminal behaviour; nurture impacting on nature. Forensic psychology has shown that quite often their motivations for murder and sex offences such as rape and paedophilia are confused with deluded beliefs about their victims. In the case of serial killers, murdering their victims serves a need and desire to dominate and inflict pain on their victims. By controlling the situation in this way, they reinforce their distorted cognition of self-importance. As we have seen in Chapter 12, it is through serial murder that serial killers are motivated to reduce or eliminate any negative thoughts that others might have of them (real or fictional) until the need arises again. Similar issues are found with sex offenders who have a need for controlling their victims and targeting specific groups of people: in the case of paedophiles young vulnerable children. Rapists targeting females often believe that their victims were asking for sex and secretly wanted to be raped – these distorted cognitions often arise from past experiences with the opposite sex. For feminists, the key factor in sexual offending is the need for control and domination over women. Feminists believe that sex offenders perceive women as closeting a sexual commodity from them which they clearly desire. Psychoanalysts have similar explanations for sex offenders as feminists – the desire for control and power over women and children.

Other offenders, such as delinquents, commit crimes for a variety of reasons (see Chapter 10). They tend to come from problem families where parents and siblings have criminal records; there is violence and rejection in family dynamics and money problems. Many psychologists, criminologists and sociologists believe that the problems delinquents experience are nurture-driven. This is borne out by programme initiatives which have proven to be successful in developing moral understanding and increasing empathy among delinquents. Success at reducing reoffending demonstrates that many delinquents can be reformed if given the right help. If they are socialised appropriately then there is no reason why they should develop delinquent tendencies provided that the causes of their familial (including extended family members) offending is not biologically driven (see Chapters 4, 10 and 17). This suggests that nurture plays a strong role in the development of the delinquent. Many of the motivations for delinquent behaviours arise from the need to be away from a dysfunctional family, and to elevate their self-esteem by controlling their environment through criminal damage and antisocial actions. (It should be noted that too much self-esteem can also develop into criminal behaviour as is the case for some serial killers – US serial killer Ted Bundy is a good example of this). Those who have been nurtured by criminal parents with criminal ideas are more likely to be motivated by the desire to conform to their parents' beliefs instilled through inappropriate socialisation (see Chapters 4 and 17). For criminologists and psychologists, socialisation plays an important role in how children behave. Their familial environment influences the development of the child, and indeed as sociologists point out the family is the first informal socialising agent a child comes into contact with. As the child becomes familiar with the outside world then other informal and formal socialising agents will influence the child's behaviour. Informal socialising agents such as the parents are responsible also for the socialisation of appropriate sex roles.

Socialisation of appropriate sex roles has been used by criminologists, sociologists and social psychologists as an explanation for why girls are more likely to conform to the mores and values of society. This might be one reason why they are more likely to obey the law than their male counterparts. Criminal values and mores instilled through inappropriate socialisation has also been used as an explanation for female criminality. Coupled with socialisation, females are biologically 'designed' to bear and nurture children – and a biological perspective suggests female hormones, such as oestrogen, encourage a 'maternal instinct' and a caring personality disposition. This therefore raises the question of why and how can some females commit *mala in se* crimes (other than for purposes of self-defence or to protect offspring). Inappropriate socialisation does not fully explain this. Furthermore, socialisation, it could be argued, fails to explain the existence of women who live a crime-free life and yet follow masculine aspirations and a career at the expense of having children – hence a male-like sex role. A criminal lifestyle goes against the grain for most women. We can also consider female crime from the point of view of a biological–environmental interaction. An adolescent girl, for example, might be prone to violent behaviour as a consequence of abnormally high levels of circulating testosterone which is exacerbated by having rejecting parents. In the cases of females who commit less serious crimes such as shoplifting, fraud and prostitution, their motivations, according to sociologists, criminologists and feminists, are likely to be driven by environmental factors such as being economically marginalised. The monetary rewards attained through these types of criminal activity fulfil their motivations for acquiring much needed provisions for themselves and any offspring.

Although **white-collar crimes** are often regarded as less serious than many other types of crime, the perpetrators are just as callous and dangerous as other types of offender – the only difference being a less conspicuous *modus operandi*. Neuroscience has shown that the brain scans of white-collar criminals also show brain structure anomalies comparable to psychopaths – in particular areas associated with moral decision making (see Chapters 1, 5 and 7). In the working fields of white-collar criminals, the requirement to take risks, to be in control and to make quick decisions while under pressure is exciting for them and helps to mask their true uncaring antisocial personality traits. This type of working environment suits such individuals well, where risks and non-rational decisions are all a part of the game. According to psychologists, planning behaviour, which is an example of executive function under the control of working memory (WM), helps us to make rational decisions and plan our actions. A highly effective WM is useful when working in commerce and the business world. In the case of white-collar criminals their effective WM, coupled with a personality disposition to lack empathy, makes them thrive in an environment where high-risk decision making is a par for the course (and where sometimes ruthless decisions are required at the expense of the employees). Again there appears to be differences in brain function and structure between white-collar criminals, other criminals and non-criminals. The criminal mentality certainly applies to these offenders. Their actions, however, arise more out of finding loop-holes in systems and opportunities for illegal activities through pushing the boundaries of entrepreneurism than out of uncontrolled criminality. Rehabilitation of the white-collar criminal is likely to entail programmes designed to alter their problem solving skills and thinking styles, moral reasoning and empathy. Success at changing the thinking style of white-collar criminals depends on the purpose and motivation served by such activity and whether they can otherwise operate within legal boundaries. Psychologists such as Robert Hare consider white-collar criminals who commit serious crimes to be psychopaths. Given that treatment interventions have little effect on the rehabilitation of criminal psychopaths, it would appear that white-collar criminals would respond in a similar way.

### Food for thought

It is difficult to separate the nature and nurture factors that contribute towards criminality. This, in part, might be due to the contribution of individual differences across offenders coupled with the variety of social reasons for committing crime – thus making it difficult to understand the relationship between nature and nurture. Continuing research in to crime and criminality will help increase our knowledge-base of plausible explanations of why some individuals find committing crime and leading a criminal lifestyle fulfilling. One method is to predict who is at risk of offending; something psychologists can already do to some degree. The prediction of dangerousness and risk of reoffending is practised by many clinicians who rely on different forms of assessment. As we have seen in Chapter 11, clinicians relying on a clinical lore tend to make two types of prediction errors: false positives and false negatives. The odds against making such errors decrease when using psychometric tests and using assessments based on actuarial or statistical methods. Even with these approaches, prediction of future dangerousness and risk of reoffending is difficult. Predicting who a serial killer is, and where a serial killer can be found, is also difficult and has a host of different problems (see Chapter 12). The reliability of using **offender profiling** has been questioned on grounds of application and empirical worth. Instead many police profilers resort to geographical profiling which is based on location and temporal variables. By using the locations of victims and the times of crime events, likely hotspots for the perpetrator's residence can be calculated.

Another approach to furthering our understanding of the criminal involves the way the legal system operates and how evidence is attained. In Chapters 13–15, research into the workings of eyewitness testimony, the cognitive interview and confessions has provided police and the criminal justice system with valuable information of how to attain evidence from witnesses and suspects alike. The improved method of attaining factual information from witnesses, based on years of psychological memory research and theory, has proven fruitful in the extraction of information about criminals. Coupled with the technological developments in presenting mugshots and line-ups to witnesses, such as VIPER, police have developed means of identifying suspects without the possibility of biasing witnesses. Understanding the significance of interrogation methods on psychologically vulnerable individuals has helped police conduct ethical interviewing techniques with suspects. Using ethical interviewing techniques with suspects has helped police realise that having to gain a confession is not always the best way forward. Confessions, for example, can be false in different ways therefore compromising the whole investigation and increasing the probability of being thrown out by, for example, the Crown Prosecution Service. Forensic psychological research has helped to change police attitudes regarding the importance of obtaining a confession during an interrogation. Forensic psychologists have devised assessments to aid police detect psychologically vulnerable suspects. Armed with social science research designed to promote improved investigative techniques, police can increase their hit rate of identifying and charging the right suspect. This is an important facet of understanding crime and criminality as it is through the apprehension of and the bringing to justice of perpetrators that we can begin to learn more about them. We can further learn how they are different to non-criminals in their understanding of what is appropriate/inappropriate and licit/illicit behaviour.

This returns us to the question addressed in Chapters 1 and 2 of what is crime, criminal behaviour and criminality? In order to understand the criminal mind we need to understand what it is they do that is considered to contravene the law. Defining crime as we have seen is not straightforward. There are many definitions of what crime is. A legal definition is different from a religious or social constructionist one for example. Hopefully, a multidisciplinary approach will offer some clarity in addressing what is a difficult question disguised as a simple one.

## Future directions?

For most of the twentieth century, people have been suspicious of biological explanations of human behaviour. This suspicion may be traced back to the fact that some biological theories, such as the notion of a strong genetic contribution to intelligence, have been misused in social policy to subjugate specific 'races', religious groups and socio-economic classes in the past. It is the misunderstanding and misuse of biological or nature approaches which have created a sense of unease whenever a nature-oriented explanation is put forward to explain criminality. In fact such an aversion to biological research findings has meant that the pendulum swung in favour of environmental approaches since the end of World War II in 1945. This has remained until new advances in medical and science technology were made during the 1980s. Developments in brain scanning techniques and neuroscience have enabled researchers to obtain a glimpse of the workings of the brain. Our understanding of neurochemistry has increased and it is now becoming easier to monitor and regulate the effects of too much or too little hormone and/or neurotransmitter production in the brain. The regulation of hormone and neurotransmitter production in the body and brain will ultimately have an impact on behaviour. This form of organic treatment has been used to subdue specific criminal-related behaviour such as sex offending. Since the completion of the Human Genome Project our increased knowledge of how our genes affect us and influence our behaviour has opened the door towards the acceptance of biological explanations of why we behave the way we do. This means we can no longer merely pay lip service to the idea that biological factors are involved in crime. But we also need to understand the social arena in which these biological inputs play out their various roles. We need to explore and develop new models to explain the interactive nature of genes and environment in the development of criminality.

# Appendix

These tables are taken from thelawpages.com website and show offences with their maximum sentences, where applicable.

The table below is a quick reference guide with offences and their corresponding maximum sentences.

thelawpages.com (2011). Reproduced with kind permission from David Ferguson.

| Offence | Contrary to | Maximum penalty |
|---|---|---|
| *Homicide and related grave offences* | | |
| Murder | Common law | Life |
| Attempted Murder | Common law | Life |
| Manslaughter | Common law | Life |
| Soliciting to commit murder | Offences against the Person Act 1861 s.4 | Life |
| Child destruction | Infant Life (Preservation) Act 1929 s.1(1) | Life |
| Infanticide | Infanticide Act 1938 s.1(1) | Life |
| Causing explosion likely to endanger life or property | Explosive Substances Act 1883 s.2 | Life |
| Attempt to cause explosion, making or keeping explosive etc. | Explosive Substances Act 1883 s.3 | Life |
| *Offences involving serious violence or damage, and serious drug offences* | | |
| Destroying, damaging or endangering the safety of an aircraft | Aviation Security Act 1982 s.2 | Life |
| Endangering the safety of an aircraft | Aviation Security Act 1982 s.2(1)(b) | Life |
| Racially-aggravated arson (endangering life) | Crime and Disorder Act 1998 s.30 | Life |
| Kidnapping | Common law | Life |

| Offence | Contrary to | Maximum penalty |
|---|---|---|
| False imprisonment | Common law | Life |
| Torture | Criminal Justice Act s.134 | Life |
| Aggravated criminal damage | Criminal Damage Act 1971 s.1(2) | Life |
| Aggravated arson | Criminal Damage Act 1971 s.1(2), (3) | Life |
| Arson (where value exceeds £30,000) | Criminal Damage Act 1971 s.1(3) | Life |
| Hostage taking | Taking of Hostages Act 1982 s.1 | Life |
| Hijacking | Aviation Security Act 1982 s.1 | Life |
| Other acts endangering or likely to endanger the safety of an aircraft | Aviation Security Act 1982 s.3 | Life |
| Hijacking of ships | Aviation & Maritime Security Act 1990 s.9 | Life |
| Endangering safety at aerodromes | Aviation & Maritime Security Act 1990 s.1 | Life |
| Seizing or exercising control of fixed platforms | Aviation & Maritime Security Act 1990 s.10 | Life |
| Destroying fixed platforms or endangering their safety | Aviation & Maritime Security Act 1990 s.11 | Life |
| Other acts endangering or likely to endanger safety navigation | Aviation & Maritime Security Act 1990 s.12 | Life |
| Offences involving threats | Aviation & Maritime Security Act 1990 s.13 | Life |
| Offences relating to Channel Tunnel trains and the tunnel system | Channel Tunnel Security Order 1994 | Life |
| Genocide, crimes against humanity, war crimes and related offences other than one involving murder | International Criminal Court Act 2001 s.51 or s.52 | 30 years |
| Possession of firearm with intent to endanger life | Firearms Act 1968 s.16 | Life |
| Possession of firearm with intent to cause fear of violence | Firearms Act 1968 s.16A | 10 years |
| Use of firearm to resist arrest | Firearms Act 1968 s.17(1) | Life |
| Possession of firearm at time of committing or being arrested for offence specified in schedule 1 to that Act | Firearms Act 1968 s.17(2) | Life |
| Possession of firearm with criminal intent | Firearms Act 1968 s.18 | Life |
| Possession or acquisition of certain prohibited weapons etc. | Firearms Act 1968 s.5 | |

| Offence | Contrary to | Maximum penalty |
|---|---|---|
| Possessing or distributing prohibited weapon or ammunition (5 year minimum sentence) | Firearms Act 1968 | 10 years |
| Trespassing with firearm or imitation firearm in a building | Firearms Act 1968 | 7 years |
| Carrying firearm or imitation firearm in public place | Firearms Act 1968 | 7 years |
| Shortening a shot gun; conversion of firearm | Firearms Act 1968 | 7 years |
| Trading in firearms without being registered as firearms dealer | Firearms Act 1968 | 5 years |
| Selling firearm to person without a certificate | Firearms Act 1968 | 5 years |
| Repairing, testing etc. firearm without a certificate | Firearms Act 1968 | 5 years |
| Falsifying certificate etc. with view to acquisition of firearm | Firearms Act 1968 | 5 years |
| Carrying of any offensive weapon in a public place without lawful authority or reasonable excuse | Prevention of Crime Act 1953 s.1 | 4 years |
| Manufacture, sale, hire, offer for sale or hire, exposure or possession for the purpose of sale or hire, or lending or giving to any other person and the importation of flick knives and gravity knives (fine up to £5000) | Restriction of Offensive Weapons Act 1959 s1(1) | 6 months |
| Having an article with a blade or a sharp point in a public place without good reason or lawful authority. (An exemption applies to folding pocket knives with a blade of less than three inches). | Criminal Justice Act 1988 S139 | 2 years |
| Unlawful marketing of knives as suitable for combat, or in ways likely to stimulate or encourage violent behaviour | Knives Act 1997 | 2 years |
| Aggravated burglary | Theft Act 1968 s.10 | Life |
| Robbery or assault with intent to rob | Theft Act 1968 s.8 | Life |
| Armed robbery | Theft Act 1968 s.8(1) | Life |
| Assault with weapon with intent to rob | Theft Act 1968 s.8(2) | Life |
| Blackmail | Theft Act 1968 s.21 | 14 years |

| Offence | Contrary to | Maximum penalty |
|---|---|---|
| Riot | Public Order Act 1986 s.1 | 10 years |
| Violent disorder | Public Order Act 1986 s.2 | 5 years |
| Contamination of goods with intent | Public Order Act 1986 s.38 | Life |
| Causing death by dangerous driving | Road Traffic Act 1988 s.1 | 14 years |
| Causing death by careless driving while under the influence of drink or drugs | Road Traffic Act 1988 s.3A | 14 years |
| Aggravated vehicle taking resulting in death | Theft Act 1968 s.12A | 14 years |
| Causing danger to road users | Road Traffic Act 1988 s.22A | |
| Attempting to choke, suffocate, strangle etc. | Offences against the Person Act 1861 s.21 | Life |
| Destroying or damaging property other than an offence of arson | Criminal Damage Act 1971 s.1(2) | Life |
| Causing miscarriage by poison, instrument | Offences against the Person Act 1861 s.58 | Life |
| Making threats to kill | Offences against the Person Act 1861 s.16 | 10 years |
| Wounding or grievous bodily harm with intent to cause grievous bodily harm etc. | Offences against the Person Act 1861 s.18 | Life |
| Endangering the safety of railway passengers | Offences against the Person Act 1861 ss.32, 33, 34 | Life |
| Impeding persons endeavouring to escape wrecks | Offences against the Person Act 1861 s.17 | Life |
| Administering chloroform, laudanum etc. | Offences against the Person Act 1861 s.22 | Life |
| Administering poison etc. so as to endanger life | Offences against the Person Act 1861 s.23 | 10 years |
| Cruelty to persons under 16 | Children and Young Persons Act 1933 s.1 | 10 years |
| Aiding and abetting suicide | Suicide Act 1961 s.2 | |
| Prison mutiny | Prison Security Act 1992 s.1 | |
| Assaulting prison officer whilst possessing firearm etc. | Criminal Justice Act 1991 s.90 | |
| Producing or supplying a Class A or B drug | Misuse of Drugs Act 1971 s.4 | |
| Possession of a Class A drug with intent to supply | Misuse of Drugs Act 1971 s.5 | Life |
| Possession of a Class B or C drug with intent to supply | Misuse of Drugs Act 1971 s.5 | 14 years |
| Manufacture and supply of scheduled substances | Criminal Justice (International Co-operation) Act 1990 s.12 | |

| Offence | Contrary to | Maximum penalty |
|---|---|---|
| Fraudulent evasion of controls on Class A and B drugs | Customs and Excise Management Act 1979 s.170(2)(b), (c) | |
| Illegal importation of Class A and B drugs | Customs and Excise Management Act 1979 s.50 | |
| Offences in relation to proceeds of drug trafficking | Drug Trafficking Act 1994 ss.49, 50 and 51 | |
| Offences in relation to money laundering investigations | Drug Trafficking Act 1994 ss.52 and 53 | |
| Practitioner contravening drug supply regulations | Misuse of Drugs Act 1971 ss.12 and 13 | |
| Cultivation of cannabis plant | Misuse of Drugs Act 1971 s.6 | |
| Occupier knowingly permitting drugs offences etc. | Misuse of Drugs Act 1971 s.8 | |
| Activities relating to opium | Misuse of Drugs Act 1971 s.9 | |
| Drug trafficking offences at sea | Criminal Justice (International Co-operation) Act 1990 s.18 | |
| Firing on Revenue vessel | Customs and Excise Management Act 1979 s.85 | |
| Making or possession of explosive in suspicious circumstances | Explosive Substances Act 1883 s.4(1) | |
| Causing bodily injury by explosives | Offences against the Person Act 1861 s.28 | |
| Using explosive or corrosives with intent to cause grievous bodily harm | Offences against the Person Act 1861 s.29 | |
| Hostage taking | Taking of Hostages Act 1982 s.1 | |
| Offences against international protection of nuclear material | Nuclear Material (Offences) Act 1983 s.2 | |
| Placing explosives with intent to cause bodily injury | Offences against the Person Act 1861 s.30 | 14 years |
| Membership of proscribed organisations | Terrorism Act 2000 s.11 | |
| Support or meeting of proscribed organisations | Terrorism Act 2000 s.12 | |
| Uniform of proscribed organisations | Terrorism Act 2000 s.13 | |
| Fund-raising for terrorism | Terrorism Act 2000 s.15 | |
| Other offences involving money or property to be used for terrorism | Terrorism Act 2000 ss.16–18 | |
| Disclosure prejudicing, or interference of material relevant to, investigation of terrorism | Terrorism Act 2000 s.39 | |
| Weapons training | Terrorism Act 2000 s.54 | |
| Directing terrorist organisation | Terrorism Act 2000 s.56 | |

| Offence | Contrary to | Maximum penalty |
| --- | --- | --- |
| Possession of articles for terrorist purposes | Terrorism Act 2000 s.57 | |
| Unlawful collection of information for terrorist purposes | Terrorism Act 2000 s.58 | |
| Incitement of terrorism overseas | Terrorism Act 2000 s.59 | |
| Concealing criminal property | Proceeds of Crime Act 2002 s.327 | |
| Involvement in arrangements facilitating the acquisition, retention, use or control of criminal property | Proceeds of Crime Act 2002 s.328 | |
| Acquisition, use or possession of criminal property | Proceeds of Crime Act 2002 s.329 | |
| Failure to disclose knowledge or suspicion of money laundering: regulated sector | Proceeds of Crime Act 2002 s.330 | |
| Failure to disclose knowledge or suspicion of money laundering: nominated officers in the regulated sector | Proceeds of Crime Act 2002 s.331 | |
| Failure to disclose knowledge or suspicion of money laundering: other nominated officers | Proceeds of Crime Act 2002 s.332 | |
| Tipping off | Proceeds of Crime Act 2002 s.333 | |
| Disclosure under sections 330, 331, 332 or 333 of the Proceeds of Crime Act 2002 otherwise than in the form and manner prescribed | Proceeds of Crime Act 2002 s.339(1A) | |
| Causing or allowing the death of a child or vulnerable adult | Domestic Violence, Crime and Victims Act 2004 s.5 | 14 years |
| Female circumcision | Prohibition of Female Circumcision Act 1985 s.1 | 5 years |
| Female genital mutilation | Female Genital Mutilation Act 2003 s.1 | 14 years |
| Assisting a girl to mutilate her own genitalia | Female Genital Mutilation Act 2003 s.2 | 14 years |
| Assisting a non-UK person to mutilate overseas a girl's genitalia | Female Genital Mutilation Act 2003 s.3 | 14 years |

| Offence | Contrary to | Maximum penalty |
| --- | --- | --- |
| *Lesser offences involving violence or damage, and less serious drugs offences* | | |
| Racially-aggravated assault – ABH or GBH | Crime and Disorder Act 1998 s.29(1) | 7 years |
| Racially-aggravated common assault | Crime and Disorder Act 1998 s.29 | 2 years |

| Offence | Contrary to | Maximum penalty |
|---|---|---|
| Racially-aggravated criminal damage | Crime and Disorder Act 1998 s.30(1) | 2 years |
| Unlawful wounding | Offences against the Person Act 1861 s.20 | 5 years |
| Assault occasioning actual bodily harm | Offences against the Person Act 1861 s.47 | 5 years |
| Concealment of birth | Offences against the Person Act 1861 s.60 | 2 years |
| Abandonment of children under two | Offences against the Person Act 1861 s.27 | 5 years |
| Arson (other than aggravated arson) where value does not exceed £30,000 | Criminal Damage Act 1971 s.1(3) | |
| Criminal damage (other than aggravated criminal damage) | Criminal Damage Act 1971 s.1(1) | |
| Possession of firearm without certificate | Firearms Act 1968 s.1 | 10 years |
| Carrying loaded firearm in public place | Firearms Act 1968 s.19 | 7 years |
| Trespassing with a firearm | Firearms Act 1968 s.20 | 7 years |
| Shortening of shotgun or possession of shortened shotgun | Firearms Act 1968 s.4 | 7 years |
| Shortening of smooth bore gun | Firearms Amendment Act 1988 s.6(1) | |
| Possession or acquisition of shotgun without certificate | Firearms Act 1968 s.2 | 10 years |
| Possession of firearms by person convicted of crime | Firearms Act 1968 s.21(4) | |
| Acquisition by or supply of firearms to person denied them | Firearms Act 1968 s.21(5) | 5 years |
| Dealing in firearms | Firearms Act 1968 s.3 | 5 years |
| Failure to comply with certificate when transferring firearm | Firearms Act 1968 s.42 | |
| Permitting an escape | Common law | |
| Rescue | Common law | |
| Escaping from lawful custody without force | Common law | |
| Breach of prison | Common law | |
| Harbouring escaped prisoners | Criminal Justice Act 1961 s.22 | |
| Assisting prisoners to escape | Prison Act 1952 s.39 | |
| Fraudulent evasion of agricultural levy | Customs and Excise Management Act 1979 s.68A(1) and (2) | |

| Offence | Contrary to | Maximum penalty |
| --- | --- | --- |
| Offender armed or disguised | Customs and Excise Management Act 1979 s.86 | |
| Making threats to destroy or damage property | Criminal Damage Act 1971 s.2 | |
| Possessing anything with intent to destroy or damage property | Criminal Damage Act 1971 s.3 | |
| Child abduction by connected person | Child Abduction Act 1984 s.1 | |
| Child abduction by other person | Child Abduction Act 1984 s.2 | |
| Bomb hoax | Criminal Law Act 1977 s.51 | |
| Producing or supplying Class C drug | Misuse of Drugs Act 1971 s.4 | |
| Possession of a Class C drug with intent to supply | Misuse of Drugs Act 1971 s.5(3) | |
| Fraudulent evasion of controls on Class C drugs | Customs and Excise Management Act 1979 s.170(2)(b), (c) | |
| Illegal importation of Class C drugs | Customs and Excise Management Act 1979 s.50 | |
| Possession of Class A drug | Misuse of Drugs Act 1971 s.5(2) | |
| Failure to disclose knowledge or suspicion of money laundering | Drug Trafficking Offences Act 1986 s.26B | |
| Tipping off in relation to money laundering investigations | Drug Trafficking Offences Act 1986 s.26C | |
| Assaults on officers saving wrecks | Offences against the Person Act 1861 s.37 | 7 years |
| Attempting to injure or alarm the Sovereign | Treason Act 1842 s.2 | |
| Assisting illegal entry or harbouring persons | Immigration Act 1971 s.25 | |
| Employment of adults subject to immigration control: penalty notice | Immigration, Asylum and Nationality Act 2006 S.15(2) | £10,000 |
| Administering poison with intent to injure etc. | Offences against the Person Act 1861 s.24 | |
| Neglecting to provide food for or assaulting servants etc. | Offences against the Person Act 1861 s.26 | |
| Setting spring guns with intent to inflict grievous bodily harm | Offences against the Person Act 1861 s.31 | 5 years |
| Supplying instrument etc. to cause miscarriage | Offences against the Person Act 1861 s.59 | |
| Endeavouring to conceal a birth | Offences against the Person Act 1861 s.60 | 2 years |
| Failure to disclose information about terrorism | Terrorism Act 2000 s.19 | 5 years |

| Offence | Contrary to | Maximum penalty |
| --- | --- | --- |
| Circumcision of females | Prohibition of Female Circumcision Act 1985 s.1 | |
| Breaking or injuring submarine telegraph cables | Submarine Telegraph Act 1885 s.3 | |
| Failing to keep dogs under proper control resulting in injury | Dangerous Dogs Act 1991 s.3 | |
| Making gunpowder etc. to commit offences | Offences against the Person Act 1861 s.64 | |
| Stirring up racial hatred | Public Order Act 1986 ss.18–23 | |

*Sexual offences and offences against children*

| Offence | Contrary to | Maximum penalty |
| --- | --- | --- |
| Administering drugs to obtain intercourse | Sexual Offences Act 1956 s.4 | 2 years |
| Procurement of a woman by threats | Sexual Offences Act 1956 s.2 | 2 years |
| Procurement of a woman by false pretences | Sexual Offences Act 1956 s.3 | 2 years |
| Attempted sexual intercourse with girl under 13 | Sexual Offences Act 1956 s.5 | 7 years |
| Procurement of a defective | Sexual Offences Act 1956 s.9 | 2 years |
| Intercourse with a defective | Sexual Offences Act 1956 s.7 | 2 years |
| Incest by man with a girl under 13 | Sexual Offences Act 1956 s.10 | 7 years |
| Incest by woman with a girl under 13 | Sexual Offences Act 1956 s.11 | 7 years |
| Attempted incest by man with a girl over 13 | Sexual Offences Act 1956 s.10 | 2 years |
| Gross indecency between male of 21 or over and male under 16 | Sexual Offences Act 1956 s.13 | |
| Indecent assault on a woman | Sexual Offences Act 1956 s.14 | 10 years |
| Indecent assault on a man | Sexual Offences Act 1956 s.15 | 10 years |
| Abuse of position of trust | Sexual Offences (Amendment) Act 2000 s.3 | |
| Man living on earnings of prostitution | Sexual Offences Act 1956 s.30 | 7 years |
| Woman exercising control over prostitute | Sexual Offences Act 1956 s.31 | |
| Living on earnings of male prostitution | Sexual Offences Act 1967 s.5 | 7 years |

| Offence | Contrary to | Maximum penalty |
|---------|-------------|-----------------|
| Inciting girl under 16 to have incestuous sexual intercourse | Criminal Law Act 1977 s.54 | 2 years |
| Ill-treatment of persons of unsound mind | Mental Health Act 1983 s.127 | |
| Abduction of unmarried girl under 18 from parent | Sexual Offences Act 1956 s.19 | 2 years |
| Abduction of unmarried girl under 16 from parent | Sexual Offences Act 1956 s.20 | 2 years |
| Abduction of defective from parent | Sexual Offences Act 1956 s.21 | 2 years |
| Causing prostitution of women | Sexual Offences Act 1956 s.22 | 2 years |
| Procuration of girl under 21 | Sexual Offences Act 1956 s.23 | 2 years |
| Detention of woman in brothel | Sexual Offences Act 1956 s.24 | 2 years |
| Permitting girl under 16 to use premises for intercourse | Sexual Offences Act 1956 s.26 | 2 years |
| Permitting defective to use premises for intercourse | Sexual Offences Act 1956 s.27 | 2 years |
| Causing or encouraging prostitution of, intercourse with or indecent assault on girl under 16 | Sexual Offences Act 1956 s.28 | 2 years |
| Causing or encouraging prostitution of defective | Sexual Offences Act 1956 s.29 | 2 years |
| Soliciting by men | Sexual Offences Act 1956 s.32 | 2 years |
| Keeping a brothel | Sexual Offences Act 1956 s.33 | 6 months |
| Ill-treatment of patients | Mental Health Act 1983 s.127 | 2 years |
| Sexual intercourse with patients | Mental Health Act 1959 s.128 | 2 years |
| Sexual assault | Sexual Offences Act 2003 s.3 | Life |
| Causing sexual activity without penetration | Sexual Offences Act 2003 s.4 | Life |
| Paying for sexual services – penetration of a child aged 16 or 17 | Sexual Offences Act 2003 s.47 | 7 years |
| Engaging in sexual activity in the presence of a child | Sexual Offences Act 2003 s.11 | 10 years |
| Causing a child to watch a sexual act | Sexual Offences Act 2003 s.12 | 10 years |
| Child sex offence committed by person under 18 | Sexual Offences Act 2003 s.13 | 5 years |
| Meeting child following sexual grooming | Sexual Offences Act 2003 s.15 | 10 years |
| Abuse of trust: sexual activity with a child | Sexual Offences Act 2003 s.16 | 5 years |
| Abuse of position of trust: causing a child to engage in sexual activity | Sexual Offences Act 2003 s.17 | 5 years |

| Offence | Contrary to | Maximum penalty |
| --- | --- | --- |
| Abuse of trust: sexual activity in the presence of a child | Sexual Offences Act 2003 s.18 | 5 years |
| Abuse of position of trust: causing a child to watch sexual activity | Sexual Offences Act 2003 s.19 | 5 years |
| Engaging in sexual activity in the presence of a person with a mental disorder | Sexual Offences Act 2003 s.32 | 7 years |
| Causing a person with a mental disorder to watch a sexual act | Sexual Offences Act 2003 s.33 | 7 years |
| Engaging in sexual activity in the presence of a person with a mental disorder | Sexual Offences Act 2003 s.36 | 7 years |
| Causing a person with a mental disorder to watch a sexual act | Sexual Offences Act 2003 s.37 | 7 years |
| Care workers: sexual activity in presence of a person with a mental disorder | Sexual Offences Act 2003 s.40 | 7 years |
| Care workers: causing a person with a mental disorder to watch a sexual act | Sexual Offences Act 2003 s.41 | 7 years |
| Causing or inciting prostitution for gain | Sexual Offences Act 2003 s.52 | 7 years |
| Controlling prostitution for gain | Sexual Offences Act 2003 s.53 | 7 years |
| Administering a substance with intent | Sexual Offences Act 2003 s.61 | 10 years |
| Committing offence with intent to commit sexual offence | Sexual Offences Act 2003 s.62 | 10 years |
| Trespass with intent to commit sexual offence | Sexual Offences Act 2003 s.63 | 10 years |
| Sex with adult relative: penetration | Sexual Offences Act 2003 s.64 | 2 years |
| Sex with adult relative: consenting to penetration | Sexual Offences Act 2003 s.65 | 2 years |
| Exposure | Sexual Offences Act 2003 s.66 | 2 years |
| Voyeurism | Sexual Offences Act 2003 s.67 | 2 years |
| Intercourse with an animal | Sexual Offences Act 2003 s.69 | 2 years |
| Sexual penetration of a corpse | Sexual Offences Act 2003 s.70 | 2 years |
| Cruelty to children | s1 Children & Young Persons Act 1933 | 10 years |

| Offence | Contrary to | Maximum penalty |
|---|---|---|
| | *Burglary etc.* | |
| Burglary (domestic) | Theft Act 1968 s.9(3)(a) | 14 years |
| Aggravated burglary | Theft Act 1968 s10 | Life |
| Going equipped to steal | Theft Act 1968 s.25 | |
| Burglary with intent to inflict GBH on a person or do unlawful damage to a building or anything in it (dwelling) | Theft Act 1968 s9 | 14 years |
| Burglary with intent to inflict GBH on a person or do unlawful damage to a building or anything in it (non-dwelling) | Theft Act 1968 s9 | 10 years |
| Burglary with intent to commit rape (dwelling) | Theft Act 1968 s9 | 14 years |
| Burglary with intent to commit rape (non-dwelling) | Theft Act 1968 s9 | 10 years |
| Burglary (non-domestic) | Theft Act 1968 s.9(3)(b) | 10 years |
| | *Other offences of dishonesty* | |
| Destruction of registers of births etc. | Forgery Act 1861 s.36 | |
| Making false entries in copies of registers sent to register | Forgery Act 1861 s.37 | |
| Possession (with intention) of false identity documents | Identity Cards Act 2006 s.25(1) | |
| Possession (with intention) of apparatus or material for making false identity documents | Identity Cards Act 2006 s.25(3) | |
| Possession (without reasonable excuse) of false identity documents or apparatus or material for making false identity documents | Identity Cards Act 2006 s.25(5) | |
| Undischarged bankrupt being concerned in a company | Insolvency Act 1986 s.360 | |
| Counterfeiting notes and coins | Forgery and Counterfeiting Act 1981 s.14 | |
| Passing counterfeit notes and coins | Forgery and Counterfeiting Act 1981 s.15 | |
| Offences involving custody or control of counterfeit notes and coins | Forgery and Counterfeiting Act 1981 s.16 | |
| Making, custody or control of counterfeiting materials etc. | Forgery and Counterfeiting Act 1981 s.175 | |

| Offence | Contrary | Maximum penalty |
| --- | --- | --- |
| Illegal importation: counterfeit notes or coins | Customs and Excise Management Act 1979 s.50 | |
| Fraudulent evasion: counterfeit notes or coins | Customs and Excise Management Act 1979 s.170(2)(b), (c) | |
| VAT offences | Value Added Tax Act 1994 s.72(1–8) | |
| Fraudulent evasion of duty | Customs and Excise Management Act 1979 s.170(1)(b) | |
| Theft | Theft Act 1968 s.1 | |
| Removal of articles from places open to the public | Theft Act 1968 s.11 | |
| Abstraction of electricity | Theft Act 1968 s.13 | |
| Obtaining property by deception | Theft Act 1968 s.15 | |
| Obtaining pecuniary advantage by deception | Theft Act 1968 s.16 | |
| False accounting | Theft Act 1968 s.17 | |
| Handling stolen goods | Theft Act 1968 s.22 | |
| Obtaining services by deception | Theft Act 1978 s.1 | |
| Evasion of liability by deception | Theft Act 1978 s.2 | |
| Illegal importation: not elsewhere specified | Customs and Excise Management Act 1979 s.50 | |
| Counterfeiting Customs documents | Customs and Excise Management Act 1979 s.168 | |
| Fraudulent evasion: not elsewhere specified | Customs and Excise Management Act 1979 s.170(2)(b), (c) | |
| Forgery | Forgery and Counterfeiting Act 1981 s.1 | |
| Copying false instrument with intent | Forgery and Counterfeiting Act 1981 s.2 | |
| Using a false instrument | Forgery and Counterfeiting Act 1981 s.3 | |
| Using a copy of a false instrument | Forgery and Counterfeiting Act 1981 s.4 | |
| Custody or control of false instruments etc. | Forgery and Counterfeiting Act 1981 s.5 | |
| Offences in relation to dies or stamps | Stamp Duties Management Act 1891 s.13 | |
| Counterfeiting of dies or marks | Hallmarking Act 1973 s.6 | |
| Fraud by false representation | Fraud Act 2006 s.2 | 10 years |
| Fraud by failing to disclose information | Fraud Act 2006 s.3 | |
| Fraud by abuse of position | Fraud Act 2006 s.4 | |

| Offence | Contrary | Maximum penalty |
|---|---|---|
| Possession etc. of articles for use in frauds | Fraud Act 2006 s.6 | 5 years |
| Making or supplying articles for use in frauds | Fraud Act 2006 s.7 | |
| Participating in fraudulent business carried on by sole trader etc. | Fraud Act 2006 s.9 | |
| Obtaining services dishonestly | Fraud Act 2006 s.11 | |

Miscellaneous other offences

| Offence | Contrary | Maximum penalty |
|---|---|---|
| Breach of anti-social behaviour order | Crime and Disorder Act 1998 s.1(10) | |
| Breach of community sentences – Increase the severity of the existing sentence or Revoke the existing sentence and proceed as though sentencing for the original offence. | Criminal Justice Act 2003 | 51 weeks custody (if custody was not available for the original offence) |
| Breach of sex offender order | Crime and Disorder Act 1998 s.2(8) | |
| Racially-aggravated public order offence | Crime and Disorder Act 1998 s.31(1) | 2 years |
| Racially-aggravated harassment/ putting another in fear of violence | Crime and Disorder Act 1998 s.32(1) | |
| Having an article with a blade or point in a public place | Criminal Justice Act 1988 s.139 | 4 years |
| Breach of harassment injunction | Protection from Harassment Act 1997 s.3(6) | |
| Putting people in fear of violence | Protection from Harassment Act 1997 s.4(1) | 5 years |
| Offences in relation to certain dangerous articles | Aviation Security Act 1982 | 5 years |
| Breach of restraining order | Protection from Harassment Act 1997 s.5(5) | |
| Being drunk on an aircraft | Air Navigation Order 2005, article 75 | |
| Possession of offensive weapon | Prevention of Crime Act 1953 s.1 | |
| Affray | Public Order Act 1986 s.3 | 3 years |
| Assault with intent to resist arrest | Offences against the Person Act 1861 s.38 | 2 years |
| Unlawful eviction and harassment of occupier | Protection from Eviction Act 1977 s.1 | |

| Offence | Contrary | Maximum penalty |
|---|---|---|
| Fraudulent evasion of the prohibition on importing indecent or obscene articles | Customs & Excise Management Act 1979 s.170 | 7 years |
| Obscene articles intended for publication for gain | Obscene Publications Act 1964 s.1 | |
| Gross indecency between males (other than where one is 21 or over and the other is under 16) | Sexual Offences Act 1956 s.13 | |
| Solicitation for immoral purposes | Sexual Offences Act 1956 s.32 | |
| Buggery of males of 16 or over otherwise than in private | Sexual Offences Act 1956 s.12 | |
| Acts outraging public decency | Common law | |
| Offences of publication of obscene matter | Obscene Publications Act 1959 s.2 | |
| Keeping a disorderly house | Common law; Disorderly Houses Act 1751 s.8 | |
| Indecent display | Indecent Displays (Control) Act 1981 s.1 | |
| Presentation of obscene performance | Theatres Act 1968 s.2 | |
| Procurement of intercourse by threats etc. | Sexual Offences Act 1956 s.2 | |
| Causing prostitution of women | Sexual Offences Act 1956 s.22 | |
| Detention of woman in brothel or other premises | Sexual Offences Act 1956 s.24 | 2 years |
| Procurement of a woman by false pretences | Sexual Offences Act 1956 s.3 | |
| Procuring others to commit homosexual acts | Sexual Offences Act 1967 s.4 | 2 years |
| Trade description offences (9 offences) | Trade Descriptions Act 1968 ss.1, 8, 9, 12, 13, 14 | |
| Misconduct endangering ship or persons on board ship | Merchant Shipping Act 1970 s.27 | |
| Obstructing engine or carriage on railway | Malicious Damage Act 1861 s.36 | |
| Offences relating to the safe custody of controlled drugs | Misuse of Drugs Act 1971 s.11 | |
| Possession of Class B or C drug | Misuse of Drugs Act 1971 s.5(2) | |
| Wanton or furious driving | Offences against the Person Act 1861 s.35 | 2 years |
| Dangerous driving | Road Traffic Act 1988 s.2 | |
| Forgery and misuse of driving documents | Public Passenger Vehicles Act 1981 s.65 | |

| Offence | Contrary | Maximum penalty |
|---|---|---|
| Forgery of driving documents | Road Traffic Act 1960 s.233 | |
| Forgery etc. of licences and other documents | Road Traffic Act 1988 s.173 | |
| Mishandling or falsifying parking documents etc. | Road Traffic Regulation Act 1984 s.115 | |
| Aggravated vehicle taking | Theft Act 1968 s.12A | 14 years |
| Failing to stop or failing to report | Road Traffic Act 1988 | 6 months imprison-ment and/or £5,000 fine |
| Failing to nominate a driver at the time of an alleged offence | Road Traffic Act 1988 S.172 Amended 2007 | 6 points and a fine of £1000. |
| Forgery, alteration, fraud of licences etc. | Vehicle Excise and Registration Act 1994 s.44 | |
| Making off without payment | Theft Act 1978 s.3 | |
| Agreeing to indemnify sureties | Bail Act 1976 s.9(1) | |
| Sending prohibited articles by post | Post Office Act 1953 s.11 | |
| Impersonating Customs officer | Customs and Excise Management Act 1979 s.13 | |
| Obstructing Customs officer | Customs and Excise Management Act 1979 s.16 | |

*Offences against public justice and similar offences*

| Offence | Contrary | Maximum penalty |
|---|---|---|
| Conspiring to commit offences outside the United Kingdom | Criminal Justice (Terrorism and Conspiracy) Act 1998 s.5 | |
| Perverting the course of public justice | Common law | |
| Perjuries (7 offences) | Perjury Act 1911 ss.1–7(2) | |
| Corrupt transactions with agents | Prevention of Corruption Act 1906 s.1 | |
| Corruption in public office | Public Bodies Corrupt Practices Act 1889 s.1 | |
| Embracery | Common law | |
| Fabrication of evidence with intent to mislead a tribunal | Common law | |
| Personation of jurors | Common law | |
| Concealing an arrestable offence | Criminal Law Act 1967 s.5 | |
| Assisting offenders | Criminal Law Act 1967 s.4(1) | |
| False evidence before European Court | European Communities Act 1972 s.11 | |

| Offence | Contrary | Maximum penalty |
|---|---|---|
| Personating for purposes of bail etc. | Forgery Act 1861 s.34 | |
| Intimidating a witness, juror etc. | Criminal Justice and Public Order Act 1994 s.51(1) | |
| Harming, threatening to harm a witness, juror etc. | Criminal Justice and Public Order Act 1994 s.51(2) | |
| Prejudicing a drug trafficking investigation | Drug Trafficking Act 1994 s.58(1) | |
| Giving false statements to procure cremation | Cremation Act 1902 s.8(2) | |
| False statement tendered under section 9 of the Criminal Justice Act 1967 | Criminal Justice Act 1967 s.89 | |
| Making a false statement to obtain interim possession order | Criminal Justice and Public Order Act 1994 s.75(1) | |
| Making false statement to resist making of interim possession order | Criminal Justice and Public Order Act 1994 s.75(2) | |
| False statement tendered under section 5B of the Magistrates' Courts Act 1980 | Magistrates' Courts Act 1980 s.106 | |
| Making false statement to authorised officer | Trade Descriptions Act 1968 s.29(2) | |

## Serious sexual offences

| Offence | Contrary | Maximum penalty |
|---|---|---|
| Rape | Sexual Offences Act 1956 s.1(1) | Life |
| Sexual intercourse with girl under 13 | Sexual Offences Act 1956 s.5 | Life |
| Attempted sexual intercourse with girl under 13 | Sexual Offences Act 1956 s.5 | 7 years |
| Sexual intercourse with defective | Sexual Offences Act 1956 s.7 | Life |
| Incest by man with a girl under 13 | Sexual Offences Act 1956 s.10 | Life |
| Buggery of person under 16 | Sexual Offences Act 1956 s.12 | |
| Indecency with children under 14 | Indecency with Children Act 1960 s.1(1) | 10 years |
| Taking, having etc. indecent photographs of children | Protection of Children Act 1978 s.1 | 10 years |
| Possession of indecent photograph of a child | Criminal Justice Act 1988 s.160 | 5 years |
| Assault with intent to commit buggery | Sexual Offences Act 1956 s.16 | 10 years |
| Abduction of woman by force | Sexual Offences Act 1956 s.17 | 14 years |
| Permitting girl under 13 to use premises for sexual intercourse | Sexual Offences Act 1956 s.25 | Life |

| Offence | Contrary | Maximum penalty |
|---------|----------|-----------------|
| Allowing or procuring child under 16 to go abroad to perform | Children and Young Persons Act 1933 ss.25, 26 | |
| Abduction of unmarried girl under 16 from parent | Sexual Offences Act 1956 s.20 | Life |
| Permitting girl under 16 to use premises for intercourse | Sexual Offences Act 1956 s.26 | Life |
| Causing or encouraging prostitution of girl under 16 | Sexual Offences Act 1956 s.28 | Life |
| Rape | Sexual Offences Act 2003 s.1 | Life |
| Assault by penetration | Sexual Offences Act 2003 s.2 | Life |
| Sexual assault | Sexual Offences Act 2003 s.3 | 10 years |
| Causing a person to engage in sexual activity without consent | Sexual Offences Act 2003 s.4 | 10 years |
| Rape of child under 13 | Sexual Offences Act 2003 s.5 | Life |
| Assault of child under 13 by penetration | Sexual Offences Act 2003 s.6 | Life |
| Sexual assault of child under 13 | Sexual Offences Act 2003 s.7 | 14 years |
| Causing a child under 13 to engage in sexual activity | Sexual Offences Act 2003 s.8 | 14 years |
| Sexual activity with a child | Sexual Offences Act 2003 s.9 | 14 years |
| Causing a child to engage in sexual activity | Sexual Offences Act 2003 s.10 | 14 years |
| Arranging or facilitating commission of a child sex offence | Sexual Offences Act 2003 s.14 | 14 years |
| Sexual activity with a child family member, with penetration (Offender over 18) | Sexual Offences Act 2003 s.25 | 14 years |
| Sexual activity with a child family member, with penetration (Offender under 18) | Sexual Offences Act 2003 s.25 | 5 years |
| Inciting a child family member to engage in sexual activity (Offender over 18) | Sexual Offences Act 2003 s.26 | 14 years |
| Inciting a child family member to engage in sexual activity (Offender under 18) | Sexual Offences Act 2003 s.26 | 5 years |
| Sexual activity with a person with a mental disorder | Sexual Offences Act 2003 s.30 | 14 years |
| Causing or inciting a person with a mental disorder to engage in sexual activity | Sexual Offences Act 2003 s.31 | 14 years |

| Offence | Contrary | Maximum penalty |
|---|---|---|
| Engaging in sexual activity in the presence of a person with a mental disorder impeding choice | Sexual Offences Act 2003 s.32 | 10 years |
| Causing a person with a mental disorder impeding choice to watch a sexual act | Sexual Offences Act 2003 s.33 | 10 years |
| Inducement, threat or deception to procure sexual activity with a person with a mental disorder | Sexual Offences Act 2003 s.34 | 14 years |
| Inducing person with mental disorder to engage in sexual activity | Sexual Offences Act 2003 s.35 | 14 years |
| Engaging in sexual activity in the presence, procured by inducement, threat or deception, of a person with a mental disorder | Sexual Offences Act 2003 s.36 | 10 years |
| Causing a person with a mental disorder to watch a sexual act by inducement, threat or deception | Sexual Offences Act 2003 s.37 | 10 years |
| Care workers: sexual activity with a person with a mental disorder | Sexual Offences Act 2003 s.38 | 10 years |
| Care workers: inciting person with mental disorder to engage in sexual act | Sexual Offences Act 2003 s.39 | 10 years |
| Paying for sexual services – penetration – of a child under 13 | Sexual Offences Act 2003 s.47 | Life |
| Paying for sexual services – penetration – of a child under 16 | Sexual Offences Act 2003 s.47 | 14 years |
| Causing or inciting child prostitution or pornography | Sexual Offences Act 2003 s.48 | 14 years |
| Controlling a child prostitute | Sexual Offences Act 2003 s.49 | 14 years |
| Facilitating child prostitution | Sexual Offences Act 2003 s.50 | 14 years |
| Trafficking into UK for sexual exploitation | Sexual Offences Act 2003 s.57 | 14 years |
| Trafficking within UK for sexual exploitation | Sexual Offences Act 2003 s.58 | 14 years |
| Trafficking out of UK for sexual exploitation | Sexual Offences Act 2003 s.59 | 14 years |

- When passing a sentence of life imprisonment, the judge should make clear what the determinate sentence would have been, and then fix the specified period.
- The specified period of a life sentence should range from between one-half to two-thirds of the determinate term. The time that the offender has spent in remand should be deducted from the specified period.
- One-half should be the normal proportion, less time spent in custody. But in some cases, more than one-half will be appropriate.

- If a judge specifies a higher proportion than one-half, he or she should state the reasons for doing so.
- A 'whole life' minimum term sentence can be imposed for the most dangerous offenders, meaning there is no minimum period which can properly be set in that case.
- A life sentence average tariff is 14 years equivalent to a 28 year sentence. However, depending on the age of the offender and mitigating circumstances it can be half that.
- A 30 year minimum tariff is usually specified for serious offenders usually involving multiple murders.
- Following their release, life sentence prisoners remain 'on licence' for the rest of their lives. This means that they are subject to supervision by the Probation Service, and may be recalled to custody at any time if the terms of the licence are breached.

# Glossary

**Actus reus**   A guilty act considered to be an offence that breaks the law and that is allegedly committed by the accused.

**Adjectival law**   This is the system which enforces **substantive law** by use of the various branches of the criminal justice system. The police are usually the first law enforcers.

**Adversarial system of law**   A court procedure involving two opposing sides (the prosecution and defence) taking turns to question witnesses, expert witnesses, police and the accused to obtain evidence of the criminal case brought to the court. This system of law is commonly used in Britain and the US.

**Adverse factors**   Variables considered to have negative or adverse effects on an individual's socio-cognitive development, such as being abused, neglected or rejected by family members.

**Allele**   Correctly known as an allelomorph, this is a gene which occupies a specific location (or locus) on a chromosome. Different forms of a gene may occupy this specific locus and such gene forms are referred to as alleles for that locus.

**Assortative mating**   This refers to a mating pattern where similar individuals, in terms of their genes (**genotype**) and the way these genes are expressed (**phenotype**), choose to mate with one another more frequently than that predicted from random mating.

**Biosocial interactionism**   With reference to crime, biosocial interactionism is a product of biological and social factors influencing each other in an interactive way.

**CCTV**   Closed-circuit television.

**Chromosome**   A chromosome is a string of genes found in the nucleus of a cell. In humans there are 23 pairs of chromosomes of which one pair is the **sex chromosomes**.

**Civil law**   This is a legal system using core principles that have been codified into a referable case law ruling. Unlike Common law, however, it does not rely on case law precedents and instead is based on legislative enactments. Civil law is primarily used in cases concerning the rights of private individuals as opposed to offences deemed to be against the state per se (dealt under Common law). Examples of Civil law cases include unpaid debts and not fulfilling agreed contracts.

**Cognitive distortions**    These describe the deviant beliefs, attitudes and schemas that sex offenders use to support and condone the nature of their sexual offending behaviour. Although paedophiles and rapists have different types of cognitive distortions, the function they serve is the same.

**Cognitive Experiential Self Theory**    This was introduced by Epstein in 1985 to account for two information processing pathways that jurors might use: rational and experiential. The rational route uses factual information while the experiential route relies on intuition and prior knowledge, which is similar to non-evidential information. This is important in the context of **extra-legal defendant characteristics**.

**Co-inherited**    This refers to factors that tend to be inherited together such as being left-handed and having asthma.

**Comorbidity**    This refers to the existence of two or more disorders or conditions occurring in the same individual at the same time. For example, people with schizophrenia are also more likely to have alcohol-related problems. The interactive effects of the two are of particular interest and they are considered to be comorbid.

**Concept of dangerousness**    This refers to a long established debate which asks whether the individual or the act committed by the individual should be considered as being dangerous. The answer very much influences how the individual will be perceived (see **Mad or bad**) and treated.

**Contra-culture**    A group of individuals who adopt values, mores and beliefs that are in conflict with mainstream culture.

**Corporate crime**    This refers to a specific class of criminal activity commonly occurring within organisations. It can take the form of negligent or fraudulent acts, or breaking statutory law (see *mala prohibita*).

**Corpus delicti**    Literally meaning 'body of crime' this defines what constitutes a crime and is divided into two elements which must be proven in order to satisfy *corpus delicti*: *actus reus* and **mens rea**.

**Crime**    Actions which contravene the law and are therefore punishable.

**Crime prevention**    This is based on the philosophy that by setting up a series of crime prevention measures then individuals are deterred from committing crime. Crime prevention can be situational-based (i.e. instalment of house alarms or CCTV) or individual-based (i.e. programmes designed to help offenders boost their self-esteem, increase their empathy and develop social skills for instance) initiatives.

**Crime seriousness**    A rating system introduced by Thurstone in 1927 based on his work on the Laws of Comparative Judgement. Different offences are rated for their perceived seriousness which can then be ranked on a scale of crime seriousness.

**Crime signature**    A crime scene characteristic unique to the offender that has personal significance but plays little part in the perpetuation of the crime.

**Criminal career pathways**  This refers to the longevity of committing crime throughout an offender's lifespan. Also considered here is the onset, duration and **desistance** (or an end). Farrington defines this as 'the longitudinal sequence of offences committed by an individual offender'.

**Criminality**  This refers to a trait or characteristic of an individual considered to predispose an individual towards leading a life of crime.

**Criminal personality**  An individual who has a propensity of characteristics indicative of how most criminals think and behave. A criminal personality leaves an individual vulnerable to, and encourages, leading a criminal lifestyle.

**Criminal psychopaths**  Individuals who are psychopaths and commit crime. Psychopaths lack morality and empathy and their behaviour is considered to be antisocial.

**Culpability**  This refers to an individual's responsibility for committing a criminal act. Individuals are held accountable for their actions.

**Cyber-stalking**  A specific type of criminal offence involving computer aided communication (i.e. email) with the intention to threaten and harass the targeted victim.

**Dangerous offenders**  This refers to offenders who are considered to be dangerous (see concept of dangerousness). Often these offenders are assessed as having a severe personality disorder or a mental disorder such as schizophrenia.

**Delinquency**  A label used to describe a young offender who normally commits petty crime, although more serious crime can also be committed.

**Delinquent subculture**  Referring to a sub-section of the population who refuse to conform to mainstream society values, mores and beliefs, and who instead adopt a delinquent ideology.

**Desistance**  The ability of those with a past record of committing crime to resist further criminal activity.

**Deterrence**  An initiative such as the implementation of CCTV used to prevent an individual or individuals from committing further crime or from repeating their crimes. Deterrence can be at the level of the individual or a general form used to deter would-be criminals.

**Developmental Ecosystem Model**  Introduced by Bronfenbrenner as a means of representing how different socialising agents in society impact on the **socialisation** and development of the child.

**Discourse analysis**  The analysis of written prose and concept formation derived from spoken communication, as a means of constructing possible interpretations and hypotheses.

**DNA (Deoxyribonucleic acid)**  A large molecule encoding genetic information. Structurally DNA consists of two strands of sugar-phosphate that twist to form a double helix when held together by pairs of bases.

**Ecclesiastical courts**   Courts held as supreme governor of the Church specifically used for religious matters.

**Electrodermal activity**   This refers to an electrical response of the skin to stimulation such as emotion and anxiety. This can be measured using electrodes attached to the skin. The resulting measurement is called the electrodermal response (EDR).

**Environmentalists**   In philosophy this refers to scientists/researchers who tend to take an environmental as opposed to a heredity stance on the world. In other words our behaviour is **nurture-driven**.

**Epigenetic rules**   Epigenetic rules refer to guided learning that is adaptive or would have been adaptive in our ancient past. This concept could also be applied to moral codes, such as incest avoidance, from which legal codes in part derive.

**Equitable reciprocal exchange**   This refers to a balanced and fair social exchange between two or more individuals. A social interaction that is fair or equitable receives a fair or equitable response. If, however, the interaction is unfair then the individual on the receiving end is less likely to reciprocate with a fair response.

**Equity Theory**   Based on the perception of rewards received during social exchanges as being proportionate with the amount of effort invested, this theory seeks to explain behaviour.

**Evoked potentials**   Electrical activity recorded from neural activity evoked by a controlled stimulus; for example, in the brain and central nervous system.

**Extra-legal defendant characteristics**   This refers to a collection of non-evidential information about a defendant which is irrelevant to the court case and evidence presented such as the defendant's physical appearance or accent.

**Facet Theory**   Initially derived from a method preparing observations for multivariate investigations, Facet Theory has been applied to criminal profiling. In this case many crime scene observations can be analysed and grouped for their likely co-occurrence.

**Free-riders**   A label used to describe individuals who fail to reciprocate and cooperate with others. They are 'takers' without being 'givers'.

**Gamete**   A sex cell housing half the number of the chromosomal complement of a given species. For females this is ova (singular ovum) and for males the sperm (singular spermatozoa).

**Game Theory**   A mathematical approach to examining strategic moves.

**Gender paradox**   In the context of psychopathology, it is boys who tend to exhibit disruptive behaviour more than girls as seen in childhood conditions such as Attention Deficit Hyperactivity Disorder. When girls do exhibit disruptive behaviour, however, there is a reversal in the extent of extreme problematic behaviours portrayed. In these circumstances girls overtake boys in the level of disruptiveness exhibited.

**Genes** DNA sequences which code for proteins; each gene occupies a **locus** on a chromosome.

**Gene–environment interaction** The combination of biological and social factors in understanding behaviour.

**Genotype** The genetic constitution of an organism.

**Grooming** A strategy used by sex offenders particularly paedophiles to initiate and maintain a close relationship with their child victim before actually offending against them.

**Group Socialisation Theory** Introduced by Judith Harris to suggest that peer groups shape children's **socialisation** and personality to a greater degree than do their parents.

**Harm principle** This is central to evaluating the seriousness of a crime by considering the extent of physical or psychological harm endured by the victim of the crime in question.

**Heuristics** A solution to a problem based on a 'rule of thumb' strategy. A heuristic solution is normally based on previous solutions to similar problems encountered in the past which makes this a fast and computationally inexpensive problem-solving strategy.

**Homologous chromosomes** A matching pair of chromosomes where each chromosome (derived from one parent) contains the same sequences of genes.

**Hostile attribution** This is a negative thinking style used to account for why someone behaves in a certain way. To explain an individual's behaviour, a judgement of its causal effect or attribution is made. A hostile attribution is a negative judgement of why a person behaves the way they do even if the true cause underlying the behaviour is not negative.

**Imprinting** This term was first used in ethology to describe how certain learning in animals (including humans) is restricted, and arises soon after birth within a short period of time. The classic example is ducklings that follow the mother soon after hatching. She is the first life-form they see and they imprint on her. In humans this occurs in the form of mother attachment and face recognition.

**Inquisitorial system of law** A court procedure where a judge conducts the trial to establish the truth of the case. This is different to the adversarial system of law where two opposing sides take turns to question witnesses and the accused as a means to establishing the evidence. This inquisitorial system is commonly adopted in Europe.

**Insecure attachment styles** Based on Attachment Theory proposed by Bowlby and later modified by Ainsworth to include different types of emotional bonds established between child and carer (or attachment), insecure attachment styles is a classification within Attachment Theory. It describes a set of behaviours shown by the child that is indicative of an insecure emotional bond between carer and child.

**Intergenerational cycle** This describes the perpetuation of a set of behaviours that continue from one generation to the next. In the case of violence, it is nurtured across the generations in a cycle that is difficult to break.

**Interrogative suggestibility**   This occurs when a suspect is vulnerable to accepting the views expressed by the interviewer during police interrogation.

**Jurisprudence**   The study and theory of law and legal systems.

**Just World Hypothesis**   A concept used to describe the belief in a fair world where justice is metered appropriately in all spheres of everyday life.

**Labelling**   When an individual is labelled as being different they eventually come to believe the label and behave in a way that is consistent with the label.

**Labelling Theory**   This predicts that an individual labelled as deviant for instance will believe the label which ultimately becomes a self-fulfilling prophesy. This can take the person from primary deviancy to secondary deviancy where the behaviour becomes more problematic.

**Lex talionis**   One perspective of classical retributivism holding an extreme view of justified retribution equalling the crime committed. The adage used to describe this viewpoint is, 'an eye for an eye and a life for a life'.

**Locus**   The position of a gene on a chromosome.

**Macro-intervention**   As part of rehabilitation programmes, Palmer introduced three levels of tackling offending behaviour. Macro-intervention programmes tackle general offending behaviour.

**Macro-level explanation**   The focus of groups and organisations as an explanation for an individual's behaviour within society.

**Mad or bad**   A term used to depict the difference between an offender with a psychological problem who has committed a dangerous act from an offender who has also committed a dangerous act but instead of having a psychological problem experiences a moral deficit.

**Mala in se**   Latin term used to describe criminal acts considered to be against the human moral code. These crimes are heinous and involve extreme forms of harm against victims.

**Mala prohibita**   Latin term used to describe criminal acts considered to contravene statutes of law. These crimes constitute behaviours that are prohibited by statutory law (i.e. listing of rule-bound behaviours such as not driving above 30 miles per hour in a 30-mile-per-hour zone).

**McNaughton Rules**   A method of ascertaining an individual's state of mind to determine whether the individual is criminally insane and therefore not legally responsible for their criminal conduct.

**Meiosis**   A form of cellular division that maintains a haploid (half the) number of chromosomes in the mother cell. This form of cellular division leads to gamete (ova and sperm cells) formation.

**Megan's Law**   A US act named after a girl called Megan who became a victim of a paedophile. Under this act the whereabouts of sex offenders can be disclosed to the public.

**Mens rea**   The Latin term used to refer to a guilty mind. In law the accused has to be shown to have had an intention to commit the crime and to knowingly do so.

**Mentally disordered offender**   An offender who has a mental disease or illness. It includes those suffering from psychosis or a personality disorder.

**Micro-intervention**   Palmer introduced three levels of tackling offending behaviour as part of rehabilitation programmes. Micro-intervention programmes tackle specific behavioural and offending behaviour.

**Micro-level explanation**   The focus on the individual and how the individual interacts with other people within society.

**Modus operandi (MO)**   Refers to the method used by an offender to commit a crime. This normally includes the planning stages and committing the crime and post crime behaviour.

**Moral panics**   Expressed public concern over certain types of behaviour by a minority of individuals that run counter to dominant values, norms and beliefs in society.

**Moral reasoning**   Thinking and evaluating information of a moral nature. This is often tested by providing participants with moral dilemmas to solve.

**mRNA (messenger ribonucleic acid)**   Ribonucleic acid is a molecule comprising a sequence of four **nucleotide** bases (adenine, guanine, cytosine and uracil). mRNA passes genetic information to a ribosome ready for amino acid production.

**Multi-modal intervention**   As part of rehabilitation programmes, Palmer introduced three levels of tackling offending behaviour. Multi-modal intervention programmes tackle general and specific behavioural and offending behaviour. It combines macro- and micro-interventions.

**Multi-paraphilia**   A paraphilia is defined as a misplaced attraction towards an object or living thing other than a human. Paraphilia can take many forms ranging from necrophilia to shoe fetishes. Coercive paraphilia are against the law and considered to be crimes. An individual can indulge in more than one paraphilia known as multi-paraphilia.

**Nativists**   In philosophy this refers to scientists/researchers who tend to take an innate stance on the world. In other words our behaviour is nature-driven.

**Nature**   Characteristics or traits of an individual that are assumed to be inherited or innate.

**Nature drives nurture**   This refers to traits or characteristics that are shaped through environmental forces but, however, are ultimately influenced by inherited genes.

**Nature–nurture controversy**   A debate concerning the degree of heredity versus environmental contribution towards behavioural and personality traits.

**Neurogenetics**   The scientific study of how genes can be understood using molecular genetics.

**Neurotransmitters**   A collection of chemicals released by neurons to transmit information from one neuron to another.

**Nucleotide**   A portion of **DNA** that consists of three units, a sugar, a phosphate and a base.

**Nucleus**   An organelle at the centre of a cell which houses the cell's genetic material such as DNA.

**Nurture**   Refers to characteristics or traits of an individual that are assumed to be influenced by a host of environmental factors.

**Nurture drives nature**   This refers to traits or characteristics that are assumed to be inherited or innate but are changed and shaped through environmental forces.

**Offender profiling**   A method used to connect identifiable crime scene evidence with likely characteristics of the perpetrator. Conversely, this can also provide information about the characteristics of offenders who are likely to commit certain types of crime.

**Pairwise concordance**   Commonly applied to twins where the presence of a trait will occur in both individuals. More generally this refers to the likelihood that a pair of individuals will both have a specific trait given that one of the pair presents with the trait.

**Persistence**   The continuation of living a life of crime and having difficulty in desisting from committing further crime.

**Phenotype**   An organism's observable characteristics derived through an interaction between the genotype and environment.

**Philosophy of equity**   see Equity Theory.

**Polymorphism**   Where a particular locus on a chromosome has a number of different alleles (genes). This has a wider implication where the occurrence of different forms arises in members of a population.

**Procedural law**   This refers to the rules governing how all aspects of a court case are conducted.

**Protective factors**   This refers to a host of variables that can help to negate the effects of adverse factors leading to criminality. For example, the effects of parental neglect can be counteracted by having siblings to talk to or having a loving grandparent.

**Proximate explanation**   A type of explanation that aims to explain the immediate cause of a specific trait. This is the opposite to an ultimate level of explanation.

**Public safety**   A factor considered when deciding the type and level of punishment given to offenders. If the offender is considered to be a danger to society then the safety of the public becomes important and figures in the length of prison sentence.

**Punishment**   A legal process that is used when an offender has contravened the rights of others. It involves causing offenders to suffer (usually by loss of freedom) for the crime they committed against another but should be proportionate to the seriousness of offence committed.

**Radex Model**    This can be used to visually represent crime scene criteria from a multitude of offences by showing common crime scene criteria at a central circular point and less frequent ones as radiating out away from the centre.

**Reasonable force**    This refers to the appropriate level of effort or force used against another person in order to defend or protect oneself, one's family or property. Once this level of reasonable force is exceeded then it is deemed unnecessary and contravenes the law.

**Recidivism**    When an offender reoffends by repeating their crime. This information becomes known through reconviction figures.

**Recorded crime**    Acts or behaviours that are considered by the public to be against the law are reported to the police. The police then record these reported events which become part of police records.

**Rehabilitation**    An opportunity for prisoners to be educated and to improve moral standards. The ideology of rehabilitation is to encourage an offender to lead a normal lifestyle.

**Res gestae**    This is a legal term referring to 'things or deeds done'. It describes evidence admissible in court that is presented by witnesses whose accounts and statements concerning a criminal event are crucial to proving an event had occurred.

**Retribution**    This refers to the punishment awarded for committing a wrongful act that contravenes the law. The extent of retribution should reflect the level of wrongfulness committed. In metering out punishment offenders should be punished proportionately to the seriousness of their crime and level of harm inflicted to victims and society.

**Reuptake**    The reabsorption of a substance such as a neurotransmitter. The substance is 'taken up' by the cell that released it and reused.

**Risk factors**    Variables that can be used to predict whether an individual is likely to commit crime or to reoffend in the future.

**Routine Activities Theory**    This contextualises offending behaviour by linking the daily activities of offenders with the opportunities that arise as a consequence of their daily routines and habits.

**Securely attached**    Based on Attachment Theory proposed by Bowlby and later modified by Ainsworth to include different types of emotional bonds established between child and carer (or attachment), a secure attachment style is a classification within Attachment Theory. It describes a set of behaviours shown by the child that is indicative of a secure emotional bond between carer and child.

**Semantic-Motivation Hypothesis**    This combines the function of cognitive distortions (i.e. schemas) with implicit motivations experienced by sex offenders. These implicit motivations coupled with the self-preservation function that cognitive distortions serve help to understand why sex offenders commit sex crimes. Furthermore the **Semantic–Motivation Hypothesis** provides an understanding of how specific personality traits develop.

**Serotonin reuptake inhibitors**    A chemical substance which prevents serotonin from being reabsorbed so that it remains active.

**Sex chromosomes**    Sex chromosomes determine the sex of the developing embryo.

**Sexual buds**    Undeveloped organs which later develop into male or female sex organs depending on the sex chromosome complement (i.e. XY or XX respectively). These first appear in the embryonic stage during prenatal development but develop into sex organs in the third month of pregnancy.

**Social Identity Theory**    Introduced by Tajfel in 1979, this describes a person's sense of who they are based on their social categorisation, social identification and social comparison with one or more groups. Belonging to a group provides individuals with pride, self-esteem and social identity.

**Socialisation**    A process where the child is taught to accept and adopt society's values, mores and belief systems. The child learns to behave in a socially acceptable way and to become a law abiding citizen (they become socialised).

**Socialised**    This is said to occur when a child has gone through the process of **socialisation**.

**Status quo**    Refers to the existing condition or state of affairs at a particular time. It is commonly used with reference to the current social or political situation.

**Substantive law**    This influences the way we behave and interact with other people on a daily basis. It is very much based on knowledge of how to behave appropriately and in accordance with the law. This knowledge is derived through the socialisation process. If an individual fails to obey **substantive law**, then they are more likely to be confronted by adjectival law (i.e. the various branches of the legal system).

**Tarasoff Decision Rules**    In America therapists are required to declare to the courts any threats and risks to others that their clients may pose. This was named after Tarasoff who told his therapist that he wanted to kill a female student he was enamoured with, and who did eventually murder her.

**Tautological**    A circular argument which fails to prove anything.

**Theory of Mind**    The ability to understand and anticipate another person's perspective. Baron-Cohen introduced the term 'mindreading' to captivate the essence of Theory of Mind. He claims that through observing behaviour we can establish what the mental state of the individual is likely to be.

**Trial by Ordeal**    This is a primitive approach to determining a person's guilt or innocence by using painful tests believed to be under divine control. An accused who survives the test is considered to be a sign of innocence.

**Ultimate explanation**    A type of explanation that aims to explain the function of a specific trait in terms of fitness. This is in contrast to a proximate level of explanation.

**White-collar crime**   First introduced by Sutherland in 1939, white-collar crime describes crimes involving financially motivated non-violent acts committed illegally for monetary gain. It is used generically to describe commercial fraud, insider trading on the stock market, embezzlement, swindles and cheating and lying to consumers. The perception was that white-collar criminals were from middle and upper middle classes and their crimes were less serious and less deserving of punishment.

**Xenophobia**   A fear of strangers that may result in dislike.

**X-linked disorder**   This is caused by mutations of genes on the X chromosome (i.e. one of the **sex chromosomes**). This can be a dominant or recessive mutation. In the case of a dominant mutation, the mother has a 50 per cent chance of passing the disorder to the foetus whereas the father will only pass this on to any daughter. In the case of a recessive mutation, fathers will pass on one copy of the mutated gene to female offspring. Mothers will pass one copy of the mutated gene to female offspring who become carriers, whereas for male offspring there is a 50 per cent chance of inheriting the condition. One such example is Lesch-Nyhan syndrome.

**Youth culture**   A distinct culture which groups of youths aspire to. A criminally inclined youth subculture normally describes groups of youths who follow delinquent values and norms.

**Zeitgeist**   A German word that literally translates to mean 'spirit of the times'. It is used to characterise the expanse of ideas, philosophies, trends and political climate that comprise a culture at a given era.

**Zygote**   The result of a fusion between an ovum and sperm cell to create a fertilised egg which then continues to develop into a foetus.

# Bibliography

Abboud, B., Wadkins, T.A., Forrest, K.D., Lange, J. and Alavi, S. (2002, March). *False Confessions: Is the Gender of the Interrogator a Determining Factor?* Paper presented at the biennial meeting of the American Psychology-Law Society, Austin, TX.

Abel, G.G., Becker, J.V., Cunningham-Rathner, J., Mittelman, M. and Rouleau, J-L. (1988). Multiple paraphilic diagnoses among sex offenders. *Bulletin of American Academy of Psychiatry Law*, 16, 153–68.

Abel, G.G. Blanchard, E. and Barlow, D. (1981). Measurement of sexual arousal in several paraphilias: The effects of stimulus modality, instructional set and stimulus content. *Behaviour Research and Therapy*, 19, 25–33.

Abel, G.G. and Harlow, N. (2001). *The Stop Child Molestation Book*. Philadelphia: Xlibris.

Abel, G.G, Mittelman, M.S. and Becker, J.V. (1985). Sex Offenders: results of assessment and recommendations for treatment. In M.H. Ben-Ron, S.J. Hucker and C.J. Webster (eds.). *Clinical Criminology: The Assessment and Treatment of Criminal Behavior*. Toronto: M and M Graphics.

Abercrombie, N., Hill, S. and Turner, B.S. (2000). Social Structure. In *The Penguin Dictionary of Sociology*, (4th edn.) (pp.326–27). London: Penguin.

Abwender, D.A. and Hough, K. (2001). Interactive effects of characteristics of defendant and mock juror on US participants' judgements and sentencing recommendations. *Journal of Social Psychology*, 141(5), 603–15.

Achenbach, T.M. (1991). *Manual for the Child Behavior Checklist and 1991 Profile*. Burlington, VT: University of Vermont, Department of Psychiatry.

Adler, F. (1975). *Sisters in Crime: The Rise of the New Female Criminal*. New York: McGraw-Hill.

Adler, F., Mueller, G.O. and Laufer, W.S. (2004). *Criminology and the Criminal Justice System*. New York: McGraw-Hill.

Adolphs, R., Tranel, D., Damasio, H. and Damasio, A. (1994). Impaired recognition of emotion in facial expressions following bilateral damage to the human amygdala. *Nature*, 372, 669–72.

Aggleton, J.P. (1992). *The Amygdala*. New York: Wiley-Liss.

Aharonian, A.A. and Bornstein, B.H. (2008). Stress and Eyewitness Memory. *Encyclopedia of Psychology and Law*. Newbury Park, CA: SAGE Publications.

Ahlstrom, D. (2011). White-collar criminal has different brain, study finds. *The Irish Times*, 22 February.

Ainsworth, M.D.S. (1967). *Infancy in Uganda*. Baltimore: Johns Hopkins.

Ainsworth, M.D.S. (1973). The development of infant-mother attachment. In B.M. Caldwell and H.N. Ricciuti (eds.). *Review of Child Development Research*, vol. 3 (pp.1–94). Chicago: University of Chicago Press.

Ainsworth, M.D.S., Bell, S.M. and Stayton, D.J. (1971). Individual differences in strange-situation behavior of one-year-olds. In H.R. Schaffer (ed.) *The origins of human social relations*, (pp.17–58). London and New York: Academic Press.

Ainsworth, M.D.S., Blehar, M.C., Waters, E. and Wall, S. (1978). *Patterns of Attachment: A Psychological Study of the Strange Situation*. Hillsdale, NJ: Erlbaum.

Ainsworth, P.B. (2001). *Offender Profiling and Crime Analysis*. Devon: Willan Publishing.

Ainsworth, P.B. and Moss, K. (2000). *Perceptions and Misperceptions of Crime Amongst A Sample of British Students*. Paper presented at the conference of the European Association of Psychology and Law, Limassol, Cyprus.

Ajzen, L. (1991). The theory of planned behaviour. *Organizational Behavior and Human Decision Processes*, 50, 179–211.

Akehurst, L., Milne, R. and Köhnken, G. (2003). The effects of children's age and delay on recall in a cognitive and structured interview. *Psychology, Crime, and Law*, 9, 97–107.

Akers, R.L. (1998). *Social Learning and Social Structure: A General Theory of Crime and Deviance*. Boston: Northeastern University Press.

Akers, R.L. and Jensen, G.F. (2006). The empirical status of social learning theory of crime and deviance: the past, present, and future. In F.T. Cullen, J.P. Wright and K.R. Blevins (eds.). *Taking Stock: The Status of Criminological Theory* (pp.37–76). New Brunswick: Transaction Publishers.

Alexander, R.D. (1987). *The Biology of Moral Systems*. New York: Aldine de Gruyter.

Ali, F., Amorim, I.S. and Chamorro-Premuzic, T. (2009). Empathy deficits and trait emotional intelligence in psychopathy and Machiavellianism. *Personality and Individual Differences*, 47, 758–62.

Alison, L., Smith, M.D. and Morgan, K. (2003). Interpreting the accuracy of offender profiles. *Psychology, Crime and Law*, 9(2), 185–95.

Allen, J. (2004). Worry about crime. In S. Nicholas and A. Walker (eds.). *Crime in England and Wales 2002/2003: Supplementary vol. 2: Crime Disorder and the Criminal Justice System – Public Attitudes and Perceptions* (pp.41–54). London: Home Office.

Allen, J. (2006). *Worry about Crime in England and Wales: findings from the 2003/04 and 2004/05 British Crime Survey*. Home Office Online Report 15/06, London: HMSO.

Almandras, S. (2010). *Registration and Management of Sex Offenders Under the Sexual Offences Act 2003*. London, England: House of Commons Library.

Al-Rodham, N.R.F. (2008). *Emotional Amoral Egoism: A Neurophilosophical Theory of Human Nature and its Universal Security Implications* (p.16). Zürich: Lit Verlag.

Alvesalo, A. (1999). *Meeting the Expectations of the Local Community on Safety – What About White-Collar Crime?* Paper presented at the 27th Annual Conference of the European Group for the Study of Deviance and Social Control, Palanga, Lithuania, 2–5 September.

American Psychiatric Association (2000). *Diagnostic and Statistical Manual of Mental Disorders* (3rd edn. rev.) (p.528). Washington, DC: American Psychiatric Association.

American Psychiatric Association (2000). *Diagnostic and Statistical Manual of Mental Disorders* (4th edn. text rev.). (*DSM-IV-TR*). Washington, DC: American Psychiatric Association.

American Psychiatric Association (2013). *Diagnostic and Statistical Manual of Mental Disorders* (5th edn.). Arlington, VA: American Psychiatric Publishing.

American Psychiatric Association (2013). *APA Statement on DSM-5 Text Error*. News Release. Arlington, VA: APA. www.dsm5.org/Documents/1-7-DSM-Correction-103113.pdf.

Amir, M. (1971). *Patterns in Forcible Rape*. Chicago: University of Chicago Press, p.259.

Amnesty International (2010). *Abolitionist and Retentionist Countries*. www.amnesty.org/en/death-penalty/abolitionist-and-retentionist-countries.

Anderson, I. (2004). Explaining negative rape victim perception: homophobia and the male rape victim. *Current Research in Social Psychology*, 10(4). www.uiowa.edu/grpproc/crisp/crisp.10.4.html.

Anderson, I. and Swainson, V. (2001). Perceived motivation for rape: Gender differences in beliefs about female and male rape. *Current Research in Social Psychology*, 6(8). www.uiowa.edu/grpproc/crisp/crisp.6.8.html

Anderson, J.R. (1976). *Language, Memory and Thought*. Hillsdale, NJ: Erlbaum.

Anderson, J.R. (1983). *The Architecture of Cognition*. Cambridge, MA: Harvard University Press.

Anderson, L.T. and Ernst, M. (1994). Self-injury in Lesch-Nyhan disease. *Journal of Autism and Developmental Disorders*, 24, 67–81.

Anderson, M.C. and Spellman, B.A. (1995). On the status of inhibitory mechanisms in cognition: Memory retrieval as a model case. *Psychological Review*, 102, 68–100.

Anderson, R.C. and Pichert, J.W. (1978). Recall of previously unrecalled information following a shift in perspective. *Journal of Verbal Learning and Verbal Behavior*, 17, 1–12.

Anderson, T.J. (1999). The Netherlands criminal justice system: An audit model of decision making. In M. Malsch and I. Freckelton (eds.). Expert Bias and Partisanship: A Comparison between Australia and the Netherlands. *Psychology, Public Policy and Law*, 11(1), 42–61.

Andrews, D. and Bonta, J. (1998). *The Psychology of Criminal Conduct* (2nd edn.). Cincinnati: Anderson Publishing Co.

Andrews, D.A. and Bonta, J. (2003). *The Psychology of Criminal Conduct*. Cincinnati, OH: Anderson.

Andrews, D.A. and Bonta, J. (2006). *The Psychology of Criminal Conduct* (4th edn.). Newark, NJ: LexisNexis.

Andrews, D.A. and Bonta, J. (2010). *The Psychology of Criminal Conduct* (5th edn.). Newark, NJ: LexisNexis.

Angrilli, A., Bianchin, M., Radaelli, S., Bertagnoni, G. and Pertile, M. (2008). Reduced startle reflex and aversive noise perception in patients with orbitofrontal cortex lesions. *Neuropsychologia*, 46, 1179–84.

Appleby, L., Shaw, J., Ames, T. and McDonnell, R. (1999). Suicides within 12 months of contact with mental health services. National Confidential Survey. *British Medical Journal*, 318, 1235–9.

Araji, S.K. (2000). Child sexual abusers: A review and update. In L.B. Schlesinger (ed.). *Serial Offenders: Current Thought, Recent Findings*. New York: CRC Press, pp.23–49

Archer, B. (2007). *Cluster Bombs as Arms mala in se: An Ethical Framework for Assessing the Means and Methods of Warfare*. www.journalofinternationalservice.org.

Archer, J. (1994). *Male Violence*. London: Routledge.

Arnold-Baker, C. (2008). *The Companion to British History, s.v. 'English Law'*. London: Loncross Denholm Press, p.484.

Aronen, E.T., Vuontela, V., Steenari, M.R., Salmi, J. and Carlson, S. (2005). Working memory, psychiatric symptoms, and academic performance at school. *Neurobiology of Learning and Memory*, 83, 33–42.

Arthur, C. (2007). *When will we know whether Operation Ore was a success?* London: The *Guardian*. Retrieved on 24/05/13.

Association of Certified Fraud Examiners (ACFE) (2004). *Report to the Nation on Occupational Fraud and Abuse*. Austin, TX: Association of Certified Fraud Examiners, Inc.

Association of Chief Police (ACPO) (2003). *ACPO Investigative Interviewing Strategy*. National Crime and Operations Faculty, England.

Association of Chief Police Officer of England, Wales and Northern Ireland (2007). *It's Never Too Early … It's Never Too Late – The ACPO Strategy for Children and Young People*. London: Criminal Justice Business Area.

Atkinson, R.C. and Shiffrin, R.M. (1968). Human memory: a proposed system and its control processes. In K.W. Spence and J.T. Spence (eds.). *The Psychology of Learning and Motivation* (vol. 2). New York: Academic Press, pp.89–195.

Audit Commission (2007). *Police Data Quality 2006/07*. London: Audit Commission. www.auditcommission.gov.uk/SiteCollectionDocuments/AnnualReports/2007/policedataquality2006_07REP.pdf.

Aveline, M. (1988). *Group Therapy in Britain*. Milton Keynes: Open University Press.

Axelrod, R. (1984). *The Evolution of Co-operation*. New York: Basic Books.

Axelrod, R. and Hamilton, W.D. (1981). The evolution of co-operation. *Science*, 211, 1390–6.

Ayers, M.S. and Reder, L.M. (1998). A theoretical review of the misinformation effect: Predictions from an activation-based model. *Psychonomic Bulletin and Review*, 5(1), 1–21.

Babiak, P. (2011). *Horizon: Are You Good or Evil?* Broadcast by BBC2 on 7/9/11.

Babiak, P., and Hare, R.D. (2006). *Snakes in Suits: When Psychopaths go to Work*. New York: ReganBooks.

Baddeley, A.D. (1990). *Human Memory*. Hove, E. Sussex: Lawrence Erlbaum.

Baddeley, A.D. and Eysenck, M. (2007). *Prospective Memory: An Overview and Synthesis of an Emerging Field*. Thousand Oaks, CA: SAGE Publications.

Baddeley, A.D. and Hitch, G. (1974). Working memory. In G.H. Bower (ed.). *The Psychology of Learning and Motivation: Advances in Research and Theory (*vol. 8). New York: Academic Press, pp.47–89.

Badr, G.M. (1978). Islamic Law: Its Relation to Other Legal Systems. *The American Journal of Comparative Law*, 26(2), 187–98.

Baenninger, M. (1994). The development of face recognition: Featural or configural processing? *Journal of Experimental Child Psychology*, 57, 377–96.

Bagley, C., Wood, M. and Young, L. (1994).Victim to abuser: Mental health and behavioral sequels of child sexual abuse in a community survey of young adult males. *Child Abuse and Neglect*, 18, 683–97.

Bahrick, H.P., Bahrick, O.P. and Wittlinger, R.P. (1975). Fifty years of memory for names and faces: A cross sectional approach. *Journal of Experimental Psychology: General*, 104, 54–75.

Bailey-Beckett, S. and Turner, G. (2009). *Triangulation: How and Why Triangulated Research Can Help Grow Market Share and Profitability* (p.2). A White Paper by Beckett Advisors, Inc. www.beckettadvisors.com

Baillargeon, R. (1994). Physical reasoning in young infants: Seeking explanations for impossible events. *British Journal of Developmental Psychology*, 12(1), 9–33.

Baillargeon, R. (2004). Infants' reasoning about hidden objects: Evidence for event-general and event-specific expectations. *Developmental Science*, 7, 391–424.

Bain, S.A. and Baxter, J.S. (2000). Interrogative suggestibility: The role of interviewer behaviour. *Legal and Criminological Psychology*, 5, 123–33.

Baird, F.E. and Kaufmann, W. (2008). *From Plato to Derrida*. Upper Saddle River, Pearson Prentice Hall.

Balch, R.W. (1972). The police personality: Fact or fiction. *Journal of Criminal Law, Criminology and Police Science*, 63(1), 106–19.

Bandura, A. (1977). Self-efficacy: Toward a unifying theory of behavioral change. *Psychological Review*, 84, 191–215.

Bandura, A. (2003). Role of mechanisms of selective moral disengagement in terrorism and counterterrorism. In F.M. Moghaddam and A.J. Marsella (eds.). *Understanding Terrorism*. Washington, DC: APA, pp.121–50.

Bandura, A. Ross, D. and Ross, S.A (1961). Transmission of aggression through the imitation of aggressive models. *Journal of Abnormal and Social Psychology*, 63, 575–82.

Bandura, A. and Walters, R.H. (1959). Adolescent Aggression. New York: Ronald.

Baldwin, J. (1993). Police interviewing techniques: Establishing truth or proof? *The British Journal of Criminology*, 33, 325–52.

Baldwin, J. (2003). Evaluating the Effectiveness of Enforcement Procedures in Undefended Claims in the Civil Courts. *London: Lord Chancellor's Department Research Series*.

Banks, T. and Dabbs, J.M. (1996). Salivary testosterone and cortisol in a delinquent and violent urban subculture. *Journal of Social Psychology*, 136, 49–56.

Barbaree, H.E. (1990). Stimulus control of sexual arousal: Its role in sexual assault. In W.L. Marshall, D.R. Laws and H.E. Barbaree (eds.). *Handbook of Sexual Assault: Issues, Theories and Treatment of the Offender*. New York: Plenum.

Barbosa, M.F.S. and Monteiro, L.M.C. (2008). Recurrent Criminal Behaviour and Executive Dysfunction. *The Spanish Journal of Psychology*, 11(1), 259–65.

Barford, V. (2008). Iran's diagnosed transsexuals. *BBC News*, first broadcast 25 February, 21.00 GMT. http://news.bbc.co.uk/1/hi/world/middle_east/7259057.stm.

Barkataki, I., Kumari, V., Das, M., Taylor, P. and Sharma, T. (2006). Volumetric structural brain abnormalities in men with schizophrenia or antisocial personality disorder. *Behavioural Brain Research*, 169, 239–47.

Barker, M. and Beech, T. (1993). Sex offender treatment programmes: A critical look at the cognitive-behavioural approach. *Issues in Criminological and Legal Psychology*, 19, 37–42.

Barkley, R.A. (1997). *ADHD and the Nature of Self-control*. New York: Guilford.

Barkley, R.A. (2006). *Attention-deficit Hyperactivity Disorder: A Handbook for Diagnosis and Treatment*. New York: Guilford Press.

Barkow, J.H. (2006). *Missing the Revolution: Darwinism for Social Scientists*. Oxford: Oxford University Press.

Baron-Cohen, S. (1995). *Mindblindness*. Cambridge: MIT Press.

Baron-Cohen, S. (2003). *The Essential Difference: Men, Women and the Extreme Male Brain*. New York: Basic Books.

Baron-Cohen, S. (2004). *The Essential Difference: Male and Female Brains and the Truth about Autism*. New York: Basic Books, p.1.

Baron-Cohen, S., Jolliffe, T., Mortimore, C. and Robertson, M. (1997). Another advanced test of theory of mind: evidence from very high functioning adults with autism or Asperger syndrome. *Journal of Child Psychology and Psychiatry*, 38, 813–22.

Baron-Cohen, S., Wheelwright, S., Hill, J., Raste, Y. and Plumb, I. (2001). The 'Reading the Mind in the Eyes' Test revised version: a study with normal adults, and adults with Asperger syndrome or high-functioning autism. *Journal of Child Psychological Psychiatry*, 42(2), 241–51.

Baron de Montesquieu, C-L. (1756). The Spirit of the Laws. Geneva: Barrillot, http://archive.org/stream/spiritoflaws01montuoft#page/vi/mode/2up.

Barr, R. and Pease, K. (1990). Crime Placement, Displacement and Deflection. In M. Tonry and N. Morris (eds.). *Crime and Justice: A Review of Research*, vol. 12. Chicago, IL: University of Chicago Press.

Barrera, M.E. and Maurer, D. (1981). Recognition of mother's photographed face by the three-month-old infant. *Child Development*, 52, 714–6.

Barrett, K.C. (1995). A functionalist approach to shame and guilt. In J.P. Tangney and K.W. Fischer (eds.). *Self-conscious Emotions: the Psychology of Shame, Guilt, Embarrassment, and Pride* (pp.25–63). New York: Guilford Press.

Bartlett, A. (1932). *Remembering*. Cambridge: Cambridge University Press.

Bartlett, J.C. and Searcy, J. (1993). Inversion and configuration of faces. *Cognitive Psychology*, 23, 281–316.

Bauman, Z. (2000). *Liquid Modernity*. Cambridge: Polity.

Baumeister, R.F. (2001). *Social Psychology and Human Sexuality*. Philadelphia, PA: Psychology Press (Taylor and Francis).

Baumrind, D. (1972). An exploratory study of socialisation effects on Black children: Some Black-White comparisons. *Child Development*, 43, 261–7.

Baumrind, D. (1993). The average expectable environment is not good enough: A response to Scarr. *Child Development*, 64, 1299–317.

Baxter, J.S. and Bain, S.A. (2002). Faking interrogative suggestibility: The truth machine. *Legal and Criminological Psychology*, 7, 219–25.

Baxter, J.S. and Boon, J.C.W. (2000). Interrogative suggestibility: The importance of being earnest. *Personality and Individual Differences*, 28, 753–62.

BBC (2007). Crime 'stable' but robbery rises. *BBC News*. Available at http://news.bbc.co.uk/1/hi/uk/6905769.stm.

Beail, N. (2002). Interrogative suggestibility, memory and intellectual disability. *Journal of Applied Research in Intellectual Disabilities*, 15(2), 129–37.

Beccaria, C. (1764). On Crimes and Punishments. In E. Richard Bellamy (ed.). *On Crimes and Punishments and other Writings*. New York: Cambridge University Press, 1995.

Beccaria, C. (1963). *On Crimes and Punishments*. Trans. Henry Paolucci. Englewood Cliff, NJ: Prentice Hall.

Beccaria, C. (1764/1986). *On Crimes and Punishments* (p.12). Indianapolis: Hackett Publishing.

Bechara, A., Damasio, H. and Damasio, A.R. (2000). Emotion, decision making, and the orbitofrontal cortex. *Cerebral Cortex*, 10, 295–307.

Bechara, A., Damasio, A.R., Damasio, H. and Anderson, S. (1994). Insensitivity to future consequences following damage to human prefrontal cortex. *Cognition*, 50, 7–15.

Becker, G.S. (1968). Crime and punishment: an economic approach. *Journal of Political Economy*, 76(2), 169–217.

Becker, H.S. (1963). *Outsiders: A Study in the Sociology of Deviance.* Glencoe: Free Press.

Bell, R. (2013). *Willing to Die: Palestinian Suicide Bombers. Crime Library, Criminal Minds and Methods.* Turner: A Time Warner Company. www.trutv.com/library/crime/terrorists_spies/terrorists/palestinians/12.html.

Bem, S.L. (1974). The measurement of psychological androgyny. *Journal of Consulting and Clinical Psychology,* 42, 155–62.

Benda, B.B. (2003). Survival analysis of criminal recidivism of boot camp graduates using elements from general and developmental explanatory models. *International Journal of Offender Therapy and Comparative Criminology,* 47, 89–110.

Bender, R.H., Wallsten, T.S. and Ornstein, P.A. (1996). Age differences in encoding and retrieving details of a paediatric examination. *Psychonomic Bulletin and Review,* 3(2), 188–98.

Benioff, S. (1997). *A Second Chance: Developing Mentoring and Education Projects for Young People.* London: Dalston Youth Project/Crime Concern.

Bennett, T., Holloway, K. and Williams, T. (2001). *Drug Use and Offending: Summary Results of the First Year of the NEW-ADAM Research Programme.* Home Office Research Findings No. 148. London: Home Office.

Bentham, J. (1781). An Introduction to the Principles of Morals and Legislation. In J.H. Burns and H.L.A. Hart (eds.). *An Introduction to the Principles of Morals and Legislation.* London: The Athlone Press, 1970.

Berenbaum, S. and Hines, M. (1992). Early androgens are related to childhood sex-typed toy preferences. *Psychological Science,* 3, 203–6.

Berger, P. L. and Luckmann, T. (1966). *The Social Construction of Reality: A Treatise in the Sociology of Knowledge.* Garden City, NY: Anchor Books.

Berman, G. (2011). Knife Crime Statistics. Standard Note: SN/SG/4304 for Members of Parliament. *Social and General Statistics,* 2 Feb 2011.

Berman, J.S., Read, S.J. and Kenny, D.A. (1983). Processing inconsistent social information. *Journal of Personality and Social Psychology,* 45(6), 1211–24.

Bertillon, A. (1886). *De l'identification par les signalements anthropométriques.* In B. Innes (ed.). *Bodies of Evidence.* Kettering, Northhants: Index, 2001.

Bichard, M. (2004). *The Bichard Inquiry Report (HC653).* London: The Stationary Office.

Biederman J. (2005). Attention-deficit/hyperactivity disorder: a selective overview. *Biological Psychiatry,* 57(11), 1215–20.

Biederman, J., Newcorn, J. and Sprich, S. (1991). Comorbidity of attention deficit hyperactivity disorder with conduct, depressive, anxiety, and other disorders. *American Journal Psychiatry,* 148(5), 564–77.

Bilefsky, D. (2009). Europeans Debate Castration of Sex Offenders. *The New York Times.* Europe: Czech Republic.

Birbaumer, N., Veit, R., Lotze, M., Erb, M., Hermann, C., Grodd, W. and Flor, H. (2005). Deficient fear conditioning in psychopathy. *Archives of General Psychiatry,* 62(7) 799–805.

Birtchnell, J. (1996). Detachment. In C.G. Costello (ed.). *Personality Characteristics of the Personality Disordered.* New York: Wiley.

Birtchnell, J. and Shine, J. (2000). Personality disorders and the interpersonal octagon. *British Journal of Medical Psychology,* 73, 433–48.

Bjorkqvist, K., Lagerspetz, K.M.J. and Kaukiainen, A. (1992). Do girls manipulate and boys fight? Developmental trends in regard to direct and indirect aggression. *Aggressive Behavior,* 18, 117–27.

Black, D. A. (1982). A five year follow up of male patients discharged from Broadmoor Hospital. In J. Gunn and D.P. Farrington (eds.). *Abnormal Offenders, Delinquency and the Criminal Justice System*. Chichester, UK: Wiley.

Black, H.C., Nolan, J.M. and Nolan-Haley, J.M. (1990). *Black's Law Dictionary* (6th edn.). (p.960). St. Paul MN: West.

Blackburn, R. (1975). An empirical classification of psychopathic personality. *British Journal of Psychiatry*, 127, 456–60.

Blackburn, R. (1995). *The Psychology of Criminal Conduct: Theory, Research and Practice*. Chichester, UK: John Wiley and Sons.

Blackburn, R. (1996). What is forensic psychology?. *Legal and Criminological Psychology*, 1(1), 3–16.

Blackburn, R. (1997). *The Psychology of Criminal Conduct: Theory, Research and Practice*. Chichester, UK: John Wiley and Sons.

Blackburn, R. (2000). Treatment or incapacitation? Implications of research on personality disorders for the management of dangerous offenders. *Legal and Criminological Psychology*, 5, 1–21.

Blackburn, R. and Coid, J.W. (1998). Psychopathy and the dimensions of personality disorder in violent offenders. *Personality and Individual Differences*, 25, 129–45.

Blackburn, R. and Coid, J.W. (1999). Empirical clusters of DSM-III personality disorders in violent offenders. *Journal of Personality Disorders*, 13(1), 18–34.

Blackburn, R., Donnelly, J.P., Logan. C. and Renwick, S.J.D. (2004). Convergent and discriminative validity of interview and questionnaire measures of personality disorder in mentally disordered offenders: A multitrait-multimethod analysis using confirmatory factor analysis. *Journal of Personality Disorders*, 18(2), 129–50.

Blackstone, W. (1765–1769). *Commentaries on the Laws of England: A Facsimile of the First Edition of 1765–1769*, vol. 1. (1979). Chicago: The University of Chicago Press.

Blair, R.J.R. (1995). A cognitive developmental approach to morality: Investigating the psychopath. *Cognition*, 57, 1–29.

Blair, R.J.R. (1999). Responsiveness to distress cues in the child with psychopathic tendencies. *Personality and Individual Differences*, 27, 135–45.

Blair, R.J.R. (2007). Aggression, psychopathy, and free will from a cognitive neuroscience perspective. *Behavioural Sciences and the Law*, 25, 321–31.

Blair, R.J.R. and Blair, K.S. (2009). Empathy, morality, and social convention: evidence from the study of psychopathy and other psychiatric disorders. In J. Decety and W. Ickes (eds.). *The Social Neuroscience of Empathy*. Cambridge, MA: Bradford/MIT Press, pp.139–152.

Blair, R.J.R., Colledge, E., Murray, L.K. and Mitchell, D.G.V. (2001). A selective impairment in the processing of sad and fearful expressions in children with psychopathic tendencies. *Journal of Abnormal Child Psychology*, 29(6), 491–8.

Blair, R.J.R., Morris, J.S., Frith, C.D., Perrett, D.I. and Dolan, R.J. (1999). Dissociable neural responses to facial expressions of sadness and anger. *Brain*, 122, 883–93.

Blakemore, S-J. and Frith, C.D. (2003). Self-awareness and action. *Current Opinion in Neurobiology*, 13, 219–24.

Blanchard, R. and Barbaree, H.E. (2005). The strength of sexual arousal as a function of the age of the sex offender: Comparisons among pedophiles, hebephiles, and teleiophiles. *Sexual Abuse: A Journal of Research and Treatment*, 17, 441–56.

Blanchard, R., Barbaree, H.E, Bogaert, A.F., Dickey, R., Klassen, P., Kuban, M.E. and

Zucker, K.J. (2000). Fraternal birth order and sexual orientation in pedophiles. *Archives of Sexual Behavior*, 29, 463–78.

Blassingame, J.W. (1972). *The Slave Community: Plantation Life in the Antebellum South*. New York: Oxford University Press. (rev. edn. 1979, p.11).

Blassingame, J.W. (1975). Using the Testimony of Ex-Slaves: Approaches and Problems. *Journal of Southern History*, 41, 490.

Blauner, R. (1972). *Racial Oppression in America*. New York: Harper and Row.

Blauner, R. (1989). *Black Lives, White Lives: Three Decades of Race Relations in America*. Berkeley: University of California Press.

Bloom, B., and Chesney-Lind, M. (2000). Women in Prison: Vengeful Equity. In Roslyn Muraskin (ed.). *It's a Crime: Women and Justice*. Upper Saddle River, NJ: Prentice Hall.

Blud, L., Travers, R., Nugent, F. and Thornton, D.M. (2003). Accreditation of offending behaviour programmes in HM Prison Service: 'What Works' in practice. *Legal and Criminological Psychology*, 8, 69–81.

Blum, R. (1969). Drugs and violence. In D.J Mulvihill, Turnin, M.M. et al. (eds.). *Causes of Violence*. A staff report submitted to the National Commission on the Causes and Prevention of Violence. Washington, DC: US Government Printing Office, pp.1461–523.

Bocij, P. (2003). Victims of Cyberstalking: An Exploratory Study of Harassment Perpetuated via the Internet. *First Monday: Peer-Reviewed Journal on the Internet*, 8(10).

Bocij, P., Griffiths, M. and McFarlane, L. (2002). Cyberstalking: A new challenge for criminal law, *Criminal Lawyer*, 122, 3–5.

Bocij, P. and McFarlane, L. (2002). Cyberstalking: Genuine problem or public hysteria? *Prison Service Journal*, 140, 32–5.

Bogaert, A. F. (2001). Handedness, criminality, and sexual offending. *Neuropsychologia*, 39, 465–9.

Bogaerts, S., Vanheule, S. and Declercq, F. (2005). Recalled parental bonding, adult attachment style, and personality disorders in child molesters: A comparative study. *The Journal of Forensic Psychiatry and Psychology*, 16(3), 445–58.

Bogaerts, S., Vervaeke, G. and Goethals, J. (2004). A comparison of relational attitude and personality disorders in the explanation of paedophilia. *Sexual Abuse: A Journal of Research and Treatment*, 16, 37–47.

Bohlander, M. (2008). *The German Criminal Code: A Modern English Translation*. Oxford: Hart Publishing.

Bohman, M. (1978). Some genetic aspects of alcoholism and criminality: A population of adoptees. *Archives of General Psychiatry*, 35(3), 269–76.

Bohon, D. (2013). Psychiatric Group Backtracks on Pedophilia Classififcation. Alex Jones Prison Planet. www.prisonplanet.com/psychiatric-group-backtracks-on-pedophilia-classification.html.

Bond, G.D. (2008). Deception Detection Expertise. *Law and Human Behavior*, 32, 339–51.

Bonta, J., Law, M. and Hanson, K. (1998). The prediction of criminal and violent recidivism amongst mentally disordered offenders: A meta-analysis. *Psychological Bulletin*, *123*, 123–42.

Bonta, J., Wallace-Capretta, S. and Rooney, J. (2000). Can electronic monitoring make a difference? An evaluation of three Canadian programs. *Crime and Delinquency*, 46, 61–75.

Boon, J.C.W. and Baxter, J.S. (2000). Minimising interrogative suggestibility. *Legal and Criminological Psychology*, 5, 303–14.

Borod, J. C. (1992). Interhemispheric and intrahemispheric control of emotion: a focus on unilateral brain damage. *Journal of Consulting and Clinical Psychology*, 60, 339–48.

Borum, R. (2004). *Psychology of Terrorism*. Tampa: University of South Florida.

Bottcher, J. (1995). Gender as social control: A qualitative study of incarcerated youths and their siblings in greater Sacramento. *Justice Quarterly*, 12, 33–57.

Bottomly, A.K. and Pease, K. (1986). *Crime and Punishment: Interpreting the Data*. Milton Keynes: Open University Press.

Bottoms, A.E. (1977). Reflections on the Renaissance of dangerousness. *The Howard Journal of Criminal Justice*, 16(2), 70–96.

Bottoms, A.E. and Brownsword, R. (1982). The dangerousness debate after the Floud Report. *British Journal of Criminology*, 22, 229–54.

Bowden, J. (2010). Deliberately inflicted powerlessness. *Inside Time*, Issue July.

Bower, G. (1967). A multicomponent theory of a memory trace. *Psychology of Learning and Motivation*, 1, 230–325.

Bowling, B. (1999). The rise and fall of New York murder: Zero tolerance or crack's decline? *British Journal of Criminology*, 39(4), 531–54.

Bowlby, J. (1944). Forty-four juvenile thieves. *International Journal of Psychoanalysis*, 25, 1–57.

Bowlby, J. (1958). The nature of the child's tie to his mother. *International Journal of Psychoanalysis*, 39, 350–73.

Bowlby, J. (1969). *Attachment and Loss: Attachment* (vol. 1). New York: Basic Books.

Bowlby, J. (1973). *Attachment and Loss: Separation, Anxiety and Anger* (vol. 2). New York: Basic Books.

Bowlby, J. (1979). *The Making and Breaking of Affectional Bonds* (p.129). London: Tavistock.

Box, S. (1983). *Power, Crime and Mystification*. London: Tavistock.

Boxford, S. (2006). *Schools and the Problem of Crime*. Cullompton: Willan.

Boyd, N. (2000). *The Beast Within: Why Men Are Violent*. Vancouver, BC: Greystone Books.

Brace, N.A., Pike, G.E., Kemp, R.I. and Turner, J. (2009). Eyewitness identification procedures and stress: A comparison of live and video identification procedures. *International Journal of Police Science and Management*, 11(2), 183–92.

Bradley, R. and Terry, M. (1952). Rank analysis of incomplete block designs I: The method of paired comparisons. *Biometrika*, 39, 324–45.

Brainerd, C.J. and Reyna, V.F. (1998). Fuzzy-trace theory and children's false memories. *Journal of Experimental Child Psychology*, 71, 81–129.

Brainerd, C.J. and Reyna, V.F. (2002). Fuzzy-trace theory and false memory. *Current Directions in Psychological Science*, 11(5): 164–9.

Brainerd, C.J. and Reyna, V.F. (2004). Fuzzy-trace theory and memory development. *Developmental Review*, 24(4), 396–439.

Brannon, L. (2011). *Gender: Psychological Perspectives*. (6th edn.). Boston: Allyn and Bacon.

Bratton, W.J. (1996). New strategies for combatting crime in New York City. In B.E. Harcourt (ed.). The collapse of the harm principle. *Journal of Criminal Law and Criminology*, 1–65.

Brennan, K.A. and Shaver, P.R. (1998). Attachment styles and personality disorders: Their connections to each other and to parental divorce, parental death, and perceptions of parental care giving. *Journal of Personality*, 66, 835–78.

Bretherton, I. (1985). Attachment theory: Retrospect and prospect. In I. Bretherton and E. Waters (eds.). *Growing points of attachment theory and research* (vol. 50, pp.3–35). Chicago: Monographs of the Society for Research in Child Development, Nos. 1–2, Seial No. 209.

Brewer, N. and Palmer, M.A. (2010). Eyewitness identification tests. *Legal and Criminological Psychology*, 15(1), 77–96.

Brigham, J.C., Maass, A., Martinez, D. and Whittenberge, G. (1983). The effect of arousal on facial recognition. *Basic and Applied Social Psychology*, 4(3), 279–93.

British Psychological Society (2013). *What is Forensic Psychology?* http://careers.bps.org.uk/area/forensic.

Brizer, D.A. (1988). Psychopharmacology and the management of violent patients. *Psychiatric Clinics of North America*, 11, 551–68.

Broadbent, D. (1958). *Perception and Communication*. London: Pergamon Press.

Brock, P., Fisher, R.P. and Cutler, B.L.(1999). Examining the cognitive interview in a double-test paradigm. *Psychology, Crime and Law*, 5, 29–45.

Bronfenbrenner, U. (1971). *Two Worlds of Childhood: US and USSR* (p.116). London: George Allen and Unwin.

Bronfenbrenner, U. (1977). Toward an experimental ecology of human development. *American Psychologist*, 32(7), 513–31.

Bronfenbrenner, U. (1979). *The Ecology of Human Development*. Cambridge, MA: Harvard University Press.

Brown, C.L. and Geiselman, R.E. (1990). Eyewitness testimony of mentally retarded: Effect of the Cognitive Interview. *Journal of Police and Criminal Psychology*, 6, 14–22.

Brown, S.A., Gleghorn, A., Schuckit, M., Myers M.G. and Mott, M.A. (1996). Conduct disorder among adolescent substance abusers. *Journal Study of Alcohol*, 57, 314–24.

Browne, K. (2013). Working at the cutting edge. *The Psychologist*, 26(6), 424–6.

Brownmiller, S. (1973). *Against Our Will: Men, Women and Rape*. Harmondsworth: Penguin.

Brownmiller, S. (1975). *Against Our Will: Men, Women and Rape*. New York: Bantam.

Bruce, V. (1982). Changing faces: Visual and non-visual coding processes in face recognition. *British Journal of Psychology*, 73, 105–16.

Bruce, V., Dench, N. and Burton, M. (1993). Effects of distinctiveness, repetition and semantic priming on the recognition of face familiarity. *Canadian Journal of Experimental Psychology*, 47(1), 38–60.

Brugman, D. and Aleva, E. (2004). Developmental delay or regression in moral reasoning by juvenile delinquents? *Journal of Moral Education*, 33, 321–38.

Brunner, H.G., Nelen, M., Breakefield, X.O., Ropers, H.H. and van Oost, B.A. (1993). Abnormal behaviour associated with a point mutation in the structural gene for mono-amine oxidase A. *Science*, 262(5133), 578–80.

Brussel, J.A. (1968). *Casebook of a Crime Psychiatrist* (p.4). New York: Bernard Geis Associates.

Bryden, M.P. and MacRae, L. (1998). Dichotic laterality effects obtained with emotional words. *Neuropsychiatry, Neuropsychology and Behavioral Neurology*, 1, 171–6.

Buckhout, R. (1982). Eyewitness Testimony. In U. Neisser (ed.). *Memory observed: Remembering in natural contexts*. San Francisco, CA: Freeman.

Bull, R. (1992). Obtaining information expertly. *Expert Evidence*, 1, 5–12.

Bull, R. (1995). Interviewing witnesses with communicative disability. In R. Bull and D. Carson (eds.). *Handbook of Psychology in Legal Contexts* (p.248). Chichester, UK: Wiley.

Bull, R. and Cherryman, J. (1995). *Helping to Identify Skills Gaps in Specialist Investigative Interviewing: Literature Review.* Home Office: London.

Bull, R. and Cherryman, J. (1996). *Helping to Identify Skills Gaps in Specialist Investigative Interviewing: Enhancement of Professional Skills.* London: Home Office Police Department.

Bull, R. and Soukara, S. (2010). Four studies of what really happens in police interviews. In G.D. Lassiter and C.A. Meissner (eds.). *Police Interrogations and False Confessions: Current Research, Practice, and Policy Recommendations* (pp.81–95). Washington: American Psychological Association.

Bullock, H.A. (1961a). Consumer Motivations in Black and White (I). *Harvard Business Review*, 39, 89–104.

Bullock, H.A. (1961b). Consumer Motivations in Black and White (II). *Harvard Business Review*, 39, 110–24.

Bulman-Fleming, M.B. and Bryden, M.P. (1994). Simultaneous verbal and affective laterality effects. *Neuropsychologia*, 32, 787–97.

Bureau of Justice Statistics (2000). *Prisoners in 1999.* Washington, DC: US Department of Justice, Office of Justice Programs.

Bureau of Justice Statistics (2003). *Reporting Crime to the Police, 1992–2000.* Washington, DC: US Department of Justice.

Burgess, A.W., Hartman, C.R., Ressler, R.D., Douglas, J.E. and McCormack, A. (1986). Sexual homicide: A motivational model. *Journal of Interpersonal Violence*, 1, 251–72.

Burgess, W.A. and Baker, T. (2002). Cyberstalking. In: J. Boon and L. Sheridan (eds.). *Stalking and Psychosexual Obsession: Psychological Perspectives for Prevention, Policing and Treatment.* London: Wiley, pp.201–19.

Burr, A. (1987). Chasing the dragon – heroin misuses, delinquency and crime in the context of South London culture. *British Journal of Criminology*, 27(4), 333.

Burr, V. (2003). *An Introduction to Social Constructionism.* London: Routledge.

Burton, D. (2003). Male adolescents: Sexual victimisation and subsequent sexual abuse. *Child and Adolescent Social Work Journal*, 20(4), 277–96.

Burton, V., Cullen, F., Evans, T.D., Dunaway, R.G., Kethineni, S. and Payne, G. (1995). The impact of partial controls on delinquency. *Journal of Criminal Justice*, 23, 111–26.

Burton, D., Miller, D. and Shill, C.T. (2002). A social learning theory comparison of the sexual victimization of adolescent sexual offenders and non-sexual offending male delinquents. *Child Abuse and Neglect*, 26(9), 893–907.

Burton, D. and Smith-Darden, J. (2001). *The 2000 Safer Society Survey Report.* Rutland, VT: Safer Society Press.

Bushnell, I.W.R., Sai, F. and Mullin, J.T. (1989). Neonatal recognition of the mother's face. *British Journal of Developmental Psychology*, 7, 3–15.

Buss, D.M. (1999). *Evolutionary Psychology: The New Science of the Mind.* Boston: Allyn and Bacon.

Buss, D.M. (2005). *The Handbook of Evolutionary Psychology.* Hoboken, NJ: Wiley.

Bussey, K. (1992). Lying and truthfulness: Children's definitions, standards and evaluative reactions. *Child Development*, 63(1), 129–37.

Bussey, K. and Grimbeek, E.J. (2000). Children's conceptions of lying and truth-telling: Implications for child witnesses. *Legal and Criminological Psychology*, 5(2), 187–99.

Byrnes, J.P., Miller, D.C. and Schafer, W.D. (1999). Gender differences in risk taking. *Psychological Bulletin*, 125(33), 367–83.

Campbell, A. (1981). *Girl Delinquents*. Oxford: Blackwell.

Campbell, A. (1995). A few good men: The evolutionary psychology of female adolescent aggression. *Ethology and Sociobiology*, 16, 99–123.

Campos, L. and Alonso-Quecuty, M. (1999). The cognitive interview: Much more than simply 'try again'. *Psychology, Crime, and Law*, 5, 47–60.

Candel, I., Merckelbach, H., Loyen, S. and Reyskens, H. (2005). 'I hit the Shift-key and then the computer crashed': Children and false admissions. *Personality and Individual Differences*, 38, 1381–7.

Cann, A. and Ross, D.A. (1989). Olfactory stimuli as context cues in human memory. *American Journal of Psychology*, 102(1), 91–102.

Cannon, W.B. (1927). The James-Lange theory of emotion: A critical examination and an alternative theory. *American Journal of Psychology*, 39, 10–124.

Canter, D.V. (1994). *Criminal Shadows: Inside the Mind of the Serial Killer* (pp.50–2). London: Harper Collins.

Canter, D.V. (2000). Offender profiling and criminal differentiation. *Legal and Criminological Psychology*, 5(1), 23–46.

Canter, D.V. (2003). *Mapping Murder: The Secrets of Geographical Profiling*. Virgin Publishing.

Canter, D.V. (2007). Doing psychology that counts: George Kelly's influence. *Personal Construct Theory and Practice*, 3, 27–38. www.pcpnet.org/journal/pctp07/canter07.html.

Canter, D.V., Alison, L.J., Alison, E. and Wentink, N. (2004). The organized/disorganized typology of serial murder: Myth or model? *Psychology, Public Policy, and Law*, 10(3), 293–320.

Canter, D.V. and Larkin, P. (1993). The environmental range of serial rapists. *Journal of Environmental Psychology*, 13, 63–9.

Canter, D.V. and Wentink, N. (2004). An empirical test of Holmes and Holmes' serial murder typology. *Criminal Justice and Behavior*, 31(4), 489–515.

Canter, D.V. and Youngs, D. (2009). *Investigative Psychology: Offender Profiling and the Analysis of Criminal Action*. Chichester, UK: John Wiley and Sons Ltd.

Cantor, J.M., Blanchard, R., Christensen, B.K., Dickey, R., Klassen, P.E., Beckstead, A.L., Blak, T. and Kuban, M.E. (2004). Intelligence, memory, and handedness in pedophilia. *Neuropsychology*, 18, 3–14.

Cantor, J.M., Blanchard, R., Robichaud, L.K. and Christensen, B.K. (2005). Quantitative reanalysis of aggregate data on IQ in sexual offenders. *Psychological Bulletin*, 131, 555–68.

Cantor, J.M., Kabani, N., Christensen, B.K., Zipursky, R.B., Barbaree, H.E., Dickey, R., Klassen, P.E., Mikulis, D.J., Kuban, M.E., Blak, T., Richards, B.A., Hanratty, M.K. and Blanchard, R. (2008). Cerebral white matter deficiencies in pedophilic men. *Journal of Psychiatric Research*, 42, 167–83.

Cantor, J.M., Klassen, P.E., Dickey, R., Christensen, B.K., Kuban, M.E., Blak, T., Williams, N.S. and Blanchard, R. (2005). Handedness in pedophilia and hebephilia. *Archives of Sexual Behavior*, 34, 447–59.

Caplow, T. and Simon, J. (1999). Understanding prison policy and population trends. In N. Morris and M. Tonry (eds.). *Crime and Justice: A Review of Research*, 26. Chicago: University of Chicago Press.

Caputo, A.A., Frick, P.J. and Brodsky, S.L. (1999). Family violence and juvenile sex offending: The potential mediating role of psychopathic traits and negative attitudes toward women. *Criminal Justice and Behavior*, 26, 338–56.

Carey, G. (1992). Twin imitation for antisocial behavior: Implications for genetic and family environment research. *Journal of Abnormal Psychology*, 101(1), 18–25.

Carey, S. and Diamond, R. (1994). Are faces perceived as configurations more by adults than by children? *Visual Cognition*, 1, 253–74.

Carkhuff, R.R. (1993). *The Art of Helping*. Amherst, Massachusetts: Human Resourse Development Press, Inc.

Carlen, P. (1983). *Women's Imprisonment* (p.67). London: Routledge and Kegan Paul.

Carlen, P. and Worrall, A. (1987). *Gender, Crime and Justice*. Milton Keynes: Open University Press.

Carpendale, J.I.M. and Lewis, C. (2004). Constructing an understanding of mind: The development of children's social understanding within social interaction. *Behavioral and Brain Sciences*, 27(1), 79–96.

Carroll, J.S. (1978). A psychological approach to deterrence: the evaluation of crime opportunities. *Journal of Personality and Social Psychology*, 36(12), 1512–20.

Carter, D.L., Prentky, R.A., Knight, R.A., Vanderveer, P.L. and Boucher, R.J. (1987). Use of pornography in the criminal and developmental histories of sexual offenders. *Journal of Interpersonal Violence*, 2, 196–211.

Carter, H. (2009). Family threatened in £1.7m Lowry raid, court told. *The Guardian*, February 18. www.theguardian.com/uk/2009/feb/18/lowry-art-robbery.

Cashmore, J. and Bussey, K. (1996). Judicial views of child witness competence. *Law and Human Behavior: Special Issue on Childrens Capacities in Legal Contexts*, 20, 313–34.

Cassese, A. (1999). The Statute of the International Criminal Court: Some Preliminary Reflections. *EJIL,* 10, 144–71.

Caspi, A., McClay, J., Moffitt, T.E., Mill, J., Martin, J., Craig, I.W., Taylor, A. and Poulton, R. (2002). Role of genotype in the cycle of violence in maltreated children. *Science*, 297, 851–4.

Cavadino, M. and Digman, J. (2007). *The Penal System: An Introduction* (4th edn.). London: SAGE Publications.

Ceci, S.J. and Bruck, M. (1993). The suggestibility of the child witness: a historical review and synthesis. *Psychology Bulletin*, 113, 403–39.

Ceci, S.J., Bruck, M. and Battin, D.B. (2000). The suggestibility of children's testimony. In D.F. Bjorklund (Ed.). *False-memory Creation in Children and Adults.* (pp.169–201). Mahwah, NJ: Erlbaum.

Centre for Investigative Skills (CFIS) (2004). *Practical Guide to Investigative Interviewing* (p.16). Central Police Training and Development Authority: England.

Chadee, D., Austen, L. and Ditton, J. (2007). The relationship between likelihood and fear of criminal victimisation. *The British Journal of Criminology*, 47(1), 133–53.

Chance, J.E. and Goldstein, A.G. (1981). Depth of processing in response to own and other race faces. *Personality and Social Psychology Bulletin*, 7(3), 475–80.

Chandler, M. (1973). Egocentrism and antisocial behaviour: the assessment and training of social perspective-taking skills. *Developmental Psychology*, 9, 326–32.

Chaplin, R., Flatley, J. and Smith, K. (2011). Crime in England and Wales 2010/11: Findings from the British Crime Survey and police recorded crime. *Home Office Statistical Bulletin*, 10/11. London: Home Office.

Chapman, A.J. and Perry, D.J. (1995). Applying the cognitive interview procedure to children and adult eyewitnesses of road accidents. *Applied Psychology: An International Review*, 44, 283–94.

Chen, C.A. and Howitt, D. (2007). Different crime types and moral reasoning development in young offenders compared with non-offender controls. In D. Howitt (ed.) (2012). *Introduction to Forensic and Criminal Psychology* (p.94). Harlow: Pearson.

Chen, X. and French, D.C. (2007). Children's social competence in cultural context. *Annual Review of Psychology*, 59, 591–616.

Chen, X., Chang, I. and He, Y. (2003). The peer group as a context: Mediating and moderating effects on the relations between academic achievement and social functioning in Chinese children. *Child Development*, 74, 710–27.

Chermak, S.M. (1995). *Victims in the News: Crime and the American News Media*. Boulder, CO: Westview Press.

Cherry, E.C. (1953). Some experiments on the recognition of speech with one and with two ears. *Journal of the Acoustical Society of America*, 25, 975–9.

Cherryman, J. and Bull, R. (2000). Investigative interviewing. In F. Leishman, S. Savage and B. Loveday (eds.). *Core Issues in policing* (2nd edn.). London: Longman.

Cherryman, J., Bull, R. and Vrij, A. (2000). How police officers view confessions: Is there still a confession culture? *European Conference on Psychology and Law*, Cyprus, March 2000.

Chesney-Lind, M., and Bloom, B. (1997). Feminist criminology: Thinking about women and crime. In B. MacLean and D. Milovanovic (eds.) *Thinking Critically About Crime* (pp.45–55). Vancouver, Canada: Collective Press.

Christiansen, K.O. (1977). A review of studies of criminality among twins. In S.A. Mednick and K.O. Christiansen (eds.). *Biosocial Bases of Criminal Behavior* (pp.45–88). New York: Gardner Press.

Christianson, S.A. (1992). Emotional stress and eyewitness memory: A critical review. *Psychological Bulletin*, 112, 284–309.

Christianson, S.A. and Hubinette, B. (1993). Hands up! A study of witnesses' emotional reactions and memories associated with bank robberies. *Applied Cognitive Psychology*, 7, 365–79.

Christie, N. (2004). *A Suitable Amount of Crime*. London: Routledge.

Cipriani, D. (2009). Children's Rights and the Minimum Age of Criminal Responsibility: A Global Perspective and the Justice for Children. *Briefing No. 4, The Minimum Age of Criminal Responsibility*. www.penalreform.org.

Ciucci, E. and Menesini, E. (2004). Emotional competence in bullies and victims. In I. Grazzani Gavazzi (Ed.). *Emotional Competence. Studies and Researches in the Life Span* (pp.37–59). Milano: Unicopli.

Clare, I.C.H. and Gudjonsson, G.H. (1993). Interrogative suggestibility, confabulation, and acquiescence in people with mild learning disabilities (mental handicap): Implications for reliability during police interrogations. *British Journal of Clinical Psychology*, 32(3), 295–301.

Clark, L., Bechara, A., Damasio, H., Aitken, M.R.F., Sahakian, B.J. and Robbins, T.W. (2008). Differential effects of insular and ventromedial prefrontal cortex lesions on risky decision-making. *Brain*, 131, 1311–22.

Clark, L. and Lewis, D. (1977). *Rape: the Price of Coercive Sexuality*. Toronto, Ontario, Canada: Women's Press.

Clark, S.E. and Davey, S.L. (2005). The target-to-foils shift in simultaneous and sequential lineups. *Law and Human Behavior*, 29(2), 151–72.

Clark, S.E. and Tunnicliff, J.L. (2001). Selecting lineup foils in eyewitness identification: experimental control and real world simulation. *Law and Human Behavior*, 25, 199–216.

Clarke, C. and Milne, R. (2005). *National Evaluation of the PEACE Investigative Interviewing Course*. London: Home Office.

Clarke, R. V. and Cornish, D.B. (1985). Modeling offenders' decisions: a framework for research and policy. In M. Tonry and N. Morris (eds.). *Crime and Justice: An Annual Review of Research*, 6, 147–85. Chicago: University of Chicago Press.

Clarke-Stewart, K.A. and Hevey, C.M. (1981). Longitudinal relations in repeated observations of mother–child interaction from 1 to 2 1/2 years. *Developmental Psychology*, 17, 127–45.

Cleare, A.J. and Bond, A.J. (1997). Does central serotonergic function correlate inversely with aggression? A study using D-fenfluramine in healthy subjects. *Psychiatry Research*, 69, 89–95.

Cleckley, H. (1941). *The Mask of Sanity*. St. Louis, MO: Mosby.

Cleckley, H. (1988). *The Mask of Sanity* (5th edn.). St. Louis, MO: Mosby.

Clifford, B.R. and George, R. (1996). A field evaluation of training in three methods of witness/victim investigative interviewing. *Psychology, Crime, and Law*, 2, 231–48.

Clifford, B.R. and Gwyer, P. (1999). The effects of the cognitive interview and other methods of context reinstatement on identification. *Psychology, Crime, and Law*, 5, 61–80.

Clingempeel, W.G. and Henggeler, S.W. (2003). Aggressive juvenile offenders transitioning into emerging adulthood: Factors discriminating persistors and desistors. *American Journal of Orthopsychiatry*, 73(3), 310–23.

Cloninger, C.R., Bohman, M. and Sigvardsson, S. (1981). Inheritance of alcohol abuse: cross-fostering analysis of adopted men. *Archives of General Psychiatry*, 38, 861–9.

Cloninger, C.R., Christiansen, K.O., Reich, T. and Gottesman, I.J. (1978). Implications of sex differences in the prevalence of antisocial personality, alcoholism, and criminality for familial transmission. *Archives of General Psychiatry*, 35, 941–51.

Cloward, R.A. and Ohlin, L.E. (1960). *Delinquency and Opportunity: A Theory of Delinquent Gangs*. New York: The Free Press.

Coccaro, E.F., Beresford, B., Minar, P., Kaskow, J. and Geracioti, T. (2007). CSF testosterone: relationship to aggression, impulsivity, and venturesomeness in adult males with personality disorder. *Journal of Psychiatric Research*, 41(6), 488–92.

Cocozza, J.J. and Steadman, H.J. (1978). Prediction in psychiatry: An example of misplaced confidence in experts. *Social Problems*, 25, 265–76.

Cohen, A.K. (1955). *Delinquent Boys: The Culture of the Gang*. Glencoe, IL: The Free Press.

Cohen, B. (1969). The delinquency of gangs and spontaneous groups. In T. Sellin and M.E. Wolfgang (eds.). *Delinquency: Selected Studies* (pp.61–111). New York: John Wiley and Son.

Cohen, C.E. (1981). Person categories and social perception: Testing some boundaries of the processing effects of prior knowledge. *Journal of Personality and Social Psychology*, 40(3), 441–52.

Cohen, G. and Faulkner, D. (1989). Age differences in source forgetting: Effects on reality monitoring and on eyewitness testimony. *Psychology and Ageing*, 4, 10–7.

Cohen, J.D., Perlstein, W.M., Braver, T.S., Nystrom, L.E., Noll, D. C., Jonides, J. et al. (1997). Temporal dynamics of brain activation during a working memory task. *Nature*, 386, 604–8.

Cohen, L.B. (1998). An information-processing approach to infant perception and cognition. In F. Simion and G. Butterworth (eds.). *The Development of Sensory, Motor, and Cognitive Capacities in Early Infancy* (pp.277–300). Hove, UK: Psychology Press.

Cohen, L. and Felson, M. (1979). Social change and crime rate trends: A routine activities approach. *American Sociological Review*, 44, 588–8.

Cohen, L.J. and Galynker, I.I. (2002). Clinical features of pedophilia and implications for treatment. *Journal of Psychiatric Practice*, 8, 276–89.

Cohen, L.J., Garfalo, R.F., Boucher, R. and Seghorn, T. (1971). The psychology of rapists. *Seminars in Psychiatry*, 3, 307–27.

Cohen, M. J. (1982). *Charles Horton Cooley and the Social Self in American Thought*. New York: Garland Publishers.

Cohen, M., Seghorn, T. and Calmas, W. (1969). Sociometric study of the sex offender. *Journal of Abnormal Psychology*, 74, 249–55.

Cohen, P. (1972). Subcultural Conflict and Working Class Community. *Working Papers in Cultural Studies*, 2, 5–51.

Cohen, P. and Flory, M. (1998). Issues in the disruptive behavior disorders: attention deficit disorder without hyperactivity and the differential validity of oppositional defiant and conduct disorders. In T. Widiger (ed.). *DSM-IV Sourcebook*, Vol 4 (pp.455–63). Washington, DC: American Psychiatric Press.

Cohen, S. (1972). *Folk Devils and Moral Panics: The Creation of the Mods and Rockers*. New York: St Martin's Press.

Coid, J.W. (1992). DSM-III diagnosis in criminal psychopaths: A way forward. *Criminal Behaviour and Mental Health*, 2, 78–9.

Coie, J.D. and Dodge, K.A. (1997). Aggression and antisocial behavior. In W. Damon and N. Eisenberg (eds.). *Handbook of Child Psychology (vol. 3): Social, Emotional and Personality Development* (pp.779–862). New York: Wiley.

Colledge, J. and Blair, R.J.R. (2001). The relationship in children between the inattention and impulsivity components of attention deficit and hyperactivity disorder and psychopathic tendencies. *Personality and Individual Differences*, 30, 1175–87.

College of Policing (2013). *Investigative interviewing*. https://www.app.college.police.uk/app-content/investigations/investigative-interviewing/

*Collins Compact English Dictionary* (1994). Glasgow: Harper Collins Publishers.

Colwell, K., Hiscock-Anisman, C., Memon, A., Taylor, L. and Prewett, J. (2007). Assessment criteria indicative of deception (ACID): An integrated system of investigative interviewing and detecting deception. *Journal of Investigative Psychology and Offender Profiling*, 4, 167–80.

Comptroller and Auditor General, N. A. O. (2006). *The Electronic Monitoring of Adult Offenders*. London: The Stationery Office.

Connell, R.W. (1987). *Gender and Power*. Cambridge: University Press.

Connellan, J., Baron-Cohen, S., Wheelwright, S., Batki, A. and Ahluwalia, J. (2000). Sex differences in human neonatal social perception. Infant Behaviour and Development, 23, 113–8.

Conner, K.R., Meldrum, S., Wieczorek, W.F., Duberstein, P.R. and Welte, J.W. (2004). The association of irritability and impulsivity with suicidal ideation among 15- to 20- year-old males. *Suicide Life-Threatening Behavior*, 34, 363–73.

Constitution of the United States, Amendment 4 (1789). www.usconstitution.net/constamrat.html.

Constitution of the United States, Amendment 5 (1789). www.usconstitution.net/constamrat.html.

Constitution of the United States, Amendment 14 (1866). www.usconstitution.net/constamrat.html.

Contagious Diseases Act (1864). Passed by Parliament of the UK. www.legislation.gov.uk.

Cook, E.H., Stein, M.A., Ellison, T., Unis, A.S. and Leventhal, B.L. (1995). Attention deficit hyperactivity disorder and whole-blood serotonin levels: Effects of comorbidity. *Psychiatry Res*, 57(1), 13–20.

Coombs, C.H. (1967). Thurstone's measurement of social values revisited forty years later. *Journal of Personality and Social Psychology*, 6, 85–91.

Cooper, R.P. and Werner, P.D. (1990). Predicting violence in newly admitted inmates: A lens model analysis of staff decision making. *Criminal Justice and Behavior*, 17, 431–47.

Copas, J., and Marshall, P. (1998). The offender group reconviction scale: A statistical reconviction score for use by probation officers. *Applied Statistics*, 47, 159–71.

Copeland, T.F. and Parish, T.S. (1979). Attempt to enhance moral judgements of offenders. *Psychological Reports*, 45, 831–4.

Corbin, R.M. (1980). Decisions that might not get made. In T.S. Wallsten (ed.). *Cognitive Processes in Choice and Decision Behavior* (pp.47–67). Hillsdale, NJ: Erlbaum.

Cornish, D.B. and Clarke, R.V. (1986). *The Reasoning Criminal: Rational Choice Perspectives on Offending*. New York: Springer-Verlag.

Costa, P.T. and McCrae, R.R. (1992). *NEO PI-R Professional Manual*. Odessa, FL: Psychological Assessment Resources, Inc.

Costa, P.T., Terracciano, A. and McCrae, R.R. (2001). Gender differences in personality traits across cultures: Robust and surprising findings. *Journal of Personality and Social Psychology*, 81(2), 322–31.

Council of Europe Report on the Czech Republic. (2009). www.cpt.coe.int.

Courtenay-Smith, N. (2011). My adopted boys had perfect childhoods. Now both are heroin addicts and in jail – just like their birth mother. *Daily Mail*. www.dailymail.co.uk/femail/article-1352387/My-adopted-boys-perfect-childhoods-Now-heroin-addicts.html.

Covington, S.S. and Bloom, B.E. (2003). Gendered Justice: Women in the Criminal Justice System. In B.E. Bloom (ed.). *Gendered Justice: Addressing Female Offenders*. Durham, NC: Carolina Academic Press.

Cowburn, M. (1990). Work with male sexual offenders in groups. *Groupwork*, 3(2), 157–71.

CPTU (Central Planning and Training Unit) (1992a). *A Guide to Interviewing*. Harrogate: Metropolitan Police.

CPTU (Central Planning and Training Unit) (1992b). *The Interviewer's Rule Book*. Harrogate: Metropolitan Police.

CPTU (Central Planning and Training Unit) (1992c). *The Interview Workbook*. Harrogate: Metropolitan Police.

Craig, M.C., Catani, M., Deeley, Q., Latham, R., Daly, E., Kanaan, R., Picchioni, M., McGuire, P.K., Fahy, T. and Murphy, G.G.M. (2009). Altered connections on the road to psychopathy. *Molecular Psychiatry*, 14, 946–53.

Craik, F.I. and Tulving, E. (1975). Depth of processing and the retention of words in episodic memory. *Journal of Experimental Psychology: General*, 104(3), 268–94.

Craven, S., Brown, S.and Gilchrist, E. (2007). Current responses to sexual grooming: Implications for prevention. *Howard Journal of Criminal Justice*, 46, 60–71.

Crawford, A. (1998). *Crime Prevention and Community Safety: Politics, Policies and Practices*. London: Longman.

Crick, N.R. and Dodge, K.A. (1996). Social information-processing mechanisms in reactive and proactive aggression. *Child Development*, 67, 993–1002.

Crick, N.R. and Rose, A.J. (2000). Toward a gender-balanced approach to the study of socio-emotional development: A look at relational aggression. In M. Cole, S.R. Cole and C. Lightfoot (eds.). *The Development of Children*. New York: Worth Publishers.

Crime and Disorder Act (1998). www.legislation.gov.uk/ukpga/1998/37/contents.

Crime Sentences Act (1997). www.legislation.gov.uk.

Criminal Code of Canada: Sentencing – Imprisonment for Life (2012). http://laws.justice.gc.ca (assessed 15/02/2011).

Criminal Justice Act (2003, 1991). www.legislation.gov.uk.

Criminal Justice and Immigration Act (2008) www.legislation.gov.uk.

Criminal Justice and Licensing (Scotland) Act (2010). www.legislation.gov.uk/asp/2010/13/section/52.

Criminal Justice and Police Bill (2005). www.publications.parliament.uk/pa/pabills/200506/police_and_justice.htm.

Criminal Justice and Public Order Act (1994). www.legislation.gov.uk/ukpga/1994/33/contents.

Crookes, D. (2012). Anti-piracy download laws around the world explained. BBC News. www.bbc.co.uk/newsbeat/16839637.

Crosson-Tower, C. (2005). *Understanding Child Abuse and Neglect*. Boston: Allyn and Bacon.

Crowell, J.A. and Feldman, S.S. (1991). Mothers' working models of attachment relationships and mother and child behavior during separation and reunion. *Developmental Psychology*, 27, 597–605.

Crowell, J.A., Treboux, D., Gao, Y., Fyffe, C., Pan, H. and Waters, E. (2002). Assessing secure base behavior in adulthood: Development of a measure, links to adult attachment representations and relations to couples communication and reports of relationships. *Developmental Psychology*, 38, 679–93.

Crowther, C. (2007). *An Introduction to Criminology and Criminal Justice*. Basingstoke: Palgrave MacMillan.

Cullen, E. (1992). *The Grendon Reconviction Study*. Unpublished document, Psychology Department, HMP Grendon.

Cunningham, M. (2006). Special issues in capital sentencing. *Applied Psychology in Criminal Justice*, 2(3), 205–36.

Cusson, M. and Pinsonneault, P. (1986). The decision to give up crime. In D.B. Cornish and R.V. Clarke (eds.). *The Reasoning Criminal: Rational Choice Perspectives on Offending*. New York: Springer-Verlag.

Cutler, B.L. and Penrod, S.D. (1989). Forensically relevant moderators of the relation between eyewitness identification accuracy and confidence. *Journal of Applied Psychology*, 74, 650–53.

Cutler, B.L., Penrod, S.D. and Dexter, H.R. (1990). Juror sensitivity to eyewitness identification evidence. *Law and Human Behavior*, 14, 185–91.

Dabbs, J.M., Carr, T.S., Frady, R.l. and Riad, J.K. (1995). Testosterone, crime, and misbehavior among 692 male prison inmates. *Personality and Individual Differences*, 18, 627–33.

Dabbs, J.M. and Morris, R. (1990). Testosterone, social class, and antisocial behavior in a sample of 4,462 men. *Psychological Science*, 1, 209–11.

Dadds, M.R., Perry, Y., Hawes, D.J., Merz, S., Riddell, A.C., Haines, D.J. et al. (2006). Attention to the eyes and fear-recognition deficits in child psychopathy. *The British Journal of Psychiatry*, 189, 280–81.

Dalton, K. (1961). Menstruation and crime. *British Medical Journal*, 2, 1752–3.

Daly, K. (1989). Gender and varieties of white-collar crime. *Criminology*, 27, 769–94.

Daly, K. (1994). *Gender, Crime and Punishment*. New Haven, CT: Yale University Press.

Daly, M. and Wilson, M.I. (1985). Child abuse and other risks of not living with both parents. *Ethology and Sociobiology*, 6, 197–210.

Daly, M. and Wilson, M.I. (1988). Homicide. In J. Archer (ed.). *Male Violence*. (p.274). London: Routledge.

Daly, M. and Wilson, M. (1990). Killing and Competition: Female/Female and Male/Male Homicide. *Human Nature*, 1, 81–107.

Daly, M. and Wilson, M. (1994). Evolutionary psychology of male violence. In J. Archer (ed.). *Male Violence* (pp.253–88). London: Routledge.

Damasio, A.R., Grabowski, T.J., Bechara, A., Damasio, H., Ponto, L.L., Parvizi, J. and Hichwa, R.D. (2000). Subcortical and cortical brain activity during the feeling of self-generated emotions. *Natural Neuroscience*, 3(10), 1049–56.

Damon, W. (1977). *The Social World of the Child*. San Francisco, CA: Jossey-Bass.

Damon, W. (1988). *The Moral Child: Nurturing Children's Natural Moral Growth*. New York: Free Press.

Dando, C.J. and Milne, R. (2009). The cognitive interview. In R. Kocsis (ed.). *Applied Criminal Psychology: A Guide to Forensic Behavioral Sciences* (pp.5–9). Sydney: Charles Thomas Publishers.

Dando, C. J., Wilcock, R. and Milne, R. (2008). The cognitive interview: Inexperienced police officers' perceptions of their witness interviewing behaviour. *Legal and Criminological Psychology*, 13, 59–70.

Dando, C.J., Wilcock, R. and Milne, R. (2009a). The cognitive interview: The efficacy of a modified mental reinstatement of context procedure for frontline police investigators. *Applied Cognitive Psychology*, 23, 138–47.

Dando, C.J., Wilcock, R. and Milne, R. (2009b). Novice police officers application of the Cognitive Interview procedure. *Psychology, Crime, and Law*, 15, 679–96.

Dando, C.J., Wilcock, R., Milne, R. and Henry, L. (2009). An adapted Cognitive Interview procedure for frontline police investigators. *Applied Cognitive Psychology*, 23, 698–716.

Darling, S., Valentine, T. and Memon, A. (2008). Selection of line up foils in operational contexts. *Applied Cognitive Psychology*, 22, 159–69.

Darwin, C. (1859). *On the Origins of Species by Means of Natural Selection*. Buffalo, NY: Prometheus Books.

Darwin, C. (1871). *The Descent of Man and Selection in Relation to Sex* (1st edn.). London: John Murray.

Das, G. and Bezbaruah, A.K.R. (2011). Social transition and status of women among the Khasi Tribe of Meghalaya by survey method. *Global Research Methodology Journal*, 2nd Issue.

Daube, D. (1969). *Roman Law: Linguistic, Social and Philosophical Aspects*. Edinburgh: Edinburgh University Press.

Daugherty, T.K. and Quay, H.C. (1991). Response preservation and delayed responding in childhood behaviour disorders. *Journal of Child Psychology and Psychiatry*, 32, 453–61.

Davidson, R.J and Fox, N.A. (1989). Frontal brain asymmetry predicts infants' response to maternal separation. *Journal of Abnormal Psychology*, 98, 127–31.

Davidson, P., Turiel, E. and Black, A. (1983). The effect of stimulus familiarity on the use of criteria and justifications in children's social reasoning. *British Journal of Developmental Psychology*, 1, 49–65.

Davies, G.M. and Flin, R.H. (1988). The accuracy and suggestibility of child witnesses. In G.M. Davies and J. Drinkwater (eds.). *The Child Witness. Do the Courts Abuse Children?* Leicester: BPS Publications.

Davies, G.M. and Milne, A. (1985). Eyewitness composite production: A function of mental or physical reinstatement of context. *Criminal Justice and Behavior*, 12, 209–20.

Davis, M. (2006). Crimes Mala in Se: An Equity-Based Definition. *Criminal Justice Policy Review*, 17, 270–89.

Dawkins, R. (1976). *The Selfish Gene*. New York: Oxford University Press.

Day, R. and Wong, S. (1996). Anomalous perceptual asymmetries for negative emotional stimuli in the psychopath. *Journal of Abnormal Psychology*, 105, 648–52.

Dean, C., Mann, R.E., Milner, R. and Maruna, S. (2007). Changing child abusers cognitions. In T.A. Gannon, T. Ward, A.R. Beech and D. Fisher (eds.). *Aggressive Offender Cognitions: Theory, Research and Practice* (pp.117–34). Chichester, UK: John Wiley and Sons.

Death Penalty Information Center (2012). *Facts about the death penalty*. www.deathpenaltyinfo.org.

Decety, J. and Jackson, P.L. (2004). The functional architecture of human empathy. *Behavioral and Cognitive Neuroscience Reviews*, 3, 71–100.

Decuyper, M., De Fruyt, F. and Buschman, J. (2008). A five-factor model perspective on psychopathy and comorbid Axis-II disorders in a forensic-psychiatric sample. *International Journal of Law and Psychiatry*, 31(5), 394–406.

Deffenbacher, K.A., Bornstein, B.H., Penrod. S.D. and McGorty, E.K. (2004). A meta-analytic review of the effects of high stress on eyewitness memory. *Law and Human Behavior*, 28, 687–706.

de Haan, M. (2001). The neuropsychology of face processing during infancy and childhood. In C. A. Nelson and M. Luciana (eds.). *Handbook of Developmental Cognitive Neuroscience*. (pp.381–98). Cambridge, MA: MIT Press.

de Haan, M., Humphreys, K. and Johnson, M. H. (2002). Developing a brain specialised for face perception: A converging methods approach. *Developmental Psychobiology*, 40, 200–12.

Del Fabbro, G.A. (2006). *A Family Systems Understanding of Serial Murder* (p.15). Unpublished PhD Thesis. Pretoria: University of Pretoria.

DeLisi, M. (2001). It's All in the Record: Assessing Self-Control Theory with an Offender Sample. *Criminal Justice Review*, 26, 1–16.

DeLisi, M. and Vaughn, M.G. (2007). The Gottfredson-Hirschi critiques revisited: reconciling self-control theory, criminal craeers, and career criminals. *International Journal of Offender Therapy and Comparative Criminology*, 20(10), 1–18.

DeLisi, M. and Vaughn, M.G. (2011). The importance of neuropsychological deficits relating to self-control and temperament to the prevention of serious antisocial behavior. *International Journal of Child, Youth and Family Studies 1 and 2*, 12, 12–35.

de Rosnay, M. and Harris, P.L. (2002). Individual differences in children's understanding of emotion: The roles of attachment and language. *Attachment Human Development*, 4(1), 39–54.

De Waal, F.B.M. (2007). Putting the Altruism Back into Altruism: The Evolution of Empathy. *Annual Review of Psychology*, 59, 279–300.

Denham, S.A., Zoller, D. and Couchoud, E.A. (1994). Socialization of preschoolers' emotion understanding. *Developmental Psychology*, 30, 928–36.

Denscombe, M. (2001). Uncertain identities: The value of smoking for young adults in late modernity. *British Journal of Sociology*, 52(1), 157–78.

Dent, H.R. (1986). Experimental study of the effectiveness of different techniques of questioning mentally handicapped child witnesses. *British Journal of Child Psychology*, 25, 13–7.

Departmental Committee on Prisons (1985). *The 'Gladstone Committee'– report and minutes of evidence*. Public Record, The National Archives, Kew. http://discovery.nationalarchives. gov.uk/

Department of Health and Ministry of Justice National Personality Disorder Strategy (2011). Report for Consideration by Cabinet on 29th November 2011. Cabinet Report Budget Strategy 2012/13.

Dessecker, A. (2004). *Gefahrlichkeit und Verhaltnismassigkeit: Eine Untersuchungzum Massregelrecht*. Berlin: Duncker and Humblot.

Deutsch, J. and Deutsch, D. (1963). Attention: Some theoretical considerations. *Psychology Review*, 70, 80–90.

Devaud, C., Jeannin, A., Narring, F., Ferron, C. and Michaud, P.A. (1998). Eating disorders among female adolescents in Switzerland: Prevalence and associations with mental and behavioral disorders. *International Journal of Eating Disorders*, 24, 207–16.

Devlin, P. (1965). *Morals and the Criminal Law: The Enforcement of Morals*. London: OUP.

Diamond, J. (1997). *Why is Sex Fun?* New York: Basic Books.

Diamond, A., Barnett, W.S., Thomas, J. and Munro, S. (2007). Preschool program improves cognitive control. *Science*, 318(5855), 1387–8.

Diamantopoulou, S., Verhulst, F.C. and van der Ende, J. (2011). Gender differences in the development and adult outcome of co-occurring depression and delinquency in adolescence. *Journal of Abnormal Psychology*, 120(3), 644–55.

DiCenso, C. (1992). The adolescent sexual offender: Victim and perpetrator. In E. Viano (ed.). *Critical Issues in Victimology: International Perspectives* (pp.190–200). New York: Springer.

Digital Economy Act (2010). Act of Parliament of the UK. www.legislation.gov.uk/ ukpga/2010/24/contents

Dion, K., Berscheid, E. and Walster, E. (1972). What is beautiful is good. *Journal of Personality and Social Psychology*, 24, 285–90.

Dixon, L., Browne, K. and Hamilton-Giachritsis, C. (2005). Risk factors of parents abused as children: A mediational analysis of the intergenerational continuity of child maltreatment (Part I). *Journal of Child Psychology and Psychiatry,* 46(1), 47–57.

Dodge, M. and Pogrebin, M.R. (2001). Collateral Costs of Imprisonment for Women: Complications of Reintegration. *Prison Journal*, 81(1), 42–54.

Dolan, M. (2004). Psychopathic personality in young people. *Advances in Psychiatric Treatment*, 10, 466–473

Dolan, M. and Park, I. (2002). The neuropsychology of antisocial personality disorder. *Psychological Medicine*, 32, 417–27.

Donohue, J.J. (1998). Understanding the time path of crime. *Journal of Criminal Law and Criminology*, 88(4), 1423–52.

Doran, B.J. and Lees, B.G. (2005). Investigating the spatiotemporal links between disorder, crime, and the fear of crime. *The Professional Geographer* 57(1), 1–12.

Dorling, D., Gordon, D., Hillyard, P., Pantazis, C., Pemberton, S. and Tombs, S. (2008). *Criminal Obsessions: Why Harm Matters More Than Crime*. Centre for Crime and Justice Studies: London.

Douglas, J.E., Burgess, A.W., Burgess, A.G. and Ressler, R.K. (1992). *Crime Classification Manual: A Standard System for Investigating and Classifying Violent Crime* (p.21). New York: Simon and Schuster.

Douglas, J.E., Burgess, A.W. and Ressler, R.K. (1995). *Sexual Homicide: Patterns and Motives*. New York: The Free Press.

Douglas, J. and Olshaker, M. (1998). *Obsession* (p.90). London: Simon and Schuster.

Dowler, K. (2003). Media consumption and public attitudes toward crime and justice: The relationship between fear of crime, punitive attitudes and perceived police effectiveness. *Journal of Criminal Justice and Popular Culture*, 10(2), 109–26.

Downes, D. (1966a). *The Delinquent Solution*. London: Routledge and Kegan Paul.

Downes, D. (1966b). The gang myth. *The Listener*, 75, 534–37.

Downes, D. and Rock, P. (2003). *Understanding Deviance: A Guide to the Sociology of Crime and Rule Breaking*. Oxford: Oxford University Press.

Doyle, J. (2012). Crime age should be raised from 10 to 14 to protect children, say MPs. MailOnLine. www.dailymail.co.uk/news/article-2111315/Crime-age-raised-10–14-protect-children-say-MPs.html.

Doyle, M. and Dolan, M. (2006). Predicting community violence from patients discharged from mental health services. *British Journal of Psychiatry*, 189, 520–6.

Dugdale, R.L. (1877). *The Jukes: A Study in Crime, Pauperism, and Heredity*. New York: Putnam.

Dunn, B.D., Dalgleish, T. and Lawrence, A.D. (2006). The somatic marker hypothesis: A critical evaluation. *Neuroscience and Biobehavioral Reviews*, 30, 239–71.

Dunn, J. and Brown, J. (1994). Affect expression in the family, children's understanding of emotions, and their interactions with others. *Merrill-Palmer Quarterly*, 40, 120–37.

Dunning, D. and Perretta, S. (2002). Automaticity and eyewitness accuracy: A 10–12 second rule for distinguishing accurate from inaccurate positive identifications. *Journal of Applied Psychology*, 87, 951–62.

Durkheim, E. (1925). *Moral Education: A Study in the Theory and Application of the Sociology of Moral Education*. In E.K. Wilson and H. Schnurer, trans 1961. New York: Free Press.

Eagly, A.H. and Chaiken, S. (1993). *The Psychology of Attitudes*. Fort Worth, TX: Harcourt Brace Jovanovich.

East, P.L. (1989). Early adolescents' perceived interpersonal risks and benefits: Relations to social support and psychological functioning. *Journal of Early Adolescence*, 9(4), 374–95.

East, P.L. and Rook, K.S. (1992). Compensatory patterns of support among children's peer relationships: A test using school friends, nonschool friends, and siblings. *Developmental Psychology*, 28, 163–72.

Eaves, D., Tien, G. and Wilson, D. (2000). Offenders with major affective disorders. In S. Hodgins and R. Müller-Isberner (eds.). *Violence, Crime and Mentally Disordered Offenders* (pp.131–52). Chichester, UK: Wiley.

Ebbesen, E. and Flowe, S. (2002). Simultaneous versus sequential lineups: what do we really know? www.psy.uesd.edu/%7eeebbesen/SimSeq.htm.

Ede, R. and Shepherd, E. (2000). *Active Defence* (2nd ed.). London: Law Society Publishing.

Edelhertz, H. (1970). *The Nature, Impact and Prosecution of White Collar Crime* (pp.3–4). Washington, D.C.: National Institute of Law Enforcement and Criminal Justice.

Edens, J.F., Marcus, D.K., Lilienfeld, S.O. and Poythress, N.G. (2006). Psychopathic, not psychopath: Taxometric evidence for the dimensional structure of psychopathy. *Journal of Abnormal Psychology*, 115(1), 131–44.

Egan, V. (2013). Are terrorists conservative? *The Psychologist*, 26(3), 226.

Egger, S. (1990). *Serial Murder: An Elusive Phenomenon*. New York: Preager Publishers.

Ehrenkranz, J., Bliss, E. and Sheard, M.H. (1974). Plasma testosterone: Correlation with aggressive behavior and social dominance in man. *Psychosomatic Medicine*, 36( 6), 469–75.

Eisenberg, N., Fabes, R.A., Shepard, S.A., Murphy, B.C., Jones, J. and Guthrie, I.K. (1998). Contemporaneous and longitudinal prediction of children's sympathy from dispositional regulation and emotionality. *Developmental Psychology*, 34, 910–24.

Eisenberg, N. and McNally, S. (1993). Socialisation and mothers' and adolescents' empathy-related characteristics. *Journal of Research on Adolescence*, 3, 171–91.

Eisenstein, Z. (1988). *The Female Body and the Law* (p.8). Berkeley, CA: University of California Press.

Ekman, P. (1992). Facial expressions of emotion: New findings, new questions. *Psychological Science*, 3(1), 34–8.

Ekman, P. (1996). Why don't we catch liars? *Social Research*, 63(3), 801–17.

Ekman, P. and Friesen, W.V. (1986). A new pan-cultural facial expression of emotion. *Motivation and Emotion*, 10(2), 159–68.

Elbogen, E.B., Patry, M. and Scalora, M.J. (2003). The impact of community notification laws on sex offender treatment attitudes. *International Journal of Law and Psychiatry*, 26, 207–19.

Eley, T.C., Lichtenstein, P. and Stevenson, J. (1999). Sex differences in the etiology of aggressive and nonaggressive antisocial behavior: Results from two twin studies. *Child Development*, 70(1), 155–68.

El-Gamal, M.A. (2006). *Islamic Finance: Law, Economics, and Practice* (p.16). Cambridge: Cambridge University Press.

Elliott, M., Browne, K. and Kilcoyne, J. (1995). Child sexual abuse prevention: What offenders tell us. *Child Abuse and Neglect*, 19, 579–94.

Ellis, H.D., Davies, G.M. and Shepherd, J.W. (1975). An investigation of the use of the Photo-fit technique for recalling faces. *British Journal of Psychology*, 66, 29–37.

Ellis, L. (1991). Monoamine oxidase and criminality: Identifying an apparent biological marker for antisocial behavior. *Journal of Research on Crime and Delinquency*, 28, 227–51.

Ellis, P.L. (1982). Empathy: A factor in antisocial behavior. *Journal of Abnormal Child Psychology*, 2, 123–33.

Ellsworth, P.C. (1989). Are 12 heads better than one? *Law and Contemporary Problems*, 52, 205–24.

Emde, R.N., Wolf, D.P. and Oppenheim, D. (2003). *Revealing the Inner Worlds of Young Children: The MacArthur Story Stem Battery and Parent-Child Narratives*. New York: Oxford University Press.

Eme, R. (1992). Selective female affliction in the developmental disorders: A literature review. *Journal of Clinical Child Psychology*, 21, 354–64.

Epstein, S. (1985). The implications of cognitive-experiential self-theory for research in social psychology and personality. *Journal for the Theory of Social Behaviour*, 15, 283–310.

Epstein, S. (1994). Integration of the cognitive and the psychodynamic unconscious. *American Psychologist*, 49, 709–24.

Epstein, S. (2003). Cognitive-experiential self-theory of personality. In T. Millon and M.J. Lerner (eds.). *Handbook of Psychology, vol. 5 Personality and Social Psychology* (pp.159–84). Hoboken, NJ: Wiley.

Erikson, K. (1966). *Wayward Puritans: A Study in the Sociology of Deviance*. New York: John Wiley and Sons.

Eriksrud, R.H. and Trana, J. (2010). *Death Penalty Bulletin*, No. 4. Norway: Amnesty International.

Eron, L.D. and Huesmann, L.R. (1984). *Advances in the study of aggression*. Orlando, FL: Academic Press.

Eron, L.D. and Huesmann, L.R. (1986). The role of television in the development of antisocial and prosocial behavior. In D. Olweus, J. Block and M. Radke-Yarrow (eds.). *Development of Antisocial and Prosocial Behavior: Research, Theories and Issues*. New York: Academic Press.

Evans, G. and Webb, M. (1993). High profile – but not that high profile: interviewing of young persons. In E. Shepherd (ed.). *Aspects of Police Interviewing*. Leicester: British Psychological Society.

Evans, J.R. and Park, N.S. (1997). Quantitative EEG findings among men convicted of murder. *Journal of Neurotherapy*, 2(2), 31–9.

Evans, M. (2012). Sam Hallam's murder conviction quashed by seven-year-old evidence. Crime Correspondent for the Telegraph. *The Telegraph*. Telegraph Media Group Limited. www.telegraph.co.uk/news/uknews/crime/9272365/Sam-Hallams-murder-conviction-quashed-by-seven-year-old-evidence.html.

Evans, R. (1993). *The Conduct of Police Interviews with Juveniles*. Royal Commission on Criminal Justice Report. London: HMSO.

Evans, W.P., Brown, R. and Killian, E. (2002). Decision making and perceived post-detention success among incarcerated youth. *Crime and Delinquency*, 48, 553–67.

Fagan, J. (1990). Intoxication and aggression in drugs and crime. In M. Tonry and J.Q. Wilson (eds.). *Crime and Justice: A Review of Research* (pp.241–320). Chicago: University of Chicago Press.

Fallon, J. (2011). *Horizon: Are You Good or Evil?* Broadcast by BBC2 on 7/9/11.

Falshaw, L., Browne, K. and Hollin, C. (1996). Victim to offender: A review. *Aggression and Violent Behavior*, 1(4), 389–404.

Fanslow, J.L., Robinson, E.M., Crengle, S. and Perese, L. (2007). Prevalence of child sexual abuse reported by a cross-sectional sample of New Zealand women. *Child Abuse and Neglect*, 31(9), 935–45.

Fantz, R.L. (1961). The origin of form perception. *Scientific American*, 204(5), 66–72.

Fantz, R.L. (1963). Pattern vision in newborn infants. *Science*, 140, 296–7.

Fantz, R.and Miranda, S. (1975). Newborn Infant Attention to Form of Contour. *Child Development*, 46, 224–8.

Farrington, D.P. (1972). Delinquency begins at home. *New Society*, 21, 495–7.

Farrington, D.P. (1986). Stepping stones to adult criminal careers. In D. Olweus, J. Block and M. Radke-Yarrow (eds.). *Development of Antisocial and Prosocial Behavior: Research, Theories and Issues.* Orlando: Academic Press.

Farrington, D.P. (1989). Early predictors of adolescent aggression and adult violence. *Violence and Victims,* 4, 79–100.

Farrington, D.P. (1990a). Age, period, cohort, and offending. In D.M. Gottfredson and R.V. Clarke (eds.). *Policy and Theory in Criminal Justice: Contributions in Honour of Leslie T. Wilkins* (pp.51–75). Aldershot: Gower.

Farrington, D.P. (1990b). Implications of criminal career research for the prevention of offending. *Journal of Adolescence,* 13, 93–113.

Farrington, D.P. (1992). Expanding the beginning, progress, and ending of antisocial behaviour from birth to adulthood. In J. McCord (ed.). *Facts, Frameworks and Forecasts: Advances in Criminological Theory, Volume 3.* (pp.521, 532). New Brunswick: Transactional Publishers.

Farrington, D.P. (1993). Childhood origins of teenage antisocial behaviour and adult social dysfunction. *Journal of the Royal Society of Medicine,* 86, 13–7.

Farrington, D.P. (1994). Childhood, adolescent and adult features of violent males. In L.R. Huesmann (ed.). *Aggressive Behavior: Current Perspectives* (pp.215–40). New York: Plenum.

Farrington, D.P. (1995a). The development of offending and antisocial behaviour from childhood: Key findings from the Cambridge Study in Delinquent Development. *Journal of Child Psychology and Psychiatry and Allied Disciplines,* 36(6), 929–64.

Farrington, D.P. (1995b). The psychology of crime: influences and constraints on offending. In R. Bull and D. Carson (eds.). *Handbook of Psychology in Legal Contexts* (pp.291–314). Chichester, UK: John Wiley.

Farrington, D.P. (1996). Self Reported Delinquency and a Combined Delinquency Seriousness Scale Based on Boys, Mothers, and Teachers: Concurrent and Predictive Validity for African-Americans and Caucasians. *Criminology,* 34(4), 493–518.

Farrington, D.P., Coid, J.W., Harnett, L., Jolliffe, D., Soteriou, N., Turner, R. and West, D.J. (2006). *Criminal Careers and Life Success: New Findings from the Cambridge Study in Delinquent Development.* Research, Development and Statistics Directorate: Home Office, 281.

Farrington, D.P. and Hawkins, J.D. (1991). Predicting participation, early onset and later persistence in officially recorded offending. *Criminal Behaviour and Mental Health,* 1, 1–33.

Farrington, D.P., Jolliffe, D., Loeber, R., Stouthamer-Loeber, M. and Kalb, L.M. (2001). The concentration of offenders in families, and family criminality in the prediction of boys' delinquency. *Journal of Adolescence,* 24, 579–96.

Farrington, D.P., Lambert, S. and West, D.J. (1998). Criminal careers of two generations of family members in the Cambridge Study in Delinquent Development. *Studies on Crime and Crime Prevention,* 7, 85–106.

Farrington, D.P. and Loeber, R. (1999). Transatlantic replicability of risk factors in the development of delinquency. In E.J. Palmer (2003b). *Offending Behaviour: Moral Reasoning, Criminal Conduct and the Rehabilitation of Offenders.* Cullompton: Willan Publishing.

Farrington, D.P., Loeber, R., Yin, Y. and Anderson, S. (2002). Are within-individual causes of delinquency the same as between-individual causes? *Criminal Behaviour and Mental Health,* 12, 53–68.

Farrington, D.P. and West, D.J. (1990). The Cambridge Study in Delinquent Development: A long-term follow-up of 411 London males. In E.J. Palmer (2003b). *Offending Behaviour: Moral Reasoning, Criminal Conduct and the Rehabilitation of Offenders*. Cullompton: Willan Publishing.

Faulds, H. (1880/2005). On the skin furrows of the hand. In I.K. Pepper (ed.). *Crime Scene Investigation* (pp.78–9). Maidenhead: Open University Press, McGraw-Hill Education.

Fazel, S. and Danesh, J. (2002). Serious mental disorder in 23000 prisoners: A systematic review of 62 surveys. *Lancet*, 359(9306), 545–50.

Federal Bureau of Investigation (2005). *Serial Murder: Multi-Disciplinary Perspectives for Investigators* (p.9). Quantico, V.A: Behavioral Analysis Unit-2, National Centre for the Analysis of Violent Crime, Critical Incident Response Group, Federal Bureau of Investigation.

Federal Bureau of Investigation (2008). Crime in the U.S.: The Uniform Crime Report. Washington, DC: GPO.

Feild, H.S. (1979). Rape trials and jurors' decisions: A psycholegal analysis of the effects of victim, defendant, and case characteristics. *Law and Human Behavior*, 3(4), 261–84.

Feldner, Y. (2000). 'Honor' murders – why the perps get off easy. *Middle East Quarterly*, 7(4), 41–50.

Ferguson, T. (1952). *The Young Delinquent in His Social Setting*. London: Oxford University Press.

Fernandez, Y.M. and Marshall, W.L. (2003). Victim empathy, social self-esteem and psychopathy in rapists. *Sexual Abuse: A Journal of Research and Treatment*, 15, 11–26.

Fernandez, Y.M., Shingler, J. and Marshall, W.L. (2006). Putting 'behaviour' back into the cognitive-behavioural treatment of sexual offenders (pp.211–24). In W.L. Marshall, Y.M. Fernandez, L.E. Marshall et al. (eds.). *Sexual Offender Treatment: Controversial Issues*. Chichester, UK: John Wiley and Sons.

Ferraro, K. (1995). *Fear of Crime: Interpreting Victimisation Risk*. Albany: State University of New York Press.

Field, J.L., Johnson. L., Kim, S., and Salfati, C.G. (2006). *Examining Expressiveness and Instrumentality in Serial Murder and Distances Travelled by Offenders*. Poster presented at American Society of Criminology Conference, Los Angeles, USA.

Field, T., Diego, M., Dieter, J., Hernandez-Reif, M., Schanberg, S., Kuhn, C. et al. (2004). Prenatal depression effects on the fetus and the newborn. *Infant Behavior and Development*, 27, 216–29.

Field, T., Diego, M., Hernandez-Reif, M., Salman, F., Schanberg, S., Kuhn, C. et al. (2002). Prenatal anger effects on the fetus and neonate. *Journal of Obstetrics and Gynecology*, 22, 260–6.

Figueira-McDonough, J. (1984). Feminism and delinquency: In search of an illusive link. *British Journal of Criminology*, 24(4), 325–42.

Fine, C. and Kennett, J. (2004). Mental impairment, moral understanding and criminal responsibility: Psychopathy and the purposes of punishment. *International Journal of Law and Psychiatry*, 27(5), 425–43.

Finger, E.C., Marsh, A.A., Mitchell, D.G., Reid, M.E., Sims, C., Budhani, S., Kosson, D.S., Chen, G., Towbin, K.E., Leibenluft, E., Pine, D.S. and Blair, J.R. (2008). Abnormal ventromedial prefrontal cortex function in children with psychopathic traits during reversal learning. *Archives of General Psychiatry*, 65(5), 586–94.

Finkelhor, D. (1994). The international epidemiology of child sexual abuse. *Child Abuse and Neglect*, 18(5), 409–17.

Finkelhor, D., Moore, D. Hamby, S. L. and Straus, M.A. (1997). Sexual abused children in a national survey of parents: Methodological issues. *Child Abuse and Neglect*, 21, 1–9.

Finney, A. (2006). *Domestic Violence, Sexual Assault and Stalking findings from the 2004/05 British Crime Survey*. London: Home Office.

Fisher, B.S., Cullen, F.T. and Turner, M.G. (2000). *The Sexual Victimization of College Women* (p.28). Research Report. National Institute of Justice. US Department of Justice.

Fisher, D., Beech, A. and Browne, K. (1999). Comparison of sex offenders to nonoffenders on selected psychological measures. *International Journal of Offender Therapy and Comparative Criminology*, 43(4), 473–91.

Fisher, R.P. and Geiselman, R.E. (1992). *Memory Enhancing Techniques for Investigative Interviewing: The Cognitive Interview*. Springfield III: Charles C. Thomas.

Fisher, R.P., Geiselman, R.E. and Amador, M. (1989). Field test of the cognitive interview: Enhancing the recollection of actual victims and witnesses of crime. *Journal of Applied Psychology*, 74(5), 722–7.

Fisher, R.P., Geiselman, R.E. and Raymond, D.S. (1987). Critical analysis of police interviewing techniques. *Journal of Police Science and Administration*, 15, 177–85.

Fisher, R.P., Geiselman, R.E., Raymond, D.S., Jurkevich, L. and Warhaftig, M.L. (1987). Enhancing enhanced eyewitness memory: Refining the cognitive interview. *Journal of Police Science and Administration*, 15, 291–7.

Fisher, R.P. and Price-Roush, J. (1986). *Question Order and Eyewitness Memory*. Unpublished Manuscript, Department of Psychology, Florida International University, USA.

Fitzpatrick, A., Grant, C., Bolling, K., Owen, R. and Millard, B. (2010). *Extending the British Crime Survey to Children: A Report on the Methodological and Development Work*. London: TNS-BMRB and the Home Office.

Flatley, J., Kershaw, C., Smith, K., Chaplin, R. and Moon, D. (2010). *Crime in England and Wales 2009/10*. Home Office Statistical Bulletin 12/10. London: Home Office.

Flavell, J.H. (2000). Development of children's knowledge about the mental world. *International Journal of Behavioral Development*, 24, 15–23.

Flavell, J.H. (2004). Theory-of-mind development: Retrospect and prospect. *Merrill-Palmer Quarterly*, 50, 274–90.

Flesch, R. (1948). A new readability yardstick. *Journal of Applied Psychology*, 32(3), 221–33.

Flin, R.H. (1995). Psychology on trial. In M. Zaragoza (ed.). *Child Witnesses. Research and Practice*. New York: SAGE.

Flin, R.H., Boon, J., Knox, A. and Bull, R. (1992). The effect of a five-month delay on children's and adults' eyewitness memory. *British Journal of Psychology*, 83, 323–36.

Floud, J. and Young, W. (1981). *Dangerousness and Criminal Justice*. London: Heinemann Educational Books.

Flor, H., Birbaumer, N., Hermann, C., Ziegler, S. and Patrick, C.J. (2002). Aversive Pavlovian conditioning in psychopaths: peripheral and central correlates. *Psychophysiology*, 39, 505–18.

Foley, L.A. and Chamblin, M.H. (1982). The effect of race and personality on mock jurors' decisions. *The Journal of Psychology*, 112, 47–51.

Fonagy, P., Target, M., Steele, M., Steele, H., Leigh, T., Levinson, A. and Kennedy, R. (1997). Morality, disruptive behavior, borderline personality disorder, crime and their relationship to security of attachment. In L. Atkinson and K.J. Zucker (eds.). *Attachment and Psychopathology* (pp.223–74). New York: Guilford Press.

Forrest, K.D., Wadkins, T.A. and Miller, R.L. (2002). The role of pre-existing stress on false confessions: An empirical study. *The Journal of Credibility Assessment and Witness Psychology*, 3, 23–45.

Forsman, M., Lichtenstein, P., Andershed, H. and Larsson, H. (2010). A longitudinal twin study of the direction of effects between psychopathic personality and antisocial behaviour. *Journal of Child Psychology and Psychiatry*, 51(1), 39–47.

Foster, R.A., Libkuman, T.M., Schooler, J.W. and Loftus, E.F. (1994). Consequentiality and eyewitness person identification. *Applied Cognitive Psychology*, 8(2), 107–21.

Fox, B.H., Farrington, D.P., Chitwood, M. and Janes, E. (2013). Developing a profile for burglary. *Criminal Investigation Review*, 78–91.

Freedman, L. (2002). *Superterrorism Policy Responses*. Malden, MA: Blackwell Publishing.

Freeman-Longo, R.E., Bird, S., Stevenson, W.F. and Fiske, J.a. (1995). *1994 Nationwide Survey of Treatment Programs and Models: Serving Abuse Reactive Children and Adolescent and Adult Sexual Offenders*. Brandon, VT: Safer Society Press.

Frei, A., Vollom, B., Graf, M. and Dittmann, V. (2006). Female serial killing: Review and case report. *Criminal Behaviour and Mental Health*, 16(33), 167–76.

Freud, S. (1920). *A General Introduction to Psychoanalysis*. New York: Basic Books.

Freund, K., Scher, H. and Hucker, S.J. (1983). The courtship disorders. *Archives of Sexual Behavior*, 12, 769–79.

Friedrich-Cofer, L. and Huston, A.C. (1986). Television violence and aggression: The debate continues. *Psychological Bulletin*, 100, 363–71.

Friendship, C., Blud, L., Erikson, M., Travers, R. and Thornton, D.M. (2003). Cognitive-behavioural treatment for imprisoned offenders: An evaluation of HM Prison Service's cognitive skills programmes. *Legal and Criminological Psychology*, 8, 103–14.

Friendship, C., Mann, R. and Beech, A. (2003). *The Prison-based Sex Offender Treatment Programme – An Evaluation*. London Home Office Development and Statistics Directorate Research Findings No. 205. www.homeoffice.gov.uk/rds/pdfs2/r205.pdf.

Frith, U. (2001). Mind blindness and the brain in autism. *Neuron*, 32, 969–79.

Frodi, A., Dernevik, M., Sepa, A., Philipson, J. and Bragesjo, M. (2001). Current attachment representations of incarcerated offenders varying in degree of psychopathy. *Attachment and Human Development*, 3, 269–83.

Fromont, M. (2001). *Grands systèmes de droit étrangers*, (4th edn.). Paris: Dalloz.

Frowd, C.D., Bruce, V. and Hancock, P.J.B. (2008). Changing the face of criminal identification. *The Psychologist*, 21(8), 670–2.

Frowd, C.D., Bruce, V., Ness, H., Thomson-Bogner, C., Paterson, J., McIntyre, A. and Hancock, P.J.B. (2007). Parallel approaches to composite production. *Ergonomics*, 50, 562–85.

Fry, E. (1998). *The Legal Aspects of Readability*. Presented at meeting of the International Reading Association, New Orleans, LA (revised). (ERIC Document No. ED 416 466).

Frye, J.G. (1998). Supreme Court of Alabama Rutledge v. State, 482 So. 2nd 1250, 1983 Alaska Criminal Appeal. *LEXIS*, 4703

Fuller, R. (1996). Fluoxetine effects on serotonin function and aggressive behavior. *Ann NY Academy of Science*, 794, 90–7.

Furnham, A. (2003). Belief in a just world: research progress over the past decade. *Personality and Individual Differences*, 34: 795–817.

Gabbert, F., Hope, L. and Fisher, R.P. (2009). Protecting eyewitness evidence: Examining the efficacy of a self-administered interview tool. *Law and Human Behavior*, 33, 298–307.

Gabbert, F., Hope, L. and Jamieson, K. (2010). In *the Field: Trials of Self-administered Interview Recall Tool with Witnesses to Serious Crime*. Paper Presented at the American Psychology Law Society Meeting, Vancouver.

Gall, F.J. and Spurzheim, J.G.(1810). *The Anatomy and Physiology of the Nervous System in General, and of the Brain in Particular*. London: Aldwin, Cradock, and Joy.

Galton, F. (1888). Personal identification and description. In I.K. Pepper (ed.). *Crime Scene Investigation* (p.79). Maidenhead: Open University Press, McGraw-Hill Education, 2005.

Galton, F. (1892). Finger Prints. In I.K. Pepper (ed.). *Crime Scene Investigation* (p.79). Maidenhead, UK: Open University Press, McGraw-Hill Education, 2005.

Gannon, T.A., Beech, A.R. and Ward, T. (2008). Does the polygraph lead to better risk prediction for sexual offenders? *Aggression and Violent Behavior*, 13, 29–44.

Gao, Y. and Raine, A. (2010). Successful and unsuccessful psychopaths: A neurobiological model. *Behavioral Sciences and the Law*, 28, 194–210.

Gao, Y., Raine, A., Chan, F., Venables, P.H. and Mednick, S.A. (2010). Early maternal and paternal bonding, childhood physical abuse and adult psychopathic personality. *Psychological Medicine*, 40(6), 1007–16.

Garber, J. and Mardin, N.C. (2002). Negative cognitions in offspring of depressed parents: Mechanisms of risk. In S.H. Goodmana dn I.N. Gotlib (eds.). *Children of Depressed Parents* (pp.121–54). Washington, DC: American Psychological Association.

Garfinkel, H. (1967). *Studies in Ethnomethodology*. Englewood Cliffs, NJ: Prentice Hall.

Garfinkel, H. (2002). *Ethnomethodology's Program*. New York: Rowman and Littlefield.

Garrido, E. and Masip, J. (1999). How good are police officers at spotting lies? *Forensic Update*, 58, 14–21

Geberth, V. (1981). Psychological profiling. *Law and Order Magazine*, 29, 46–9.

Geberth, V. (1995). The Signature Aspect in Criminal Investigation. *Law and Order Magazine*, 43, 45–9.

Geberth, V. (1996). The Staged Crime Scene. *Law and Order Magazine*, 44, 89–93.

Geis, G. (1972). *Not the Law's Business: An Examination of Homosexuality, Abortion, Prostitution, Narcotics and Gambling in the United States*. Washington: US Department of Health and Welfare.

Geiselman, R.E and Callot, R. (1990). Reverse versus forward order recall of script based texts, *Applied Cognitive Psychology*, 4, 141–4.

Geiselman, R.E., Fisher, R.P., MacKinnon, D.P. and Holland, H.L. (1985). Eyewitness memory enhancement in the police interview: Cognitive retrieval mnemonics versus hypnosis. *Journal of Applied Psychology*, 70, 401–12.

Geiselman, R.E., Fisher, R.P., Mackinnon, D.P. and Holland, H.L. (1986). Enhancement of eyewitness memory with the cognitive interview. *American Journal of Psychology*, 99, 354–401.

Gelfand, D.M., Jensen, W.R. and Drew, C.J. (1997). *Understanding Child Behavior Disorders* (3rd edn.). Fort Worth, TX: Harcourt Brace.

Gemignani, M. and Peña, E. (2007/2008). Postmodern Conceptualizations of Culture in Social Constructionism and Cultural Studies. *Journal of Theoretical and Philosophical Psychology*, 27(2), 2007 and 28(1), 2008.

Gendreau, P. and Ross, R.R. (1987). Revivication of rehabilitation: Evidence from the 1980s. *Justice Quarterly*, 4, 349–407.

Gendreau, P., Little, T. and Goggin, C. (1996). A meta-analysis of the predictors of adult offender recidivism: What works! *Criminology*, 34(4), 575–608.

General Medical Council (1993). *Professional Conduct and Discipline: Fitness to Practise*. London: GMC.

George, C. and West, M. (1999). Developmental vs. social personality models of adult attachment and mental ill health. *British Journal of Medical Psychology*, 72, 285–303.

Gerbner, G. and Gross, L. (1976). Living with television: The violence profile. *Journal of Communication*, 26, 173–99.

Gerhardt, S. (2004). *Why Love Matters: How Affection Shapes a Baby's Brain*. Hove, Sussex: Brunner-Routledge.

Gibbs, J.C. (2003). *Moral Development and Reality: Beyond the Theories of Kohlberg and Hoffman*. Thousand Oaks, CA: SAGE Publication.

Gibbs, J.C., Arnold, K.D., Ahlborn, H.H. and Cheesman, F. (1984). Facilitation of socio-moral reasoning in delinquents. *Journal of Consulting and Clinical Psychology*, 52, 37–45.

Gibbs, J.C. and Potter, G.B. (1992). *A Typology of Criminogenic Cognitive Distortions*. Unpublished manuscript, Ohio State University, Columbus.

Giles, M. (1990). *Nutshells Criminal Law in a Nutshell* (2nd edn.). London: Sweet and Maxwell Ltd.

Gilbert, R., Widom, C.S., Browne, K., Fergusson, D., Webb, E. and Janson, S. (2009). Burden and consequences of child maltreatment in high-income countries. *Lancet*, 373(9657), 68–81.

Gillies, V., Ribbens McCarthy, J. and Holland, J. (2001) *Pulling Together, Pulling Apart: the Family Lives of Young People*. London: Family Policy Studies Centre/Joseph Rowntree Foundation.

Gilligan, A. (2011). Ken Livingstone: the rioters need someone to 'care about them and speak for them'. *The Telegraph*, Telegraph Media Group Ltd, 9 August.

Gilligan, C. (1982). *In a Different Voice: Psychological Theory and Women's Development*. Cambridge, MA: Harvard University Press.

Ginsburg, H., Wright, L.S., Harrell, P.M. and Hill, D.W. (1989). Childhood victimisation: desensitisation effects in the later lifespan. *Child Psychiatry Human Development*, 20(1), 59–71.

Glaister, D. (2009). China accused of global cyberspying. *The Guardian Weekly*, 180(16), 5.

Glassner, B. (1999). *The Culture of Fear*. New York: Basic Books.

Glenn, A.I. and Raine, A. (2009). Psychopathy and instrumental aggression: Evolutionary, neurobiological, and legal perspectives. *International Journal of Law and Psychiatry*, 32, 253–58.

Glenn, A.I., Raine, A. and Schug, R.A. (2009). The neural correlates of moral decision-making in psychopathy. *Molecular Psychiatry*, 14, 5–6.

Glicksohn, J., Ben-Shalom, U. and Lazar, M. (2004). Elements of unacceptable risk taking in combat units: An exercise in offender profiling. *Journal of Research in Personality*, 38, 203–15.

Glover, N. (1999). *Risk Assessment and Community Care in England and Wales*. Liverpool: Faculty of Law, University of Liverpool.

Glueck, S. and Glueck, E. (1950). *Unravelling Juvenile Delinquency*. New York: Harper and Row.

Gneezy, U. and List, J. (2013). *The Why Axis: Hidden Motives and the Undiscovered Economics of Everyday Life*. New York: PublicAffairs.

Godden, D.R. and Baddeley, A.D. (1975). Context-dependent memory in two natural environments: On land and under water. *British Journal of Psychology*, 66, 325–31.

Godwin, M. and Canter, D. (1997). Encounter and death: The spatial behaviour of US serial killers. *Policing: International Journal of Police Strategy and Management*, 20, 24–38.

Goldfried, M.R. and Sprafkin, J.N. (1976). *Behavioural personality assessment*. Morristown, NJ: General Learning Press.

Goldstein, J.M., Jerram, M., Poldrack, R., Anagnoson, R., Breiter, H.C., Makris, N., Goodmman, J.M., Tsuang, M.T. and Seidman, L.J. (2005). Sex differences in prefrontal cortical brain activity during fMRI of auditory verbal working memory. *Neuropsychology*, 19, 509–19.

Goode, E. and Ben-Yehuda, N. (1994). *Moral Panics: The Social Construction of Deviance*. Cambridge, MA: Blackwell.

Goodey, J. (1997). Boys Don't Cry: Masculinities, Fear of Crime and Fearlessness. *The British Journal of Criminology*, 37(3), 401–18.

Goodey, J. (2005). *Victims and Victimology: Research, Policy and Practice*. Harlow: Pearson Education Ltd.

Goodman, G.S., Aman, C. and Hirschman, J. (1987). Child sexual and physical abuse: Children's testimony. In S.J. Ceci, M.P. Toglia and D.F. Ross (eds.). *Children's Eyewitness Memory* (p.79). New York: Springer-Verlag.

Goodman, R. and Stevenson, J. (1989). A twin study of hyperactivity: An examination of hyperactivity scores and categories derived from Rutter Teacher and Parent Questionnaires. *The Journal of Child Psychology and Psychiatry*, 30(5), 671–89.

Gorby, B.L. (2000). *Serial Murder: A Cross-national Descriptive Study*. Fresno, CA: California State University.

Gordon, A.M. (1973). Patterns of delinquency in drug addiction. *The British Journal of Psychiatry*, 122, 205–10.

Gordon, D.A. and Arbuthnot, J. (1987). Individual, group, and family interventions. In H.C. Quay (ed.). *Handbook of Juvenile Delinquency*. New York: Wiley.

Gordon, H.L., Baird, A.A. and End, A. (2004) Functional differences among those high and low on a trait measure of psychopathy. *Biological Psychiatry*, 56, 516–21.

Gosavi, S.R., Gajbe, U.L., Meshram, S.W. and Chimurkar, V.K. (2009). Cytogenetic study in criminals (murderers): Role of XYY chromosome in criminality. *Journal of Clinical and Diagnostic Research*, 3(6), 1911–4.

Gottfredson, M. (1984). Victims of Crime: The Dimensions of Risk. *Home Office Research Study*, 81. London: HMSO.

Gottfredson, M.R. (2006). The empirical status of control theory in criminology. In F. Cullen, J.P. Wright and K.R. Blevins (eds.). *Taking Stock: The Status of Criminological Theory* (pp.77–100). New Brunswick: Transaction Publishers.

Gottfredson, M.R. and Hirschi, T. (1990). *A General Theory of Crime*. Stanford, CA: Stanford University Press.

Götz, M.J., Johnstone, E.C. and Ratcliffe, S.G. (1999). Criminality and antisocial behaviour in unselected men with sex chromosome abnormalities. *Psychological Medicine*, 29(4), 953–62.

Gould, P. (2005). Life of crime (part 1). *BBC News*. http://news.bbc.co.uk/hi/english/static/in_depth/uk/2001/life_of_crime/yob_culture.stm

Graham, J. and Bowling, B. (1995). *Young People and Crime*. London: Home Office.

Granhag, P.A. and Spjut, E. (2001) Childrens's recall of the unfortunate fakir: A further test of the Enhanced Cognitive Interview. In R. Roesch, R.R. Corrado and R.J. Dempster (eds.). *Psychology in the Courts: International Advances in Knowledge* (pp.209–22). London: Routledge.

Granhag, P-A. and Stromwall, L. (2004). *The Detection of Deception in Forensic Contexts.* Cambridge, MA: Cambridge University Press.

Gray, N.S., Hill, C., McGleish, A., Timmons, D., MacCulloch, M.J. and Snowden, R.J. (2003). Prediction of violence and self-harm in mentally disordered offenders: a prospective study of the efficacy of HCR–20, PCL–R and psychiatric symptomology. *Journal of Consultancy Clinical Psychology*, 71, 443–51.

Gray, N.S., Snowden, R.J., MacCulloch, S., Phillips, H., Taylor, J. and MacCulloch, M.J. (2004). Relative efficacy of criminological, clinical and personality measures of future risk of offending in mentally disordered offenders: a comparative study of HCR-20, PCL:SV and OGRS. *Journal of Consultancy Clinical Psychology*, 72, 523–30.

Gray, N.S., Taylor, J. and Snowden, R.J. (2008). Predicting violent reconvictions using the HCR–20. *The British Journal of Psychiatry*, 192, 384–7.

Gray, P., Campbell, B., Marlowe, F., Lipson, S. and Ellison, P. (2004). Social variables predict between-subject but not day-to-day variation in testosterone of US men. *Psychoneuroendocrinology* 29, 1153–62.

Greene, E. and Drew, E. (2008). *Resources for teaching undergraduate psychology and law courses (p.3).* Fort Collins, CO: University of Colorado at Colorado Springs.

Greene, J. and Haidt, J. (2002). How (and where) does moral judgment work? *Trends in Cognitive Science*, 6, 517–23.

Greene, J.D., Sommerville, R.B., Nystrom, L.E., Darley, J.M. and Cohen, J.D. (2001). An fMRI investigation of emotional engagement in moral judgment. *Science*, 293(5537), 2105–8.

Greenberg, D.M., Bradford, J. and Curry, S. (1995). Infantophilia – A New Subcategory of Pedophilia?: A Preliminary Study. *Bulletin of American Academy of Psychiatric Law*, 23(1), 63–71.

Greenberg, M.T., Kusche, C. and Mihalic, S.F. (2006). *Promoting Alternative Thinking Strategies (PATHS): Blueprints for Violence Prevention* (Book Ten). Boulder, CO: Centre for the Study and Prevention of Violence.

Greenwald, G. (2009). *'Preventive Detention' And Prisoners of War.* TalkLeft the politics of crime. 22 May 2009 www.talkleft.com/story/2009/5/22/112959/706/detainees/-Preventive-Detention-And-Prisoners–Of-War.

Gresswell, D.M. and Hollin, C.R. (1994). Multiple murder: A review. *British Journal of Criminology*, 34(1), 1–13.

Grevatt, M., Thomas-Peter, B. and Hughes, G. (2004). Violence, mental disorder and risk assessment: can structured clinical assessments predict the short-term risk of inpatient violence? *Journal of Forensic Psychiatric Psychology*, 15, 278–92.

Griffin, R. (2012). *Terrorist's Creed: Fanatical Violence and the Human Need for Meaning.* Basingstoke: Palgrave Macmillan.

Griffiths A. (2008). *An Examination into the Efficacy of Police Advanced Investigative Interview Training* (p.72). Unpublished PhD thesis, University of Portsmouth, UK.

Grimland, M., Apter, A. and Kerkhof, A. (2006). The phenomenon of suicide bombing: a review of psychological and nonpsychological factors. *Crisis*, 27(3), 107–18.

Gross, C.A. and Hansen, N.E. (2000). Clarifying the experience of shame: The role of attachment style, gender, and investment in relatedness. *Personality and Individual Differences*, 28, 897–907.

Groth, A.N. (1983). Treatment of the sexual offender in a correctional institution. In J.G. Greer and I.R. Stuart (eds.). *The Sexual Aggressor*. New York: Van Nostrand Reinhold.

Groth, A.N. and Birnbaum, H.J. (1978). Adult sexual orientation and attraction to underage persons. *Archives of Sexual Behavior*, 7(3), 175–81.

Groth, A.N. and Burgess, A.W. (1977a). Rape: A sexual deviation. *American Journal of Orthopsychiatry*, 47, 400–6.

Groth, A.N. and Burgess, A.W. (1977b). Motivational intent in the sexual assault of children. *Criminal Justice and Behavior*, 4, 253–71.

Grove, W.M., Eckert, E.D., Heston, L., Bouchard, T.J., Segal, N. and Lykken, D.T. (1990). Heritability of substance abuse and antisocial behavior: A study of monozygotic twins reared apart. *Biological Psychiatry*, 27, 1293–304.

Grubin, D. (1996b). Silence in court: psychiatry and the Criminal Justice and Public Order Act 1994. *Journal of Forensic Psychiatry*, 7(3), 647–52.

Grubin, D. (1998). Sex offending against children: Understanding the risk. *Police Research Series Paper*, 99, London: Home Office.

Gruneberg, M.M. and Sykes, R.N. (1993). The generalizability of confidence-accuracy studies in eyewitnessing. *Memory*, 1(3), 185–9.

Guardian News (2011). *Manchester Rioter's Sentence Is Halved*. www.guardian.co.uk/uk/2011/oct/06/manchester-rioter-sentence-halved.

Gudjonsson, G.H. (1984). A new scale of interrogative suggestibility. *Personality and Individual Differences*, 5, 303–14.

Gudjonsson, G.H. (1988). Interrogative suggestibility: Its relationship with assertiveness, social evaluative anxiety, state anxiety and method of coping. *British Journal of Clinical Psychology*, 27, 159–66.

Gudjonsson, G.H. (1989). Compliance in an interrogation situation: A new scale. *Personality and Individual Differences*, 10, 535–40.

Gudjonsson, G.H. (1997). *The Gudjonsson Suggestibility Scales Manual*. Hove, UK: Psychology Press.

Gudjonsson, G.H. (1999). *The Psychology of Interrogations, Confessions and Testimony*. Chichester, UK: Wiley and Sons.

Gudjonsson, G.H. (2003). *The Psychology of Interrogations and Confessions*. Chichester, UK: Wiley.

Gudjonsson, G.H. and Clark, N.K. (1986). Suggestibility in police interrogation: A social psychological model (p.84). *Social Behaviour*, 1, 83–104.

Gudjonsson, G.H. and Lister, S. (1984). Interrogative suggestibility and its relationship with perceptions of self-concept and control. *Journal of the Forensic Science Society*, 29, 264–9.

Gudjonsson, G.H., Murphy, G.H. and Clare, I.C.H. (2000). Assessing the capacity of people with intellectual disabilities to be witnesses in court. *Psychological Medicine*, 30, 307–14.

Gudjonsson, G.H. and Sigurdsson, J.F. (1999). The Gudjonsson Confession Questionnaire-Revised (GCQ-R). Factor structure and its relationship with personality. *Personality and Individual Differences*, 27, 953–68.

Gudjonsson, G.H., Sigurdsson, J.F., Bragason, O.O., Einarsson, E. and Valdimarsdottir, E.B. (2004). Confessions and denials and the relationship with personality. *Legal and Criminological Psychology*, 9, 121–33.

Gunn, J., Robertson, G., Dell, S. and Way, C. (1978). *Psychiatric Aspects of Imprisonment*. London: Academic Press.

Gunnell, J. and Ceci, S.J. (2010). When emotionality trumps reason: A study of individual processing style and juror bias. *Behavioral Science and Law*, 28, 850–77.

Gunning, K.F. (1993). *Statistics on the Netherland. President, Dutch National Committee on Drug Prevention.* Rotterdam, Holland (22nd September).

Guo, G. and Adkins, D.E. (2008). How is a statistical link established between a human outcome and a molecular genetic variant? *Sociological Methods and Research*, 37, 201–26.

Guo, G., Ou, X-M. Roettger, M. and Shih, J.C. (2008). The VNTR 2-Repeat in *MAOA* and Delinquent Behavior in Adolescence and Young Adulthood: Associations and *MAOA* Promoter Activity. *European Journal of Human Genetics*, 16(5), 626–34.

Guo, G., Roettger, M. and Shih, J.C. (2007). Contributions of the *DAT1* and *DRD2* Genes to Serious and Violent Delinquency among Adolescents and Young Adults. *Human Genetics*, 121(1), 125–36.

Gupta, L. (2008). *Forcing the issue*. London: *The Guardian*. www.guardian.co.uk/commentisfree/2008/jan/09/forcingtheissue.

Gurucharri, C., Phelps, E. and Selman, R. (1984). Development of interpersonal understanding: a longitudinal and comparative study of normal and disturbed youths. *Journal of Consulting and Clinical Psychology*, 52, 26–36.

Guterman, S.L. (1990). *The Principle of the Personality of Law in the Germanic Kingdoms of Western Europe from the Fifth to the Eleventh Century.* New York: P. Lang.

Guttman, L. (1982). Facet theory, smallest space analysis and factor analysis. *Perceptual and Motor Skills*, 54(2), 491–3.

Guyer, B.M. (2012). A measuring rod: Canon Law in the life of the church. *The Living Church*, 12–13. www.scribd.com/doc/95849670/Measuring-Rod.

Habermas, J. (1989). *The Structural Transformation of the Public Sphere: An Inquiry into a Category of Bourgeois Society* (trans. Thomas Burger). Cambridge, MA: The MIT Press.

Häfner, H. and Böker, W. (1982). *Crimes of Violence by Mentally Abnormal Offenders.* Cambridge, MA: Cambridge University Press.

Hagan, F.E. (1998). *Introduction to Criminology: Theories, Methods and Criminal Behavior* (4th edn.). Chicago, IL: Nelson-Hall.

Hagerty, B.B. (2010). Can your genes make you murder? *Special Series, Inside the Criminal Brain.* NPR. www.npr.org/templates/story/story.php?storyId=128043329.

Haidt, J., Koller, S.H. and Dias, M.G. (1993). Affect, culture, and morality, or, is it wrong to eat your dog? *Journal of Personality and Social Psychology*, 65(4), 613–28.

Hakim, S. and Rengert, G.F. (1981). Introduction. In: S. Hakim and G.F. Rengert (eds.). *Crime Spillover.* Beverly Hills, CA: SAGE.

Häkkänen, H. and Laajasalo, T. (2006). Homicide crime scene actions in a Finnish sample of mentally ill offenders. *Homicide Studies*, 10, 33–54.

Häkkänen-Nyholm, H. and Hare, R.D. (2009). Psychopathy, homicide, and the courts: Working the system. *Criminal Justice and Behavior*, 36(8), 761–77.

Häkkänen-Nyholm, H. and Nyholm, J-O. (2012). *Psychopathy and Law: A Practitioner's Guide* (p.193). Chichester, UK: Wiley-Blackwell.

Häkkänen-Nyholm, H., Repo-Tiihonen, E., Lindberg, N., Salenius, S. and Weizmann-Henelius, G. (2009). Finnish sexual homicides: Offence and offender characteristics. *Forensic Science International*, 188, 125–30.

Hale, S. (2004). *The Discourse of Court Interpreting.* Amsterdam/Philadelphia: John Benjamins.

Hall, J. (2012). Sir Jimmy Savile cannot be posthumously stripped of knighthood in the wake of sexual abuse allegations despite hints from Prime Minister David Cameron. London: *The Independent*, October 9.

Hall, J. and Rawlinson, K. (2013). Oxford child paedophile gang: Council chief Joanna Simons insists shes will not resign as seven men are found guilty of child rape, trafficking and organising prostitution. London: *The Independent*, 15 May.

Hall, S. (1974). Deviance, Politics and the Media. In P. Rock and M. McIntosh (eds.). *Deviance and Social Control*. London: Tavistock.

Hall, S. (1980). *Drifting Into a Law and Order Society*. London: Cobden Trust.

Hall, S., Critcher, C., Jefferson, T., Clarke, J. and Roberts, B. (1978). *Policing the Crisis: Mugging, the State and Law and Order*. London: Macmillan.

Hallevy, G. (2008). Culture-based crimes against women in societies absorbing immigrants – rejecting the 'mistake of law' defence and imposing harsher sentencing. *Cardozo Journal of Law and Gender*, 16, 439–67.

Halpern, D.F. (1997). Sex differences in intelligence: Implications for education. *American Psychologist*, 52, 1091–102.

Halpern, D.F. (2000). *Sex Differences in Cognitive Abilities*. Mahwah, NJ: Erlbaum.

Halperin, J.M., Newcorn, J.H., Kopstein, I., McKay, K.E., Schwartz, S.T., Siever, L.J. and Sharma, V. (1997). Serotonin, aggression, and parental psychopathology in children with attention-deficit hyperactivity disorder. *Journal of the American Academy of Child and Adolescent Psychiatry*, 36(10), 1391–8.

Hannerz, U. (1969). *Soulside: Inquiries into Ghetto Culture and Community*. New York: Columbia University Press.

Hansard Parliamentary Notes (2009). *Speaker Mr Alan Campbell on Antisocial Behaviour Orders*. 10 November 2009 col. 330W. www.parliament.uk

Hansard Parliamentary Notes (2011). *Speaker Mr David Cameron (Prime Minister) on Public Disorder*. 11 August 2011 col. 1051. www.parliament.uk.

Hanson, R.K. (1997). *The Development of a Brief Actuarial Risk Scale for Sexual Offense Recidivism*. User Report No. 1997–04. Ottawa: Department of the Solicitor General of Canada.

Hanson, R.K. (2000). What is so special about relapse prevention? In D.R. Laws, S.M. Hudson and T. Ward (eds.). *Remaking Relapse Prevention with Sex Offenders* (pp.27–38). Thousand Oaks, CA: SAGE.

Hanson, R. K. and Bussière, M. T. (1998). Predicting relapse: A meta-analysis of sexual offender recidivism studies. *Journal of Consulting and Clinical Psychology*, 66, 348–62.

Hanson, R.K., Gordon, A., Harris, A.J., Marques, J.K., Murphy, W., Quinsey, V.L., Seto, M.C. (2002). First report of the Collaborative Outcome Project on the effectiveness of psychological treatment for sex offenders. *Sexual Abuse: A Journal of Research and Treatment*, 14, 159–94.

Hanson, R. K. and Thornton, D. (2003). *Notes on the Development of Static-2002*. (Corrections Research User Report No. 2003–01). Ottawa: Department of the Solicitor General of Canada.

Happe, F. (1995). The role of age and verbal ability in the theory of mind task performance of subjects with autism. *Child Development*, 66, 843–55.

Harbort, S. and Mokros, A. (2001). Serial murderers in Germany from 1945 to 1995: A Descriptive Study. *Homicide Studies*, 5(4), 311–34.

Harcourt, B.E. (1999). The collapse of the harm principle. (p.3). *Journal of Criminal Law and Criminology*, 90(1), 1–65.

Harding, D. (2003). Jean Valjean's dilemma: The management of ex-convict identity in the search for employment. *Deviant Behavior*, 24(6), 571–96.

Hare, R.D. (1980). A research scale for the assessment of psychopathy in criminal populations. *Personality and Individual Differences*, 1, 111–19.

Hare, R.D. (1990). *Development of an Instrument for the Assessment of Psychopathy in the Mentally Disordered*. Progress Report.

Hare, R.D. (1991). *Manual for the Psychopathy Checklist-Revised*. Toronto, ON: Multi-Health Systems.

Hare, R.D. (1993). *Without Conscience: The Disturbing World of the Psychopaths Among Us*. New York: Guilford Press.

Hare, R.D. (2005). Without Conscience: Understanding and Treating Psychopaths. *Seminar Presentation at Lancaster, Pennsylvania*. July 7–8.

Hare, R.D. and Jutai, J.W. (1988). Psychopathy and cerebral asymmetry in semantic processing. *Personality and Individual Differences*, 9, 329–37.

Hare, R.D. and McPherson, L M. (1984). Psychopathy and perceptual asymmetry during verbal dichotic listening. *Journal of Abnormal Psychology*, 93, 141–9.

Hare, R.D. and Neumann, C.S. (2006). The PCL-R assessment of psychopathy. In C.J. Patrick (ed.). *Handbook of Psychopathy*. New York: The Guilford Press.

Hargreaves, D.H. (1967). *Social Relations in a Secondary School*. London: Tinling.

Hargreaves, D.H. (1980). Classrooms, schools, and juvenile delinquency. *Educational Analysis*, 2, 75–87.

Harlow, H.F. (1958). The Nature of Love. *American Psychologist*, 13, 673–85.

Harlow, H.F. (1962). Development of affection in primates. In E.L. Bliss (ed.). *Roots of Behavior* (pp.157–66). New York: Harper.

Harris, J.R. (1995). Where is the child's environment? A group-socialisation theory of development. *Psychological Review*, 102(3), 458–89.

Harris, J.R. (1998). *The Nurture Assumption: Why Children Turn Out the Way They Do*. New York: Simon and Schuster.

Harris, M. (1985). *Good to Eat: Riddles of Food and Culture*. New York: Simon and Schuster.

Harris, P.L. (1989). *Children and emotion*. New York: Cambridge University Press.

Harris, Z.S. (1952). Discourse analysis. *Language*, 28(1), 1–30.

Hart, H.L.A. (1963). *Law, Liberty and Morality*, Oxford: Oxford University Press.

Hart, S. and Dempster, R. (1997). Impulsivity and psychopathy. In C. Webster and M. Jackson (eds.). *Impulsivity: Theory, Assessment and Treatment* (pp.212–32). New York: The Guilford Press.

Hart, C.H., Ladd, G.W. and Burleson, B.R. (1990). Children's expectations of the outcomes of social strategies: relations with sociometric status and maternal disciplinary styles. *Child Development*, 61, 127–37.

Harter, S. (1990). Adolescent self and identity development. In S.S. Feldman and G.R. Elliot (eds.). *At the Threshold: The Developing Adolescent* (pp.352–87). Cambridge, MA: Harvard University Press.

Hashibe, M., Morgenstern, H., Cui, Y., Tashkin, D.P., Zhang, Z.F., Cozen, W., Mack, T.M. and Greenland, S. (2006). Marijuana use and the risk of lung and upper aerodigestive tract cancers: Results of a population-based case-control study. *Cancer Epidemiology Biomarkers Prevention*, 15(10), 1829–34.

Hastie, R. and Pennington, N. (2000). Explanation-based decision-making. In T. Connolly and H.R. Arkes (eds.). *Judgement and Decision-Making: An Interdisciplinary Reader*. New York: Cambridge University Press.

Hatcher, R. (2008). Psychological skills in working with offenders. In G.M. Davies, C.R. Hollin and R. Bull (eds.). *Forensic Psychology*. Chichester, UK: John Wiley and Sons.

Hatcher, R.M., Palmer, E.J., McGuire, J., Housome, J.C., Bilby, C.A.I. and Hollin, C.R. (2008). Aggression replacement training with adult male offenders within community settings: A reconviction analysis. *Journal of Forensic Psychiatry and Psychology*, 19(4), 517–32.

Hatz, J.L. and Bourgeois, M.J. (2010). Anger as a cue to truthfulness. *Journal of Experimental Social Psychology*, 46, 680–3.

Hauser, M.D., Cushman, F.A., Young, L., Kang-Xing, K. and Mikhail, J. (2007). A dissociation between moral judgements and justifications. *Mind and Language*, 22(1), 1–21.

Hauser, M.D., Young, L. and Cushman, F.A. (2008). Reviving Rawl's linguistic analogy. In W. Sinnott-Armstrong (ed.). *Moral Psychology and Biology*. New York: Oxford University Press.

Hay, D.A., McStephen, M. and Levy, F. (2001). The developmental genetics of ADHD. In F. Levy and D. Hay (eds.). *Attention, Genes, and ADHD* (pp.58–79). Philadelphia, PA: Taylor and Francis.

Hedderman, C. (1987). Children's Evidence: The Need for Corroboration, *Home Office Research and Planning Unit*, 41. London: Home Office.

Heidensohn, F.M. (1985). *Women and Crime* (p.42). London: Macmillan Press.

Heidensohn, F.M. (1986). Models of justice: Portia or Persephone? Some thoughts on equality, fairness and gender in the field of criminal justice. *International Journal of the Sociology of Law*, 14, 287–98.

Heider, F. (1944). Social perception and phenomenal causality. *Psychological Review*, 51, 358–74.

Hennigan, K.M., Del Rosario, M.L., Heath, L., Cook, T.D., Wharton, J.D. and Calder, B.J. (1982). Impact of the introduction of television crime in the United States: Empirical findings and theoretical implications. *Journal of Personality and Social Psychology*, 42, 461–77.

Hepper, P.G., Shahidullah, S. and White, R. (1991). Handedness in the human foetus. *Neuropsychologia*, 29, 1107–11.

Hepper, P.G., Wells, D.L. and Lynch, C. (2005). Prenatal thumb sucking is related to postnatal handedness. *Neuropsychologia*, 43, 313–5.

Herrnstein, R.J. and Murray, C. (1994). *The Bell Curve*. New York: The Free Press.

Herschel, W.J. (1880). Skin Furrows of the Hand. *Nature*, 23, 76.

Herschel, W.J. (1894). Fingerprints. *Nature*, 51, 77.

Heston, L.L. (1966). Psychiatric disorders in foster home reared children of schizophrenic mothers. *British Journal of Psychiatry*, 112(489), 819–25.

Hiatt, K.D., Lorenz, A.R. and Newman, J.P. (2002). Assessment of emotion and language processing in psychopathic offenders: results from a dichotic listening task. *Personality and Individual Differences*, 32, 1255–68

Hickey, E.W. (1991). *Serial Murderers and Their Victims*. Pacific Grove, CA: Brooks/Cole.

Hickey, E.W. (2002). *Serial Murderers and their Victims* (3rd edn.). Belmont: Wadsworth.

Hickey, E.W. (2006). *The Male Serial Murderer: Serial Murderers and their Victims* (4th edn.). Belmont, CA: Wadsworth Group.

Hickey, J.E. (1972). The effects of guided moral discussion upon youthful offenders' level of moral reasoning. *Dissertation Abstracts International*, 33, 1551A.

Hickey, J.E. and Scharf, P.L. (1980). *Towards a Just Correctional System*. San Francisco, CA: Jossey-Bass.

Hildebrand, M. and de Ruiter, C. (2004). PCL-R psychopathy and its relation to DSM-lV Axis l and Axis ll disorders in a sample of male forensic psychiatric patients in the Netherlands. *International Journal of Law and Psychiatry*, 27, 233–48.

Hill, C., Memon, A. and McGeorge, P. (2008). The role of confirmation bias in suspect interviews: A systematic evaluation. *Legal and Criminological Psychology*, 13, 357–71.

Hillyard, P. and Tombs, S. (2007). From crime to social harm. *Crime, Law and Social Change*, 48(1–2), 9–25.

Hillyard, P. and Tombs, S. (2008). Beyond criminology. In P. Hillyard, C. Pantazis, S. Tombs, and D. Gordon (eds.). *Beyond Criminology: Taking Harm Seriously*. London: Pluto Press.

Hindelang, M.J. (1973). Causes of delinquency: A partial replication and extension. *Social Problems*, 20, 471–87.

Hinson, J.M., Jameson, T.L. and Whitney, P. (2003). Impulsive decision making and working memory. *Journal of Experimental Psychology: Learning, Memory, and Cognition*, 29, 298–306.

Hirschi, T. (1969). *Causes of Delinquency* (p.16). CA: University of California Press.

Hirschi, T. (1971). *Causes of Delinquency*. Berkeley: University of California Press.

Hirschi, T. and Gottfredson, M. (1988). Towards a general theory of crime. In W. Buikhuisen and S.A. Mednick (eds.). *Explaining Criminal Behaviour*. Leiden: Brill.

Hobbs, G., Vignoles, A. and the ALSPAC Study Team Centre for the Economics of Education (2007). *Is Free School Meal Status A Valid Proxy For Socio-Economic Status (In Schools Research)?* Brief no.CEE03–07, May. London: DfES.

Hobbes, T. (1651). *Leviathan, or the Matter, Forme, and Power of a Commonwealth, Ecclesiastical and Civil*. 1982 reprint, New York: Viking Press.

Hobson, J. and Shine, J. (1998). Measurement of psychopathy in a UK prison population referred for long-term psychotherapy. *British Journal of Criminology*, 38, 504–15.

Hodge, S.A. (2000). Multivariate model of serial sexual murder. In D. Canter (ed.). Offender profiling and criminal differentiation. *Legal and Criminological Psychology*, 5, 23–46.

Hodgins, S. (1997). An overview of research on the prediction of dangerousness. *Nordic Journal of Psychiatry*, 51, 33–38 and 73–95.

Hodgins, S. (2004). Criminal and antisocial behaviours and schizophrenia: a neglected topic. In W.F. Gattaz and H. Häfner (eds.). *Search for the Causes of Schizophrenia* (vol.5, pp.315–41). Darmstadt, Germany: Steinkopff Verlag.

Hodgins, S. (2008). Criminality among persons with severe mental illness. In K. Soothill, M. Dolan and P. Rogers (eds.). *Handbook of Forensic Mental Health*. (Chap.16). Devon, UK: Willan Publishing.

Hodgins, S. and Côté, G. (1993). Major mental disorder and APD: a criminal combination. *Bulletin of American Academy of Psychiatry Law*. 21, 155–60.

Hodgins, S. and Müller-Isberner, R. (2004). Preventing crime by people with schizophrenic disorders: the role of psychiatric services. *British Journal of Psychiatry*, 185, 245–50.

Hodgskiss, B. (2001). *A Multivariate Model of the Offence Behaviours of South African Serial Murderers*. Unpublished MA (Research Psychology) Thesis. Grahamstown: Rhodes University.

Hodgskiss, B. (2004). Lessons from serial murder in South Africa. *Journal of Investigative Psychology and Offender Profiling*, 1, 67–94.

Hoffman, H., Janssen, E. and Turner, S.L. (2004). Classical conditioning of sexual arousal in women and men: Effects of varying awareness and biological relevance of the conditioned stimulus. *Archives of Sexual Behavior*, 33, 43–53.

Hoffman, M.L. (1971). Father absence and conscience development. *Developmental Psychology*, 4, 400–6.

Hoffman, M.L. (1975). Altruistic behavior and the parent-child relationship. *Journal of Personality and Social Psychology*, 31, 937–43.

Hoffman, M.L. (1977). Moral internalisation: Current theory and research. In L. Berekowitz (ed.). *Advances in Experimental Social Psychology* (vol. 10). New York: Academic Press.

Hoffman, M.L. (1979). Development of moral thought, feeling, and behavior. *American Psychologist*, 34(10), 958–66.

Hoffman, M.L. (1982). Development of prosocial motivation: Empathy and guilt. In N. Eisenberg (ed.). *The Development of Prosocial Behavior*. New York: Academic Press.

Hoffman, M.L. and Saltzstein, H.D. (1967). Parent discipline and the child's moral development. *Journal of Personality and Social Psychology*, 5, 45–57.

Hogan, R.A. (1969). Development of an empathy scale. *Journal of Consulting and Clinical Psychology*, 33, 307–16.

Hogan, R.A. (1970). A dimension of moral judgement. *Journal of Consulting and Clinical Psychology*, 35, 205–12.

Hogg, M.A. and Vaughan, G.M. (2002). *Social Psychology* (3rd ed.). London: Prentice Hall.

Hohfeld, W.N. (1923). Fundamental legal conceptions. In A.A. Zuckerman (ed.). *The Principles of Criminal Evidence*. Oxford: Claredon Press, 1989.

Holliday, R.E. (2003). Reducing misinformation effects in children with cognitive interviews: Dissociating recollection and familiarity. *Memory*, 74, 728–51.

Hollin, C.R. (1992). *Criminal Behaviour: A Psychological Approach to Explanation and Prevention*. London: Falmer Press.

Holmberg, U. and Christianson, S. (2002). Murderers' and sexual offenders' experiences of police interviews and their inclination to admit or deny crimes. *Behavioral Sciences and the Law*, 20, 31–45.

Holmes, R.M. and De Burger, J. (1985). Profiles in terror: The serial murderer. *Probation*, 49, 29–34.

Holmes, R.M. and De Burger, J. (1988). *Serial Murder*. London: SAGE.

Holmes, R.M. and Holmes, S.T. (1998). Serial Murder. In D.V. Canter and N. Wentink (eds.). An Empirical Test of the Holmes and Holmes Serial Murder Typology. *Criminal Justice and Behavior*, 3 1(4), 489–515.

Holmes, R.M. and Holmes, S.T. (2001). *Serial Murder* (3rd edn.). Thousand Oaks, CA: SAGE.

Holmes, R.M. and Holmes, S.T. (2002). *Profiling Violent Crimes: An Investigative Tool* (p.124). Thousand Oaks, CA: SAGE.

Holt, T.J., Burruss, G.W. and Bossler, A.M. (2010). Social learning and cyber deviance: Examining the importance of a full social learning model in the virtual world. *Journal of Crime and Justice*, 33(2), 31–61.

Home Office (1998). *Draft Guidance Document: Anti-Social Behaviour Orders*. London: Home Office.

Home Office (1999a). *Criminal Statistics England and Wales 1998*. (Cm. 4649), London: Stationery Office.

Home Office (1999b). *Probation Service Performance Monitor*. Probation Circular No. 8/1999, London: Home Office Probation Unit.

Home Office Statistical Bulletin (2003). *Crime in England and Wales 2002/2003*. London: Home Office.

Home Office (2005a). *National Offender Management Service – Corporate Plan 2005–06 to 2007–08.* London: Home Office.

Home Office (2006a). Criminal Statistics 2005: England and Wales. *Statistical Bulletin,* 19/06. London: Home Office.

Home Office (2006b). *The NOMS Offender Management Model.* London: Home Office.

Home Office Statistical Bulletin (2007a). *Crime in England and Wales 2006/2007* (4th edn.). London: Home Office.

Home Office (2007b). *Child Sex Offender Review.* London: Home Office.

Home Office (2008). *Keeping our Communities Safe: Managing Risk through MAPPA.* London: Home Office.

Home Office (2011a). *Crime in England and Wales: Quarterly Update to September 2011.* London: Home Office.

Home Office (2011b) *Home Office Counting Rules for Recorded Crime.* London: Home Office. www.homeoffice.gov.uk/science-research/researchstatistics/crime/counting-rules/

Home Office (2011c). *User Guide to Home Office Crime Statistics.* London: Home Office.

Home Office (2013). *An Overview of Sexual Offending in England and Wales.* London: Home Office.

Home Office and Department of Health and Social Security (1975). *Report of the Committee on Mentally Abnormal Offenders (Butler Report) Cmnd. 6244.* London: HMSO.

Home Office Statistical Bulletin (2011). *Crime in England and Wales: Quarterly Update* (Sept 2010). London: Home Office.

Honourable Sir Thomas, R.J.L. and Turner, R.T. (1992). Mirror Group Newspapers plc. Investigations under Sections 432(2) and 442 of the Companies Act 1985. The National Archives. http://webarchive.nationalarchives.gov.uk/+/http:/www.dti.gov.uk/cld/mirrorgroup/summary.htm.

Hoptman, M.J., Volavka, J., Weiss, E.M., Czobor, P., Szeszko, P.R., Gerig, G., Chakos, M., Blocher, J., Citrome, L.L., Lindenmayer, J.P., Sheitman, B., Lieberman, J.A. and Bilder, R.M. (2005). Quantitative MRI measures of orbitofrontal cortex in patients with chronic schizophrenia or schizoaffective disorder. *Psychiatry Research: Neuroimaging,* 140, 133–45.

Horgan, J. (2003). The search for the terrorist personality. In A. Silke (ed.). *Terrorists, Victims and Society* (pp.3–27). West Sussex, UK: John Wiley and Sons Ltd.

Horgan, J. and Taylor, M. (2001). The making of a terrorist. *Jane's Intelligence Review,* 13(12), 16–18.

Horgan, J. (2005). *The Psychology of Terrorism.* USA: Routledge.

Horrowitz, S.W. (2009). Direct mixed and open questions in child interviewing: An analog study. *Legal and Criminological Psychology,* 14(1), 135–47.

Horselenberg, R., Merckelbach, H. and Josephs, S. (2003). Individual differences and false confessions: A conceptual replication of Kassin and Kiechel (1996). *Psychology, Crime and Law,* 9, 1–8.

Hough, M. and Mayhew, P. (1985). Taking Account of Crime: Key findings from the second British Crime Survey. *Home Office Research Study,* 85. London: HMSO.

House of Commons (11th August 2012). Public Disorder Parliament. *Hansard Official Report* www.parliament.uk.

House of Commons Home Affairs Committee (2009). *Knife Crime.* Seventh Report of Session 2008–09. London: HMSO.

House of Commons Justice Committee (2015). *Crime Reduction Policies: A Co-ordinated Approach.* First Report of Session 2014–15. London: HMSO.

Howells, K. (1986). Social skills training and criminal and antisocial behaviour in adults. In C.R. Hollin and P. Trower (eds.). *Handbook of Social Skills Training* (vol. 1). Oxford: Pergamon Press.

Howells, K. and Day, A. (2007). Readiness for treatment in high risk offenders with personality disorders. *Psychology, Crime and Law*, 13, 47–56.

Howells, K. and Hollin, C.R. (1993). *Clinical Approaches to the Mentally Disordered Offender*. Chichester: Wiley.

Howes, H. and Workman, L. (2007). Male and female brains. *Psychology Review*, 12(3), 17–20.

Howitt, D. (1998). *Crime, the Media and the Law*. Chichester, UK: John Wiley.

Howitt, D. (2002). *Forensic and Criminal Psychology*. Harlow: Pearson Education Limited.

Howitt, D. (2011). *Introduction to Forensic and Criminal Psychology* (4th edn.), (pp.272, 281). Harlow: Pearson Education Limited.

Howitt, D. (2012). *Introduction to Forensic and Criminal Psychology* (4th edn.). Harlow: Pearson Education Limited.

Howlett, J., Hanfland, K. and Ressler, R. (1986). The violent criminal apprehension program. *FBI Law Enforcement Bulletin*, 55, 14–19.

Hrdy, S.B. (2011). *Mothers and Others: The Evolutionary Origins of Mutual Understanding*. Cambridge, MA. Belknap Press.

Hu, E., Vik, P., Dasher, N. and Fowler, B. (2011). Social inference, history of conduct disorder, and the OFC. *Archival Clinical Neuropsychology*, 26(6), 470–567.

Hucker, S.J. and Bain, J. (1990). Androgenic hormones and sexual assault. In W.L. Marshall, D.R. Laws and H.E. Barbaree (eds.). *Handbook of Sexual Assault: Issues, Theories and Treatment of the Offender*. New York: Plenum.

Hudson, B. (2003). *Understanding Justice: An Introduction to Ideas, Perspectives and Controversies in Modern Penal Theory* (p.115). Buckinghamshire and Philadelphia, PA: Open University Press.

Huesmann, L.R. (1988). An information processing model for the development of aggression. *Aggressive Behavior*, 14,13–24.

Huesmann, L.R. and Taylor, L.D. (2006). Media effects in middle childhood. In A.C. Huston and M.N. Ripke (eds.). *Developmental Contexts in Middle Childhood*. New York: Cambridge University Press.

Hughes, C., Deater-Deckard, K. and Cutting, A.L. (1999). 'Speak roughly to your little boy'? Sex differences in the relations between parenting and preschoolers' understanding of mind. *Social Development*, 8, 143–60.

Hughes, M. (2011). Ken Livingstone blames Tottenham riot on spending cuts. *The Telegraph*, Telegraph Media Group Ltd (7 August).

Hulsman, L.H.C. (1986). Critical Criminology and the Concept of Crime. *Contemporary Crises*, 10(3–4), 63–80.

Human Rights Watch (2007). *No Easy Answer: Sex offender laws in the US Part V1*. Public access to information on sex offenders. www.hrw.org/reports/2007/us0907/6.htm

Humes, E. (2004). Experts say false confessions come from leading questions, young suspects, high-pressure interrogations. In R. Bell (ed.). *Coerced False Confessions during Police Interrogations*. True TV Crime Library: Criminal Minds and Methods. Turner: A Time Warner Company. Knight Ridder/Tribune News Service.

Husak, D.N. (2005). Limitations on criminalisation and the general part of criminal law. In G. Hallevy (ed.). Culture-based crimes against women in societies absorbing immigrants –

rejecting the 'mistake of law' defence and imposing harsher sentencing (2008). *Cardozo Journal of Law and Gender*, 16, 439–67.

Huson, R.A. (1999). *The Sociology and Psychology of Terrorism: Who Becomes a Terrorist and Why?* A report prepared under an interagency agreement by the Federal Research Division, Library of Congress.

Hutchings, B. and Mednick, S.A. (1975). Registered criminality in the adoptive and biological parents of registered male criminal adoptees. In R.R. Fieve, D. Rosenthal and H. Brill (eds.). *Genetic Research in Psychiatry* (pp.105–16). Baltimore, MD : Johns Hopkins University Press.

Hutt, C. (1972). *Males and Females*. Harmondsworth, UK: Penguin Books.

Igloo Books (2011). *Serial Killers: A Shocking History* (p.28). Sywell, Northamptonshire: Igloo Books.

Inbau, F.E., Reid, J., Buckley, J.P. and Jayne, B.C. (2001). *Criminal interrogations and confessions* (4th edn.). Gaithersburg, MD: Aspen.

India Today (2013). Rape highest reported crime in matrilineal Meghalaya. Living Media India Limited.

Innes, M. (2004). Crime as a Signal, Crime as a Memory. *Journal for Crime, Conflict and the Media*, 1(2), 15–22.

Innocence Project. (2012). Innocence Project. Accessed February 11, 2012, www.innocenceproject.org (2012).

International Criminal Law Services (ICLS) (2011). International Criminal Law and Practice Training Materials, Modes of Liability: Commission and Participation. Part of the OSCE ODIHR/ICTY/UNICRI Project Supporting the Transfer of Knowledge and Materials of War Crimes Cases from the ICTY to National Jurisdictions. EU Funded.

International Covenant on Civil and Political Rights, art.27, Mar. 23, 1976, 6 U.S.T. 3316, 75 U.N.T.S. 135. In G. Hallevy (ed.). Culture-based crimes against women in societies absorbing immigrants – rejecting the 'mistake of law' defence and imposing harsher sentencing (2008). *Cardozo Journal of Law and Gender*, 16, 439–67.

International Criminal Court Act (1998, 2001). www.legislation.gov.uk.

IRIN (2007). *Liberia: Trial by Ordeal Makes the Guilty Burn but 'Undermines Justice'*, IRIN Global: UN Office for the Coordination of Humanitarian Affairs. www.irinnews.org/fr/Report/75111/LIBERIA-Trial-by-ordeal-makes-the guilty-burn-but-undermines-justice

Isabella, R.A., Belsky, J. and von Eye, A. (1989). Origins of infant-mother attachment: An examination of interactional synchrony during the infant's first year. *Developmental Psychology*, 25, 12–21.

Ishikawa, S.S., Raine, A., Lencz, T., Bihrle, S. and LaCasse, L. (2001). Autonomic stress reactivity and executive functions in successful and unsuccessful criminal psychopaths from the community. *Journal of Abnormal Psychology*, 110, 423–32.

Islam-Zwart, K.A., Heath, N.M. and Vik, P.W. (2005). Facial recognition performance of female inmates as a result of sexual assault history. *Journal of Traumatic Stress,* 18(3), 263–6.

Jackson, C. and Tinkler, P. (2007). 'Ladettes' and 'Modern Girls': Troublesome young femininities. *The Sociological Review*, 55(2), 251–72.

Jackson, J. (2006). Introducing Fear of Crime to Risk Research. (p.343). *Risk Analysis*, 26(1), 253–64.

Jackson, J.L. and Bekerian, D.A. (1997). *Offender Profiling: Theory, Research and Practice*. Chichester, UK: Wiley.

Jackson, P.L., Meltzoff, A.N. and Decety, J. (2005). How do we perceive the pain of others? A window into the neural processes involved in empathy. *NeuroImage*, 24, 771–9.

Jacobs, P.A., Brunton, M., Melville, M.M., Brittain, R.P. and McClemont, W.F. (1965). Aggressive behaviour, mental subnormality and the XYY male. *Nature*, 208(5017), 1351–2.

Jacobson, J. and Hough, M. (2010). *Unjust Deserts: Imprisonment for Public Protection*. London: Prison Reform Trust ISBN: 0946209 93 6.

Jacobson, L. (2012). Extraordinary rendition officially ruled out, but secrecy makes its elimination hard to prove. *Tampa Bay Times*. www.politifact.com/truth-o-meter/promises/obameter/promise/176/end-the-use-of-extreme-rendition/

James, P. and D'Orban, P.T. (1970). Patterns of delinquency among British heroin addicts (p.19). *Bulletin on Narcotics*, 22, UNODC.

Jamieson, L. (1998). *Intimacy: Personal Relationships in Modern Societies*. Cambridge, UK: Polity Press.

Janssen, W., Koops, E., Anders, S., Kuhn, S. and Püschel, K. (2005). Forensic aspects of 40 accidental autoerotic death in Northern Germany. *Forensic Science International*, 147, 61–4.

Janssens, J.M.A.M. and Deković, M. (1997). Child rearing, prosocial moral reasoning, and prosocial behavior. *International Journal of Behavioral Development*, 20, 509–27.

Jaspers, J.M. and Fraser, C. (1984). Attitudes and social representations. In R.M. Farr and S. Moscovici (eds.). *Social Representations*. Cambridge, UK: Cambridge University Press.

Jefferson, T. and Holloway, W. (2000). The role of anxiety in fear of crime. In T. Hope and R. Sparks (eds.). *Crime, Risk and Insecurity*. London: Routledge.

Jeffery, C.R. (1957). Development of Crime in Early English Society. *Journal of Criminal Law and Criminology*, 47(6), 647–66.

Jew, C.C., Clanon, T.L. and Mattocks, A.L. (1972). The effectiveness of group psychotherapy in a correlational institution. *American Journal of Psychiatry*, 129, 602–5.

Johnson, E.J. and Russo, J.E. (1984). Product familiarity and learning new information. *Journal of Consumer Research*, 11, 542–50.

Johnson, J.T. (1984). *Can Modern War Be Just?* New Haven, CT: Yale University Press.

Johnson, J.T. (2011). *Ethics and the Use of Force: Just War in Historical Perspective*. Surrey: Ashgate.

Johnson, M.H. (2000). Functional brain development in infants: elements of an interactive specialization framework. *Child Development*, 71, 75–81.

Johnson, M.H., Dziurawiec, S., Ellis, H.D. and Morton, J. (1991). Newborns' preferential tracking of face-like stimuli and its subsequent decline. *Cognition*, 40, 1–19.

Johnson, M.H. and Morton J. (1991). *Biology and Cognitive Development: The Case of Face Recognition*. Oxford, England: Blackwells.

Johnson, M.K. (1997). Source monitoring and memory distortion (p.1733). *Philosophy Transactions of the Royal Society Lond B: Biological Sciences*, 352(1362), 1733–45.

Johnson, M.K., Hashtroudi, S. and Lindsay, D.S. (1993). Source monitoring. *Psychological Bulletin*, 114(1), 3–28.

Johnstone, J.W. (1981). Youth gangs and black suburbs. *Pacific Sociological Review*, 24, 355–75.

Jones, A. (2010). *Genocide: A Comprehensive Introduction*. New York: Routledge.

Jones, T., Maclean, B. and Young, J. (1986). *The Islington Crime Survey: Crime, Victimization and Policing in Inner City London*. Aldershot: Gower.

Jonsson, G. (1967). *Delinquent Boys, their Parents and Grandparents*. Copenhagen: Munksgaard.

Joseph, J. (2006). *The Missing Gene: Psychiatry, Heredity, and the Fruitless Search for Genes*. New York: Algora Publishing.

Joyal, C.C., Black, D.N. and Dassylva, B. (2007). The neuropsychology and neurology of sexual deviance: A review and pilot study. *Sexual Abuse*, 19(2), 155–73.

Junger-Tas, J., Terlouw, G-J., and Klein, M.W. (1994). Delinquent Behaviour Among Young People in the Western World: First Results of the International Self-Report Delinquency Study. Amsterdam, the Netherlands: Kugler Publications.

Jutai, J., and Hare, R. D. (1983). Psychopathy and selective attention during performance of a complex perceptual-motor task. *Psychophysiology*, 20, 146–51.

Kafka, M.P. (1997). A monoamine hypothesis for the pathophysiology of paraphilic disorders (p.346). *Archives of Sexual Behavior*, 26(4), 343–58.

Kafka, M.P. (2003). Sex offending and sexual appetite: the clinical relevance of hypersexual desire. *International Journal of Offender Therapy and Comparative Criminology*, 47, 439–51.

Kahneman, D.and Tversky, A. (1972). Subjective probability: A judgement of representativeness. *Cognitive Psychology*, 3, 430–54.

Kahneman, D. and Tversky, A. (1973). On the psychology of prediction. *Psychological Review*, 80, 237–51.

Kahneman, D. and Tversky, A. (1979). Prospect theory: An analysis of decisions under risk. *Econometrica*, 4(2), 263–91.

Kalin, N. (1999). Primate models to understand human aggression. *Journal of Clinical Psychiatry*, 60, 29–32.

Kalnia, R.K. (1964). Diazepam: its role in a prison setting. *Diseases of the Nervous System*, 25, 101–7.

Kamphuis, J.H. and Emmelkamp, P.M.G. (2000). Stalking: A contemporary challenge for forensic and clinical psychiatry. *British Journal of Psychiatry*, 176, 206–9.

Kaplan, J. (1970). *Marijuana: the new prohibition*. New York: World Publishing Company.

Kaplan, M.F. and Kemmerick, G.D. (1974). Juror judgement as information integration: Combining evidential and non-evidential information. *Journal of Personality and Social Psychology*, 30, 493–9.

Kaplan, P. (1967). In C. Hutt (ed.). *Males and Females* (p.25). Harmondsworth, UK: Penguin Books, 1972.

Karmiloff-Smith, A. (1996). *Beyond Modularity: A Developmental Perspective on Cognitive Science*. Cambridge, MA: MIT Press.

Karmiloff-Smith A. (1998). Development itself is the key to understanding developmental disorders. *Trends in Cognitive Sciences*, 2(10), 389–8.

Karpman, B. (1941). On the need for separating psychopathy into two distinct clinical types: symptomatic and idiopathic. *Journal of Clinical Psychopathology*, 3, 112–37.

Kassin, S.M., Ellsworth, P.C. and Smith, V.L. (1989). The 'general acceptance' of psychological research on eyewitness testimony: A Survey of Experts. *American Psychologist*, 44(8), 1089–98.

Kassin, S. and Gudjonsson, G. (2004). The psychology of confessions: A review of the literature and issues. *Psychological Science in the Public Interest*, 5, 33–67.

Kassin, S.M. and Kiechel, K.L. (1996). The social psychology of false confessions: Compliance, internalization, and confabulation. *Psychological Science*, 7, 125–8.

Kassin, S.M., Meissner, C.A. and Norwick, R.J. (2005). I'd know a false confession if I saw one: A comparative study of college students and police investigators. *Law and Human Behavior*, 29(2), 211–27.

Katz, J.E. (1994). Empirical and theoretical dimensions of obscene phone calls to women in the United States (p.155). *Human Communication Research*, 21(2), 155–82.

Kauer, J.A. and Malenka, R.C. (2007). Synaptic plasticity and addiction. *Nature Reviews, Neuroscience*, 8(11), 844–58.

Keasey, C.B. (1971). Social participation as a factor in the moral development of preadolescents. *Developmental Psychology*, 5, 216–20.

Kebbell, M.R. and Hatton, C. (1999). People with mental retardation as witnesses in court: A review. *Mental Retardation*, 37(3), 179–87.

Kebbell, M.R., Hurren, E. and Mazerolle, P. (2006). An investigation into the effective and ethical interviewing of suspected sex offenders. In D. Walsh and R. Bull (eds.). How do interviewers attempt to overcome suspects' denials? *Psychiatry, Psychology and Law*, 19(2), 1–18.

Kebbell, M.R., Wagstaff, G.F. and Covey, J.A. (1996). The influence of item difficulty on the relationship between eyewitness confidence and accuracy. *British Journal of Psychology*, 87, 653–62.

Kelleher, M.D. and Kelleher, C.L. (1998). *Murder Most Rare: The Female Serial Killer*. Wesport, CT: Praeger.

Kennedy, L. (1989). Europe v England: The Advantages of the Inquisitorial over the Adversary System of Criminal Justice. In M. Schollum (ed.). *Investigative Interviewing: The Literature* (p.22). New Zealand Police. Wellington: Office of the Commissioner of Police.

Keppel, R.D., Weis, J.G., Brown, K.M. and Welch, K. (2005). The Jack the Ripper murders: A modus operandi and signature analysis of the 1888–1891 Whitechapel murders (p.14). *Journal of Investigative Psychology and Offender Profiling*, 2, 1–21.

Kershaw, C., Nicolas, S. and Walker, A. (2007). *Crime in England and Wales 2006/2007*. London: HMSO.

Kiehl, K.A., Smith, A.M., Hare, R.D., Mendrek, A., Forster, B.B., Brink, J. and Liddle, P.F. (2001). Limbic abnormalities in affective processing by criminal psychopaths as revealed by functional magnetic resonance imaging. *Biological Psychiatry*, 50, 677–84.

Kimura, D. (1999). *Sex and Cognition*. Cambridge, MA: MIT Press.

Kindlon, D., Mezzakappa, E. and Earls, F. (1995). Psychometric properties of impulsivity measures: Temporal stability, validity and factor structure. *Journal of Child Psychology and Psychiatry*, 36, 645–61.

Kinsey, A.C., Pomeroy, W.B. and Martin, C.E. (1948). *Sexual Behavior in the Human Male*. Philadelphia, PA: W.B. Saunders.

Kinsey, R. (1984). *Merseyside Crime and Policing Survey*. Merseyside: Merseyside County Council.

Kirchner, L. (2014). Breaking Down the Broken Windows Theory. Pacific Standard Newsletter. www.psmag.com/navigation/politics-and-law/breaking-broken-windows-theory-72310/

Kitsuse, J.I. and Dietrick, D. (1958). The delinquent subculture: An alternative formulation. *The Pacific Sociological Review*, 1(2), 85.

Kitsuse, J.I. and Dietrick, D. (1959). Delinquent boys: A critique. *American Sociological Review*, 24(2), 208–15.

Knapska, E., Radwanska, K., Werka, T. and Kaczmarek, L. (2007). Functional internal complexity of amygdala: Focus on gene activity mapping after behavioral training and drugs of abuse. *Physiological Review*, 87, 1113–73.

Knight, R.A. and Prentky, R.A. (1990). Classifying sexual offenders. The development and corroboration of taxonomic models. In W.L. Marshall, D.R. Laws and H.E. Barbaree (eds.). *Handbook of Sexual Assault: Issues, Theories and Treatment of the Offender*. NewYork: Plenum.

Knight, R.A. and Prentky, R.A. (1993). Exploring characteristics for classifying juvenile sex offenders. In H.E. Barbaree, W.L. Marshall and S.M. Hudson (eds.). *The Juvenile Sex Offender* (pp.25–44). New York: The Guilford Press.

Koch, C. (2013). Where women rule the world: Matriarchal communities from Albania to China. *Metro*. http://metro.co.uk/2013/03/05/where-women-rule-the-world-matri archal-communities-from-albania-to-china-3525234/

Koch, J.L. (1891). *Die psychopathischen Minderwertigigkeiten*. Ravensburg, Germany: Maier.

Kochanska, G. (1992). Children's interpersonal influence with mothers and peers. *Developmental Psychology*, 28, 491–9.

Kochanska, G., Aksan, N. and Nichols, K.E. (2003). Maternal power assertion in discipline and moral discourse contexts: Commonalities, differences, and implications for children's moral conduct and cognition. *Developmental Psychology*, 39, 949–63.

Kocsis, R.N. and Irwin, H.J. (1997). An analysis of spatial patterns on Australian offences of serial, rape, arson and burglary: The utility of the circle theory of environmental range for psychological profiling. *Psychiatry, Psychology and Law*, 4, 195–206.

Kocsis, R.N., Middledorp, J. and Karpin, A. (2008). Taking stock of accuracy in criminal profiling: The theoretical quanddary for investigative psychology. *Journal of Forensic Psychology Practice*, 8(3), 244–61.

Koehn, C.E., Fisher, R.P. and Cutler, B.L. (1999). Using cognitive interviewing to construct facial composites. In D. Canter and L. Alison (eds.). *Psychology and Criminal Detection* (pp.41–63). Brookfield: Dartmouth.

Kohlberg, L. (1958). *The Development of Modes of Moral Thinking and Choice in the Years Ten to Sixteen*. Unpubublished Doctoral Dissertation, University of Chicago.

Kohlberg, L. (1969). Stage and sequence: The cognitive-developmental approach to socialization. In D. Goslin (ed.). *Handbook of Socialization Theory and Research* (pp.347–480). Chicago, IL: Rand McNally.

Köhnken, G., Milne, R., Memon, A. and Bull, R. (1999). The cognitive interview: A meta-analysis. *Psychology, Crime, and Law*, 5, 3–27.

Köhnken, G., Thurer, C. and Zoberbier, D. (1994). The cognitive interview: Are the investigators' memories enhanced too? *Applied Cognitive Psychology*, 8, 13–24.

Kolvin, I., Miller, F.J., Fleeting, M. and Kolvin, P.A. (1988). Social and parenting factors affecting criminal-offence rates: Findings from the Newcastle Thousand Family Study (1947–1980). *British Journal of Psychiatry*, 152, 80–90.

Koss, M.P. (1992). The under detection of rape: Methodological choices influence incidence estimates (p.61). *Journal of Social Issues*, 48(1), 61–75.

Krafft-Ebing, R. (1886). *Psychopathia Sexualis* (English trans. by F.J. Rebman). New York: Physicians and Surgeons Book Co.

Krakowsky, M., Volavka, J. and Brizer, D. (1986). Psychopathology and violence: A review of the literature. *Comprehensive Psychiatry*, 27, 131–48.

Kramer, T.H., Buckhout, R., Fox, P., Widman, E. and Tusche, B. (1991). Effects of stress on recall. *Applied Cognitive Psychology*, 5(6), 483–8.

Kraepelin, E. (1915). *Psychiatrie: Ein Lehrbuch* (8th edn., vol 4). Leipzig: Barth.

Krebs, D.L. (1998). The evolution of moral behaviour. In C. Crawford and D.L. Krebs (eds.). *Handbook of Evolutionary Psychology: Ideas, Issues, and Applications* (pp.337–68). Hillsdale, NJ: Erlbaum.

Kruesi, M.J.P., Schmidt, M.E., Donnelly, M., Hibbs, E.D. and Hamburger, S.D. (1989). Urinary free cortisol output and disruptive behavior in children. *Journal of American Academy of Child Adolescent Psychiatry*, 28, 441–3.

Krug, K. (2007). The relationship between confidence and accuracy: Current thoughts of the literature and a new area of research. *Applied Psychology in Criminal Justice*, 3(1), 7–41.

Kruger, A.C. (1992). The effect of peer and adult-child transactive discussions on moral reasoning. *Merrill-Palmer Quarterly*, 38, 191–211.

Krus, D., Sherman, J. and Kennedy, P. (1977). Changing values over the last half-century: The story of Thurstone's crime scales. *Psychological Reports*, 40, 207–11.

Kubik, E.K. and Hecker, J.E. (2005). Cognitive distortions about sex and sexual offending: A comparison of sex offending girls, delinquent girls, and girls from the community. *Journal of Child Sexual Abuse*, 14, 43–70.

Kurtz, C.J. and Hunter, R.D. (2004). *Dark Truths: Modern Theories of Serial Murder*. London: Virgin Books.

Labuschagne, G.N. (2001). *Serial Murder Revisited: A Psychological Exploration of Two South African Cases*. Unpublished Doctoral Thesis. Pretoria, University of Pretoria.

Lacey, N. (1994). *State Punishment: Political Principles and Community Values*. London: Routledge.

Lacourse, E., Nagin, D.S., Vitaro, F., Côté, S., Arseneault, L. and Tremblay, R.E. (2006). Prediction of early-onset deviant peer group affiliation: A 12-year longitudinal study. *Archives of General Psychiatry*, 63(5), 562–8.

Lader, D., Singleton, N. and Meltzer, H. (2000). *Psychiatric Morbidity Among Young Offenders in England and Wales*. London: ONS.

Ladner, J. (1971). *Tomorrow's Tomorrow: The Black Woman*. New York: Doubleday.

Ladner, J. (1973). *Introduction: The Death of White Sociology*. Baltimore, MD: Black Classic Press.

La Fave, W. (1965). Arrest: The decision to take a suspect into custody. In H. Williams (ed.). *Criminology and Criminal Justice*. London: Butterworths, 1982.

LaFree, G. (1998). *Losing Legitimacy: Street Crime and the Decline of Social Institutions in America*. Boulder, CO: Westview.

LaGrange, R. and Raskin White, H. (1985). Age Differs in Delinquency: A test of theory. *Criminology*, 23, 19–45.

Lahey, B.B., Piacentini, J.C., McBurnett, K., Stone, P., Hartdagen, S. and Hynd, G. (1988). Psychopathology in the parents of children with conduct disorder and hyperactivity. *Journal of the American Academy of Child and Adolescent Psychiatry*, 27, 163–70.

Lakatos, K., Nemoda, Z., Birkas, E., Ronai, Z., Kovacs, E., Ney, K., Toth, I., Sasvari-Szekely, M. and Gervai, J. (2003). Association of D4 dopamine receptor gene and serotonin transporter promoter polymorphisms with infants' response to novelty. *Molecular Psychiatry, 8,* 90–7.

Lakatos, K., Toth, I., Nemoda, Z., Ney, K., Sasvari-Szekely, M. and Gervai, J. (2000). Dopamine D4 receptor (DRD4) gene polymorphism is associated with attachment disorganization in infants. *Molecular Psychiatry*, 5(6), 633–7.

Lampel, A. and Anderson, N.H. (1968). Combining visual and verbal information in an impression-formation task. *Journal of Personality and Social Psychology*, 9, 1–6.

Landsinger, K.L. (2002). Effects of stress on prospective memory. *Journal of Undergraduate Study and Independent Research*, 3, 24–9.

Lane, B. and Gregg, W. (1992). *The New Encyclopaedia of Serial Killers* (p.1). Surrey: Headline.

Lange, J.S. (1931). *Crime and Destiny*. London: Allen and Unwin.

Langelüddeke, A. (1963). *Castration of Sexual Criminals*. Berlin: de Gruyter.

Latessa, E.J. and Lowenkamp, C. (2005). What are criminogenic needs and why are they important? *For the Record*, 4th Quarter, 15–16.

Lattimore, P.K. and Witte, A. (1986). Models of Decision-making under uncertainty: The criminal choice. In D.B. Cornish and R.V. Clarke (eds.). *The Reasoning Criminal: Rational Choice Perspectives on Offending* (pp.129–55). New York: Springer-Verlag.

Laughery, K.R., Duval, C. and Wogalter, M.S. (1986). Dynamics of facial recall. In H.D. Ellis, M.A. Jeeves, F. Newcombe and A. Young (eds.). *Aspects of Face Processing*. Netherlands: Martinus Nijhoff Publishers.

Lawrence, E. and Kubie, S. (1959). Implications for legal procedure of the fallibility of human memory, 108 *U. PA. L. REV*, 59.

Laycock, G. (1991). Operation identification, or the power of publicity? *Security Journal*, 2(2), 67–72.

Leapman, B. (2008). Violent youth crime up a third. *The Telegraph*. www.telegraph.co.uk/news/uknews/1576076/Violent-youth-crime-up-a-third.html

Le Blanc, M. and Loeber, R. (1998). Developmental criminology updated. In N. Morris and M. Tonry (eds.). Crime and Justice. *A Review of Research*, 23. Chicago: University of Chicago Press.

Le Bon, G. (1895, trans. 1947). *The Crowd: A Study of the Popular Mind*. London: Ernest Benn.

Lee, J. H. (1999). *The Treatment of Psychopathic and Antisocial Personality Disorders: A Review*. Clinical Decision Making Support Unit: Broadmoor Hospital.

Lee, M. and Prentice, N.M. (1988). Interrelations of empathy, cognition and moral reasoning with dimensions of juvenile delinquency. *Journal of Abnormal Child Psychology*, 16, 127–39.

Lee, R.B. (1979). *The !Kung San. Men, Women and Work in Foraging Society*. Cambridge: Cambridge University Press.

Lehman, J. and Phelps, S. (2005). *West's Encyclopedia of American Law: Mala in Se* (2). Gale Group, Inc. www.enotes.com/wests-law-encyclopedia/mala-se.

Lehman, J. and Phelps, S. (2005). *West's Encyclopedia of American Law: Mala Prohibita (2)*. Gale Group, Inc. www.enotes.com/wests-law-encyclopedia/mala-prohibita.

Lemert, E. M. (1951). *Social Pathology* (pp.75–6). New York: Mcgraw-Hill.

Lemert, E. (1967). *Human Deviance, Social Problems, and Social Control* (2nd edn.). Englewood Cliffs, NJ: Prentice Hall.

Lemert, E. (1969). Primary and Secondary Deviation. In D.R. Cressey and D.A. Ward (eds.). *Delinquency, Crime and Social Process* (p.604). New York, Evanston and London: Harper and Row.

Leo, R. (1996). Inside the interrogation room. *Journal of Criminal Law and Criminology*, 86, 266–303.

Lerner, E. (2011). Can science predict criminal behavior? *Penn Current: Research*. Philadelphia, PA: University of Pennsylvania Press.

Lerner, M. (1966). The unjust consequences of the need to believe in a just world. In B.D.

Sales (ed.). *Perspectives in Law and Psychology: Volume 2. The Jury, Judicial and Trial Processes.* New York: Plenum.

Lerner, M. (1980). *The Belief in a Just World: A Fundamental Delusion.* New York: Plenum.

Leslie, A.M. (1991). The theory of mind impairment in autism. In A. Whiten (ed.). *Natural Theories of Mind: Evolution, Development, and Simulation of Everyday Mindreading* (pp.63–78). Oxford: Blackwell.

Leslie, A.M. (1994). ToMM, ToBY, and Agency: Core architecture and domain specificity. In L.A.Hirschfeld and S.A. Gelman (eds.). *Mapping the Mind: Domain Specificity in Cognition and Culture* (pp.119–48). Cambridge, UK: Cambridge University Press.

Leung, R. (2009). The Confession. *CBS News* (Feb 11th 2009). www.cbsnews.com/2100–18559162–649381.html

Levenson, J.S. (2006). Residence restrictions and their impact on sex offender reintegration, rehabilitation and recidivism. *ATSA Forum*, XVIII(2).

Levenson, R.W. and Ruef, A.M. (1992). Empathy: A physiological substrate. *Journal of Personality and Social Psychology*, 63(2), 234–46.

Leventhal, G. and Krate, R. (1977). Physical attractiveness and severity of sentencing. *Psychological Reports*, 40, 315–8.

Leventhal, G., Weiss, T. and Long, G. (1969). Equity, reciprocity and reallocating rewards in the dyad. *Journal of Personality and Social Psychology*, 13, 300–5.

Levesque, R.J.R. (1999). *Sexual Abuse of Children: A Human Rights Perspective.* Bloomington: Indiana University Press.

Levi, M. (1993). *Drugs and Crime. A Report by the WCDM.* Cardiff: Welsh Office.

Levi, M. and Jones, S. (1985). Public and police perception of crime seriousness in England and Wales. *British Journal of Criminology*, 25, 234–50.

Leyton, E. (1986). *Hunting Humans: The Rise of the Modern Multiple Murderer* (p.18). Toronto: McClelland and Stewart.

Liberal Democratic Party (2009). *Victimless crimes.* http://ldp.org.au/policies/1166-victimless-crimes.

Liebowitz, M.R., Stone, M.H. and Turkat, I.D. (1986). Treatment of personality disorders. In A.J. Frances and R.E. Hales (eds.). *American Psychiatric Association Annual Review*, 5, Washington, DC: American Psychiatric Press.

Lilienfeld, S.O. (1998). Methodological advances and developments in the assessment of psychopathy. *Behaviour Research and Therapy*, 36(1), 99–125.

Lindamood-Bell. (1998). *Sensory Cognitive Solutions: Definitions and Terminology Resource.* www.lblp.com/definitions.

Lindsay, D.S. and Johnson, M.K. (1991). Recognition memory and source monitoring. *Psychological Bulletin*, 29(3), 203–5.

Lindsay, R.C.L. and Wells, G.L. (1985). Improving eyewitness identification from lineups: Simultaneous versus sequential lineup presentations. *Journal of Applied Psychology*, 70, 556–64.

Linden, M.G. and Bender, B.G. (2002). Fifty-one prenatally diagnosed children and adolescents with sex chromosome abnormalities. *American Journal of Medical Genetics*, 110, 11–8.

Liotti, M. and Tucker, D.M. (1995). Emotion in asymmetrical corticolimbic networks. In R.J. Davidson and K. Hugdahl (eds.). *Brain Asymmetry* (pp.389–423). Cambridge, MA: The MIT Press.

Livesey, C. and Lawson, T. (2009). *Crime and Deviance: Different Theories of Crime, Deviance,*

*Social Order and Social Control, Pt 1.* onlineclassroom.tv. www.ecclesbourne.derbyshire. sch.uk.

Lockmuller, M., Beech, A. and Fischer, D. (2008). Sexual offenders with mental health problems: epidemiology, assessment and treatment. In K. Soothill, P. Rogers and M. Dolan (eds.). Handbook of Forensic Mental Health. (pp.446–79) Cullompton, Devon: Willan Publishing.

Loeber, R. and Keenan, K. (1994). Interaction between conduct disorder and its comorbid conditions: Effects of age and gender. *Clinical Psychology Review*, 14, 497–523.

Loeber, R. and Stouthamer-Loeber, M. (1998). Development of juvenile aggression and violence: Some common misconceptions and controversies. *American Psychologist*, 53, 242–59.

Loftus, E.F. (1975). Leading questions and the eyewitness report. *Cognitive Psychology*, 7, 560–72.

Loftus, E.F. (2004). The devil in confessions. In S.M. Kassin and G. Gudjonsson (eds.). The psychology of confessions. *Psychological Science in the Public Interest*, 5(2), 1–2.

Loftus, E.F. (2005). Planting misinformation in the human mind: A 30-year investigation of the malleability of memory. *Learning and Memory*, 12(4), 361–6.

Loftus, E.F., Miller, D.G. and Burns, H.J. (1978). Semantic integration of verbal information into a visual memory. *Human Learning and Memory*, 4, 19–31.

Loftus, E.F. and Palmer, J.C. (1974). Reconstruction of auto-mobile destruction: An example of the interaction between language and memory. *Journal of Verbal Learning and Verbal Behavior*, 13, 585–9.

Lombroso, C. (1911). *Crime: Its Causes and Remedies*. Boston: Little, Brown and Co.

London Borough of Newham (1987). *The Newham Crime Survey*. London: London Borough of Newham.

London, E.D., Ernst, M., Grant, S., Bonson, K. and Weinstein, A. (2000). Orbitofrontal cortex and human drug abuse: Functional imaging. *Cerebral Cortex*, 10, 334–42.

London, K., Bruck, M. and Melnyk, L. (2009). Post-event information affects children's autobiographical memory after one year. *Law and Human Behavior*, 33, 344–55.

Long, D.E. (1990). *The Anatomy of Terrorism*. New York: The Free Press.

Looman, J., Abracen, J. and Nicholaichuk, T.P. (2000). Recidivism among treated sexual offenders and matched controls: Data from the Regional Treatment Centre (Ontario). *Journal of Interpersonal Violence*, 15, 279–90.

Loranger, A. (1999). Dimensional approaches to personality disorder assessment and diagnosis. In C. Cloniger (ed.). *Personality and Psychopathology* (pp.201–17). Washington, DC: American Psychiatric Press.

Lorenz, K. (1935). Der Kumpan in der Umwelt des Vogels: Der Artgenosse als auslösendes Moment sozialer Verhaltensweisen. *Journal für Ornithologie*, 83, 137–215.

Lorenz, A.R. and Newman, J.P. (2002). Deficient response modulation and emotion processing in low-anxious Caucasian psychopathic offenders: Results from a lexical decision task. *Emotion*, 2, 91–104.

Lösel, F. and Schmucker, M. (2005). The effectiveness of treatment for sexual offenders: A comprehensive meta-analysis. *Journal of Experimental Criminology*, 1, 117–46.

Luna, K. and Martin-Luengo, B. (2010). New advances in the study of the confidence-accuracy relationship in the memory for events. *The European Journal of Psychology Applied to Legal Context*, 2(1), 55–71.

Luntz, B.K. and Widom, C.S. (1994). Antisocial personality disorder in abused and neglected children grown up.*American Journal of Psychiatry*, 151(5), 670–4.

Lutchmaya, S., Baron-Cohen, S. and Raggatt, P. (2002). Foetal testosterone and eye contact in 12-month-old human infants. *Infant Behaviour and Development*, 25, 327–35.

Luu, T.N. and Geiselman, R.E. (1993). Cognitive retrieval techniques and order of feature construction in the formation of composite facial images. *Journal of Police and Criminal Psychology*, 9, 34–9.

Luus, C.A.E. and Wells, G.L. (1991). Eyewitness identification and the selection of distractors for lineups. *Law and Human Behavior*, 15, 43–57.

Lykken, D.T. (1957). A study of anxiety in the sociopathic personality. *Journal of Abnormal Social Psychology*, 55, 6–10.

Lykken, D.T. (1995). *The Antisocial Personalities*. Mahwah, NJ: Erlbaum.

Lynam, D.R. (2002). Psychopathy from the perspective of the five-factor model of personality. In P.T. Costa and T.A. Widiger (eds.). *Personality Disorders and the Five-Factor Model of Personality* (pp.325–48). Washington, DC: American Psychological Association.

Lynam, D.R., Caspi, A., Moffitt, T.E., Loeber, R. and Stouthamer-Loeber, M. (2007). Longitudinal evidence that psychopathy scores in early adolescence predict adult psychopathy. *Journal of Abnormal Psychology*, 116(1), 155–65.

Lynam, D.R. and Widiger, T.A. (2001). Using the five-factor model to replicate the DSM-IV personality disorders: An expert consensus approach. *Journal of Abnormal Psychology*, 110, 401–12.

Lyons, H.A. and Harbinson, H.J. (1979). A comparison of political and non-political murderers in Northern Ireland, 1974–1984. *Medicine, Science and the Law*, 26, 193–8.

Maccoby, E.E. and Martin, J.A. (1983). Socialisation in the context of the family: Parent-child interaction. In E.M. Hetherington (ed.). *Handbook of Child Psychology*, vol. 4. New York: Wiley.

Macdonald, J. (1998). Disclosing shame. In P. Gilbert and B. Andrews (eds.). *Shame: Interpersonal Behavior, Psychopathology, and Culture* (pp.141–60). New York: Oxford University Press.

Macfarlane, M. (2015). ISIS: Two runaway teenage girls believed to be terror group's latest recruits. Mirror. www.mirror.co.uk/news/world-news/isis-two-runaway-teenage-girls-5312603.

Mackintosh, N. (2011). In A. Jha (ed.). *Age of criminal responsibility is too low, say brain scientists. The Guardian*. www.guardian.co.uk/science/2011/dec/13/age-criminal-responsibility-brain-scientists.

McLeod, E. (1982). *Women Working: Prostitution Now*. London: Croom Helm.

MacLeod, M. (2002). Retrieval-induced forgetting in eyewitness memory: Forgetting as a consequence of remembering. *Applied Cognitive Psychology*, 16, 135–49.

Maguire, M. (2003). Criminal investigation and crime control. In T. Newburn (ed.). *Handbook of Policing* (pp.363–93). Cullompton: Willan Publishing.

Main, M. (1985). *Attachment: A Move to the Level of Representation*. Symposium presented at the meeting of the Society for Research in Child Development, Toronto, Canada.

Mair, G. and May, C. (1997). Offenders on Probation. *Home Office Research Study*, 167, London: Home Office.

Maiuro, R.D., O'Sullivan, M.C. and Vitaliano P.P. (1989). Anger, hostility and depression in assaultive vs. suicide-attempting males. *Journal of Clinical Psychology*, 45, 531–41.

Makdisi, J.A. (1999). The Islamic Origins of the Common Law. *North Carolina Law Review*, 77 (5), 1635–739.

Mail Online (2011). Afghan mother and daughter stoned and shot dead after Taliban accused them of 'moral deviation and adultery'. *Daily Mail*. www.dailymail.co.uk/news/article-2060380/Afghan-mother-daughter-stoned-shot-dead-Taliban-accused-moral-deviation-adultery.html.

Maletzky, B.M. (1980). Self-referred versus court-referred sexually deviant patients: Success with assisted covert sensitisation. *Behaviour Therapy*, 11, 306–14.

Maletzky, B.M. (1991). *Treating the Sex Offender*. Newbury Park, CA: SAGE.

Malpass, R.S., Lavigueur, H. And Weldon, D.R. (1973). Verbal and visual training in face recognition. *Perception and Psychophysics*, 14(2), 285–92.

Malsch, M. and Freckelton, I. (2005). Expert bias and partisanship: A comparison between Australia and the Netherlands. *Psychology, Public Policy and Law*, 11(1), 42–61.

Mammarella, N., Russo, R. and Avons, S.E. (2002). Spacing effects in cued-memory tasks for unfamiliar faces and non-words. *Memory and Cognition*, 30(8), 1238–51.

Mann, R.E. and Beech, A.R. (2003). Cognitive distortions, schemas, and implicit theories. In T. Ward, D.R. Laws and S.M. Hudson (eds.). *Sexual Deviance: Issues and Controversies* (pp.135–53). Thousand Oaks, CA: SAGE Publications.

Mann, S., Vrij, A. and Bull, R. (2004). Detecting true lies: Police officers' ability to detect suspects' lies. *Journal of Applied Psychology*, 89, 137–49.

Mangold, T. (1997). *Predators*. BBC, Panorama, 3 March.

Mantyla, T. and Cornoldi, C. (2002). Remembering changes: Repetition effects in face recollection. *Acta Psychologica*, 109(1), 95–105.

Marikkar, F.A. (2009). Crime and Capital Punishment in Japan: How does the Japanese Society Respond? *Crime and Punishment in Japan*, 37, 95–104.

Markus, H.R. and Kitayama, S. (1991). Culture and self: Implications for cognition, emotion and motivation. *Psychological Review*, *98*, 224–53.

Marsh, A.A., Finger, E., Buzas, B., Kamel, N., Richell, R., Vythilingham, M., Pine, D.S., Goldman, D. and Blair, R.J.R. (2006). Impaired recognition of fear facial expressions in 5-HTTLPR S-polymorphism carriers following tryptophan depletion. *Psychopharmacology*, 189, 387–94.

Marshall, L. and Cooke, D. (1995). The role of childhood experiences in the aetiology of psychopathy. *Issues in Criminological and Legal Psychology*, 24, 107–8.

Marshall, L. and Cooke, D.J. (1996). The role of childhood experiences in the aetiology of psychopathy. In D.J. Cooke, A.E. Forth, J.P. Newman and R.D. Hare (eds.). *Issues in Criminological and Legal Psychology: No. 24. International Perspectives on Psychopathy* (pp.107–8). Leicester, England: British Psychological Society.

Marshall, W.L. (1996). Assessment, treatment and theorizing about sex offenders. Development during the past twenty years and future directions. *Criminal Justice and Behavior*, 23, 162–99.

Marshall, W.L. (1997). The relationship between self-esteem and deviant sexual arousal in nonfamilial child molesters. *Behavior Modification*, 21, 86–96.

Marshall, W.L. (2005). Therapist style in sexual offender treatment: Influence on indices of changes. *Sexual Abuse: A Journal of Research and Treatment*, 17, 109–16.

Marshall, W.L., Anderson, D. and Fernandez, Y.M. (1999). *Cognitive Behavioural Treatment of Sexual Offenders*. Chichester, UK: John Wiley and Sons.

Marshall, W.L. and Barbaree, H.E. (1988). The long-term evaluation of a behavioural treatment program for child molesters. *Behaviour Research Therapy*, 26(6), 499–511.

Marshall, W.L. and Barbaree, H.E. (1990). An integrated theory of the etiology of sexual offending. In W.L. Marshall, D.R. Laws and H.E. Barbaree (eds.). *Handbook of Sexual Assault: Issues, Theories and Treatment of the Offender*. New York: Plenum.

Marshall, W.L., Barbaree, H.E. and Butt, J. (1988). Sexual offenders against male children: sexual preferences. *Behaviour Research and Therapy*, 26(5), 383–91.

Marshall, W.L., Champagne, F., Brown, C. and Miller, S. (1997). Empathy, intimacy, loneliness and self-esteem in nonfamilial child molesters: A brief report. *Journal of Child Sexual Abuse*, 6(3), 87–98.

Marshall, W.L., Champagne, F., Sturgeon, C. and Bryce, P. (1997). Increasing the self-esteem of child molesters. *Sexual Abuse: A Journal of Research and Treatment*, 9, 321–33.

Marshall, W.L., Cripps, E., Anderson, D. and Cortoni, F.A. (1999). Self-esteem and coping strategies in child molesters. *Journal of Interpersonal Violence*, 14, 955–62.

Marshall, W.L. and Eccles, A. (1993). Pavlovian conditioning processes in adolescent sex offenders. In H. Barbaree, W. Marshall, and S. Hudson (eds.). *The Juvenile Sex Offender* (pp.118–42). New York: The Guilford Press.

Marshall, W.L., Hamilton, K. and Fernandez, M. (2001). Empathy deficits and cognitive distortions in child molesters. *Sexual Abuse: A Journal of Research and Treatment*, 13, 123–31.

Marshall, W.L., Jones, R., Hudson, S.M. and McDonald, E. (1993). Generalised empathy in child molesters. *Journal of Child Sexual Abuse*, 2(4), 61–8.

Marshall, W.L., Marshall, L.E. and Serran, G.a. (2007). *A Large Scale Evaluation of the Long-term Effects of the Rockwood Sexual Offenders; Treatment Program*. Ontario: Rockwood Psychological Services.

Marshall, W.L., Marshall, L.E., Serran, G.A. and O'Brien, M.D. (2009). Self-esteem, shame, cognitive distortions and empathy in sexual offenders: Their integration and treatment implications. *Psychology, Crime and Law*, 15(2/3), 217–34.

Marshall, W.L. and Mazzucco, A. (1995). Self-esteem and parental attachments in child molesters. *Sexual Abuse: A Journal of Research and Treatment*, 7, 279–85.

Martin, S.E., Sechrest, L.B. and Redner, R. (1981). *New Directions in the Rehabilitation of Criminal Offenders*. Washington, DC: National Academy Press.

Martinson, R. (1974). What works? Questions and answers about prison reform. *The Public Interest*, 35, 22–54.

Marx, K. and Engels, F. (1848). Manifesto of the Communist Party. In *The Revolutions of 1848: Political Writings*, vol. I (pp.62–98). Harmondsworth: Penguin, 1973.

Marx, K. and Engels, F. (1954). *Marx and Engels on Malthus*. New York: International.

Marx, K. and Engels, F. (1955). *Selected Correspondence*. Moscow: Progress, (2nd edn. 1965).

Maslow, A.H. (1954). *Motivation and Personality*. New York: Harper and Row.

Matthews, J.K., Matthews, R. and Speltz, K. (1991). Female sexual offenders: A typology. In M.Q. Patton (ed.). *Family Sexual Abuse: Frontline Research and Evaluation* (pp.199–219). Newbury Park, CA: SAGE Publications.

Matza, D. (1964). *Delinquency and Drift*. New York: Wiley.

Matza, D. (1969). *Becoming Deviant*. New Jersey: Prentice Hall.

Matza, D. and Sykes, G.M. (1961). Delinquency and subterranean values. *American Sociological Review*, 27, 712–9.

Mayer, J. (2005). Outsourcing Torture: The secret history of America's 'extraordinary rendition' program. *The New Yorker* (14 February 2005).

Maynard-Smith, J. (1974). The theory of games and the evolution of animal conflicts. *Journal of Theoretical Biology*, 47, 209–21.

McBurnett, K. (1992). Psychobiological theories of personality and their application to child psychopathology. In B.B. Lahey and A. Kazdin (eds.). *Advances in Child Clinical Psychology*, 14 (pp.107–64). New York: Plenum Press.

McCabe, D. (2002). Rethinking the war on crime. *McGill Reporter*, 34(13). www.mcgill. ca/reporter/34/.

McCaffrey, B. (1998). Legalization would be the wrong direction. *Los Angeles Times*, 27 July.

McCaffrey, B. (1999). *The destructive impact of drugs on the United States: How the legalization of drugs would jeopardize the health and safety of the American people and our nation*. Washington: Office of National Drug Control Policy, Executive Office of the President.

McCauley, C. (1991). *Terrorism Research and Public Policy*. London: Frank Cass.

McCauley, C. and Moskalenko, S. (2008). Mechanisms of political radicalisation: Pathways toward terrorism. *Terrorism and Political Violence*, 20, 415–33.

McClatchey, C. (2011). HMP Grendon: Therapy for dangerous prisoners. *BBC News*. www.bbc.co.uk/news/uk-11947481.

McCloskey, M. and Zaragoza, M.S. (1985). Misleading postevent information and memory for events: Arguments and evidence against memory impairment hypotheses. *Journal of Experimental Psychology: General*, 114, 1–16.

McClure, E. (2000). A meta-analytic review of sex differences in facial expression processing and their development in infants, children and adolescents. *Psychological Bulletin*, 126, 242–53.

McCord, J. (1977). A comparative study of two generations of native Americans. In R.F. Meiser (ed.). *Theory in Criminology* (pp.83–92). Beverly Hills, CA: SAGE.

McCord, J. (1979). Some child rearing antecedents of criminal behavior in adult men. *Journal of Personality and Social Psychology*, 37, 1477–86.

McCord, J. (1986). Instigation and insulation: How families affect antisocial aggression. In D. Olweus, J. Block and M. Radke-Yarrow (eds.). *Development of Antisocial and Prosocial Behavior: Research, Theories and Issues*. New York: Academic Press.

McCord, J. (1992). *Facts, Frameworks and Forecasts: Advances in Criminological Theory*, Volume 3. (pp.521, 532). New Brunswick: Transactional Publishers.

McCrae, R.R. and Costa, P.T. (1990). *Personality in Adulthood*. New York: Guilford Press.

McDaniel, M., Robinson, B. and Einstein, P. (1998). Prospective remembering: Perceptually driven or conceptually driven processes? *Memory and Cognition*, 26, 121–34.

McDermott, R. (2001). The psychological ideas of Amos Tversky and their relevance for political science. *Journal of Theoretical Politics*, 13(1), 5–33.

McEllistrem, J.E. (2004). Affective and predatory violence: A bimodal classification system of human aggression and violence. *Aggression and Violent Behavior*, 10, 1–30.

McGuire, J. (2004). *Understanding Psychology and Crime: Perspectives on Theory and Action*. Maidenhead: Open University Press.

McGuire, J. (2008). What's the point of sentencing? Psychological aspects of crime and punishment. In G.M. Davies, C.R. Hollin and R. Bull (eds.). *Forensic Psychology* (pp.265–91). Chichester, UK: John Wiley and Sons.

McGuire, R.J., Carlisle, J.M. and Young, B.G. (1965). Sexual deviation as a conditioned behavior: A hypothesis. *Behavioral Research and Therapy*, 2, 185–90.

McGuire, J. and Hatcher, R. (2001). Offence-focused problem solving: Preliminary evaluation of a cognitive skills program. *Criminal Justice and Behavior*, 28, 564–87.

McLeod, S.A. (2010). *Simply Psychology: Cognitive Interview*. Accessed 14 April 2012. www. simplypsychology.org/cognitive-interview.html

McLuhan, M. (1962). *The Gutenberg Galaxy: The Making of Typographic Man*. Toronto: University of Toronto Press.

Mcluhan, M. (1964). *Understanding Media: The Extensions of Man*. New York: McGraw-Hill.

McVeigh, K. (2011). Cyberstalking 'now more common' than face-to-face stalking. First study of its kind shows complete strangers target victims, of whom nearly 40% are men. London: *The Guardian*. www.guardian.co.uk

Mead, G.H. (1934). *Mind, Self, and Society*. Chicago, IL: University of Chicago Press.

Meadows, S. (2006). *The Child as Thinker*. London: Routledge.

Meadows, S. (2010). *The Child as Social Person*. London: Routledge.

Mealey, L. (1995). Primary sociopathy (psychopathy) is a type, secondary is not. *Behavioral and Brain Sciences*, 19, 579–99.

Mednick, S.A., Gabrielli, W.F. Jr. and Hutchings, B. (1984). Genetic influences in criminal convictions: Evidence from an adoption cohort. *Science*, 224, 891–3.

Mednick, S.A., Machon, R.A., Huttunen, M.O. and Bonett, D. (1988). Adult schizophrenia following prenatal exposure to an influenza epidemic. *Archives General Psychiatry*, 45(2), 189–92.

Meehl, P.E. and Rosen, A. (1955). Antecent probability and the efficiency of psychometric signs, patterns, or cutting scores. *Psychological Bulletin*, 52, 194–216.

Megargee, E.I. (1976). The prediction of dangerous behavior. *Criminal Justice and Behavior*, 3, 1–22.

Meikle, A., Stringham, J., Bishop, D. and West, D. (1988). Quantitating genetic and nongenetic factors influencing androgen production and clearing rates in men. *Journal of Clinical Endocrinology and Metabolism*, 67, 104–9.

Meins, E., Fernyhough, C., Wainwright, R., Das Gupta, M., Fradley, E. and Tuckey, M. (2002). Maternal mind-mindedness and the attachment security as predictors of theory of mind understanding. *Child Development*, 73, 1715–26.

Memon, A., Cronin, O., Eaves, R. and Bull, R. (1996). An empirical test of the mnemonic components of the Cognitive Interview. In G.M. Davies, Lloyd-Bostock, S., McMurran, M. and Wilson, J.C. (eds.). *Psychology and Law: Advances in Research* (pp.135–45). Berlin: De Gruyter.

Memon, A., Holley, A., Wark, L., Bull, R. and Köhnken, G. (1996). Reducing suggestibility in child witness interviews. *Applied Cognitive Psychology*, 10, 503–18.

Memon, A., Meissner, C.A. and Fraser, J. (2010). The Cognitive Interview: A meta-analytic review and study space analysis of the past 25 years. *Psychology, Public Policy, and Law*, 16(4), 340–72.

Memon, A., Milne, R., Holley, A., Bull, R. and Köhnken, G. (1994). Towards understanding the effects of interviewer training in evaluating the cognitive interview. *Applied Cognitive Psychology*, 8, 641–59.

Memon, A., Vrij, A. and Bull, R. (2003). *Psychology and Law: Truthfulness, Accuracy and Credibility*. London: Jossey-Bass.

Memon, A. Wark, L., Bull, R. and Köhnken, G. (1997). Isolating the effects of the cognitive interview. *British Journal of Psychology*, 88, 179–97.

Menesini, E. and Camodeca, M. (2008). Shame and guilt as behaviour regulators: Relationships with bullying, victimization and prosocial behaviour. *British Journal of Developmental Psychology*, 26(2), 183–96,

Mental Deficiency Act (1913). Act of Parliament of the United Kingdom.

Mental Health Act (2007). *Guidance on the Extension of Victims' Rights Under the Domestic Violence, Crime and Victims Act 2004*. Department of Health Mental Health Act Implementation Team and Ministry of Justice Mental Health Unit and NOMS Public Protection Unit. www.dh.gov.uk/publications.

Merton, R.K. (1938). Social structure and anomie. *American Sociological Review*, 3, 672–82.

Merton, R.K. (1949). *Social Theory and Social Structure.* New York: Free Press.

Merton, R.K. (1957). *Social Theory and Social Structure.* New York: Free Press.

Meyer, B., Pilkonis, P.A., Proietti, J.M., Heape, C.L. and Egan, M. (2001). Attachment styles and personality disorders as predictors of symptom course. *Journal of Personality Disorders*, 15, 371–89.

Michaud, S.G. (1983). When one murders: Ted Bundy talks about the unthinkable. *Esquire*, 99, 76–84.

Michaud, S.G. and Aynesworth, H. (1999). *The Only Living Witness: The True Story of Serial Sex Killer Ted Bundy* (p.21). Irving, TX: Authorlink Press.

Milhailides, S., Devilly, G.J. and Ward, T. (2004). Implicit cognitive distortions and sexual offending. *Sexual Abuse: A Journal of Research and Treatment*, 16(4), 333–50.

Mill, J.S. (1859). *On Liberty.* (2nd edn.). London: John W. Parker and Son.

Miller, J.D. and Lynam, D.R. (2003). Psychopathy and the five-factor model of personality: A replication and extension. *Journal of Personality Assessment*, 81(2), 168–78.

Miller, J.D., Lynam, D.R., Widiger, T.A. and Leukefeld, C. (2001). Personality disorders as extreme variants of common personality dimensions. Can the five-factor model of personality adequately represent psychopathy? *Journal of Personality*, 69, 253–76.

Miller, M., Schreck, C. and Tewksbury, R. (2006). *Criminological Theory.* Boston, MA: Allyn and Bacon.

Miller, P.H. and Bjorklund, D.F. (1998). Contemplating fuzzy-trace theory: The gist of it. *Journal of Experimental Child Psychology,* 71(2), 184–93.

Miller, W.B. (1958). Inter-institutional conflict as a major impediment to delinquency prevention. *Human Organization*, 17, 20–3.

Miller, W.B. (1958). Lower class culture as a generating milieu of gang delinquency. *Journal of Social Issues*, 14, 5–19.

Millington, T. and Sutherland Williams, M. (2007). *Millington and Sutherland Williams on The Proceeds of Crime* (3rd edn.). Oxford: Oxford University Press.

Millon, T. (2004). *Personality Disorders in Modern Life* (p.4). Hoboken, NJ: Wiley and Sons.

Millon, T. (2011). *Disorders of Personality: Introducing a DSM/ICD Spectrum from Normal to Abnormal* (3rd edn.). Hoboken, NJ: Wiley and Sons.

Millon, T. and Davis, R.D. (1998). Ten subtypes of psychopathy. In T. Millon, E. Simonsen, M. Birket-Smith and R.D. Davis (eds.). *Psychopathy: Antisocial, Criminal and Violent Behavior* (Chapter 10). New York: The Guilford Press.

Millon, T., Simonsen, E., Birket-Smith, M. and Davis, R.D. (1998). *Psychopathy: Antisocial, Criminal and Violent Behavior.* New York: The Guilford Press.

Mills, H. and Roberts, R. (2012). *Reducing the Numbers in Custody: Looking Beyond Criminal Justice Solutions.* Centre for Crime and Justice Studies.

Milne, R. and Bull, R. (1999). *Investigative Interviewing: Psychology and Practice.* Chicester, UK: Wiley.

Milne, R. and Bull, R. (2001). Interviewing witnesses with learning disabilities for legal purposes. *British Journal of Learning Disabilities*, 29, 93–7.

Milne, R. and Bull, R. (2002). Back to basics: A componential analysis of the original cognitive interview mnemonics with three age groups. *Applied Cognitive Psychology,* 16, 743–53.

Milne, R. and Bull, R. (2003). Does the cognitive interview help children to resist the effects of suggestive questioning? *Legal and Criminological Psychology*, 8(1), 21–38.

Milne, R. and Bull, R. (2006). Interviewing victims of crime, including children and people with intellectual difficulties. In M.R. Kebbell and G.M. Davies (eds.). *Practical Psychology for Forensic Investigations.* Chichester, England: Wiley.

Milne, R., Bull, R., Koehnken, G. and Memon, A. (1995). The cognitive interview and suggestibility. In G.M. Stephenson and N.K. Clark (eds.). Criminal behaviour: Perceptions, attributions and rationality (pp.21–7). *Division of Criminological and Legal Psychology Occasional Papers*, 22. Leicester, UK: British Psychological Society.

Milne, R., Clare, I.C.H. and Bull, R. (1999). Using the cognitive interview with adults with mild learning disabilities. *Psychology, Crime and Law*, 5(1–2), 81–99.

Ministry of Justice (2009). *Statistics on Women and the Criminal Justice System: A Ministry of Justice publication under Section 95 of the Criminal Justice Act 1991*. London: Ministry of Justice.

Ministry of Justice (2010). *Compendium of Reoffending Statistics and Analysis Tables*. www.justice.gov.uk/statistics/reoffending/compendium-of-reoffending-statistics-and-analysis.

Ministry of Justice (2010). *Breaking the Cycle: Effective Punishment, Rehabilitation and Sentencing of Offenders* (pp.1 and 9). UK: HMSO.

Ministry of Justice (2011). *Breaking the Cycle: Government Response* (p.11). UK: HMSO.

Ministry of Justice (2012). *Comparing International Criminal Justice Systems*. London: National Audit Office.

Ministry of Justice (2012). *Statistics on Women and the Criminal Justice System 2011*. A Ministry of Justice publication under Section 95 of the Criminal Justice Act 1991. www.justice.gov.uk/downloads/statistics/criminal-justice-stats/women-cjs-2011/statistics-women-cjs-2011-v2.pdf.

Ministry of Justice (2013). *An Overview of Sexual Offending in England and Wales*. Statistics Bulletin: Ministry of Justice, Home Office and the Office for National Statistics.

Mirror News (2012). Freed from a seven-year nightmare: Innocent man jailed for murder has his conviction overturned. *Mirror News*, 17th May 2012. Mirror Online. www.mirror.co.uk/news/uk-news/sam-hallam-freed-innocent-man-837508

Modestin, J. and Ammann, R. (1996). Mental disorder and criminality: Male schizophrenia. *Schizophrenia Bulletin*, 22(1), 69–82.

Moffitt, T.E. (1987). Parental mental disorder and offspring criminal behavior: An adoption study. *Psychiatry*, 50, 346–60.

Moffitt, T.E. (1990). The neuropsychology of juvenile delinquency: A critical review. In M. Tonry and N. Morris (eds.). *Crime and Justice: An Annual Review of Research* (vol. 12; pp.99–169). Chicago, IL: University of Chicago Press.

Moffitt, T.E. (1993). The neuropsychology of conduct disorder. *Developmental Psychopathology*, 5, 135–51.

Moffitt, T.E., Brammer, G.L., Caspi, A., Fawcett, J.P., Raleigh, M., Yuwiler, A. and Silva, P. (1998). Whole blood serotonin relates to violence in an epidemiological study. *Biological Psychiatry*, 43, 446–57.

Moffitt, T. E. and Caspi, A. (2001). Childhood predictors differentiate life-course persistent and adolescence-limited antisocial pathways among males and females. *Development and Psychopathology*, 13, 355–75.

Moffitt, T.E., Caspi, A., Dickson, N., Silva, P. and Stanton, W. (1996). Childhood-onset versus adolescent-onset antisocial conduct problems in males: natural history from ages 3 to 18 years. *Developmental Psychopathology*, 8, 399–424.

Moffitt, T.E., Caspi, A., Rutter, M. and Silva, P.A. (2001). *Sex Differences in Antisocial Behaviour: Conduct Disorder, Delinquency, and Violence in the Dunedin Longitudinal Study*. Cambridge, UK: Cambridge University Press.

Moilanen, I. (1987). Dominance and submissiveness between twins. I. Perinatal and developmental aspects. *Acta Genet Med Gemellol*, 36, 249–55.

Mojo Law (2008). Criminal Law: Crimes Mala in Se – Crime Classification (¶1). www. mojolaw.com/info/cl018

Moir, A., and Jessel, D. (1995). *A Mind to Crime: The Controversial Link Between the Mind and Criminal Behaviour* (p.31). London: Michael Joseph Ltd; Penguin.

Moll, J., Eslinger, P.J. and Oliveira-Souza, R. (2001). Frontopolar and anterior temporal cortex activation in a moral judgment task: Preliminary functional MRI results in normal subjects. *Arq Neuropsiquiatr*, 593-B.

Moll, J., de Oliveira-Souza, R., Eslinger, P.J., Bramati, I.E., Mourao-Miranda, J., Andreiuolo, P.A. and Pessoa, L. (2002). The neural correlates of moral sensitivity: a functional magnetic resonance imaging investigation of basic and moral emotions. *Journal of Neuroscience*, 22(7), 2730–6.

Monahan, J. (1981). *Predicting Violent Behavior: An Assessment of Clinical Techniques*. Beverly Hills, CA: SAGE.

Monahan, J., Steadman, H.J., Silver, E., Appelbaum, P., Robbins, P., Mulvey, E., Roth, L., Grisso, T. and Banks, S. (2001). *Rethinking Risk Assessment: The MacArthur Study of Mental Disorder and Violence*. Oxford: Oxford University Press.

Monckton-Smith, J., Adams, T., Hart, A. and Webb, J. (2013). *Introducing Forensic and Criminal Investigation*. London: SAGE.

Moore, S. (1996). *Investigating Crime and Deviance*. London: Collins Educational.

Moore, S. and Shepherd, J. (2007). The elements and prevalence of fear. *The British Journal of Criminology*, 47(1), 154–62.

Moore, T.H., Zammit, S., Lingford-Hughes, A., Barnes, T.R., Jones, P.B., Burke, M. and Lewis, G. (2007). Cannabis use and risk of psychotic or affective mental health outcomes: A systematic review. *Lancet*, 370 (9584), 319–28.

Morgan, D. and Stephenson, G. (1994). Suspicion and silence: The right to silence in criminal investigations. In M. Schollum (ed.). *Investigative Interviewing: The Literature* (p.18). New Zealand Police. Wellington: Office of the Commissioner of Police.

Morgan, C. A., Hazlett, G., Doran, A., Garrett, S., Hoyt, G., Thomas, P., Baranoski, M. And Southwick, S.M. (2004). Accuracy of eyewitness memory for persons encountered during exposure to highly intense stress. *International Journal of Law and Psychiatry*, 27, 265–79.

Morgan, J.E. (2006). A classic for the 21st century: Defining the Zeitgeist of contemporary neuropsychology. [Review of the book Neuropsychological Assessment]. *The Clinical Neuropsychologist*, 20, 602–6.

Morris, C. (1866). The making of Man. *American Naturalist*, 20, 493–504.

Morris, R.G. and Higgins, G.E. (2010). Criminological theory in the digital age: The case of social learning theory and digital piracy. *Journal of Criminal Justice*, 38, 470–80.

Morrison, I., Lloyd, D., di Pellegrino, G. and Roberts, N. (2004). Vicarious responses to pain in anterior cingulate cortex: Is empathy a multisensory issue? *Cognitive Affective, and Behavioral Neuroscience*, 4(2), 270–8.

Morton, J. and Johnson, M.H. (1991). CONSPEC and CONLERN: A two-process theory of infant face recognition. *Psychological Review*, 98, 164–81.

Moscovici, S. (1984). The phenomenon of social representations. In R.M. Farr and S. Moscovici (eds). *Social Representations* (pp. 3–69). Cambridge, UK: Cambridge University Press.

Moscovici, S. (1988). Notes towards a description of social representations. *Journal of European Social Psychology*, 18 (3), 211–50.

Moston, S. and Engleberg, T. (1993). Police questioning techniques in tape recorded interviews with criminal suspects. *Policing and Society*, 3, 223–37.

Moston, S., Stephenson, G.M. and Williamson, T.M. (1990). Police interrogation styles and suspect behaviour. In F. Lösel, D. Bender and T. Bliesener (eds.). *Psychology and Law International Perspectives*. New York: Walter de Gruyter, 1992.

Mouras, H. and Stoléru, S. (2007). Functional neuroanatomy of sexual arousal. In F.R. Kandeel, T.F. Lue, J.L. Pryor and R.S. Swerdloff (eds.). *Male Sexual Dysfunction: Pathophysiology and Treatment* (pp.39–54). New York: Informa Healthcare.

Mourato, S., Saynor, B. and Hart, D. (2004). Greening London's black cabs: A study of driver's preferences for fuel cell taxis. In G. Vanderveen (2006). *Interpreting Fear, Crime, Risk and Unsafety*, The Hague: BJU Legal Publishers.

Moyes, T. Tennent, T.G. and Bedford, A.P. (1985). Long-term follow-up of a ward based behaviour modification programme for adolescents with acting out and conduct problems. *British Journal of Psychiatry*, 147, 300–5.

MSN Encarta (2007). *Crime* (4). http://encarta.msn.com/encyclopedia_761559497/crime.html.

Mueller, G. and Adler, F. (1995). The emergence of criminal justice: Tracing the route to Neolithic times. In J. McCord and J. Laub (eds.). *Contemporary Masters in Criminology* (pp.59–75). New York: Plenum.

Mueller-Johnson, K. (2009). Elderly in Court. In A. Jamieson and A. Moenssens (eds.). *Wiley Encyclopedia of Forensic Science*. Chichester, England: Wiley.

Mulvey, E.P. and Lidz, C.W. (1984). Clinical considerations in the prediction of dangerousness in mental patients. *Clinical Psychology Review*, 4, 379–401.

Münsterberg, H. (1908). *On the Witness Stand*. New York: Doubleday, Page and Company.

Murphy, W.D. (1990). Assessment and modification of cognitive distortions in sex offenders. In W.L. Marshall, D.R. Laws and H.E. Barbaree (eds.). *Handbook of Sexual Assault: Issues, Theories and Treatment of the Offender*. New York: Plenum.

Murray, J.B. (2000). Psychological profile of paedophiles and child molesters. *The Journal of Psychology*, 134(2), 211–24.

Myers, J.E.B. (1987). *Child Witness Law and Practice* (p.5 and p.66). New York: John Wiley and Sons.

Myers, J.E.B., Saywitz, K. and Goodman, G.S. (1996). Psychological research on children as witnesses: Practical implications for children's interviews and courtroom testimony. *Pacific Law Review*, 28, 1–91.

Myers, M.G., Stewart, D.G. and Brown, S.A. (1998). Progression from conduct disorder to antisocial personality disorder following treatment for adolescent substance abuse. *American Journal of Psychiatry*, 155, 479–85.

Myhill, A. and Allen, J. (2002). Rape and sexual assault of women: Findings from the British Crime Survey. *Home Office Research Study*, 159, 1–6.

Nadelmann, E. (1999). Learning to live with drugs. In B.E. Harcourt (ed.). The collapse of the harm principle. *Journal of Criminal Law and Criminology*, 90(1), 1–65. http://findarticles.com.

Nagin, D.S. and Farrington, D.P. (1992). The stability of criminal potential from childhood to adulthood. *Criminology*, 30, 235–60.

Nasby, W., Hayden, B. and DePaulo, B.M. (1979). Attributional bias among aggressive boys to interpret ambiguous social stimuli as displays of hostility. *Journal of Abnormal Psychology*, 89, 459–68.

Nash, Jr., J.F. (1950a). Equilibrium points in n-person games. *Proceedings National Academy of Sciences*, 36, 48–9.

Nash, Jr., J.F. (1950b). *Non-cooperative Games*. Ph.D. thesis, Mathematics Department, Princeton University.

Nash, Jr., J.F. (1950c). The bargaining problem. *Econometrica*, 18, 155–62.

Nash, Jr., J.F. (1951). Non-cooperative games. *Annals of Mathematics*, 54, 286–95.

Nash, Jr., J.F. (1953). Two-person cooperative games. *Econometrica*, 21, 128–40.

Nathanson, R., Crank, J.N. and Saywitz, K. (2002). *Enhancing Narrative Discourse in Children with Learning Disabilities*. Manuscript submitted for publication.

National Association for the Care and Resettlement of Offenders (NACRO) (1993). *Opening the Doors. The Resettlement of Prisoners in the Community*. London: NACRO.

National District Attorneys Association. (2007). *Residency Restrictions for Sexual Offenders*. Alexandria, VA: Author.

National Hi-Tech Crime Unit (2001). Serious Organised Crime Agency: Association of Chief of Police Officers (ACPO). www.soca.gov.uk.

National Investigative Interviewing Strategy. (2009). *National Policing Improvement Agency (NPIA), Professional Practice.* www.npia.police.uk/en/docs/National_Investigative_Interviewing_Strategy_09.pdf.

Naylor, T. (2002). *Wages of Crime: Black Markets, Illegal Finance and the Underworld Economy*. Montreal: McGill-Queen's University Press.

Neill, S.R.St.J. (2005) Knives and other weapons in London schools, *The International Journal on School Disaffection*, 3(2), 27–32.

Neill, S.R.St.J. (2008) *Disruptive Pupil Behaviour. A survey analysed for the National Union of Teachers*. Institute of Education: University of Warwick.

Neitzel, M. (1979). *Crime and its Modification: A Social Learning Perspective* (p.350). Elmsford, NY: Pergamon.

Nellis, M. (2006). Surveillance, rehabilitation, and electronic monitoring: Getting the issues clear. *Criminology and Public Policy*, 5, 103–8.

Nelson, J.R., Smith, D.J. and Dodd, J. (1990). The moral reasoning of juvenile delinquents: A meta-analysis. *Journal of Abnormal Child Psychology*, 18, 231–9.

Neville, H. (1995). Developmental specificity in neurocognitive development in humans. In M. Gazzaniga (ed.). *The Cognitive Neurosciences* (pp.219–31). Cambridge, MA: Bradford.

Newburn, T. (2003). *Handbook of Policing*. Cullompton: Willan Publishing.

Newman, J.P., Schmitt, W.A. and Voss, W.D. (1997). The impact of motivationally neutral cues on psychopaths: Assessing the generality of the response modulation hypothesis. *Journal of Abnormal Psychology*, 106, 563–75.

Nezu, A.M., Nezu, C.M. and Lombardo, E. (2004). *Cognitive-Behavioral Case Formulation and Treatment Design: A Problem-Solving Approach*. New York: Springer Publishing Company.

NHS England (2013). NHS Standard Contract for Medium and Low Secure Mental Health Services (Adults). *NHS England/CO3/S/a*.

Nicholaichuk, T., Gordon, A., Deqiang, G. and Wong, S. (2000). Outcome of an institutional sexual offender treatment program: A comparison between treated and matched untreated offenders. *Sexual Abuse: A Journal of Research and Treatment*, 12, 139–154.

Nielsen, J., Sørensen, A., Theilgaard, A., Frøland, A. and Johnsen, S.G. (1969). A psychiatric-psychological study of 50 severely hypogonadal male patients, including 34 with Klinefelter's syndrome, 47,XXY. *Acta Jutlandica*, XLI(3).

Price, M.E., Cosmides, L. and Tooby, J. (2002). Punitive sentiment as an anti-free rider psychological device. *Evolution and Human Behavior*, 23, 203–31.

Prichard, J.C. (1835). *A Treatise on Insanity and Other Disorders Affecting the Mind*. London: Sherwood, Gilbert and Piper.

Priestley, G. and Pipe, M.E. (1997). Using toys and models in interviews with young children. *Applied Cognitive Psychology*, 11, 69–87.

Protess, D. (1993). *Hate Crimes and the Press: A Refracted Mirror*. Chicago, IL: North Western University.

Prothrow-Stith, D. and Spivak, H. (1999). America's Tragedy. *Psychiatric Times*, 16(6), 1–7.

Purcell, C.E., and Arrigo, B.A. (2006). *The Psychology of Lust Murder: Paraphilia, Sexual Killing, and Serial Homicide*. San Diego, CA: Elsevier/Academic Press.

Puri, B.K., Counsell, S.J., Saeed, N., Bustos, M.G., Treasaden, I.H. and Bydder, G.M. (2008). Regional grey matter volumetric changes in forensic schizophrenia patients: An MRI study comparing the brain structure of patients who have seriously and violently offended with that of patients who have not. *BioMed Central Psychiatry*, 8 Suppl.1:S6.

Purkinje, J.E. (1823). Commentary on the physiological examination of the organs of vision and the cutaneous system. In A. McRoberts and D. McRoberts (eds.). *The Fingerprint Sourcebook* (Chapter 5). Washington, DC: National Institute of Justice, 2012.

Quay, H.C. (1988). Attention deficit disorder and the behavioural inhibition system: The relevance of the neuropsychological theory of Jeffrey A. Gray. In L.M. Bloomingdale and J.A. Sergeant (eds.). *Attention Deficit Disorder: Criteria: Cognition, Intervention*. (pp.117–26). Oxford: Pergamon Press.

Quinn, K. (1986). Competency to be a witness: A major child forensic issue. *The Bulletin of the American Academy of Psychiatry and the Law*, 14, 311–21.

Quinney, R. (1970). *The Problem of Crime*. New York: Dodd, Mead, and Company.

Quinsey, V.L. (1984). Sexual aggression: Studies of offenders against women. In D. Weisstub (ed.). *Law and Mental Health: International Perspectives, Volume 1*. New York: Pergamon.

Quinsey, V.L. (2002). Evolutionary theory and criminal behaviour. *Legal and Criminological Psychology*, 7(1), 1–13.

Quinsey, V.L. and Earls, C.M. (1990). The modification of sexual preferences. In W.L. Marshall, D.R. Laws and H.E. Barbaree (eds.). *Handbook of Sexual Assault: Issues, Theories, and Treatment of the Offender*. New York: Plenum.

Rachman, S. (1966). Sexual fetishism: An experimental analogue. *Psychological Record*, 16, 293–6.

Rada, R.T. (1978). *Clinical Aspects of the Rapist*. New York: Grune and Stratton.

Radelet, R. and Lacock, T. (2009). Do executions lower homicide rates? The views of leading criminologists. *Journal of Criminal Law and Criminology*, 99(2), 489–508.

Radke-Yarrow, M. and Zahn-Waxler, C. (1986). The role of familial factors in the development of prosocial behavior: Research findings and questions. In D. Olweus, J. Block and M. Radke-Yarrow (eds.). *Development of Antisocial and Prosocial Behavior: Research, Theories and Issues* (207–33). New York: Academic Press.

Rafter, N. (1990). The social construction of crime and crime control. *Journal of Research in Crime and Delinquency*, 27(4), 376–89.

Raikes, H.A. and Thompson, R.A. (2006). Family emotional climate, attachment security, and young children's emotion knowledge in a high-risk sample. *British Journal of Developmental Psychology*, 24, 89–104.

Raine, A. (1993). *The Psychopathology of Crime: Criminal Behavior as a Clinical Disorder.* San Diego, CA: Academic Press.

Raine, A. (2002). The biological basis of crime. In J.Q. Wilson and J.Petersilia (eds.). *Crime: Public Policies for Crime Control* (pp.43–74). Oakland, CA: ICS Press.

Raine, A. (2002a). Biosocial studies of antisocial and violent behavior in children and adults: A review. *Journal of Abnormal Child Psychology*, 30, 311–26.

Raine, A. (2002b). Annotation: The role of prefrontal deficits, low autonomic arousal, and early health factors in the development of antisocial and aggressive behavior in children. *Journal of Child Psychology and Psychiatry*, 43, 417–34.

Raine, A. (2013). *The Anatomy of Violence: The Biological Roots of Crime.* New York: Pantheon.

Raine, A., Buchsbaum, M. and LaCasse, L. (1997). Brain abnormalities in murderers indicated by positron emission tomography. *Biological Psychiatry*, 42, 495–508.

Raine, A., Buchsbaum, M.S., Stanley, J., Lottenberg, S., Abel, L. and Stoddard, S. (1994). Selective reductions in prefrontal glucose metabolism in murderers. *Biological Psychiatry*, 36, 365–73.

Raine, A., Laufer, W., Yang, Y., Narr, K.L., Thompson, P. and Toga, A.W. (2012). Increased executive functioning, attention, and cortical thickness in white-collar criminals. *Human Brain Mapping*, 33(12), 2932–40.

Raine, A., Lencz, T., Bihrle, S., LaCasse, L. and Colletti, P. (2000). Reduced prefrontal gray matter volume and reduced autonomic activity in antisocial personality disorder. *Archives of General Psychiatry*, 57, 119–27.

Raine, A., Lencz, T., Taylor, K., Hellige, J., Bihrle, S., Lacasse, L., Lee, M., Ishikawa, S. and Colletti, P. (2003). Corpus callosum abnormalities in psychopathic antisocial individuals. *Archives of General Psychiatry*, 60(11) 1134–42.

Raine, A., Liu, J., Venables, P.H., Mednick, S.A. and Dalais, C. (2010). Cohort Profile: The Mauritius Child Health Project. *International Journal of Epidemiology*, 39, 1441–51.

Raine, A., Meloy, J.R., Bihrle, S., Stoddard, J., LaCasse, L. and Buchsbaum, M.S. (1998). Reduced prefrontal and increased subcortical brain functioning assessed using positron emission tomography in predatory and affective murderers. *Behavioural Sciences and the Law*, 16, 319–32.

Raine, A., O'Brien, M., Smiley, N., Scerbo, A. and Chan, C.J. (1990). Reduced lateralization in verbal dichotic listening in adolescent psychopaths. *Journal of Abnormal Psychology*, 99, 272–7.

Raine, A., Park, S., Lencz, T., Bihrle, S., LaCasse, L., Spatz-Widom, C., Al Dayeh, L. and Singh, M. (2001). Reduced right hemisphere activation in severely abused violent offenders during a working memory task as indicated by fMRI. *Aggressive Behavior, 27*(2), 111–29.

Raine, A., Reynolds, C., Venables, P.H., Mednick, S.A. and Farrington, D.P. (1998). Fearlessness, stimulation-seeking, and large body size at age 3 years as early predispositions to childhood aggression at age 11 years. *Archives of General Psychiatry*, 55, 745–51.

Raine, A., Venables, P.H. and Williams, M. (1990). Relationships between central and autonomic measures of arousal at age 15 years and criminality at 24 years. *Arch Gen Psychiatry*, 47, 1003–7.

Raine, A., Venables, P.H. and Williams, M. (1990a). Autonomic orienting responses in 15 year old male subjects and criminal behavior at age 24. *American Journal of Psychiatry*, 147, 933–7.

Ramchand, R., MacDonald, J., Haviland, A. and Morral, A. (2009). A developmental approach for measuring the seriousness of crimes. (p.14). *Journal of Quantitative Criminology*, 25(2), 129–53.

Ramchand, R., Morral, A.R. and Becker, K. (2009). Seven-year life outcomes of adolescent offenders in Los Angeles. *American Journal of Public Health*, 99(5), 863–70.

Ramchandani, P.G., Domoney, J., Sethna, V., Psychogiou, L., Vlachos, H. and Murray, L. (2013). Do early father–infant interactions predict the onset of externalising behaviours in young children? Findings from a longitudinal cohort study. *Journal of Child Psychology and Psychiatry, and Allied Disciplines*, 54(1), 56–64.

Ramsay, M. (1989). Downtown drinkers: The perceptions and fears of the public in a city Centre. *Crime Prevention Unit*, Paper 19. London: HMSO.

Randall, V. (2007). *Ignorance or Mistake*. MPC §2.04. http://academic.udayton.edu/legaled/crimlaw/02-Elements/07MPC2–04.htm.

Rankin, J.H. and Kern, R. (1994). Parental attachments and delinquency. *Criminology*, 32, 195–215.

Rape Crisis for England and Wales (2014). Common myths about rape. www.rapecrisis.org.uk/commonmyths2.php.

Rapoport, A. and Chummah, A.M. (1965). *Prisoner's Dilemma*. Ann Arbor: University of Michigan Press.

Rawls, J. (1971). *A Theory of Justice*. Oxford: Oxford University Press.

Ray, A. (2011). Honor killing cases among South Asians in the UK rising. *The Indian Times*.

Rayner, G. and Gardner, B. (2015). Men must prove a woman said 'Yes' under tough new rape rules. *The Telegraph*. Telegraph Media Group Limited. www.telegraph.co.uk/news/uknews/law-and-order/11375667/Men-must-prove-a-woman-said-Yes-under-tough-new-rape-rules.html.

Rector, N. and Bagby, R.M. (1993). The effect of prejudice and judicial ambiguity on defendant guilt ratings. *Journal of Social Psychology*, 133(5), 651–6.

Redondo, S., Sanchez-Meca, J. and Garrido, V. (1999). The influence of treatment programmes on the recidivism of juvenile and adult offenders: A European meta-analytic review. *Psychology, Crime and Law*, 5, 251–78.

Redondo, S., Sánchez-Meca, J. and Garrido, V. (2002). Crime treatment in Europe: A review of outcome studies. In J. McGuire (ed.). *Offender Rehabilitation and Treatment: Effective Programmes and Policies to Reduce Reoffending* (pp.113–41). Chichester, UK: John Wiley and Sons.

Redondo, S., Luque, E. and Funes, J. (1996). Social beliefs about recidivism in crime. In G. Davies, S. Lloyd-Bostock, M. McMurran and C. Wilson (eds.). *Psychology, Law and Criminal Justice: International Developments in Research and Practice* (pp.394–400). Berlin: Walter de Gruyter.

Reiman, J. (1998). *The Rich Get Richer and the Poor Get Prison: Ideology, Class and Criminal Justice* (5th, edn.). Boston, MA: Allyn and Bacon.

Reiner, W. G. and J. P. Gearhart (2004). Discordant sexual identity in some genetic males with cloacal exstrophy assigned to female sex at birth. *New England Journal of Medicine* 350(4), 333–41.

Reno, J. (1999). *Cyberstalking: A New Challenge for Law Enforcement and Industry*. www.usdoj.gov/criminal/cybercrime/cyberstalking.htm.

Renzema, M. and Mayo-Wilson, E. (2005). Can electronic monitoring reduce crime for moderate to high-risk offenders? *Journal of Experimental Criminology*, 1, 215–37.

Ressler, R.K. and Burgess, A.W. (1985). Crime Scene and Profile Characteristics of Organized and Disorganized Murders (1985), *FBI Law Enforcement Bulletin*, 54, 18–25.

Ressler, R.K., Burgess, A.W., Douglas, J.E., Hartman, C.R. and D'Agnostino, R.B. (1986). Sexual killers and their victims: Identifying patterns through crime scene analysis. *Journal of Interpersonal Violence*, 1, 288–308.

Reynolds, J. (2004). Spite? It's All Down to the Nasty Genes. *The Scotsman*. http://news.scotsman.com/scitech.cfm?id=1035142004;.

Rhodes, G., Brake, S. and Atkinson, A. (1993). What's lost in inverted faces? *Cognition*, 47, 25–57.

Rider, E.A. (2005). *Our Voices: Psychology of Women*. (2nd edn.). Hoboken, NJ: Wiley.

Rimé, B., Bouvy, H., Leborgne, B. and Rouillon (1978). Psychopathy and nonverbal behavior in an interpersonal situation. *Journal of Abnormal Psychology*, 87(6), 636–43.

Ringgold v. Black Entertainment Television, Inc., *126 F.3d 70 (2d Cir. 1997)*. http://fairuse.stanford.edu/overview/fair-use/four-factors/#sthash.sAnpAIb7.dpuf.

Roberts, D. (2009). Social harm and crime at a global level. London: *Centre for Crime and Justice Studies Briefing*, 9, 1–6.

Robertson, G. (1981). The extent and pattern of crime amongst mentally handicapped offenders. *Journal of the British Institute of Mental Handicap*, 9, 100–3.

Robertson, G., Pearson, R. and Gibb, R. (1996). Police interviewing and the use of appropriate adults. *Journal of Forensic Psychiatry*, 7(2), 297–309.

Robins, J. (1974). *Deviant Children Grown Up: A Sociological and Psychiatric Study of Sociopathic Personality*. New York: Krieger, Huntington.

Robins, L.N. (1979). Sturdy childhood predictors of adult outcomes: Replications from longitudinal studies. In J.E. Barrett, R.M. Rose and G.L. Klerman (eds.). *Stress and Mental Disorder* (pp.219–35). New York: Raven Press.

Robins, L.N. and Price R.K. (1991). Adult disorders predicted by childhood conduct problems: Results from the NIMH Epidemiologic Catchment Area Project. *Psychiatry*, 54, 116–32.

Robins, L.N., West, P.A. and Herjanic, B.L. (1975). Arrests and delinquency in two generations: A study of black urban families and their children. *Journal of Child Psychology and Psychiatry*, 16, 125–40.

Robinson, J. (2010). Britons 'downloaded 1.2bn illegal tracks this year'. *The Guardian*. www.guardian.co.uk/media/2010/dec/16/illegal-music-downloading-online-piracy.

Robinson, J. and McGuire, J. (2006). Suggestibility and children with mild learning disabilities: The use of the cognitive interview. *Psychology, Crime and Law*, 12, 537–56.

Robinson-Riegler, B. and Robinson-Riegler, G. (2004). *Cognitive Psychology: Applying the Science of the Mind* (p.313). Boston, MA: Allyn and Bacon.

Robson, S. (2015). ISIS: 'About 20' teenage girls fled Britain to join terror group in Syria in 2014. Mirror. www.mirror.co.uk/news/uk-news/isis-about-20-teenage-girls-5252686.

Rose, N. (1989). *Governing the Soul: The Shaping of the Private Self*. London: Routledge.

Rose, N. (1996). Authority and the genealogy of subjectivity. In P. Heelas, S. Lash and P. Morris (eds.). *Detraditionalization: Critical Reflections on Authority and Identity* (p.305). Oxford: Blackwell.

Rosenbaum, D.P., Bickman, L., Christenholtz, C., Chaitin, N. and Roth, T.S. (1979). *National Evaluation Program Phase I Assessment of Shoplifting and Employee Theft Programs: Interim Report*. Evanston, IL: Westinghouse Evaluation Institute, May, (Prepared for the 26 National Institute of Justice).

Rosenfield, R. (2002). Crime Decline in Context. *Contexts*, 1, 25–34.

Roshier, B. (1989). *Controlling Crime: The Classical Perspective in Criminology* (p.16). Philadelphia, PA: Open University Press.

Rosman, J.P. and Resnick, P.J. (1989). Sexual attraction to corpses: A psychiatric review of necrophilia. *Bulletin of the American Academy of Psychiatry and the Law*, 17(2), 153–63.

Ross, E.A. (1907). *Sin and Society: An Analysis of Latter-Day Iniquity*. Boston, MA: Houghton-Mifflin.

Ross, R.R. and Fabiano, E.A. (1985). *Time to Think: A Cognitive Model of Delinquency Prevention and Offender Rehabilitation*. Johnson City, TN: Institute of Social Sciences and Arts.

Ross, R.R., Fabiano, E.A. and Ewles, C.D. (1988). Reasoning and rehabilitation. *International Journal of Offender Therapy and Comparative Criminology*, 32, 29–36.

Rossano, M.J. (2003). Expertise and the evolution of consciousness. *Cognition*, 89, 207–36.

Rossi, P.H., Waite, E., Bose, C. and Berk, R. (1974). The seriousness of crimes: Normative structure and individual differences. (p.224). *American Sociological Review*, 39, 224–37.

Rossmo, D. K. (2000). *Geographic Profiling*. Boca Raton, FL: CRC Press.

Rothbaum, F. and Trommsdorf, G. (2007). Do roots and wings complement or oppose one another? The socialisation of relatedness and autonomy in cultural context. In J.E. Grusec and P.D. Hastings (eds.). *Handbook of Socialisation*. New York: Guilford.

Rubin, R.T. (1987). The neuroendocrinology and neurochemistry of antisocial behaviour. In S.A. Mednick, T.E., Moffitt and S.A. Stack (eds.). *The Causes of Crime: New Biological Approaches*. Cambridge, UK: Cambridge University Press.

Rubin, Z. and Peplau, L.A. (1973). Belief in a just world and reactions to another's lot: A study of participants in the national draft lottery. *Journal of Social Issues*, 29, 73–93.

Rudebeck, P.H., Bannerman, D.M. and Rushworth, M.F.S. (2008). The contribution of distinct sub-regions of the ventromedial frontal cortex to emotion, social behaviour, and decision making. *Cognitive, Affective and Behavioral Neuroscience*, 8, 485–97.

Ruma, E.H. and Mosher, D.I. (1967). Relationship between moral judgement and guilt in delinquent boys. *Journal of Abnormal Psychology*, 72, 122–7.

Rumbelow, D. (2004). *The Complete Jack the Ripper*. London: Penguin UK.

Rumelhart, D.E. (1975). Notes on a schema for stories. In D.G. Bobrow and A. Collins (eds.). *Representation and Understanding: Studies in Cognitive Science* (pp.185–210). New York: Academic Press.

Rumelhart, D.E. and Normam, D.A. (1975). The active structural network. In D.A. Norman, D.E. Rumelhart and the LNR Research Group (eds.). *Explorations in Cognition*. San Francisco: Freeman.

Rumelhart, D.E. and Norman, D.A. (1983). *Representation in Memory*. Centre for Human Information Processing. University of California, San Diego. Report no. ONR 8302. UCSD Chip 116. June 1983. 117.

Rupley, W.H. and Blair, T.R. (1983). *Reading Diagnosis and Remediation: Class and Clinic*. Boston, MA: Houghton-Mifflin.

Rusche, G. (1933). Labour market and penal sanctions: Thoughts on the sociology of punishment. In T. Platt and P. Takagi (eds.). *Punishment and Penal Discipline*. Berkeley, CA: Crime and Social Justice Associates.

Ruse, M. and Wilson, E. (1985). The evolution of morality. *New Scientist*, 1478, 108–28.

Rush, B. (1812). *Medical Inquiries and Observations Upon the Diseases of the Mind*. Philadelphia, PA: Kimber and Richardson.

Rushton, J.P., Fulker, D.W., Neale, M.C., Nias, D.K.B. and Eysenck, H.J. (1986). Altruism and aggression: The heritability of individual differences. *Journal of Personality and Social Psychology*, 50, 1192–8.

Russ, E., Heim, A. and Westen, D. (2003). Parental bonding and personality pathology assessed by clinical report. *Journal of Personality Disorders*, 17, 522–36.

Russano, M.B., Meissner, C.A., Narchet, F.M. and Kassin, S.M. (2005). Investigating true and false confessions within a novel experimental paradigm. *Psychological Science*, 16(6), 481–6.

Russell, D.E.H. (1975). *The Politics of Rape: The Victim's Perspective*. New York: Stein and Day.

Russo, R., Parkin, A.J., Taylor, S.R. and Wilks, J. (1998). Revising current two-process accounts of spacing effects in memory. *Journal of Experimental Psychology: Learning, Memory, and Cognition*, 24, 161–72.

Rustein E.H. and Goldberg, L. (1973). The effects of aggressive stimulation on suicidal patients: An experimental study of the psychoanalytic theory of suicide. In I. Rubinstein (ed.). *Psychoanalysis and Contemporary Sciences* (vol. 2). (pp.157–74). New York: Macmillan.

Rutter, M. and Giller, H. (1983). *Juvenile Delinquency: Trends and Perspective*. Harmondsworth: Penguin.

Rutter, M., Maughan, B., Mortimore, P. and Ouston, J. (1979). *Fifteen Thousand Hours: Secondary Schools and Their Effects on Children*. London: Open Books.

Rycroft, C. (1968). *A Critical Dictionary of Psychoanalysis*. New York: Basic Books.

Rypma, B., Berger, J.S. and D'Esposito, M. (2002). The influence of working-memory demand and subject performance on prefrontal cortical activity. *Journal of Cognitive Neuroscience*, 14, 721–31.

Safron, A., Barch, B., Bailey, J.M., Gitelman, D.R., Parrish, T.B. and Reber, P.J. (2007). Neural correlates of sexual arousal in homosexual and heterosexual men. *Behavioral Neuroscience*, 121, 237–48.

Sahebjam, F. (1990). The stoning of Soraya M. In G. Hallevy (ed.). Culture-based crimes against women in societies absorbing immigrants – rejecting the 'mistake of law' defence and imposing harsher sentencing (2008). *Cardozo Journal of Law and Gender*, 16, 439–67.

Salfati, C.G. and Bateman, A.L. (2005). Serial homicide: An investigation of behavioural consistency. *Journal of Investigative Psychology and Offender Profiling*, 2, 121–44.

Salfati, C.G. and Canter, D. (1999). Differentiating stranger murders: Profiling offender characteristics from behavioural styles. *Behavioral Sciences and the Law*, 17, 391–406.

Salfati, C.G. and Dupont, F. (2006). Canadian homicide: An investigation of crime-scene actions. *Homicide Studies*, 10(2), 118–39.

Salfati, C.G. and Haratsis, E. (2001). Greek homicide: A behavioral examination of offender crime scene actions. *Homicide Studies*, 5, 363–87.

Samenow, S. (1984). *Inside the Criminal Mind*. New York: Crown Publishers.

Samenow, S. (1991). Correcting errors of thinking in the socialization of offenders. *Journal of Correctional Education*, 42(2), 56–8.

Samuelson, P. (1938). A note on the pure theory of consumers' behaviour. *Economica*, 5, 61–71.

Sanchez-Martin, J.R., Fano, E., Ahedo, L., Cardas, J., Brain, P.F. and Azpiroz, A. (2000). Relating testosterone levels and free play social behavior in male and female preschool children. *Psychoneuroendocrinology*, 8, 773–83.

Sander, J-J. (2003). *Exploring the Criminal Mind*. Oslo: Jens-Jacob Sander.

Sandoval v. New Line Cinema Corp., 147 F.3d 215 (2d Cir. 1998) http://fairuse.stanford. edu/overview/fair-use/four-factors/#sthash.sAnpAIb7.dpuf.

Santtila, P., Canter, D., Elfgren, T. and Häkkänen, H. (2001). The structure of crime scene actions in Finnish homicides. *Homicide Studies*, 5, 363–87.

Sasaki, M. (2005). Amending the Juvenile Law in Japan: Ignoring the UN Committee on the Rights of the Child Recommendations. *FOCUS*, 40, 5–7.

Saunders, J. and MacLeod, M.D. (2006). Can inhibition resolve retrieval competition through the control of spreading activation? *Memory and Cognition*, 34, 307–22.

Saxe, R. and Wexler, A. (2005). Making sense of another mind: The role of the right temporo-parietal junction. *Neuropsychologia*, 43(10), 1391–9.

Saywitz, K.J., Geiselman, R.E. and Bornstein, G.K. (1992). Effects of the cognitive interview and practice on children's recall performance. *Journal of Applied Psychology*, 77, 744–56.

Scarr, S. (1996). Family policy dilemmas in contemporary nation-states: Are women benefitted by family-friendly governments? In S. Gustavsson and L. Lewin (eds.). *The Future of the Nation State: Essays on Cultural Pluralism and Political Integration* (pp.107–29). London: Routledge.

Schachter, F.F. and Stone, R.K. (1985). Difficult sibling, easy sibling: Temperament and the within-family environment. *Child Development*, 56(5), 1335–44.

Schalling, D. and Rosén, A.S. (1968). Porteus maze differences between psychopathic and non-psychopathic criminals. *British Journal of Social Clinical Psychology*, 7, 224–8.

Schank, R. and Abelson, R.P. (1977). *Scripts, Plans, Goals, and Understanding*. Hillsdale, NJ: Lawrence Erlbaum.

Scharf, P.L. and Hickey, J.E. (1976). The prison and the inmate's conception of legal justice: An experiment in democratic education. *Criminal Justice and Behavior*, 3, 107–22.

Scheper-Hughes, N. (2014). Human traffic: Exposing the brutal organ trade. *New Internationalist Magazine: People, ideas and action for global justice*, 472. http://newint.org/ features/2014/05/01/organ-trafficking-keynote/.

Schiffer, B., Krueger, T., Paul, T., de Greiff, A., Forsting, M., Leygraf, N., Schedlowski, M. and Gizewski, E. (2008). Brain response to visual sexual stimuli in homosexual pedophiles. *Journal of Psychiatry and Neuroscience*, 33(1), 23–33.

Schiffer, B., Peschel, T., Paul, T., Gizewski, E., Forsting, M., Leygraf, N., Schedlowski, M. and Tillmann H.C. Kruger (2007). Structural brain abnormalities in the frontostriatal system and cerebellum in pedophilia. *Journal of Psychiatric Research*, 41(9), 753–62.

Schiltz, K., Witzel, J., Northoff, G., Zierhut, K., Gubka, U., Fellmann, H., Kaufmann, J., Tempelmann, C., Wiebking, C. and Bogerts, B. (2007). Brain pathology in pedophilic offenders evidence of volume reduction in the right amygdala and related diencephalic structures. *Archives of General Psychiatry*, 64, 737–46.

Schlesinger, L.B. (2004). *Sexual Murder: Catathymic and Compulsive Homicides*. Boca Raton, FL: CRC Press.

Schnitzspahn, K.M. and Kliegel, M. (2009). Age effects in prospective memory performance within older adults: the paradoxical impact of implementation intentions. *European Journal of Ageing*, 6, 147–55.

Schneider, H.J. (2001). Victimological developments in the world during the past three decades: A Study of comparative victimology. *International Journal of Offender Therapy and Comparative Criminology*, 45, 449–68.

Schober, J.M., Kuhn, P.J., Kovacs, P.G., Earle, J.H., Byrne, P.M. and Fries, R.A. (2005).

Leuprolide acetate suppresses pedophilic urges and arousability. *Archives of Sexual Behavior*, 34(6), 691–705.

Schollum, M. (2005). *Investigative Interviewing: The Literature*. New Zealand Police. Wellington: Office of the Commissioner of Police.

Schreiber, F-R. (1983). *The Shoe Maker: Anatomy of a Psychotic*. New York: Simon and Schuster.

Schur, E.M. (1976). *Crimes without Victims: Deviant Behavior and Public Policy*. Englewood Cliffs, NJ: Prentice Hall.

Schur, E.M. (1980). *The Politics of Deviance: Stigma Contests and the Uses of Power*. Englewood Cliffs, NJ: Prentice Hall.

Schwartz, B.K. (2008). *The Sex Offender: Offender Evaluation and Program Strategies (Volume V1)*. Kingston, NJ: Civic Research Institute, Inc.

Schwartz, B.K. and Cellini, H.R. (1997). *The Sex Offender: New Insights, Treatment Innovations and Legal Developments*. Kingston, NJ: Civic Research Institute.

Schwartz, B.K. and Cellini, H.R. (2005). *The Sex Offender: Issues in Assessment, Treatment and Supervision of Adult and Juvenile Populations*. Kingston, NJ: Civic Research Institute.

Schwartz, J. and Steffensmeier, D. (2008). Nature of Female Offending: Patterns and Explanation. In R.T. Zaplin (ed.). *Female Offenders: Critical Perspectives and Effective Interventions* (2nd edn.). (p.43–75). Sudbury, MA: Jones and Bartlett Publishers.

Schweinhart, L.J., Barnes, H.V. and Weikart, D.P. (1993). *Significant Benefits: The HighScope Perry Preschool Study Through Age 27* (Monographs of the HighScope Educational Research Foundation, 10). Ypsilanti: HighScope Press.

Sear, I. and Williamson, T. (1999). British and American interrogation strategies. In D. Canter and L. Alison (eds.). *Interviewing and Deception* (pp.67–81). Dartmouth: Ashgate.

Searcy, J.H. and Bartlett, J.C. (1996). Inversion and processing of component and spatial– relational information in faces. *Journal of Experimental Psychology: Human Perceptual Performance*, 22, 904–15.

Searcy, J.H., Bartlett, J.C. and Memon, A. (1999). Age differences in accuracy and choosing rates on face recognition and eyewitness identification tasks. *Memory and Cognition*, 27, 538–52.

Searcy, J. H., Bartlett, J. C. and Memon, A. (2000). Relationship of availability, lineup conditions and individual differences to false identification by young and older eyewitnesses. *Legal and Criminological Psychology*, 5, 219–36.

Searcy, J.H., Bartlett, J.C., Memon, A. and Swanson, K. (2001). Aging and lineup performance at long retention intervals: Effects of metamemory and context reinstatement. *Journal of Applied Psychology*, 86, 207–14.

Sedikides, A. (1989). *Relations Between Role-Taking Opportunities and Moral Judgement Development*. Unpublished PhD thesis. Ohio: Ohio State University.

Seguin, J.R., Boulerice, B., Harden, P.W., Tremblay, R.E. and Pihl, R.O. (1999). Executive functions and physical aggression after controlling for attention deficit hyperactivity disorder, general memory, and IQ. *Journal of Child Psychology and Psychiatry*, 40, 1197–208.

Seguin, J.R., Nagin, D., Assaad, J.M. and Tremblay, R.E. (2004). Cognitive neuropsychological function in chronic physical aggression and hyperactivity (p.604). *Journal of Abnormal Psychology*, 113, 603–13.

Sellin, T. and Wolfang, M.E. (1964). *The Measurement of Delinquency*. New York: Wiley.

Selman, R.L. (1971). The relation of role taking to the development of moral judgement in children. *Child Development*, 42, 79–91.

Sentencing Guidelines Council (2008). *Dangerous Offenders: Guide for Sentencers and Practitioners* (version 2). Sentencing Guidelines Council, Crown Copyright.

Serber, M. (1970). Shame aversion therapy. *Journal of Behavior Therapy and Experimental Psychiatry*, 1(3), 213–5.

Seto, M.C. and Barbaree, H.E. (1999). Psychopathy, treatment behavior, and sex offender recidivism. *Journal of Interpersonal Violence*, 14, 1235–48.

Sexual Offences Act (1967). Act of Parliament of the UK. www.legislation.gov.uk/ukpga/1967/60/section/1.

Sexual Offences Act (2000). Act of Parliament of the UK. www.legislation.gov.uk/ukpga/1967/60/section/1.

Sexual Offences Act (2003). Act of Parliament of the UK. www.legislation.gov.uk/ukpga/1967/60/section/1.

Shamay-Tsoory, S.G., Aharon-Peretz, J. and Perry, D. (2009). Two systems for empathy: a double dissociation between emotional and cognitive empathy in inferior frontal gyrus versus ventromedial prefrontal lesions. *Brain*, 132, 617–27.

Shamay-Tsoory, S.G., Harari, H., Aharon-Peretz, J. and Levkovitz, Y. (2010). The role of the orbitofrontal cortex in affective theory of mind deficits in criminal offenders with psychopathic tendencies. *Cortex*, 46(5), 668–77.

Sharrock, R. and Gudjonsson, G.H. (1993). Intelligence, previous convictions and interrogative suggestibility: A path analysis of alleged false-confession cases. *British Journal of Clinical Psychology*, 32, 169–75.

Shaw, J., Appleby, L., Ames, T., McDonnell, R., Harris, C., McCann, K., Kiernan, K., Davies, S., Biddy, H. and Parsons, R. (1999). Mental disorder and clinical care in people convicted of homicide: National clinical survey. *British Medical Journal*, 318, 1240–4.

Shea, W.M. (1996). Personality characteristics of child molesters, non-sex offending criminal child abuse controls, and normals as differentiated by the Millon Clinical Multiaxial Inventory-II. *Dissertation Abstracts International: Section B: The Sciences and Engineering*, 56, 5184.

Sheldon, W.H. (1942). *The Varieties of Temperament: A Psychology of Constitutional Differences*. New York: Harper and Row.

Shepherd, E. (1993). Resistance in interviews: The contribution of police perceptions and behaviour. In E. Shepherd (ed.). Aspects of police interviewing (p.7). *Issues in Criminological and Legal Psychology*, 18. Leicester: The British Psychological Society.

Sheybani, M-M. (1987). Cultural defence: One person's culture is another's crime. In G. Hallevy (ed.). Culture-based crimes against women in societies absorbing immigrants – rejecting the 'mistake of law' defence and imposing harsher sentencing (2008). *Cardozo Journal of Law and Gender*, 16, 439–67.

Shover, N. and Honaker, D. (1992). The socially bounded decision making of persistent property offenders. *Howard Journal of Criminal Justice* 31(4), 276–93.

Shover, N. and Hochstetler, A. (2006). *Choosing White-Collar Crime*. Cambridge: Cambridge University Press.

Shye, S. and Elizur, D. (1994). *Introduction to Facet Theory: Content Design and Intrinsic Data Analysis in Behavioral Research* (p.179). Thousand Oaks, CA: SAGE.

Siegel, L. (1992). *Criminology* (4th edn.). (p.148). St Paul, MN: West Publishing.

Siegel, L. (2006). *Criminology* (9th edn.). Belmont, CA: Thomson Wadsworth.

Siegal, M. and Peterson, C.C. (1998). Children's understanding of lies and innocent and negligent mistakes. *Developmental Psychology*, 34, 332–43.

Sigall, H. and Ostrove, N. (1975). Beautiful but dangerous: Effects of offender attractiveness and nature of the crime on juridic judgement. *Journal of Personality and Social Psychology*, 31, 410–4.

Sigelman, C.K., Budd, E.C., Spanhel, C.L. and Schoenrock, C.J. (1981). Asking questions of mentally retarded persons: A comparison of yes-no and either-or formats. *Applied Research in Mental Retardation*, 2, 347–57.

Sigurdsson, J.F. and Gudjonsson, G.H. (1996). The psychological characteristics of false confessors. A study among Icelandic prison inmates and juvenile offenders. *Personality and Individual Differences*, 20, 321–9.

Sigurdsson, J.F. and Gudjonsson, G.H. (2001). False confessions: The relative importance of psychological, criminological and substance abuse variables. *Psychology, Crime and Law*, 7, 275–89.

Sigvardsson, S., Bohman, M. and Cloninger, C.R. (1996). Replication of the Stockholm Adoption Study of alcoholism: Confirmatory cross-fostering analysis. *Archives of General Psychiatry*, 53, 681–7.

Silva, J.A., Leong, G.B. and Ferrari, M.M. (2004). A neuropsychiatric developmental model of serial homicidal behavior. *Behavioral Science and the Law*, 22, 787–99.

Simmons, J., Legg, C. and Hosking, R. (2003). *National Crime Recording Standard (NCRS): An Analysis of the Impact on Recorded Crime. Companion Volume to Crime in England and Wales 2002/2003*. Home Office Online Report March 31. London: Home Office. http://webarchive.nationalarchives.gov.uk.

Simon, H.A (1957). *Models of Man. Social and Rational Mathematical Essays on Rational Human Behavior in a Social Setting*. New York: Wiley.

Simon, R.J. (1975). *Women and Crime*. Lexington: Lexington Books.

Simon, R.J. and Landis, J. (1991). *The Crimes Women Commit, the Punishments they Receive*. Lexington: Lexington Books.

Simons, K.W. (2011). Ignorance and Mistake of Criminal Law, Noncriminal Law, and Fact. *Ohio State Journal of Criminal Law*, Boston Univ. School of Law, Public Law Research Paper No. 11-46. http://ssrn.com/abstract=1935409.

Simons, W. (2011). Ignorance and mistake of criminal law, noncriminal law, and fact. *Ohio State Journal of Criminal Law*, 9(1), 1–57.

Simpson, B. (2006). Rational choice theories. In G. Ritzer (ed.) *Blackwell Encyclopedia of Sociology*. New York: Blackwell.

Singh, S. (2011). *Short notes on mistake of free consent*. www.preservearticles. com/2012012621501/short-notes-on-mistake-of-free-consent.html.

Singleton, N., Meltzer, H. and Gatward, R. (1998). *Psychiatric Morbidity Among Prisoners in England and Wales* London: HMSO.

Skeem, J.L., Poythress, N., Edens, J.F., Lilienfeld, S.O. and Cale, E.M. (2003). Psychopathic personality or personalities? Exploring potential variants of psychopathy and their implications for risk assessment. *Aggression and Violent Behavior*, 8, 513–46.

Skinner, B.F. (1938). *The Behavior of Organisms: An Experimental Analysis*. New York: Appleton-Century.

Skinner, B.F. (1953). *Science and Human Behavior*. New York: Macmillan.

Skolnick, J. (1966). *Justice Without Trial: Law Enforcement in Democratic Society*. London: Wiley and Sons Inc.

Sky News (2002). *Icon of Modern Evil.* (p.28). www.sky.com.skynews/ article/0,,30100–12169839,00.html.

Sky News (2012). *Esther Rantzen: Rumours Followed Jimmy Savile.* http://news.sky.com/story/991538/esther-rantzen-rumours-followed-jimmy-savile.

Slack, J. (2009). A decade of delinquency: Teen robberies, violence and drug crime soar to record levels. *Daily Mail.* www.dailymail.co.uk/news/article-1159834/A-decade-delinquency-Teen-robberies-violence-drug-crime-soar-record-levels.html.

Small, M. (1993). Legal psychology and therapeutic jurisprudence. *St. Louis University Law Journal,* 37, 675–700.

Smallbone, S.W. and Dadds, M.R. (2000). Attachment and coercive sexual behavior. *Sexual Abuse: A Journal of Research and Treatment,* 12, 3–15.

Smart, C. (1979). The new female offender: reality or myth? *British Journal of Criminology,* 19(1), 50–9.

Smetana, J. (1981). Preschool children's conceptions of moral and social rules. *Child Development,* 52 , 1333–6.

Smetana, J.G. (1990). Morality and conduct disorders. In M. Lewis and S.M. Miller (eds.). *Handbook of Developmental Psychopathology.* New York: Plenum Press.

Smetana, J., Kelly, M. and Twentyman, C. (1984). Abused, neglected, and nonmaltreated children's conceptions of moral and social-conventional transgressions. *Child Development,* 55, 277–87.

Smeulers, A. (2006). Towards a criminology of international crimes. Newsletter – *Criminology and International Crimes,* 1(1), 2–4.

Smith, A. (2006). *Crime Statistics: An Independent Review.* Independent Report. London: Home Office. http://webarchive.nationalarchives.gov.uk.

Smith, E.D. and Hed, A. (1969). Effects of offenders' age and attractiveness on sentencing by mock juries. *Psychological Reports,* 44, 691–4.

Smith, K. and Gudjonsson, G.H. (1986). Investigation of the responses of 'fakers' and 'non-fakers' on the Gudjonsson Suggestibility Scale (GSS). *Medicine, Science and the Law,* 26, 66–71.

Smith, P. (2003). Brenton Butler didn't do it. *The New York Times Upfront 2003.* www.upfrontmagazine.com.

Smith, P., Goggin, C. and Grendreau, P. (2002). *The Effects of Prison Sentences on Recidivism: General Effects and Individual Differences.* Ottawa, ON: Correctional Services of Canada.

Smith, P.B. and Pederson, D.R. (1988). Maternal sensitivity and patterns of infant-mother attachment. *Child Development,* 59, 1097–101.

Smith, R.E. and Bayen, U. (2004). A multinomial model of event-based prospective memory. *Journal of Experimental Psychology: Learning, Memory and Cognition,* 30, 756–77.

Smith, R.E., Bayen, U. and Martin, C. (2010). The cognitive processes underlying event-based prospective memory in school-age children and young adults: A formal model-based study. *Developmental Psychology,* 46(1), 230–44.

Snook, B., Cullen, R.M., Mokros, A. and Harbort, S. (2005). Serial murderers' spatial decisions: Factors that influence crime location choice. *Journal of Investigative Psychology and Offender Profiling,* 2, 147–64.

Snook, B., Eastwood, J., Gendreau, P. and Bennell, C. (2010). The importance of knowledge cumulation and the search for hidden agendas: A reply to Kocsis, Middledorp and Karpin (2008). *Journal of Forensic Psychology Practice,* 10(3), 214–23.

Snowden, R. (2006). *Teach Yourself Freud.* New York: McGraw-Hill.

Snyder, H.N. (2000). *Sexual Assault of Young Children as Reported to Law Enforcement: Victim, Incident, and Offender Characteristics*, NIBRS Statistical Report. Washington, DC: US Department of Justice, Office of Justice Programs Bureau of Justice Statistics.

Social Exclusion Unit (SEU) (2005). *Transitions: Young adults with complex needs*. London: HMSO.

Soloman, G.S. and Ray, J.B. (1984). Irrational beliefs of shoplifters. *Journal of Clinical Psychology*, 40, 1075–7.

Solomon, S. C., Lee, J. and Batchelder, J. S. (2007). The effects of registration and notification on offenders and the community. *Sex Offender Law Report*, 8(5), 65, 75–80.

Sorochinksi, M. and Salfati, C.G. (2010). The consistency of inconsistency in serial homicide: Patterns of behavioural change across series. *Journal of Investigative Psychology and Offender Profiling*, 7(2), 109–36.

Soudek, D. and Laroya, P. (2008). Longer Y chromosome in criminals. *Clinical Genetics*, 6(3), 225–9.

Speicher, B. (1994). Family patterns of moral judgment during adolescence and early adulthood. *Developmental Psychology*, 30, 624–32.

Spry, W.B. (1984). Schizophrenia and crime. In M. Craft and A. Craft (eds.). *Mentally Abnormal Offenders* (pp.125–137). London: Bailliere Tindall.

Stalenheim, E.G., Eriksson, E., von Knorring, L. and Wide, L. (1998). Testosterone as a biological marker in psychopathy and alcoholism. *Psychiatry Research*, 77, 79–88.

Stamms, G.J.M.M., Brugman, D., Dekovic, M., van Rosmalen, L., van der Iaan, P. and Gibbs, J.C. (2006). The moral judgement of juvenile delinquents: A meta-analysis. *Journal of Abnormal Child Psychology*, 34, 697–713.

Stanny, C.J. and Johnson, T.C. (2000). Effects of stress induced by a simulated shooting on recall by police and citizen witnesses. *American Journal of Psychology*, 113(3), 359–86.

Statistical Bulletin (2015). *Crime in England and Wales, Quarterly First Release to April 2015*. London: Office for National Statistics.

Staut, C.C. and Naidich, T.P. (1998). Urbach-Wiethe disease (lipoid proteinosis). *Pediatric Neurosurgery*, 28, 212–4.

Steadman, H.J. and Cocozza, J.J. (1974). Some refinements in the measurement and prediction of dangerous behavior. *American Journal of Psychiatry*, 131(9), 1012–4.

Steblay, N. and Dysart, J. (2003). Eyewitness accuracy rates in sequential and simultaneous lineup presentations: a meta-analytic comparison. *Law and Human Behavior*, 25(5), 459–73.

Steblay, N.M., Dysart, J., Fulero, S. and Lindsay, R.C.L. (2001). Eyewitness accuracy rates in sequential and simultaneous lineup presentations: A meta-analytic comparison. *Law and Human Behavior*, 25, 459–74.

Steen, R.G. (1996). *DNA and Destiny, Nature and Nurture in Human Behavior* (p.234). New York: Plenum Press.

Steffensmeier, D. and Ulmer, J. (2005). *Confessions of a Dying Thief: Understanding Criminal Careers and Illegal Enterprise*. New Brunswick, NJ: Aldine-Transaction.

Stein, L.M. and Memon, A. (2006). Testing the efficacy of the cognitive interview in a developing country. *Applied Cognitive Psychology*, 20, 597–605.

Stein, S. (2009). Obama's Preventive Detention Policy Compared To 'Minority Report'. *Huffington Post: US*. www.huffingtonpost.com/2009/05/22/obamas-preventive-denti-n-206810.html

Stephen, J.F. (1873). Liberty, Equality, Fraternity. In R.J. White (ed.). *Fraternity*. Cambridge, UK: Cambridge University Press, 1967.

instrument. *National Adult Literacy Database (NALD)*. www.nald.ca/fulltext/report4/rep31–35/REP34–01.HTM.

Taylor, P. and Chaplin, R. (2011). Crimes detected in England and Wales 2010/11. *Home Office Statistical Bulletin*, 11/11. London: Home Office.

Taylor, P. J. (1986). Psychiatric disorder in London's life-sentenced offenders. *British Medical Journal*, 289, 9–12.

Taylor, P. J. and Gunn, J. (1999). Homicides by people with mental illness: myth and reality. *British Journal of Psychiatry*, 174, 9–14.

Taylor, S.E. and Crocker, J. (1980). Schematic bases of information processing. In C.E. Cohen (ed.). Person categories and social perception: Testing some boundaries of the processing effects of prior knowledge. *Journal of Personality and Social Psychology*, 40(3), 441–52.

Taylor, S.R. (1990). *Improving Facial Memory*. Unpublished Thesis, Brighton: University of Sussex.

Taylor, S.R. (2009). Gender. In M. Cardwell, L. Clark, C.Meldrum and A. Wadeley (eds.). *Psychology A2 for AQAA* (4th edn.) (pp.190–225). London: HarperCollins Publishers Limited.

Taylor S.R. (2015) *Forensic Psychology: The Basics*. Abingdon, Oxon: Routledge.

Taylor, S.R. and Butcher, M. (2007). Extra-legal Defendant Characteristics and Mock Juror Ethnicity Re-examined. In *Proceedings of the BPS*, 11(2), 272.

Taylor, S.R. and Hartley, R. (2009). Watching crime TV increases fear of crime. BPS: *Book of Abstracts*, Annual Conference 2009, p.81.

Taylor, S.R., Lambeth, D., Green, G., Bone, R. and Cahillane, M. (2012). Cluster Analysis Examination of Serial Killer Profiling Categories: A Bottom-Up Approach. *Journal of Investigative Psychology and Offender Profiling*, 9, 30–51.

Taylor, S.R. and Workman, L. (2007). Electronic house arrest: What the public think. *The Psychologist in Wales*, BPS, 20, 6–17.

Tellegen, A., Lykken, D.T., Bouchard, T.J.Jr., Wilcox, K.J., Segal, N.L. and Rich, S. (1988). Personality similarity in twins reared apart and together. *Journal of Personality and Social Psychology*, 54(6), 1031–9.

Tennent, G., Tennent, D., Prins, H. and Bedford, A. (1993). Is psychopathic disorder a treatable condition? *Medicine, Science and the Law*, 33, 63–6.

Teti, D.M., Gelfand, D.M., Messinger, D.S. and Isabella, R. (1995). Maternal depression and the quality of early attachment: An examiniation of infants, pre-schoolers, and their mothers. *Developmental Psychology*, 31(3), 364–76.

Thayer, J.B. (1898). A preliminary treatise on evidence at Common Law. In A.A. Zuckerman (ed.). *The Principles of Criminal Evidence*. Oxford: Claredon Press, 1989.

The Daily Oklahoman (1995). Michael Fortier: Factual statement in support of plea petition. *Oklahoma Publishing Company*.(8–13–95). www.handwriting.org/michael-fortier.html.

*The Economist* (1997). The Guinness Affair: Bitter end. The Economist Newspaper. www.economist.com/node/107492.

The House of Lords and the Judges' 'Rules' 1843. (1977). In D.J. West and A. Walk (eds.). *Daniel McNaughton: His Trial and the Aftermath* (pp.74–81). Ashford: Gaskell Books.

The Independent (2012). Janet Street-Porter heard about Jimmy Savile abuse claims. London: *The Independent*, 9 October. www.independent.co.uk

thelawpages (2011). *A Quick Reference Guide With Offences and Their Corresponding Maximum Sentences*. www.thelawpages.com.

The OpenLearn Team (2010). Eyewitness. *OU on the BBC*, Open University, 18th April 2010. Shiers, K (Producer). (2010). Eyewitness. London: BBC / Open University.

The Scottish Government (2010). *Violent Crime – Homicide. High Level Summary of Statistics Trend*. www.scotland.gov.uk/Topics/Statistics/Browse/Crime-Justice/TrendHom.

The Wolfenden Committee Report (1957). *Report of the Committee on Homosexual Offences and Prostitution*. London: HMSO.

Thijssen, J. and de Ruiter, C. (2011). Instrumental and expressive violence in Belgian homicide perpetrators. *Journal of Investigative Psychology and Offender Profiling*, 8(1), 58–73.

Thomas, D. and Loader, B. (2002). *Cybercrime: Law Enforcement, Security and Surveillance in the Information Age*. London: Routledge.

Thompson, R.A. (1998). Early sociopersonality development. In W. Damon (series ed.) and N. Eisenberg (vol ed.). Handbook of child psychology: vol. 3. *Social, Emotional, and Personality Development* (5th edn.) (pp.25–104). New York: Wiley.

Thompson, R.A. (2000). The legacy of early attachments. *Child Develpoment*, 71, 145–52.

Thornhill, R. and Palmer, C.T. (2000a). *A Natural History of Rape: Biological Bases of Sexual Coercion*. Cambridge, MA: Massachusetts Institute of Technology.

Thornhill, R. and Palmer, C.T. (2000b). Why men rape. *The Sciences*, 40, 30–6.

Thorton, D.M. and Reid, R.L. (1982). Moral reasoning and type of criminal offence. *British Journal of Social Psychology*, 21, 231–8.

Thrasher, F. (1927). *The Gang*. Chicago, IL: University of Chicago Press.

Thurstone, L.L. (1927a). A law of comparative judgement. *Psychological Review*, 34, 278–86.

Thurstone, L.L. (1927b). The method of paired comparisons for social values. *Journal of Abnormal and Social Psychology*, 21, 384–400.

Tice, D.M. (1991). Esteem protection or enhancement? Self-handicapping motives and attributions differ by trait self-esteem. *Journal of Personality and Social Psychology*, 60, 711–25.

Tice, D.M. and Baumeister, R.F. (1990). Self-esteem, self-handicapping, and self-presentation: The strategy of inadequate practice. *Journal of Personality*, 58, 443–64.

Tiersma, P.M. (1999). *Legal language* (p.5). Chicago, IL: University of Chicago Press.

Toates, F. (2011). *Biological Psychology* (3rd edn.). Harlow: Pearson Education Ltd.

Tollison, C.D. and Adams, H. (1979). *Sexual Disorders: Treatment, Theory and Research*. New York: Gardner.

Tombs, S. (1995). Law, resistance and reform: 'Regulating' safety crimes in the UK. *Social and Legal Studies*, 4(3), 343–65.

Tombs, S. (2008). Corporations and Health and Safety. In J. Minkes and L. Minkes (eds.). *Corporate and White-Collar Crime (pp.18–38)*. London: SAGE.

Topping, A. (2011). Knife crime and gang violence on the rise as councils reduce youth services. *The Guardian*. www.guardian.co.uk/uk/2011/jul/29/gang-violence-rises-as-councils-cut-youth-services.

Travis, A. (2011). Convicted offenders committed 510,000 crimes within a year. *The Guardian*. www.guardian.co.uk/society/2011/oct/27/convicted-offenders-crime-figures

Treisman, A. (1964). Selective attention in man. *British Medical Bulletin*, 20, 12–6.

Trivers, R.L. (1972). Parental investment and sexual selection. In B. Campbell (ed.). *Sexual Selection and the Descent of Man* (pp.139–79). Chicago, IL: Aldine.

Trivers, R.L. (1985). *Social Evolution*. Menlo Park, CA: Benjamin/Cummings.

Tuckey, M.R. and Brewer, N. (2003). How schemas affect eyewitness memory over repeated retrieval attempts. *Applied Cognitive Psychology*, 17(7), 785–800.

Tullett, T. (1987). *Clues to Murder.* London: Bodley Head Ltd.

Tulving, E. (1983). *Elements of Episodic Memory.* Oxford, England: Oxford University Press.

Tulving, E. and Thompson, D.M. (1973). Encoding specificity and retrieval processes in episodic memory. *Psychological Review,* 80, 352–73.

Turk, A. (1969). *Criminality and the Social Order.* Chicago, IL: Rand McNally.

Turk, V. and Brown, H. (1992). Sexual Abuse and Adults with Learning Disabilities. *Journal of the British Institute of Mental Handicap,* 20(2), 56–8.

Turtle, J., Lawrence, C. and Leslie, V. (1994). *Exercising Cognitive Interview Skills With Police: A Research/Training Success Story.* Paper presented at the APLS Mid-Year Conference, Santa Fe.

Tversky, A. and Kahneman, D. (1973). Availability: A heuristic for judging frequency and probability. *Cognitive Psychology,* 5, 207–32.

Ugwuegbu, D.C.E. (1979). Racial and evidential factors in juror attribution of legal responsibility. *Journal of Experimental Social Psychology,* 15, 133–46.

UK Statistics Authority (2009). *Overcoming Barriers to Trust in Crime Statistics England and Wales.* Monitoring Report 5: Interim Report.

Unis, A.S., Cook, E.H., Vincent, J.G., Gjerde, D.K., Perry, B.D., Mason, C. and Mitchell, J. (1997). Platelet serotonin measures in adolescents with conduct disorder. *Biological Psychiatry,* 42(7), 553–9.

United Nations Office on Drugs and Crime (UNOCD). Statistics: Crime: Sexual Violence. Rape at the national level, number of police-recorded offences. www.unodc.org.

United States Supreme Court (1966). *Miranda v. Arizona,* 384 U.S. 436.

U.S.S.G.5A (2009). *Federal Sentencing Guidelines.* www.ussc.gov/2009guid/5a_SenTab. htm(assessed 02/02/2011).

Valenti-Hein, D.C. and Schwartz, L.D. (1993). Witness competency in people with mental retardation: Implications for prosecution of sexual abuse. *Sexuality and Disability,* 11(4), 287–94.

Valentine, T. and Mesout, J. (2009). Eyewitness identification under stress in the London Dungeon. *Applied Cognitive Psychology,* 23, 151–61.

Valier, C. (2000). Looking daggers: A Psychoanalytical reading of the scene of punishment. *Punishment and Society,* 2(4), 379–94.

Valier, C. (2002). *Theories of Crime and Punishment.* (p.122). Harlow: Pearson Education Ltd.

Vallender, E.J. and Lahn, B.T. (2004). How mammalian sex chromosomes acquired their peculiar gene content. *Bioessays,* 26, 159–69.

Vanderveen, G. (2006). *Interpreting Fear, Crime, Risk and Unsafety,* The Hague: BJU Legal Publishers.

van den Bos, K. and Maas, M. (2009). On the why of the belief in a just world: Exploring experiential and rationalistic paths to victim blaming. *Personality and Social Psychology Bulletin,* 35, 1567–78.

van de Wiel, N.M.H., van Goozen, S.H.M., Matthys, W., Snoek, H. and van Engeland, H. (2004). Cortisol and treatment effect in children with disruptive behavior disorders: a preliminary study. *Journal of American Academy of Child Adolescent Psychiatry,* 43(8), 1011–18.

van Dijk, J., van Kesteren, J. and Smit, P. (2007). *Criminal Victimisation in International Perspective. Key findings from the 2004–2005 ICVS and EU.* Tilburg University: Wetenschappelijk Onderzoeken Documentatiecentrum.

van Gijseghem, H. (2011). *Minutes of Proceedings February 14, 2011.* Standing Committee on

Justice and Human Rights, Number 048. Parliament of Canada. www.parl.gc.ca/HousePublications/Publication.aspx?DocId=4959361&Language=E&Mode=1.

van Goozen, S.H.M., Cohen-Kettenis, P.T., Snoek, H., Matthys, W., Swaab-Barneveld, H. and van Engeland, H. (2004). Executive functioning in children: a comparison of hospitalised ODD and ODD/ADHD children and normal controls. *Journal of Child Psychology and Psychiatry*, 45(2), 284–92.

van Goozen, S.H., Matthys, W., Cohen-Kettenis, P.T., Buitelaar, J.K. and van Engeland, H. (2000). Hypothalamic-pituitary-adrenal axis and autonomic nervous system activity in disruptive children and matched controls. *Journal of American Academy of Child Adolescent Psychiatry*, 39(11), 1438–45.

van Goozen, S.H.M., Matthys, W., Cohen-Kettenis, P.T., Gispen-de Wied, C., Wiegant, V.M. and van Engeland, H. (1998). Salivary cortisol and cardiovascular activity during stress in oppositional defiant disorder boys and normal controls. *Biological Psychiatry*, 43, 531–9.

van Goozen, S.H.M., Snoek, H., Matthys, W., van Rossum, I. and van Engeland, H. (2004). Evidence of fearlessness in behaviourally disordered children: A study on startle reflex modulation. *Journal of Child Psychology and Psychiatry*, 45(4), 884–92.

van Ijzendoorn, M., Feldbrugge, J., Derks. F., de Ruiter, C., Verhagen, M., Philipse, M., van der Staak, C.P. and Riksen-Walraven, J.M. (1997). Attachment representations of personality-disordered criminal offenders. *American Journal of Orthopsychiatry*, 67(3), 449–59.

Veneziano, C., Veneziano, L. and LeGrand, S. (2000). The relationship between adolescent sex offender behaviors and victim characteristics with prior victimisation. *Violence and Victims*, 15(4), 363–74.

Virkkunen, M. (1988). Cerebrospinal fluid: Monoamine metabolites among habitually violent and impulsive offenders. In T.E. Moffitt and S.A. Mednick (eds.). *Biological Contributions to Crime Causation*. Dordrecht: Martinus Nijhoff.

Virkkunen, M., De Jong, J., Bartko, J., Goodwin, F.K. and Linnoila, M. (1989). Relationship of psychobiological variables to recidivism in violent offenders and impulsive fire setters. *Archives of General Psychiatry*, 46, 600–3.

von Neumann, J. and O. Morgenstern (1944). *Theory of Games and Economic Behavior*. Princeton, NJ: Princeton University Press.

Voyer, D., Voyer, S. and Bryden, M.P. (1995). Magnitude of sex differences in spatial abilities: A meta-analysis and consideration of critical variables. *Psychological Bulletin*, 117, 250–70.

Vrij, A. (2004). Why professionals fail to catch liars and how they can improve. *Legal and Criminological Psychology*, 9, 159–81.

Vrij, A. and Mann, S. (2001). Telling and detecting lies in a high-stake situation: The case of a convicted murderer. *Applied Cognitive Psychology*, 15, 187–203.

Vrij, A., Mann, S., Fisher, R.P., Leal, S., Milne, R. and Bull, R. (2008). Increasing cognitive load to facilitate lie detection: The benefit of recalling an event in reverse order. *Law and Human Behavior*, 32, 253–65.

*W v. Edgell* [1990] 1 All ER 835. In B. Dolan (2004). Medical records: Disclosing confidential clinical information. *Psychiatric Bulletin*, 28, 53–6.

Wadsworth, M. (1979). *National Survey of Health and Development 1946 Cohort*. MRC

Waldman, I. (1988). *Relationships Between Non-social Information Processing, Social Perceptual Deficits and Biases, and Social Status in 7- to 12-Year-Old Boys*. Unpublished Dissertation, Waterloo, Ontario, Canada:University of Waterloo.

Walker, I.J. and Taylor, J.H. (1991). Family interactions and the development of moral reasoning. *Child Development*, 62, 264–93.

Walklate, S. (2011). *Criminology the basics* (2nd edn.). London: Routledge, Taylor and Francis Group.

Walsh, D.W. and Bull, R. (2010). How do interviewers attempt to overcome suspects' denials? *Psychiatry, Psychology and Law*, 19(2), 1–18.

Walsh, D.W. and Bull, R.H. (2010a). Interviewing suspects of fraud: An analysis of interviewing skills. *The Journal of Psychiatry and Law*, 38, 99–135.

Walsh, D.W. and Bull, R.H. (2010b). What really is effective in interviews with suspects? A study comparing interview skills against interview outcomes. *Legal and Criminological Psychology*, 15, 305–21.

Walsh, D. and Bull, R. (2011). Benefit fraud investigative interviewing: Investigation professionals' beliefs concerning practice. *Journal of Investigative Psychology and Offender Profiling*, 8, 189–202.

Walsh, D. and Milne, R. (2007). Giving PEACE a chance. *Public Administration*, 85, 525–40.

Walters, S.B. (2002). Principles of kinesic interview and interrogation (2nd edn.). Washington, DC: CRC Press.

Walzer, M. (2000). *Just and Unjust Wars* (3rd edn.). New York: Basic Books.

Ward, T. (2000). Sexual offenders' cognitive distortions as implicit theories. *Aggression and Violent Behavior*, 5, 491–507.

Ward, T. and Beech, A.R. (2006). An integrated theory of sexual offending. *Aggression and Violent Behavior*, 11, 44–63.

Ward, T. and Hudson, S.M. (1998). The construction and development of theory in the sexual offending area: A metatheoretical framework. *Sexual Abuse: A Journal of Research and Treatment*, 10, 47–63.

Ward, T. and Hudson, S.M. (2000). A self-regulation model of relapse prevention. In D.R. Laws, S.M. Hudson and T. Ward (eds.). *Remaking Relapse Prevention with Sex Offenders: A Sourcebook* (pp.79–101). Thousand Oaks, CA: SAGE.

Ward, T., Hudson, S.M. and Marshall, W.L. (1996). Attachment style in sex offenders: A preliminary study. *The Journal of Sex Research*, 33, 17–26.

Ward, T. and Keenan, T. (1999). Child molesters' implicit theories. *Journal of Interpersonal Violence*, 14, 821–38.

Watkins, M.J., Ho, E. and Tulving, E. (1976). Context effects in recognition memeory for faces. *Journal of Verbal Learning and Verbal Behavior*, 15, 505–17.

Watson, J.B. (1913). Psychology as the behaviorist views it. *Psychological Review*, 20, 158–77.

Watson, J.B. and Rayner, R. (1920). Conditioned emotional reactions. *Journal of Experimental Psychology*, 3(1), 1–14.

Weathers, H. (2011). I'm not a hostage to the past any more: Stephanie Slater reveals how – 20 years after being kidnapped and raped – she's finally able to move on. *Mail Online*. www.dailymail.co.uk/femail/article-2080489/Stephanie-Slater-finally-able-20-years-kidnapped raped.

Weber, N., Brewer, N. and Wells, G.L. (2004). *Is There a Magical Decision Latency That Discriminates Correct from Incorrect Eyewitness Identifications?* Paper presented at 14th conference of the European Association of Psychology and Law, Krakow, Poland.

Webster, C.D., Douglas, K.S., Eaves, S.D. and Hart, S.D. (1997). Assessing risk of violence to others. In C.D. Webster and M.A. Jackson (eds.). *Impulsivity: Theory, Assessment, and Treatment* (pp.251–77). New York: Guilford.

*Webster's New World Law Dictionary* (2010). Hoboken, NJ: Wiley Publishing Inc.

Weiss, B., Dodge, K.A., Bates, J.E. and Pettit, G.S. (1992). Some consequences of early harsh discipline: child aggression and a maladaptive social information processing system. *Child Development*, 63, 1321–35.

Weiten, W. (2010). *Psychology Themes and Variations* (p.292). Belmont, CA: Cengage Learning.

Weitzer, R. and Kubrin, C.E. (2004). Breaking news: How local TV news and real world conditions affect fear of crime. *Academy of Criminal Justice Sciences*, 21, 3.

Welch, M., Fenwick, M. and Roberts, M. (1997). Primary definitions of crime and moral panic: A content analysis of experts' quotes in feature newspaper articles on crime. *The Journal of Research in Crime and Delinquency*, 34(4), 474–94.

Wells, G.I. (1978). Applied eyewitness testimony research system variables and estimator variables. *Journal of Personality and Social Psychology*, 36, 1546–57.

Wells, G.L. (1984). The psychology of lineup identifications. *Journal of Applied Social Psychology*, 14, 89–103.

Wells, G.L. (1993). What do we know about eyewitness identifications? *American Psychology*, 48, 553–71.

Wells, G.L. and Hryciw, B. (1984). Memory for faces: Encoding and retrieval operations. *Memory and Cognition*, 12, 338–44.

Wells, S. (2003). *The Journey of Man: A Genetic Odyssey*. Princeton, NJ: Princeton University Press.

Wentlink, N. (2001). *Serial Sexual Murder: Classification and Development Over a Series of Offences*. Unpublished Masters Thesis. Liverpool, UK: University of Liverpool.

West, D.J. (1982). *Delinquency: Its Roots, Careers and Prospects*. London: Heinemann Educational Books Ltd.

West, D.J. and Farrington, D.P. (1973). *Who Becomes Delinquent?* London: Heinemann.

West, D.J. and Farrington, D.P. (1977). *The Delinquent Way of Life*. London: Heinemann.

Westcott, H.L., Davies, G.M. and Bull, R.H.C. (2002). *Children's Testimony: A Handbook of Psychological Research and Forensic Practice*. Chichester, UK: Wiley.

Wexler, S. (2010). Aristotle on equity, mens rea and actus reus: Some problems with translation. *International Zeitschrift (IZ)*, 6(3), 1–8. www.zeitschrift.co.uk/indexv6n3.

Whitehead, T. (2009). Sex offences advisor backs castration. London: *The Daily Telegraph*.

Whittaker, M.K., Brown, J., Beckett, R. and Gerhold, C. (2006). Sexual knowledge and empathy: A comparison of adolescent child molesters and non-offending adolescents. *Journal of Sexual Aggression*, 12, 143–54.

Whitten, A. and Byrne, R.W. (1988). Tactical Deception in Primates. *Behavioral and Brain Sciences*, 11: 223–73.

Widiger, T.A. (1996). Personality disorder dimensional models. In T.A. Widiger, A.J. Frances, H.A. Pincus, R. Ross, M.B. First and W.W. Davis (eds.). *DSM-IV Sourcebook* (vol. 2, pp.789–98). Washington, DC: American Psychiatric Association.

Widom, C.S. (1979). Female offenders: Three assumptions about self-esteem, sex-role identity and feminism. *Criminal Justice and Behavior*, 6, 365–82.

Widom, C.S. (1989a). Does violence beget violence? A critical examination of the literature. *Psychological Bulletin*, 106, 3–28.

Widom, C.S. (1989b). The cycle of violence. *Science*, 244, 160–6.

Wilkins L.T. (1980). *The Principles of Guidelines for Sentencing*. Washington: US Department of Justice.

Wilkins, L.T. (1983). *Consumerist Criminology*. London: Heinemann.